The Kingfisher
Children's
Illustrated
Dictionary
and
Thesaurus

KINGFISHER

BOSTON

Dictionary Editor	Heather Crossley
Dictionary Editorial Consultants	John Grisewood and Anne Soukhanov
Dictionary Editorial Development	Angela Crawley
Dictionary Definitions	Allene Tuck, Penny Stock, Anne Soukhanov, and Elizabeth Longley
Dictionary Pronunciation Consultant	Sheila Dignen
Thesaurus Author	George Marshall
Thesaurus Editor	John Grisewood
Thesaurus Revised By	John Bollard
Designer	Malcolm Smythe
Photographers	Tim Ridley, Nick Goodall, Steve Gorton
Cover Design	Tracey McNerney
Art Archivists	Wendy Allison, Steve Robinson
Artwork Researcher	Vicky Guilder
Prop Organizer	Sarah Wilson
Production Managers	Susan Wilmot and Oonagh Phelan

KINGFISHER
a Houghton Mifflin Company imprint
222 Berkeley Street
Boston, Massachusetts 02116
www.houghtonmifflinbooks.com

Material in this edition previously published by
Kingfisher Publications Plc as *The Kingfisher Illustrated Junior Dictionary*
and *The Kingfisher Illustrated Thesaurus*

2 4 6 8 10 9 7 5 3 1

1TR/0403/TIM/PIC/115GPM

LIBRARY OF CONGRESS CATALOGING-IN-PUBLICATION DATA
has been applied for.

ISBN 0-7534-5653-2

Printed in China

Contents

Your guide to the dictionary

How to find a word

All headwords (entries) in this dictionary are listed in the order of the alphabet. Words that begin with **A** are followed by those which begin with **B**, and so on until you reach **Z**. All the words under each letter of the alphabet are themselves in alphabetical order, so **admit** follows **admire**; **form** follows **fork**, and **vampire** follows **value**.

guide words
show first headword on left-hand page and last headword on the right-hand page.

colored headwords
begin all entries and show how the word is spelled.

entries
include headword and all its information, including any different definitions and related words.

alpha rules
help you to find the right letter section. The highlighted **b** shows that you are in the **b** section.

definition
what the word means.

different senses
Some words have more than one meaning. Each different sense or definition is numbered.

example sentences
show how a word is used to make the meaning clearer.

parts of speech
show whether the word is a noun, verb, adjective, adverb, conjunction, or preposition (see page 8), and tell what it does in a sentence.

changed forms
Spelling changes when words are used in different ways. All plurals of nouns, verb inflections, and the comparatives and superlatives of adjectives are shown.

verb tenses
These shows how each verb is written in the present, continuous present, and past tenses.

related words
belong to the same word family.

feature pages and panels
group words and pictures together by topic—birds, fruit, or space, for example. With their word boxes, these pages extend vocabulary and knowledge about the topic.

new letter section
A big, colored letter starts each section of the alphabet.

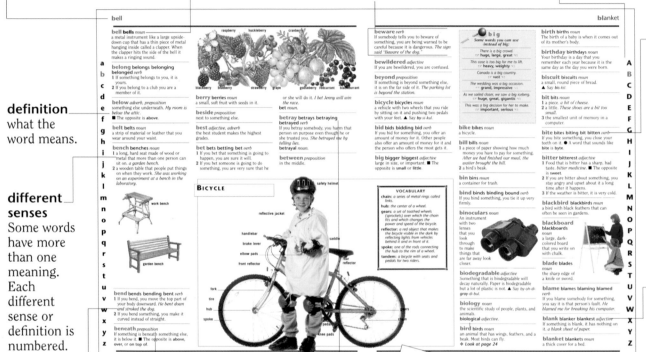

Useful features to help you explore words

thesaurus boxes
These show how you can vary and enrich your vocabulary by choosing a different word with a similar meaning to express yourself. The dictionary section of this book has thesaurus boxes for the following words:
bad, big, eat, fast, good, happy, like, nice, piece, small.

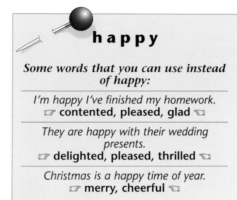

happy
Some words that you can use instead of happy:

I'm happy I've finished my homework.
☞ **contented, pleased, glad** ☜

They are happy with their wedding presents.
☞ **delighted, pleased, thrilled** ☜

Christmas is a happy time of year.
☞ **merry, cheerful** ☜

small
Some words you can use instead of small:

All small animals look sweet.
☞ *baby, young* ☜

The writing is so small you need a magnifying glass to read it.
☞ *minute, tiny* ☜

Don't worry. It's only a small mistake.
☞ *unimportant, slight, minor* ☜

homophones
Words that sound the same but have different meanings are marked with this sign ●

fair fairs *noun*
a place outside where rides and competitions are set up for people to have fun. ● A word that sounds like **fair** is **fare**.

pronunciation and rhyming words
Words that are difficult or awkward to say are marked with this sign ▲

fracture fractures *noun*
a break or crack in something, especially a bone. *Her arm is in a cast because she has a fracture.* ▲ Say *frak-cher*.

opposites
The opposite meanings for some words are shown by this sign ■

fill fills filling filled *verb*
If you fill something, you put as much into it as it can hold. *Frances filled the bottles with water.* ■ The opposite is **empty**.

How our states got their names

On page 318 you will find a list of all the 50 states, together with information about how they got their names. For example, did you know that Montana means "mountainous" in Spanish? You can learn a lot about words from their sounds.

spelling tips
If you cannot find a word under one letter, it may be under another letter. For instance, the correct spelling for "cangaroo" is "kangaroo!"

Spelling tip:
....
Some words that begin with a "co" sound are spelled with a "ko," for example, koala.

vocabulary boxes
Many topic pages have a list of special words connected to the topic.

VOCABULARY
bailey
the courtyard inside the walls.

battering ram
a heavy, wooden pole that was rammed against an enemy's castle wall or gate.

battlement
top of a castle wall with gaps through which people could fire on the enemy.

buttress
a pillar strengthening a wall.

drawbridge
a bridge over the moat that could be pulled up to stop the enemy getting into the castle.

dungeon
a prison under the castle.

keep
the main tower.

loophole
a slit in a wall for light, air, or for shooting through.

First writing

At first people would just draw a picture of a thing they wanted to record—a woman, a horse, or a bird, for instance. The people of ancient Egypt could write very complicated messages using these kinds of pictures. The people of ancient China also drew pictures of things they wanted us to know about. In time, these pictures became much simpler—just a few brush strokes known as "characters." Chinese is still written in characters to this day.

About 3,000 years ago, a way of writing was developed that used signs for each sound in a word. A letter stood for a sound. We call letters that stand for sounds an alphabet. These are the "bricks" we use to build our language.

A B C D E F G H I J K L M N O P Q R S T U V W X Y Z

A a

abandon abandons abandoning abandoned *verb*
If you abandon somebody or something, you leave them behind.

abbreviation abbreviations *noun*
a short way of writing something. *"Rd." is an abbreviation for "Road."*

ability abilities *noun*
If you have the ability to do something, you can do it.

aboard *adverb, preposition*
If you are aboard a train, bus, ship, or plane, you are on it or in it.

abolish abolishes abolishing abolished *verb*
to make an end to something. *President Lincoln abolished slavery.*

above *adverb, preposition*
higher than something. *My bedroom is above the kitchen.* ■ The opposite is **below** or **beneath**.

abroad *adverb, preposition*
in another country.

absent *adjective*
If you are absent, you are not here. *Katie was absent from school yesterday.* ■ The opposite is **present**.

absorb absorbs absorbing absorbed *verb*
When a cloth or sponge absorbs water, it soaks it up.

abuse *noun*
words or acts that hurt or injure someone.

accelerator accelerators *noun*
the pedal that makes a car go faster.

accent accents *noun*
1 the way that a person from a certain place speaks. *He spoke with a Southern accent.*

2 a mark that shows how to pronounce a word. *"Café" has an accent on the "e."*

accept accepts accepting accepted *verb*
1 to take something that somebody gives you. *She accepted the gift.*
2 to say that you will come to a party. ■ The opposite is **refuse**.

accident accidents *noun*
something bad that happens without being planned. *Ella dropped the drinks. It was an accident.* **accidentally** *adverb*.

accompany accompanies accompanying accompanied *verb*
If you accompany others, you go with them. *The teacher accompanied the children on the field trip.*

account accounts *noun*
1 If you give an account of something, you describe what happened. *He wrote an account of the bank robbery in the local newspaper.*
2 money that you keep in the bank.

accurate *adjective*
exactly right. *Is your watch accurate?* ▲ Say *ak-yoo-rit.*

accuse accuses accusing accused *verb*
If you accuse somebody, you say that person has done something wrong. *The man was accused of stealing.*

ace aces *noun*
Somebody who does something very well.

ache aches *noun*
a pain in your body that keeps on hurting, such as an earache. ▲ Rhymes with **take**.

achieve achieves achieving achieved *verb*
If you achieve something, you get it after trying very hard.

acid acids *noun*
a liquid that tastes sour, such as lemon juice or vinegar. Some strong acids can burn your skin.

acid rain *noun*
rain that has chemicals in it from factories and cars. Acid rain damages trees, rivers, and buildings.

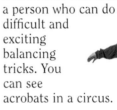

acorn acorns *noun*
the nut that grows on an oak tree.

acrobat acrobats *noun*
a person who can do difficult and exciting balancing tricks. You can see acrobats in a circus.

across *adverb, preposition*
If you walk across something such as a field, you walk from one side to the other.

act acts *noun*
1 one part of a play. *This play has three acts.*
2 something that you do. *an act of kindness.*

act acts acting acted *verb*
1 When you act, you do something. *She acted quickly to save the boy from drowning.*
2 If you act in a play or movie, you play a part in it.

action actions *noun*
something that you do. *Frankie's fast actions saved the man's life.*

active *adjective*
If you are active, you are always busy and able to do lots of things.

activity activities *noun*
1 something that you do. *Playing football is Tom's favorite activity.*
2 a lot of things happening and people doing things. *During the summer there is a lot of activity on the beach.*

actor actors *noun*
a person who acts in a play or movie.

add adds adding added *verb*
1 When you add numbers, you put them together to find an answer. *If you add 2 and 3, you get 5.* ■ The opposite is **subtract**.
2 If you add something to something else, you put the two things together. *She put coffee in a mug and added sugar.*
addition *noun*.

address addresses *noun*
Your address is the number or name of the street where you live, and the city or town where it is. *Your zip code is also part of your address.*

adjective adjectives *noun*
a word that tells you what somebody or something is like. In the sentence "Tom has a new, red bike," "new" and "red" are adjectives.

admire admires admiring admired *verb*
If you admire somebody or something, you think they are very good. *Everyone admired Katie's painting.*

admit admits admitting admitted *verb*
If you admit something, you agree that you have done something wrong. *Matthew admitted that he had broken the glass.*

adopt adopts adopting adopted *verb*
When people adopt a child, they take the child to live with them as part of their family.

adult adults *noun*
a person or an animal that is fully grown. *an adult bear.*

advance advances advancing advanced *verb*
When something advances, it moves forward. *The army advanced toward the enemy.*

advantage advantages *noun*
something that can help you to do better than other people. *In the game of basketball, it is an advantage to be tall.* ■ The opposite is **disadvantage**.

adventure adventures *noun*
something exciting that happens to you. *We got lost in the snow. It was a real adventure!*

adverb adverbs *noun*
a word that tells you more about a *verb*, *adjective*, or another *adverb*. In the sentence "Mike quickly opened the package," "quickly" is an adverb.

advertise advertises advertising advertised *verb*
If you advertise, you tell people about things that you are selling. *These toys were advertised on television.*

advertisement advertisements *noun*
information on a poster, in a newspaper, or on television that tells you about something to buy or something to do. ▲ Say ad-ver-**tize**-ment.

advice *noun*
If somebody gives you advice, they tell you what they think you should do.

advise advises advising advised *verb*
If you advise somebody, you tell them what you think they should do.

aerial *adjective*
in the air or from the air. *an aerial photograph.* ▲ Say **air**-ee-ul.

aerobics *noun*
exercises like dancing and stretching that you do regularly. ▲ Say air-**oh**-bix.

aerosol aerosols *noun*
a can with liquid inside. You press a button to send out the liquid in a spray. ▲ Say air-oh-sol.

affect affects affecting affected *verb*
If something affects you, it makes you different in some way. *Smoking affects your health.*

affection *noun*
the feeling of loving or liking somebody. *Samantha shows great affection for her little sister Joan.*
affectionate *adjective*.

afford affords affording afforded *verb*
If you can afford something, you have enough money to buy it. *I've spent my allowance and I can't afford any more candy this week.*

A B C D E F G H I J K L M N O P Q R S T U V W X Y Z

afraid *adjective*
If you are afraid, you think something bad will happen to you.

African-American *noun*
An American who has ancestors from Africa.

afternoon **afternoons** *noun*
the part of the day between midday and the evening.

again *adverb*
If you do something again, you do it once more. *Tell me that story again.*

against *preposition*
1 If you play against somebody in a game, you are on the other side.
2 next to, or touching something. *The ladder was against the wall.*
3 If you are against something, you do not agree with it. *I'm against violence in movies.*

age **ages** *noun*
1 Your age is how old you are.
2 a certain time in history.

agree **agrees agreeing agreed** *verb*
If you agree with somebody, you think the same about something. ■ The opposite is **disagree**.
agreement *noun*.

agriculture *noun*
Agriculture is keeping animals and growing plants for food.
agricultural *adjective*.

ahead *adverb*
in front of somebody or something. *We walked slowly, but the dog ran ahead.*

aim **aims aiming aimed** *verb*
1 If you aim at something, you point something such as a bow and arrow at the thing you want to hit.
2 If you aim to do something, you try to do it.

air *noun*
the mixture of gases that we breathe.

aircraft **aircraft** *noun*
any machine that can fly.

airplane *noun*
a flying machine with wings and an engine.

airport **airports** *noun*
a place where airplanes take off and land.

aisle **aisles** *noun*
a place where you can walk between rows of seats, such as in a theater or a church. *The bride and groom walked down the aisle.* ▲ Say **eye-l**.

alarm **alarms** *noun*
1 something such as a bell or a flashing light that warns you of something. *a burglar alarm.*
2 a sudden feeling of fear.

album **albums** *noun*
1 a book that you keep things such as photographs or stamps in.
2 a CD, tape, or record with several different pieces of music on it.

alcohol *noun*
Drinks such as wine, beer, and whiskey have alcohol in them. Some medicines have alcohol in them.
alcoholic *adjective*
Wine and beer are alcoholic drinks.

alien **aliens** *noun*
a creature from another planet. ▲ Say **ay-lee-un**.

alike *adjective*
If two things or people are alike, they are the same in some way. *The twins are not identical, but they are alike.*

alive *adjective*
A person, an animal, or a plant that is alive is living now. *Plants need water to stay alive.* ■ The opposite is **dead**.

allergy **allergies** *noun*
an illness caused by something that does not normally make people ill. *Some people have an allergy to dust.*
allergic *adjective*.

alley **alleys** *noun*
a narrow path between buildings.

alligator **alligators** *noun*
a large reptile similar to a crocodile but with shorter, wider jaws. Alligators live in rivers in the southern United States and in China.
See below

allow **allows allowing allowed** *verb*
If you are allowed to do something, somebody lets you do it. *I'm allowed to stay up later on weekends.*

alone *adjective, adverb*
by yourself, with nobody else. *Sophie walked home alone.*

AIRCRAFT

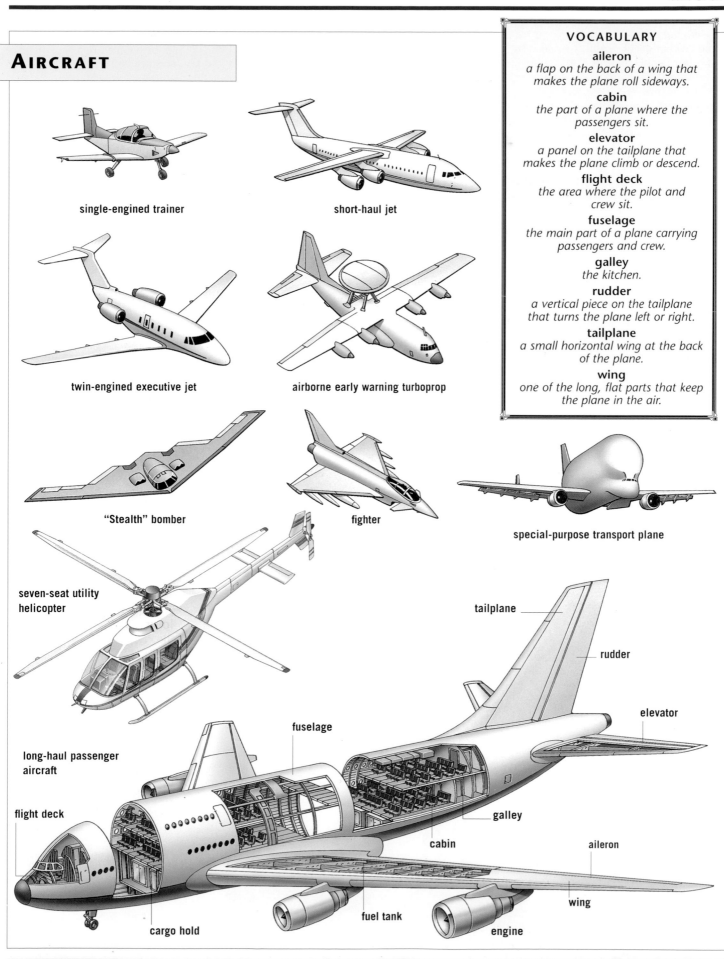

single-engined trainer

short-haul jet

twin-engined executive jet

airborne early warning turboprop

VOCABULARY

aileron
a flap on the back of a wing that makes the plane roll sideways.

cabin
the part of a plane where the passengers sit.

elevator
a panel on the tailplane that makes the plane climb or descend.

flight deck
the area where the pilot and crew sit.

fuselage
the main part of a plane carrying passengers and crew.

galley
the kitchen.

rudder
a vertical piece on the tailplane that turns the plane left or right.

tailplane
a small horizontal wing at the back of the plane.

wing
one of the long, flat parts that keep the plane in the air.

"Stealth" bomber

fighter

special-purpose transport plane

seven-seat utility helicopter

long-haul passenger aircraft

tailplane

rudder

elevator

flight deck

fuselage

galley

cabin

aileron

wing

cargo hold

fuel tank

engine

A B C D E F G H I J K L M N O P Q R S T U V W X Y Z

a
b
c
d
e
f
g
h
i
j
k
l
m
n
o
p
q
r
s
t
u
v
w
x
y
z

aloud *adverb*
If you read or speak aloud, you do it so that other people can hear. ● A word that sounds like **aloud** is **allowed**.

alphabet **alphabets** *noun*
all the letters from A to Z that we use to write words. The English alphabet has 26 letters.

A a	A α	৩	৳	A	a	ﺍ	ﺍ	
B b	B β	৮	৳	Б	б	ﺏ	ﺏ	
C c	Γ γ	৯	৬	В	в	ﺕ	ﺕ	
D d	Δ δ	ৠ	ৠ	Г	г	ﺙ	ﺙ	
E e	E ε	৫	৫	Д	д	ﺝ	ﺝ	
F f	Z ζ	৪	৪	Е	е	ﺡ	ﺡ	
G g	H η	৬	৬	Ж	ж	ﺥ	ﺥ	
H h	Θ θ	৷	৷	З	з	ﺩ	ﺩ	
I i	I ι	৹	৹	И	и	ﺯ	ﺯ	
J j	K κ	৬	৬	Й	й	ﺯ	ﺯ	
K k	Λ λ	ৣ	ৣ	К	к	ﺱ	ﺱ	
L l	M μ	৶	৶	Л	л	ﺵ	ﺵ	
M m	N ν	৬	৬	М	м	ﺱ	ﺱ	
N n	Ξ ξ	৩	৩	Н	н	ﺹ	ﺹ	

different types of alphabet

already *adverb*
before this time. *We ran to the bus stop, but the bus had already gone.*

alter **alters altering altered** *verb*
If you alter something, you change it in some way. *My father has altered his working hours so he can pick me up from school.*
alteration *noun*.

altogether *adverb*
counting everybody or everything. *My uncle gave me $5 and my aunt gave me $10, so I've got $15 altogether.*

aluminum *noun*
a light, silver-colored metal. Aluminum is used to make cans and tinfoil.
▲ Say *uh-loo-muh-num*.

amateur **amateurs** *noun*
a person who does something such as a sport because he or she enjoys it, but does not get paid for it. *Sarah is an amateur at figure skating.*
▲ Say *am-at-ur*.

amaze **amazes amazing amazed** *verb*
If something amazes you, it surprises you very much.
amazement *noun*
We watched the acrobat in amazement.
amazing *adjective*
She told us an amazing story.

ambulance **ambulances** *noun*
a special motor vehicle that takes people who are hurt or ill to the hospital.

amigo **amigos** *noun*
Spanish-speaking people say "amigo" to mean "friend."

among *preposition*
1 in the middle of. *The house stood among the trees.*
2 shared between more than two people. *She divided the candy bars among the children.*

amount **amounts** *noun*
An amount of something is how much there is. *I get the same amount of allowance as my friend.*

amphibian **amphibians** *noun*
an animal that lives on land but also in water. Newts, toads, and axolotls are amphibians. ▲ Say *am-fib-ee-un*.

amplifier **amplifiers** *noun*
a machine that makes sounds louder. CD players and cassette players have amplifiers.

amuse **amuses amusing amused** *verb*
If you amuse somebody, you make someone laugh or you keep them happy and busy. *The joke amused my sister.*
◆ *We played games to amuse ourselves on the long trip.*

ancestor **ancestors** *noun*
Your ancestors are members of your family who lived a long time ago.

anchor **anchors** *noun*
a heavy, metal hook on a long chain that you drop into the water from a ship or boat to stop it from floating away. ▲ Say *an-ker*.

ancient *adjective*
very old. *an ancient castle.*

anger *noun*
Anger is the strong feeling you have when you think something is unfair.
angrily *adverb*.

angle **angles** *noun*
the corner where two lines meet.

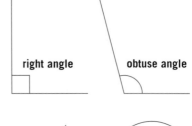

right angle   obtuse angle

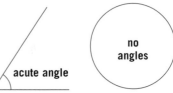

acute angle   no angles

warty newt

common toad

axolotl

angry angrier angriest *adjective*
If you are angry, you feel anger.

animal animals *noun*
a living thing that is not a plant. Birds, fish, insects, frogs, snakes, rabbits, and elephants are all animals.

ankle ankles *noun*
Your ankle is the part of your leg that joins your foot.

anniversary anniversaries *noun*
a day when you remember something special that happened on the same date in another year. *Today is my parents' 11th wedding anniversary.*

announce announces announcing announced *verb*
If you announce something, you say it in front of a lot of people. *She announced to the class that the play would open tomorrow.*

annoy annoys annoying annoyed *verb*
If you annoy somebody, you make the person angry.
annoyance *noun*

annual *adjective*
If something is annual, it happens once every year. *The fair is an annual event.*

answer answers answering answered *verb*
When you answer, you say something to somebody who has asked you a question or said something to you. *"What's the capital of France?" "Paris," she answered.* ▲ Say *an-sur.* ■ The opposite is **question**.
answer *noun.*

ant ants *noun*
a tiny insect. Ants live in groups called colonies in a "hill."

antelope antelopes *noun*
an animal like a deer with horns and long legs that can run fast. Antelopes live in Africa and parts of Asia.

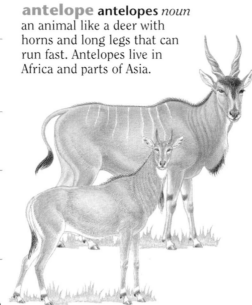

a nilgar (front) and an eland (back)

antenna antennas or antennae *noun*
1 a long, thin part on the head of an insect that it uses for touching.
2 an aerial.

antifreeze *noun*
a substance that you add to a liquid to keep it from freezing. *Dad put antifreeze into the car's radiator.*

antique antiques *noun*
a thing that is very old and often worth a lot of money. ▲ Say *an-teek.*

antiseptic antiseptics *noun*
a cream, liquid, or spray that you put on a wound in order to keep it clean and germfree.

antler antlers *noun*
one of two large horns that grow on the head of a male deer. The male deer, called a "buck" or a "stag," loses its antlers every year and grows new ones.

anxious *adjective*
If you are anxious about something, you worry about it. *Mom was anxious because we were late coming home.* ▲ Say *ang-shuss.*

ape apes *noun*
an animal like a big monkey with no tail. Gorillas, chimpanzees, and gibbons are all apes.

apologize apologizes apologizing apologized *verb*
If you apologize, you say you are sorry. *Billy apologized for being late.*
apology *noun.*

apostrophe apostrophes *noun*
1 a mark that you use in writing to show that something belongs to somebody. *Lucy's book.*
2 a mark that you use in writing to show that a letter has been left out. In the word "I'm," which is short for "I am," the apostrophe shows that the letter "a" has been left out.
▲ Say *a-poss-trof-ee.*

gibbon

orangutan

gorilla

chimpanzee

A
B
C
D
E
F
G
H
I
J
K
L
M
N
O
P
Q
R
S
T
U
V
W
X
Y
Z

apparatus *noun*
1 the pieces of equipment that you need to do a scientific experiment.
2 things such as bars and ropes that you use in gymnastics.

appear appears appearing appeared *verb*
1 to come into view. *He suddenly appeared from behind a tree.* ◆ *A black cloud appeared.* ■ The opposite is **disappear**.
2 If something appears to be a certain way, it seems to be that way. *A magnifying glass makes things appear bigger than they really are.*

appearance appearances *noun*
1 If you make an appearance, you come to a place where people can see you. *She made a television appearance.*
2 Your appearance is what you look like. *Having her hair cut really changed her appearance.*

appendix appendixes *or* appendices *noun*
Your appendix is a small, closed tube inside your body. It is part of the intestines.

appetite appetites *noun*
If you have an appetite, you are ready to eat something. *I hope you've got a good appetite, because I've cooked a really big dinner.*

applause *noun*
Applause is when people clap their hands together to show that they liked something.

apple apples *noun*
a hard, round, green, red, or yellow fruit that grows on a tree. *Apples are good for your health.*

apply applies applying applied *verb*
1 If something such as a rule applies to you, you must do what it says. *School rules apply to everyone in the school.*
2 If you apply for something such as a job, you write to somebody to ask for it.
application *noun*.

appointment appointments *noun*
a time that you have arranged to see somebody. *I have a doctor's appointment at 4 o'clock.*

appreciate appreciates appreciating appreciated *verb*
If you appreciate something, you are grateful for it. *I appreciate all your help.*
appreciation *noun*.

approach approaches approaching approached *verb*
If something approaches, it comes nearer. *The train is approaching.* ◆ *The dog approached the cat.*

approve approves approving approved *verb*
If you approve of something, you think it is good and right. *Mom doesn't approve of my new haircut.*

apricot apricots *noun*
a soft, round, orange-yellow fruit with a large pit in the middle.

apron aprons *noun*
a piece of clothing that you wear over your clothes to keep them clean when you are cooking.

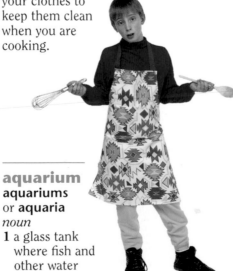

aquarium aquariums *or* aquaria *noun*
1 a glass tank where fish and other water animals are kept.
2 a building with lots of glass tanks where people can look at fish.

arch arches *noun*
a part of a bridge, building, or wall that has a curved shape. Arches support buildings and let people, trains, boats, cars, and other vehicles pass underneath.

archery *noun*
the sport of shooting with a bow and arrow. You shoot at a circular target.

area areas *noun*
1 a part of a country, a city, or the world. *My uncle comes from this area.*
2 the size of a flat place. *If a room is 20 feet wide and 40 feet long, it has an area of 800 square feet.*
3 a place that you use for something special. *a picnic area.*

area code *noun*
three numbers that show the telephone region where you live.

arena arenas *noun*
a place with rows of seats in it where you can watch sports or concerts.

argue argues arguing argued *verb*
If you argue with somebody, you speak in an angry way because you do not agree with that person.
argument *noun*.

arithmetic *noun*
working with numbers to find answers to problems.

arm **arms** *noun*
Your arm is the part of your body between your shoulder and your hand.

armed *adjective*
If somebody is armed, the person has a weapon and is ready to fight.

armor *noun*
a suit of strong metal that soldiers used to wear to protect their bodies during battles.

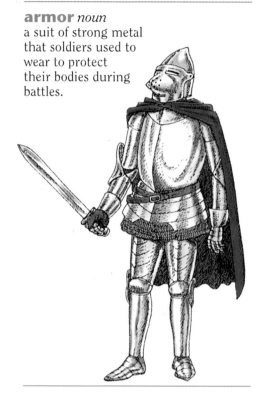

arms *noun*
Arms are guns, swords, bombs, and other weapons used in fighting.

army **armies** *noun*
a large group of soldiers who are trained to fight on land in a war.

arrange **arranges arranging arranged** *verb*
1 If you arrange something such as a party, you plan it. *We are arranging a birthday party for my sister.*
2 If you arrange things such as flowers or your belongings, you set them out in a certain way or put them in order. *We arranged the books on the shelf in alphabetical order.*
arrangement *noun*.

arrest **arrests arresting arrested** *verb*
When the police arrest somebody, they catch the person and accuse him or her of breaking the law.

arrive **arrives arriving arrived** *verb*
If you arrive somewhere, you get there. *She arrived at 3 o'clock.* ■ The opposite is **depart** or **leave**.
arrival *noun*.

arrow **arrows** *noun*
1 a thin stick with a sharp point at one end, that you shoot from a bow.
2 a sign that points to tell you the way to somewhere.

art *noun*
Art is something beautiful that somebody has made, such as a painting or a statue.

artery **arteries** *noun*
An artery is one of the large tubes that carry blood from your heart to all parts of your body.

artificial *adjective*
If something is artificial, it is made by people. ■ The opposite is **natural**.

artist **artists** *noun*
a person who draws or paints pictures or makes other beautiful things.

ash **ashes** *noun*
1 the gray powder that is left after something has been burned.
2 a tree that has gray bark and loses its leaves in winter.

ashamed *adjective*
If you are ashamed of something you have done, you are sorry and unhappy about it. *William was ashamed that he had told a lie.*

ask **asks asking asked** *verb*
1 If you ask a question, you say that you want to know something. *"What time is it?" she asked.*
2 If you ask for something, you say that you want it. *Tom asked for a bike for his birthday.*

asleep *adjective*
sleeping. *The cat was asleep by the fire.* ■ The opposite is **awake**.

assembly **assemblies** *noun*
a meeting of a big group of people for something special. *We have a school assembly every Monday.*

assist **assists assisting assisted** *verb*
If you assist, you help somebody.
assistance *noun*, **assistant** *noun*.

assorted *adjective*
If things such as candy or cookies are assorted, all different kinds are mixed together.

asthma *noun*
an illness that makes it difficult for a person to breathe. ▲ Say *azz-ma*.

astonish **astonishes astonishing astonished** *verb*
If something astonishes you, it surprises you very much. *She was astonished to see the big rainbow.*

astronaut **astronauts** *noun*
a person who travels in space.

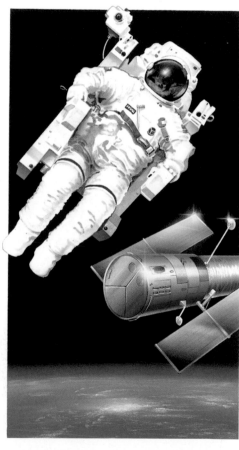

astronomy *noun*
the study of the Sun, Moon, planets, and stars.

ate past of **eat**.

athlete athletes *noun*
a person who is good at sports and games like football.

athletics *noun*
sports such as football, baseball, and ice skating.

atlas atlases *noun*
a book of maps.

atmosphere *noun*
1 the layer of gases that surrounds the Earth.
2 the feeling that a room or a place has. *The hotel has a warm, cozy atmosphere.*

atom atoms *noun*
a very tiny part of something. Everything is made of atoms. *Water is made of two kinds of atoms.*

attach attaches attaching attached *verb*
If you attach something to something else, you join or fasten them together. *We attached the rope to a tree.*

attack attacks attacking attacked *verb*
to try to hurt someone by using violence.
attack *noun*.

attempt attempts *noun*
a try. *After two attempts, I managed to ski down the hill.*
attempt *verb*.

attention *noun*
listening to somebody or watching that person carefully. *Pay attention!*

attic attics *noun*
a room or space under the roof of a house. *We keep our old toys in the attic.*

attract attracts attracting attracted *verb*
1 to like or to find somebody or something interesting. *Katie was attracted to the red car.*
2 To attract also means to make something come nearer. *Magnets attract iron.*
attraction *noun*.

attractive *adjective*
very nice to look at.

audience audiences *noun*
a group of people who are watching a play, movie, or concert.

audio *adjective*
1 relating to hearing a sound.
2 used to broadcast sounds.

aunt aunts *noun*
Your aunt is the sister of your mother or your father, or the wife of your uncle.

author authors *noun*
a person who writes stories or books.

autograph autographs *noun*
the signature of somebody famous.

automatic *adjective*
If a machine is automatic, it works by itself instead of a person doing the work.

autumn autumns *noun*
the season between summer and winter. *Leaves fall off the trees in autumn.*

avenue avenues *noun*
a street. Avenues are often wide with trees along both sides.

average *adjective*
1 usual. *She is above average height for her age.*
2 In math, to find the average of three numbers, 5, 9, and 10, add them up and divide by 3: 5 + 9 + 10 = 24, and 24 ÷ 3 = 8.

aviary aviaries *noun*
a place for keeping large numbers of birds. *I love to visit the aviary at the zoo.*

avoid avoids avoiding avoided *verb*
If you avoid something, you stay away from it. *The driver swerved to avoid the dog.*

awake *adjective*
If you are awake, you are not asleep.

award awards *noun*
a prize for something you have done well. *I won an award in swimming.*
award *verb*.

awful *adjective*
very bad. *This cake is stale. It tastes awful.*

awkward *adjective*
1 If you move in an awkward way, you are clumsy.
2 difficult or not convenient. *Our cabin is awkward to get to if you don't have a car.*

axe axes *noun*
a tool with a long handle and a sharp blade for cutting down trees and chopping wood.

B b

baboon baboons *noun*
a large African monkey with a nose and mouth the same shape as a dog's.

a family of baboons

baby babies *noun*
a very young child.

babysitter babysitters *noun*
a person who looks after children when their parents are out.
babysit *verb*.

back backs *noun*
1 Your back is the part of your body behind you, between your neck and the bottom of your waist.
2 The back of something is the opposite part from the front. ■ The opposite is **front**.

background backgrounds *noun*
The background is everything behind the main thing you are looking at. *This picture shows some camels with pyramids in the background.*

bacon *noun*
meat from the back or sides of a hog that has been prepared over smoke or treated with salt.

bacteria *noun*
Bacteria are living things so tiny that you cannot see them without a microscope. Bacteria live in air, soil, water, and inside people and animals, and some kinds can make you sick.

bad worse worst *adjective*
1 not good.
2 If you are bad at something, you cannot do it very well.
3 If food is bad, it starts to smell or to be moldy, so that you cannot eat it.

---

b a d

Some words you can use instead of bad:

The weather was very bad last week.
☞ **unpleasant, nasty** ☜

You've been a bad girl.
☞ **naughty, disobedient** ☜

Candy is bad for your teeth.
☞ **harmful, damaging** ☜

Is the pain bad?
☞ **severe** ☜

Her car is in bad condition.
☞ **poor** ☜

The food has gone bad.
☞ **rotten** ☜

---

badge badges *noun*
a piece of metal or plastic with a picture or words on it. A badge is pinned or sewn on your clothes.

badger badgers *noun*
a wild animal with gray fur, and black and white stripes on its head. Badgers live underground in holes called setts, and come out to eat at night.

badminton *noun*
a game in which players use rackets to hit a light object called a shuttlecock, or a birdie, over a high net.

bag bags *noun*
a thing that you use for carrying other things in.

bait *noun*
a piece of food that you put on a hook or put in a trap to catch fish or animals.

bake bakes baking baked *verb*
When you bake food, you cook it in an oven.

balance balances balancing balanced *verb*
If you balance, you stay steady and do not fall over. *Connie balances on the box.*

balcony balconies *noun*
a platform on the outside wall of a building upstairs, with a wall or railing around it.

bald balder baldest *adjective*
A man who is bald has no hair on his head.

bald eagle *noun*
an eagle, the symbol of the U.S.A. It is brown with a white head.

ball balls *noun*
1 a round thing that you use to play games.
2 something made into a round shape. *a ball of wool.*
3 a fancy party where people dance.

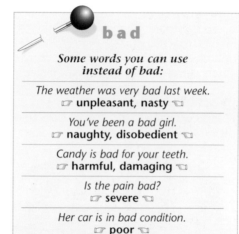

ballet *noun*
a kind of dancing to music that tells a story.
▲ Say *bal-lay*.

balloon balloons *noun*
a round bag made of rubber and filled with air or gas so that it floats.

bamboo *noun*
a tropical plant with hollow stems.

ban bans banning banned *verb*
If somebody bans something, it is not allowed. *My parents have banned us from watching TV in the morning.*

banana bananas *noun*
a long, curved fruit with yellow skin.

A B C D E F G H I J K L M N O P Q R S T U V W X Y Z

band **bands** *noun*
1 a group of people who play music .
2 a group of people who do something together. *a band of soldiers.*
3 a narrow piece of material that goes around something. *Tennis players often wear wristbands.*

bandage **bandages** *noun*
a long strip of material that can be wrapped around a part of your body that is injured in order to protect it.

bandit **bandits** *noun*
an armed robber.

bang **bangs** *noun*
a sudden and very loud noise.
bangs *noun*.
hair across the forehead cut to just above the eyebrows.

bank **banks** *noun*
1 a building where people keep money.
2 the ground at the side of a river.

banner **banners** *noun*
a long piece of cloth with writing on it that people carry in a crowd or march.

bar **bars** *noun*
1 a long, straight piece of metal.
2 a flat solid piece. *a bar of soap.*
3 a place where you can buy a drink or food. *a salad bar.*
4 one of the short groups of notes that a piece of music can be divided into. When music is written down, the bars are shown by lines between the groups of notes.

barbecue **barbecues** *noun*
a grill on which you can cook things like hot dogs over hot charcoal outdoors. ▲ Say *bar-bi-kew.*

bare **bare barest** *adjective*
1 without any clothes on. *bare feet.*
2 A bare closet or shelf is empty.
● A word that sounds like **bare** is **bear.**

bargain **bargains** *noun*
a thing being sold that is much cheaper than you expected.

barge **barges** *noun*
a long boat with a flat bottom, used on rivers and canals.

bark **barks barking barked** *verb*
When a dog barks, it makes a sudden loud noise.

bark *noun*
the rough outside covering of a tree's trunk and branches.

barley *noun*
a plant whose grain is used as food. *beef and barley soup.*

barn **barns** *noun*
a large farm building for storing crops such as hay or keeping animals inside.

barrel **barrels** *noun*
a large container with curved sides that is used for storing liquids.

barrier **barriers** *noun*
a thing like a wall or fence, that stops people or things from getting past.

base **bases** *noun*
a bottom part.

barrio **barrios** *noun*
a Spanish neighborhood.

baseball *noun*
a game played with a bat and ball by two teams of nine players. Each player has to hit the ball and run around four bases on the field before the ball is caught.

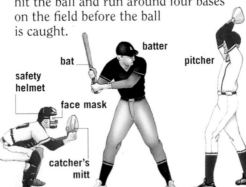

safety helmet
bat
batter
pitcher
face mask
catcher's mitt
catcher

basement **basements** *noun*
a room or rooms below the ground floor in a building.

basic *adjective*
Basic things are the important things that you cannot do without. *The one basic piece of equipment you need for soccer is a ball.*

basket **baskets** *noun*
a kind of stiff bag made from cane or wire, for carrying things.

basketball *noun*
a game played by two teams of five players. The teams have to get a large ball through a high net attached to a ring at each end of the court.

bat **bats** *noun*
1 a small animal like a mouse with wings. Bats hunt for food at night.
2 a piece of wood or metal that you use for hitting the ball in sports such as baseball. **batter** *noun.*

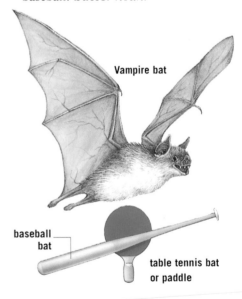

Vampire bat

baseball bat

table tennis bat or paddle

bat **bats batting batted** *verb*
When you bat, you have a turn at hitting the ball in baseball.

bath **baths** *noun*
1 a very large container for water that you get into to wash your whole body.
2 When you have a bath, you get into a bath and wash yourself.
▲ Rhymes with **path.**

battery **batteries** *noun*
a metal object that makes and stores electricity. You put batteries in radios, cameras, and flashlights.

battle battles *noun*
a fight between armies or navies.

bay bays *noun*
a part of the sea that has land curving around it on three sides.

beach beaches *noun*
the land beside the sea that is covered with sand or pebbles.

bead beads *noun*
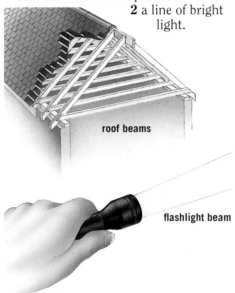
a small, round piece of glass, wood, or plastic with a hole through the middle. A piece of string can be threaded through the holes of lots of beads to make a necklace or bracelet.

beak beaks *noun*
the hard, pointed part of a bird's mouth.

beam beams *noun*
1 one of the thick, strong pieces of wood or metal that holds up a roof.
2 a line of bright light.

roof beams

flashlight beam

beam beams beaming beamed *verb*
If you are beaming, you have a big, happy smile on your face.

bean beans *noun*
a large seed that grows inside a pod. Sometimes you eat the whole pod, and sometimes you eat the seed.
green beans ◆ *baked beans.*

bear bears *noun*
a big, wild animal with thick fur. Bears are brown, black, or white.
● A word that sounds like **bear** is **bare**.

bear bears bearing bore borne *verb*
1 If you cannot bear something, you cannot put up with it. *She couldn't bear the pain any longer.*
2 If you bear something, you carry or support it. *He bore a heavy load.*
● A word that sounds like **bear** is **bare**.

beard beards *noun*
the hair on a man's chin and face.

beast beasts *noun*
a wild animal.

beat beats beating beat beaten *verb*
1 If you beat somebody in competition or game, you win.
2 To beat somebody or something means to hit them very hard again and again, especially with your hand or a stick.
3 If you beat eggs or cream, you stir them fast with a fork, electric mixer, or whisk.
4 When your heart is beating, it is pushing the blood around your body regularly and keeping you alive.

beat beats *noun*
the regular rhythm of your heart or of a piece of music. *the beat of a drum.*

beautiful *adjective*
very lovely to look at, or listen to or smell. *a beautiful painting.* ■ The opposite is **ugly**.

beaver beavers *noun*
a furry animal with strong teeth and a flat tail. Beavers live by rivers or streams where they build homes called lodges.

become becomes becoming became *verb*
1 When one thing becomes another thing, it changes into it. *Caterpillars eventually become butterflies.*
2 When you become something, you change to be it. *She became worried about her son when he didn't come home at the usual time.*

bed beds *noun*
1 the piece of furniture that you sleep on. The room where your bed is and where you sleep is called a bedroom.
2 The seabed is the bottom of the sea.

bee bees *noun*
an insect with a yellow and black body that makes honey. ● A word that sounds like **bee** is **be**.

beef *noun*
meat from a cow.

beehive beehives *noun*
a box or place where bees live.

beetle beetles *noun*
an insect with hard, shiny wings.

beet beets *noun*
a round, red vegetable that grows in the ground.

beg begs begging begged *verb*
1 If somebody begs, he or she asks people for money in the street.
2 If you beg for something, you ask for it in a way that shows you want it very badly.

begin begins beginning began begun *verb*
When something begins, it starts. ■ The opposite is **finish** or **end**.
beginning *noun*.

behave behaves behaving behaved *verb*
The way you behave is the way you act. *The children behaved very badly.*
behavior *noun*.

believe believes believing believed *verb*
1 If you believe something, you are sure that it is true or real even though you cannot prove it. *Do you believe in ghosts?*
2 If you believe somebody, you think the person tells the truth. *Mom believed my story.*
belief *noun*.

A
B
C
D
E
F
G
H
I
J
K
L
M
N
O
P
Q
R
S
T
U
V
W
X
Y
Z

bell bells *noun*

a metal instrument like a large upside-down cup that has a thin piece of metal hanging inside called a clapper. When the clapper hits the side of the bell it makes a ringing sound.

belong belongs belonging belonged *verb*

1 If something belongs to you, it is yours.
2 If you belong to a club you are a member of it.

below *adverb, preposition*

something else underneath. *My room is below the attic.*
■ The opposite is **above**.

belt belts *noun*

a strip of material or leather that you wear around your waist.

bench benches *noun*

1 a long, hard seat made of wood or metal that more than one person can sit on. *a garden bench.*
2 a wooden table that people put things on when they work. *The carpenter was working at his bench, drilling a hole in a piece of wood.*

workbench

garden bench

bend bends bending bent *verb*

1 If you bend, you move the top part of your body downward. *He bent down and stroked the dog.*
2 If you bend something, you make it curved instead of straight.

beneath *preposition*

If something is beneath something else, it is below it. ■ The opposite is **above**, **over**, or **on top of**.

raspberry   huckleberry   cranberry

blackberry   blueberry   strawberry   grape   gooseberry   red currant   blackcurrant

berry berries *noun*

a small, soft fruit with seeds in it.

beside *preposition*

next to something else.

best *adjective, adverb*

better than all others. *my best clothes.*
◆ *I like math class best.*

bet bets betting bet *verb*

1 If you bet that something is going to happen, you are sure it will.
2 If you bet someone is going to do something, you are very sure that he or she will do it. *I bet Jenny will win the race.*
bet *noun.*

betray betrays betraying betrayed *verb*

If you betray somebody, you harm that person on purpose even though he or she trusted you. *She betrayed me by telling lies.*
betrayal *noun.*

between *preposition*

in the middle.

BICYCLE

safety helmet

reflective jacket

handlebar

brake lever

elbow pads

front reflector

saddle

rear reflector

fork

tire

hub

spoke

pedal

knee pads

beware *verb*
If somebody tells you to beware of something, you are being warned to be careful because it is dangerous. *The sign said "Beware of the dog."*

bewildered *adjective*
If you are bewildered, you are confused.

beyond *preposition*
If something is beyond something else, it is on the far side of it. *The parking lot is beyond the station.*

bicycle **bicycles** *noun*
a vehicle with two wheels that you ride by sitting on it and pushing two pedals with your feet. ▲ Say **by-si-kul**.

bid **bids bidding bid** *verb*
If you bid for something, you offer an amount of money for it. Other people also offer an amount of money for it and the person who offers the most gets it.

big **bigger biggest** *adjective*
large in size, or important. ■ The opposite is **small** or **little**.

VOCABULARY

chain: *a series of metal rings called links.*

hub: *the center of a wheel.*

gears: *a set of toothed wheels (sprockets) over which the chain fits and which change the power and speed of the bicycle.*

reflector: *a red object that makes the bicycle visible in the dark by reflecting lights from vehicles behind it and in front of it.*

spoke: *one of the rods connecting the hub to the rim of a wheel.*

tandem: *a bicycle with seats and pedals for two riders.*

gears

chain

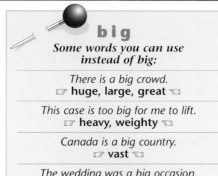

b i g
Some words you can use instead of big:

There is a big crowd.
☞ **huge, large, great** ☜

This case is too big for me to lift.
☞ **heavy, weighty** ☜

Canada is a big country.
☞ **vast** ☜

The wedding was a big occasion.
☞ **grand, impressive** ☜

As we sailed closer, we saw a big iceberg.
☞ **huge, great, gigantic** ☜

This was a big decision for her to make.
☞ **important, serious** ☜

---

bike **bikes** *noun*
a bicycle.

bill **bills** *noun*
1 a bird's beak.
2 a piece of paper money. *a $5 bill.*
3 a piece of paper showing how much money you owe for something. *After lunch, the waiter brought our bill.*

bin **bins** *noun*
a container to store things in.

bind **binds binding bound** *verb*
If you bind something, you tie it up very firmly.

binoculars *noun*
An instrument with two lenses that you look through to make things that are far away look closer.

biodegradable *adjective*
Something that is biodegradable will decay naturally. Paper is biodegradable, but a lot of plastic is not. ▲ Say **by-oh-di-gray-di-bul**.

biology *noun*
the scientific study of people, plants, and animals.
biological *adjective*.

bird **birds** *noun*
an animal that has wings, feathers, and a beak. Most birds can fly.
❖ *Look at page 24*

---

birth **births** *noun*
The birth of a baby is when it comes out of its mother's body.

birthday **birthdays** *noun*
Your birthday is a day that you remember each year because it is the same day as the day you were born.

biscuit **biscuits** *noun*
a small bread raised with baking soda. ▲ Say **bis-kit**.

bit **bits** *noun*
1 a piece. *a bit of cheese.*
2 a little. *These shoes are a bit too small.*
3 the smallest unit of memory in a computer.

bite **bites biting bit bitten** *verb*
If you bite something, you close your teeth on it. ● A word that sounds like **bite** is **byte**.

bitter **bitterest** *adjective*
1 Food that is bitter has a sharp, bad taste. *bitter medicine.* ■ The opposite is **sweet**.
2 If you are bitter about something, you stay angry and upset about it a long time after it happens.
3 If the weather is bitter, it is very cold.

blackbird **blackbirds** *noun*
a bird with black feathers that can often be seen in gardens.

blackboard **blackboards** *noun*
a large, dark-colored board that you write on with chalk.

blade **blades** *noun*
the sharp edge of a knife or sword.

blame **blames blaming blamed** *verb*
If you blame somebody for something, you say it is that person's fault. *He blamed me for breaking his computer.*

blank **blanker blankest** *adjective*
If something is blank, it has nothing on it. *a blank sheet of paper.*

blanket **blankets** *noun*
a thick cover for a bed; a thick covering. *a blanket of fog.*

A
B
C
D
E
F
G
H
I
J
K
L
M
N
O
P
Q
R
S
T
U
V
W
X
Y
Z

BIRDS

a b c d e f g h i j k l m n o p q r s t u v w x y z

Condor

secondary feathers

primary feathers

bill

tail

tail feathers

talons

feather

shaft

Toco toucan

Hummingbird

Starling

Barn owl

Great blue heron

Kiwi

Black swan

Pelican

Great crested grebe

20

blast blasts *noun*
an explosion. *One person was injured in the blast when the bomb went off.*

blaze blazes blazing blazed *verb*
When a fire blazes, it burns very strongly. *The forest fire blazed for more than a week.*

bleed bleeds bleeding bled *verb*
When a part of your body bleeds, blood flows out. *He cut his arm and it started bleeding.*

blew past of **blow**
● A word that sounds like **blew** is **blue**.

blind *adjective*
A person who is blind cannot see.

blind blinds *noun*
a roll of material that you pull down to cover a window.

blindfold blindfolds *noun*
a piece of material tied over somebody's eyes so that he or she cannot see.

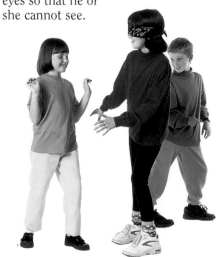

blink blinks blinking blinked *verb*
When you blink, you shut both your eyes and open them again very quickly.

blister blisters *noun*
a small bubble of liquid just under your skin that you get if something has rubbed your skin a lot or if you get burned.

blizzard blizzards *noun*
a snowstorm with very strong winds.

block blocks *noun*
1 a thick piece of something solid, with flat sides. *a block of wood.*

2 the area in a city or town within four streets is also a block.
3 an apartment block is a big building divided into apartments.

block blocks blocking blocked *verb*
If something blocks a place, it is in the way and nothing can get by.

blond blonde blonder blondest *adjective*
A person who is blond or blonde has light-colored hair. We use the spelling **blond** for men and boys, and **blonde** for women and girls.

blood *noun*
the liquid that flows all around your body through your arteries and veins.

bloom blooms blooming bloomed *verb*
When a plant blooms, its flowers come out.

blossom *noun*
flowers on a tree. *cherry blossoms.*

blot blots *noun*
a drop of ink that has spilled onto something and left a mark.

> When the clapper hits the side of the bell it makes a ringing sound.
>
> **belong** belongs belonging belonged *verb*
> 1 If something belongs to you, it is yours.
> 2 If you belong to a club or society, you are a member of it.
>
> **below** *preposition*
> If something is below something else, it is underneath it.
> ■ The opposite is **above**.
>
> **belt** belts *noun*

blouse blouses *noun*
a piece of clothing like a shirt worn by a girl or woman.

blow blows blowing blew blown *verb*
1 If you blow, you breathe a lot of air out of your mouth at once. *He blew all nine candles out with one breath.*
2 When you blow your nose, you breathe out through your nose very hard into a handkerchief.
3 If something blows somewhere, the wind is pushing it along. *Leaves were blowing around the street.*
blow up If something is blown up, it is destroyed with an explosion.

blow blows *noun*
a hard hit.

blunt blunter bluntest *adjective*
1 A blunt knife does not cut very well because it is not sharp anymore.
2 A blunt object has a rounded or flat end instead of a pointed one. *a blunt pencil.*
3 If you are blunt, you say exactly what you think even if it is not polite or kind.

blur blurs blurring blurred *verb*
When something blurs, you cannot see it clearly. *My eyes were so tired that the TV was beginning to blur.*

blush blushes blushing blushed *verb*
When you blush, your face gets red because you are embarrassed. *Mark blushed when Tina saw his baby picture.*

board boards *noun*
1 a long piece of sawn lumber.
2 a blackboard.
3 a surfboard.
● A word that sounds like **board** is **bored**.

board boarder boarding boarded *verb*
to get into a big vehicle.

A B C D E F G H I J K L M N O P Q R S T U V W X Y Z

boast boasts boasting boasted
verb
If you boast, you talk in a way that shows you are too proud of something. *John boasted about his grades.*

boat boats *noun*
Boats carry people and things across water. Some boats have engines, some have sails, and some you row by using oars or paddles.

body bodies *noun*
1 the parts of a person or of an animal that can be seen or touched.
2 a dead person.
3 a group of people. *our student body.*

boil boils boiling boiled *verb*
1 When liquid boils, it gets so hot that bubbles appear on the surface and it starts to change into steam.
2 When you boil food, you cook it in boiling water. *We boiled potatoes.*

boil boils *noun*
a big, painful spot on your skin.

bold bolder boldest *adjective*
not afraid to do dangerous things.
boldness *noun.*

bolt bolts *noun*
1 a metal bar that slides across to lock a door or window.
2 a metal pin that screws into a metal nut to fasten things together.
3 a big flash of lightning.
4 a large roll of cloth.

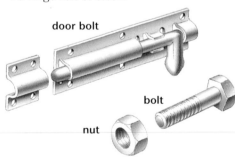

door bolt

bolt

nut

bolt bolts bolting bolted *verb*
1 When you bolt a door, you slide a bolt across it, to hold it in place, so that it cannot be opened.
2 When people or animals bolt, they suddenly run away. *The horse was frightened by the noise and bolted across the field.*

bomb bombs *noun*
a weapon containing chemicals that can be made to explode.

bone bones *noun*
A bone is one of the hard parts inside your body that make up your skeleton.

bonfire bonfires *noun*
a big fire that is made outdoors. *Campers sat around the bonfire.*

bonnet
bonnets *noun*
1 a kind of hat that is tied with strings under the chin. Babies sometimes wear bonnets.
2 Pioneer women wore sunbonnets.

book books *noun*
sheets of paper fastened together inside a cover.

book books booking booked *verb*
When you book something, you ask somebody to keep it for you. *Mom booked seats on the plane.*

boomerang
boomerangs *noun*
a curved stick that comes back to the person who throws it. The first people who lived in Australia, called Aboriginals, used the boomerang as a weapon for hunting.

boot boots *noun*
1 a shoe that covers your foot and ankle, and sometimes part of your leg. *Cowboys and cowgirls wear high-heeled boots.*

border borders *noun*
1 the line that separates two countries.
2 a strip around the edge of something that is a different color or has a different pattern.

bore bores boring bored *verb*
1 If something bores you, you are not interested in it.
2 If you bore into something, you make a hole in it using a drill. *The engineer bored a hole in the rock.*
boredom *noun,* **boring** *adjective.*

bore past of **bear**.

born *adjective*
When a baby is born, it comes out of its mother's body.

borrow borrows borrowing borrowed *verb*
If you borrow something, someone lets you have it for a time and then you give it back. *I borrowed books from the library.* ■ The opposite is **lend**.

boss bosses *noun*
The boss is the person who is in charge.

both *pronoun*
When something is true about two people or things, you can say it is true about both of them. *Both my sister and my aunt are called Mary.*

bother bothers bothering bothered *verb*
1 If something bothers you, it makes you feel worried or uncomfortable.
2 If you bother about something you care about it and take trouble with it.

bottle bottles *noun*
a tall container of glass or plastic that you keep liquid in.

bottom bottoms *noun*
1 the lowest part of something. ■ The opposite is **top**.
2 Your bottom is the part of your body that you sit on.

bought past of **buy**
▲ Say *bawt.*

boulder boulders *noun*
a very large, smooth rock.

bounce bounces bouncing bounced *verb*
When something bounces, it hits the ground or another hard surface and moves back up again. *The ball bounced off the wall.*

bound bounds bounding bounded *verb*
To bound is to move along by making big jumps. *The dog bounded up to the gate.*
bound to If something is bound to happen, it will definitely happen.

bound past of **bind**.

bouquet bouquets *noun*
a bunch of flowers. ▲ Say *boo-kay*.

bow bows bowing bowed *verb*
If you bow, you bend your head or body forward. *Actors bow at the end of a play when people clap for them.*
▲ Rhymes with **cow**.

bow bows *noun*
1 a long piece of wood with a string fastened at each end that is used to shoot arrows.
2 a knot with two loops.
3 a long, straight piece of wood with horsehair stretched along it and fastened at each end. A bow is used to play a musical instrument such as a violin.
▲ Rhymes with **no**.

different types of bow

bowl bowls *noun*
a deep, round dish for food or liquids.

bowl bowls bowling bowled *verb*
When you bowl, you roll a heavy ball down a long alley to knock over pins. **bowling** *noun, adjective*.

box boxes *noun*
a container, usually with a lid, that is used for packing or storing things.

box boxes boxing boxed *verb*
When people box, they fight with their fists as a sport called boxing.

boy boys *noun*
a male child.

brace braces *noun*
a piece of wire that a dentist can put over your teeth to make them straighter.

bracelet bracelets *noun*
a piece of jewelry that you wear around your wrist.

Braille *noun*
a form of writing made of patterns of raised dots that blind people can read by touching. *The Braille system is named after Louis Braille who invented it.*

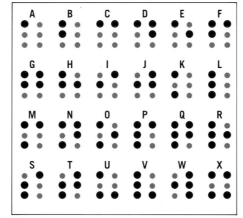

the Braille alphabet

brain brains *noun*
the part inside your head that you use to think and that controls all the parts of your body.

brake brakes *noun*
the part of a bicycle or car that you use to make it go slower or stop. ● A word that sounds like **brake** is **break**.

brake brakes braking braked *verb*
When you brake, you make a bicycle or car go slower or stop by using the brake. ● A word that sounds like **brake** is **break**.

branch branches *noun*
a part of a tree that grows out from the trunk. ▲ Rhymes with **ranch**.

brass *noun*
a yellow metal made from copper and another metal called zinc. *Trumpets and horns are made of brass.*

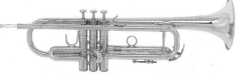

brave braver bravest *adjective*
If you are brave, you will do something frightening or dangerous without showing fear.

bread *noun*
a food made from flour and baked in an oven.

break breaks breaking broke broken *verb*
1 If you break something, you damage it so that it is in pieces or does not work anymore. *I think I've broken the CD player.* ◆ *He broke the dish.*
2 If you break a promise, you do not do what you promised you would.
3 If you break the law, you do something that is against the law.
● A word that sounds like **break** is **brake**.

break breaks *noun*
a short rest from work. *She's having a coffee break.* ● A word that sounds like **break** is **brake**.

breakfast breakfasts *noun*
the first meal of the day. *We have cereal every morning for breakfast.*

breast breasts *noun*
part of a woman's body that makes milk to feed her babies.

breath breaths *noun*
the air that goes in and out of your lungs through your nose or mouth when you breathe.

breathe breathes breathing breathed *verb*
When you breathe, you take air into your lungs through your nose or mouth and then let it out again.

breed breeds *noun*
one kind of an animal. *Spaniels and labradors are different breeds of dog.*

breed breeds breeding bred *verb*
1 If you breed animals, you keep them in order to produce young ones.
2 When animals breed, they produce young ones.

breeze breezes *noun*
a gentle wind.

A
B
C
D
E
F
G
H
I
J
K
L
M
N
O
P
Q
R
S
T
U
V
W
X
Y
Z

a b c d e f g h i j k l m n o p q r s t u v w x y z

brick bricks *noun*
a block made out of baked clay that is used for building houses and walls.

bride brides *noun*
a woman on her wedding day.

bridegroom bridegrooms *noun*
a man on his wedding day.

bridesmaid bridesmaids *noun*
a girl or young woman who accompanies the bride on her wedding day.

bridge bridges *noun*
something built over a river, railroad line, or road so that people and vehicles can travel from one side to the other.

cantilever bridge

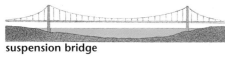
suspension bridge

arch bridge

cable-stayed bridge

brief briefer briefest *adjective*
Something that is brief lasts only a short time. *We had a brief visit.*

bright brighter brightest *adjective*
1 A bright light shines very strongly. ■ The opposite is **dim**.
2 Bright colors are clear and strong. ■ The opposite is **dull** or **dark**.
3 A bright person is smart. ■ The opposite is **stupid**.
▲ Rhymes with **kite**.
brightness *noun*.

brilliant *adjective*
1 A brilliant person is very smart.
2 Brilliant light is very bright.
3 very good. *It was a brilliant ice-skating performance.*

brim brims *noun*
1 If you fill a cup or glass to the brim, you fill it right up to the top.
2 the flat part that sticks out from the edge of a hat.

bristle bristles *noun*
1 a short, stiff hair on an animal.
2 Bristles are the stiff hairs fastened into the handle of a brush.

brittle *adjective*
If something is brittle, it is hard but easy to break. *Eggshells are brittle.*

broad broader broadest *adjective*
wide. *a broad street.* ■ The opposite is **narrow**.

broadcast broadcasts broadcasting broadcast *verb*
When a radio or TV program is broadcast, it is sent out so that you can hear it on the radio or see it on TV.

broke, broken past of **break**.

bronze *noun*
a brown metal made from a mixture of copper and tin.

brooch brooches *noun*
a piece of jewelry with a pin that you can fasten onto your clothes. ▲ Rhymes with **coach**.

brook brooks *noun*
a small stream.

broom brooms *noun*
a brush with a long handle for sweeping the floor.

brother
A person's brother is a boy or man who has the same mother and father.

brought past of **bring**. ▲ Rhymes with **caught**.

brow brows *noun*
1 a person's forehead.
2 the top of a hill.
▲ Rhymes with **cow**.

bruise bruises *noun*
a dark mark on your skin where something has hit it or you have fallen over and banged it. ▲ Say *brooz*.

brush brushes *noun*
a set of bristles fastened to a handle. You use different sizes and shapes of brushes for different jobs like painting, brushing your teeth, or sweeping the floor.

brush brushes brushing brushed *verb*
If you brush something, you clean it with a brush. *Don't forget to brush your hair.*

bubble bubbles *noun*
a little ball of air or gas that you get in soft drinks or boiling water.

bucket buckets *noun*
a large container with a handle used for carrying liquid.

buckle buckles *noun*
a fastening on a belt or strap. *My belt has a silver buckle.*

bud buds *noun*
a part of a plant that opens up to become a flower or a leaf.

Buddhist Buddhists *noun*
a person who follows a religion started by a religious teacher called Buddha. ▲ Say *buh-dist*.

buffalo buffalo or **buffaloes** *noun*
a wild member of the cattle family, with horns. The North American buffalo is called a bison.

bug bugs *noun*
1 an insect.
2 an illness such as a cold or flu.

build builds building built *verb*
When you build something, you make it by putting different parts together.

building buildings *noun*
a place that has walls and a roof like a house, a department store, or a school.

bulb bulbs *noun*
1 the thick, round root of a plant such as a daffodil or tulip that is under the ground, from which the plant grows.
2 the round glass part of a lamp or light.

bull bulls *noun*
the male of the cattle family. Male elephants and whales are also called bulls.

bulldozer bulldozers *noun*
a tractor with a wide blade in front of it that is used to move dirt or knock down buildings.

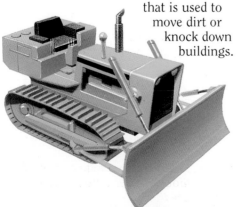

bullet bullets *noun*
a small piece of metal that is fired from a gun.

bully bullies *noun*
a person who hurts or frightens other, weaker people.

bump bumps bumping bumped *verb*
If you bump into something, you hit it by accident. *I wasn't looking where I was going, and I bumped into the wall.*

bump bumps *noun*
1 the sound that something makes when it hits something else. *She fell off the chair and landed on the floor with a loud bump.*
2 a round lump or swelling on a surface. *Dad has a bump on his head where he banged it on the ceiling.*
bumpy *adjective*.

bunch bunches *noun*
a group of things. *a bunch of flowers.* ◆ *a bunch of grapes.*

bundle bundles *noun*
a group of things tied together. *a bundle of sticks.*

bunk bunks *noun*
a small narrow bed.

bunkbeds *noun*
two beds, one above the other.

buoy buoys *noun*
a floating object fastened to the bottom of the sea or a river. A buoy shows a ship where it is dangerous to go. ▲ Say **boy** or **boo**-*ee*.

burglar burglars *noun*
a person who gets into a house or store to steal things.

burglary burglaries *noun*
getting into a house or store to steal things.

burn burns burning burned or **burnt** *verb*
1 If something is burning, it is on fire.
2 If you burn something, you damage it with fire or heat. *What's that smell? Have you burned the steak?*

burn burns *noun*
when fire or heat causes a sore place on your skin or a mark on something.

burrow burrows *noun*
a hole or tunnel under the ground where an animal lives. Prairie dogs live in burrows.

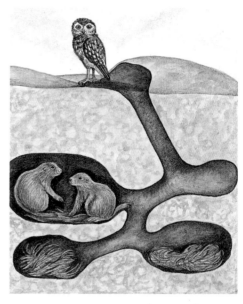

burst bursts bursting burst *verb*
When something bursts, it breaks open suddenly, especially because there is too much inside. *The little boy was crying because his balloon had burst.*

bury buries burying buried *verb*
When you bury something, you put it in a hole in the ground and cover it up. *Squirrels bury their nuts to store them for winter.* ▲ Say **bair**-*ee*.

bus buses *noun*
a large vehicle that carries a lot of passengers by road. *We ride the bus to school.*

bush bushes *noun*
1 a large plant like a small tree with a lot of branches.
2 The bush is a wild part of the countryside in Australia or Africa.

A B C D E F G H I J K L M N O P Q R S T U V W X Y Z

business businesses *noun*
1 the work of making, buying, or selling things. *The company does a lot of business with England.*
2 a company or store that makes or sells things. *a software business.*
▲ Say *biz-niss.*

busy busier busiest *adjective*
1 If you are busy, you have a lot to do.
2 A place that is busy is full of people doing things. *a busy supermarket.*
▲ Say *biz-ee.*

butcher butchers *noun*
a person whose job is to cut up meat.

butter *noun*
a yellow fat made from cream. You spread it on bread and use it in cooking.

butterfly butterflies *noun*
an insect with large white or colored wings and a thin body.

button buttons *noun*
1 a small disk for fastening clothes.
2 a small part that you press to make a machine work.

buy buys buying bought *verb*
to pay somebody money for something.
● A word that sounds like **buy** is **bye**.
▲ Rhymes with **pie**.

byte bytes *noun*
a unit of memory in a computer. One letter or one number takes up one byte.
● A word that sounds like **byte** is **bite**.

Peacock

Red Admiral

Painted Lady

Small Tortoiseshell

C c

cab cabs *noun*
1 a taxi.
2 the part of a truck, train, or bus where the driver sits.

cabbage cabbages *noun*
a large, round vegetable with green, white, or dark red leaves.
❖ *Look at page 24*

cabin cabins *noun*
1 a bedroom on a ship.
2 the part of a plane where the passengers sit.
3 a small house made of wood. *a log cabin in the woods.*

cable cables *noun*
1 a set of wires that carry electricity, television, or radio signals. *an underwater telephone cable.*
2 strong, thick wire or rope.

cable television cable televisions *noun*
a way of sending television programs using wires.

cactus cacti or cactuses *noun*
a plant with no leaves. Cacti are covered with sharp spikes. Cacti store water in their stems and grow in hot, dry places like deserts.

café cafés *noun*
a place where you can buy a drink and something to eat, and sit down to eat it.
▲ Say ka-*fay.*

cage cages *noun*
a box or room with metal bars for keeping animals or birds. *a hamster cage.*

cake cakes *noun*
a sweet food that you make by mixing flour, butter, eggs, and sugar, and baking it in the oven.

calculator calculators *noun*
a small machine for doing math quickly. You work a calculator by pressing buttons with numbers on them.

calendar calendars *noun*
a list of all the days, weeks, and months of one year.

calf calves *noun*
1 a young cow. Young elephants, whales, and seals are also called calves.
2 the thick part at the back of your leg, between your knee and your ankle.

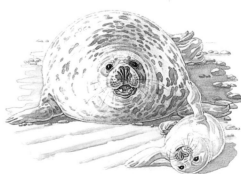

call calls calling called *verb*
1 If you call somebody, you shout. *"Dinner's ready," he called.*
2 If you call somebody something, you give that person a name. *She called the dog Spot.*
3 To telephone or go to see somebody. *Did anyone call when we were out?*
call *noun.*

calm calmer calmest *adjective*
1 quiet and not afraid. ■ The opposite is **nervous**.
2 If the sea is calm, there are no big waves on it.
▲ Say *kahm.*

camcorder camcorders *noun*
a camera that can take movies and record sound.

camel camels *noun*
an animal with one or two humps on its back. Camels are used to carry people and things in the desert because they can travel for a long time without water.

camera cameras *noun*
a machine for taking photographs or making movies.

camouflage camouflages camouflaging camouflaged *verb*
If somebody or something is camouflaged, you cannot see that one because it is the same color or shape as things around it. *Chameleons are lizards that change color and use camouflage for protection.* ▲ Say *kam-uh-flahj.*
camouflage *noun.*

a camouflaged gecko

camp camps *noun*
a place where people live or stay in tents or cabins on vacation.

camp camps camping camped *verb*
When you camp, you live in a tent or take a vacation in a tent.
go camping *We're going camping this summer.*

can cans *noun*
a metal container for food, drink, or paint. *a can of soda.*

canal canals *noun*
a long, narrow strip of water made for boats to travel along.

cancel cancels canceling canceled *verb*
If you cancel something that you have planned, you stop it from happening. *We canceled our trip because Mom was ill.*

cancer *noun*
a serious illness that makes some cells inside the body grow too fast.

candle candles *noun*
a stick made of wax with a string called a wick inside. You light the wick and the candle burns to give light.

candy candies *noun*
a sweet food that is made with sugar.

cane canes *noun*
1 the hard, hollow stem of some plants.
2 a long, thin stick.

cannon cannons *noun*
a big gun that fires heavy metal balls, or shells, that explode.

canoe canoes *noun*
a light, thin boat that you move with a paddle. ▲ Say *kun-oo.*

canopy canopies *noun*
1 a piece of material over a door or window that keeps the sun out.
2 a cover over something. *Tall trees form a canopy over the rain-forest floor.*

canvas canvases *noun*
strong material that is used for making sails, tents, or shoes.

canyon canyons *noun*
a deep, rocky valley. *The Colorado River flows through the Grand Canyon in northwestern Arizona.*

cap caps *noun*
1 a flat hat with a peak at the front.
2 the top of a jar, bottle, or pen.

cape capes *noun*
1 a piece of land that sticks out into the sea. *Cape Cod.*
2 a loose coat with no sleeves that you wrap around your shoulders.

capital capitals *noun*
1 the most important city in a country or state, where the government is. *Washington, D.C. is the capital of the United States. Springfield is the capital of Illinois.*
2 a big letter in the alphabet.

captain captains *noun*
1 the person in charge of a ship or an aircraft.
2 an officer in the army, navy, or air force.
3 the leader of a sports team.

capture captures capturing captured *verb*
If you capture an animal, you catch it and make sure it cannot escape. *The hunters captured the bear.*

A
B
C
D
E
F
G
H
I
J
K
L
M
N
O
P
Q
R
S
T
U
V
W
X
Y
Z

car cars *noun*
a machine with an engine and four wheels for traveling on the road. The driver uses the steering wheel to turn the car, and stops it by putting a foot on the brake.

caravan caravans *noun*
a group of people and animals, such as camels, that travel together. *Caravans in the desert use camels because they can travel long distances without needing water.*

carbohydrate carbohydrates *noun*
a substance in food that gives you energy.

card cards *noun*
1 a piece of stiff, thick paper with a picture and message on it. We send cards on birthdays and other special occasions. *My parents sent out over 100 cards at Christmas.*

2 one of a pack of 52 cards that you play games with.

cardboard *noun, adjective*
very thick paper. *a cardboard box.*

cardigan cardigans *noun*
a sweater with buttons down the front.

care cares caring cared *verb*
1 If you care about somebody or something, you think that one is important. *I don't care who wins.*
2 If you care for somebody or something, you look after that person or thing.

care *noun*
If you do something with care, you try not to make a mistake or break something. *Wash the glasses with care—they are very delicate.*

career careers *noun*
a job that you learn to do and then do for a long time. *a career in teaching.*

careful *adjective*
If you are careful, you think about what you are doing so that you do it safely and well. *Be careful when you cross the street.* ■ The opposite is **careless**. **carefully** *adverb*.

careless *adjective*
If you are careless, you make mistakes because you are not thinking about what you are doing. ■ The opposite is **careful**.

carnival carnivals *noun*
1 a special time when people dress up in colorful clothes and sing, dance, and play music as they move through the streets.

2 an outdoor entertainment where you can play games and go on rides. *At the carnival we rode the ferris wheel.*

carpenter carpenters *noun*
a person who makes or mends wooden things such as chairs, tables, or doors.

car pool car pools *noun*
a group of people who take turns driving to and from a place.

carriage carriages *noun*
an old-fashioned vehicle with wheels that is pulled by horses.

carrot carrots *noun*
a long, orange-colored vegetable that grows under the ground.

carry carries carrying carried *verb*
When you carry something, you pick it up and take it to another place. *Tom carried the books upstairs.*

cart carts *noun*
a wooden vehicle with two or four wheels that is pulled by an animal, such as a horse or pony.

carton cartons *noun*
1 a cardboard or plastic container for holding food or drink. *a milk carton.*
2 a box containing something.

cartoon cartoons *noun*
1 a movie that uses drawings instead of real people or animals.
2 a drawing in a newspaper or magazine that makes a joke.

cartwheel cartwheels *noun*
If you do a cartwheel, you put your hands on the ground and swing your

legs over sideways in a complete circle, ending up standing on your feet again.

carve carves carving carved *verb*
1 If you carve wood or stone, you cut it to make a shape out of it.
2 If you carve cooked meat, you cut it into slices.

case cases *noun*
1 a container such as a pencil case.
2 a crime that the police are trying to solve. *The detective was working on a murder case.*
3 a big box. *a case of sodas.*

cash *noun*
money in coins and paper bills.

cassette cassettes *noun*
a plastic box with magnetic tape inside it that you can use to record and play music and other sounds. You can record and play movies on a video cassette recorder (VCR).

cast casts *noun*
1 all the actors in a play or movie.
2 a hard plaster covering that holds a broken arm or leg in place while it is healing.

cast casts casting cast *verb*
1 If you cast something like a fishing line, you throw it.
2 If somebody in a story casts a spell, he or she uses magic to trick somebody. *The wicked witch cast a spell on the prince and changed him into a frog.*

castle castles *noun*
a large building with thick, high walls. Castles were built long ago to keep the people who lived inside them safe from their enemies.
❖ *Look at page 34.*

casual *adjective*
not fancy or formal. *We wore casual clothes to the picnic.*

casualty casualties *noun*
1 a person who is hurt or killed in an accident or a war. *There were three casualties in the traffic accident.*

cat cats *noun*
a furry mammal with sharp claws. Small cats are kept as pets. Big cats such as lions and tigers live in the wild.

catalog catalogs *noun*
1 a book listing all the things that a company or store sells.
2 a list of all the books or other things in a library.

catapult catapults *noun*
a big weapon that soldiers used to shoot heavy rocks at an enemy.

catch catches catching caught *verb*
1 If you catch a ball, you take hold of it when it is moving.

2 If you catch a person or an animal, you stop that one from running away.
3 If you catch a train or bus, you get on it.
4 If you catch an illness, you get it. *He caught a cold.*

caterpillar caterpillars *noun*
a small animal like a hairy worm that will turn into a moth or butterfly.

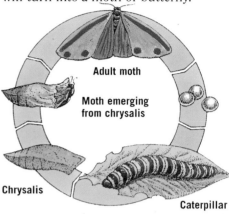

Adult moth

Moth emerging from chrysalis

Chrysalis

Caterpillar

cathedral cathedrals *noun*
a large, important church. *St. Patrick's Cathedral is in New York City.*

A B C D E F G H I J K L M N O P Q R S T U V W X Y Z

CATS

Japanese bobtails

Silver tabby

Maine coon cat

Red tabby

Black shorthair

Red Point Siamese

Egyptian maus

CASTLE

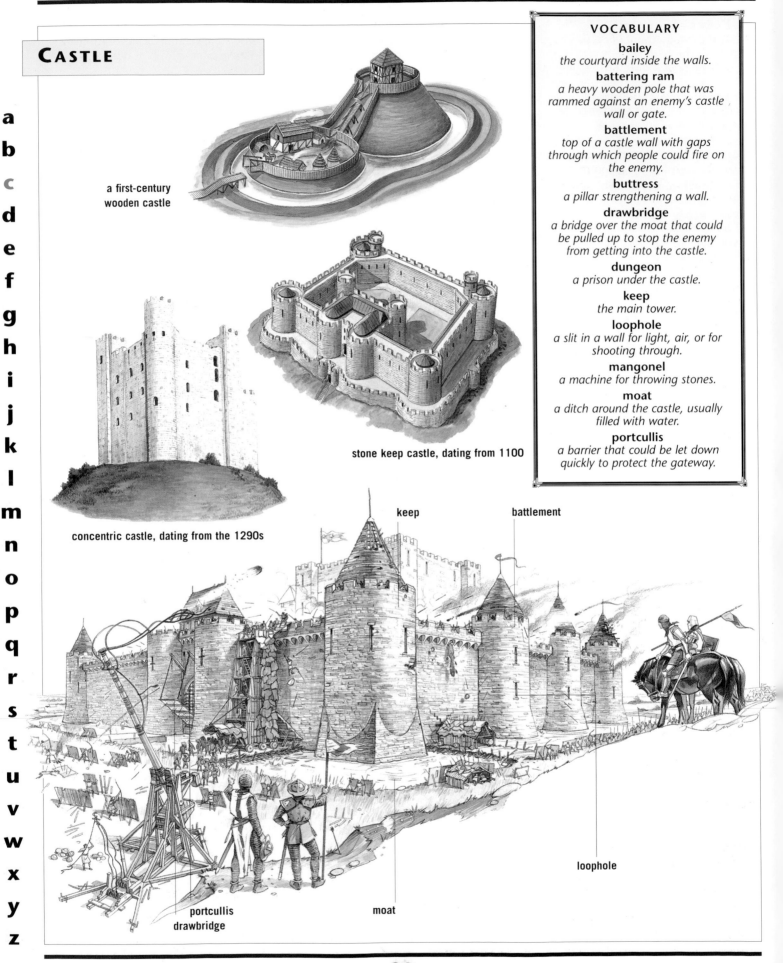

a first-century wooden castle

concentric castle, dating from the 1290s

stone keep castle, dating from 1100

keep

battlement

loophole

portcullis
drawbridge

moat

VOCABULARY

bailey
the courtyard inside the walls.

battering ram
a heavy wooden pole that was rammed against an enemy's castle wall or gate.

battlement
top of a castle wall with gaps through which people could fire on the enemy.

buttress
a pillar strengthening a wall.

drawbridge
a bridge over the moat that could be pulled up to stop the enemy from getting into the castle.

dungeon
a prison under the castle.

keep
the main tower.

loophole
a slit in a wall for light, air, or for shooting through.

mangonel
a machine for throwing stones.

moat
a ditch around the castle, usually filled with water.

portcullis
a barrier that could be let down quickly to protect the gateway.

cattle *noun*
cows and bulls. *a herd of cattle.*

caught past of **catch**.

cauliflower cauliflowers *noun*
a large, round, white vegetable with green leaves on the outside.

cause causes causing caused *verb*
If you cause something, you make it happen. *Keep your dog on a leash or you'll cause an accident.*

cautious *adjective*
If you are cautious, you are very careful because of danger.

cave caves *noun*
a big hole under the ground, or in the side of a mountain or cliff.

CD CDs *noun*
a flat, round piece of plastic that can store music or information. CD is short for **compact disc**.

CD-ROM CD-ROMs *noun*
a disk that you use with a computer or a television to show words and pictures. CD-ROM is short for **compact disc read-only memory**.

ceiling ceilings *noun*
the top part of a room over your head. *The light is hanging from the ceiling.*

celebrate celebrates celebrating celebrated *verb*
When you celebrate something, you do something that you enjoy at a special time. *Let's have a party to celebrate your birthday.*
celebration *noun*.

celery *noun*
a vegetable with a white or pale green stem that you can eat raw or cooked.

cell cells *noun*
1 one of the tiny parts that make up all animals and plants. The human body contains millions of red blood cells.

2 a small room in a prison or police station where people are locked up.
● A word that sounds like **cell** is **sell**.

cellar cellars *noun*
a room under a building where the furnace is.

cello cellos *noun*
a musical instrument like a big violin that you sit and hold between your knees. You play it by sliding a bow across the strings. ▲ Say **chel-lo**.

cement *noun*
a gray powder that becomes hard when you mix it with water and leave it to dry.

cemetery cemeteries *noun*
a place where dead people are buried.

cent cents *noun*
a coin in the U.S.A. A dollar equals 100 cents. ● A word that sounds like **cent** is **scent** or **sent**.

center centers *noun*
1 the middle of something. *The table was in the center of the room.*
2 a place where people go to do something special, such as a day-care or a shopping center.

centipede centipedes *noun*
a tiny animal like a worm but with many sets of legs.

central *adjective*
in the middle. *Central Dallas.*

century centuries *noun*
1 100 years.
2 The 20th century is the time between 1900 and the end of 1999.

cereal cereals *noun*
Cereals are plants such as rice and wheat that produce grain. We use the grain of cereal plants to make flour and bread. Breakfast cereals are made from grains such as rice and wheat. ● A word that sounds like **cereal** is **serial**.

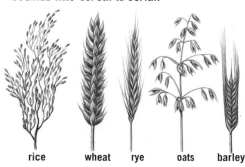

rice　wheat　rye　oats　barley

ceremony ceremonies *noun*
the actions and words that are used at a special and important event such as a wedding.

certain *adjective*
1 If you are certain about something, you are sure it is true. *I'm certain I saw him yesterday.*
2 If something happens at a certain time, it happens then and not at other times. *The swimming pool is open only at certain times.*

certificate certificates *noun*
an important piece of paper that shows that something is true. *I got a certificate for swimming 100 yards.*

chain chains *noun*
A chain is made from rings of metal joined together. *a bicycle chain.*

chair chairs *noun*
a seat with four legs and a back, for one person to sit on. ▲ Rhymes with *mare.*

chalk chalks *noun*
1 soft, white rock.
2 a soft white or colored stick used for writing on a blackboard.
▲ Say *chawk.*

challenge challenges challenging challenged *verb*
If you challenge somebody, you ask that person to try to do something better than you.

challenge challenges *noun*
If something is a challenge, it is difficult to do. *This math is a real challenge!*

champion champions *noun*
a person who is the best at a sport or game. *a world champion swimmer.*

A B C D E F G H I J K L M N O P Q R S T U V W X Y Z

chance chances *noun*
1 a time when you can do something. *It was their last chance to escape.*
2 If there is a chance that something will happen, it might happen. *There's a chance that it will rain today.*
by chance If something happens by chance, it happens without being planned.

change changes changing changed *verb*
1 When something changes, it becomes different. *Tadpoles change into frogs.*
2 If you change your clothes, you put on different ones. *Katie changed into her jeans.*

change changes *noun*
1 If there is a change in something, it is different now.
2 the money that you get back if you have paid too much for something.
3 coins like 5¢, 10¢, 25¢, and 50¢. *Do you have change for the phone?*

channel channels *noun*
1 a narrow part of a sea.
2 a television station. *Which channel is the program on?*

chapter chapters *noun*
a part of a book.

character characters *noun*
1 the way a person or thing is. *She has a kind and loving character.*
2 a person in a play, movie, or book.

charge charges charging charged *verb*
1 If somebody charges you a certain amount of money for something, he or she asks you to pay that amount. *He charged me 75¢ for the fruit.*
2 When the police charge somebody, they say that person has done something wrong.
3 If you charge at people or things, you run toward them very fast. *The bull charged at the fence.*
4 If you charge a battery, you pass an electric current through it to make it work.

charge charges *noun*
the money that you have to pay for something. *There is a charge of $5 to get into the museum.*
in charge If you are in charge, you are the leader of a group of people. *The principal is in charge of the school.*

chariot chariots *noun*
a vehicle with two wheels pulled by a horse. Chariots were used in wars, races, and hunting a long time ago.

charity charities *noun*
an organization that collects money to help people who need it.

chart charts *noun*
1 a drawing that shows important dates or numbers. *The chart shows how long different animals live.*
2 a map of the sea or the stars.

Animal lifespans

Turtle
Elephant
Chimpanzee
Lion
Dog
10 20 30 40 50 60 70 80 90 100
Numbers of years

charter charters chartering chartered *verb*
to hire an airplane or bus for a trip.

chase chases chasing chased *verb*
to run after someone and try to catch him or her.

cheap cheaper cheapest *adjective*
Something that is cheap does not cost a lot of money. ■ The opposite is **expensive**.

cheat cheats cheating cheated *verb*
If somebody cheats, he or she does something that is not fair, or that breaks the rules. *Play the game without cheating!*

check checks checking checked *verb*
When you check something, you look at it again to make sure that it is right. *Check your spellings in the dictionary.*
check *noun*
pattern of squares.

cheek cheeks *noun*
Your cheeks are the soft parts on each side of your face.

cheerful *adjective*
If you are cheerful, you feel happy. **cheerfully** *adverb*.

cheese cheeses *noun*
a white or yellow food made from milk.

cheetah cheetahs *noun*
a large, wild cat that can run very fast.

chef chefs *noun*
a person who cooks food in a restaurant. ▲ Say **sheff**.

chemical chemicals *noun*
a substance that is made by chemistry or used in chemistry.

chemical *adjective*

chemist chemists *noun*
a scientist who works with chemicals.

chemistry *noun*
the scientific study of what substances are made of and how they work together.

chemotherapy chemotherapies *noun*
Doctors treat people who have cancer with chemicals to kill the cancer cells. This is chemotherapy. We also call it "chemo."

cherry cherries *noun*
a small, round, red, yellow, or black fruit. Cherries have a small, smooth, hard seed in the middle.

chess *noun*
a game that two people play using 16 pieces each on a board with black and white squares. An expert in chess is called a "grand master."

chest chests *noun*
1 Your chest is the front part of your body between your neck and your waist.
2 a big, strong box with a lid. *The pirates stored gold in a wooden chest.*

chew chews chewing chewed *verb*
When you chew food, you use your teeth to make it soft and to break it into smaller pieces.

chicano chicanos *noun*
an American who was either born in Mexico or who has ancestors who came from Mexico.

chicken chickens *noun*
a bird that people keep on farms for its eggs and meat.

chickenpox *noun*
an illness that gives you lots of itchy spots.

chief chiefs *noun*
the leader of a group of people.

child children *noun*
1 a young boy or girl.
2 a son or daughter. *They have two children.*

childish *adjective*
If you are childish, you are being silly and acting younger than your age.

chili chilies *noun*
a small, red or green vegetable. Chilies have a very hot taste.

chilly chillier chilliest *adjective*
If you are chilly, you feel quite cold. *The cold wind made me chilly.*

chime chimes chiming chimed *verb*
When a bell or a clock chimes, it makes a ringing sound. *The clock chimed midnight.*

chimney chimneys *noun*
a large pipe above a fire or fireplace that lets smoke and gas go outside into the air.

chimpanzee chimpanzees *noun*
a small African ape. Chimpanzees are very intelligent animals.

chin chins *noun*
Your chin is the part of your face below your mouth.

china *noun*
a kind of white clay made into things such as cups and plates. It breaks easily.

chip chips *noun*
1 a very thin piece of fried, dried potato.
2 a tiny piece of a material called silicon that has an electronic circuit on it. Chips are used in computers.
3 a small piece that has broken off something, or the gap that is left. *This plate has a small chip in it.*

chip chips chipping chipped *verb*
If you chip something, you accidentally break a small part off. *a chipped plate.*

chipmunk chipmunks *noun*
a furry little animal with a stripe down its back. It looks a little like a squirrel.

chocolate chocolates *noun*
1 sweet, brown food made from cocoa.
2 a candy made of chocolate. *a box of chocolates.*

choice choices *noun*
1 all the things you can choose from. *There's a wide choice of books in the library.*
2 a person or thing that you choose. *Macaroni is my first choice for lunch.*

choir choirs *noun*
a group of singers, especially in a church. ▲ Say *kwire.*

choke chokes choking choked *verb*
If you choke, you cannot breathe because something is blocking your throat. *Tom choked on a fish bone.*

choose chooses choosing chose chosen *verb*
When you choose something, you take it because it is the thing you want.

chop chops chopping chopped *verb*
If you chop something, you cut it with a knife or an ax. *Ricky is chopping carrots with his mother.*

chord chords *noun*
a group of notes that you play at the same time in a piece of music. ▲ Say *kord.* ● A word that sounds like **chord** is **cord**.

chorus choruses *noun*
1 the part of a song that you repeat at the end of each verse.
2 a group of singers.
▲ Say *kor-uss.*

chose, chosen past of **choose**.

Christian Christians *noun*
a person who believes in and follows the teachings of Jesus Christ. *a Christian country.*
Christianity *noun*.

chrysalis chrysalides *noun*
a moth or a butterfly at the stage between a caterpillar and an adult, when it has a hard case around it. ▲ Say *kriss-e-liss.*

chuckle chuckles chuckling chuckled *verb*
When you chuckle, you laugh quietly to yourself.

church churches *noun*
a building where Christians hold religious services.

A B C D E F G H I J K L M N O P Q R S T U V W X Y Z

a b c d e f g h i j k l m n o p q r s t u v w x y z

circle **circles** *noun*
1 a flat, round shape like a ring.
2 a group of people who are interested in the same things.
circle *verb*
The plane circled the airport.

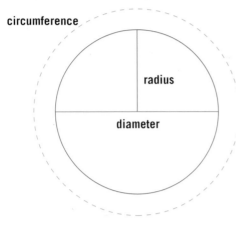
circumference
radius
diameter

circuit **circuits** *noun*
1 a complete path that an electric current can flow around.
2 a route that a judge travels to run court trials in a number of places.

circular *adjective*
round like a circle. *a circular table.*

circulation *noun*
the movement of blood around the body. Blood is pumped by the heart and travels in arteries and veins.

circumference **circumferences** *noun*
the distance around the edge of a circle.

circus **circuses** *noun*
a traveling show with people such as acrobats and clowns. A circus is held in a big, round tent.

city **cities** *noun*
a big and important town.

civilization **civilizations** *noun*
1 the way people live in a certain place and at a certain time. *We're learning about civilization in ancient Greece.*
2 living in a group with lots of laws and certain ways of doing things, not living wild in a forest.

claim **claims claiming claimed** *verb*
1 If you claim something, you say it is yours. *Nobody has claimed the watch I found.*
2 If you claim that something is true, you say it is true. *She claimed that the dog had eaten her homework.*

clap **claps clapping clapped** *verb*
When you clap, you hit your hands together to make a noise. You clap to show you have enjoyed something.

clash **clashes clashing clashed** *verb*
1 When metal objects clash, they hit together making a loud, banging sound. *Cymbals clash.*
2 If colors clash, they do not look good together. *Do you think red and orange clash?*

class **classes** *noun*
1 a group of people who learn together. *Sam and I are in the same class at school.*
2 a group of people, animals, or things that are the same in some way.

classical *adjective*
in a style that has been used for a long time because people think it is good. *classical music of the 19th century.*

classroom **classrooms** *noun*
a room in a school where you have lessons.

claw **claws** *noun*
the long, sharp nails that an animal or bird has on its feet.

clay *noun*
sticky red or gray earth that becomes hard when it is dry. Clay is used to make pots and bricks.

clean **cleaner cleanest** *adjective*
having no dirt or marks on it. ■ *The opposite is* **dirty** *or* **soiled**.

clean **cleans cleaning cleaned** *verb*
to make it clean. *You clean your teeth by brushing them.* ■ The opposite is **dirty**.

clear **clearer clearest** *adjective*
1 easy to see, hear, or understand. *a clear photograph.*
2 easy to see through.
3 free from things that are blocking the way or covering something. *A clear sky does not have any clouds.*

clear **clears clearing cleared** *verb*
When you clear something, you take away things that you do not want or need. *We cleared the snow from the driveway.*

clever **cleverer cleverest** *adjective*
A person who is clever can learn and understand things quickly.

cliff **cliffs** *noun*
the high, steep land, often by the sea or along a river.

climate **climates** *noun*
the kind of weather that a place usually has. *India has a hot climate.*

climb climbs climbing climbed *verb*
When you climb something, you move up using your hands and feet. *Ella is climbing up Louis's back.*
climber *noun*.

cling clings clinging clung *verb*
If you cling to somebody or something, you hold on tightly. *He clung to the rope because he was afraid he was going to fall.*

clinic clinics *noun*
a place where you go to see a doctor.

clip clips *noun*
a small metal or plastic object used for holding things together. *a paper clip.*

clip clips clipping clipped *verb*
If you clip something, such as a hedge or your fingernails, you cut small pieces off to make it neater.

cloak cloaks *noun*
a long, loose coat with no sleeves.

clock clocks *noun*
a machine that tells you the time.

clockwise *adjective, adverb*
If you turn clockwise, you move in the same direction as the hands on a clock. ■ The opposite is **counterclockwise**.

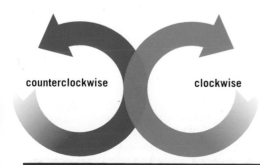

counterclockwise   clockwise

Spelling tip:
Some words that begin with a "co" sound are spelled with a "ko," for example koala.

close closes closing closed *verb*
When you close something, you shut it. *He closed the drawer quietly.* ▲ Rhymes with **nose**. ■ The opposite is **open**.

close closer closest *adjective*
1 near. *Our house is close to the train station.*
2 If you are close to someone, you like them very much. *Richard and Ray are close friends.* ▲ Rhymes with **dose**.

cloth cloths *noun*
1 material made from something such as cotton or wool, that we use to make clothes and other things.
2 a piece of material used for cleaning. *She wiped the table with a cloth.*

clothes *noun*
Clothes are things that you wear, such as jeans, skirts, shirts and blouses, and sweaters and coats.

cloud clouds *noun*
Clouds are made of millions of drops of water which sometimes fall as rain. On a cloudy day, the sky is full of white or gray clouds.

clown clowns *noun*
a person in a circus who wears funny clothes and makes people laugh.

club clubs *noun*
a group of people who meet to do something that they are all interested in. *a swimming club.* ◆ *a chess club.*

clue clues *noun*
something that helps you to find the answer to a puzzle or a mystery. *I can't guess who it is. Give me a clue.*

clump clumps *noun*
a group of plants growing together. *a clump of grass.*

clumsy clumsier clumsiest *adjective*
If somebody is clumsy, the person often falls over and drop things.
clumsily *adverb*.

clung past of cling.

clutch clutches clutching clutched *verb*
If you clutch something, you hold it tightly. *The child clutched her mother's hand.*

clutch clutches *noun*
the pedal in a car or other vehicle that you press when you switch gears.

coach coaches *noun*
1 a railroad car where passengers sit.
2 a large carriage that is pulled along by horses.
3 a person who teaches people a sport. *a tennis coach.*

coal *noun*
a hard, black substance that is dug out of the ground and burned to give heat. Coal is made from the remains of plants that died and were buried millions of years ago.

coast coasts *noun*
the part of the land that is next to the sea.

coat coats *noun*
1 You wear a coat on top of your other clothes to go outdoors when the weather is cold.
2 The fur that an animal has is called a coat. *A leopard has a spotted coat, a tiger has a striped one.*

cobweb cobwebs *noun*
a net of silky threads that a spider makes to catch insects. *The cobwebs were everywhere in the deserted house.*

cock cocks *noun*
1 a male bird.
2 a rooster.

cockpit cockpits *noun*
the front part of a plane where the pilot sits. The part of a racing car where the driver sits is also called a cockpit.

cocoa *noun*
1 a brown powder made from the beans of the cacao tree and used to make chocolate.
2 a drink made from cocoa powder mixed with hot milk or water.

coconut coconuts *noun*
a large, round fruit with a hard, hairy brown shell. Inside there is a milky juice and sweet, white "meat" you can eat. Coconuts grow on palm trees in hot countries.

coconut shell and flesh

cocoon cocoons *noun*
a bundle of silky threads that some young insects make to cover themselves while they are developing into adults.

cod cod *noun*
a large sea fish that you can eat.

code codes *noun*
1 If you write something in code, you mix up the letters or change them into special signs. Only the people who know the code can read the message.
2 a group of letters or numbers that give information about something. *The zip code for this area of Virginia is 24523–1403.*
3 a collection of laws or rules. *the criminal code.*

coffee *noun*
1 a brown powder made from the roasted and ground beans of the coffee tree. You use coffee to make drinks.
2 a hot drink you make by mixing ground coffee beans with hot water.

coffin coffins *noun*
a box in which a dead person is buried.

cog cogs *noun*
1 a wheel with teeth around the edge. Cogs are used in machines to turn other things.
2 The teeth around the edge of the wheel are also called cogs.

coil coils *noun*
a thing that is twisted around into circles. *a coil of rope.*
coil *verb*. *The snake coiled around the branch.*

coin coins *noun*
a flat, usually round piece of metal that we use as money.

coincidence coincidences *noun*
A coincidence is when two things happen at the same time or in the same place by chance. ▲ Say *koh-in-si-denss*.

cold colder coldest *adjective*
1 not hot or warm. Ice and snow are cold.
2 unfriendly. *He gave me a cold look.*

cold colds *noun*
an illness that makes you sneeze and cough. *Lucy caught a cold.*

collage collages *noun*
a picture that you make by sticking lots of bits of material or paper onto a surface. ▲ Say *kul-lazh*.

collapse collapses collapsing collapsed *verb*
1 If something collapses, it falls down suddenly. *The tent collapsed.*
2 If somebody collapses, he or she falls over because of illness. *She collapsed in the street.*

collar collars *noun*
1 the part of a shirt or coat that goes around your neck.
2 a band that you put around the neck of a pet dog or cat.

collect collects collecting collected *verb*
1 When you collect things, you bring them together. *Please collect the bags and take them to the car.*
2 If you collect things such as stamps, you keep a lot of them because you like them. *I collect shells.*
collection *noun*
a stamp collection.

college colleges *noun*
a place where people go to study when they graduate from high school.

collide collides colliding collided *verb*
If something collides with another thing, it crashes into it. *The bus collided with a truck.*
collision *noun*.

colony colonies *noun*
a group of people who go to and settle in a land.

color colors *noun*
Red, blue, yellow, and green are colors.
colorful *adjective*. ❖ *Look at page 145*

column columns *noun*
1 a tall piece of stone that holds up part of a building or stands on its own.
2 a long, thin strip of writing in a book or newspaper.

Books sell more than games again

Champions! At last!

coma comas *noun*
If somebody is in a coma, he or she is in a very deep sleep and cannot wake up for a long time. People who have had a serious accident sometimes go into a coma.

a b c d e f g h i j k l m n o p q r s t u v w x y z

comb combs *noun*
a flat piece of metal or plastic with teeth along one edge. You use it to make your hair neat. ▲ Rhymes with **home**.
comb *verb*.

combine combines combining combined *verb*
When you combine things, you join or mix them together.
combination *noun*.

combine harvester combine harvesters *noun*
a large machine that is used on a farm. It cuts, separates, and cleans grain.

comedy comedies *noun*
a funny play, movie, or TV program.

comet comets *noun*
a thing in space that looks like a star with a tail and moves around the Sun.

comfortable *adjective*
If something is comfortable, it is nice to wear, sit in, or lie on. *a comfortable bed.*
comfortably *adverb*.

comic comics *noun*
1 a magazine that tells stories in pictures.
2 a person who tells jokes and makes people laugh.

comma commas *noun*
a mark (,) that you use in writing. You put commas between words in a list. *Katie, Tom, Lucy, and I went to the park.*

command commands commanding commanded *verb*
If somebody commands you to do something, he or she tells you that you have to do it. *The general commanded the soldiers to march.*

comment comments *noun*
If you make a comment, you say what you think about something.

common *adjective*
1 If a thing is common, it exists in large numbers. *Robins and sparrows are common birds.*
2 Something that happens often is common. *These days it is common for people to have computers at home.*
■ The opposite is **rare**.

communicate communicates communicating communicated *verb*
If you communicate with somebody, you talk or write to him or her. *Pilots communicate with the airport by radio.*

communications *noun*
Communications are ways of sending information to people, or ways of moving from one place to another. Roads, railroads, and telephones are communications.

compact disc compact discs *noun*
a flat, round piece of plastic that can store music or information. Also known as a **CD**.

company companies *noun*
1 a group of people who work together to make or sell something.
2 being with others so that you are not alone. *My grandmother lives alone, but she has a cat for company.*

compare compares comparing compared *verb*
When you compare two things, you look at them both together so that you can see in what ways they are the same or different. *When you have finished the test, compare your answers with the ones in the back of the book.*
comparison *noun*.

compartment compartments *noun*
1 a space with walls. *a baggage compartment.*
2 a part of a container. *My bag has a separate compartment for my pencil case.*

compass compasses *noun*
1 a compass helps hikers and sailors tell which direction they are going in. It has a magnetic needle that always points north.

North
West | East
South

2 a tool that you use for drawing circles. One arm has a sharp point and the other holds a pencil. You hold the pointed arm still and move the other around it.

competition competitions *noun*
a game or test that people try to win. *Sophie won first prize in the skating competition.*

complain complains complaining complained *verb*
If you complain about something, you say that you are not happy about it or that it makes you angry. *He complained about having to clean his room.*
complaint *noun*.

complete *adjective*
1 If something is complete, it has no parts missing. *a complete pack of cards.*
2 in every way. *a complete surprise.*
completely *adverb*, **complete** *verb*.

complicated *adjective*
If something is complicated, it is difficult to do or understand. *The story had a very complicated plot.*

compliment compliments *noun*
If somebody pays you a compliment, he or she says something nice about you.

compose composes composing composed *verb*
To compose means to write music or poetry. *Beethoven composed nine symphonies.*
composer *noun*.

computer computers *noun*
a machine that can solve problems quickly, store information, or control other machines. *Mom uses the computer to design new buildings.*
compute computes computing *verb*.

A B C D E F G H I J K L M N O P Q R S T U V W X Y Z

a b c d e f g h i j k l m n o p q r s t u v w x y z

conceal conceals concealing concealed *verb*
If you conceal something, you hide it. *She concealed the box under her bed.*

concerned *adjective*
If you are concerned about something, you worry about it.

concert concerts *noun*
a performance of music to a big group of people.

conclusion conclusions *noun*
1 the end of something. *The story had a sad conclusion.*
2 If you come to a conclusion about something, you decide what happened and why it happened. *We came to the conclusion that she went home because she was sick.*

concrete *noun*
a building material made from cement, sand, and small stones mixed with water that gets hard when it dries.

condition conditions *noun*
1 how somebody or something is. *The car is old, but it's still in good condition.*
2 how things are around you. *The animals in the zoo lived in good conditions.*
3 something that you must do before you are allowed to do something else. *You may go out on condition that you clean your room first.*

condor condors *noun*
a big bird that lives in the Andes mountains and western North America. It is the biggest flying bird in the world.

conductor conductors *noun*
a person who stands in front of a group of musicians and controls how they play a piece of music.

cone cones *noun*
1 a solid shape that is pointed at the top and rounded at the bottom.
2 the hard fruit of a pine or fir tree.

confess confesses confessing confessed *verb*
If you confess something, you say that you have done something wrong. *Luke confessed that he had broken the fence.* **confession** *noun*.

confidence *noun*
the feeling that you can do something well. *She climbed the tree with confidence.*
confident *adjective*, **confidently** *adverb*.

confuse confuses confusing confused *verb*
1 If you confuse people, you mix up their ideas so that they cannot understand. *My sister tried to explain the rules of the game to me but she spoke too quickly and I got confused.*
2 If you confuse two things, you mix them up so that you cannot tell the difference between them. *I always confuse the words "there" and "their" because they sound the same.*
confusing *adjective*, **confusion** *noun*.

congratulate congratulates congratulating congratulated *verb*
When you congratulate people, you tell them that you are pleased about something they have done. *I congratulated Lucy on passing her arithmetic test.*
congratulations *noun*.

Congress *noun*
the two groups, the U.S. Senate and House of Representatives, that make laws in Washington D.C.

conjunction conjunctions *noun*
a word that joins words or groups of words in a sentence. "And," "but," "if," and "yet" are conjunctions.

conjurer conjurers *noun*
a person who does magic tricks to entertain people at a show.

connect connects connecting connected *verb*
To connect things is to join them. *They are connecting parts of a toy.* **connection** *noun*.

conquer conquers conquering conquered *verb*
If an army conquers its enemies, it wins the war and takes control of them. **conqueror** *noun*.

conscience consciences *noun*
Your conscience is a feeling inside you that tells you about right and wrong. *Natalie didn't steal any candy; she has a clear conscience.* ▲ Say *kon-shunss*.

conscious *adjective*
If you are conscious, you are awake and you know what is happening around you. ▲ Say *kon-shuss*. ■ The opposite is **unconscious**.

consider considers considering considered *verb*
When you consider something, you think carefully about it. *We must consider what to do next.*

considerate *adjective*
If you are considerate, you think about other people's feelings and you are not selfish.

consist consists consisting consisted *verb*
If something consists of different things, it is made up of those things.

consonant consonants *noun*
any letter except *a, e, i, o* or *u*, and sometimes *y*, which are vowels.

Constitution *noun*
a paper that lists the basic laws and rules of the U.S.A.

construct constructs constructing constructed *verb*
If you construct something, you build or put it together. *Tara is constructing a tractor.*

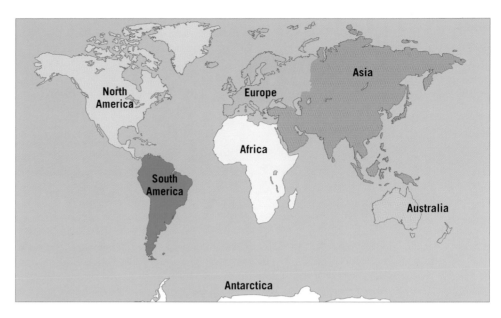

contact contacts contacting contacted *verb*
If you contact somebody, you write or telephone that person.

contact *noun*
If two things make contact, they touch each other. *The spaceship made contact with the Moon.*

contain contains containing contained *verb*
To contain something is to have something inside. *This can contains coffee.*

container containers *noun*
A container is something that you put things in. Boxes, bottles, and cans are containers.

content *adjective*
If you are content, you feel happy. ▲ Say kon-**tent**.

contents *noun*
The contents of something are all the things inside. *Joanne dropped her bag, and all the contents fell out onto the floor.* ▲ Say kon-**tents**.

contest contests *noun*
a competition or game that people try to win. *a judo contest.*

continent continents *noun*
one of the seven big pieces of land in the world. The continents are: Africa, Asia, Europe, North America, South America, Australia, and Antarctica.

continue continues continuing continued *verb*
When you continue doing something, you keep on doing it. *We continued playing outside until it got dark.*

contract contracts *noun*
a written agreement between two people or groups.

control *noun*
If you have control over somebody or something, you can make that person or thing do what you want. *You should have more control over your dog and not let it run into the road.*
control *verb*.

convenient *adjective*
If something is convenient, it is easy to do or use. *The theater is very convenient; it is just around the corner.* ■ The opposite is **inconvenient**.

conversation conversations *noun*
If you have a conversation with others, you talk to them. *Hank and Toby are having a conversation.*

convince convinces convincing convinced *verb*
to make somebody believe something.

cook cooks cooking cooked *verb*
When you cook food, you prepare and heat it, ready to eat.

cook cooks *noun*
a person who prepares and cooks food.

cookie cookies *noun*
a small, round, sweet cake. *I helped my mother to bake four dozen chocolate chip cookies.*

cool cooler coolest *adjective*
If something like water or the weather is cool, it is cold, but not very cold. ■ The opposite is **warm**.

cool cools cooling cooled *verb*
When something cools, it becomes colder. *Take the cake out of the oven and leave it to cool.*

copper *noun*
a reddish-brown metal that is dug out of the ground. Copper wire is used to carry electricity.

copy copies copying copied *verb*
1 If you copy others, you try to do the same things or look the same as them. *Lucy copied her sister's way of talking.*
2 If you copy something, you write or draw something that is exactly the same as another thing. *The teacher asked us to copy the examples from the blackboard.*

A B C D E F G H I J K L M N O P Q R S T U V W X Y Z

a b c d e f g h i j k l m n o p q r s t u v w x y z

copy copies *noun*
a thing that is made to look exactly the same as another thing.

coral *noun*
Coral is found in shallow seawater, near the shore. It is the skeletons of tiny creatures that are left when they have died. Most coral is pink, white, or red.

cord cords *noun*
strong, thick string. ● A word that sounds like **cord** is **chord**.

core cores *noun*
1 the middle part of some kinds of fruit that has seeds inside it. *an apple core.*
2 the center of the Earth. *The Earth's core is very hot.*

corn *noun*
a tall green plant that has ears, or corncobs. The yellow or white grains on the ears, called "kernels," are used for food. *I love corn on the cob with butter.*

corner corners *noun*
the place where two walls, roads, or edges meet.

corral corrals *noun*
an area with a fence around it that is used for horses, cattle, and sheep. **corral** *verb.*

correct *adjective*
If something is correct, it is right and there are no mistakes. *Are all your spellings correct?* **correction** *noun.*

corridor corridors *noun*
a long, narrow space inside a building such as a hotel, with rooms opening on each side of it.

cost costs *noun*
the amount of money that you must pay to buy something. *The cost of the tickets was $6.00 each.*

cost costs costing cost *verb*
If something costs $5, you have to pay $5 to buy it. *How much did it cost?*

costume costumes *noun*
the clothes that actors wear or that people wear at special times. *We all wore costumes to the party.*

cot cots *noun*
a small narrow bed. *We slept on cots last summer while we were camping.*

cottage cottages *noun*
a small house in the country.

cotton *noun*
material that is made by weaving the soft white fibers of the cotton plant.

cough coughs coughing coughed *verb*
When you cough, you make a sudden loud noise in your throat. *The smoke made me cough.*
cough *noun*
I've got a bad cough.
▲ Say **koff**.

council councils *noun*
a group of people who are chosen to plan and decide things for other people.

count counts counting counted *verb*
1 When you count, you say numbers one after another in the right order. *I can count from one to a million!*
2 to add things up to find out how many there are. *Can you count the spoons and see if we have enough?*

counter counters *noun*
1 a long, high table in a store or bank between the people who work there and the people who want to buy things.
2 a small, round piece of plastic that you use in some games.

counterclockwise *adjective, adverb*
if you turn counterclockwise, you move in the opposite direction as the hands on a clock. ■ The opposite is **clockwise**.

countertop *noun*
a counter used as a work surface in a kitchen.

country countries *noun*
1 an area of land in the world with its own people and government. *France, Spain, and Japan are countries.*
2 the land outside towns and cities.

country and western *noun*
country music.

county counties *noun*
one of the parts of a U.S. state that can make some rules for the people who live in it. *Broward county, Florida.*

couple couples *noun*
1 two people who are together.
2 two things. *a couple of oranges.*

courage *noun*
If you show courage, you are brave. **courageous** *adjective.*

course courses *noun*
1 an area of ground used for some games and sports. *People play golf on a golf course.*
2 a set of lessons that you have when you learn something new. *I'm taking a course in Italian.*
3 one of the parts of a meal. *We had chicken for the main course.*

court courts *noun*
1 a place where a group of people, called a jury, and a judge, decide if a person has done something wrong and what the punishment should be.
2 a piece of ground where you can play a certain sport. *a tennis court.*
3 a place where a king or queen lives.

courtyard courtyard *noun*
an area surrounded by walls.

cousin cousins *noun*
Your cousin is the child of your aunt or uncle.

cover covers *noun*
1 a thing that you put over another thing. *She got into bed and pulled the covers over her head.*
2 the outside of a book or magazine.

cover covers covering covered *verb*
1 to put something over something else to hide it or keep it warm.
2 When something covers another thing, it is all over it. *Snow covered the grass.*

cow cows *noun*
a big female farm animal that gives us milk. Female whales, seals, and elephants are also called cows. ▲ Rhymes with **now** and **brow**.

coward cowards *noun*
a person who is easily frightened.

cowboy
cowboys
cowgirl
cowgirls *noun*

a person whose job is to look after cattle.

cozy cozier coziest *adjective*
If a place is cozy, it is warm and comfortable. *Birds build nests that are cozy for their eggs.*

crab crabs *noun*
a sea animal with a flat, hard shell, and ten legs. The two front legs have big claws called pincers on the end.

crack cracks *noun*
1 a thin line on something where it has nearly broken. *This cup has a tiny crack in it.*
2 a sudden loud noise. *a crack of thunder.*

crack cracks cracking cracked *verb*
If something cracks, it has a thin split in it, but it does not break into pieces. *Hot water will crack the glasses.*

cracker crackers *noun*
a thin, dry, crisp biscuit.

cradle cradles *noun*
a small wooden bed for a baby, it usually rocks.

craft crafts *noun*
work or a hobby where you make things with your hands. Pottery and wood carving are crafts.

crane cranes *noun*
1 a tall machine that lifts and moves heavy things.

2 a large waterbird with a long neck and long legs.

crash crashes *noun*
1 an accident when something that is moving hits another thing.
2 a loud noise like the sound of thunder. *There was a loud crash as he dropped the plates on the floor.*

crash crashes crashing crashed *verb*
When something crashes, it hits another thing very hard and makes a loud noise.

crate crates *noun*
a wooden or plastic box for carrying things in. *a crate of bananas.*

crater craters *noun*
1 a huge hole in the ground that is made by something like a bomb or meteor landing on it.
2 the hole at the top of a volcano where fire and hot, liquid rock called lava comes out.

crawl crawls crawling crawled *verb*
When a baby crawls, it moves slowly along the ground on its hands and knees. When an insect crawls, it moves with its body close to the ground.

The baby is crawling across the floor.

crayon crayons *noun*
a colored pencil or wax stick that you draw with.

creak creaks creaking creaked *verb*
If something like a door creaks, it makes a strange squeaking sound. *The old floor creaked.*

cream *noun*
the thick, pale yellow liquid that is a part of milk. It contains a lot of fat.

crease creases creasing creased *verb*
If you crease something, you put lots of lines in it by crushing it, or not folding it carefully. *If you sit on your coat you will crease it.*

create creates creating created *verb*
If you create something, you make something new.
creator *noun*, **creation** *noun*.

A B C D E F G H I J K L M N O P Q R S T U V W X Y Z

creature creatures *noun*
any animal. *Elephants are very big creatures.*

creep creeps creeping crept *verb*
If something creeps along, it moves slowly and quietly. *The cat crept toward the bird.*

crescent crescents *noun*
the curved shape of a new Moon.

crew crews *noun*
all the people who work on a ship or an airplane.

cricket *noun*
1 an insect like a grasshopper with wings and long legs that can jump high.
2 a British game played by two teams of 11 players with bats and a ball.

cried past of **cry.**

crime crimes *noun*
something that is against the law. *Murder is a crime.*

criminal criminals *noun*
a person who does something that is against the law.

crisp crisper crispest *adjective*
If something like a cracker is crisp, it is hard, crunchy, and easy to break.

criticize criticizes criticizing criticized *verb*
If somebody criticizes you, that person says you have done something badly or wrong. ■ The opposite is **praise.**

croak croaks croaking croaked *verb*
To croak is to make a deep rough sound like a frog makes. *"I've got a sore throat," she croaked.*

crocodile crocodiles *noun*
a large reptile with a long body and sharp teeth. Crocodiles live in rivers in some hot countries.
◆ See below.

crocus crocuses *noun*
a tiny plant with bright red, purple, yellow, or white flowers. It blooms in spring or fall.

crooked *adjective*
not straight. *a crooked path through the trees.* ▲ Say *krook-id.*

crops *noun*
Crops are plants that farmers grow as food. Wheat, rice, and oats all are crops.

cross crosses *noun*
a mark like this **+** or this **x**.

cross crosses crossing crossed *verb*
When you cross something such as a road or a river, you go from one side to the other.

cross crosser crossest *adjective*
If you are cross, you are angry about something.

crouch crouches crouching crouched *verb*
When you crouch, you bend your knees so that your body is close to the ground. *Hank crouched to look at the plant.*

crow crows *noun*
a big, black bird that makes a loud noise.

crow crows crowing crowed *verb*
To crow means to make a noise like a rooster makes in the early morning.

crowd crowds *noun*
a lot of people together in one place. *There was a huge crowd at the football game.*

crowded *adjective*
If a place is crowded, it is full of people. *The swimming pool gets very crowded in hot weather.*

crown crowns *noun*
a ring of precious metal and jewels that kings and queens wear on their heads.

cruel crueler cruelest *adjective*
A person who is cruel hurts people or animals on purpose.

cruise cruises *noun*
If you go on a cruise, you have a vacation on a ship that stops at lots of different places.

crumb crumbs *noun*
a tiny piece of bread, cake, or cookie.

crunch crunches crunching crunched *verb*
If you crunch something hard and firm like a cracker, you make a loud noise when you eat it. *She crunched a carrot.* **crunchy** *adjective.*

crush crushes crushing crushed *verb*
If you crush something, you press it hard so that you break or squash it.

a Nile crocodile

42

crust crusts *noun*
1. the hard layer on the outside of something like very cold snow.
2. The Earth's crust is the thin outer layer.

crutches *noun*
two long sticks that fit under or around your arms to help you walk if you have hurt your foot or leg.

cry cries crying cried *verb*
1 When you cry, you have tears falling from your eyes. *The baby is crying because he is hungry.*
2 To cry also means to shout or make a loud noise. *"Help!" she cried.*

crystal crystals *noun*
1 a hard kind of rock that looks like glass.
2 a small, hard piece of something such as salt or ice that has a regular shape.
▲ Say **kriss**-tal.

cub cubs *noun*
a young bear, lion, tiger, fox, or wolf.

cube cubes *noun*
a solid shape with six square sides. *a cube of sugar.*

cuckoo cuckoos *noun*
a bird that makes a sound like its name. Cuckoos lay their eggs in the nests of other birds.

cucumber cucumbers *noun*
a long vegetable that is dark green on the outside and pale green inside. You can eat it raw in salads.

cuddle cuddles cuddling cuddled *verb*
When you cuddle somebody, you put your arms around and hold the person. *Dad cuddled the baby.*

cup cups *noun*
1 a small container with a handle. You drink liquids such as tea and coffee from a cup.
2 a metal container with two handles, that you can win as a prize. *He won a silver cup for winning the race.*

cupboard cupboards *noun*
a piece of furniture with shelves and doors where you can keep things.
▲ Say **kub**-erd.

cupcake cupcakes *noun*
a small round cake with icing.

cure cures curing cured *verb*
If something cures somebody, it makes an illness go away.
cure *noun*.

curious *adjective*
If you are curious about something, you want to know more about it. *I was curious to know what the noise was.*

curl curls *noun*
a piece of hair in a curved shape.
▲ Rhymes with **pearl**.
curly *adjective*

curl curls curling curled *verb*
If something curls or curls up, it bends into a curved shape. *The porcupine curled up into a ball.*

currant currants *noun*
a small, dried grape. ● A word that sounds like **currant** is **current**.

current currents *noun*
1 air or water that is moving. *It is too dangerous to swim here because of the strong currents.*
2 electricity that is passing through a wire.
● A word that sounds like **current** is **currant**.

cursor cursors *noun*
a little sign on a computer screen that shows you where to type the next letter.

curtain curtains *noun*
Curtains are pieces of cloth that you pull across a window or the front of the stage in a theater to cover it.

curve curves *noun*
a line that bends smoothly.

curved *adjective*
having the shape of a curve.

cushion cushions *noun*
a pad filled with soft material that you put on a chair to make it comfortable.

custom customs *noun*
something that people usually do. *It is the custom to give people presents on their birthdays.*

customer customers *noun*
a person who buys something from a store.

cut cuts cutting cut *verb*
1 You use scissors or a knife to cut things into pieces.
2 If you cut yourself, you hurt yourself by accident with something sharp.
cut *noun*.

cute cuter cutest *adjective*
If something like a kitten is cute, you like it because it looks pretty and sweet.

cyberspace *noun*
If you use your computer to communicate with lots of other people, you are in cyberspace.

cycle cycles *noun*
a bicycle. *a cycle shop.*

cycle cycles cycling cycled *verb*
When you cycle, you ride a bicycle.
cyclist *noun*.

cylinder cylinders *noun*
a long, round shape like a tube or a can.

cymbals *noun*
two round metal plates that you use as a musical instrument. Cymbals make a loud clashing sound when you hit them together.

A B C D E F G H I J K L M N O P Q R S T U V W X Y Z

D d

daffodil daffodils *noun*
a bright yellow, trumpet-shaped flower that blooms in the spring.

dagger daggers *noun*
a short sword with two sharp edges.

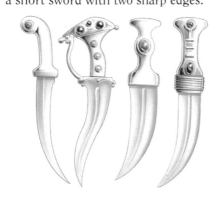

daily *adjective, adverb*
every day. *a daily newspaper.*

dainty daintier daintiest *adjective*
small and neat. *The doll's face is dainty.*

dairy dairies *noun*
a company that sells milk and other foods made from milk, such as butter and ice cream. A dairy farm produces milk.

dairy *adjective*
Dairy foods are milk, butter, and cheese, and other foods made from milk.

daisy daisies *noun*
a small flower with narrow, white petals around a yellow center.

dam dams *noun*
a wall built across a river to hold back the water.

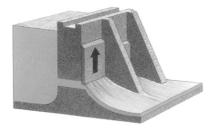

damage damages damaging damaged *verb*
If you damage something, you break it or harm it. *A car hit the wall and*

damaged it. ▲ Say *dam-ij.*
damage *noun.*

damp damper dampest *adjective*
a little wet.

dance dances dancing danced *verb*
When you dance, you move your body in time to music.
dance *noun.*

dandelion dandelions *noun*
a wild flower with a lot of bright yellow petals.

danger dangers *noun*
1 If you are in danger, you are in a situation where something bad could happen to you. *The sign on the electric fence said: "DANGER! Keep out!"*
2 something that might harm you. *Smoking cigarettes is a danger to your health.*

dangerous *adjective*
Something that is dangerous might harm you. *It's dangerous to go near the edge of the cliff.* ■ The opposite is **safe**.

dare dares daring dared *verb*
1 If you dare to do something, you are brave enough to do it even though it is dangerous. *Sheila wouldn't dare get near the angry bull.*
2 If you dare somebody, you ask that person if he or she is brave enough to do something. *I dare you to walk along the top of that wall.*

dark darker darkest *adjective*
1 without any light. *Open the curtains. It's dark in here.* ■ The opposite is **light** or **bright**.
2 Dark colors are nearer to black than to white. *Ricky is wearing a dark blue T-shirt.* ■ The opposite is **light**, **pale**, or **fair**.
darkness *noun.*

dart darts *noun*
a short arrow that you throw at a round target called a dartboard in a game called darts.

dart darts darting darted *verb*
If you dart somewhere, you run there very quickly and suddenly. *Dad darted into the store and came out with ice cream cones for everybody.*

dash dashes dashing dashed *verb*
If you dash somewhere, you run there very quickly. *She put her umbrella up and dashed across the street.*

data *noun*
facts and information. Information stored in a computer is called data. ▲ Say **day**-ta.

date dates *noun*
1 the day, the month, and sometimes the year when something happens. *What's the date today?*
2 a brown, sticky fruit with a pit inside. Dates grow on a type of palm tree.

daughter daughters *noun*
A person's daughter is a girl or woman who is his or her child. ▲ Say **daw**-ter.

dawdle dawdles dawdling dawdled *verb*
If you dawdle, you walk very slowly.

dawn dawns *noun*
the beginning of the day when the Sun is just starting to come up.

day days *noun*
1 the time when it is light. ■ The opposite is **night**.
2 a measure of time. The 24 hours of a day start at midnight and end the next midnight.

daze *noun*
If you are in a daze, you cannot think clearly and you are confused. *He hit his head and he's in a daze.*

dazzle dazzles dazzling dazzled *verb*
If a light dazzles you, it shines straight in your eyes so that you cannot see.

dead *adjective*
no longer alive. ■ The opposite is **alive**.

deaf *adjective*
A person who is deaf cannot hear very well or cannot hear at all.

dear dearer dearest *adjective*
If someone or something is dear to you, you love it and think it is very special. ● A word that sounds like **dear** is **deer**.

death deaths *noun*
the end of a life, when a person or animal dies.

debt debts *noun*
money that you owe somebody and have to pay back. ▲ Say *det*.

decade decades *noun*
a measure of time. There are ten years in a decade.

decay decays decaying decayed *verb*
When something decays, it becomes bad or rotten. *Eating candy can make your teeth decay.*

deceive deceives deceiving deceived *verb*
If you deceive people, you trick them by making them believe something that is not true. *It is dishonest if you deceive your parents by sneaking out at night.*

decide decides deciding decided *verb*
If you decide something, you make up your mind about what you are going to do. *I'm trying to decide what to buy my brother for his birthday.*

deciduous *adjective*
A deciduous tree loses its leaves in the winter and gets new ones in the spring. ▲ Say *de-sid-yoo-uss*. ■ The opposite is **evergreen**.

decimal decimals *noun*
a fraction that you write as a number, with amounts less than one written after the dot, called a decimal point. 2.5 is a decimal. It is the same as $2\frac{1}{2}$.

decision decisions *noun*
If you make a decision, you make up your mind about what you are going to do. *Have you made a decision yet?*

deck decks *noun*
1 a floor on a ship.
2 a platform with a railing that is part of a house. *We eat on the deck in summer.*

declare declares declaring declared *verb*
If you declare something, you say something important to a lot of people. *I declare that the winner is Ben Watson.*

decorate decorates decorating decorated *verb*
1 If you decorate something, you add things to it to make it look more beautiful. *Sam decorated the cake.*
2 If you decorate a room, you paint it or put wallpaper on the walls.
decoration *noun*.

decrease decreases decreasing decreased *verb*
If something decreases, it gets smaller or less. *The number of trees in the rain forests of South America has decreased over the last few years.*
■ The opposite is **increase**.

Rain-forest losses

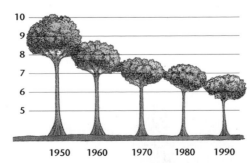

deep deeper deepest *adjective*
1 Something that is deep goes a long way down from the top. *The river is very deep.* ■ The opposite is **shallow**.
2 A deep sleep is sleep that is hard to wake somebody from.
3 A deep voice is very low. *Men's voices are usually deeper than women's.*

deer deer *noun*
a wild animal that eats grass and can run very fast. Male deer have big horns called antlers on their heads. ● A word that sounds like **deer** is **dear**.

defeat defeats defeating defeated *verb*
If you defeat people, you beat them in a game, competition, or battle.
defeat *noun*.

defend defends defending defended *verb*
When you defend somebody or something, you protect them when somebody else is attacking them. *Jack defended the goal.*
defense *noun*.

definite *adjective*
certain and not likely to change. *We haven't set a definite date for the trip.*
definitely *adverb*
I'm definitely going to do my homework on time tonight.

defrost defrosts defrosting defrosted *verb*
To defrost is to thaw frozen food.

degree degrees *noun*
1 a measurement of temperature. Degree is sometimes written as °. *10°F is ten degrees Fahrenheit.*
2 a measurement of angles. *A right angle is 90°.*
3 a qualification that you get after studying at a college or university.

A B C D E F G H I J K L M N O P Q R S T U V W X Y Z

delay delays delaying delayed *verb*
1 If you delay doing something, you put it off until later. *We had to delay our vacation for a week because my sister was very sick.*
2 To delay somebody is to make him or her late.

delete deletes deleting deleted *verb*
If you delete something, you remove it from a piece of writing or from a computer's memory.

deliberate *adjective*
If something you do is deliberate, you do it on purpose.

delicate *adjective*
1 Something that is delicate is small and lovely but it can be broken or damaged quite easily. *A spider's web is very delicate.*
2 A person who is delicate gets ill quite easily. *He's a delicate child.*

delicious *adjective*
Food that is delicious tastes very nice. ▲ Say *di-li-shuss.*

delight delights delighting delighted *verb*
If something delights you, it makes you feel very pleased.

deliver delivers delivering delivered *verb*
When you deliver something, you take it to the person it is supposed to go to. *A mail carrier delivers letters and packages to your home.*

delta deltas *noun*
muddy or sandy land shaped like a triangle that sits at the mouth of a river. *the Mississippi Delta.*

demand demands demanding demanded *verb*
If you demand something, you ask for it very strongly. *My father demanded to know why I was so late getting home from school.*
demand *noun.*

demolish demolishes demolishing demolished *verb*
To demolish something is to destroy it completely.
demolition *noun.*

den dens *noun*
the home of a wild animal such as a lion.

dent dents denting dented *verb*
If you dent something that is made of metal, you damage it so that part of it is pushed in slightly instead of flat. *He dropped the can and dented it.*

dentist dentists *noun*
a person whose job is to look after people's teeth.

deny denies denying denied *verb*
If you deny something, you say it is not true. *Tom denied taking the money.*

depart departs departing departed *verb*
If you depart, you leave. *The plane departs at 6:25.* ■ The opposite is **arrive**.
departure *noun.*

depend depends depending depended *verb*
1 If you depend on people or things, you need them. *The school depends on parents to raise money for school trips.*
2 If you depend on people, you trust them to do what they say they will. *I'm depending on you to help me.*
3 To depend also means to be decided by something. *I don't know if we'll have a picnic tomorrow. It depends on the weather.*

depth depths *noun*
The depth of something is how deep it is. *What is the depth of the lake?*

deputy deputies *noun*
a person who does another person's job when that person is not there. *a deputy sheriff.*

descend descends descending descended *verb*
If something descends, it goes down. *We watched as the parachute slowly descended before landing.* ▲ Say *di-send.*

describe describes describing described *verb*
When you describe something, you say what it is like.
description *noun*
The woman gave the police a description of the man she had seen.

desert deserts *noun*
an area where it is very dry and hardly any plants can grow. ▲ Say *dez-ert.*

deserted *adjective*
If a place is deserted, there is nobody there. *The house was deserted.*

deserve deserves deserving deserved *verb*
If you deserve something, it is fair that it should happen to you. *He trained very hard and he deserved to win the medal.*

design designs designing designed *verb*
If you design something, you decide what it will be like and then you draw it to show how it should be made. ▲ Say *di-zine.*

design designs *noun*
a pattern. *Each of these sweaters has a different design.* ▲ Say *di-zine.*

desire desires *noun*
a very strong wish for something. *She had a great desire to become an artist.*
desirable *adjective*
worth having. *a desirable house.*

desk desks *noun*
a table where you sit to write or read. Desks often have drawers.

despair despairs despairing despaired *verb*
If you despair, you feel no hope that something good will happen.

desperate *adjective*
If you are desperate, you are in a very bad situation and you will do almost anything to change it.

destination destinations *noun*
the place where you are going.

destroy destroys destroying destroyed *verb*
If you destroy something, you damage it or break it so badly that it cannot be fixed. *Fire destroyed the house.*
destruction *noun*
The storm caused a lot of destruction.

detail details *noun*
one of many small pieces of information about something.

detective detectives *noun*
a person who tries to find out who did a crime.

detention detentions *noun*
If the teacher keeps you after school for bad behavior, that's detention.

detergent *noun*
a powder or liquid that you use to clean clothes or dishes.

determined *adjective*
If you are determined to do something, you are going to do it and nothing can stop you. *Alex had trained very hard; he was determined to win the race.*

detest detests detesting detested *verb*
to hate somebody or something very much.

develop develops developing developed *verb*
When something develops, it changes as it grows. *A photograph is developing.*
development *noun*
The new housing development.

dew *noun*
Small drops of water that form in the night on grass and plants. ● A word that sounds like **dew** is **due**.

diagonal *adjective*
a line that slants from one corner of something to the opposite corner.

diagram diagrams *noun*
a simple picture that explains something.

dial dials *noun*
the part of something such as a clock or speedometer that has numbers and a pointer on it.

diameter diameters *noun*
a line drawn straight across a circle, through the center.
❖ *Look at page 38.*

diamond diamonds *noun*
1 a very hard, clear jewel.
2 a shape like a square turned so that it is standing on one of its corners.

diary diaries *noun*
a book where you can write what has happened during the day or what you plan to do.

dice *noun*
small cubes with a different number of dots on each side. You use dice when you play some games. The word for one of the dice is a **die**.

dictionary dictionaries *noun*
a book that gives the meanings of words and how to spell them in alphabetical order.

die dies dying died *verb*
When a person, an animal, or a plant dies, that one comes to the end of life and stops living. ■ The opposite is **live**. ● A word that sounds like **die** is **dye**.
death *noun*.

diesel *noun*
a kind of oil that is used as fuel in bus and truck engines. Some cars use diesel oil. ▲ Say **dee**-zil.

diet diets *noun*
1 Your diet is the food that you normally eat. *A healthy diet includes plenty of fresh fruit and vegetables.*
2 If you go on a diet, you eat only certain foods either because you have an illness or because you are trying to lose weight.

different *adjective*
If something is different from another thing, it is not like it. ■ The opposite is **same**.
difference *noun*
Can you tell the difference between these two horses?

difficult *adjective*
hard to do. ■ The opposite is **easy** or **simple**.
difficulty *noun*.

dig digs digging dug *verb*
If you dig, you use something such as a spade or shovel to move dirt or make a hole in the ground. Animals dig using their claws.

digest digests digesting digested *verb*
When you digest food, it passes through your body and gets broken up so that your body can use it to make energy.
digestion *noun*.

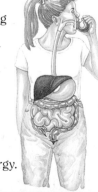

A B C D E F G H I J K L M N O P Q R S T U V W X Y Z

digit digits *noun*
1 one of the numbers from 0 to 9.
2 a finger or a toe.

dilute dilutes diluting diluted *verb*
When you dilute a liquid, you make it weaker by adding water.
dilution *noun*.

dim dimmer dimmest *adjective*
not very strong or bright. ■ The opposite is **bright**.

dinghy dinghies *noun*
a small, open boat that you row or sail.
▲ Say *ding-gi*.

dinner
dinners *noun*
the main meal that you eat usually in the evening, sometimes in the middle of the day.

dinosaur dinosaurs *noun*
a large reptile that lived millions of years ago and then became extinct.

dip dips dipping dipped *verb*
1 If you dip something into a liquid, you put it in for a moment. *He dipped his brush into the paint.*
2 If something dips, it slopes down. *The road dipped suddenly after the bridge.*
■ The opposite is **rise**.

direct *adjective*
The direct way to go somewhere is by the shortest way and without stopping.

direct directs directing directed *verb*
1 If you direct people to a place, you tell them the way to go.
2 A person who directs a movie or television program tells the actors what to do.

direction
directions *noun*
1 the way that something is pointing or moving. *Am I going in the right direction for the museum?*
2 Directions are instructions telling you how to do something.

dirt *noun*
mud, dust, or marks on something.

dirty dirtier dirtiest *adjective*
covered with dirt or marks. ■ The opposite is **clean**.

Word Builder

Dis – is a little word called a prefix that you can add to the beginning of certain words, often to change their meaning.
1 Not, or the opposite of — disloyal.
2 To do the opposite of — disagree, dislike.

---

disabled *adjective*
A disabled person has a part of the body that does not work properly.
disability *noun*.

disagree disagrees disagreeing disagreed *verb*
When people disagree, they do not think the same way about something. *My brother and I often disagree about what to watch on TV.*
■ The opposite is **agree**.

disappear disappears disappearing disappeared *verb*
If something disappears, it goes out of sight. *We waved at the boat until it disappeared in the distance.* ■ The opposite is **appear**.
disappearance *noun*.

disappointed *adjective*
You feel disappointed when something you were looking forward to does not happen or when what happens is not as good as you had hoped.
disappointment *noun*.

disaster disasters *noun*
a really terrible thing that happens. *An earthquake is a natural disaster.*

disc discs *noun*
a flat plastic case with a magnetic metal part inside that stores information from a computer.

discover discovers discovering discovered *verb*
If you discover something, you find out about it or see it for the first time. *We discovered a secret hiding place.*
discovery *noun*.

discuss discusses discussing discussed *verb*
If you discuss something, you talk about it with other people.
discussion *noun*.

disease diseases *noun*
an illness.

disguise
disguises *noun*
something that you do to change the way you look so that other people do not know who you are. ▲ Say *dis-gize*.

disgust *noun*
a very strong feeling of not liking something that is really nasty or bad.
disgusting *adjective*

dish dishes *noun*
a plate or a bowl used for cooking or for putting food on.

dishonest *adjective*
If you steal, lie, or cheat, you are a dishonest person.

disk *noun*
a round, flat object.

dislike dislikes disliking disliked *verb*
to not like somebody or something.

distance distances *noun*
Distance is how far apart two things are.
distant *adjective*.

distract distracts distracting distracted *verb*
If something distracts you, it takes your attention away from what you are doing. *I can't do my homework with the radio on because I get distracted by it.*
distraction *noun*.

disturb disturbs disturbed disturbing *verb*
If you disturb somebody, you stop them doing something such as working or sleeping. *Don't disturb her; she's asleep.*

ditch ditches *noun*
a long hole in the ground that has been dug along the side of a road so that water can drain away.

a b c d e f g h i j k l m n o p q r s t u v w x y z

dive dives diving dived or dove
verb
1 When you dive, you jump into water with your arms and head first.
2 to swim underwater with special breathing equipment.
3 To dive is to go underwater. *We watched the submarine dive.*
diver *noun*.

divide divides dividing divided
verb
1 If you divide something, you separate it into smaller parts. *He is dividing the liquid into four equal amounts.*
2 You divide one number by another number to see how many times the smaller number goes into the larger one. When you write this you use a

division sign: ÷. *8÷2=4.* ■ The opposite is **multiply**.
division *noun*.

divorce divorces *noun*
the ending of a marriage.
divorce *verb*
She divorced her husband.

dizzy dizzier dizziest *adjective*
If you feel dizzy, you feel as if everything is spinning around and you are going to fall over.

dock docks *noun*
a place where ships stop to load or unload cargo or to be repaired.
dock *verb*.

doctor doctors *noun*
a person whose job is to help people who are sick to get better, by giving them medicines or advice. *M.D.* comes after a doctor's name.

document documents *noun*
a piece of paper with important information on it.

dog dogs *noun*
an animal that is often kept as a pet or for hunting or guarding things. A young dog is called a puppy. ❖ *Look below.*

doll dolls *noun*
a toy in the shape of a person.

DOGS

Labrador retriever

Dogue de Bordeaux

Basenji

Bull terrier

Black and tan coonhound

Beagle

A B C D E F G H I J K L M N O P Q R S T U V W X Y Z

dollar dollars *noun*
an amount of money equal to 100 cents.

dolphin dolphins *noun*
a mammal that lives in the sea but breathes air. Dolphins look like very large fish. ▲ Say *dol-fin*.

domino dominoes *noun*
Dominoes are small, rectangular blocks of wood or plastic with different numbers of dots on them, used to play a game.

donkey donkeys *noun*
an animal like a small horse but with longer ears.

door doors *noun*
a large piece of wood or glass that moves to open and close the way into a room, building, or closet.

dose doses *noun*
an amount of medicine that you have to take at one time.

dot dots *noun*
a small, round spot. *a blue shirt with white dots.*

double *adjective*
twice as large or twice as many. *Josh has double the number of blocks that Natasha has.* ▲ Say *dub-ul*.

doubt doubts *noun*
If you have a doubt about something, you are not sure about it. ▲ Say *dowt*.

dough *noun*
a mixture of flour, water, and other things that you cook to make bread, cakes or pastry. ▲ Say *doh*.

dove doves *noun*
a kind of pigeon. ▲ Say *duv*.

dozen dozen *noun*
twelve. *We made two dozen sandwiches for the party.*
▲ Say *duz-un*.

draft drafts *noun*
cold air coming into a room because there is a slight gap between a window or door and the wall.
drafty *adjective*.

drag drags dragging dragged *verb*
If you drag something, you pull it along the ground. *Freddy dragged his coat across the floor.*

dragon dragons *noun*
a very large animal in stories with a long body covered in scales. Dragons have wings and can breathe fire.

dragonfly dragonflies *noun*
an insect with a long, thin body and two sets of wings. Dragonflies live near ponds and rivers.

drain drains draining drained *verb*
1 When water drains away, it flows slowly away.
2 When you drain food, you pour away the water that it cooked in. *Drain the spaghetti and serve with a spicy tomato sauce.*

drain drains *noun*
a pipe that carries water away. A sewer pipe is a large drain.

drama dramas *noun*
1 a serious play.
2 an interesting or exciting thing.

drank past of **drink**.

drastic *adjective*
severe or harsh.

draw draws drawing drew drawn *verb*
1 When you draw, you use a pencil, pen, or crayon to make a picture of something or someone.
2 If you draw the drapes, you move them together by pulling.
drawing *noun*.

drawbridge drawbridges *noun*
a bridge that opens to let ships pass underneath.

drawer drawers *noun*
a wooden box that slides in and out of a piece of furniture and holds things like clothes or paper and pens.

dream dreams dreaming dreamed or **dreamt** *verb*
1 When you dream, you see pictures and hear sounds in your mind while you are sleeping. *Last night I dreamed that I could fly.*
2 When you dream of something, you think about how much you would love to be able to do it. *Madeleine dreams of becoming a world-famous ballet dancer.*
dream *noun*.

dress dresses dressing dressed *verb*
When you dress you put on clothes.
■ The opposite is **undress**.

dress dresses *noun*
a piece of clothing that a woman or girl wears. A dress has a top part and a skirt joined together.

drew past of **draw**.

drift drifts drifting drifted *verb*
When something drifts, it is carried slowly along by the wind or by the movement of water. *She stopped the engine and let the boat drift.*

drill drills *noun*
a tool that is used for making holes.
drill *verb*.

drink drinks drinking drank drunk *verb*
When you drink, you take liquid into your mouth and swallow it.
drink *noun*.

drip drips dripping dripped *verb*
When liquid drips, it falls in drops. *Rain dripped off the roof.*

drive drives driving drove driven *verb*
to control something such as a car or bus and make it go where it is supposed to.

drizzle *noun*
light rain in very small drops.

droop droops drooping drooped *verb*
When something droops, it hangs or bends down because it is weak or tired. *The flower drooped because it had no water.*

drop drops *noun*
a tiny amount of liquid.

drop drops dropping dropped *verb*
If you drop something, you let it fall. *I dropped the plate.*

drought droughts *noun*
a long period of time when there is no rain. ▲ Rhymes with **out**.

drove past of **drive**.

drown drowns drowning drowned *verb*
to die because someone cannot breathe under water.

drug drugs *noun*
1 medicine that a doctor gives you to treat a sickness.
2 an illegal pill or chemical.

druggist druggists *noun*
a person who prepares and sells medicine.

drugstore drugstores *noun*
a store where you can buy medicines and personal items.

drum drums *noun*
a musical instrument that you beat with a stick or your hands.

drunk *adjective*
When somebody is drunk, they have drunk too much alcohol.

drunk past of **drink**.

dry drier driest *adjective*
If something is dry, there is no water or liquid in it. ■ The opposite is **wet**.

dry dries drying dried *verb*
If you dry something, you make it dry. *Hal is drying himself with a towel.*

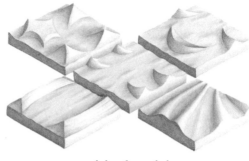

duck ducks *noun*
a water bird with webbed feet and a flat, broad beak. A male duck is called a drake, and a young duck is called a duckling.

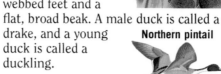

Northern pintail

Steller's eider

Garganey

Shelduck

Mandarin

due *adjective*
When something is due at a particular time, it should happen at that time. *They are due to arrive at 10 o'clock.* ● A word that sounds like **due** is **dew**.

duffle coat *noun*
a long, warm jacket made from thick wool. It usually has a hood and long wooden buttons called toggles.

dug past of **dig**.

dull duller dullest *adjective*
1 A dull color is not very bright. ■ The opposite is **bright**.
2 A dull day is cloudy and the Sun is not shining.
3 If something such as a movie or book is dull, it is not interesting.
4 not sharp. *a dull ache.*

dumb *adjective*
1 completely unable to speak.
2 stupid.

dump dumps dumping dumped *verb*
If you dump something, you put it down quickly and carelessly. *My parents get angry when my sister just dumps her clothes on the floor.*

dune dunes *noun*
a low hill of sand by the sea or in a desert.

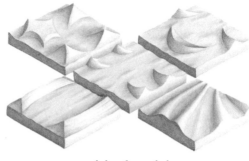

models of sand dunes

dungarees *noun*
pants made out of a very strong cotton material, such as blue denim.

dungeon dungeons *noun*
an underground prison in a castle. ▲ Say **dun**-jun.

dusk *noun*
the time in the evening when it is nearly dark but not quite.

dust *noun*
dirt that is like powder. *The furniture was covered with dust.*
dusty *adjective*.

duty duties *noun*
a job that you have to do. *The dog belongs to my brother, so it's his duty to take it for walks.*

dwell dwells dwelling dwelled or dwelt *verb*
When you dwell somewhere, you live there.
dwelling *noun*.

dye dyes *noun*
a liquid that you soak cloth or your hair in to change its color. ● A word that sounds like **dye** is **die**.
dye *verb*.

dyslexia *noun*
a learning difficulty that causes problems with reading and spelling.
dyslexic *adjective*. ▲ Say dis-**lex**-ee-uh.

A B C D E F G H I J K L M N O P Q R S T U V W X Y Z

E e

eager *adjective*
If you are eager to do something, you want to do it very much. *Ben was eager to help with the cooking.*

eagle **eagles** *noun*
a large bird with a curved beak and broad wings. Eagles are called birds of prey because they catch and eat small animals and other birds.

ear **ears** *noun*
Your ears are the part of your body that you hear with.

early **earlier earliest** *adjective, adverb*
1 near the beginning of a period of time. *Early cars had solid tires.*
2 before the usual time or the time that you are expected. *We went to the swimming pool early before it got crowded.*
■ The opposite is **late**.

earn **earns earning earned** *verb*
If you earn money, you get money for work that you do. *Lauren sometimes earns extra allowance by washing her mother's car.*

earring **earrings** *noun*
a piece of jewelry that you wear on your ear.

earth *noun*
1 The Earth is the planet that we live on. Our Earth moves around the Sun.
2 the ground that plants grow in.

earthquake **earthquakes** *noun*
An earthquake happens when part of the ground suddenly begins to shake. Earthquakes happen when rocks deep beneath the surface of the Earth move.

easel **easels** *noun*
a stand for a blackboard or an artist's painting.

east *noun*
1 the direction from which the Sun rises.
2 the East is where countries such as China and Japan are.
east *adjective*, **eastern** *adjective*
■ The opposite is **west**, **western**.

easy **easier easiest** *adjective*
not difficult. *These arithmetic problems are easy!*
■ The opposite is **hard** or **difficult**.

eat **eats eating ate eaten** *verb*
When you eat something, you chew food in your mouth and swallow it.

e a t

Some words you can use instead of eat:

Rabbits eat carrots.
☞ **nibble** ☜

Apples make a crunchy sound when you eat them.
☞ **chew, munch, bite** ☜

We ate at the new Italian restaurant.
☞ **dined** ☜

echo **echoes** *noun*
An echo is the sound that comes back to you when you shout in a place such as a cave. ▲ Say *eck-oh*.

eclipse **eclipses** *noun*
1 An eclipse of the Sun happens when the Moon comes between the Earth and the Sun so that you cannot see all Sun's light (a).

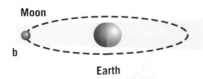

2 An eclipse of the Moon happens when the Earth comes between the Sun and the Moon so that you cannot see all the Moon's light (b).

edge **edges** *noun*
An edge is the end or side of something. *Don't stand on the edge of the cliff.*

education *noun*
Education is teaching people to read, write, and learn about all kinds of things in a school or college.

eel **eels** *noun*
a long, thin fish that lives in rivers or in the sea.

effect **effects** *noun*
An effect is a change that is caused by somebody or something. *The trash in the river had a bad effect on the fish.*

effort **efforts** *noun*
If you make an effort, you try hard to do something. *It takes a lot of effort to try to pull Kirsty off the floor.*

egg **eggs** *noun*
1 Birds, fish, some reptiles, and some other animals lay eggs. The young of these animals live inside the eggs until they are ready to hatch.
2 a hen's egg with a hard shell that you can cook and eat.

elastic *adjective*
A material that stretches when you pull it is elastic.

elbow **elbows** *noun*
Your elbow is the joint in the middle of your arm where it bends.

elderly *adjective*
rather old. *an elderly man.*

election **elections** *noun*
An election is when people choose who they want to be their leader by voting. *an election for a new President.*

electric *adjective*
A machine that is electric works by using electricity. *an electric fan.*

electricity *noun*
the form of energy that travels along wires. Rubbing a balloon on hair creates a form of electricity called "static electricity."
electrical *adjective*.

electronic *adjective*
An electronic machine, such as a computer, uses a piece of material called a silicon chip that has a tiny electric circuit on it.

elephant **elephants** *noun*
a very big, gray animal with a long trunk and two long teeth called tusks. Elephants live in Africa and Asia. They eat grass and parts of trees that they tear off with their trunks.

elevator **elevators** *noun*
a small room that can carry people from floor to floor in a building.

E-mail *noun*
electronic messages or mail that you send on a computer.

embroider *verb*
to decorate cloth with tiny stitches.
embroidery *noun*.

embryo **embryos** *noun*
a tiny person or animal that has only just begun to develop inside its mother and has not been born yet. ▲ Say *em-bree-oh.*

emerald **emeralds** *noun*
a bright green jewel.

emergency **emergencies** *noun*
An emergency is when somebody is in danger and needs help immediately. *In an emergency, you should call 911.*

emotion **emotions** *noun*
a strong feeling such as love, anger, or sadness. ▲ Say *em-oh-shun.*

emperor **emperors** *noun*
a man who rules over a group of countries, called an empire.

a Chinese emperor

employ **employs employing employed** *verb*
If you employ somebody, you pay that one to work for you.

empress **empresses** *noun*
a woman who rules over a group of countries, called an empire.

empty *adjective*
If something is empty, there is nothing in it. *She drank all the milk and left the empty glass on the table.*
■ The opposite is **full**.

empty **empties emptying emptied** *verb*
If you empty something, you take out or throw away everything that is in it. *He emptied the whole pitcher.*
■ The opposite is **fill**.

enchanted *adjective*
A place that is enchanted has been put under a magic spell. *The story is about an enchanted wood where the trees come to life.*

encourage **encourages encouraging encouraged** *verb*
If you encourage people, you make them feel that what they are doing is good. *We encouraged the smaller kids to swim the length of the pool.*
encouragement *noun*.

encyclopedia **encyclopedias** *noun*
a book that tells you about all kinds of facts and subjects from A to Z. ▲ Say *en-sy-clo-**pee**-dee-uh.*

end **ends** *noun*
1 the last part of something. *I'm almost at the end of my book.* ■ The opposite is **beginning** or **start**.
2 one of the short edges of something long. *They sat at opposite ends of the table.*

end **ends ending ended** *verb*
When something ends, it finishes. *What time does the movie end?* ■ The opposite is **begin** or **start**.

enemy **enemies** *noun*
An enemy is a person who hates someone else or is a country that another country fights in a war.

A B C D E F G H I J K L M N O P Q R S T U V W X Y Z

energy *noun*
1 Energy is the power that makes machines work and gives us heat and light. Electricity is one kind of energy.
2 Your energy is the strength that your body has to do things. *You need a lot of energy to run 1,000 yards.*
energetic *adjective.*

engaged *adjective*
1 If two people are engaged, they have agreed to get married.
2 If somebody is engaged in doing something like a job, he or she is busy doing it. *He is engaged in fixing the furnace.*

engine **engines** *noun*
1 a machine that makes things move. *a car engine.*
2 the front part of a train that pulls it along.

enjoy **enjoys enjoying enjoyed** *verb*
If you enjoy something, you like doing it. *I enjoy playing football.*
enjoyable *adjective,* **enjoyment** *noun.*

enormous *adjective*
very, very big. *China is an enormous country.* ■ The opposite is **tiny.**

enough *adjective, adverb, noun*
If you have enough of something, you have as much as you need. *Have you had enough to eat?*

enter **enters entering entered** *verb*
1 If you enter a place, you go into it. *She entered the room quietly.*
2 If you enter a race or competition, you take part in it. *Did you enter the bicycle race?*

entertain **entertains entertaining entertained** *verb*
If you entertain people, you do things that they find interesting or amusing. *The clown entertained the crowd while the acrobats changed their costumes.*
entertainment *noun.*

enthusiasm *noun*
a strong feeling of liking something or wanting to do something. *The children were full of enthusiasm for the party.*
enthusiastic *adjective.*

entrance **entrances** *noun*
the way into a place. *I'll meet you at the entrance to the store.* ■ The opposite is **exit.**

envelope **envelopes** *noun*
a folded paper cover for a letter or card. You write the address of the person you are writing to on the front of the envelope.

environment *noun*
The environment is the air, water, land, and all the plants and animals around us. *We must all try to protect the environment.*
environmental *adjective.*

envy **envies envying envied** *verb*
to wish you had the same things others have.
envious *adjective.*

episode **episodes** *noun*
An episode is one part of a long story on television or radio that you watch or listen to in several parts. *The television movie had seven separate episodes.*

equal *adjective*
If things are equal, they are the same in size, amount, or number. *The children had an equal number of candies each.*
equally *adverb.*

equator *noun*
The equator is an imaginary line on maps that goes around the Earth at an equal distance between the North and South Poles. Countries near the equator are very hot.

equipment *noun*
all the things you need to do something. *sports equipment.* ◆ *kitchen equipment.*

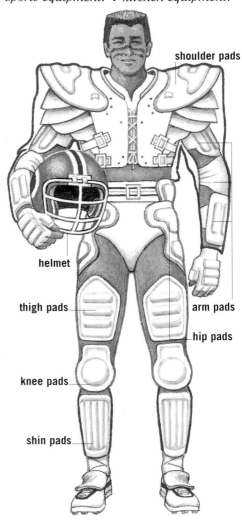

shoulder pads

helmet

thigh pads

arm pads

hip pads

knee pads

shin pads

error **errors** *noun*
a mistake.

erupt **erupts erupting erupted** *verb*
When a volcano erupts, it explodes and very hot liquid rock called lava shoots out of the top.
eruption *noun.*

escalator **escalators** *noun*
a staircase with moving steps.

escape **escapes escaping escaped** *verb*
A person or an animal that escapes, gets away from somebody or something. *The bird has escaped from its cage.*

especially *adverb*
most of all. *I especially like cats.*

essential *adjective*
If something is essential, it is absolutely necessary.

ethnic *adjective*
having to do with people who have the same country, language, and way of life.

evaporate **evaporates evaporating evaporated** *verb*
When a liquid evaporates, it changes into a gas or vapor and seems to disappear. *Hot water evaporates.*
evaporation *noun*.

even *adjective*
1 flat and smooth. *an even floor.* ■ The opposite is **uneven**.
2 Even numbers can be divided exactly by two. *2, 4, 6, and 8 are even numbers.* ■ The opposite is **odd**.

evening **evenings** *noun*
the part of the day between afternoon and night.

event **events** *noun*
something that happens, especially something important or unusual. *The school field day is a big event.*

eventually *adverb*
after a very long time. *I waited for ages, then eventually the bus came.*

evergreen *adjective*
An evergreen tree does not lose its leaves in the winter. Pine trees are evergreen. ■ The opposite is **deciduous**.

evidence *noun*
proof of something that happened. *The paw marks were evidence that the cat had jumped on the table.*

evil *adjective*
A person who is evil is very bad and cruel. *an evil emperor.*

exact *adjective*
correct. *What is the exact time?*
exactly *adverb*.

exaggerate **exaggerates exaggerating exaggerated** *verb*
If you exaggerate, you pretend something is bigger, better, or worse than it really is. *Tom was exaggerating when he said he saw a spider as big as a cat.*
▲ Say *eks-**zaj**-uh-rate*.

exam **exams** *noun*
a short word for examination. *a math exam.* ◆ *a ballet exam.*

examination **examinations** *noun*
1 an important test that you are given to see how much you have learned.
2 looking at somebody or something closely and carefully. *a medical examination.*

examine **examines examining examined** *verb*
If you examine something, you look at it closely and carefully. *Freddie examined the fossil with a magnifying glass.*

example **examples** *noun*
a thing that shows what other things of the same kind are like. *At the school open house, we showed our parents examples of our work.*

excellent *adjective*
Something that is excellent is very good. *We had an excellent vacation.*

except *preposition*
but not. *Everybody except Lee passed the history test.*
exception *noun*.

exchange **exchanges exchanging exchanged** *verb*
If you exchange something, you give one thing and get something else in return. *At the end of camp we exchanged addresses with our new friends.*

excited *adjective*
If you are excited, you are so happy that you cannot keep quiet or calm. *Freddie is so excited that he is jumping for joy!*
excitement *noun,*
exciting *adjective*.

exclaim **exclaims exclaiming exclaimed** *verb*
To exclaim means to say something in a loud voice because you are surprised or angry. *"What a mess!" she exclaimed.*
exclamation *noun*
He gave an exclamation of surprise when he saw the huge snake.

exclamation point **exclamation points** *noun*
a mark (**!**) that you use in writing. You put an exclamation mark to show that somebody is surprised or angry. *Oh no!*

excuse **excuses** *noun*
If you make an excuse, you try to explain why you did something wrong. *What's your excuse for being late this time?*
▲ Say *ex-**kyoos**.*

excuse **excuses excusing excused** *verb*
If you excuse people, you forgive them for something that they did wrong. *I'll excuse you for forgetting your homework this time.*
▲ Say *ex-**kyooz**.*

exercise **exercises** *noun*
1 Exercise is something such as running or jumping that you do to keep your body strong and well. *The children are doing different kinds of exercise.*
2 An exercise is a piece of work that you do to help you learn something. *Our teacher asked us to finish Exercise 2 for homework.*

exhausted *adjective*
very tired. *After running all the way up the hill, I was exhausted.*

exhibition **exhibitions** *noun*
a collection of things in a place such as a museum or gallery for people to come and look at. ▲ Say *ex-i-**bish**-un.*

A B C D E F G H I J K L M N O P Q R S T U V W X Y Z

exist exists existing existed *verb*
If something exists, you can find it in the real world now. *Do you think ghosts really exist?*
existence *noun*.

exit exits *noun*
the way out of a building. *The exit is at the back of the theater.* ■ The opposite is **entrance**.

expand expands expanding expanded *verb*
If something expands, it gets bigger. *When you blow air into a balloon it expands.*

expect expects expecting expected *verb*
If you expect something to happen, you think it will happen. *I expect that they will be here soon.*

expedition expeditions *noun*
a long journey to find or do something special. *Admiral Byrd led an expedition to the South Pole.*

expensive *adjective*
Something that is expensive costs a lot of money. ■ The opposite is **cheap**.

experience experiences *noun*
1 An experience is something that has happened to you. *What's the most frightening experience you've had?*
2 Experience is knowing about something because you have done it for a long time. *I can cycle to school when I've had more experience riding my bike on the road.*

experiment experiments *noun*
a test that you do to find out something. *We did an experiment to see which objects are magnetic.*

expert experts *noun*
a person who knows a lot about something. *a computer expert.*

explain explains explaining explained *verb*
1 If you explain how to do something, you tell somebody about it so that he or she can understand it. *My brother explained to me how to mend my bike.*
2 If you explain something that happened, you give reasons why it happened. *We explained that we were late because we had missed the bus.*
explanation *noun*.

explode explodes exploding exploded *verb*
If something such as a bomb explodes, it bursts suddenly with a very loud noise.
explosion *noun*.

explore explores exploring explored *verb*
When you explore, you look carefully around a place you have never seen before.
exploration *noun*.

express expresses expressing expressed *verb*
If you express what you think or feel, you show it in words or actions.

expression expressions *noun*
Your expression is the look on your face that shows how you feel. *A smile is a happy expression.*

expressway expressways *noun*
a big road with many lanes.

extinct *adjective*
An animal or plant that is extinct does not exist now. *Dinosaurs became extinct millions of years ago.*
extinction *noun*.

extinguish extinguishes extinguishing extinguished *verb*
If you extinguish a fire, you put it out. *He extinguished the flames with a bucket of water.* ▲ Say ex-**ting**-gwish.

extra *adjective*
more than you usually have. *I wore an extra sweater because I was cold.*

extraordinary *adjective*
very special or unusual. *I read an extraordinary story about a horse that could talk.*

extremely *adverb*
very. *Elephants are extremely big animals.*

eye eyes *noun*
Your eyes are the parts of your face that you use to see with. In the middle of the eye is a hole called a pupil that lets light onto the lens behind. ● A word that sounds like **eye** is **I**.

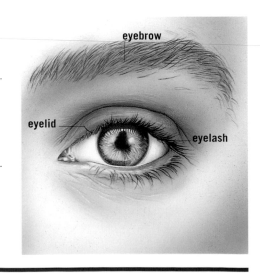
eyebrow
eyelid
eyelash

a b c d e f g h i j k l m n o p q r s t u v w x y z

F f

fable fables *noun*
a story, usually about animal characters, that teaches you something.

face faces *noun*
Your face is the front part of your head where your eyes, nose, and mouth are.

fact facts *noun*
something that is known to be true. *It's a fact that we live in San Jose.*

factory factories *noun*
a building where people use machines to make things. *a car factory.*

fade fades fading faded *verb*
1 If something fades, it becomes paler.
2 If a sound fades away, it slowly becomes quieter.

Fahrenheit *adjective*
having to do with a way of measuring temperature that shows the freezing point of water at 32 degrees and its boiling point at 212 degrees.
failure *noun*.

fail fails failing failed *verb*
If you fail at something, you do not succeed in doing it.
failure *noun*.

faint faints fainting fainted *verb*
If you faint, you become unconscious for a short time. *Sam fainted when he saw blood coming from the cut on his finger.*

faint fainter faintest *adjective*
Something that is faint is not very strong or clear. *There is a faint smell of smoke.*

fair fairer fairest *adjective*
1 A person who is fair has light-colored hair and skin. ■ The opposite is **dark**.
2 Something that is fair seems right or treats everybody the same. *It's not fair that I have to go to bed when Ben is allowed to stay up.* ■ The opposite is **unfair**.
● A word that sounds like **fair** is **fare**.

fair fairs *noun*
a place outside where rides and competitions are set up for people to have fun. ● A word that sounds like **fair** is **fare**.

fairy fairies *noun*
in stories, a magical creature like a very small person with wings.

faith *noun*
If you have faith in somebody, you trust that person to do what he or she says.

faithful *adjective*
If you are faithful to somebody who trusts you, you do not do anything to hurt that person; loyal. *She's very faithful to her friends.*

fake *adjective*
looking like the real thing. *It's a fake diamond.* ■ The opposite is **real**.

fall falls falling fell fallen *verb*
When something falls, it goes down or drops from a higher to a lower place. *Sam fell off the skateboard.*
fall *noun*.

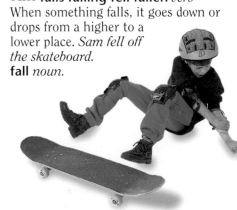

false *adjective*
1 not true. *The man gave a false name.* ■ The opposite is **true**.

2 not the real thing. *Tom is wearing a false beard and glasses.*

fame *noun*
being famous.

familiar *adjective*
If something is familiar to you, you know it well. *Her face was familiar but I couldn't remember her name.* ■ The opposite is **unfamiliar** or **strange**.

family families *noun*
1 a group of people made up of parents, grandparents, and children. Aunts, uncles, and cousins are also part of your family.
2 a group of animals or plants that are like each other in certain ways. *Polar bears are members of the bear family.*

Grizzly bear
Black bear
Sun bear   Asiatic black bear   Polar bear

famine famines *noun*
a time when there is not enough food for the people in a country to eat.
▲ Say *fam-in*.

famous *adjective*
known by lots of people. *a famous movie star.* ▲ Say *fay-muss*.

fan fans *noun*
1 a machine with blades that turn around fast to keep a room cool in hot weather.
2 a flat object, often made of paper, that you wave in front of your face to keep you cool in hot weather.
3 a person who really admires somebody famous such as a singer or an actor, or who likes a certain sport very much. *football fans.*

fancy fancier fanciest *adjective*
Something that is fancy has a lot of decoration on it. *My fanciest dress has a lace collar and a ruffled hem.* ■ The opposite is **plain**.
fancily *adverb*, **fanciness** *noun*.

A B C D E F G H I J K L M N O P Q R S T U V W X Y Z

fang fangs *noun*
a long, sharp, pointed tooth. Some snakes have fangs.

fantastic *adjective*
amazing or really good.

far *adjective*
a long distance from something or somebody. ■ The opposite is **near**.

fare fares *noun*
the money that you pay to go on a bus, train, or plane. ● A word that sounds like **fare** is **fair**.

farm farms *noun*
a place where people grow crops or raise animals to sell as food.
farmer *noun*.

fascinate fascinates fascinating fascinated *verb*
If something fascinates you, you feel very interested in it. *Snakes fascinate me.* ▲ Say *fas-in-ate.*
fascination *noun*, **fascinating** *adjective*.

fashion fashions *noun*
a way of dressing or behaving that is very popular for a time.

fast faster fastest *adjective*
1 very quick. *She's a fast runner.*
2 If a watch or clock is fast, it shows a time that is later than the real time. ■ The opposite is **slow**.
fast *adverb*.

fast

Some words you can use instead of fast:

We ate in a fast-food restaurant.
☞ **quick service** ☜

She's a very fast talker.
☞ **quick, rapid** ☜

The news spread fast.
☞ **quickly, swiftly, speedily, rapidly** ☜

fasten fastens fastening fastened *verb*
If you fasten something, you fix it firmly. *Fasten your seat belt.* ▲ Say *fa-sun.*

fat fatter fattest *adjective*
A person or animal with a large, heavy body. ■ The opposite is **thin**.

---

fat fats *noun*
oil, butter, or margarine that you can use to cook with.

father fathers *noun*
a male parent.

faucet faucets *noun*
a thing that you turn when you want water to come out of a pipe or when you want the water to stop.

fault faults *noun*
1 a mistake.
2 If something bad is your fault, it happened because of you.

favor favors *noun*
a kind and helpful thing that you do for somebody. *Could you do me a favor and carry this box for me?*

favorite *adjective*
Your favorite thing is the one you like best.

fax faxes *noun*
1 a machine that sends a picture or message along a telephone wire to another machine that prints it out.
2 a message or picture sent on a fax machine.

an original document and a fax copy

fear *noun*
the feeling that you have when you are afraid. *He has a fear of heights.*

feast feasts *noun*
a large, special meal for a lot of people.

feather feathers *noun*
one of the light, soft parts that cover a bird's body.

---

federal *adjective*
If a government of a country is a group of states joined under one control, it is a federal government.

feed feeds feeding fed *verb*
1 If you feed others, you give them food. *We fed the ducks.*
2 When an animal feeds, it eats.

feel feels feeling felt *verb*
1 When you feel something, you touch it and know what it is like against your skin. *Feel my bear—it's so soft.*
2 If you feel sad, happy or angry, you are that way at the moment. *I feel really hungry.*

feeling feelings *noun*
A feeling is what you feel, like happiness.

feet plural of **foot**.

fell past of **fall**.

felt past of **feel**.

female *adjective*
A female person or animal belongs to the sex that can have babies or lay eggs. Girls and women are female. ■ The opposite is **male**.

fence fences *noun*
a wall of wood or wire around land such as a garden or field. *a wooden fence.*

fern ferns *noun*
a plant that has leaves like feathers and no flowers.

Ferris wheel Ferris wheels
noun
a big, high wheel with seats around the edge. People ride on Ferris wheels at carnivals and amusement parks.

ferry ferries *noun*
a large boat that carries passengers and cars across a river or a narrow piece of sea.

fertile *adjective*
Fertile land is where plants grow well.

festival
festivals
noun
a special or religious holiday when people celebrate.

fetch
fetches
fetching
fetched *verb*
When you fetch something, you go to get it and bring it back. *Our dog fetches the newspaper.*

fever fevers *noun*
an illness that makes the temperature of your body higher than usual.

few *adjective*
not many. ■ The opposite is **numerous**.

fiber fibers *noun*
a thread of wool, cotton, nylon, or something similar that is used to make cloth.

fiction *noun*
stories that have been made up by somebody and are not about people who really exist or things that really happen.

field fields *noun*
an area of land where farmers grow crops or keep animals.

fierce fiercer fiercest *adjective*
An animal that is fierce is likely to attack you. *a fierce bull.*

fight fights fighting fought *verb*
When people or animals fight, they attack and try to hurt each other. *Lions sometimes fight over a kill.*
fight *noun*.

figure figures *noun*
1 one of the signs that we use to write numbers, such as 1, 2, and 3.
2 the shape of a person. *I could just make out the figure of a tall man in the fog.*

file files *noun*
1 a box or cardboard cover where you can keep papers.
2 a set of information on a computer.
3 a tool with a rough surface that you use to make things smooth. *a nail file.*
single file a line of people or animals, one behind the other. *The children walked single file into the cafeteria.*

different types of file

fill fills filling filled *verb*
If you fill something, you put as much into it as it can hold. *Frances filled the bottles with water.* ■ The opposite is **empty**.

film films *noun*
1 a movie. *Mom and Dad took me to see a foreign film.*
2 a long, thin strip of plastic that you put in a camera for taking photographs. *I need new film for my camera.*

fin fins *noun*
A fin is one of the thin, flat parts on a fish's body that help it to swim and balance.

final *adjective*
last. *the final episode of the TV series.*
finally *adverb*.

find finds finding found *verb*
When you find something, you see it again after it has been lost or you did not know where it was. *I've found my sneakers.* ■ The opposite is **lose**.

fine finer finest *adjective*
1 healthy. *"How are you?" "I'm fine."*
2 bright and sunny. *The weather is fine for sailing.*
3 good enough. *There's nothing wrong with your work—it's fine.*
4 very thin.
5 very good. *She's a fine athlete.*

fine fines *noun*
Money that you have to pay as a punishment.

finger fingers *noun*
Your fingers are the long, thin parts at the end of your hands.

fingernail fingernails *noun*
the hard material over the tips of your fingers.

fingerprint
fingerprints *noun*
the mark made by the tip of your finger showing the lines on your skin. *The police couldn't find any fingerprints because the thief had worn gloves during the robbery.*

finish finishes finishing finished *verb*
When you finish something, you come to the end of it. ■ The opposite is **start** or **begin**.
finish *noun*.

fir firs *noun*
an evergreen tree with cones and leaves that are the shape of needles. ● A word that sounds like **fir** is **fur**.

fire fires *noun*
the hot, bright flames that come from something that is burning.

fire fires firing fired *verb*
1 to shoot bullets from a gun. *The thief fired at the police officer.*
2 to dismiss somebody from a job. *He was fired for stealing.*

A
B
C
D
E
F
G
H
I
J
K
L
M
N
O
P
Q
R
S
T
U
V
W
X
Y
Z

fire engine fire engines *noun*
a large truck with hoses and ladders that firefighters ride in to get to a fire.

fire extinguisher
fire extinguishers *noun*
a metal container full of special chemicals that you use to put out a fire.

firefighter firefighters *noun*
a person whose job is to put out dangerous fires and to rescue people who are in danger.

fireplace fireplaces *noun*
a hole in a wall in a room beneath a chimney where you can light a fire.

fireworks *noun*
small objects containing chemicals that explode noisily and make brightly colored sparks when you light them.

firm firmer firmest *adjective*
1 Something that is firm is quite hard and does not change its shape when you press it. *Bananas are firm when they are green but get soft when they are ripe.*
2 If you are firm about something, you are sure and you are not going to change your mind. *We haven't made a firm decision yet about where we are going on vacation.*

firm firms *noun*
a business company. *Dad works for a large law firm.*

first aid *noun*
medical help or treatment that is given to a sick or hurt person before he or she sees a doctor.

fish fish or fishes *noun*
an animal that lives in water and breathes through gills. A fish has fins and a tail for swimming, and its body is covered in scales. ❖ *Look opposite*

fish fishes fishing fished *verb*
To try to catch fish. *My uncle taught us how to fish with a fishing rod.*

fishery fisheries *noun*
a place where fish are raised.

fist fists *noun*
You make a fist when you curl your fingers and thumb into your palm. *The boxers were punching each other with their fists.*

fit fits fitting fitted *verb*
1 If a thing fits, it is the right size or shape. *These jeans don't fit me any more.*
2 If you fit things together, you join one thing to another. *I fitted the pieces of the puzzle together.*

fit fitter fittest *adjective*
If you are fit, your body is well and strong. *My parents exercise to keep themselves fit.*

fix fixes fixing fixed *verb*
1 When you fix something that was broken, you make it useful again. *I've fixed your bike.*
2 When you fix something to another thing, you join the two things firmly. *She fixed the shelf to the wall.*

fizzy fizzier fizziest *adjective*
full of small bubbles.

flag flags *noun*
a piece of cloth with a pattern on it, on the end of a pole. Each country has its own flag.

flake flakes *noun*
a small, thin, light piece of something. *a snowflake.*

flame flames *noun*
the hot, bright, burning gas that comes from a fire.

flap flaps flapping flapped *verb*
When a bird flaps its wings, it moves them up and down quickly.

flap flaps *noun*
a flat piece that hangs down to cover an opening. *a tent flap.*

flare flares *noun*
a bright flame or light used as a signal.

flash flashes *noun*
a sudden, bright light that lasts a short time. *a flash of lightning.*

flashlight flashlights *noun*
a small tube with a lightbulb that gets power from batteries. When you press a switch it lights up.

flat flatter flattest *adjective*
1 level and completely smooth and even, with no parts that are higher than the rest. *A table has to have a flat top so that things do not slide around.*
2 A flat tire does not have enough air in it. *My bike has a flat tire.*

flattery *noun*
too much praise. It can be insincere.

flavor
flavors *noun*
The flavor of something is what it tastes like. *different flavors of ice cream.*

flea fleas *noun*
a tiny jumping insect with no wings. Fleas bite animals and people.

flesh *noun*
1 the soft part of your body that is under your skin, covering your bones.
2 the soft part of fruit or vegetables.

flew past of **fly**
● A word that sounds like **flew** is **flu**.

flight flights *noun*
1 a journey in a plane. *It is a long flight from Chicago to Tokyo.*
2 flying through the air. *Have you ever seen geese in flight?*
3 A set of stairs. *We ran up six flights.*

float floats floating floated *verb*
1 When something floats in a liquid, it stays on the top and does not sink. *an experiment to see what floats.*
2 When something floats in air, it moves along gently in the air without falling to the ground. *We watched our balloon float through the backyard and over the fence.*

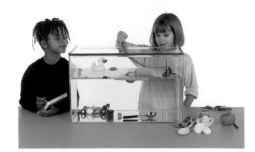

flock flocks *noun*
a group of animals of one kind. *a flock of sheep.* ◆ *a flock of geese.*

flood floods *noun*
A flood happens when a lot of water covers an area that is usually dry.

floodlight floodlights *noun*
very bright lights that light up a sports stadium or a building at night.

floor floors *noun*
1 the flat part that you walk on inside a building.
2 a level of a building.

floppy disk floppy disks *noun*
a magnetic disk in a square box that stores information from a computer.

floss flosses flossing flossed *verb*
to clean between your teeth with a special string.

flour *noun*
white or brown powder that is made by grinding grains such as wheat. We use flour to make bread, cakes, and pastry.
● A word that sounds like **flour** is **flower**.

flow flows flowing flowed *verb*
When a liquid flows, it moves smoothly along. *Many rivers flow into seas.* ◆ *The water flowed down the drain.*

flower flowers *noun*
the part of a plant at the end of the stem that has colored or white petals. ● A word that sounds like **flower** is **flour**.

flown past of **fly**.

flu *noun*
an illness that gives you a high temperature and makes your body ache all over. Flu is short for **influenza**. ● A word that sounds like **flu** is **flew**.

fluffy fluffier fluffiest *adjective*
soft and light like wool or hair. *Baby chickens are fluffy.*

fluid fluids *noun*
a substance that flows. *Liquids and gases are fluids.*

fluorescent *adjective*
A fluorescent object glows in the dark when you shine a light on it. *Cyclists wear fluorescent strips so that car drivers can see them in the dark more easily.* ▲ Say flor-**es**-ent.

flush flushes flushing flushed *verb*
1 If you flush, your face gets red. *Thomas flushed with embarrassment.*
2 When you flush the toilet, you make a lot of water flow through it to clean it.

flute flutes *noun*
a musical instrument like a long, thin pipe. You hold it sideways and blow into the end, covering its holes with your fingers to play different notes.

flutter flutters fluttering fluttered *verb*
When something flutters, it makes quick, light, flapping movements. *A moth was fluttering against the window.*

fly flies *noun*
a small insect with two wings.

fly flies flying flew flown *verb*
1 When something flies, it moves through the air. *A flock of geese was flying overhead.*
2 When you fly, you take a trip in a plane.

foal foals *noun*
a young horse.

foam *noun*
a mass of small air bubbles. *Liquid detergent makes a lot of foam.*

focus focuses focusing focused *verb*
When you focus a camera, a telescope, or binoculars, you move a part of it so that what you see through it is clear.

fog *noun*
a kind of thick cloud near the ground that makes it difficult to see things. **foggy** *adjective*.

foil *noun*
a very thin sheet of metal used to wrap food.

fold folds folding folded *verb*
When you fold something, you bend one part so that it covers another. *Fred folded his sweater before putting it in his suitcase.* ■ The opposite is **unfold**.

follow follows following followed *verb*
1 If you follow others, you go along behind them. ■ The opposite is **lead**.
2 If one thing follows another, it comes after it. *Night always follows day.*

fond fonder fondest *adjective*
If you are fond of somebody, you like that person very much and care about what happens to him or her.

food *noun*
all the things that people and animals can eat.

foolish *adjective*
very silly. ■ The opposite is **sensible**.

foot feet *noun*
Your foot is the part of your body at the bottom of your leg that you stand on.

football footballs *noun*
1 a game played by two teams who try to get a ball into the other team's end zone. *high-school football team.*
2 the ball that you use to play football.

footprint footprints *noun*
the mark that your foot or shoe leaves on a surface.

footstep footsteps *noun*
the sound that a person who is walking makes when each foot touches the ground. *I could hear footsteps coming up the path.*

forbid forbids forbidding forbade forbidden *verb*
If somebody forbids you to do something, he or she is telling you that you cannot do it. *Our teacher forbade us to bring pets to school.* ■ The opposite is **permit** or **allow**.

force forces forcing forced *verb*
1 If somebody forces you to do something, he or she makes you do it. *He forced me to sit down.*
2 If you force something somewhere, you use your strength to make it go there. *She tried to force a package through the letter slot.*

force forces *noun*
power or strength. *A lot of trees were blown down by the force of the wind.*

forecast forecasts forecasting forecast or forecasted *verb*
If you forecast something, you say it is going to happen in the future. *She forecasts that the weather will become warmer by the weekend.*
forecast *noun*
the weather forecast.

forehead foreheads *noun*
Your forehead is the part of your face above your eyes and below your hair.

foreign *adjective*
A person or thing that is foreign belongs to a country that is not your own. *Jane collects foreign stamps.* ▲ Say **for-en**.

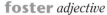

forest forests *noun*
a very large group of trees.

forge forges forging forged *verb*
If somebody forges something, such as money, the person makes an exact copy of it to deceive people. *He was put in jail for forging another person's signature on checks.* ▲ Say **forj**.
forgery *noun*.

forget forgets forgetting forgot forgotten *verb*
When you forget something, you do not remember it. *Don't forget your keys.*

forgive forgives forgiving forgave forgiven *verb*
When you forgive somebody, you do not mind anymore about something bad that he or she did to you. *Lily finally forgave me for losing her pen.*

fork forks *noun*
1 a tool with long, pointed parts called prongs, or tines, at one end. You use a fork for putting food in your mouth.
2 the place where something divides into two parts. *a fork in the road.*

form forms *noun*
1 the shape of something. *a birthday cake in the form of a dog.*
2 a kind of something. *Gas and coal are forms of fuel.*
3 a printed paper that has questions and spaces for you to write the answers.

form forms forming formed *verb*
1 When things form a certain shape, they are arranged in that shape. *The chairs formed a semicircle.*
2 When something forms, it starts to appear. *A crowd was forming outside the theater.*

fort forts *noun*
an army base.

fortress fortresses *noun*
a big, strong building such as a castle that can be defended against enemies.

fortune fortunes *noun*
1 good or bad luck.
2 a lot of money. *They made a fortune on the movie.*

fossil fossils *noun*
what remains of a plant or animal that died millions of years ago and that has become part of a piece of rock.
fossilized *adjective*.

foster *adjective*
giving care to someone else's child for a while. *foster parents of orphans.* ◆ *a foster family.*

fought past of **fight**.

found past of **find**.

fountain fountains *noun*
an object that sprays water up into the air.

fox foxes *noun*
a wild animal that looks like a small dog with red-brown fur and a long, thick tail.

fraction fractions *noun*
1 a part of a whole number. $1/2$ and $2/5$ are fractions.
2 a tiny part. *She opened the cage only a fraction but the hamster escaped.*

fracture fractures *noun*
a break or crack in something, especially a bone. *Her arm is in a cast because she has a fracture.* ▲ Say **frak-cher**.
fracture *verb*.

fragile *adjective*
Something that is fragile can break easily. *Be careful not to drop that vase; it's very fragile.* ▲ Say **fraj-il**.

frame frames *noun*
1 an edge around something such as a picture or window.
2 the shape of something such as a building or vehicle that is built first out of metal or wood, so that the rest can be built over it.
frame *verb*.

freckle freckles *noun*
a small brown spot on a person's skin.

free *adjective*
1 If you are free, you are able to do what you want or go where you want without anybody stopping you.
2 Something that is free does not cost any money.
3 Free also means not busy. *I'm busy now but I'll be free after dinner.*
freedom *noun*.

freeway freeways *noun*
an expressway.

freeze freezes freezing froze frozen *verb*
1 When water freezes, it gets so cold that it turns into ice.
2 When you freeze food, you make it very cold by storing it at a very low temperature so that it will stay fresh for a long time.
3 If you are freezing, you are very cold.

freezer freezers *noun*
a large metal chest or part of a refrigerator that freezes food so that it stays fresh for a long time.

freight *noun*
things that a truck, train, ship, or plane is carrying. ▲ Rhymes with *late.*

french fries *noun*
long, thin pieces of potato fried until they are crisp.

frequent *adjective*
Something that is frequent happens or comes often. *There are frequent buses to the city from here.*

fresh fresher freshest *adjective*
1 Food that is fresh has been made or picked recently and is not old or spoiled. *fresh eggs.* ◆ *fresh fruit.*
2 Fresh air is air that is clean and good to breathe. *We went outside to get some fresh air.*
3 Freshwater is water that is not salty.

freshman freshmen *noun*
a student who is in his or her first year at a high school or college.

friend friends *noun*
a person you like a lot. *Jane, Ali, and Rachel are friends.*
friendship *noun*.

friendly friendlier friendliest *adjective*
A friendly person gets to know other people easily and acts like a friend toward them. *Erica is friendly to everybody.*

fright frights *noun*
a feeling of great fear. *The explosion caused fright among the people.*

frighten frightens frightening frightened *verb*
If you frighten others, you make them feel afraid. *Tom frightened me with his Halloween costume.*
frightened *adjective*, **frightening** *adjective*.

frigid *adjective*
very cold. *Frigid weather conditions meant that the roads were icy.*

frijole frijoles *noun*
beans served with Mexican meals. They usually look mashed or mushy.

fringe fringes *noun*
a strip of hanging threads decorating the edge of something. *The cushion was trimmed with a fringe.*

frog frogs *noun*
a small animal with long, powerful back legs that it uses to jump. Frogs lay their eggs in water and these eggs develop into tadpoles.

front fronts *noun*
the part of something that faces forward or that you usually see first. ■ The opposite is **back** or **rear**.
in front of not behind. *There is a flower bed in front of our house.*

frost *noun*
a layer of ice crystals like white powder that forms at night when the weather is very cold.
frosty *adjective*.

froth *noun*
a mass of small bubbles on the surface of a liquid.
frothy *adjective*.

frown frowns frowning frowned *verb*
When you frown, you pull your eyebrows down and make your forehead wrinkle, often because you are angry or worried. *The teacher frowned at Richard when he wouldn't stop talking.*

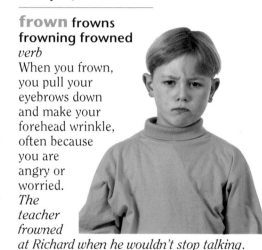

froze, frozen past of freeze.

fruit fruits *noun*
the part of a plant that contains seeds or a pit. You can eat many kinds of fruit.
❖ *Look opposite*

fry fries frying fried *verb*
When you fry food, you cook it in hot fat. You fry food in a frying pan.

fuel fuels *noun*
something such as coal, wood, or gasoline that we burn to make heat or power. *Cars and airplanes cannot run without fuel.*

full fuller fullest *adjective*
If something is full, there is so much inside it that there is no room for any more. *The bus was full of people.* ■ The opposite is **empty**.

fumble fumbles fumbling fumbled *verb*
If a player fumbles a football, he drops it.

fumes *noun*
smelly or poisonous smoke or gases that come from something that is burning or from chemicals. *gasoline fumes.*

fun *noun*
When you have fun, you enjoy yourself.

fund funds *noun*
an amount of money that is going to be used for a special purpose. *The school is raising funds to build a new gym.*

funeral funerals *noun*
a ceremony in which a dead body is buried or burned.

fungus
fungi *noun*
a kind of plant that is not green and does not have leaves or flowers. Fungi grow in damp, dark places. Mushrooms and toadstools are common kinds of fungi.

funnel funnels *noun*
1 a tube that is wide at one end and narrow at the other. A funnel is used for pouring liquid into a narrow container such as a bottle.
2 a chimney on a ship.

funny funnier funniest *adjective*
1 If something is funny, it makes you laugh or smile. *a funny story.*
2 Funny also means strange. *There was a funny smell coming from the kitchen.*

fur *noun*
the soft, thick hair that covers the body of many animals such as cats. ● A word that sounds like **fur** is **fir**.
furry *adjective*.

a furry hamster

furious *adjective*
very angry.

furniture *noun*
large things such as sofas, tables and chairs, beds, and desks that people have in their homes or offices.

fuse fuses *noun*
a small piece of wire or a tiny metal strip in electrical equipment that melts if too much electricity flows through it. This stops the power and means that the wiring can't get too hot. Fuses are for safety and stop fires from starting. *When a fuse melts and the power stops we say that the fuse has blown.*

fuss *noun*
If you make a fuss about something, you keep worrying and talking about it. *It would be better if you stopped making a fuss and actually did something.*

future *noun*
the time that has not happened yet. *Nobody can be sure what will happen in the future.* ■ The opposite is **past**.

G g

gadget gadgets *noun*
a tool that you use to do a special job.

useful kitchen gadgets

gain gains gaining gained *verb*
1 To gain means to get or win something. *By the end of the game, our team had gained 10 points.*
2 To gain also means to get more of something. *The bicycle gained speed as it went down the hill.*

galaxy galaxies *noun*
a very large group of stars and planets in space. *The Earth is part of one galaxy.*

gale gales *noun*
a very strong wind. *Gales can blow down trees and damage buildings.*

galleon galleons *noun*
a big sailing ship that was used a long time ago.

a large galleon carrying treasure

gallery galleries *noun*
a place where you can go to look at paintings, sculptures, or photographs.

gallon gallons *noun*
four quarts of a liquid. You use about 10 gallons of water if you stay in the shower for two minutes.

gallop gallops galloping galloped *verb*
When a horse gallops, it runs very fast.
gallop *noun*.

game games *noun*
A game is something that you play for fun. Games often have rules. *It rained so we spent most of the day at home playing games.*

gang gangs *noun*
a group of people who do things together. *a railroad gang.*

gap gaps *noun*
a space between two things.

garage garages *noun*
1 a building where somebody can keep a car.
2 a place that sells gasoline and where people repair cars.

garbage *noun*
pieces of food and trash that you put into cans and bags and throw away.

garden gardens *noun*
a piece of land near a house, where people grow flowers and vegetables.

garlic *noun*
a plant similar to a small onion with a very strong taste and smell. Garlic is used in cooking.

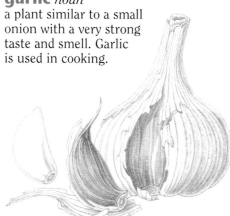

gas gases *noun*
A gas is something like air that is not liquid or solid and that you cannot see. Air is made of several gases mixed together. We use another kind of gas for cooking and heating.

gasoline *noun*
a liquid fuel that comes from petroleum. Gasoline makes cars and trucks run. We also call it "gas."

gate gates *noun*
a gate is a kind of door in a wall or fence. *a garden gate.*

gather gathers gathering gathered *verb*
1 If you gather things, you collect them. *The Scouts gathered wood for the campfire.*
2 If people gather, they come together in a group. *The children gathered around the ice-cream truck.*

gaze gazes gazing gazed *verb*
If you gaze at something, you look at it for a long time. *He stood on the shore gazing out to sea.*

gear gears *noun*
1 a set of wheels that work together in a car, bicycle, or model to make it go faster or slower.
2 the special clothes or things that you need for something. *camping gear.*

geese plural of **goose**.

gem gems *noun*
a precious stone or jewel.

gene genes *noun*
Genes are the tiny parts of the cells of plants and animals that control what they look like. Genes are passed from parents to children. ▲ Say *jeen.*

general *adjective*
Something that is general has to do with most people or things. *The general feeling is that exercise is good for you.* **generally** *adverb.*

generation generations *noun*
all the people who were born at about the same time. *This photo shows three different generations of my family: my grandparents, my parents, and me.*

generous *adjective*
If you are generous, you are kind and always ready to give money and other things to other people. **generosity** *noun.*

model helicopter gears

genius geniuses *noun*
an unusually smart, intelligent person. ▲ Say *jee-nee-uss.*

gentle gentler gentlest *adjective*
a gentle person is kind and careful. *Be very gentle when you pick up the baby.* ■ The opposite is **rough**.

genuine *adjective*
real, not fake. *Is this a genuine dinosaur fossil?* ▲ Say *jen-yoo-in.*

geography *noun*
the study of the countries of the world, and of its mountains and rivers.

gerbil gerbils *noun*
a small furry animal with long back legs. Some people keep gerbils in cages as pets.

germ germs *noun*
a very small living thing that can make you sick. *flu germs.*

ghost ghosts *noun*
the figure of a dead person that some people say they have seen.

A
B
C
D
E
F
G
H
I
J
K
L
M
N
O
P
Q
R
S
T
U
V
W
X
Y
Z

giant giants *noun*
a very big, strong person in stories.

gift gifts *noun*
1 a present. *birthday gifts.*
2 If you have a gift for something, you are very good at it. *Harry has a gift for music.*

gigantic *adjective*
very, very big. *a gigantic mountain.*
▲ Say *jy-gan-tik.*

giggle giggles giggling giggled *verb*
If you giggle, you laugh in a silly way. *We couldn't stop giggling at our teacher's funny shoes.*

gill gills *noun*
Gills are the parts of a fish that it breathes through. A fish has a pair of gills, one on each side of its head.

ginger *noun*
a plant that has a strong, hot taste. You can use the root or powder that is made from the root in cooking things.
gingersnaps ◆ *gingerbread.*

giraffe giraffes *noun*
a tall African animal with a very long neck. Giraffes feed on leaves and twigs from trees.

girl girls *noun*
a female child or a young woman.

ice fields

ice moves downward, creating cracks called crevasses

ice falls from the slope of the glacier and melts to form rivers

glacier glaciers *noun*
a huge mass of ice that moves very slowly down a mountain valley.
▲ Say *glay-shur.*

glad *adjective*
happy. *I'm glad you can come to my birthday party.*

glance glances glancing glanced *verb*
If you glance at something, you look at it quickly. *She glanced at her watch.*

gland glands *noun*
one of the parts of your body that make the chemicals that your body needs. *Sweat glands produce sweat to help your body cool down when you are hot.*

glare glares glaring glared *verb*
If you glare at people, you look at them in a very angry way.

glass glasses *noun*
1 Glass is a hard material that you can see through and that breaks easily. Windows and bottles are made of glass. *A greenhouse is made of glass.*
2 A glass is a container that you drink from, made of glass.

glasses *noun*
Glasses are two pieces of special glass, called lenses, in a frame. Some people wear glasses to help them see better. *She wears glasses to help her see more clearly.*

gleam gleams gleaming gleamed *verb*
To gleam means to shine with a soft light. *The lake gleamed in the moonlight.*

glide glides gliding glided *verb*
If something glides, it moves smoothly along. *The dancers glided gracefully around the floor.*

glider gliders *noun*
a very light aircraft that does not have an engine. Gliders fly by floating on currents of air.

glimpse glimpses glimpsing glimpsed *verb*
If you glimpse people or things, you see them only for a very short time. *We just glimpsed the rabbit as it ran into the woods.*

glitter glitters glittering glittered *verb*
If something glitters, it shines brightly with lots of flashes of light. *The fresh snow glittered like diamonds.*
glitter *noun.*

globe globes *noun*
a ball with a map of the world on it.

gloomy gloomier gloomiest
adjective
1 If a room or a day is gloomy, it is dark and dull.
2 If you are gloomy, you feel sad.

glossy glossier glossiest *adjective*
shiny. *a dog with a glossy coat.*

glove gloves *noun*
a piece of clothing that you wear on your hand. *woolen gloves.*

glow glows glowing glowed *verb*
If something glows, it shines with a steady light. *The fire glowed in the dark.*

glue *noun*
a thick liquid that you use for sticking things together. *Janice and Marina used glue to fix the broken pottery.*
glue
verb.

gnat gnats *noun*
a small, flying insect that bites people. ▲ Say *nat*.

gnaw gnaws gnawing gnawed
verb
If you gnaw something hard, you keep biting it for a long time. *The dog was gnawing at a bone.* ▲ Say *naw*.

gnome gnomes *noun*
a little old man in fairy tales who lives underground. Gnomes usually have long beards and pointed hats. ▲ Say *nome*.

goal goals *noun*
1 A goal is the place where you have to make the ball go to score points in games such as soccer or hockey.
2 A goal is the point or points you score when the ball goes into the goal.
3 A goal can also be something important that you want to do in your life. *My goal is to run the marathon in the Olympic Games.*

goat goats
noun
an animal with horns and short, rough hair. A male goat is called a billy goat, a female is a nanny goat, and a young goat is a kid.

gobble gobbles gobbling gobbled
verb
If you gobble food, you eat it very quickly and greedily. *She gobbled up all the cookies and cakes before anyone else could eat them.*

god gods *noun*
a being that people believe controls them and nature. Some people pray to many different gods. *Brahma, Vishnu, and Shiva are the three main gods of the Hindu religion.*

goggles *noun*
special glasses that you wear to protect your eyes from water or dust. *He wears goggles when he's making models.*

go-kart go-karts *noun*
a small, low, open racing car. *go-kart racing.*

gold *noun*
a shiny, yellow metal that is used to make rings and other jewelry.

goldfish goldfish or goldfishes
noun
a small, orange fish you keep as a pet.

golf *noun*
a game that you play by using long sticks called golf clubs to hit a ball into holes around a golf course.

gong gongs *noun*
a round piece of metal that you hit to make a loud noise.

good better best *adjective*
1 If something is good, people like it. *a good story.*
2 If you are good, you do as you are told.
3 If you are good at something, you can do it well. *Chris is good at spelling.*
4 If something is good for you, it makes you healthy. *Fruit is good for you.*

---

g o o d

Some words you can use instead of good:

We need a good plumber to fix the broken pipes.
☞ **skilled, expert** ☜

He's a good pianist.
☞ **talented** ☜

The weather is good today.
☞ **marvelous** ☜

---

goods *noun*
things that can be bought and sold.

goose geese *noun*
a large bird with a long neck and webbed feet that lives near water. Some geese are wild but others are kept on farms for their eggs, meat, and feathers. A male goose is called a gander, and a young goose is a gosling.

Canada goose

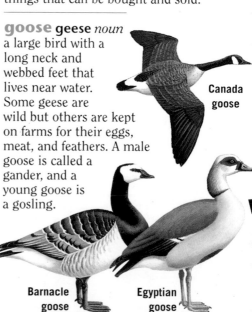

Barnacle goose

Egyptian goose

A B C D E F G H I J K L M N O P Q R S T U V W X Y Z

a b c d e f g h i j k l m n o p q r s t u v w x y z

gorge gorges *noun*
a deep, narrow valley. *The river runs through the gorge.*

gorgeous *adjective*
very beautiful. *a gorgeous day.* ◆ *a gorgeous view of the sea.* ▲ Say **gor**-*juss.*

gorilla gorillas *noun*
a very big African ape with dark fur.

gossip *noun*
stories about others that people repeat.

government governments *noun*
a group of people who are in charge of a country. ▲ Say **guv**-er-ment.

governor governors *noun*
the person the people of a state elect as their leader.

gown gowns *noun*
1 a long dress that women wear at special times. *a ball gown.*
2 a long, loose piece of clothing that judges wear.

grab grabs grabbing grabbed *verb*
If you grab something, you take it quickly and roughly. *The robber grabbed the money and ran away.*

graceful *adjective* beautiful or pleasing. *a graceful skater.*

grade grades *noun* a mark that a teacher gives you to show how good your work is. *I got grade A for my story and B for art.*

gradual *adjective*
If something is gradual, it happens slowly and steadily. *I'm making gradual progress at swimming.*

graduate graduates graduating graduated *verb*
to pass tests and get a diploma from a school.

graffiti *noun*
writing and drawing on walls in public places. ▲ Say *gra-**fee**-tee.*

grain grains *noun*
1 Grain is the seeds of plants such as wheat and rice that we eat.
2 Grains are tiny, hard bits of something such as salt, sugar, or sand.

grandchild grandchildren *noun*
A grandchild is the child of a person's son or daughter.

grandparent grandparents *noun*
The mother or father of your mother or father.

grape grapes *noun*
a small green, red, or black fruit that grows in bunches on a vine. Wine is made from grapes.

grapefruit grapefruit *noun*
a large, round yellow fruit that is similar to an orange but not as sweet.

graph graphs *noun*
a diagram that shows how numbers and amounts compare with each other. *We drew a graph to show how much rain there was in each month of the year.*

grasp grasps grasping grasped *verb*
If you grasp something, you hold it tightly. *She grasped the child's hand as they crossed the street.*

grass grasses *noun*
the thin, green leaves that cover fields and lawns. *Sheep, horses, and cows eat grass.*
grassy *adjective.*

grasshopper grasshoppers *noun*
a jumping insect with strong back legs and two pairs of wings. Grasshoppers feed on plants.

grate grates grating grated *verb*
If you grate food, you rub it over a metal tool called a grater to shred it into very small pieces. *grated cheese.* ● A word that sounds like **grate** is **great.**

grateful *adjective*
If you feel grateful to people, you want to thank them because they have done something for you. *I was very grateful to her for finding my purse.* ■ The opposite is **ungrateful.**
gratefully *adverb.*

grave graves *noun*
a hole in the ground where a dead person is buried.

grave graver gravest *adjective*
very serious and important. *a grave mistake.* ◆ *a grave illness.*

gravel *noun*
small stones that are used to cover roads and driveways.

gravity *noun*
the natural force that pulls everything down toward the Earth.

gravy *noun*
a sauce made from the juices that come out of meat when you cook it.

graze grazes grazing grazed *verb*
1 When animals graze, they move around eating grass. *The sheep were grazing in the field.*
2 If you graze your skin, you cut it slightly by scraping it against something. *When she fell over she grazed her knee badly.*

grease *noun*
thick oil or soft fat. *You will need very hot water to wash the grease off those dirty pots.*
greasy *adjective.*

great greater greatest *adjective*
1 very good. *a great movie.*
2 very important. *a great king.*
3 very big. *a great crowd of people.*
● A word that sounds like **great** is **grate.**

greedy greedier greediest *adjective*
People who are greedy want more of something than they really need. *Don't be so greedy—leave some cake for your brother and sister.*

greenhouse greenhouses *noun*
a building made of glass, used for growing plants.

greet greets greeting greeted *verb*
When you greet somebody, you do something friendly when you meet them, such as saying "hello" or shaking hands. *She greeted me with a friendly smile.*

greeting greetings *noun*
words such as "hello," "good morning," or "Happy New Year" that you say when you meet somebody.

grew past of **grow.**

grief *noun*
great sadness. *She was filled with grief when her dog died.*

grill grills grilling grilled *verb*
If you grill food, you cook it on metal bars under or over strong heat. *We grilled hot dogs outside.*
grill *noun.*

grin grins grinning grinned *verb*
If you grin, you have a big smile. *She grinned at me when I said hello.*
grin *noun.*

grind grinds grinding ground *verb*
If you grind something, you crush it into tiny pieces or into a powder. *grinding peppercorns.*

grip grips gripping gripped *verb*
If you grip something, you hold it very firmly. *She gripped the branch and swung from it.*

groan groans groaning groaned *verb*
To groan is to make a long, deep sound because you are unhappy or in pain.

groom grooms *noun*
1 a person who looks after horses.
2 a man on his wedding day.

groom grooms grooming groomed *verb*
If you groom an animal, you clean and brush it. *The children are grooming their horse before riding it.*

groundbreaker groundbreakers *noun*
A groundbreaker is a person or a process that achieves something new. *a groundbreaking discovery.*

grouchy grouchier grouchiest *adjective*
If you are grouchy, you are in a bad mood and you feel like grumbling.

groove grooves *noun*
a long, thin line that is cut into a flat surface.

ground grounds *noun*
1 The ground is what you walk on when you are outside. *We sat on the ground to eat our picnic lunch.*
2 a piece of land that is used for something special. *a camping ground.*

ground past of **grind.**

group groups *noun*
1 a number of people or things that are together in one place. *A group of children stood near the corner.*
2 a group of musicians who play or sing together.

grow grows growing grew grown *verb*
1 When something grows, it gets bigger or more. *The puppy is growing very fast. The crowd grew.*
2 If you grow something, you plant it so that it will develop. *Flora grew this plant from a seed.*
3 To grow also means to become. *We are all growing older.*

growl growls growling growled *verb*
To growl is to make the low, rough noise that a dog or a bear makes when it is angry or frightened.

A B C D E F G H I J K L M N O P Q R S T U V W X Y Z

growl *noun.*

grown-up **grown-ups** *noun*
an adult. *Parents are grown-ups.*

growth *noun*
the result of growing. *We measured the tree's growth every month.*

grumble **grumbles grumbling grumbled** *verb*
If you grumble, you complain about something in an angry way. *She grumbled about having to do her homework.*

grunt **grunts grunting grunted** *verb*
To grunt is to make the short, deep, rough sound that a pig makes.

guacamole *noun*
a dip made from mashed avocado and seasonings. ▲ Say *gwahk-uh-moh-lee.*

guarantee **guarantees** *noun*
1 a promise made by the makers of something, that they will fix or replace it if it breaks.
2 a promise that something will happen.
▲ Say *ga-ran-tee.*
guarantee *verb.*

guard **guards** *noun*
a person who keeps somebody or something safe, or who stops people from escaping. *a Swiss guard.*

guardian **guardians** *noun*
a person who is told by a court to take care of someone else, usually a child.

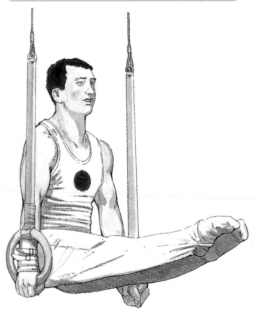

guava *noun*
a sweet, tropical fruit with pink flesh.

guess **guesses guessing guessed** *verb*
When you guess, you try to give an answer to something when you do not really know if it is right. *Sometimes you can guess what is inside a box by looking at its shape.*

guess *noun.*
Take a guess at how much the birthday cake weighs.

guest **guests** *noun*
a person who is staying in your home because you have invited him or her. *We have guests staying with us this weekend.* ▲ Rhymes with **best.**

guide **guides guiding guided** *verb*
If you guide people, you show them where to go or what to do. *Her job is to guide people around the city.* ▲ Rhymes with **wide.**
guide *noun.*

guilty *adjective*
1 If you are guilty, you have done something wrong. ■ The opposite is **innocent.**
2 If you feel guilty, you feel sorry because you have done something wrong. *She felt guilty for being rude to her aunt.*

guinea pig **guinea pigs** *noun*
a small, furry animal with short ears and no tail. Some people keep guinea pigs as pets. ▲ Say *gih-nee pig.*

guitar **guitars** *noun*
a musical instrument with six strings that you play with your fingers.

gulf **gulfs** *noun*
a big part of the sea that has land partly around it.

gull **gulls** *noun*
a large, gray or white seabird.

gulp **gulps gulping gulped** *verb*
If you gulp, you swallow something very quickly. *Katie gulped down the orange juice because she was thirsty.*

gum **gums** *noun*
1 Your gums are the firm, pink flesh around your teeth.
2 chewing gum.

gun **guns** *noun*
a weapon that shoots bullets. *She aimed the gun and fired at the target.*

gutter **gutters** *noun*
an open pipe along the edge of a roof for carrying away rainwater. *We cleaned leaves out of the gutters.*

gym **gyms** *noun*
a large room where you can do exercises, often using special equipment. Gym is short for **gymnasium.**

gymnast **gymnasts** *noun*
a person who does difficult and carefully controlled movements with the body in competitions. *an Olympic gymnast.*

gymnastics *noun*
1 exercises for your body.
2 a sport in which people do difficult and carefully controlled movements with their bodies in competitions.

a b c d e f g h i j k l m n o p q r s t u v w x y z

H h

habit habits *noun*
something that you do often, usually without thinking about it.

habitat habitats *noun*
The habitat of an animal or a plant is the kind of place where it lives.

hacienda haciendas *noun*
a big farm in the southwest United States.
▲ Say *hah-see-en-dah.*

hail *noun*
frozen rain falling as little balls of ice.

hair hairs *noun*
Hair is lots of thin threads that grow on your head and other parts of your body.
● A word that sounds like **hair** is **hare.**

straight, curly, and wavy hair

hairdresser hairdressers *noun*
a person whose job is to cut and arrange people's hair.

hairy hairier hairiest *adjective*
covered with hair. *The book is about a big hairy monster.*

half halves *noun*
one of two equal parts of something. You can write *half* as ¹/₂. *Half of ten is five.*
◆ *Two halves make a whole.*

hall halls *noun*
1 the part just inside the door of a house or apartment building with doors leading to rooms.
2 a large room or a building where events such as concerts and meetings take place. *our town hall.*

halt halts halting halted *verb*
When something halts, it stops. *The truck halted at the stoplight.*

halve halves halving halved *verb*
If you halve something, you divide it into two equal parts. *Halve the fruit and remove the pit.*

ham *noun*
meat from a hog's leg that has been treated with salt so it can be kept for a long time. *a ham and cheese sandwich.*

hamburger hamburgers *noun*
chopped beef pressed into a flat, round shape and eaten in a bun.

hammer hammers *noun*
a tool with a heavy part at one end that you use for hitting nails into things.

hammock hammocks *noun*
a bed made of canvas or pieces of rope that is hung at each end from something such as a tree or post.

hamster hamsters *noun*
a small animal that is often kept as a pet. It is similar to a large mouse with a very short tail. Hamsters can store food in pouches inside their cheeks.

hand hands *noun*
Your hand is the part of your body at the end of your arm.

hand hands handing handed *verb*
If you hand something to somebody, you give it to him or her.

handicap *noun*
something that makes it more difficult to do things. *Being tall can be a handicap in getting into small cars.*

handkerchief handkerchiefs *noun*
a small square of cloth or paper tissue that you use for blowing your nose.
▲ Say *hang-kur-chief.*

handle handles *noun*
1 The handle of something such as a cup or a bag is the part that you take in your hand to carry it or pick it up.
2 The handle of a door is the lever or knob that you move with your hand to open and close it.

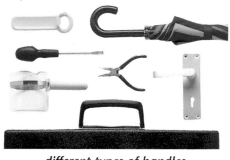
different types of handles

handlebar handlebars *noun*
the curved bar at the front of a bicycle or a motorcycle that you use for steering.

handsome *adjective*
A man who is handsome has an attractive face.

handwriting *noun*
Your handwriting is the way you write with a pen or pencil.

hang hangs hanging hung *verb*
If you hang something somewhere, you fasten it from the top to something above it. *Hang your coat in the closet.*

hang glider hang gliders *noun*
a kind of large kite with a harness underneath, in which you fly through the air in the sport of hang gliding.

happen happens happening happened *verb*
1 Something that happens or occurs takes place. *The accident happened because she was not paying attention.*
2 If you happen to do something, you do it by chance. *I happened to find your ball when I was in the garden.*

A B C D E F G H I J K L M N O P Q R S T U V W X Y Z

happy happier happiest *adjective*
If you are happy, you feel good because something nice has happened or because you are enjoying yourself. ■ The opposite is **unhappy** or **sad**.
happily *adverb*, **happiness** *noun*.

happy

Some words that you can use instead of happy:

I'm happy I've finished my homework.
☞ **contented, pleased, glad** ☜

They are happy with their wedding presents.
☞ **delighted, pleased, thrilled** ☜

Christmas is a happy time of year.
☞ **merry, cheerful** ☜

harbor harbors *noun*
an area of sea by the coast where ships can tie up.

hard harder hardest *adjective*
1 If something is hard, you cannot break, cut, or bend it easily. *Stones, nuts, and bolts are hard.* ■ The opposite is **soft**.
2 hard to do. *a hard puzzle.* ■ The opposite is **easy**.

hard harder hardest *adverb*
Hard means a lot. *Stephanie has worked very hard this semester.*

hard disk hard disks *noun*
the part inside a computer where a large amount of information is stored.

harden hardens hardening hardened *verb*
When something hardens, it becomes hard. *Hold the pieces together until the glue has hardened.* ■ The opposite is **soften**.

hare hares *noun* an animal that looks like a large rabbit

with long ears and long legs. ● A word that sounds like **hare** is **hair**.

harm harms harming harmed *verb*
1 If you harm people, you hurt them. *The dog won't harm you.*
2 If you harm something, you damage it.

harmful *adjective*
If something is harmful, it could hurt you or make you ill. *Looking straight at the Sun is harmful to your eyes.* ■ The opposite is **harmless**.

harmless *adjective*
If something is harmless, it will not hurt you. *Our dog is harmless—it wouldn't bite anybody.* ■ The opposite is **harmful**.

harmony harmonies *noun*
a group of musical notes that sound nice when you hear them together.

harness harnesses *noun*
1 a set of straps and metal parts that go around a horse's head or body so that you can control it.
2 a set of straps for fastening something such as a parachute to a person's body.

harp harps *noun*
a musical instrument. It has a large frame with strings that you play (pluck) with your fingers.
harpist *noun*

harsh harsher harshest *adjective*
1 If people behave in a harsh way, they are cruel or unkind. *That was a very harsh punishment.*
2 A harsh winter is very cold and difficult.
3 Harsh sounds are loud and unpleasant. *a harsh voice.*

harvest harvests *noun*
the time when farmers pick or cut their crops because they are ripe.

hat hats *noun*
a covering that you wear on your head.

hatch hatches hatching hatched *verb*
When a baby bird or other animal hatches, it breaks out of its egg.

hatchet hatchets *noun*
a small ax.

hate hates hating hated *verb*
If you hate somebody or something, you have a very strong feeling of not liking that one. *I hate getting up early in the morning.* ■ The opposite is **love**.

haunted *adjective*
If a place is haunted, there is supposed to be a ghost there. *a haunted house.*
▲ Say *hawn-ted*.

hawk hawks *noun*
a large bird with a curved beak and strong claws, that eats other birds and small animals.

hay *noun*
grass that has been cut and dried and is used to feed horses and cattle in the winter months.

hazard hazards *noun*
a danger or risk. *Patches of oil on the sea from leaking tankers are a hazard to seabirds and fish.*
hazardous *adjective*.

head heads *noun*
1 Your head is the top part of you.
2 the person who is in charge of a group. *the head of a large company.*
▲ Rhymes with **tread**.

headache headaches *noun*
a pain in your head.

headlight headlights *noun*
the lights on the front of a car.

headline headlines *noun*
words in larger print at the top of a story in a newspaper.

DAILY GLOBE
BOOKS STILL REIGN SUPREME!
by John Grisewood
Dictionary Correspondent

Good books still sell

Champions! At last!

headphones *noun*
small speakers for a stereo or radio that fit on your ears and that are joined together by a band over the top of your head. Headphones let you hear music and other sounds without other people hearing them.

headquarters *noun*
the building where the people in charge of an organization work.

head start *noun*
an advantage that you get when you are allowed to start a race first.

heal heals healing healed *verb*
If something heals, it gets better after being ill or injured. ● A word that sounds like **heal** is **heel**.

health *noun*
Your health is how well you are. If your health is bad, you are ill. If your health is good, you are well. ▲ Say **helth**.

healthy healthier healthiest *adjective*
1 If you are healthy, you are fit and well.
2 Something that is healthy is good for you and helps you to stay well. *Fresh fruit and vegetables are healthy foods.*
▲ Say **helth**-y. ■ The opposite is **unhealthy**.

heap heaps *noun*
a large, messy pile of things. *She left her clothes in a heap on the floor.*

hear hears hearing heard *verb*
When you hear a sound, you notice it through your ears. ● A word that sounds like **hear** is **here**.

heart hearts *noun*
Your heart is the part of you, inside your chest, that pumps the blood around your body.
▲ Say **hart**.

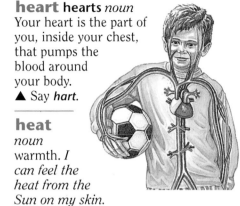

heat *noun*
warmth. *I can feel the heat from the Sun on my skin.*

heat heats heating heated *verb*
If you heat something, you make it hot. *He heated some water to make soup.*

heave heaves heaving heaved *verb*
If you heave something somewhere, you use a lot of energy to lift, push, or pull it. *Ben and Joe heaved the rope together in a tug-of-war.*

heavy heavier heaviest *adjective*
Something that is heavy weighs a lot. *The suitcase was too heavy for me to lift.* ■ The opposite is **light**.

hedge hedges *noun*
a line of bushes or small trees growing close together at the edge of a garden, yard, or road.

heed heeds heeding heeded *verb*
If you heed, you pay close attention. *Heed my advice.*

heel heels *noun*
1 Your heel is the back part of your foot.
2 the part of a shoe or boot that is under the back part of your foot.
● A word that sounds like **heel** is **heal**.

height heights *noun*
The height of something is how high it is from the bottom to the top.
▲ Rhymes with **kite**.

held past of **hold**.

helicopter helicopters *noun*
an aircraft without wings that is kept in the air by long blades that are attached to its roof and turn around very fast.

hello *interjection*
People say hello when they answer the phone or meet and greet others. ■ The opposite is **good-bye**.

helmet helmets *noun*
a hard hat that protects your head.

help helps helping helped *verb*
If you help people, you make it easier for them to do something. *Amy helped me with my arithmetic homework.*
help *noun*.

helpful *adjective*
1 If you are helpful, you do what you can to help other people.
2 Something that is helpful is useful. *Thank you for your helpful advice.*

helpless *adjective*
If you are helpless, you cannot look after yourself. *A baby is completely helpless when it is born.*

hem hems *noun*
the edge of a piece of material that is folded over and sewn flat in order to make it neat.

A B C D E F G H I J K L M N O P Q R S T U V W X Y Z

hen hens *noun*
1 a female chicken that lays eggs that we eat.
2 any female bird.

herb herbs *noun*
a plant that we use to give flavor to food or to make medicines. *Marjoram, yarrow, and mint are all herbs.*

yarrow

marjoram

herd herds *noun*
a large group of animals of one kind that live together. *Elephants live in herds.*

hero heroes *noun*
1 a person who is very brave or very good.
2 the main male character in a book, play, or movie.

heroine heroines *noun*
1 a woman who is very brave or very good.
2 the main female character in a book, play, or movie.
▲ Say *hair-oh-in.*

heron herons *noun*
a large, gray bird with long legs and a long neck. Herons live near water and eat fish.

hesitate hesitates hesitating hesitated *verb*
If you hesitate, you stop for a short time before you do something, often because you are not sure what to do. *She hesitated before answering me.*
hesitation *noun.*

hexagon hexagons *noun*
a flat shape with six sides.
❖*Look at page 145*
hexagonal *adjective.*

hibernate hibernates hibernating hibernated *verb*
When an animal hibernates, it stays in a deep sleep all through the winter. *Bears hibernate.*
hibernation *noun.*

Dormice hibernate.

hiccup hiccups *noun*
a sudden, short breath in and a noise that sounds like "hic," that you cannot help making. You sometimes get hiccups when you eat or drink too quickly.
hiccup *verb.*

hickory hickories *noun*
a tall tree with hard wood and nuts that taste good.

hide hides hiding hid hidden *verb*
1 If you hide, you go where nobody can find you.
2 If you hide something, you put it where nobody can find it.

hieroglyphic *adjective*
a kind of writing that uses pictures instead of letters to make up words. Hieroglyphic writing was used in ancient Egypt. ▲ Say *hie-ro-glif-ik.*
hieroglyph *noun.*

high higher highest *adjective*
1 Something that is high goes up a long way from the bottom to the top.
2 High also means a long way above the ground. ■ The opposite is **low.**

high school high schools *noun*
a school for students from the ninth through the twelfth grades.

hijack hijacks hijacking hijacked *verb*
If people hijack a plane or ship, they take control of it by threatening the passengers and crew and then try to make it go where they want it to.
hijacker *noun.*

hill hills *noun*
an area of land that is higher than the land around it.

Hindu Hindus *noun*
a person who follows a religion called Hinduism. Hindus worship several different gods and believe that after you die you are born again in a different body.

hinge hinges *noun*
a piece of metal that holds a door to its frame at one side, so that it can open and close.

hint hints hinting hinted *verb*
When you hint, you let somebody know something without actually saying exactly what you mean.

hip hips *noun*
Your hips are at the side of your body between your waist and the top of your legs.

hippopotamus hippopotamuses *noun*
a large animal with a thick, dark gray skin and very short legs. Hippopotamuses live by lakes and rivers in Africa, and are sometimes called **hippos** for short. *Hippopotomuses have only four toes on each foot.*

African hippo

Pygmy hippo

hire hires hiring hired *verb*
If you hire someone, you pay him or her to work for you for a certain time. *Dad hired a person to paint our house.*

Hispanic Hispanics *noun*
an American who has ancestors from Spain, Mexico, or Latin America.

history *noun*
the study of things that happened in the past. *At school we are learning about the history of our state.*
historical *adjective*.

hit hits hitting hit *verb*
When you hit something, you touch it quickly and with force. *I hit the ball with the bat.*

hive hives *noun*
a special box for bees to live in where you can collect their honey.

hoarse hoarser hoarsest *adjective*
If you are hoarse, your voice sounds rough. *He yelled at the top of his voice all through the match until he was hoarse.* ● A word that sounds like **hoarse** is **horse**.

hobble hobbles hobbling hobbled *verb*
If you hobble, you walk with difficulty because your feet hurt. *He was hobbling because his feet were covered in blisters.*

hobby hobbies *noun*
something that you enjoy doing in your spare time. *My hobbies are swimming, reading, and collecting shells.*

hockey *noun*
a game played outdoors, or indoors on ice, by two teams of eleven players who try to get a puck or ball into a goal by hitting it with a long, curved stick.

hog hogs *noun*
a grown-up pig.

hold holds holding held *verb*
1 If you hold something, you have it in your hand or hands. *I held up the picture so that my sister could see it.*
2 If a container holds a certain amount, it can have that amount in it but no more. *A one-pint measuring cup holds up to 16 ounces.*

hole holes *noun*
a gap or space in something. *These jeans have a hole in the knee.* ● A word that sounds like **hole** is **whole**.

holiday holidays *noun*
a time when you do not have to go to school or work. *New Year's Day is a holiday.*

hollow *adjective*
Something that is hollow has an empty space inside it. ■ The opposite is **solid**.

holly *noun*
a tree that has red berries and leaves with sharp points.

holy holier holiest *adjective*
Something that is holy is very special because it has to do with religion.

homage *noun*
an act that is performed to show respect to someone.

home homes *noun*
Your home is the place where you live.

homeless *adjective*
a homeless person has no place to live.

homeroom homerooms *noun*
a schoolroom where you sit before classes start.

homework *noun*
work that a teacher gives to pupils to do at home.

honest *adjective*
If you are honest, you tell the truth.
▲ Say **on**-est.
■ The opposite is **dishonest**.

honey *noun*
a sweet, sticky food that is made by bees.
▲ Rhymes with *funny*.

hood hoods *noun*
a part of a coat or jacket that you can pull over your head.

hoof　　　　　horseshoe

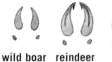

water
deer　　deer　　wild boar　reindeer　　elk

horse　　　rhino　　　tapir

hoof hooves *or* hoofs *noun*
the hard covering on the foot of some animals such as a horse or deer.

hook hooks *noun*
a curved piece of metal or plastic that is used for hanging things on or for holding or fastening things.

hoop hoops *noun*
a large ring made of wood, metal, or plastic.

hoot hoots hooting hooted *verb*
1 To hoot is to make the long "oo" sound that an owl makes.
2 When people hoot, they make a loud noise to show dislike for someone or something. *The crowd hooted loudly at the opposing team.*

hop hops hopping hopped *verb*
1 If you hop, you jump on one leg.
2 When an animal or insect hops, it moves along by jumping. *The frog hopped away.*

hope hopes hoping hoped *verb*
If you hope something will happen, you want it to happen and you think it probably will. *I hope you will be able to come to my party.*
hope *noun*, **hopeless** *adjective*

a b c d e f g h i j k l m n o p q r s t u v w x y z

hopeful *adjective*
If you are hopeful, you think that what you want will probably happen. *The police are hopeful that they will soon be able to solve the crime.*

horizon horizons *noun*
the line in the far distance where the land or the sea seems to meet the sky. ▲ Say *hor-eye-zon.*

horizontal *adjective*
Something that is horizontal goes from side to side, parallel to the ground, not up and down. *The top of the table is horizontal with the floor.* ■ The opposite is **vertical**.
horizontally *adverb*

horn horns *noun*
1 Horns are the hard, pointed, bony parts that grow out of the head of some animals such as cows, goats, and some sheep.
2 A horn is a brass musical instrument that you blow into to make sounds.
3 A horn is also an instrument in a car or other vehicle that the driver uses to make a loud noise as a warning to other drivers or to pedestrians.

horrible *adjective*
terrible, or very unpleasant. *What a horrible thing to say!*
horribly *adverb.*

horror *noun*
1 a feeling that you get when you are very shocked and upset at something terrible. *We were filled with horror at the news of the famine in Africa.*
2 A horror story is a story that is meant to frighten you.

horse horses *noun*
a large animal with a long tail and a mane. People ride horses or use them to pull carts or carriages. A female horse is called a mare, a male horse is a stallion, and a young horse is a foal. ● A word that sounds like **horse** is **hoarse**.

horse chestnut
noun
a large tree with white flowers that produces a large nut.

hose hoses *noun*
a long, plastic pipe that is used for spraying water. *You can use a hose to water the garden.*

HORSES

Clydesdale horse

Przewalski's horse

Wild ass

Arab stallion

Shetland pony

> ### VOCABULARY
> **aids**
> *the signals a rider gives to tell the horse what to do.*
>
> **bit**
> *the metal or rubber device attached to the bridle and placed in the horse's mouth.*
>
> **bridle**
> *the part of saddle that is placed over a horse's head and to which the bit and reins are attached.*
>
> **colt**
> *a male foal.*
>
> **filly**
> *a female foal.*
>
> **gait**
> *the pace of a horse.*

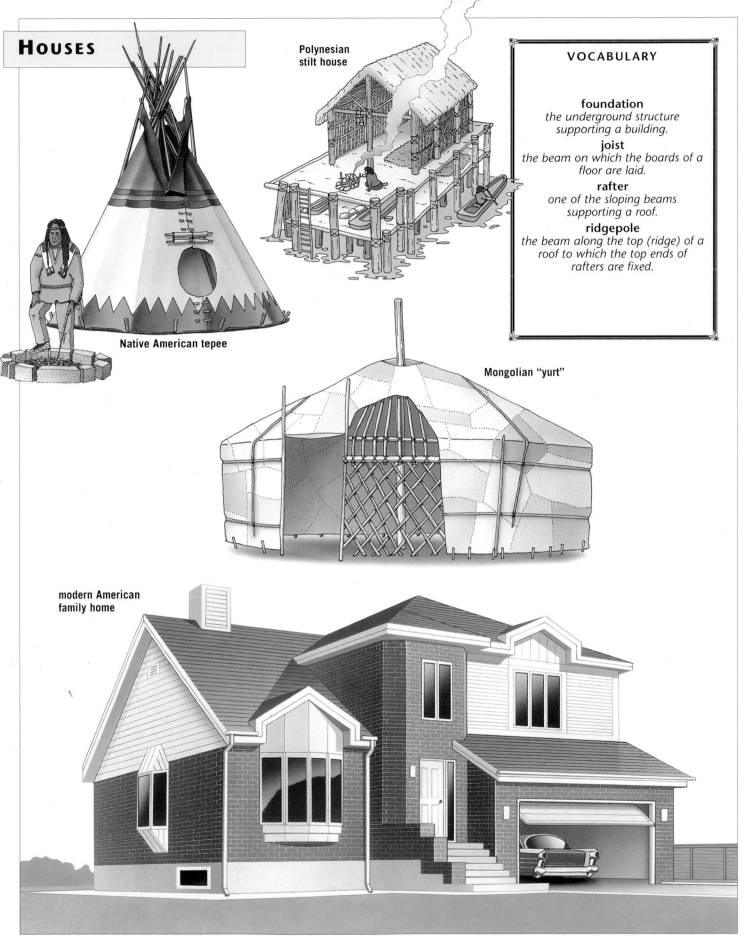

HOUSES

Polynesian stilt house

Native American tepee

VOCABULARY

foundation
the underground structure supporting a building.

joist
the beam on which the boards of a floor are laid.

rafter
one of the sloping beams supporting a roof.

ridgepole
the beam along the top (ridge) of a roof to which the top ends of rafters are fixed.

Mongolian "yurt"

modern American family home

A B C D E F G H I J K L M N O P Q R S T U V W X Y Z

hospital hospitals *noun*
a building where doctors and nurses take care of people who are sick or injured.

host hosts *noun*
a person who invites guests and looks after them when they arrive.

hostage hostages *noun*
a person who is held prisoner by those who threaten to hurt or kill the prisoner if they do not get what they want.

hot hotter hottest *adjective*
1 Something that is hot has a high temperature. *Careful! That oil is very hot!*
2 Hot foods have a strong taste and make your mouth feel like it is burning when you eat them. *Some spices are hot.*

hotel hotels *noun*
a building with bedrooms where people pay to stay for a few nights.

hour hours *noun*
a period of 60 minutes. There are 24 hours in a day. ▲ Rhymes with *tower*. ● A word that sounds like **hour** is **our**.

house houses *noun*
a building where people live.
❖ *Look at page 83*

House of Representatives *noun*
One of the two branches of Congress. Its members serve for two years.

hover hovers hovering hovered *verb*
If something hovers, it stays in one place in the air. *A rescue helicopter hovered over the boat.*

howl howls howling howled *verb*
When an animal howls, it makes a long, loud, crying sound. *Wolves were howling.*

hug hugs hugging hugged *verb*
When you hug people, you put your arms around them and hold them tight.
hug *noun.*

huge *adjective*
very, very big. ■ The opposite is **tiny**.

hum hums humming hummed *verb*
When you hum, you make a singing sound with your lips closed. *He was humming a tune while he worked.*

human humans *noun*
a person. *A lot of animals are afraid of humans.*

humid *adjective*
Humid weather is hot, sticky, and damp. ▲ Say **hyoo-mid**.

humor *noun*
the ability to make people laugh or to see when something is funny. *She has a good sense of humor.* ▲ Say **hyoo-mer**.
humorous *adjective.*

hump humps *noun*
1 a large round lump on a camel's back, for example.
2 a bump in the road.

a dromedary camel (one hump)   a Bactrian camel (two humps)

hung past of **hang**.

hungry hungrier hungriest *adjective*
If you are hungry, you want to eat.
hunger *noun.*

hunt hunts hunting hunted *verb*
1 To hunt is to chase and catch wild animals to kill them, either to eat or as a sport.
2 If you hunt for something, you look everywhere for it. *I've been hunting for my watch all morning.*
hunt *noun.*

hurl hurls hurling hurled *verb*
If you hurl something, you throw it as far and as hard as you can. *She hurled the stone into the lake.*

hurricane hurricanes *noun*
a powerful storm with winds that are strong enough to blow down trees or damage roofs.

hurry hurries hurrying hurried *verb*
If you hurry, you try to get somewhere or do something as quickly as possible. *You'd better hurry or you'll miss the game.*
hurry *noun.*

hurt hurts hurting hurt *verb*
1 If you hurt yourself, you cause pain to a part of your body. *Did you hurt yourself when you fell over?*
2 If a part of your body hurts, it feels pain. *I've got a sore knee. It really hurts.*
3 To hurt people is also to upset them. *I think she was hurt when you didn't invite her to your party.*

husband husbands *noun*
A woman's husband is the man she is married to.

hut huts *noun*
a small building, usually with one room.

hutch hutches *noun*
a wooden and wire cage for a rabbit.

hydrogen *noun*
a gas that is lighter than air. Oxygen and hydrogen together make up water.

hyphen hyphens *noun*
a mark in writing (-) to show that two parts of a word belong together. *self-esteem.* ▲ Say **hie-fen**.

I i

ice *noun*
frozen water. *There was ice on the pond last winter.*
icy *adjective.*

iceberg **icebergs** *noun*
a huge piece of ice floating in the sea. Icebergs are dangerous to ships because most of the ice is under the water where you cannot see it.

ice cream *noun*
a sweet, frozen food that is made from cream or milk.

ice skating *noun*
sliding on ice in special boots called ice skates that have thin, metal blades on the bottom.

icicle **icicles** *noun*
a hanging, pointed piece of ice made of dripping water that has frozen.

icing *noun*
a smooth, sweet covering for cakes that is made of sugar mixed with other things.

icy **icier iciest** *adjective*
very cold. *an icy wind.*

idea **ideas** *noun*
1 a new thought about something. *I've got an idea. Let's go to the beach!*
2 a picture in your mind. *The movie gives you a good idea of what India is like.*

ideal *adjective*
If something is ideal, it is perfect and just what you want. *The weather was ideal for a picnic.*
ideally *adverb.*

identical *adjective*
exactly the same. *Ben and Jason are identical twins.*

identify **identifies identifying identified** *verb*
If you identify others, you know who or what they are and can name them. *Can you identify this wildflower and that bird?*
identification *noun.*

idle *adjective*
lazy, or not working.

igloo **igloos** *noun*
a round house, built by Inuit people out of blocks of hard snow and ice.

ignorant *adjective*
not knowing about something.
ignorance *noun.*

ignore **ignores ignoring ignored** *verb*
If you ignore people, you take no notice of them. *She ignored me when I said hello.*

ill *adjective*
If you are ill, you are sick. *I didn't go to school today because I was ill.*

illegal *adjective*
If something is illegal, it is not allowed by law. ■ The opposite is **legal.**

illness **illnesses** *noun*
something such as measles or a cold that makes you feel unwell.

illusion **illusions** *noun*
something that you think you can see, but that is not really there.

illustration **illustrations** *noun*
a picture in a book or magazine. *This dictionary has lots of illustrations.*

image **images** *noun*
1 a picture on paper, on a screen, or in a mirror. *A ghostly image appeared in the mirror.*
2 a picture in your mind. *I have an image of how I want to look when I'm a grown-up.*

imaginary *adjective*
Something that is imaginary is not real and exists only in your mind. *I read a story about a boy who had an imaginary friend.* ▲ Say *i-maj-in-ar-ee.*

imagination *noun*
Your imagination is your ability to think of new ideas or create pictures in your mind. *Use your imagination and draw whatever you like.*
imaginative *adjective.*

imagine **imagines imagining imagined** *verb*
When you imagine something, you create a picture of it in your mind. *Can you imagine living in a cave like people in the Stone Age?*

imitate **imitates imitating imitated** *verb*
If you imitate others, you copy the way they talk or act. *Chet is imitating Nick taking a photograph of the magician.*
imitation *noun*
It is not a real Christmas tree, but a plastic imitation.

immediately *adverb*
now. *The ambulance arrived immediately after we called it.*

immigrant **immigrants** *noun*
a person who comes to live in one country from another.

immune *adjective*
If you are immune to a disease, you cannot catch it.

impatient *adjective*
If you are impatient, you do not like waiting for things. ■ The opposite is patient.
impatience *noun*.

important *adjective*
1 If something is important, it matters a lot. *It is important to look both ways before you cross the street.*
2 One who is important has power. *Our President is an important man.*
importance *noun*.

impossible *adjective*
If something is impossible, you cannot do it, or it cannot happen. ■ The opposite is **possible**.

impress impresses impressing impressed *verb*
If you impress people, they think that what you have done is very good. *Her drawings impressed us.*

impression impressions *noun*
1 thoughts and feelings that you have about somebody or something. *My first impressions of the new school were that it was very large and noisy.*
2 If you make an impression on people, they remember what you are like and what you have done. *The ballet dancer made a great impression on all of us.*

impressive *adjective*
If something is impressive, people admire it, especially because it is very good or very big. *an impressive fort.*

improve improves improving improved *verb*
If something improves, it gets better.
improvement *noun*.

include includes including included *verb*
To include is to have somebody or something as part of a group or as part of the whole thing. *Dan was pleased to be included on the football team.*

inconvenient *adjective*
If something is inconvenient, it is hard to do or use. ■ The opposite is **convenient**.

increase increases increasing increased *verb*
If something increases, it gets bigger in size or amount. ■ The opposite is **decrease**.
increase *noun*.

incredible *adjective*
If something is incredible, it is difficult to believe. *an incredible story.*

incubator incubators *noun*
1 a container where babies who are born early are kept until they grow bigger and stronger.
2 a container where eggs are kept warm until they hatch.

independent *adjective*
If you are independent, you do not want or need help from other people.
independence *noun*.

index indexes *noun*
a list of words from A to Z at the end of a book. The index tells you what things are in the book and where they are.

Indian Indians *noun*
a person from India or South America.
❖ *Look at Native American.*

indigestion *noun*
an uncomfortable feeling that you have in your stomach when you have eaten too much or eaten the wrong food.

individual *adjective*
to do with one person or thing, not a whole group. *individual voters.*

individual individuals *noun*
one person. *Every individual is different.*

indoors *adverb*
inside a building. *We went indoors when it started to rain.* ■ The opposite is **outdoors**.

industry industries *noun*
the work of making things in factories. *the car industry.*
industrial *adjective*

infant infants *noun*
a baby or young child.

infection infections *noun*
sickness that is caused by germs. *a throat infection.*

infectious *adjective*
If an illness is infectious, it travels easily from one person to another. *Measles is a very infectious disease.*

inflate inflates inflating inflated *verb*
If you inflate something such as a balloon or a tire, you blow it up with air or gas.
inflatable *adjective*.

influence *noun*
If somebody or something has an influence over you, that one has a certain effect on you so that you change the way you think or act. *My parents don't like me to play with Dan because they say he is a bad influence on me.*
influence *verb*, **influential** *adjective*.

inform informs informing informed *verb*
If you inform people about something, you tell them about it. *The teacher informed us that there would be a history test next week.*

information *noun*
the facts about something. *This dictionary gives you information about words and how to spell them.*

ingredient ingredients *noun*
Ingredients are all the things that you put in when you make something. *The ingredients for making a cake are butter, sugar, flour, and eggs.*

inhabitant inhabitants *noun*
The inhabitants of a place are the people or animals that live there. *The inhabitants of the island are mainly fishermen and their families.*
inhabit *verb*.

initial initials *noun*
the first letters of each of your names. *Tom Jackson's initials are T.J.*

injection injections *noun*
If a doctor or nurse gives you an injection, he or she puts medicine into your body through a needle.
inject *verb*.

injure injures injuring injured *verb*
If you injure yourself, you hurt a part of your body. *He injured his leg playing football.*
injury *noun*.

ink *noun*
a colored liquid that is used for writing or printing. *The words on this page were printed with ink.*

inland *adjective, adverb*
toward the middle of a country, away from the sea. *an inland lake.*

inner *adjective*
1 in the middle of a place. *He lives in the inner city.*
2 inside something. *A bicycle tire has an inner tube.*
■ The opposite is **outer**.

innocent *adjective*
If you are innocent, you have not done anything wrong. *The police have accused him of stealing the money but he says that he is innocent.* ■ The opposite is **guilty**.
innocence *noun*.

inquire inquires inquiring inquired *verb*
If you inquire about something, you ask about it. *We inquired about the flights to Dallas.*
inquiry *noun*
an official inquiry into the disaster.

insect insects *noun*
a small creature with six legs and a body that is divided into three sections. Many insects have wings. *Ants, grasshoppers, and butterflies are insects.*
❖ *Look at page 89*

insert inserts inserting inserted *verb*
If you insert a thing into something else, you put it inside it. *She inserted the key into the lock and opened the door.*

insist insists insisting insisted *verb*
If you insist on doing something, you say very firmly that you want to do it so that no one can stop you. *Eleanor insisted on wearing her new sneakers.*
insistence *noun*.

inspect inspects inspecting inspected *verb*
to look at something carefully.
inspection *noun*.

instant *adjective*
If something is instant, it happens very quickly, or you can make it very quickly.

instead *adverb*
in the place of somebody or something else. *I don't like ice cream. May I have fruit instead?*

instinct instincts *noun*
something that makes people and animals do things without having to think or learn about them. *Birds build their nests by instinct.*

instructions *noun*
words that tell you how to do something. *She gave us instructions on how to look after the puppies.*

instrument instruments *noun*
1 a thing that is used for doing a special job. *A telescope is an instrument for looking at things, such as stars.*
2 A musical instrument is something that you play to make music. *Recorders and pianos are instruments.*

telescope

recorder

insult insults insulting insulted *verb*
If somebody insults you, that one upsets you by saying rude things to you.
insult *noun*.

integrate integrates integrating integrated *verb*
to open something like a school to all people of all races.

intelligent *adjective*
A person who is intelligent is able to learn and understand things quickly.
intelligence *noun*.

intend intends intending intended *verb*
If you intend to do something, you plan to do it. *What do you intend to do now?*
intention *noun*.
My intention is to make all A's.

interest interests interesting interested *verb*
If something interests you, you like it and want to know more about it. *Football doesn't interest Mom at all.*
interesting *adjective*.

interior *noun*
The interior of something is the part inside it. *The interior of the room was dark and gloomy.*

international *adjective*
If something is international, it has to do with more than one country. *an international flight.*

interrupt interrupts interrupting interrupted *verb*
If you interrupt people, you stop them while they are saying or doing something. *Please don't interrupt me.*
interruption *noun*.

intersection intersections *noun*
the place where streets cross.

interview interviews *noun*
a meeting when you answer questions about yourself. *The senator gave a television interview.*

intestine intestines *noun*
Your intestine is the long tube inside your body that carries food from your stomach.

introduce introduces introducing introduced *verb*
If you introduce two people who have never met before, you tell them each other's names so they can get to know one another. *Tim introduced me to Bob.*
introduction *noun*.

Inuit Inuits *noun*
a person or a people whose ancestors were the first people who lived in Alaska or the northern part of Canada.

invade invades invading invaded *verb*
When an army invades, it goes into another country to attack it.
invasion *noun*.

A
B
C
D
E
F
G
H
I
J
K
L
M
N
O
P
Q
R
S
T
U
V
W
X
Y
Z

invent invents inventing invented *verb*
If you invent something, you make something that has never been made or thought of before.
invention *noun*.

inventor inventors *noun*
a person who invents something.

investigate investigates investigating investigated *verb*
When you investigate something, you try to find out all about it. *The police investigated the accident.*
investigation *noun*.

invisible *adjective*
If something is invisible, you cannot see it. ■ The opposite is **visible**.

invitation invitations *noun*
If somebody gives you an invitation, the person writes or speaks to you to ask you to go somewhere.

invite invites inviting invited *verb*
If you invite people, you ask them to come to your house, to a party or a meal.

involve involves involving involved *verb*
1 If you are involved in something, you take part in it. *Are you involved in the school play?*
2 If something is involved in an activity, it is part of it. *Tennis involves a lot of skill.*

iron *noun*
1 Iron is a strong, hard metal that is found in rocks. Iron is used for making tools, gates, and other things.
2 An iron is an electric tool that you use to make clothes smooth.
▲ Say **eye**-urn.

irritate irritates irritating irritated *verb*
If something irritates you, it annoys you.
irritation *noun*.

Islam *noun*
the religion that Muslims follow.

island islands *noun*
a piece of land with water all around it.
▲ Say **eye**-land.

itch itches itching itched *verb*
When a part of your body itches, you have a feeling on your skin that you want to scratch it.
itch *noun*, **itchy** *adjective*.

ivy ivies *noun*
a plant with shiny pointed leaves that stay green in winter. Ivy climbs up walls and trees.

J j

jacket jackets *noun*
a short coat.

jack-o'-lantern jack-o'-lanterns *noun*
a pumpkin with a face cut in it. *Roy put a candle in the jack-o'-lantern.*

jack rabbit jack rabbits *noun*
a big rabbit with strong legs.

jaguar jaguars *noun*
a wildcat that has brown and yellow fur with black spots. Jaguars live in North and South America.

jail jails *noun*
a prison.

jam *noun*
1 a food made by cooking fruit with sugar. *Billie loves strawberry jam on toast.*
2 a traffic jam is a large number of vehicles unable to move.

jam jams jamming jammed *verb*
If something jams, it cannot move. *The paper has jammed in the printer.*

jar jars *noun*
a glass container for jam or other foods. *a jar of pickles.*

jaw jaws *noun*
Your jaws are the two large bones in your mouth that hold your teeth. Your jaws move up and down when you speak and eat.

jealous *adjective*
If you are jealous, you want what somebody else has and it makes you angry and unhappy. *Joe was jealous of his little sister because she always seemed to get what she wanted.*
▲ Say **jel**-uss.
jealousy *noun*.

jeans *noun*
pants made from thick, strong, cotton material called denim. ● A word that sounds like **jeans** is **genes**.

jelly jellies *noun*
a clear, slightly wobbly food with a fruit flavor.

jellyfish jellyfish or jellyfishes *noun*
a sea animal that has a clear, round body and long tentacles that sting.

jerk jerks jerking jerked *verb*
To jerk is to make a sudden, sharp movement. *She jerked her hand away from the flame.*

jet jets *noun*
1 a fast plane with an engine that sucks air in and then forces it out at the back.
2 a fast, thin stream of liquid. *A jet of water was coming out of the burst pipe.*

Jew Jews *noun*
a person who belongs to the race of people who in ancient times lived in Israel, or a person who follows the religion called Judaism.
Jewish *adjective.*

jewel jewels *noun*
a beautiful and valuable stone such as a diamond, ruby, or emerald.

jewelry *noun*
rings, bracelets, necklaces, brooches, and other things that people wear to decorate their bodies. Jewelry is often made of valuable metals such as gold or silver, and jewels such as diamonds or rubies.

jigsaw
jigsaws *noun*
a puzzle made up of a lot of small pieces of wood or thick cardboard that fit together to make a picture.

job jobs *noun*
1 the work that a person does to get money. *My mother is looking for a job at the moment.*
2 a piece of work that you have to do. *My sister and I were given the job of washing the car.*

jockey jockeys *noun*
a person who rides a horse in races.

jog jogs jogging jogged *verb*
If you jog, you run quite slowly, for exercise.

join joins joining joined *verb*
1 When you join things, you put them together. *I joined the pieces of the jigsaw puzzle.*
2 If you join a group, you become a member of it. *Maria has joined the school band.*

joint joints *noun*
a part of your body where two bones are joined together, such as your elbow or wrist or your knee or ankle.

joke jokes *noun*
something that somebody says or does to make people laugh.

journalist journalists *noun*
a person who writes news and stories for newspapers or television. ▲ Say *jer-na-list.*
journalism *noun.*

journey journeys *noun*
When you go on a journey, you travel from one place to another. *It's a three-hour journey by car from here to the beach.* ▲ Say *jer-nee.*

joy *noun*
a feeling of great happiness. ■ The opposite is **sorrow.**
joyful *adjective.*

Judaism *noun*
the religion of the Jews.

judge judges *noun*
1 A judge is the person who controls what happens in a court of law and who decides what a guilty person's punishment should be.
2 a person who decides who is the winner in a competition.

judo *noun*
a sport from Japan in which two people try to throw each other to the ground using various special movements.

jug jugs *noun*
a large pitcher; a container with a handle and a shaped part at the top that is used for pouring liquids.

juggle juggles juggling juggled *verb*
If you juggle, you throw several things into the air and catch them, one after another, so that there is more than one thing in the air at once. *Chris is juggling.*
juggler *noun.*

juice juices *noun*
the liquid from fruit, vegetables, or meat. *orange juice.* ◆ *carrot juice.*
juicy *adjective.*

jump jumps jumping jumped *verb*
When you jump, you push your body quickly and suddenly up into the air.
jump *noun.*

jungle jungles *noun*
a thick forest in a tropical country.

junior *adjective*
younger. ■ The opposite is **senior.**

junior juniors *noun*
a student who is in his or her third year at a high school or college.

jury juries *noun*
a group of 12 ordinary people in a court of law who have to hear all the evidence and to decide whether the person on trial is guilty or innocent.

justice *noun*
a way of treating people that is both fair and right.

juvenile *adjective*
young.

A
B
C
D
E
F
G
H
I
J
K
L
M
N
O
P
Q
R
S
T
U
V
W
X
Y
Z

K k

kaleidoscope **kaleidoscopes**
noun
a tube that you look through and see lots of colored patterns as you turn it. ▲ Say *ku-lie-du-skope*.

kangaroo **kangaroos** *noun*
a wild animal that lives in Australia. It has strong back legs and moves by making long jumps. A female kangaroo has a kind of pocket called a pouch at the front where she keeps her baby.

a kangaroo and its mother

karate *noun*
a sport from Japan in which two people fight with their hands and feet using special movements. ▲ Say *ku-rah-tee*.

kayak **kayaks** *noun*
a canoe that is covered on top. It has a small opening where the paddler sits. *The Inuit use kayaks.*

kennel **kennels** *noun*
a small house for a dog.

ketchup *noun*
a thick red sauce made with tomatoes. *We put ketchup on our hamburgers and french fries.*

kettle **kettles** *noun*
a container with a handle and a spout, that is used for heating water.

key **keys** *noun*
1 a piece of metal that is shaped so that when you turn it, it locks or unlocks something such as a door or padlock.

2 The keys of a piano are the parts that you press when you play to make different musical notes.
3 The keys of a computer are the parts with letters and numbers that you press when you work at the computer.
4 The key to a map is a list that tells you what the symbols on the map mean.

keyboard **keyboards** *noun*
1 the part of a computer with buttons, called keys, that have letters and numbers on them.
2 the row of keys on a piano or other musical instrument.
3 an electronic keyboard makes musical sounds.

kick **kicks kicking kicked** *verb*
If you kick something, you hit it with your foot. *Ben kicked the ball.*

kid **kids** *noun*
1 a young goat.
2 a child.

kidnap **kidnaps kidnapping kidnapped** *verb*
When people kidnap another person, they take them away and hide them so that their family or friends will have to pay money to free them.

kidney **kidneys** *noun*
Your kidneys are the two parts inside your body that help to clean your blood.

kill **kills killing killed** *verb*
To kill somebody or something means to make that one die.

kind **kinder kindest** *adjective*
A person who is kind is friendly and gentle and likes to help other people. ■ The opposite is **unkind**.

kind **kinds** *noun*
a sort or type. *There are thousands of different kinds of insects.*

kindergarten **kindergartens**
noun
a class or a school for children who are four to six years old.

king **kings** *noun*
A king is a man who leads his people and who is a member of a royal family.

kiss **kisses kissing kissed** *verb*
When you kiss people, you touch them with your lips in a friendly way.
kiss *noun*.

kit **kits** *noun*
1 all the things that you need to do something. *a tool kit.*
2 pieces that you put together to make something. *a model airplane kit.*

kitchen **kitchens** *noun*
a room where food is kept and cooked.

kite **kites** *noun*
a toy that you fly in the wind. It is made of a light frame covered with paper or plastic, attached to a long piece of string.

kitten **kittens** *noun*
a very young cat.

knee **knees** *noun*
Your knees are the parts in the middle of your legs where they bend. *He fell over and grazed his knee.* ▲ Say **nee**.

kneel **kneels kneeling knelt** or **kneeled** *verb*
to go down on your knees. ▲ Say **neel**.

knew past of **know**
● A word that sounds like **knew** is **new**.

knife **knives** *noun*
A knife is a tool for cutting. It has a handle and a long, sharp piece of metal called a blade. ▲ Say **nife**.

knight **knights** *noun*
a soldier who wore armor and rode a horse hundreds of years ago. Knights fought in battles for their king or queen. ● A word that sounds like **knight** is **night**.

knit **knits knitting knitted** *verb*
When you knit, you use yarn and two long needles to make clothes. *My grandmother knitted this sweater for me.* ▲ Say **nit**.

knob knobs *noun*
1 a round handle that you use to open a door or a drawer.
2 A knob is also a button that you turn or press to make a machine work. ▲ Say **nob**.

knock knocks knocking knocked *verb*
1 If you knock on something such as a door, you hit it hard so that people will hear you.
2 If you knock something over, you hit it so that it falls. *I knocked over the vase and it broke.* ▲ Say **nock**.

knot knots *noun*
a place where a piece of string, thread, or rope is tied. *Can you undo this knot?*
● A word that sounds like **knot** is **not**.

know knows knowing knew known *verb*
1 If you know something, you have it in your mind and you are sure that it is true because you have learned it. *Do you know what the capital of Texas is?*
2 If you know people, you have met them before. *I know them because they are in my class.*
● A word that sounds like **know** is **no**.

knowledge *noun*
what you know and understand about something. *She has a good knowledge of computers.* ▲ Say **nol**-*edge*.

different types of knot

knuckle knuckles *noun*
Your knuckles are the bony parts in the middle of your fingers and where they bend. ▲ Say **nuk**-*ul*.

koala
koalas *noun*
an animal that looks like a small bear with thick, gray fur. It lives in trees in Australia, and feeds on their leaves and bark. A female koala has a kind of pocket called a pouch at the front where she keeps her baby.

L l

label labels *noun*
a small piece of paper put onto something that gives you information about it. *The label on the dress gives its price and size.*

laboratory laboratories *noun*
a room where scientists work and do experiments using special equipment. ▲ Say **lab**-*ruh-tor-ee*.

lace *noun*
thin, delicate material with a pretty pattern of tiny holes in it. *a pair of lace gloves.*

laces *noun*
pieces of cord or string that you use to tie shoes.

lack *noun*
If there is a lack of something, it is missing or there is not enough of it. *The lack of rain meant that the crops did not grow properly.*

ladder ladders *noun*
two long metal or wooden poles with bars, called rungs, between them that you can use to climb up or down. *The firefighter climbed up the ladder to rescue our cat from the tree.*

ladle ladles *noun*
a big, deep spoon with a long handle, used for serving soup.

ladybug ladybugs *noun*
a small, round beetle. Ladybugs are usually orange or red with black spots on their wings. They eat aphids, which are harmful to plants.

laid past of lay.

lake lakes *noun*
a large area of water with land all around it. *Lake Tahoe is a popular vacation spot.*

lamb lambs *noun*
1 a young sheep.
2 meat from a young sheep.

lame *adjective*
If a person or an animal is lame, that one cannot walk properly because a leg has been hurt. *The dog was lame in one leg.*

lamp lamps *noun*
an object that uses electricity, gas, or oil to give light.

land lands *noun*
1 the solid, dry part of the world that is not covered by sea. *The sailors were glad to be on land again after spending three months at sea.*
2 a country. *He told the children tales of the foreign lands he had visited.*

land lands landing landed *verb*
When a plane lands, it comes down to the ground and stops. ■ The opposite is **take off**.

lane lanes *noun*
1 a narrow road.
2 part of a main road or expressway that is wide enough for one car at a time. *Drivers should always signal before they change lanes.*
● A word that sounds like **lane** is **lain**.

A B C D E F G H I J K L M N O P Q R S T U V W X Y Z

language languages *noun*
the words that people use to talk and write to each other. *These books are written in different languages.* ▲ Say *lang-gwij.*

lantern lanterns *noun*
a light inside a glass and metal case that you can carry.

lap laps *noun*
1 Your lap is the top half of your legs when you are sitting down.
2 one journey around a racetrack.

laptop laptops *noun*
a small computer that you can open and use on your lap.

large larger largest *adjective*
big in size or amount. ■ The opposite is **small** or **little**.

larva larvae *noun*
an insect after it has come out of an egg but before it has become an adult.

laser lasers *noun*
a machine that produces a very powerful beam of light. People use laser beams for many different things such as surgery.

lasso lassos *noun*
a piece of rope with a large loop at one end that you can make bigger or smaller. Cowboys use lassos to catch cattle. ▲ Say *lass-oh.*

last *adjective*
coming after everybody or everything else.

late later latest
adjective, adverb
If you are late, you come after the time that you were supposed to. ■ The opposite is **early**.

laugh laughs laughing laughed *verb*
When you laugh, you make sounds that show that you find something funny. *All the children laughed and laughed at the funny clowns in the circus.* ▲ Say *laff.*

laughter *noun*
the sound of somebody laughing. ▲ Say *laff-ter.*

launch launches launching launched *verb*
1 When people launch a ship or boat, they make it go into the water.
2 When a rocket or missile is launched, it is sent up into the sky.

laundry laundries *noun*
1 dirty clothes.
2 dirty clothes that you have just washed.
3 a place where people's dirty laundry is washed. *We picked up the clean sheets and towels from the laundry.*

lava *noun*
hot, liquid rock that flows from a volcano when it erupts.

lavatory lavatories *noun*
a bathroom. ▲ Say *lav-uh-tor-ee.*

law laws *noun*
a rule or a set of rules made by a government that everybody in a country has to obey. *Stealing is against the law.*

lawn lawns *noun*
an area of short grass in front of a house.

lawyer lawyers *noun*
a person who advises people about the law and speaks for them in court. *Two lawyers defended the man accused of robbery.*
▲ Say *loy-yer.*

lay lays laying laid *verb*
1 If you lay something down, you put it down carefully.
2 When you lay a table, you put knives, forks, spoons, and other things on it, ready for a meal.
3 When a hen lays an egg, it produces it.

lay past of **lie**.

layer layers *noun*
a flat piece of something that lies between two other pieces of it or that lies on the top. *A sandwich usually has three layers, two slices of bread and the filling in between — this one has five!*

layoff layoffs *noun*
a time when people are dismissed from their jobs because there is not enough work for them to do.

lazy lazier laziest *adjective*
Somebody who is lazy does not want to work or do very much. *She gets a ride to school every morning because she's too lazy to walk.*

lead leads leading led *verb*
1 If you lead others, you go in front of them to show them the way. *Follow me and I'll lead you to the church.* ■ The opposite is **follow**.
2 If you lead a group of people, you are in charge of them. *The general led the troops into battle.*
3 If you are leading in a race or game, you are winning at the time *John was leading for most of the race.*
▲ Say *leed.*
leader *noun*.

lead *noun*
a soft, heavy, gray metal. ▲ Rhymes with *bed.* ● A word that sounds like **lead** is **led**.

leaf leaves *noun*
Leaves are the thin, flat parts of a plant that grow from the stem or from branches or twigs. Leaves are usually green.

league leagues *noun*
a group of sports teams. *a hockey league.*

leak leaks leaking leaked *verb*
If something leaks, liquid or gas escapes from it through a crack or hole. *The washing machine is leaking, and there's water all over the floor.*

lean leans leaning leaned *verb*
1 If you lean against something, you rest against it so that part of your weight is on it. *She leaned against the wall.*
2 If you lean somewhere, you bend your body in that direction. *Ray leaned across the table to talk to me.*

leap leaps leaping leaped or **leapt** *verb*
If you leap, you jump high or a long way. *The dog leaped over the fence.*
leap *noun.*

leap year leap years *noun*
a year that has an extra day, February 29, so that the year has 366 days instead of 365. Leap years happen once every four years.

learn learns learning learned or **learnt** *verb*
When you learn something, you find out about it or how to do it.

leash leashes *noun*
a long, thin piece of leather or a chain that you attach to a dog's collar to stop it from running away.

leather *noun*
a strong material made from an animal's skin. Leather is used to make shoes.

leave leaves leaving left *verb*
1 When you leave, you go away from somewhere. ■ The opposite is **arrive**.
2 When you leave something, you let it stay where it is.

led past of **lead**.
● A word that sounds like **led** is **lead**, the metal.

left *noun, adjective*
When you write the word "left," the "l" is to the left of the "e." *Carla writes with her left hand.* ■ The opposite is **right**.

leg legs *noun*
1 Your legs are the two long parts of your body that you use for walking.
2 The legs of a table or chair are the long, narrow parts that stand on the floor and support the top part.

legal *adjective*
If something is legal, the law says you can do it. ▲ Say **lee-gul.** ■ The opposite is **illegal**.

legend legends *noun*
a story from long ago that may or may not be true. ▲ Say **lej-end.**

legislature legislatures *noun*
A legislature is elected by the people. It makes laws.

lemon lemons *noun*
a bright yellow fruit with sour juice.

lend lends lending lent *verb*
If you lend something to others, you let them have it for a while and then they give it back to you. *Can you lend me a pen?* ■ The opposite is **borrow**.

length *noun*
The length of something is how long it is. *My desk is three feet in length.*
lengthen *verb*
to make or become longer.

lens lenses *noun*
a curved piece of glass or transparent plastic used in a camera, a pair of glasses, a telescope, or something similar to help you see more clearly.

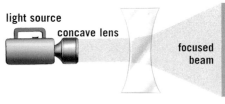
light source concave lens focused beam

light source convex lens focused beam

lent past of **lend**.

leopard leopards *noun*
a wild cat that has yellow fur with black spots. Leopards live in Africa and South Asia. ▲ Say **lep-erd.**

leotard leotards *noun*
a tight piece of clothing that covers you from your shoulders to your thighs, made of material that stretches. Dancers wear leotards. ▲ Say **lee-o-tard.**

lesson lessons *noun*
a period of time when you are taught something by a teacher.

let lets letting let *verb*
If you let somebody do something, you do not stop that person from doing it. *Will you let me try on your jewelry?*

letter letters *noun*
1 one of the signs that we use to write words, such as a, b, and c.
2 a written message that you send or receive by mail.

lettuce lettuces *noun*
a plant with large green leaves that we eat raw in salads. ▲ Say **let-iss.**

level *adjective*
flat and not sloping.

lever levers *noun*
1 a long bar that you put under something heavy at one end so that you can lift the heavy object by pushing on the bar at the other end of the bar.
2 a long handle like a stick that you use to make a machine work.
▲ Say **leh-ver.**

liar liars *noun*
a person who does not tell the truth.

library libraries *noun*
a building or room that has books, tapes, CDs, and videos for people to borrow.

A
B
C
D
E
F
G
H
I
J
K
L
M
N
O
P
Q
R
S
T
U
V
W
X
Y
Z

license licenses *noun*
an official piece of paper that gives you permission to do something. *a driver's license.* ▲ Say **lie-sense.**

lick licks licking licked *verb*
If you lick something, you move your tongue over it. *The dog licked my hand.*

lid lids *noun*
a cover for a box, pot, can, or jar.

lie lies lying lied *verb*
If you lie, you say something that you know is not true.
lie *noun.*

lie lies lying lay lain *verb*
When you lie down, you rest your body in a flat position, for example on the floor or on a bed.

life lives *noun*
A person's or an animal's life is the time that one is alive, until death. *I'll remember today for the rest of my life.*

lifeboat lifeboats *noun*
a boat that is used for rescuing people who are in danger at sea.

lift lifts lifting lifted *verb*
If you lift something, you pick it up or raise it. *I can't lift this suitcase—it's too heavy.*

lift lifts *noun*
1 If somebody gives you a lift, he or she takes you somewhere in a car. *Can you give me a lift home from the party?*
2 a very happy feeling. *Your comments on my concert gave me a lift.*

light lights *noun*
1 Light is the bright rays that come from the Sun, the Moon, or from a lamp, that lets you see things.
2 A light is a thing that produces light. *Can you turn on the light?*

light lighter lightest *adjective*
1 Something that is light does not weigh very much and you can pick it up easily. *A feather is light.* ■ The opposite is **heavy.**
2 Light also means not dark. *My room is very light because it has two big windows.*
3 Light also means pale in color. *light green.* ■ The opposite is **dark.**

light lights lighting lit *verb*
If you light something, you make it start burning. *Mom lit the candles on the birthday cake.*

lighthouse lighthouses *noun*
a tower with a very bright light on top that flashes to warn ships that they are near rocks or to show them the safe way to go.

lightning *noun*
a flash of very bright light that you see in the sky when there is a storm.

like likes liking liked *verb*
1 If you like others, you think that they are nice.
2 If you like doing something, you enjoy it. *I like swimming more than any other sport.*
■ The opposite is **dislike.**

---

like

Some words you can use instead of like:

I like firefighters because they help people.
☞ **admire, respect** ☜

I would like an ice cream.
☞ **enjoy, want** ☜

He's a vet because he likes animals.
☞ **is fond of, loves** ☜

---

like *preposition*
very similar to somebody or something. *Jack looks just like his dad.* ■ The opposite is **unlike.**

likely likelier likeliest *adjective*
If something is likely, it is probably going to happen. ■ The opposite is **unlikely.**

limb limbs *noun*
an arm or a leg. ▲ Rhymes with **him.**

lime limes *noun*
a fruit similar to a lemon, with green skin and sour juice.

limit limits *noun*
the largest amount of something that is allowed. *The speed limit on this road is 55 miles per hour.*

limp limps limping limped *verb*
If a person or an animal limps, that one walks in an uneven way because a leg or foot has been hurt.

line lines *noun*
1 a long, thin mark on something. *Draw a line under the title of the book.*
2 a number of people or things next to each other or one behind the other. *There was a long line of people waiting to get into the theater.*
3 a long piece of rope or string. *He's hanging the clean sheets on the line to dry.*

link links *noun*
1 a ring in a chain.
2 a connection between things or people. *The police believe there is a link between the two crimes.*

lion lions *noun*
a large wild cat that has light brown fur and lives in parts of Africa and Asia. The male lion has a large mane. A female lion is called a lioness and a young lion is a cub.

lip lips *noun*
Your lips are the two soft parts that form the edges of your mouth.

liquid liquids *noun*
water or anything else that flows like water. ■ The opposite is **solid.**
liquid *adjective.*

list lists *noun*
a line of things that are written down one under the other. *a shopping list.*
list *verb.*

listen listens listening listened *verb*
When you listen, you pay attention to sounds so you can hear them. *Listen carefully to the instructions.*

lit past of **light.**

litter *noun*
1 trash such as pieces of paper and cans that are thrown away in the street or in a public place instead of being put in a trash can.
2 a group of baby animals that are born at the same time to one mother. *Our cat had a litter of four kittens.*

little *adjective*
1 small in size. ■ The opposite is **big** or **large**.
2 A little child is a young child. *I loved drawing when I was little.*
3 small in amount.

live **lives living lived** *verb*
1 To live means to be alive. ■ The opposite is **die**.
2 If you live somewhere, that is where your home is. *I live with Granny.*
▲ Rhymes with **give**.

live *adjective*
1 A live animal is alive. *Have you ever seen a real, live crocodile?* ■ The opposite is **dead**.
2 A live TV or radio program is being broadcast as it is happening.
▲ Rhymes with **five**.

lively **livelier liveliest** *adjective*
full of energy or excitement. *The old man is lively for his age.*

liver **livers** *noun*
Your liver is a large organ of your body that helps to clean your blood.

living *noun*
When you do something for a living, you earn money by doing it. *She earned her living as a journalist.*

lizard **lizards** *noun*
a reptile with four very short legs, rough skin, and a long tail.

a thorny devil lizard

load **loads** *noun*
something that is being carried somewhere. *The truck carried a very heavy load of wood.*

load **loads loading loaded** *verb*
1 If you load a car or other vehicle, you put a lot of things into it to take somewhere. *The men loaded the furniture into the truck.* ■ The opposite is **unload**.
2 If you load a gun, you put bullets in it.
3 If you load a camera, you put film in it.

4 If you load a computer, you put information or a program into it.

loaf **loaves** *noun*
bread that is cooked in one piece and then cut up into slices.

loan **loans** *noun*
money or something else that somebody lends you and that you have to pay or give back later.

lobster **lobsters** *noun*
a sea animal with a hard shell, eight legs, and two large claws in front. Lobsters can be eaten.

local *adjective*
close to where you live.
locally *adverb*.

lock **locks** *noun*
an object that fastens a door or lid so that you cannot open it without a key.

lock **locks locking locked** *verb*
If you lock something such as a door, you fasten it with a key. ■ The opposite is **unlock**.

locomotive **locomotives** *noun*
a railroad engine.

locust **locusts** *noun*
Locusts are grasshoppers that move from place to place and eat plants.

log **logs** *noun*
a piece of a thick branch cut from a tree. *We need some logs to put on the fire.*

lonely **lonelier loneliest** *adjective*
If you are lonely, you are sad because you are on your own or because you do not have any friends. *Patsy feels lonely in her new school.*

long **longer longest** *adjective*
1 far between one end and the other. *a long bridge.*
2 for more time than usual. *The movie was very long and we got bored.*
■ The opposite is **short**.

long **longs longing longed** *verb*
If you long for something, you want it very much. *She longed to have a pony of her own.*

longhorn **longhorns** *noun*
a cow with big horns that grow far out on each side of its head.

look **looks looking looked** *verb*
1 When you look at something, you use your eyes to see it.
2 If somebody looks a certain way, they seem that way to you. *You look tired and sleepy.*
3 If you look for something, you try to find it.
4 If you look after somebody or something, you take care of them. *Dad looked after us while Mom was in the hospital.*

loop **loops** *noun*
a circle made in a piece of string, rope, thread, or wire.

loose **looser loosest** *adjective*
1 not fixed firmly in place. *a loose tooth.*
2 too big to fit properly. *My pants are loose.* ■ The opposite is **tight**.

lose **loses losing lost** *verb*
1 If you lose something, you do not know where to find it. ■ The opposite is **find**.
2 If you lose a competition, game, or fight, you do not win it.
3 If you have lost weight, you now weigh less than you did before.

loss **losses** *noun*
The loss of something is not having it anymore. *Emily felt sad about the loss of her necklace.*

lot **lots** *noun*
1 a large number. *There were lots of people at the concert.*
2 a piece of land. *Dad and Mom bought a big lot on the beach.*

loud **louder loudest** *adjective*
Something that is loud makes a lot of noise. *loud music.* ■ The opposite is **quiet** or **soft**.
loudness *noun*.

A
B
C
D
E
F
G
H
I
J
K
L
M
N
O
P
Q
R
S
T
U
V
W
X
Y
Z

loudspeaker loudspeakers *noun*
a piece of equipment that makes sounds louder. When a singer sings into a microphone, the audience can hear his or her voice through loudspeakers.

love loves loving loved *verb*
to have a very strong feeling of liking for somebody or something. ■ The opposite is **hate**.

lovely lovelier loveliest *adjective*
beautiful, or very pleasant. *The park looks lovely in the spring when all the flowers are in bloom.*

low lower lowest *adjective*
1 not very far from the ground. *There was a low wall between the houses.*
2 deep in sound. *He has a very low voice.*
■ The opposite is **high**.

lower lowers lowering lowered *verb*
If you lower something, you bring it slowly down. *They lowered the flag.*
■ The opposite is **raise**.

loyal *adjective*
If you are loyal to somebody, you always support him or her. *Janice has always been a very loyal friend.*
■ The opposite is **disloyal**.
loyally *adverb*.

luck *noun*
1 Luck is when something happens by chance instead of when you plan it or make it happen. *There is no skill needed to play this game. It's just luck whether you win or not.*
2 Luck is also good things that happen to you by chance. *Wish me luck for my piano exam!*

lucky luckier luckiest *adjective*
If you are lucky, you have good things happening to you by chance. *What is your lucky number?* ■ The opposite is **unlucky**.

luggage *noun*
all the bags and suitcases that you take with you when you are traveling. ▲ Say *lug-ij*.

luminous *adjective*
Something that is luminous glows in the dark. *My watch has a luminous dial.*

lump lumps *noun*
1 a solid bit of something. *a lump of cheese.* ◆ *This sauce has lumps in it.*
2 a swelling. *I've got a lump on my head where I banged it.*
lumpy *adjective*

lunch lunches *noun*
a meal that you eat in the middle of the day.

lung lungs *noun*
Your lungs are the two parts like bags inside your chest that fill up when you breathe in and then empty again when you breathe out.

luxury luxuries *noun*
something that is expensive and very nice to have, but that you do not need. *Mom says we can't afford the luxury of a new car this year.* ▲ Say *luk-sher-ee*.
luxurious *adjective*.

M m

macaroni *noun*
hollow tubes of a flour dough that we cook and eat. *a macaroni and cheese casserole.*

machine machines *noun*
a thing with parts that move to do work or to make something. We use machines in the home to help us sew, cook, and clean. A washing machine cleans our clothes and a machine called a vacuum cleaner sucks up dirt from rugs.
machinery *noun*.

mad madder maddest *adjective*
A person who is mad at someone or about something is angry.

magazine magazines *noun*
a thin book with pictures, stories, and information about things in it. Most magazines come out every week or every month.

maggot maggots *noun*
a creature that looks like a worm and grows up to become a fly. Maggots are found in dead flesh.

magic *noun*
1 a power that some people think makes strange and wonderful things happen. *The witch made the frog disappear by magic.*
2 the skill of doing clever tricks, such as making things disappear.
magic *adjective*

magical *adjective*
1 produced by magic. *a magical hat that makes you disappear.*
2 strange or very exciting. *a magical fireworks display.*

magician magicians *noun*
a person who can do magic tricks.

magnet magnets *noun*
a piece of metal that makes iron or steel move toward it.
magnetic *adjective*.

magnificent *adjective*
very beautiful or grand. *a magnificent view.*

magnify magnifies magnifying magnified *verb*
When you magnify something, you make it look bigger. *We magnified the insect under the microscope.*

magnifying glass *noun*
a special piece of glass called a lens that can makes things look bigger.

mail *noun*
letters, postcards, and packages that you send by the postal service. ● A word that sounds like **mail** is **male**.

main *adjective*
most important. *the main entrance.* ● A word that sounds like **main** is **mane**.

major *adjective, noun*
1 large, important, or serious. *Miami is a major city.* ■ The opposite is **minor**.
2 an officer in the army, air force, or marines.

make makes making made *verb*
1 If you make something, you put things together so that you have a new thing. *Sandy is making a cake.*
2 to cause something to happen. *The balloon made a loud bang when it burst.*
3 to do something. *I made a mistake.*
4 If you make somebody do something, you force him or her to do it. *Dad makes me go to bed early.*

makeup *noun*
special powders, paints, and creams that women and actors put on their faces. Eye shadow and lipstick are kinds of makeup.

male males *adjective*
a person or animal that belongs to the sex that cannot have babies or lay eggs. Boys and men are male. ■ The opposite is **female**. ● A word that sounds like **male** is **mail**.

mammal mammals *noun*
an animal that drinks milk from its mother's body when it is young. People, horses, and whales are all mammals.

man men *noun*
a grown-up male person.

manage manages managing managed *verb*
1 If you manage to do something difficult, you do it well. *Those problems were hard, but I managed to do them.*
2 If you manage people at work, you tell them what to do.

manager managers *noun*
a person whose job is to run or control such things as a bank, a store, or a hotel.

mane manes *noun*
the long hair on the neck of a horse or a male lion.

manner manners *noun*
1 the way that you do something. *She smiled in a friendly manner.*
2 Your manners are the way you behave when you are eating or talking to other people. *It's bad manners to talk with your mouth full.*

many more most *adjective*
a large number of people or things.

map maps *noun*
a drawing that shows you what a place looks like from above. Maps show things such as roads, mountains, and rivers. *Will you draw me a map of how to get to your house?*

A B C D E F G H I J K L M N O P Q R S T U V W X Y Z

MAMMALS

water shrew

blue whale

greater horseshoe bat

weasel (winter coat, below)

walrus

raccoon

bison

wolf

American mink

marathon marathons *noun*
a race when people have to run a very long way. *He won the Boston marathon.*

marble *noun*
a kind of very hard stone that can be polished until it is shiny. Marble is used to make statues and buildings.

marbles *noun*
small colored glass balls that you use in some games.

march marches marching marched *verb*
When you march, you walk like a soldier with regular steps.
march *noun.*

margarine *noun*
a soft, yellow fat that looks like butter, but is not made from milk.

margin margins *noun*
a space around the writing or printing on a page.

mark marks *noun*
1 a spot, stain, or line on something that spoils it. *Your shoes have left a dirty mark on the rug.*
2 Marks are numbers or letters that your teacher gives you to show how good your work is. *Ben got the highest marks in the class.*
mark *verb.*

market markets *noun*
a place, usually in the open air, with lots of little shops where you can buy things such as fruit and vegetables.

marmalade *noun*
a jam made from oranges or lemons.

marriage marriages *noun*
1 the special ceremony or wedding when a man and a woman become husband and wife.
2 the time a man and woman live together as husband and wife. *Grandma and Grandpa have had a long and happy marriage; they have four children and seven grandchildren.*

marry marries marrying married *verb*
When a man and a woman marry, they become husband and wife.

marsh marshes *noun*
an area of land that is soft and wet.

marsupial marsupials *noun*
a mammal, the female of which has a pouch for carrying her babies. Opossums and koalas are marsupials.

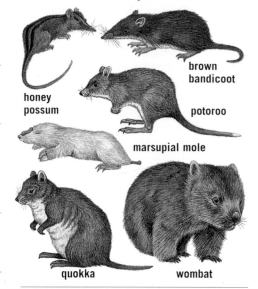

honey possum
brown bandicoot
potoroo
marsupial mole
quokka
wombat

marvelous *adjective*
very good, wonderful. *We had a marvelous day at the seaside.* ◆ *What a marvelous idea!*

mascot mascots *noun*
a person or thing that is supposed to bring good luck. *Our team's mascot is a donkey.*

mask masks *noun*
something you wear on your face to hide it or to protect it.

mass masses *noun*
1 a large number of people or things.
2 a large amount of something solid. *a mass of rock.*
3 A Mass is a service in the Catholic Church.

massacre massacres *noun*
the violent killing of a lot of people. *Hundreds were massacred in the battle.*

massive *adjective*
very big, strong, and heavy. *massive castle walls.*

mast masts *noun*
a tall pole that holds a flag or the sails on a boat.

mat mats *noun*
1 a small carpet. *Please wipe your feet on the mat at the door.*
2 a piece of wood or material that you put on the table under a plate. *Put the dishes on the place mats.*

match matches matching matched *verb*
If two things match, they are the same color, shape, or pattern, or they look good together. *Chris's hat and scarf match.*

match
matches *noun*
1 a small, thin stick of wood or cardboard that makes fire when you rub it against something rough. *My father struck a match and lit the bonfire.*
2 a game that is played between two teams or two players. *a soccer match.* ◆ *a tennis match.*

mate mates *noun*
1 a merchant marine officer. *a third mate.*
2 one of two animals that have come together to have young ones. *Most birds choose a mate in the spring.*
mate *verb.*

material materials *noun*
1 things that you use to make other things with. Glass, wood, and stone are materials that we use to build houses.
2 a cloth that we use to make things such as clothes. *Jack bought material to make new curtains.*

maternal *adjective*
to do with being a mother. *Mothers have maternal feelings.*

math *noun*
adding, subtracting, multiplying, and dividing numbers.

a b c d e f g h i j k l m n o p q r s t u v w x y z

matter *noun*
1 something that you must talk about or do. *Mom said there were some important matters she had to discuss.*
2 a problem or difficulty. *What's the matter with your computer?*
3 a thing that you can see or touch. *The world is made of matter.*

matter matters mattering mattered *verb*
If something matters, it is important. *Ben has lost my ruler, but it doesn't matter because I have another one.*

mattress mattresses *noun*
the thick part of the bed that you lie on.

mature *adjective*
If you are mature, you have grown up, or you behave in a grown-up way.

maximum *noun*
the most you can have of something. *We have a maximum of $5 to spend on Zack's present.*
maximum *adjective*
What's the maximum speed of this car?
■ The opposite is **minimum**.

mayonnaise *noun*
a thick sause for salads or sandwiches. It is made of oil, eggs, lemon juice or vinegar, and mustard.

mayor mayors *noun*
a person who is in charge of the government of a city or town.

meadow meadows *noun*
a field of grass. Wildflowers often grow in meadows. ▲ Say *med-oh.*

meal meals *noun*
the food that you eat at certain times of the day. Breakfast, lunch, and dinner are all meals.

mean *adjective*
Somebody who is mean does not like other people and is not good or kind to others.

mean means meaning meant *verb*
1 If you ask what something means, you want somebody to explain it so that you can understand it. *What does this word mean?*
2 If you mean to do something, you plan and want to do it. *I meant to clean my room, but I forgot.*
meaning *noun*.

meanwhile *adverb*
If something happens meanwhile, it happens at the same time as something else, or before something else happens. *I'm getting a new bike next week; meanwhile, I'll have to borrow my sister's bike.*

measles *noun*
an illness that gives you little red spots all over your skin. *Jim wasn't at school today; he has measles.*

measure measures measuring measured *verb*
When you measure something, you find out how big, tall, long, wide, or heavy it is. *Angela is being measured by Susan.*

measurement *noun*.

meat *noun*
the part of an animal that we eat.

mechanical *adjective*
If something is mechanical, it is done, made, or works by a machine. *a mechanical clock.*

medal medals *noun*
a kind of badge that somebody gives you when you win something or when you do something very brave or special. *She won a gold medal in the swimming meet.*

bronze, silver, and gold medals

meddle meddles meddling meddled *verb*
If you meddle with something, you touch or move it when you have been told not to. *The teacher told us not to meddle with the computer.*

media *noun*
newspapers, radio, and television.

medicine medicines *noun*
the tablets, liquid, and drugs a doctor gives you when you are sick to make you feel better.

medium *adjective*
not large or small but a size in between. *Do you want a small, medium, or large shirt?*

meet meets meeting met *verb*
When you meet people, you go to the same place at the same time as them. **meeting** *noun*.

meet meets *noun*
a sports contest.

melody melodies *noun*
a tune that you sing or play.

melon melons *noun*
a big, round, yellow or green fruit with lots of seeds inside.

melt melts melting melted *verb*
When something melts, it changes into a liquid. *Fran's ice cream is beginning to melt in the sun.*

member members *noun*
a person who belongs to something such as a club or a sports team. *Bill is a member of the school football team.*

memorize memorizes memorizing memorized *verb*
To memorize is to learn something so that you can remember it exactly. *Have you memorized the names of all the players on the team?*

A B C D E F G H I J K L **M** N O P Q R S T U V W X Y Z

a b c d e f g h i j k l m n o p q r s t u v w x y z

memory memories *noun*
1 being able to remember things. *It is easy to learn spellings, if you have a good memory.*
2 Your memories are the things that happened to you a long time ago and that you can still remember. *My grandmother has lots of happy memories of her childhood.*
3 the part of a computer where it stores information.

men plural of **man**.

mend mends mending mended *verb*
When you mend something, you make it useful again. *Katie is mending her sweater.*

mental *adjective*
If something is mental, it is in your mind or you do it in your mind. *mental arithmetic.*

mention mentions mentioning mentioned *verb*
If you mention something, you say a little bit about it. *Did Jay mention where they were going?*

menu menus *noun*
1 a list of things that you can eat in a restaurant.
2 a list on a computer that tells you what you can do.

Menu
Breakfast
Fruit Juice
Toast
Boiled eggs
Cereal
Tea or coffee

mercury *noun*
a metal that has a silver color and is usually liquid. Mercury is used in thermometers.

Style
Edit ▼
File ○ ○
New... ○ W
Open... ○ S
Close ○+S
Save
Save As... ○ E
Revert to Saved ○+E
Get Text... ○+❶E
Save Text...
Save Page...

mercy *noun*
If you show mercy to people, you do not hurt them or punish them.

mermaid mermaids *noun*
a sea creature in stories that has the head and body of a woman and the tail of a fish.

merry merrier merriest *adjective*
happy and full of fun. *Merry Christmas!*

merry-go-round merry-go-rounds *noun*
1 A fairground machine with wooden animals and seats that go round and round.
2 a playground ride.

mesa mesas *noun*
a high hill with a flat top. ▲ Say *may-suh*.

mess *noun*
Things are a mess when they are dirty or not where they belong. *Your bedroom is in a mess—please clean it up!*
messy *adjective*.

message messages *noun*
words that you say or write when the person you want to speak to is not there. *Tom isn't in. Leave a message for him.*

messenger messengers *noun*
a person who brings a message.

met past of **meet**.

metal metals *noun*
a hard material that is used in making things such as cars and airplanes. Metal becomes soft or liquid when it is heated. Silver, iron, and copper are different kinds of metals.

meteor meteors *noun*
a piece of rock or metal that travels in space and burns when it nears the Earth.

meteorite meteorites *noun*
a piece of rock or metal from space that has landed on the Earth.

meter meters *noun*
an instrument that measures how much gas, electricity, or water has been used. *a gas meter.* ◆ *a parking meter.*

method methods *noun*
a way of doing something. *Baking, frying, and boiling are methods of cooking.*

mice plural of **mouse**.

microphone microphones *noun*
an instrument that is used to record sound or to makes sounds louder than they really are. *She sang with a microphone.*

microscope microscopes *noun*
an instrument that makes very small things look much bigger. *We looked at the insect under the microscope.*

microwave oven microwave ovens *noun*
a kind of oven that cooks food very quickly using waves called electromagnetic waves.

midday *noun*
12 o'clock in the middle of the day. ■ The opposite is **midnight**.

middle *noun*
the part of something that is not near the outside edges. *There is a vase of flowers in the middle of the table.*

midnight *noun*
12 o'clock in the middle of the night. ■ The opposite is **midday** or **noon**.

migrate migrates migrating migrated *verb*
When birds and animals migrate, they move to another part of the country for part of the year so that they can find food. *Ducks and geese migrate to Florida from Maine in the winter.*
migration *noun*.

milk *noun*
the white liquid that mothers and female mammals make in their bodies to feed their babies. People drink the milk that cows make.
milky *adjective*.

mill mills *noun*
1 a factory for making things such as steel, paper, or materials such as wool or cotton.
2 a building where a machine grinds grain into flour.
3 a small tool that grinds or crushes things. *a pepper mill.*

millionaire millionaires *noun*
a very rich person who has more than a million dollars.

mime mimes miming mimed *verb*
If you mime something, you use actions but you do not speak. *Tom mimed blowing up a balloon and we had to guess what he was doing.*

mind minds *noun*
Your mind is the part of you that thinks, feels, learns, and remembers things.

mind minds minding minded *verb*
If you mind about something, you feel unhappy or angry about it. *Do you mind if I borrow your bike? No. I don't mind.*

mine mines *noun*
1 a place where people dig under the ground to get things such as coal, gold, or diamonds. *a coal mine.*
2 a bomb put in water, or under the ground.

mineral minerals *noun*
Minerals are things such as coal, gold, salt, or oil that are found in rocks or under the ground.

miniature miniatures *noun*
a very small copy of something much bigger.
miniature *adjective*
miniature furniture. ▲ Say *min-at-cher.*

minimum *noun*
the smallest amount you can have of something. *We need a minimum of four people to play this game.*
minimum *adjective*
Sixteen is the minimum age for driving in this state. ■ The opposite is **maximum.**

minister ministers *noun*
a person who holds services in a church.

minnow minnows *noun*
a very tiny fish that lives in fresh water.

minor *adjective*
not very serious or important. *a minor injury.* ■ The opposite is **major.**

minor minors *noun*
If you are a minor, you are too young to decide and do things like an adult.

mint *noun*
1 a plant called an herb. It is used to add flavor to things such as meat, toothpaste, and candy.
2 a piece of candy with a strong mint flavor.
3 the place where coins are made by the government.

minus *noun, preposition*
1 You use the minus sign (-) to show that you have taken one number away from another. *Seven minus four is three (7 - 4 = 3).*
2 Minus also means below zero. *The temperature was minus ten degrees.*

minute minutes *noun*
a measure of time. There are 60 seconds in a minute and 60 minutes in an hour. ▲ Say *min-it.*

minute *adjective*
very, very small. *a minute insect.* ▲ Say *my-newt.*

mirror mirrors *noun*
a piece of special glass that you can see yourself in. Mirrors reflect light.

Some mirrors can make you look funny.

mischief *noun*
bad or annoying behavior.
mischievous *adjective*
Mike played a mischievous trick on his uncle.

miserable *adjective*
If you are miserable, you feel very unhappy or sad. *Katie is miserable because she can't go on vacation.*

miss misses missing missed *verb*
1 If you miss a ball, you do not hit or catch it.
2 If you miss a bus or a train, you are not there in time to catch it.
3 If you miss somebody, you are sad because that person is not there. *I really missed my friend when he moved out of town.*

mist mists *noun*
a low cloud of tiny drops of water that is difficult to see through. *In the early morning, the fields were covered with mist.*

mistake mistakes *noun*
something that you do wrong. *I only made one spelling mistake.*

mix mixes mixing mixed *verb*
1 When you mix things, you stir them or put them together so that sometimes they make something new. *If you mix blue and red paint, you get purple.* ◆ *Oil and water do not mix.*
2 When people mix, they come together and talk to each other. *I mix with lots of different people at school.*

mixture mixtures *noun*
something that is made when two or more things are mixed together. *There are butter, flour, and sugar in this cake mixture.*

moan moans moaning moaned *verb*
1 When a person or an animal moans, that one makes a low, sad sound because of being in pain or unhappy. *The dog was moaning because it was locked in the pen.*
2 If you moan, you keep complaining about something that you do not like. *He was moaning about having to study so long.*

A B C D E F G H I J K L M N O P Q R S T U V W X Y Z

mobile *adjective*
If something is mobile, it can move or you can move it easily. *a mobile phone.*

mock mocks mocking mocked *verb*
If you mock others, you make fun of them.

model models *noun*
1 a small copy of something. *a model ship.*
2 a person who sits or stands so that an artist can draw him or her.
3 a person who wears new clothes so that people can see what the clothes look like before they buy them.

modern *adjective*
new or happening now. *We live in a modern house.*

modest *adjective*
If you are modest, you do not boast about how good or smart you are.

moist *adjective*
damp or a little wet. *The ground was moist after the rain.*
moisten *verb.*

moisture *noun*
small drops of water on something or in the air.

mole moles *noun*
a small animal with dark fur that lives under the ground and digs tunnels with its strong claws. Where moles have been digging they leave piles of earth called molehills.

moment moments *noun*
a very short time. *I'll be back in a moment.*

money *noun*
the coins and bills that we use to buy things with.

mongrel mongrels *noun*
a dog whose mother and father are of different types of dogs.

monk monks *noun*
Monks are a group of men who obey rules and live and pray together in a building called a monastery because of the religion that they believe in.

monkey monkeys *noun*
an animal with long arms and legs and a long tail that lives mainly in trees in hot countries.

monster monsters *noun*
a big, frightening creature that you can read about in stories.

month months *noun*
a measure of time. There are twelve months in a year. *January is the first month of the year.*
monthly *adjective, adverb*
a monthly magazine.

monument monuments *noun*
a large statue or building that people have made to remember an important person or event. *The Washington Monument is in Washington, D.C.*

mood moods *noun*
the way that you feel at different times. *Joe was in an angry mood today, but Sara was in a cheerful mood.*

moon moons *noun*
The Moon is a small satellite that travels around the Earth once every four weeks. You can often see it in the sky at night.

moose mooses *noun*
a big animal that is related to deer, but that is heavier and has much bigger antlers.

mop mops *noun*
a mop is a tool with a long handle for washing floors.

morning mornings *noun*
the early part of the day before midday. *What time do you get up in the morning?*

mosque mosques *noun*
a building where Muslims go to pray. ▲ Say *mosk.*

mosquito mosquitoes *noun*
a small flying insect that lives in hot, wet places. Female mosquitoes bite people and animals. People can get a serious illness called malaria from mosquito bites. ▲ Say *mos-kee-toe.*

moss mosses *noun*
a soft, green plant like a rug that grows on trees and damp ground.

moth moths *noun*
an insect that looks like a butterfly but that usually flies around at night.

mother mothers *noun*
a woman who has children.

motion *noun*
movement or the way of moving. *The motion of the boat on the rough sea made him feel sick.*

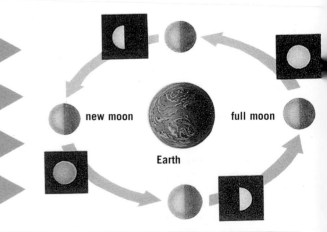

sunlight

new moon   full moon

Earth

motor motors *noun*
the part inside a machine that makes it move or work. Washing machines have electric motors.

a small motor for a model

motorbike motorbikes *noun*
a kind of bicycle with an engine.

motorcycle motorcycles *noun*
a two-wheeled vehicle with a motor and handlebars that is heavier and faster than a motorbike.

mountain mountains *noun*
a very high piece of ground. The highest mountain in the world is Mount Everest.

mountain lion mountain lions *noun*
a big yellow wildcat. It is also called a *cougar* or a *puma*.

mouse mice *noun*
1 a small furry animal with sharp teeth and a long tail. Mice are rodents.
2 a small instrument on your desk that you use to make the cursor on your computer screen move.

mouth mouths *noun*
1 the part of your face that you open and close to talk and to eat.
2 The mouth of a cave is the way into it.
3 The mouth of a river is the place where it enters the sea.

move moves moving moved *verb*
1 When you move, you go from one place to another. *Don't move—I want to take your picture.*
2 If you move something, you put it in another place. *We moved the piano into the living room.*
movement *noun*.

movie movies *noun*
a story in moving pictures that you watch in a theater or on TV.

mow mows mowing mowed *verb*
When you mow grass, you cut it with a machine called a lawnmower. ▲ Rhymes with *low*.

mud *noun*
soft wet dirt. *After playing football, Tom was covered with mud.*
muddy *adjective*.

mug mugs *noun*
a big, tall cup that you use without a saucer. *a mug of hot chocolate.*

mule mules *noun*
an animal whose parents are a female horse and a male donkey.

multiply multiplies multiplying multiplied *verb*
When you multiply a number, you add the number to itself several times. Four multiplied by three is twelve
$(4 + 4 + 4 = 12$ or $4 \times 3 = 12)$.
■ The opposite is **divide**.
multiplication *noun*.

mumps *noun*
a sickness you can get from others that makes your neck and jaws swell and hurt.

munch munches munching munched *verb*
When you munch something hard, you bite and chew it in a noisy way. *Cal was munching an apple.*

murder murders murdering murdered *verb*
To murder somebody means to kill somebody on purpose.
murder *noun*, **murderer** *noun*.

murmur murmurs murmuring murmured *verb*
If you murmur, you say something softly and quietly.
murmur *noun*.

muscle muscles *noun*
Your muscles are the parts inside your body that stretch so that you can bend and move. Muscles are attached to your bones.
muscular *noun*.

museum museums *noun*
a building where lots of interesting things are kept for people to look at. *We saw a model of a dinosaur at the museum.*

mushroom mushrooms *noun*
a small plant without leaves that looks like a tiny umbrella. People can eat some kinds of mushrooms; some other kinds are poisonous. A mushroom is a fungus.

music *noun*
the sounds that come from somebody singing or playing a musical instrument, like a piano, flute, or guitar.
musical *adjective*.

musical instrument musical instruments *noun*
something that you play to make music. Violins are musical instruments.
❖ *Look at page 106*

musician musicians *noun*
a person who plays a musical instrument well. *six musicians in the band.*

Muslim Muslims *noun*
a person who follows the religion of Islam. The religion is based on the teachings of the prophet Muhammad.

mustache mustaches *noun*
hair that grows above a man's top lip.
▲ Say **mus**-*tash*.

mutter mutters muttering muttered *verb*
If you mutter, you speak in a quiet and angry way. *"I don't want to go home,"* she muttered.

muzzle muzzles *noun*
1 the nose and mouth of an animal such as a dog or a fox.
2 something that you can put over a dog's mouth to stop it from biting.

mystery mysteries *noun*
something strange that has happened and that you cannot explain.

myth myths *noun*
1 a very old story with a special meaning. Greek myths are about gods and goddesses.
2 a story that is not true.

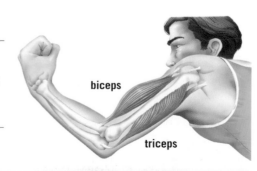

biceps

triceps

A B C D E F G H I J K L M N O P Q R S T U V W X Y Z

MUSICAL INSTRUMENTS

a b c d e f g h i j k l m n o p q r s t u v w x y z

tabla drums

tuned stones

timpani

Chinese stick fiddle

bull roarer

hurdy-gurdy

Korean piba

lira da braccio

Wagner tuba

recorder

square piano

N n

nail nails *noun*
1 a thin piece of metal with one pointed end and a flat end, like a very large pin. *She's hammering a nail into the wall to hang the picture.*
2 Your nails are the hard part at the end of your fingers and toes.

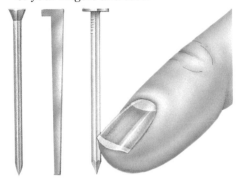

name names *noun*
the word we use to call somebody or something. *The dog's name is Spot. Her last name is Jones.*

nap *noun*
a short sleep.

napkin napkins *noun*
a piece of paper or cloth that you use to wipe your fingers and mouth when you eat food.

narrator narrators *noun*
a person who tells a story out loud or explains to somebody how something happened. ▲ Say *nar-ate-or.*

narrow narrower narrowest *adjective*
If something is narrow, it is thin and does not measure very much from one side to the other. *A narrow path leads to the sand dunes.* ■ The opposite is **broad** or **wide**.
narrowness *noun*.

nasty nastier nastiest *adjective*
1 horrible or not nice. *a nasty smell.*
2 unkind or cruel. *He was really nasty to me.*
nastily *adverb*, **nastiness** *noun*.

nation nations *noun*
a country with its own laws and government. The people of a nation share the same history and language.

national *adjective*
to do with the whole of a nation or the people in a nation. *the national news.*

Native American Native Americans *noun*
a person who is descended from the original peoples who lived in North America before the explorers and European settlers came.

natural *adjective*
If something is natural, it is made by nature and not by human beings. ■ The opposite is **artificial**.
naturally *adverb*.

nature *noun*
animals, plants, and all the things that are not made by human beings. ▲ Say *nay-cher.*

navigate navigates navigating navigated *verb*
If you navigate a ship or aircraft, you find out and say which way to go.
navigator *noun*.

navy navies *noun*
the ships and the sailors that are used to defend a country or fight an enemy.

near nearer nearest *adjective, preposition*
close by or a short distance from something or somebody. *Where's the nearest subway station?* ◆ *In the picture, I'm standing near the statue.* ■ The opposite is **far**.

nearly *adverb*
almost but not quite. *She nearly won.*

neat neater neatest *adjective*
clean and tidy with everything in its proper place.

necessary *adjective*
If something is necessary, it is needed or has to happen. *It is necessary to have a passport when you go abroad.*
necessarily *adverb*.

neck necks *noun*
The neck is the part of a person or animal that joins the head to the body. *The giraffe has a very long neck.*

necklace necklaces *noun*
a piece of jewelry such as a chain that you wear around your neck.

nectar *noun*
a sweet liquid in flowers that insects collect and that bees make into honey.

need needs needing needed *verb*
If you need something, you have to have it in order to live or to do a job. *People and animals need air and water or they die.* ◆ *I need some more green thread to finish my sewing.*

needle needles *noun*
1 a thin, pointed piece of metal with a hole at one end for thread that is used for sewing.
2 a long, thin stick used for knitting.
3 a long, thin leaf on a pine tree.
4 a short tube with a thin, sharp point at one end that doctors use to give injections.

negative *adjective, noun*
1 meaning "no." *She gave a negative answer.*
2 A negative number is less than zero. *–20*
3 film from a camera from which photographs are printed. ■ The opposite is **positive**.

neglect neglects neglecting neglected *verb*
1 If you neglect people or things, you do not look after them and give them the time and attention they need. *He neglected the garden.*
2 to fail to do something. *He neglected to answer the letter.*

A B C D E F G H I J K L M N O P Q R S T U V W X Y Z

neighbor neighbors *noun*
a person who lives near or next to you.
We have very friendly neighbors.
▲ Say *nay-ber*.

neighborhood neighborhoods
noun
the area where you live. *I've lived in this neighborhood all my life.* ▲ Say *nay-ber-hood*.

nephew nephews *noun*
the son of your brother or sister.
▲ Say *nef-you*.

nerve nerves *noun*
1 Your nerves are the long, thin parts inside your body that link your brain to other parts of your body. They carry the messages to and from your brain that make your body move and feel.
2 brave and calm when something is difficult or frightening.

nervous *adjective*
1 worried about something that is going to happen. *I'm nervous about the test.*
2 easily frightened. *a nervous horse.*
■ The opposite is **calm**.

nest nests *noun*
a home made by birds, squirrels, wasps, and other animals for their babies.

net nets *noun*
1 material made of thread, string, or rope joined with knots so as to leave small holes between.
2 the long barrier that you string between two poles so that you can play tennis, volleyball, or badminton. *Jill hit the ball over the net.*

nettle nettles *noun*
a wild plant with hairy leaves that sting you if you touch them. *Johnny got caught in the stinging nettle.*

network networks *noun*
1 a system of things that are connected at many different points. *a railroad network.*
2 a company or group of companies that broadcast the same radio or television programs.

never *adverb*
at no time ever in the past or the future. *It is a beautiful horse but it has never won a race.*

new newer newest *adjective*
1 If something is new, it has only just been made, or you have only just bought it. *I got some new games for my birthday.*
2 different from somebody or something you knew before. *We've got a new teacher.*
■ The opposite is **old**.

news *noun*
information about what is going on or has just happened.

newspaper newspapers *noun*
sheets of paper folded over that have news stories and pictures and other information printed on them.

newt newts *noun*
a small amphibian with short legs and a long tail that lays its eggs in water.

nib nibs *noun*
the pointed part of a pen that touches the paper when you write.

nibble nibbles nibbling nibbled
verb
If you nibble, you eat something slowly, taking very small bites of it.

nice nicer nicest *adjective*
1 If you think something is nice, you like it or enjoy it.
2 kind and easy to like. *a nice person.*

🖈 **n i c e**

Some words you can use instead of nice:

We had a nice supper.
☞ **delicious, tasty** ☜

The woman next door is nice.
☞ **kind, friendly, likable** ☜

We had a nice time on vacation.
☞ **enjoyable, pleasant, wonderful** ☜

What nice weather we are having.
☞ **good, fine, beautiful, mild** ☜

---

nickname nicknames *noun*
a short or special name that people call you instead of your real name.

niece nieces *noun*
the daughter of your brother or sister.
▲ Say *neess*.

night nights *noun*
the time when it is dark and most people are asleep. ■ The opposite is **day**. ● A word that sounds like **night** is **knight**.

nightmare nightmares *noun*
a frightening dream.

nocturnal *adjective*
awake and active mostly at night rather than during the day. *The owl is a nocturnal animal.*

nod nods nodding nodded *verb*
When you nod, you move your head up and down to show you agree with something or to say "yes."

noise noises *noun*
1 a sound. *I heard a strange noise.*
2 sounds that are too loud and unpleasant. *Please stop making so much noise!*
■ The opposite is **silence**.
noisily *adverb*, **noisy** *adjective*.

noodle noodles *noun*
a long, thin strip of pasta. *Do you want rice or noodles with your meal?*

noon *noun*
12 o'clock in the middle of the day.
■ The opposite is **midnight**.

noose nooses *noun*
a loop made in rope with a special knot that gets smaller when you pull on the rope.

normal *adjective*
ordinary, the same as usual. *Cold weather is normal in winter.* ■ The opposite is **unusual**.
normally *adverb*
I normally go to bed at 9 o'clock.

north *noun*
a direction that is to your left if you face the Sun as it is rising in the morning.
north *adjective*, **northern** *adjective*
a north wind. ◆ *a northern accent.*
■ The opposite is **south**, **southern**.

nose noses *noun*
Your nose is the part sticking out in the middle of your face that you use for breathing and smelling. At the end of your nose there are two holes called nostrils. ❖ *Look below*

note notes *noun*
1 a few words that you write down to remind yourself of something. *I've made a note of your phone number.*
2 a short letter. *I'll send a note to the school to explain that you have to go to the dentist.*
3 a single sound in music or a symbol written to show a sound. *Some opera singers can sing very high notes.*

notice notices noticing noticed *verb*
If you notice something, you start to see it or hear it or smell it. *I suddenly noticed that there were lots of people in the yard.*

Spelling tip:
....
Some words that begin with an "n" sound are spelled with "gn" or "kn" such as gnat, gnome, knee, knight.

---

notice notices *noun*
a written message that is put in a public place so that many people will be able to read it. *I saw the notice about the town council meeting.*

notify notifyer notifying notified *verb*
to tell somebody about something.

noun nouns *noun*
a word that gives the name of a thing, a state, a feeling, an idea, a person, or a place. *Table, talent, happiness, sadness, Ben, and Texas are all different nouns.*

nourishment *noun*
food that is good for you and makes you strong and healthy. ▲ Say *nu-rish-ment.*
nourishing *adjective*.

novel novels *noun*
a long written story that has been made up by somebody about people and events that do not really exist.
novelist *noun*.

nudge nudges nudging nudged *verb*
If you nudge somebody, you push him or her with your elbow to make that person notice something. *Cindy stayed quiet but nudged Michael and pointed to the deer.*

---

nuisance nuisances *noun*
a person or something that annoys you. ▲ Say **new-sense**.

numb *adjective*
unable to feel anything in a part of your body. *It was so cold that my feet were numb.* ▲ Say **num**.

number numbers *noun*
a word or sign that shows you how many of something there are.

Digital	Roman	Binary	Mayan
1	I	1	•
2	II	10	••
3	III	11	•••
4	IV	100	••••
5	V	101	——
6	VI	110	•
7	VII	111	••
8	VIII	1000	
9	IX	1001	
10	X	1010	====
15	XV	1111	
20	XX	10100	
50	L		
100	C		
500	D		
1000	M		

numerous *adjective*
very many. *Numerous people were invited.* ■ The opposite is **few**.

nun nuns *noun*
Nuns are a group of women who obey rules and live and pray together in a building called a convent because of the religion that they believe in.

nurse nurses *noun*
a person whose job is to look after people who are sick or injured.

nursery nurseries *noun*
1 a place where young children can go during the day when they are too young to start school.
2 a place where plants and flowers are grown to be sold.

nut nuts *noun*
the fruit of a tree that has a seed inside with a hard shell.

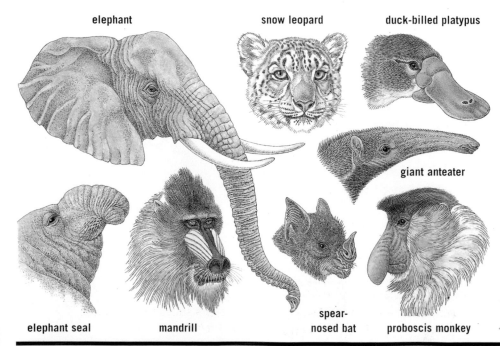

elephant

snow leopard

duck-billed platypus

giant anteater

elephant seal

mandrill

spear-nosed bat

proboscis monkey

O o

oak oaks *noun*
1 a large tree that acorns grow on.
2 the wood from this tree.

oar oars *noun*
a long pole with one flat end that you use to row a boat. ▲ Say *or*.

oasis oases *noun*
a place in a desert with water, plants, and trees. ▲ Say *oh-ay-sis*.

oats *noun*
Oats are plants that farmers grow for their seeds called grain.

obey obeys obeying obeyed *verb*
If you obey a person, you do what he or she tells you to do. ■ The opposite is **disobey**.
obedient *adjective*.

object objects *noun*
1 a thing that you can see and touch. *The box was full of objects of all shapes and sizes.*
2 the purpose or thing that you are trying to achieve. *Her object was to win the contest.*
3 in the sentence, *"Jim hit the ball,"* the object of the sentence is *ball*.
▲ Say *ob-jekt*

object objects objecting objected *verb*
If somebody objects to something, he or she does not like it or agree with it. *The teacher objects to fighting.*
▲ Say *ob-jekt*.

oblong oblongs *noun*
a shape with two long, opposite sides and two short, opposite sides.
oblong *adjective*
The pages of this dictionary are oblong.

observe observes observing observed *verb*
When you observe somebody or something, you watch carefully. *We observed a bird feeding its babies.*

obstacle obstacles *noun*
something that is in your way and stops you from doing something. *The fallen tree was an obstacle in the road.*

obstinate *adjective*
An obstinate person does not like to change what he or she thinks, or do what other people want. *Rod is so obstinate that he will only do what he wants to do.*

obvious *adjective*
If something is obvious, it is easy to see or understand. *The answers to the quiz were obvious.*

occasion occasions *noun*
a time when something happens. *A wedding is an important occasion.*

occasionally *adverb*
If something happens occasionally, it happens but not very often. *I usually walk to school, but occasionally I go by bicycle.*

occupant occupants *noun*
somebody who lives or works in a place.

occupy occupies occupying occupied *verb*
1 If you occupy a house, you live in it.
2 If somebody or something occupies a space, they are in it. *All the parking spaces were occupied.*
3 If you are occupied, you are busy.
occupation *noun*

occur occurs occurring occurred *verb*
1 When something occurs, it happens. *The storm occurred last night.*
2 If something occurs to you, you suddenly think about it. *It occurred to me that I had been very rude to my aunt.*

ocean oceans *noun*
any of the very large areas of sea. *the Atlantic Ocean.*

ocelot ocelots *noun*
a big wildcat with yellow and black fur. It lives in Mexico and South America.

octagon octagons *noun*
a shape with eight straight sides.

octopus octopuses *noun*
an animal that lives in the sea. It has eight long arms called tentacles.

odd odder oddest *adjective*
1 strange or unusual.
2 Odd things do not belong together in a pair or a set. *Tom is wearing odd socks; one is green and the other one is brown.*
3 An odd number is any number that ends in 1, 3, 5, 7, or 9. You cannot divide these numbers by two without carrying something over. ■ The opposite is **even**.

odds and ends *noun*
1 a number of things. *The eraser was in the odds and ends in the drawer.*
2 things you still have to do. *Debbie had some odds and ends to take care of.*

odor odors *noun*
a strong smell. *Domenic's socks have a strong odor!*

offend offends offending offended *verb*
If you offend somebody, you upset that one and hurt the person's feelings. *Her mean remarks offended me.*
offense *noun*, **offensive** *adjective*
offensive behavior.

offer offers offering offered *verb*
1 If you offer people something, you ask them if they would like it. *She offered me a cookie.*
2 If you offer to do something, you say you are willing to do it. *He offered to do the dishes.*

office offices *noun*
1 a place where people go to work. Offices have things such as desks, chairs, computers, and telephones.
2 a place where you can buy something or get information. *the post office.*

officer officers *noun*
1 a person in the army, navy, air force, marines, or coast guard who gives orders to other people.
2 a member of a police force. *police officer.*

official *adjective*
If something is official, it is important and people must believe it or do it. *an official report from the government.*
▲ Say oh-**fish**-al.

oil *noun*
1 a smooth, thick liquid that comes from the ground. You can burn oil to make heat or to make machines work.
2 Oil is also a smooth liquid that comes from plants and animals. Some people use it for cooking.
oily *adjective.*

ointment *noun*
a cream that you put on a cut or on sore skin to heal it.

old older oldest *adjective*
1 Somebody who is old has lived for a long time. *My great-grandfather is very old—he is ninety!*
■ The opposite is **young**.
2 Something that is old was made a long time ago. *This castle is very old—it was built five hundred years ago.*
■ The opposite is **new**.
3 having a certain age.
4 You also use old to talk about something that you had before. *Yesterday I saw an old friend while I was out shopping.*

olive olives *noun*
a small green or black fruit. Olives are used to make olive oil, which is used in cooking.

Olympic *adjective*
of the Olympic Games or the Olympics, international sports contests held every four years in a different country.

onion onions *noun*
a round vegetable with a strong taste and smell that grows under the ground. *I like onions in a salad.*

only *adjective, adverb, conjunction*
1 with no others. *This is the only photo I have of her.*
2 no more than. *I've only got one brother.* ◆ *It will only take five minutes to prepare the food.*
3 but. *This is a good story, only it's too long.*

open *adjective*
1 not closed or covered. *The dog escaped through the open gate.*
2 ready for people to come in. *The store is open at nine o'clock.*

open opens opening opened *verb*
1 If you open a door, you let people or things go through.
2 To open means to move something so that it is not closed or covered. *Open your eyes!* ◆ *He opened the box and found a present inside.* ■ The opposite is **shut**.
3 If you open a store or office, you make it ready for people to come in.
opening *noun.*

open house open houses *noun*
a reception for visitors, as at a school.

opera operas *noun*
a play where actors sing most of the words. *"The Magic Flute" is an opera by Mozart.*

operate operates operating operated *verb*
1 When surgeons operate, they take away or mend part of patients' bodies to make them well again.
2 If you operate a machine, you use it or make it work. *Can you operate this computer?*

operation operations *noun*
When somebody has an operation, a surgeon takes away or mends a part of the person's body.

opportunity opportunities *noun*
a time or chance that is right for doing something. *On vacation, we had the opportunity to go sailing.*

opposite opposites *noun*
something that is different from another thing in every way. *Bad is the opposite of good.*

opposite *adjective, adverb*
1 different in every way. *North is in the opposite direction to South.*
2 across or on the other side. *The women stood opposite each other.*

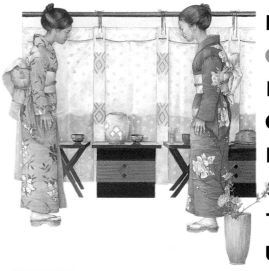

optician opticians *noun*
a person who tests your eyes to see if you need glasses.

orbit orbits *noun*
the invisible path that something such as a planet or a spaceship follows as it travels around the Earth, another planet, or the Sun.
orbit *verb.*

a b c d e f g h i j k l m n o p q r s t u v w x y z

orchard orchards *noun*
an area of land where fruit trees grow.

orchestra orchestras *noun*
a group of people who play different musical instruments together.
▲ Say *or-kess-tra.*

order orders *noun*
1 Order means the way that things follow one another. *The letters of the alphabet always come in the same order.*
2 An order is something that you must do because somebody tells you to do it. *The officer gave the soldiers an order to march.*

order orders ordering ordered *verb*
1 If you order something, you say you would like it. *We ordered bacon, sausages, and eggs.*
2 If you order somebody to do something, you say that the person must do it. *The doctor ordered Tom to stay in bed for a week.*

ordinary *adjective*
not exciting or special. *Yesterday was my birthday, but today is just an ordinary day.*

organ organs *noun*
1 An organ is a part of your body that does something special. Your heart, liver, and kidneys are all organs.
2 a big musical instrument like a piano with pipes that air goes through to make sounds. *a church organ.*

organization organizations *noun*
a group of people who work together.

organize organizes organizing organized *verb*
If you organize something you arrange or plan it. *The school has organized a trip to New York City.*

origin origins *noun*
1 the beginning of something and how and why it began. *We are learning about the origins of life on Earth.*
2 where somebody or something came from. *a statue of African origin.*

original *adjective*
1 Something that is original is the first to be made. *This is an original painting. All the others are copies.*
2 Original also means different and exciting. *What an original idea!*

a gamelan orchestra from Indonesia

ornament ornaments *noun*
an object that you like and use to make a place look pretty. *china ornaments.*

orphan orphans *noun*
a child whose mother and father are dead.

ostrich ostriches *noun*
a very large bird with long legs and a long neck that lives in Africa. Ostriches can run fast, but they cannot fly.

otter otters *noun*
a small animal with brown fur. Otters can swim well and catch fish to eat.

ought *verb*
If you ought to do something, you should do it because it is important. *You ought to brush your teeth before you go to bed.*

outdoors *adverb*
outside a building. *We went outdoors when the sun came out.* ■ The opposite is **indoors**.

outer *adjective*
1 not in the middle of a place. *I live in the outer suburbs of Houston.*
2 the outside of something. *His outer clothing was covered with mud.*
■ The opposite is **inner**.

outing outings *noun*
a short trip that you go on to enjoy yourself.

outline outlines *noun*
1 a line around the edge of something that shows its shape.
2 a drawing where you just draw a line to show the shape of something.
3 a list of topics that you want to write about. *Zeke made an outline before he wrote his essay.*

oval ovals *noun*
An oval is a shape like an egg.
oval *adjective*

oven ovens *noun*
the part like a box inside a stove where you cook food. *Chris baked a chocolate cake in the oven.*

overalls *noun*
clothes that you wear to keep your other clothes clean when you do things such as painting.

overflow overflows overflowing overflowed *verb*
If something like a bathtub overflows, the water comes over the top of it. *I forgot to turn off the faucet and the tub overflowed so much that water came out of the bathroom and ran down the stairs!*

overgrown *adjective*
If a garden is overgrown, it is covered with weeds and the plants look messy.

overhead *adjective, adverb*
above your head. *an overhead light.*
◆ *A plane flew overhead.*

overhear **overhears overhearing overheard** *verb*
When you overhear something, you hear what somebody says when he or she is speaking to someone else. *I overheard Lee say that she liked me.*

overlap **overlaps overlapping overlapped** *verb*
When two things overlap, part of one thing covers part of the other thing. *The shingles on the roof overlap.*

overseas *adverb*
across an ocean. *We flew overseas to London and Paris for our summer vacation.*

owe **owes owing owed** *verb*
If you owe money, you have to give the money back to the person who lent it to you. *I owe you 50¢ for the candy.*

owl **owls** *noun*
a bird with large eyes that can see well in the dark and hunts small animals, such as mice, at night.

own **owns owning owned** *verb*
If you own something, you have something that belongs to you. *Do you own that bike or did you borrow it?*

owner **owners** *noun*
a person who has or owns something. *Who is the owner of this pencil box?*

ox **oxen** *noun*
a bull that is used in some countries for pulling carts.

oxygen *noun*
a gas in the air we breathe. People, animals, and plants need oxygen to live and things cannot burn without it.

oyster **oysters** *noun*
a sea animal that lives inside a pair of shells. A few oysters produce a pearl inside their shells.

ozone *noun*
a gas in the air. Ozone forms a layer, called the ozone layer, around the Earth. It protects us from the harmful rays of the Sun.
ozone-friendly not harmful to the ozone layer. *We buy only ozone-friendly aerosols.*

P p

pace *noun*
the speed at which something happens or moves. *They started off at a fast pace.*

pack **packs packing packed** *verb*
When you pack, you put clothes and other things you need in a suitcase or box to take away with you.

package **packages** *noun*
1 Something wrapped in paper so that you can mail it. *Mom wrapped up Grandma's birthday present and mailed the package to her.*
2 a box or bag of something. *a package of cheese.*

pad **pads** *noun*
1 a thick piece of soft material that can be used to protect something.
2 a lot of pieces of paper to write or draw on that are held together at one edge.
3 the soft part on the underneath of an animal's paw.

paddle **paddles paddling paddled** *verb*
1 If you paddle, you walk in the shallow water at the edge of the sea or a lake.
2 When you paddle a canoe, you move it through the water.

paddle **paddles** *noun*
a short, flat oar for a boat or canoe. *Hold the paddle in both hands.*

padlock **padlocks** *noun*
a small, metal block with a bar in the shape of a U at the top that you can use to lock things such as gates and bicycles and some doors.

page **pages** *noun*
one side of a piece of paper in a book or newspaper. *This dictionary has lots of pages.*

paid past of **pay**.

pain *noun*
the feeling that you have in a part of your body when it hurts. *I have a bad pain in my lower back.* ● A word that sounds like **pain** is **pane**.

painful *adjective*
When something is painful, it hurts a lot. *I fell over and my knee is quite painful.*
painfully *adverb*.

paint **paints** *noun*
a liquid that you use to make colored pictures or to give a new color to the walls and ceilings in a house.
paint *verb*
I am going to paint a picture.

painter **painters** *noun*
1 a person whose job it is to put paint on walls, doors, and window frames.
2 an artist who paints pictures. *Monet was a French painter.*

painting **paintings** *noun*
a picture made using paint. *We hung our painting on the wall.*

A B C D E F G H I J K L M N O P Q R S T U V W X Y Z

pair pairs *noun*
1 two things that go together or that you use together. *a pair of gloves.*
2 We also talk about pairs of things such as pants, scissors, or binoculars that have two parts the same joined together. ● A word that sounds like **pair** is **pear**.

pajamas *noun*
pants and a jacket that you wear in bed.

palace palaces *noun*
a large building for a king or queen.

pale paler palest *adjective*
Something that is pale is almost white. *pale blue.* ■ The opposite is **dark**.

palm palms *noun*
1 a tree with no branches but that has long leaves that grow from the top of the trunk.
2 the flat part inside your hand between your wrist and your fingers.

European fan palm

coconut palm

date palm

pan pans *noun*
a container with a handle that you use for cooking food. *a frying pan.*

pancake pancakes *noun*
a flat cake made from flour, baking powder, eggs, and milk and fried in a pan.

panda pandas *noun*
a large animal that looks like a black and white bear. *Pandas live in China and are very rare.*

black and white panda

red panda

pane panes *noun*
a flat piece of glass. *a windowpane.* ● A word that sounds like **pane** is **pain**.

panel panels *noun*
a long, flat piece of wood or glass that is part of a door or fence.

panic panics panicking panicked *verb*
If you panic, you feel so worried or afraid that you do not know what to do and you cannot act or think in a sensible or calm way.
panic *noun.*

pant pants panting panted *verb*
If people or animals pant, they breathe quickly with their mouth open. *Dogs pant when they get hot in order to cool themselves.*

panther panthers *noun*
a black leopard.

pantomime pantomimes *noun*
a play with a story that is told by actors who do not speak but use arm and other body movements.

pants *noun*
a piece of clothing that you wear to cover all or part of your legs. Pants have two holes for your legs to go through.

paper *noun*
1 thin material that you use for writing on or wrapping things in and that books, newspapers, and magazines are printed on.
2 a newspaper.

parable parables *noun*
a story that teaches people something.

parachute parachutes *noun*
a large piece of cloth held to a person with ropes that opens up like an umbrella so that the person can jump from a plane and float safely to the ground. ▲ Say *pair-a-shoot.*

parade parades *noun*
a lot of people marching along, often with decorated vehicles and music to celebrate something special. *There was a big parade to celebrate July 4th.*

paragraph paragraphs *noun*
several sentences about the same idea that are written or printed together. The first sentence of a paragraph starts on a new line. ▲ Say *pair-a-graf.*

parallel *adjective*
Parallel lines are straight and always the same distance from each other. *Railroad lines are parallel.*

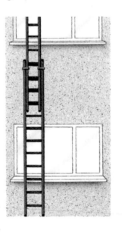

paralyzed *adjective*
If part of your body is paralyzed, you cannot move it or feel anything in it. *She is paralyzed from the waist down but is able to move around in a wheelchair.*

parcel parcels *noun*
a package. *At Christmas we mailed many parcels.*

parchment *noun*
a material made from the skin of a sheep or goat that was used for writing on in the past.

pardon pardons pardoning pardoned *verb*
If you pardon people, you forgive them. *The governor pardoned the criminal.*

parent parents *noun*
a mother or a father.

park parks *noun*
an area of land, usually in a town, with grass and plants where people can go to walk and children can play.

park parks parking parked *verb*
to leave a car somewhere.

parliament parliaments *noun*
a group of people who meet to discuss or make new laws for a country. ▲ Say *parl-e-ment*.

parrot parrots *noun*
a tropical bird with brightly colored feathers and a curved beak. Parrots can be taught to copy human speech.

part parts *noun*
1 one piece or bit of something.
2 If you have a part in a play, you act as one of the characters in the play.

part parts parting parted *verb*
1 to divide. *hair parted in the middle.*
2 to separate. *We parted at the crossroads.*

particular *adjective*
A particular thing or person is the one that you mean and not anything or anybody else. *I don't want any old kitten; I want that particular one over there.*

partner partners *noun*
A partner is somebody who does something with another person. *She's my favorite partner when we go square dancing.*

party parties *noun*
1 a group of people who get together to have fun. *a birthday party.*
2 a group of people who have the same ideas about politics. *the Democratic Party.* ◆ *the Republican Party.*

pass passes passing passed *verb*
1 If you pass something, you go by it without stopping.
2 If you pass an exam, you do it well enough to succeed.
3 If you pass something to others, you give or hand it to them. *Pass us that pair of scissors, please.*
● A word that sounds like **passed** is **past**.

pass passes *noun*
a ticket or card that allows you to do something, such as travel free or enter a building.

passage passages *noun*
a narrow place with walls on each side like a corridor.

passenger passengers *noun*
a person who is traveling in a vehicle but not driving it.

passport passports *noun*
a small book or document that you take when you travel to another country that shows who you are and what country you come from.

password passwords *noun*
a secret word that you have to know to get into a place or, sometimes, to be able to work on a computer.

past *noun*
the time up until now. *In the past there was no gas or electricity.*
■ The opposite is **future**. ● A word that sounds like **past** is **passed**.

past *preposition*
further on than something, or after it. *Go past the church and then turn left.*
● A word that sounds like **past** is **passed**.

pasta *noun*
a food made from flour that is formed into different shapes. Spaghetti and macaroni are kinds of pasta.

paste *noun*
1 a thick, soft glue.
2 a thick, soft mixture of food.

pastel pastels *noun*
a special colored crayon that looks like chalk that you use for drawing.

pastime pastimes *noun*
a hobby or sport that you do when you are not working.

pastry *noun*
a mixture of flour, fat, and water that is rolled flat and used for making pies.

pasture pastures *noun*
a field with grass for animals such as cows and sheep to eat.

pat pats patting patted *verb*
If you pat something, you hit it gently with your hand. *He patted the dog.*

patch patches *noun*
1 a piece of material that you put over a hole to mend it. *Lee's jeans had patches on the knees.*
2 a small area that is different from the rest. *a patch of white fur.*

path paths *noun*
a narrow piece of ground where people can walk to get somewhere. *There's a path across the field.*

patience *noun*
If you have patience, you stay calm when something takes a long time or is very difficult.
▲ Say *pay-shenss*.

patient *adjective*
If you are patient, you stay calm and do not complain when something takes time. ■ The opposite is **impatient**.
patiently *adverb*.

types of pasta

A B C D E F G H I J K L M N O P Q R S T U V W X Y Z

patient patients *noun*
a person who is being treated by a doctor or a dentist. *The doctor sees 30 patients a day.* ▲ Say **pay**-*shent.*

patrol patrols *noun*
a group of soldiers, guards, or police officers who regularly go around an area to protect it and make sure there is no trouble or danger.

pattern patterns *noun*
a design or arrangement of colors and shapes on something. *It is fun to make patterns using different colors and shapes.*

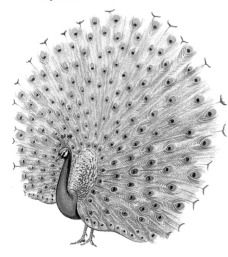

pause pauses pausing paused *verb*
If you pause, you stop what you are doing for a short time before you go on with it.
pause *noun*
● A word that sounds like **pause** is **paws.**

pavement pavements *noun*
the hard surface of a road or sidewalk. *The pavement was covered with ice.*

paw paws *noun*
an animal's foot. ● A word that sounds like **paws** is **pause.**

pay pays paying paid *verb*
When you pay people, you give them money for something you have bought or for work they have done. *How much did you pay Don to wash your car?*

pea peas *noun*
a small, round, green vegetable that grows in a pod.

peace *noun*
1 a time when people are not fighting. ■ The opposite is **war.**
2 a time when there is no noise or no worry.
peaceful *adjective.*

peach peaches *noun*
a soft, round fruit with a pale, furry orange skin and a large pit inside.

peacock peacocks *noun*
a large male bird with a tail made of blue and green feathers that it can spread out like a fan. The female is called a peahen.

peak peaks *noun*
1 the pointed top of a mountain.
2 the front top part of a cap.

peanut peanuts *noun*
a light brown, oily seed that grows in a pod. The pod ripens underground.

pear pears *noun*
a sweet fruit that is round at the bottom but narrower at the top where the stalk is. ● A word that sounds like **pear** is **pair.**

pearl pearls *noun*
a small, hard, round, white ball that is used as jewelry and that grows inside the shell of an oyster. *a pearl necklace.* ▲ Rhymes with **curl.**

pebble pebbles *noun*
a small, smooth stone.

pecan pecans *noun*
a flat nut that is good to eat. *salted pecans.*

peck pecks pecking pecked *verb*
When a bird pecks, it pushes its beak at something and picks it up. *The hens were pecking at the food scattered on the ground.*

pedal pedals *noun*
a part on a machine that you push with your foot. You push the pedals around on a bicycle to make it move. You push the pedals down in a car to make the car go faster or slower.

pedestrian pedestrians *noun*
a person who is walking across or along a street.

peel peels peeling peeled *verb*
If you peel a fruit or vegetable you take off the skin. *She is peeling an apple.*

peel *noun*
the outside skin of a fruit or vegetable. *orange peel.*

peep peeps peeping peeped *verb*
If you peep, you look quickly at something. *The movie was so frightening, he just peeped at it.*

peer peers peering peered *verb*
You peer at something when it is difficult to see, so you have to look hard to see it. ● A word that sounds like **peer** is **pier.**

peg pegs *noun*
a piece of wood, plastic, or metal that is used to hold something down or to hang something up. *tent pegs.* ◆ *a peg to hang your coat on.*

pelican pelicans *noun*
a large waterbird with a long, narrow beak with a pouch under it that it uses for holding fish.

pen pens *noun*
a long, narrow object with a point called a nib at one end that you use for writing with ink.

penalty penalties *noun*
a punishment given if you do not obey a rule or do something wrong.

pencil pencils *noun*
a long, thin stick made of wood with a substance called graphite in the middle that you use for writing or drawing.

pendulum pendulums *noun*
a weight on the end of a rod inside some clocks. It swings from side to side to make the clock work.

penguin penguins *noun*
a large black and white bird that swims but cannot fly. Penguins mostly live in the Antarctic, the very cold land and sea in the far south of the world. Penguins feed on fish.

penitentiary penitentiary *noun*
a federal or state prison for people guilty of bad crimes.

penknife penknives *noun*
a knife with blades that fold back into the handle.

pennant pennants *noun*
a flag in the shape of a triangle.

penny pennies *noun*
In the United States and Canada 100 pennies make one dollar.

pen pal pen pals *noun*
a person who lives far away whom you get to know by writing letters back and forth. *Lucy met her pen pal after writing for six years.*

pentagon pentagons *noun*
a shape with five sides.

people *noun*
men, women, and children. *A lot of people were waiting at the bus stop.*

pepper peppers *noun*
1 a spice with a hot taste that is ground to a powder and put on food. *black pepper.*
2 a green, red, or yellow vegetable that is hollow inside.

different types of pepper

percent *noun*
a number of parts of something in every hundred. *Eight percent of people or eight people in every hundred travel to work by bus.* The sign for percent is % *(8 %).* ▲ Say *per sent.*

perch perches *noun*
1 a place for a bird to stand.
2 a fish that lives in freshwater.
perch *verb*
The birds perched on the fence.

percussion *noun*
all the different musical instruments such as drums that you play by hitting them.

perfect *adjective*
A perfect thing has no mistakes or faults.
perfection *noun,* **perfectly** *adverb.*

perform performs performing performed *verb*
1 If actors perform, they act, sing, dance, or tell jokes in front of an audience.
2 to do or carry out. *The surgeon performed an operation.*
performer *noun.*

perfume perfumes *noun*
a liquid with a pleasant smell that you put on your skin to make you smell nice. *a bottle of perfume.*

perimeter perimeters *noun*
the outside edge of something. *the perimeter of the circle.* ▲ Say *per-imi-ter.*

period periods *noun*
1 an amount of time.
2 a particular time in history.
3 a dot that you put at the end of a full sentence.

periscope periscopes *noun*
a tube with mirrors inside that are arranged so that when you look in one end of the tube you can see things through the top that you would not be able to see normally. Periscopes are used in submarines to see what is happening above the surface of the water.

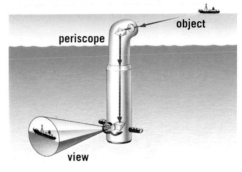

permanent *adjective*
lasting forever or for a very long time.
■ The opposite is **temporary**.

permission *noun*
If people give you permission to do something, they say you are allowed to do it. *My teacher gave me permission to go home early.*

permit permits permitting permitted *verb*
If people permit you to do something, they allow you to do it. *My parents permit me to stay up late on Friday and Saturday nights.* ■ The opposite is **forbid**.

person *noun*
a man, woman, or child.

personal *adjective*
belonging to one person.

persuade persuades persuading persuaded *verb*
If you persuade somebody to do something, you manage to make him or her do it.
▲ Say *per-swade.*

pest pests *noun*
1 an insect or animal that damages plants or is harmful to people.
2 a person who is annoying or causes trouble.

A B C D E F G H I J K L M N O P Q R S T U V W X Y Z

pet pets *noun*
a tame animal that you keep in the house and look after.

petal petals *noun*
one of the white or colored parts that make the outside of a flower.

petroleum *noun*
a yellow-black oil under the ground that people use to make gasoline and other fuel.

phantom phantoms *noun*
a ghost. ▲ Say *fan-tom*.

pharmacy pharmacies *noun*
the part of a drugstore that sells medicines. ▲ Say *far-ma-see*.

phone phones *noun*
a telephone. ▲ Say *fone*.
phone *verb*

photo photos *noun*
a photograph or picture that you make by using a camera. ▲ Say *foh-toh*.

photocopy photocopies *noun*
a copy of a document made by a machine called a photocopier.

physical *adjective*
to do with people's bodies rather than their minds. ▲ Say *fiz-i-cul*.
physically *adverb*

piano pianos *noun*
a large musical instrument with a row of black and white keys. When you press a key, a small hammer inside the piano hits a string to make a sound.
pianist *noun*.

pick picks picking picked *verb*
1 When you pick something, you take it from a group of things because it is the one that you want. *Pick your favorite tape and we'll buy it.*
2 If you pick a fruit or a flower, you take it off the plant. *We're going to the farm tomorrow to pick strawberries.*
3 When you pick something up, you lift it from where it is lying. *Can you pick those bags up and bring them into the house?*
4 If you pick at something, you eat a little bit of it. *He wasn't very hungry and only picked at his food.*

pickle pickles *noun*
a vegetable that has been kept in a vinegar. *I like cucumber pickles.*

picnic picnics *noun*
a meal that you take somewhere with you and eat outside.

picture pictures *noun*
a drawing, painting, or photograph.

pie pies *noun*
a piece of pastry with fruit or custard, meat, fish, or vegetables cooked inside it.

piece pieces *noun*
1 a part or bit that is cut off something bigger. *Cut the pie into four equal pieces.*
2 a single thing. *a piece of paper.*

piece
Some words you can use instead of piece:

May I have a piece of cake?
☞ **slice, portion** ☜

She tore the paper into pieces.
☞ **bits, scraps** ☜

There were huge pieces of meat in the soup.
☞ **chunks, lumps** ☜

On this piece of land we grow roses.
☞ **part, section** ☜

pier piers *noun*
a long platform built out over the sea where people can walk or where boats can be tied up. ● A word that sounds like **pier** is **peer**.

pierce pierces piercing pierced *verb*
When a sharp object pierces something, it makes a hole in it. *Have you had your ears pierced?*

pig pigs *noun*
a farm animal with a flat nose, short legs, and a short curly tail. Male pigs are called boars and female pigs are called sows. The meat of pigs is eaten as bacon, pork, and ham.

pigeon pigeons *noun*
a gray bird with a fat body. Some pigeons have been trained to carry messages and some are used for racing.

pile piles *noun*
a lot of things that have been put one on top of the other. *a pile of books.*

pill pills *noun*
A pill is a medicine that has been made into a small round object that you swallow.

pillar pillars *noun*
a tall, round column made of stone or brick that holds up part of a building. *The Lincoln Memorial has tall, white marble pillars.*

pillow pillows *noun*
a soft cushion that you put your head on when you are in bed.

pilot pilots *noun*
a person who flies an aircraft.

pin pins *noun*
a small, thin, metal stick with a sharp point at one end that you use for holding two pieces of cloth or paper in place.
pin *verb*
She pinned the badge to her dress.

pinch pinches pinching pinched *verb*
1 If you pinch somebody, you squeeze a little bit of the person's skin with your thumb and finger.

pine pines *noun*
a tall evergreen tree that has narrow, pointed leaves called needles and has its seeds held in cones.

pineapple pineapples *noun*
a large, sweet fruit that is yellow inside and has a thick, prickly skin and leaves growing out of the top.

pint pints *noun*
sixteen ounces of a liquid. *Two cups equal one pint.*

pipe pipes *noun*
a tube, usually made of metal or plastic, that carries things like water and gas.

pirate pirates *noun*
a person who attacks and robs ships and private boats.

pistol pistols *noun*
a small gun that is held in the hand.

pit pits *noun*
1 a large hole in the ground.
2 a large fruit seed.

pitch pitches *noun*
1 a way of throwing a ball, as in softball or baseball.
2 The pitch of a sound is how low or high the sound is. *Her voice rose in pitch.*
pitch *verb*.

pity *noun*
If you feel pity for people, you feel sorry for them. *He feels pity for children who do not have enough to eat.*
pity *verb*.

pixie pixies *noun*
a small fairy.

pizza pizzas *noun*
a round piece of flat dough with things on top such as tomatoes and cheese that is baked in the oven. ▲ Say *pee-tsa*.

place places *noun*
1 an area or building. *Show me the place on your leg that hurts.*
2 a position in a race. *He was in third place.*

plague plagues *noun*
a serious disease that spreads quickly. *Plague can be spread by rats and fleas.*

plain plainer plainest *adjective*
1 something that is plain has no pattern or marks on it. *Take a piece of plain paper and write the essay title at the top.* ◆ *He wore a plain red tie.*
2 A plain person is ordinary and not beautiful. *She had a plain face but she was very kind.*
3 If something is plain to you, it is clear and easy to understand. *She made it plain that she expected good behavior at all times.*
● A word that sounds like **plain** is **plane**.

plait plaits *verb*
to divide into strands and weave one over the other until a smooth line like a rope is formed. *She plaited her thick hair into two long braids.* ▲ Rhymes with *cat*.

plan plans
noun
a set of ideas that show how you are going to do something.

plan plans planning planned
verb
When you plan something, you work out what you are going to do and how you are going to do it.

plane planes *noun*
an airplane that takes people to places by air.
● A word that sounds like **plane** is **plain**.

planet planets *noun*
a very big round object in space, such as Venus, Mars, or the Earth, that moves around a star such as the Sun.

plank planks *noun*
a long, flat piece of wood. *The floors are made of planks.*

plant plants *noun*
a tree, flower, bush, or other living thing that grows in one place and has roots, a stem, and leaves.
❖ *Look at page 120*

plant plants planting planted *verb*
When you plant things such as flowers or trees, you put them into the ground where you want them to grow. *The garden club has planted trees on both sides of the street.*

plaster plasters *noun*
1 a wet material that a doctor puts around a broken arm or leg and that becomes hard. A cast made of plaster keeps the part from moving.
2 a soft, wet mixture that you use to cover walls and ceilings inside a house. It becomes hard and smooth and you can paint or wallpaper over it.

plastic *noun*
a material that is made in a factory for a lot of different uses. It is light in weight and does not break easily.

plate plates *noun*
a flat dish that you put food on.

platform platforms *noun*
1 the part of a railroad station where you get on and off the trains.
2 a flat area that is built higher than the floor so that the people on it can be seen more easily.
3 a flat structure that is higher than the ground or built over water. *an offshore oil platform.*

play plays playing played *verb*
1 When you play, you do things that you enjoy doing such as games.
2 If you play a musical instrument, you use it to make music. *She plays the clarinet.*

play plays *noun*
a story that is performed in the theater, on television, or on the radio. *a school play by our class.*

playful *adjective*
liking to play and have fun.

playground playgrounds *noun*
an area of land where children can play. *Freddie plays in the school playground.*

A B C D E F G H I J K L M N O P Q R S T U V W X Y Z

PLANTS

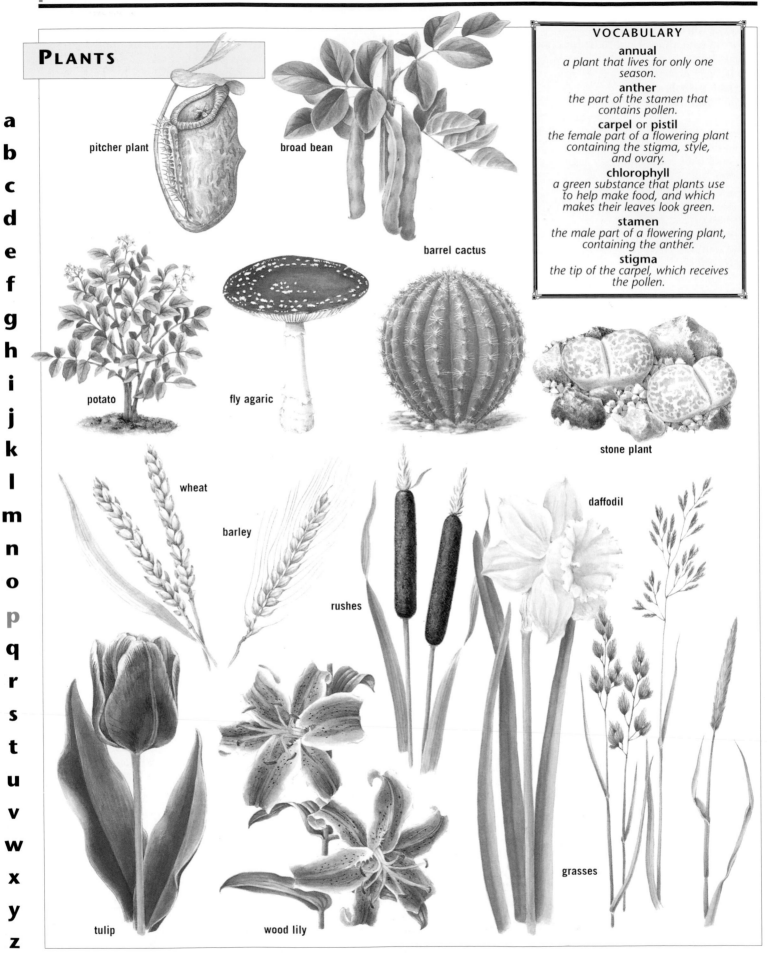

pitcher plant

broad bean

barrel cactus

potato

fly agaric

stone plant

wheat

barley

rushes

daffodil

tulip

wood lily

grasses

a b c d e f g h i j k l m n o p q r s t u v w x y z

plead pleads pleading pleaded or
pled *verb*.
If you plead with somebody, you strongly
ask the person to do something. *She
pleaded to be allowed to go home.*

pleasant pleasanter pleasantest
adjective
A pleasant thing is something you enjoy
or like. *We had a pleasant afternoon at
the beach.*

please *interjection*
You say "please" to be polite when you
are asking for something. *Would you
pass me that magazine, please?*
please *verb*.

pleasure *noun*
the feeling you get when you are happy
and enjoying something. ▲ Say *plesh*-ur.

plenty *noun*
a large amount of something and more
than is needed. *There's plenty of cake, so
you can all have a piece.*

plot plots *noun*
1 a secret plan by a group of people to
   do something, usually wrong.
2 the story in a book, film, or TV
   program.
3 a small area of ground. *a vegetable
   plot*.

plow plows *noun*
a tool that is used for turning over the
soil to make it ready for planting seeds.
It is pulled along by a tractor or an
animal. ▲ Rhymes with **cow**.
plow *verb*.

pluck plucks plucking plucked *verb*
1 When you pluck a musical instrument
   such as a guitar, you pull on the
   strings in order to make the notes
   sound.
2 When you pluck a flower or fruit, you
   pick it from the place where it was
   growing.

plug plugs *noun*
1 a round object that you put into the
   hole of a bathtub or basin to stop the
   water from running out.
2 a thing at the end of a wire on a
   machine that fits into a socket on the
   wall so that the machine can be
   connected to the power supply.

plum plums *noun*
a soft, purple or yellow fruit with a thin
skin and a pit in the center.

plumber plumbers *noun*
a person whose job is to put in water
pipes in a house and to fix them when
they break. *The plumber has come to fix
the drain.* ▲ Say *plum*-er.

plump plumper plumpest *noun*
nicely fat. *The baby had plump cheeks.*
■ The opposite is **slim**.

plural plurals *noun*
the form of a word that you use when
you are talking about two or more
things instead of just one. The plural of
"desk" is "desks" and the plural of
"mouse" is "mice." ▲ Say *pler-rel*. ■ The
opposite is **singular**.

plus *preposition*
You use the word plus to talk about
adding numbers together. In arithmetic,
you can use the sign + to mean plus. *Six
plus five equals eleven is the same as*
$6 + 5 = 11$.

pocket pockets *noun*
a part like a flat bag in your clothes that
you can put things in.

pocket money *noun*
allowance; money that is given each
week to a child to spend.

pod pods *noun*
a long, narrow part of some plants that
seeds grow inside. Peas and beans grow
in pods.

poem poems *noun*
a piece of writing arranged in short
lines. The words in the lines make a
rhythm and sometimes the words at the
ends of the lines rhyme.

some poetry books

poet poets *noun*
a person who writes poetry.

poetry *noun*
poems are poetry.

point points *noun*
1 the end of something sharp like a
   needle or a pencil.

2 a particular place or time. *At this
   point, she suddenly saw that
   everybody had left the room.*
3 a score that somebody gets in a game
   or competition.
4 the purpose of doing something.
   *What's the point in taking your coat
   off if you're going right out again?*

point points pointing pointed *verb*
If you point, you show where something
is by using your finger.

pointed *adjective*
A pointed thing has a point at one end.

poison *noun*
a substance that will make you sick or
kill you if it gets into your body.
poisonous *adjective*.

poke pokes poking poked *verb*
To poke somebody is to push something
into that one. *She poked me in the back
with her finger.*

polar bear polar bears *noun*
a large white bear that lives near the
North Pole.

pole poles *noun*
1 a long, narrow, round piece of wood or
   metal. *a telephone pole.*
2 a point at each end of the Earth that is
   furthest from the Equator. *the North
   Pole and the South Pole.*

police *noun*
those whose job is to protect people and
make sure that everybody obeys the law.
policeman *noun*, **policewoman** *noun*,
police officer *noun*.

polish polishes polishing polished
verb
If you polish something, you rub it to
make it shine.
*David is
polishing his
shoes.*
polish *noun*.

A
B
C
D
E
F
G
H
I
J
K
L
M
N
O
P
Q
R
S
T
U
V
W
X
Y
Z

polite politer politest *adjective*
If you are polite, you behave well toward other people and think about how to make them feel comfortable. *It is polite to say "thank you" and "please."*
■ The opposite is **rude**.
politely *adverb*.

politics *noun*
all the activities to do with the government of a country.
political *adjective*.

pollen *noun*
a fine powder inside flowers that the wind or insects take to other flowers of the same kind so that they can produce seeds.

pollution *noun*
poisonous chemicals and other forms of dangerous dirt that cause damage to the air, water, and environment.

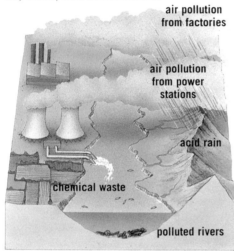

air pollution from factories

air pollution from power stations

acid rain

chemical waste

polluted rivers

pond ponds *noun*
a small area of water.

pony ponies *noun*
a small kind of horse.

pool pools *noun*
1 a small area of water.
2 a swimming pool.

poor poorer poorest *adjective*
1 A person who is poor has very little money. ■ The opposite is **rich**.
2 not good enough. *My spelling is very poor.*
3 unlucky or in a bad situation. *Poor John failed his driver's test.*

pop pops *noun*
1 modern, popular music.
2 a short, sharp sound.

popcorn *noun*
corn that you cook in hot oil to make it pop open.

popular *adjective*
liked by a lot of people. *a popular song.*
◆ *a popular girl.*
popularly *adverb*.

population populations *noun*
all the people who live in a particular area or country.

porch porches *noun*
a floor with a roof that is attached to the front, back, or sides of a house. *I love to sit on the porch and watch the sun set.*

porcupine porcupines *noun*
an animal that has stiff hairs on its back, called quills.

pork *noun*
meat from a hog.

port ports *noun*
a place or town beside a large river or the sea where ships can stay and load and unload.

portable *adjective*
Something that is portable is small enough or light enough to be carried around easily. *a portable computer.* ◆ *a portable television.*

portion portions *noun*
an amount of food for one person. *a portion of peas.*

portrait portraits *noun*
a picture of a person.

position positions *noun*
1 the place where something is. *I'm not sure where we are, can you check our position on the map?*
2 the way you are sitting, standing, or lying down. *Get into a comfortable position.*

positive *adjective*
1 certain about something. *I'm positive I saw him.*
2 A positive number is higher than zero. ■ The opposite is **negative**.

possess possesses possessing possessed *verb*
If you possess something, you own it and it belongs to you. *Do you possess a TV and a stereo?*
possession *noun*.

possible *adjective*
If something is possible, it can be done or it can happen. *Come as soon as possible.* ■ The opposite is **impossible**.
possibility *noun*

post posts *noun*
a long, thick, strong pole or piece of wood fixed in the ground. *a fence post.*

post posts posting posted *verb*
When you post a notice, you put it on a wall in a public place.

postal service *noun*
the government department that sells stamps, picks up and delivers the mail.

postcard postcards *noun*
a small piece of card, usually with a picture on one side, that you can use to send a short message to somebody.

poster posters *noun*
a large picture, notice, or advertisement that is put up on a wall.

post office post offices *noun*
1 a place where you can send letters and packages and buy stamps.
2 a local organization or group of people who collect, sort, and deliver people's letters and parcels.

postpone postpones postponing postponed *verb*
If you postpone something, you put it off until later. *The race was postponed because of bad weather.*

pot pots *noun*
1 a round container. *a pot of hot chocolate.*
2 a container for plants to grow in made of plastic or clay.

potato potatoes *noun*
a white vegetable with a thin, brown skin that grows under the ground.

pottery *noun*
dishes and other objects made out of clay and then baked hard in a special oven called a kiln.

a b c d e f g h i j k l m n o p q r s t u v w x y z

pouch pouches *noun*
1 a small bag.
2 a bag of skin that female kangaroos and some other female animals have on their stomach and that they use for carrying their babies.

pounce pounces pouncing pounced *verb*
To pounce is to jump forward suddenly and catch hold of something. *The kitten pounced on the ball of wool.*

pound pounds *noun*
A pound of something weighs sixteen ounces.

pour pours pouring poured *verb*
When you pour a liquid, you tilt a container such as jug or bottle so that the liquid flows out.

poverty *noun*
People who live in poverty are very poor.

powder *noun*
tiny, dry grains that you get when you crush or grind something well.

power *noun*
1 the ability to do something. *Human beings have the power of speech.*
2 the force or strength of something. *The power of the wind knocked the trees down.*
3 A person who has power can control what happens to a lot of people.

powerful *adjective*
A powerful person or thing has a lot of power. *a powerful king.* ◆ *a powerful engine.* ■ The opposite is **weak**.

practical *adjective*
1 to do with actually working or doing something rather than knowing or having ideas about it. *Do you have practical training in using computers?*
2 sensible, useful, and likely to work. *a practical suggestion.*
practically *adverb*
almost. *I've practically finished eating.*

practice *noun*
doing something again and again until you can do it well. *guitar practice.*

practice practices practicing practiced *verb*
If you practice something, you keep doing it until you can do it well.

prairie prairies *noun*
flat land with lots of tall grass and few trees.

prairie dog prairie dogs *noun*
Prairie dogs live in burrows. They can stand on their hind legs. They have brown fur and they can bark.

praise praises praising praised *verb*
When you praise somebody, you say how well they have done something. *Everybody praised the brave firefighters.* ■ The opposite is **criticize**.

pray prays praying prayed *verb*
If you pray, you talk to God or Allah.
● A word that sounds like **pray** is **prey**.

prayer prayers *noun*
the words somebody says when they are talking to God or Allah.

precious *adjective*
very valuable or very important to you.
▲ Say **pre-shus**.

predict predicts predicting predicted *verb*
If you predict something, you say that you think it is going to happen. *The weather forecast predicts rain for the weekend.*
prediction *noun*.

prefer prefers preferred *verb*
If you prefer one thing to another thing,

you like it better. *Would you prefer an apple or a peach?*

prehistoric *adjective*
belonging to a very long time ago before history was remembered and written down. *Dinosaurs lived in prehistoric times.* ❖ *Look at page 125*

prepare prepares preparing prepared *verb*
When you prepare something, you make it ready. *Len helped his dad prepare lunch.*
preparation *noun*.

preposition prepositions *noun*
a word you use for such things as where and how. "Down," "on," and "in" are prepositions used in the following sentences. "He ran down the hill." "The phone was on the table." "The milk is in the bottle." Prepositions show how the words before and after it are related.

prescription prescriptions *noun*
the piece of paper that a doctor uses to write down the medicines or pills you need to get from the drugstore.

present *adjective*
1 being in a place or being there. *Many people were present at the concert.*
■ The opposite is **absent**.
2 happening now. *the present time.*

present presents *noun*
1 a thing that you give to somebody. *What presents did you get?*
2 the time now. *We've had no trouble up to the present.*

preserve preserves preserving preserved *verb*
1 If you preserve something, you keep it the way it is without changing it. *Most people want to preserve the old buildings, though the city council wants new ones.*
2 If you preserve food, you do something to it so that it will not spoil.

president presidents *noun*
A person who is chosen to lead a country that does not have a king or queen.

press presses pressing pressed *verb*
If you press something, you push hard on it. *You press a button and the door slides open.*

pressure *noun*
the force of one thing pressing or pushing on another. *If you use pressure on that cut, it will stop bleeding.* ▲ Say *presh-ur.*

pretend pretends pretending pretended *verb*
If you pretend, you try to make other people believe something that is not true. *David's pretending to be a tree!*

pretty prettier prettiest *adjective*
attractive and nice to look at. *Flowers are pretty.*

prevent prevents preventing prevented *verb*
If you prevent something, you stop it from happening. *Shut the gate to prevent the horse from running away.*

previous *adjective*
The previous thing is the thing that came before or earlier. *I went over to Jane's house on Wednesday like we had arranged on the phone the previous day.* ▲ Say *pree-vee-us.*
previously *adverb.*

prey *noun*
any animal that is hunted for food. *Mice are the owl's natural prey.* ▲ Rhymes with *may.* ● A word that sounds like **prey** is **pray**.

price prices *noun*
the amount of money you have to pay to buy something. *What's the price of that pair of sneakers?*

prick pricks pricking pricked *verb*
If you prick something, you make a small hole in it with something sharp. *Domenic said he'd prick the balloon with a pin.*

prickle prickles *noun*
a sharp point or thorn. *Be careful of this bush; it's covered with prickles.*
prickly *adjective.*

pride *noun*
the good feeling you get when you are proud and have done something well or somebody you love or admire has done something well.

priest priests *noun*
a specially trained person in the Christian religion who leads people in services. ▲ Say **preest.**

primary *adjective*
1 first and most important. *Our primary need is to make sure everybody has enough to eat.*
2 to do with teaching children who are in kindergarten and grades one through four.

prime *adjective*
first and most important. *A matter of prime importance.*

prime number *noun*
a number that can only be divided exactly by itself or one. 7 and 17 are prime numbers.

prince princes *noun*
the son of a king or queen or a man or boy who is a member of a royal family.

princess princesses *noun*
the daughter of a king or queen or a woman or girl who is a member of a royal family.

principal principals *noun*
a person who is in charge of an elementary or high school.

principle principles *noun*
an important rule that you have about what is right and wrong. *It's against my principles to take drugs.*

print prints printing printed *verb*
1 When people print a book, magazine, or newspaper, they make copies of it on paper using a machine called a printer.
2 If you print something out from a computer, you use a machine called a printer to put information in the computer on paper.
3 If you print words, you write using letters that are not joined up.
printer *noun.*

prison prisons *noun*
a building where people who have broken the law are kept locked up.
prisoner *noun.*

private *adjective*
Something that is private is for only one person or one small group of people and not for everybody. *You can't see my letter; it's private.* ■ The opposite is **public.**
privately *adverb.*

prize prizes *noun*
a thing that you are given for winning a competition or for doing good work.

probably *adverb*
Something will be sure or likely to happen if you think it is probably true or will probably happen.

problem problems *noun*
A problem is something that is difficult to work out, understand, or do.

procession processions *noun*
a number of people walking or driving in a public place as part of a ceremony. *A brass band led the procession.*

prod prods prodding prodded *verb*
If you prod something, you push at it with something such as a stick or a finger. *I prodded him in the ribs.*

PREHISTORIC ANIMALS

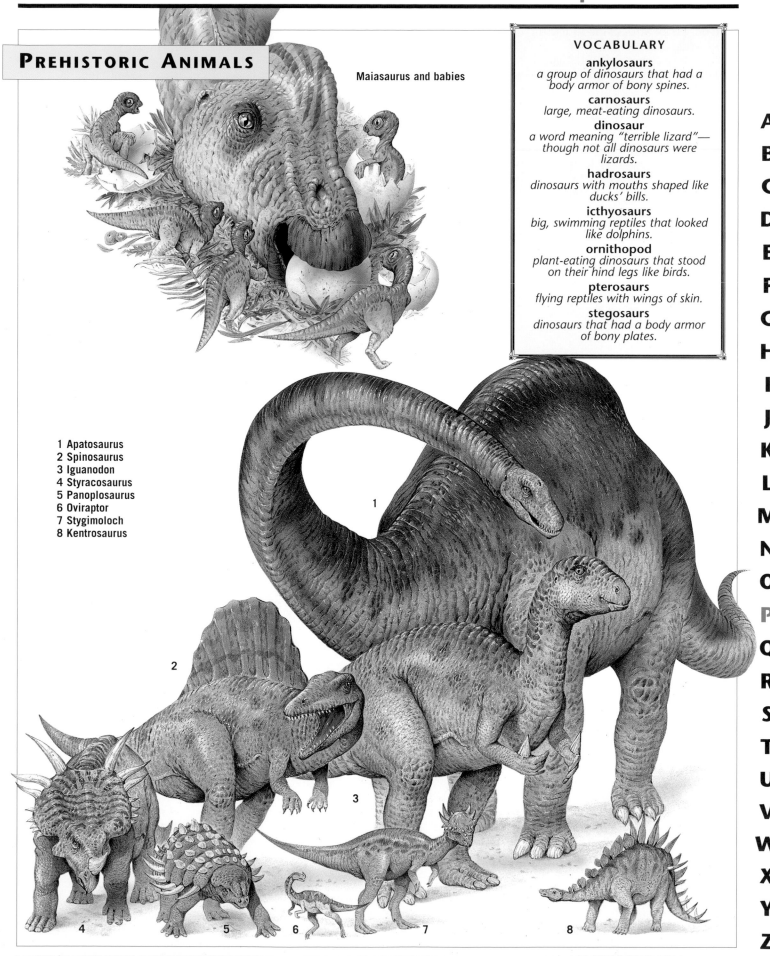

Maiasaurus and babies

1 Apatosaurus
2 Spinosaurus
3 Iguanodon
4 Styracosaurus
5 Panoplosaurus
6 Oviraptor
7 Stygimoloch
8 Kentrosaurus

A B C D E F G H I J K L M N O P Q R S T U V W X Y Z

produce produces producing produced *verb*
1 To produce something is to make it. *The factory produces hundreds of new cars a week.*
2 If you produce something, you take it out and show it. *She peered in her bag and produced a clean handkerchief.*
3 To produce a play, movie, or TV program is to organize the people making it and get it ready to show to the public.
▲ Say *pruh-dooss*.

product products *noun*
a thing that is made to be sold. *Maple syrup is a product of Canada.*

profession professions *noun*
a job that needs special knowledge and training, such as being a doctor or a teacher.

professor professors *noun*
a person who is a teacher at a college or university. *My cousin is a professor at Iowa State University.*

profit profits *noun*
money that you get when you sell something for more than it cost to buy or make.

program programs *noun*
1 a television or radio show.
2 a printed piece of paper that gives you information about such things as a play, a concert, a ballet, or a football game.
3 a list of instructions that makes a computer work.

progress progresses *noun*
the way something or someone moves forward or gets better. *Jennifer is making good progress learning Spanish.*

project projects *noun*
a piece of work you do in which you find out as much as you can about a subject. *We're doing a project on World War II at school.*

prom proms *noun*
a fancy school dance.

promise promises promising promised *verb*
When you promise you will do something, you say you will do it and you really mean it. *Pam promised not to make a noise.*

prompt *adjective*
When you are prompt, you do something quickly or immediately, without delay.

pronoun pronouns *noun*
a word like "you," "her," or "one" that you use when you know the person or thing that is being talked about. "Her," "me," "I," "it," and "one" are pronouns in the following sentences. *Jane tossed me the ball and I threw it back to her.* ◆ *I don't want the red crayon; I want the green one.*

pronounce pronounces pronouncing pronounced *verb*
When you pronounce a word right, you say the sound of the word in the correct way. *Some English words are hard for French people to pronounce correctly.*
pronunciation *noun.*

proof *noun*
To have proof of something is to have all the facts that show it is true.

prop props propping propped *verb*
If you prop something, you put it or lay it against something. *She propped her bike against the wall.*

propeller propellers *noun*
a set of blades that spin around to make a ship, plane, or helicopter move.

proper *adjective*
The proper way to do something is the right or correct way to do it.

property properties *noun*
1 things that you own. *Those books don't belong to the school; they're my property.*
2 a building and the land around it.

prosecute prosecutes prosecuting prosecuted *verb*
To prosecute people is to accuse them of crimes and make them go to court. *Trespassers will be prosecuted.*

prospector prospectors *noun*
a person who hunts for valuable minerals like gold.

protect protects protecting protected *verb*
If you protect others, you try to keep them from being hurt.

protest protests protesting protested *verb*
If you protest, you say that you think something is wrong and should be changed.

proud *adjective*
feeling good or pleased because you or someone else has done something very well. *I got better grades and I was really proud of myself.*
proudly *adverb.*

prove proves proving proved *verb*
When you prove something, you show that it is true. ▲ Rhymes with *move.*

provide provides providing provided *verb*
If you provide something, you get it and make sure that you give it when it is needed. *I'll provide the sandwiches.*

prune prunes pruning pruned *verb*
When you prune a tree or bush, you cut back its branches to keep it healthy or keep it from getting too big.

public *adjective*
for everybody to use or see. *a public phone booth.* ◆ *public transportation.*
■ The opposite is **private**.

public school public schools *noun*
a school in a city, town, or county that you attend free.

publish publishes publishing published *verb*
To publish a book, magazine, or newspaper is to have it printed and ready for people to buy copies.

puck pucks *noun*
a hard rubber disk that ice hockey players push with long sticks.

a b c d e f g h i j k l m n o p q r s t u v w x y z

puddle puddles *noun*
a pool or small area of water left on the ground after it has rained.

pueblo pueblos *noun*
a Native American village in the Southwest that has stone and adobe buildings.

puff puffs *noun*
a small amount of moving air, smoke, or wind. *a puff of smoke.*

pull pulls pulling pulled *verb*
When you pull something, you hold it and move it toward you.

pulp *noun*
the soft part inside a fruit or vegetable.

pulse *noun*
the regular beat or throbbing that your blood makes as it goes through your body. You can feel your pulse by putting your fingers on your wrist.

pump pumps *noun*
a machine that is used to push air, liquid, or gas into or out of something.

pump pumps pumping pumped *verb*
to force air or liquid with a pump.

pumpkin pumpkins *noun*
a large, round orange vegetable that grows on the ground.

pun puns *noun*
a joke that works because a word has two meanings. "Two pears make one pair."

punch punches punching punched *verb*
1 If you punch somebody, you hit him or her with your fist.
2 If you punch something, you make a hole in it. *The guard inspected everybody's tickets and punched them.*

punctual *adjective*
arriving on time.
punctually *adverb*.

punctuation *noun*
marks such as periods, commas, and quotation marks that you use when you are writing.

puncture punctures *noun*
a hole in a bicycle tire or a car tire.
▲ Say *punk-cher.*

punish punishes punishing punished *verb*
To punish somebody is to make that one hurt or suffer because he or she has done something wrong.
punishment *noun*.

pupa pupae *noun*
a stage in an insect's life after it is a larva but before it is an adult insect with wings. ▲ Say *pew-pa.*

pupil pupils *noun*
1 a person who is studying at school.
2 the small, round, black part at the center of the eye.

puppet puppets *noun*
a kind of doll that you can make move by pulling strings that are fixed to the different parts of the puppet, or by putting your hand inside the puppet and moving it with your fingers.

puppy puppies *noun*
a young dog.

purchase purchases purchasing purchased *verb*
If you purchase something, you buy it.

pure purer purest *adjective*
Something that is pure is not mixed with anything else. *pure apple juice.*
▲ Say *pyuer.*

Puritan Puritans *noun*
a person in America in the 1600s who wanted simple religious ceremonies.

purpose purposes *noun*
the reason that something is being done or what it is meant to do. *The purpose of the trip is to see some famous places.*
on purpose If you do something on purpose, you intend to do it.

purr purrs purring purred *verb*
When a cat purrs, it makes a low sound to show that it is pleased.

push pushes pushing pushed *verb*
If you push something, you move it away from you. *When the car broke down all the family had to get out and push it off the road.*

pussy willow pussy willows *noun*
a bush that has small flowers with silky fibers on them.

puzzle puzzles *noun*
a question, problem, or game that is hard to work out the answer to.

pyramid pyramids *noun*
1 a solid shape with triangular sides that meet in a point at the top.
2 a building with four triangular sides that meet at the top. *There are pyramids in Egypt and Mexico, and the ancient Egyptians buried some of their dead kings, called Pharaohs, in them.*

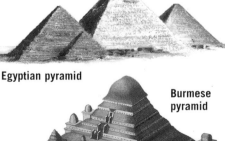

Egyptian pyramid

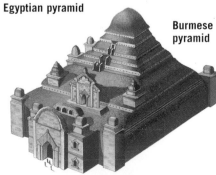

Burmese pyramid

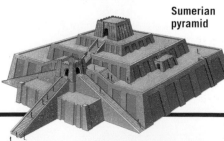

Sumerian pyramid

A B C D E F G H I J K L M N O P Q R S T U V W X Y Z

Q q

quack quacks quacking quacked
verb
To quack is to make the sound that a duck makes.
quack *noun.*

quaint quainter quaintest *adjective*
pretty and unusual. *a quaint old cottage.*

qualify qualifies qualifying qualified *verb*
1 If you qualify, you pass a test that allows you to do a job. *She qualified as a teacher.*
2 You qualify if you win part of a competition and are able to go on to the next part. *Our team qualified for the championship.*
qualification *noun.*

quality *noun*
1 how good or bad something is. *a dress made from material of good quality.*
2 what makes something what it is. *One quality of lemons is that they are sour.*

quantity quantities *noun*
an amount of something. *Birds need large quantities of twigs to make a nest.*

quarrel quarrels quarreling quarreled *verb*
If you quarrel with others, you have an angry argument with them.

quarry quarries *noun*
a place where things such as stone are dug out of the ground.

quart quarts *noun*
A quart equals two pints. Four quarts equal one gallon.

Spelling tip:
· ·
Words that begin with "qu" sound like they are spelled with "cw" or "kw."

quarter quarters *noun*
1 one of four equal parts of something.
2 a coin worth twenty-five cents.

quay quays
a place in a harbor where boats are tied up to be loaded or unloaded.

queen queens *noun*
a woman who rules a country or who is the wife of a king and who is a member of a royal family.

queer *adjective*
very strange. *queer sounds.*

query queries *noun*
a question. *Does anyone have any queries?*

quest quests *noun*
a long and hard search for something important. *a quest for a cure for cancer.*

question questions *noun*
You ask a question when you want to find out about something. *I asked my teacher a question about the computer.* ■ The opposite is **answer.**

question mark question marks
noun
a mark (**?**) that you use in writing. You put a question mark at the end of a sentence to show that somebody has asked a question. *What did you say?*

quick quicker quickest *adjective*
1 fast. *If you're not quick, we'll miss the bus.*
2 done in a short time. *We had a quick breakfast before we went out.*
quickly *adverb*
Go as quickly as you can.

quiet quieter quietest *adjective*
making no noise or very little noise. *She played quiet music.* ■ The opposite is **loud.**

quill quills *noun*
1 a large, stiff feather from a bird's wing or tail.
2 the sharp spines of a porcupine.

quilt quilts *noun*
a soft, light cover for a bed made from two layers of cloth filled with padding.

quintuplet quintuplets *noun*
one of five babies that are born all at the same time to one mother.

quit quits quitting quit *verb*
If you quit, you stop doing something. *I am going to quit studying German.*

quite *adverb*
1 more than a little. *He's quite tall.*
2 completely. *You're quite right.*

quiver quivers *noun*
a case for carrying arrows.

quiz quizzes *noun*
a short test.

quotation quotations *noun*
words that you say or write that somebody else has said before. *"We the people" is a quotation from the Constitution.*

quotation mark quotation marks *noun*
marks (**" "**) that you use in writing. You put quotation marks before and after the words that somebody has said. *"What did you say?" he asked.*

quote quotes quoting quotes
verb
1 to say or write something that somebody else has said before.
2 to name a price. *He quoted a price of $100.*

R r

rabbi rabbis *noun*
a teacher of the Jewish religion and the leader of a synagogue.

rabbit rabbits *noun*
a small, wild animal with soft fur and long ears. Rabbits live in burrows.

rabies *noun*
Rabies is a disease that kills dogs and some other animals.

raccoon raccoons *noun*
a small animal that has mask-like black markings on its face and black rings around its tail.

race races *noun*
1 a competition to see who is the fastest.
2 a large number of human beings whose ancestors all came from the same area and who look alike in some way, for example in skin color.

race races racing raced *verb*
If you race, you go very fast. *She was racing along the bicycle path.*

rack racks *noun*
a frame or set of shelves that you can put things on or hang things on.

plate rack
wine rack
shoe rack

racket rackets *noun*
a bat with an oval frame for hitting a ball in tennis or badminton.

radar *noun*
a device that shows on a screen the exact position and speed of a plane or ship that cannot be seen.

> **Spelling tip:**
> ....
> *Some words that begin with an "r" sound are spelled "wr" such as wrong, wriggle, wrestle.*

radiator radiators *noun*
a flat, metal object against a wall that steam or hot water runs through to heat a room. ▲ Say *ray-di-ay-ter.*

radio radios *noun*
a machine that receives sounds sent through the air so that you can hear them. You turn on a radio to listen to music, news and other programs.

radius radiuses *noun*
a straight line from the center of a circle to the edge. ❖ *Look at page 38*

raft rafts *noun*
a flat boat made of rubber or wood.

rag rags *noun*
an old piece of material that you can use to clean things.

rage *noun*
very great anger. *He was purple with rage.*

raid raids *noun*
a sudden attack on a place. *a raid by soldiers on a village.*

rail rails *noun*
1 a bar for people to hold onto or to stop them from falling. *She held onto the rail as she climbed the stairs.*
2 the long, parallel metal bars (lines) that trains run on.
3 a railroad system. *We traveled all around Europe by rail.*
railings *noun.*

---

railroad railroads *noun*
the system of trains, stations, and tracks used when people travel by train.

rain *noun*
water that falls to the ground from clouds in small drops.
rain *verb,* **rainy** *adjective.*
rainy weather.

rainbow rainbows *noun*
an arc or curve of light of different colors that you can sometimes see in the sky when there are rain and sunshine at the same time.

rain forest rain forests *noun*
an area of thick, tropical forest where a lot of rain falls. Most are in Central and South America, Africa, and Southeast Asia.

raise raises raising raised *verb*
If you raise something, you lift it up or move it so that it is higher. *Raise your hand if you know the answer.* ■ The opposite is **lower.**

raisin raisins *noun*
a dried grape.

rake rakes *noun*
a garden tool with a long handle and a row of metal teeth like a comb that you use to make the dirt level or to gather leaves into a pile.
rake *verb.*

rally rallies *noun*
1 a large public meeting.
2 a car or motorcycle race that takes place over a long distance.

ram rams *noun*
a male sheep.

ran past of **run.**

A B C D E F G H I J K L M N O P Q R S T U V W X Y Z

a b c d e f g h i j k l m n o p q r s t u v w x y z

ranch ranches *noun*
a very large farm for cattle, horses, or sheep. ▲ Rhymes with **branch**.

rang past of **ring**.

range ranges *noun*
1 a choice of things of the same kind. *The store stocks a wide range of sneakers.*
2 a long line of mountains.
3 the area or distance over which something can be used.
4 a big area of land where animals feed.

ransom ransoms *noun*
money demanded in return for letting a kidnapped person go free.

rap raps *noun*
1 a short, sharp sound like a single knock on a door.
2 a kind of music where the words are spoken in rhythm, not sung.

rapid *adjective*
very quick. *a rapid heartbeat.*
rapidly *adverb*.

rare rarer rarest *adjective*
not often seen or done. ■ The opposite is **common**.

rash rashes *noun*
a lot of small red spots that you get on your skin if you have an illness like measles.

raspberry raspberries *noun*
a small, sweet, red fruit that grows on a bush.
❖ *Look at page 22.*

rat rats *noun*
an animal that is like a very large mouse with a long tail.

a black rat

rate rates *noun*
1 the speed at which something happens. *Scientists are worried by the rate at which rain forests are being cut down.*

2 the amount of money that you pay for a service. *You pay a cheaper rate for phone calls in the evenings and on weekends.*

rattle rattles rattling rattled *verb*
When something rattles, it makes the noise of things knocking together.

rattlesnake rattlesnakes *noun*
a snake with a poisonous bite. It has hard rings on its tail that rattle.

raw *adjective*
Food that is raw has not been cooked. *raw cabbage.* ◆ *raw meat.*

ray rays *noun*
a line of light. *the Sun's rays.*

razor razors *noun*
a tool with a very sharp blade for shaving.

reach reaches reaching reached *verb*
1 When you reach a place, you get there. *When we reach Denver, we'll stop and have lunch.*
2 When you reach for something, you stretch out your arm toward it. *I'm not tall enough to reach the books on the top shelf.*

react reacts reacting reacted *verb*
When you react to something, you behave in a certain way because of that thing and as a kind of answer to it. *Rose is tapping Freddie's knee to see if his leg reacts.*
reaction *noun*.

read reads reading read *verb*
When you read something, you look at written words and understand what they mean. ● A word that sounds like **read** is **reed**.

ready *adjective*
When you are ready, you are prepared and can do something right away. *Are you ready to go yet?* ▲ Say **red**-ee.

real *adjective*
1 really existing and not made up. *Do you think that unicorns were real?*
2 not a copy. *real leather.*
■ The opposite is **fake**.

realize realizes realizing realized *verb*
When you realize something, you start to know or understand it. *I realize I can't have everything I want.*

reap reaps reaping reaped *verb*
When you reap crops such as wheat, you cut them and gather them up.

rear *noun*
the back of something. *There's a large garden at the rear of the house.* ■ The opposite is **front**.

reason reasons *noun*
a fact that explains why something happens. *The reason I'm afraid of snakes is that I was once bitten by one.*

rebel rebels rebelling rebelled *verb*
When people rebel, they refuse to obey the people who are in charge.
▲ Say ri-**bell**.

receipt receipts *noun*
a piece of paper that shows how much money you paid for something. ▲ Say ree-**seet**.

receive receives receiving received *verb*
If you receive something, you get it when it has been given or sent to you. *Connie and Ted received a cup for winning the school spelling bee.* ▲ Say *ree-seev*.

recent *adjective*
from or happening a short time ago. *a recent photo of my brother.* **recently** *adverb*.

reception receptions *noun*
a big party to honor or introduce somebody. *We attended the reception after my sister's wedding.*

recess recesses *noun*
a short period to relax. *We played soccer at noon recess.* ◆ *The judge announced a short recess.*

recipe recipes *noun*
a list of things you need to cook something and the instructions on how to cook it. ▲ Say *res-i-pee*.

recognize recognizes recognizing recognized *verb*
If you recognize people, you know who they are because you have seen them before. *You look so different that I didn't recognize you at first.*

recommend recommends recommending recommended *verb*
If you recommend something, you say that you think it is good. *I recommend the apple pie and cream.*

record records recording recorded *verb*
1 If you record something, you write down what happened. *Every night, before he went to bed, Ray recorded the day's events in his diary.*
2 To record something is to store it on film, tape, a compact disk, or a record so that it can be played or shown again.
▲ Say *re-kord*.

record records *noun*
1 a written list of what has happened. *I kept a record of everything I spent while we were on vacation.*
2 a round, black piece of plastic that has music or other sounds recorded on it in a special sound studio.
3 the best performance so far. *She holds the record for the high jump.*
▲ Say *rek-erd*.

recorder recorders *noun*
a machine that records sounds, such as music.

recover recovers recovering recovered *verb*
1 When you recover from an illness, you get better. *He's recovering from the flu.*
2 If you recover something, you get it back after it has been lost or stolen.

recreation *noun*
a way of exercising, relaxing, and having fun.

rectangle rectangles *noun*
a shape with four sides and four corners. Each side of a rectangle is the same length as the side opposite to it. **rectangular** *adjective*.

recycle recycles recycling recycled *verb*
To recycle things is to make them into something new after they have already been used instead of throwing them away. *recycled paper.*

reduce reduces reducing reduced *verb*
To reduce is to make something smaller or less. *I'm trying to reduce the amount of chocolate that I eat.*

reed reeds *noun*
a plant with long, hollow stems that grows near water. ● A word that sounds like **reed** is **read**.

reef reefs *noun*
a long line of rocks, sand, or coral in the sea. *In very bad weather, ships sometimes hit the reef and sink.*

reel reels *noun*
a round object that you wrap film, tape, or fishing line around.

referee referees *noun*
a person who makes sure that everybody playing in a game obeys the rules. *The referee's decision was final.*

reference book reference books *noun*
a book with facts and information in it.

reflect reflects reflecting reflected *verb*
1 If a surface reflects light, the light hits the surface and bounces back, rather than passing through it.
2 A mirror reflects something in front of it and shows what it looks like. **reflection** *noun*.

refrigerator refrigerators *noun*
a metal cabinet where you can put food to keep it cold and fresh. ▲ Say *re-frij-er-ay-ter*.

refugee refugees *noun*
If you are a refugee, you have been forced out of your country and you are looking for a new place to live.

refuse refuses refusing refused *verb*
If you refuse to do something, you will not do it. *Jill refused to wash the dishes and said that somebody else would have to do it.* ■ The opposite is **accept**.

regard regards regarding regarded *verb*
If you regard something in a certain way, that is what you think about it. *She regarded the uniform as old-fashioned.*

region regions *noun*
an area of land or part of a country. *a mountain region.* ▲ Say *ree-jun*.

register registers *noun*
a book containing a list of names or important information. *The teacher checked her register at the beginning of the class.*

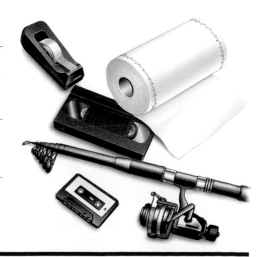

regret regrets regretting regretted *verb*
If you regret something, you are sorry about it and wish that you had not done it or that it had not happened.

regular *adjective*
Regular things have exactly the same amount of time between them. *When you exercise your pulse gets faster but it stays regular.*
regularly *adverb*.

rehearse rehearses rehearsing rehearsed *verb*
If you rehearse, you practice something before doing it for an audience. *We rehearsed the play every night for a week.* ▲ Say *re-hurse*.
rehearsal *noun*.

reign reigns reigning reigned *verb*
To reign is to be the king or queen of a country. ▲ Rhymes with *pain*. ● A word that sounds like **reign** is **rain**.

reindeer *noun*
a large deer with very large antlers that lives in northern countries where it is very cold. ▲ Say *rain-deer*.

rein reins *noun*
Reins are long leather straps that you use to guide a horse. ▲ Say *rain*.

reject rejects rejecting rejected *verb*
If you reject something, you will not accept it. *He rejected my advice.*

related *adjective*
If you are related to people, you are in the same family.

relation relations *noun*
a link between things. *the relation between smoking and cancer.*

relative relatives *noun*
a person who is in your family.

relax relaxes relaxing relaxed *verb*
When you relax, your body becomes less tense and you feel calm and less worried.

relay relays *noun*
a race between teams of runners. Each member of the team takes a turn to run a part of the race. A special stick called a baton is passed to the person whose turn it is to run.

release releases releasing released *verb*
When you release somebody or an animal that has been held in some way, you set them free. *Robert released the bird after it was caught in a bush.*

reliable *adjective*
If somebody is reliable, you can trust and depend on that person. ▲ Say *re-lie-uh-bul*.

relief *noun*
the good feeling that you get when you can stop worrying. *It was a great relief when I was told that I'd passed the test.* ▲ Say *re-leef*.

religion religions *noun*
believing in God or gods and a way of worshiping.
religious *adjective*.

rely relies relying relied *verb*
If you can rely on people, you know you can trust them and depend on them. ▲ Say *re-lie*.

remain remains remaining remained *verb*
1 If people remain in a place, they stay there. *He did not go out to play but remained in the house all day.*

2 If something remains, it is still there. *The roof has gone, but most of the rest of the building remains.*

remark remarks *noun*
a thing that you say about someone or something. *She made a nice remark about my dress.*

remedy remedies *noun*
1 an answer to a problem.
2 a way of curing an illness.
remedy *verb*.

remember remembers remembering remembered *verb*
When you remember something, you have it in your mind or bring it into your mind again. *Can you remember what you did on vacation last year?*

remind reminds reminding reminded *verb*
1 If you remind somebody, you tell the person something again in case he or she has forgotten. *Will you remind me to phone David?*
2 If something reminds you, it makes you remember something.
3 If somebody reminds you of somebody else, that person is like the other person in some way.

remote remoter remotest *adjective*
very far away.

remote control remote controls *noun*
an electronic device you use to turn a TV on and off and choose channels.

remove removes removing removed *verb*
to take something away.

renew renews renewing renewed *verb*
1 When you renew something, you arrange for it to go on longer. *You*

have to renew your subscription to the magazine.

2 When you renew something, you start doing it again. *He renewed his efforts to spell better.*

3 If you renew a book you have borrowed from the library, you ask to keep it longer.

rent rents *noun*

money that you pay to live in a place or to use something that you do not own yourself. *The rent for this apartment is $1,500 a month.*
rent *verb.*

repair repairs repairing repaired *verb*

If you repair something that is broken or does not work, you mend it.

repeat repeats repeating repeated *verb*

If you repeat something, you say it or do it again. *Will you repeat the question?*
repetition *noun.*

replace replaces replacing replaced *verb*

1 If you replace something, you put it back where it came from. *She replaced the book on the shelf.*

2 When you replace something, you get a new one instead of the old one. *The school is replacing all the computers with more modern ones.*

reply replies replying replied *verb*

When you reply, you give an answer. *"Must I reply to this letter?" "I don't know," he replied.*

report reports *noun*

Something that someone says or writes that tells you about something that has happened.

report card report cards *noun*

a written report that teachers give to parents to say how well a pupil has done in school.

represent represents representing represented *verb*

If one thing represents another thing, it is a picture or symbol of it.

representative representatives *noun*

a person who speaks for people, as in a legislature.

reproduction reproductions *noun*

1 a copy of something old.

2 making new young animals or plants.

reptile reptiles *noun*

an animal with cold blood that has scales on its skin. Female reptiles lay eggs. Snakes, crocodiles, turtles, and lizards are reptiles.

❖ *Look at page 134*

request requests requesting requested *verb*

to ask for something politely.

require requires requiring required *verb*

to need something or ask for it.

rescue rescues rescuing rescued *verb*

If you rescue people, you save them from danger.

The man was rescued by the mountain climbers.

reserve reserves reserving reserved *verb*

To reserve is to ask for something to be kept for you to use later. *Tom reserved a table for six at the restaurant.*
reservation *noun.*

reservoir reservoirs *noun*

a lake used to hold water that is sent through pipes to people's houses. ▲ Say *rez-er-vwar.*

resist resists resisting resisted *verb*

If you resist something, you fight against it or try to stop it from happening.

resort resorts *noun*

a place where people go to have fun. *an ocean resort.*

resources *noun*

things that are found naturally in a country, such as gas or oil, that can make the country richer.

respect *noun*

the feeling that you have for somebody you like and admire because he or she is good, knows a lot, or is smart.

respond responds responding responded *verb*

If you respond to somebody, you answer that person.
response *noun.*

responsible *adjective*

1 A responsible person is sensible and can be trusted.

2 If you are responsible for somebody or something, you are in charge.

rest *noun*

1 a time when you are quiet and do not work or do anything energetic. *Hal was having a rest reading a book.*

2 everything or everybody that is left over. *Jim and his friends went home but the rest went swimming.*

◆ *What shall we do for the rest of the afternoon?*

restaurant restaurants *noun*

a place where you can pay to eat a meal. ▲ Say *rest-er-ont.*

A B C D E F G H I J K L M N O P Q R S T U V W X Y Z

a b c d e f g h i j k l m n o p q r s t u v w x y z

REPTILES

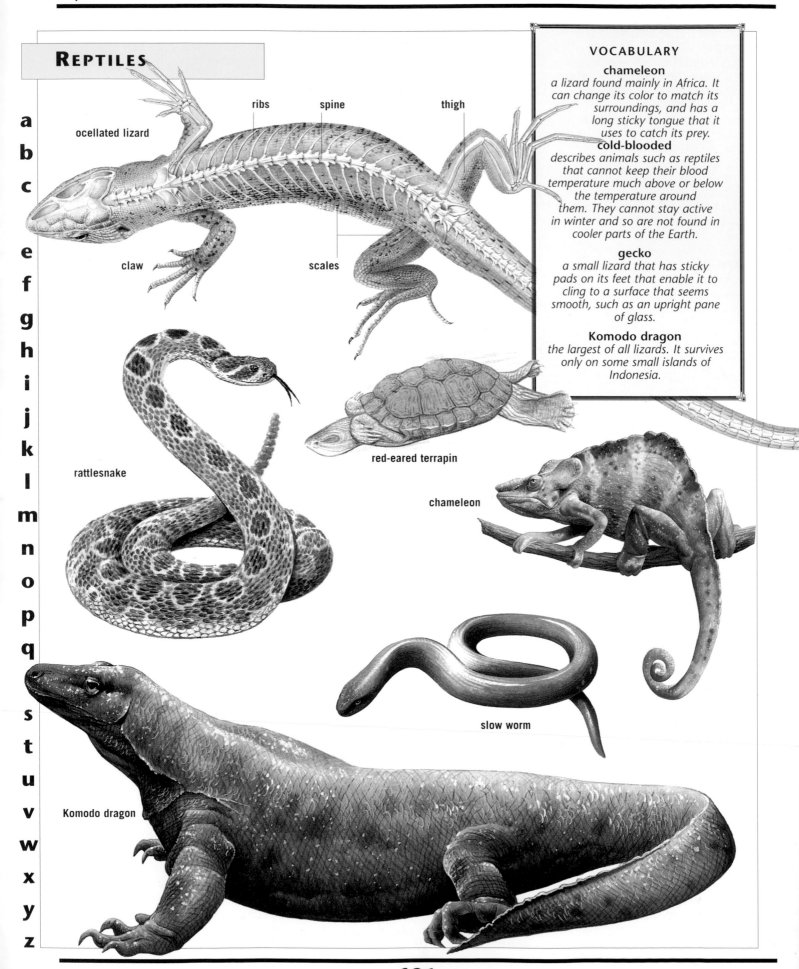

ocellated lizard

ribs

spine

thigh

claw

scales

rattlesnake

red-eared terrapin

chameleon

slow worm

Komodo dragon

restrict restricts restricting restricted *verb*
If you restrict something, you keep it within a limit so it is not too large. *The hall isn't very big so we have to restrict the number of people coming to the concert.*

result results *noun*
1 a thing that happens because of something else. *The fence fell down as a result of the storm.*
2 the score at the end of a contest. *the election results.*

retire retires retiring retired *verb*
When somebody retires, the person gives a job up, usually because of getting old. **retirement** *noun*.

retreat retreats retreating retreated *verb*
If people retreat, they move back from something dangerous.

return returns returning returned *verb*
1 If you return to a place after going away, you come back or go back there.
2 If you return something, you give it back. *James returned his library books after he had read them.*

revenge *noun*
a thing that one person does to hurt somebody else for being horrible to him or her.

reverse reverses *noun*
The opposite of something else. *"Fast" is the reverse of "slow."* **reverse** *verb*.

review reviews *noun*
something that somebody says or writes in a newspaper or on radio or television telling people what a new movie, book, or TV program is like and whether it is good or bad.

revolution revolutions *noun*
a fight to get a new kind of government. **revolutionary** *noun*.

revolver revolvers *noun*
a small gun that can be fired several times before it needs to be loaded again.

reward rewards *noun*
a nice thing that you are given because you have done something very well or been very helpful.
reward *verb*.

rewind rewinds rewinding rewound *verb*
To rewind a tape or video is to make it go backward so that it can be played again.

rhinoceros rhinoceroses *noun*
a large, heavy, wild animal with thick skin. It has one or two horns on its nose. Rhinoceroses live in Africa and Asia. They are called **rhinos** for short. ▲ Say *reye-noss-er-us*.

rhyme rhymes *noun*
a set of words that sound the same as other words except for the first letters. ▲ Say *rime*.

rhythm rhythms *noun*
a pattern of repeated sounds that are regular. Music and poetry have rhythm. ▲ Say *rith-um*.

rib ribs *noun*
Your ribs are the bones that curve around your chest to protect your heart and lungs.

ribbon ribbons *noun*
a strip of colored material that you can use to tie hair or for decorating things.

rice *noun*
white or brown grains that you cook and eat. Rice plants grow in wet ground in hot regions. *China and India produce the biggest rice crops in the world.*

rich richer richest *adjective*
A person who is rich has a lot of money. ■ The opposite is **poor**.

rid rids ridding rid *verb*
to free somebody or something from something harmful or annoying.
get rid of to throw something away. *Get rid of those old comics.*

riddle riddles *noun*
a question that is a puzzle and has a clever or funny answer. *"What goes up when the rain comes down?"* Answer: *"An umbrella."*

A B C D E F G H I J K L M N O Q R S T U V W X Y Z

ride rides *noun*
a trip in a car or on a horse, bicycle, bus, or train.

ride rides riding rode ridden *verb*
1 When you ride a horse or a bicycle or motorcycle, you sit on it and travel along.
2 When you ride in something such as a car or bus, you travel in it.

rifle rifles *noun*
a long gun.

right *adjective*
1 When you write the word "right," the "i" is to the right of the "r." *I write with my right hand.* ■ The opposite is **left**.
2 If something is right, it is correct. *Congratulations, that's the right answer!* ■ The opposite is **wrong**.
● A word that sounds like **right** is **write**.

right *adverb*
correctly. *Did I guess right?* ■ The opposite is **wrong**. ● A word that sounds like **right** is **write**.

right angle right angles *noun*
an angle of 90 degrees like the corners of a square.

rigid *adjective*
If something is rigid, you cannot bend or stretch it. *You can't bend a rigid metal bar.*

rim rims *noun*
the edge around the top of such things as a glass, a jar, or cup. *The rim had a chip.*

ring rings *noun*
1 a round piece of metal that you wear on your finger.
2 a circle with an empty center.
3 the noise of a bell.

ring rings ringing rang rung *verb*
When something rings, it makes the sound of a bell. *The phone rang.* ◆ Has the phone rung this morning?

rinse rinses rinsing rinsed *verb*
to wash in clean water, not using soap.

rip rips ripping ripped *verb*
If you rip something, you tear it. *He ripped his shirt on a nail.*

ripe riper ripest *adjective*
When a fruit is ripe, it is ready to eat. *The banana isn't ripe yet—it's green.*

ripple ripples *noun*
a very small wave or movement on the surface of water.

rise rises rising rose risen *verb*
To rise is to move upward. *The smoke was rising. The bread dough has risen.* ■ The opposite is **dip**.

risk risks *noun*
a danger that something bad or harmful will happen. *She took a risk when she rushed into the burning house.* **risk** *verb*, **risky** *adjective*.

rival rivals *noun*
someone who is trying to win the same thing as you are.

river rivers *noun*
a large amount of water flowing across the land towards the sea or a lake.

road roads *noun*
a long piece of hard ground that cars, bicycles, and trucks can travel on. ● A word that sounds like **road** is **rode**.

roam roams roaming roamed *verb*
To roam is to wander about without trying to go anywhere. *Cattle roamed the big fields.*

roar roars roaring roared *verb*
To roar is to make a very loud noise. *The lion roared.* ◆ The car engine roared.

roast roasts roasting roasted *verb*
When you roast food, you cook it in an oven. *Dad roasted the chicken for dinner.*

rob robs robbing robbed *verb*
To rob people is to steal from them. **robber** *noun*, **robbery** *noun*.

robe robes *noun*
a long, loose piece of clothing.

robin robins *noun*
a small brown bird with red feathers on the front of its body.

European Robin

American Robin

robot robots *noun*
a machine controlled by a computer that can do jobs that people would otherwise do. *In factories, robots now do a lot of work.* ▲ Say **roh**-bot.

rock rocks *noun*
1 stone; the material that mountains and hard ground are made of.
2 a large piece of stone.
3 pop music with a very strong rhythm.

rock rocks rocking rocked *verb*
When you rock, you move or move something gently from side to side or backward and forward. *He was rocking the baby in his arms.*

rocket rockets *noun*
1 an engine in a tall metal tube that is used to send spacecraft into space or to carry bombs.

a b c d e f g h i j k l m n o p q r s t u v w x y z

2 a firework that is sent high up into the air and then explodes in different colors.

rod rods *noun*
a long, thin, round piece of wood or metal. *a fishing rod.*

rode past of **ride**.
● A word that sounds like **rode** is **road**.

rodent rodents *noun*
a small animal with sharp front teeth that gnaws things. Mice, rats, and squirrels are all rodents.

rodeo rodeos *noun*
a show in which cowboys and cowgirls ride horses and rope cattle.

roll rolls *noun*
1 a very small round loaf of bread.
2 a long thin tube made by rolling a piece of paper or material around.

roll rolls rolling rolled *verb*
1 When something rolls, it goes along the ground turning over and over.
2 To roll something is to wrap it around itself several times in the shape of a long thin tube.

roller coaster roller coasters *noun*
a high railroad in an amusement park that has steep bends and turns.

roof roofs *noun*
the top of a building or of a car.

room rooms *noun*
1 a part inside a building that is separated from the other parts inside the building by walls.
2 space. *There's not enough room in our car for ten people!*

rooster roosters *noun*
a grown male chicken.

root roots *noun*
1 a part of plant that grows underground and takes in water and food from the soil.
2 the part of a tooth or hair growing under the gum or skin that you cannot see.

rope ropes *noun*
very thick, strong string that is used for tying things.

rose roses *noun*
a garden flower that has lots of petals and sharp-pointed parts on its stem called thorns.

cultivated rose   wild prairie rose

rose past of **rise**.

rot rots rotting rotted *verb*
When something rots, it spoils or starts to get soft and weak. *The tomatoes were rotting on the ground.* ◆ *Wood rots in water.*

rotate rotates rotating rotated *verb*
If something rotates, it turns around and around like a wheel. *The Earth rotates as it goes around the Sun.*

rotten *adjective*
If something is rotten, it has rotted and is so spoiled that it cannot be used. *That fruit is rotten.*

rough rougher roughest *adjective*
1 bumpy or uneven, not smooth. *A cat's tongue is very rough.*
2 not exact. *a rough guess.*
3 using a lot of force. *Soccer is a rough game.* ■ The opposite is **gentle**.
▲ Say *ruff*.
roughly *adverb*, **roughness** *noun*.

This sandpaper is rough.

round *adjective*
shaped like a circle or a ball. *Most coins are round.*

round trip round trips *noun*
a trip you take from one place to another and back.

roundup roundups *noun*
When cowboys and cowgirls gather cattle to ship them to market, it's a roundup.

rout routs *verb*
To cause complete disorganization or defeat. *Our football team routed the opposing side.*
▲ Rhymes with **out**.

route routes *noun*
the way you go from one place to another place on a trip. *Please work out the best route on the map before we leave.* ▲ Rhymes with **boot**.

row rows *noun*
things or people in a line. *a row of jars.*

row rows rowing rowed *verb*
When you row a boat, you make it move by pushing against the water with oars.
▲ Rhymes with **low**.

royal *adjective*
belonging to a king or queen. *a royal family.* ◆ *a royal palace.*

rub rubs rubbing rubbed *verb*
1 If you rub something, you move your hand up and down it. *She yawned and rubbed her eyes.*
2 To rub is to press one thing backward and forward against another. *People say that you can make a fire by rubbing two sticks together but I've never been able to do it.*

rubber *noun*
a strong, waterproof material that stretches and bounces. *Tires are made of black rubber.*

rubber band rubber bands *noun*
a strand of rubber in a circle that stretches.

ruby rubies *noun*
a valuable red jewel. *a necklace of rubies.* ▲ Say *roo-by*.

A B C D E F G H I J K L M N O P Q R S T U V W X Y Z

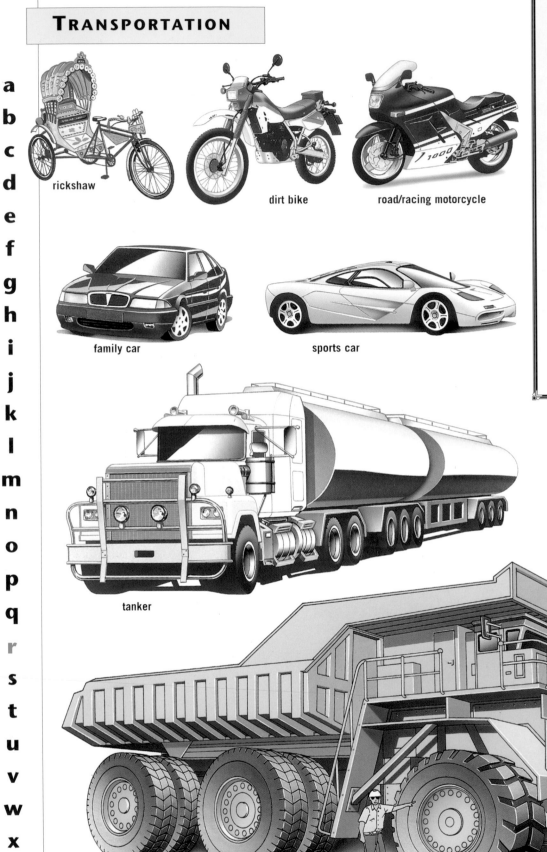

TRANSPORTATION

rickshaw

dirt bike

road/racing motorcycle

family car

sports car

tanker

Terex "Titan"

a b c d e f g h i j k l m n o p q r s t u v w x y z

VOCABULARY

by-pass
a road built around a busy town so that traffic does not pass though it.

crosswalk
parallel white lines painted on a road to show where people may cross and where traffic must stop.

freeway
a wide road with several lanes on which traffic can travel faster than on other roads.

intersection
a place where two or more roads cross one another.

lane
the part of a road used by vehicles going in the same direction.

on-ramp/off-ramp
ramp by which one joins or leaves a freeway.

overpass
a highway or bridge crossing over another highway.

stop lights
lights of changing color for controlling traffic at intersections and crosswalks.

rucksack rucksacks *noun*
a bag for carrying things in that you wear on your back. *We need rucksacks to take on our hike.*

rude ruder rudest *adjective*
If somebody is rude, the person behaves in a bad way and is not polite. ■ The opposite is **polite**.

rug rugs *noun*
a small piece of thick, heavy material that you put on the floor.

rugby *noun*
a game played mostly in England between two teams using an oval ball. Players score points by trying to carry the ball over a line or kicking it over a bar.

ruin ruins ruining ruined *verb*
To ruin something is to spoil it completely. *The rain ruined our picnic.* ▲ Say *roo-in.*

ruins *noun*
the parts of a building left after the rest has fallen down or been destroyed. *the ruins of a castle.* ▲ Say *roo-ins.*

rule rules ruling ruled *verb*
To rule a country is to be in charge of it.

rule rules *noun*
something that says what you are allowed to do and what you are not allowed to do. *the rules of soccer.*

ruler rulers *noun*
1 a long, narrow piece of wood, metal, or plastic that you use for drawing straight lines and for measuring.
2 a person who rules a country.

rumble rumbles rumbling rumbled *verb*
When something rumbles, it makes a long, low sound like thunder. *The trucks rumbled past.*

run runs running ran run *verb*
1 When a person or animal runs, it goes on its feet much faster than when it walks.
2 If you run something, you are in charge of it, and you make sure that it works properly.
3 When liquid runs, it flows. *Tears were running down her face.*

rung past of **ring**.

runway runways *noun*
the long, level strip of land at an airport on which airplanes take off and land.

rush rushes rushing rushed *verb*
If you rush, you are going somewhere or doing something very quickly. *He was rushing to get to the bus stop before the bus arrived.*

rust *noun*
a reddish-brown substance that covers iron or steel after it has gotten wet. *He left the tool outside in the rain and it got covered in rust.*
rusty *adjective*.

rustle rustles rustling rustled *verb*
To rustle is to make the soft sound that leaves make as they move together in the wind. ▲ Say *russ-el.*

S s

sabotage *noun*
When someone destroys enemy property during a war, it is sabotage.

sack sacks *noun*
a large, strong bag that you put things such as coal, potatoes, or trash in.

sad sadder saddest *adjective*
unhappy. ■ The opposite is **happy**.

saddle saddles *noun*
1 a seat for a rider on a horse.
2 a seat on a bicycle.

safe *adjective*
1 If you are safe, you are unharmed. *The lost kitten was found safe and well hiding in the garage.*
2 not harmful or dangerous. ■ The opposite is **dangerous**.
safety *noun*.

safe safes *noun*
a strong box with a lock that you keep money or jewels in.

said past of **say**.

sail sails *noun*
A sail is a big piece of cloth on a boat. When the wind blows against the sail, the boat moves along.

sail sails sailing sailed *verb*
To sail means to move along in a boat using its sails. *Sam went sailing on the river.*

sailor sailors *noun*
a person who works on a ship or boat.

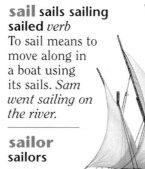

salad salads *noun*
a cold food made of raw vegetables such as lettuce, tomato, and cucumber.

salary salaries *noun*
the money that people are paid for the work that they do. *Teachers' salaries are paid regularly every month.*

sale sales *noun*
a time when a store sells things at a cheaper price than usual. *Mom bought some shoes in the sale.*

saliva *noun*
the liquid in your mouth.

salmon salmon *noun*
a fish with silver skin and pink flesh that you can eat. ▲ Say *sa-mun.*

salt *noun*
a white powder that you put on food to give it a stronger taste. Seawater has salt in it.
salty *adjective*
The soup that I made was too salty.

a
b
c
d
e
f
g
h
i
j
k
l
m
n
o
p
q
r
s
t
u
v
w
x
y
z

salute salutes saluting saluted *verb*
When soldiers salute, they make a sign by lifting their right hand to their forehead as a greeting or to show respect to somebody. *She saluted the general.*

same *adjective*
exactly alike. ■ The opposite is **different**.

sample samples *noun*
a small amount of something that shows what the rest of it is like.

sand *noun*
a white or yellow substance that is made from lots of tiny pieces of rock.

sandal sandals *noun*
a light shoe made of a sole with straps that go over your foot.

sandwich sandwiches *noun*
two slices of bread with food in between.

sang past of **sing**.

sank past of **sink**.

sap *noun*
the sticky liquid inside the stems of plants and the trunks of trees. Sap carries food to all parts of the plant.

sapphire sapphires *noun*
a bright blue jewel.

sari saris *noun*
a long piece of material that many Indian women and girls wrap around the body like a dress.

sat past of **sit**.

satellite satellites *noun*
1 a natural object in space, like a moon, that moves around a larger object, like a planet.
2 A satellite is also a machine that is sent into space to pick up and send back signals and information. Satellite television comes to us by satellite.
▲ Say *sat-il-ite*.

satisfy satisfies satisfying satisfied *verb*
If you satisfy people, you please them and give them what they want or need. *Nothing I ever do satisfies you.*

sauce *noun*
a thick liquid that you pour over food to add to its flavor. *Do you like sauce on your steak?*

saucepan saucepans *noun*
a metal pot with a handle and a lid for cooking food.

saucer saucers *noun*
A saucer is a kind of small plate for putting a cup on.

sausage sausages *noun*
meat that is cut up into very small pieces and made into a long, thin shape like a tube.

savannah *noun*
a flat, grassy plain that has only a few trees.

save saves saving saved *verb*
1 If you save somebody, you take them away from danger. *The man saved the child from drowning.*
2 If you save money or something else, you keep it somewhere to use later. *I'm saving my allowance for a new computer game.*

saw past of **see**.

saw saws *noun*
a tool for cutting wood. It has a metal blade with sharp points called teeth along one edge.
saw *verb*.

saxophone saxophones *noun*
a musical instrument made of brass that you play by blowing into it.
saxophonist *noun*.

say says saying said *verb*
If you say something you speak words. *My uncle said that he didn't like eating meat very often.*

s a y

Some words you can use instead of say:

I heard her say that she has read the book.
☞ **remark, comment, mention** ☜

How do you say "last"?
☞ **pronounce** ☜

She said that I would have to work much harder.
☞ **explained, announced** ☜

Other ways of saying things:
chat, exclaim, have a conversation, murmur, mutter, scream, shout, shriek, talk, tell, whisper

scab scabs *noun*
a piece of dried blood that forms over a cut in your skin when it is healing.

scald scalds scalding scalded *verb*
If you scald yourself, you burn yourself with very hot liquid or steam.

scale scales *noun*
1 a row of marks on something such as a ruler that is used to measure things.
2 a way of showing distances between places on a map. *This map has a scale of one inch to one mile.*
3 one of the small, hard pieces of skin that cover the body of a fish or reptile.
4 A scale is also a series of musical notes. *You play or sing the notes of a scale one after the other.*

0   10   30
map scale

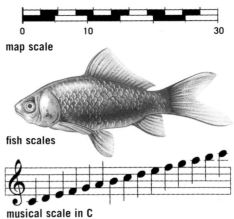

fish scales

musical scale in C

scales *noun*
You use scales to find out how heavy you are, or to weigh things such as fruit and vegetables.

scar scars *noun*
a mark on your skin left by a cut that has healed.

scarce scarcer scarcest *adjective*
If things are scarce, they are difficult to find because there are only a few of them. *Flowers are scarce in winter.*
scarcely *adverb*
I was so happy I could scarcely speak.

scare scares scaring scared *verb*
If something scares you, it frightens you. *That ghost story really scared me.*

scarecrow scarecrows *noun*
a thing that looks like a person dressed in old clothes. Farmers put scarecrows in their fields when crops are growing to frighten off birds.

scarf scarves *noun*
a long piece of material or knitted wool that you wear around your neck.

scatter scatters scattering scattered *verb*
1 If animals or things scatter, they move quickly in different directions. *The loud noise frightened the squirrels and they scattered in many different directions.*
2 If you scatter things, you throw them around in different directions. *Ben scattered some bread for the ducks.*

scene scenes *noun*
1 what you see in the countryside around you. *a mountain scene.*
2 a place where something happens. *the scene of the murder.*
3 a part of a play. *Does the hero get killed in the last scene?*

scenery *noun*
1 what you see around you in the countryside, such as mountains, forests, rivers, and lakes.
2 the things on the stage of a theater that make a play more real to the audience.

scent scents *noun*
1 a nice smell. *a beautiful scent.*
2 a liquid that you can put on your skin to make you smell nice.
● Words that sound like **scent** are **sent** and **cent**.

school schools *noun*
a place where children go to learn.
▲ Say *skule*.

school schools *noun*
a group of fish that swim together. *a school of minnows.*

science sciences *noun*
finding out about things such as animals, plants, and natural materials.
scientific *adjective*

scientist scientists *noun*
a person who finds out about animals, plants, and other things in the world by looking at them closely, writing down information about them, and doing experiments.

scissors *noun*
a small tool for cutting paper and other things. A pair of scissors has two sharp blades that are joined together.

scoop scoops scooping scooped *verb*
To scoop is to lift something up using your hands or with a kind of spoon called a scoop. *Nick scooped some ice cream out of the tub.*

scooter scooters *noun*
1 a motorbike with a small engine.
2 a kind of child's bicycle with a board you stand on with one foot and push the ground with the other foot.

scorch scorches scorching scorched *verb*
If you scorch something like a piece of material, you burn it a little, leaving a brown mark.

score scores *noun*
In a game, the score is how many points each side has.

score scores scoring scored *verb*
To score means to get a point in a game.

scorpion scorpions *noun*
an animal related to spiders. It has a poisonous stinger on its tail.

scout scouts *noun*
a Boy or Girl Scout.

scowl scowls scowling scowled *verb*
If you scowl, you have an angry, bad-tempered look on your face.

scramble scrambles scrambling scrambled *verb*
If you scramble over rocks or rough ground, you use your hands and feet to help you move quickly.

scrap scraps *noun*
a small piece of something such as paper or material.

scrapbook scrapbooks *noun*
a book with blank pages that you can paste pictures, postcards, or clippings in.

scrape scrapes scraping scraped *verb*
1 If you scrape your knee, you hurt it by rubbing it against something hard or rough.
2 If you scrape mud off your shoes, you get it off with a thing such as a knife.

A B C D E F G H I J K L M N O P Q R S T U V W X Y Z

scratch scratches scratching scratched *verb*
1 If you scratch your skin, you make thin cuts on it by rubbing something sharp against it. *Sarah scratched her hand on the thorns.*
2 If you scratch yourself, you rub your nails across your skin because it itches.
scratch *noun*.

scream screams screaming screamed *verb*
If you scream, you shout in a very loud, high voice because you are excited or frightened. *Sophie screamed when she went on the big ride at the fairground.*

screen screens *noun*
1 the flat part of a TV or computer where you see the pictures or words.
2 the place on the wall where the movie is shown in a theater.

screw screws *noun*
a thin piece of metal like a nail with a sharp point at one end and a slot in the top. Screws are used to join things such as pieces of wood together. You use a screwdriver to turn the screw into the piece of wood.

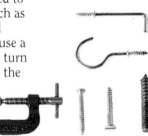

screw screws screwing screwed *verb*
1 to join things together using screws. *He screwed the shelf to the wall.*
2 If you screw things up, you squeeze them into a ball. *She screwed up the paper and threw it away.*

scribble scribbles scribbling scribbled *verb*
to write quickly and without care.

script scripts *noun*
all the words that have been written for the actors to say in a play or movie.

scrub scrubs scrubbing scrubbed *verb*
If you scrub something, you rub it hard to clean it. *Paul scrubbed the floor with a stiff brush.*

scruffy *adjective*
messy and dirty. *scruffy clothes.*

sculpture sculptures *noun*
1 a person, an animal, or a shape that has been made of stone, wood, or metal by an artist called a sculptor.
2 Sculpture is the art of carving or modeling things.

scurry scurries scurried *verb*
to move in a hurried, confused way. *We tried to catch my hamster, but each time we got near it, it scurried away.*

sea seas *noun*
a large area of salt water; an ocean. *We went swimming in the sea.*

sea horse sea horses *noun*
a tiny fish with a head shaped like a horse's head and a long curling tail.

seal seals *noun*
an animal with short, gray fur that lives near the sea. Seals spend a lot of time in the sea and catch fish to eat.

seam seams *noun*
a line made where two pieces of material are sewn together. *These two pieces of fabric are joined with a seam.*

search searches searching searched *verb*
If you search for people or things, you look very carefully for them. *We searched everywhere for the lost kitten.*

season seasons *noun*
one of the four parts of the year. They are spring, summer, fall, and winter.
seasonal *adjective*
seasonal vegetables.

seat seats *noun*
a thing you sit on. Buses and cars have seats. *We sat in the front seats at the theater.*

seaweed *noun*
a red, green, or brown plant that grows in the sea. *After the storm, the beach was covered with seaweed from the ocean.*

second seconds *noun*
a very short measure of time. There are 60 seconds in a minute.

second *adjective*
Second means next after the first. *Tom won the race and Wil came second.*

secret secrets *noun*
something that only a few people know about. *I'm not telling you what you're getting for your birthday—it's a secret!*

secretary secretaries *noun*
a person who works in an office. Secretaries answer the phone, make appointments, and type letters.

section sections *noun*
one of the separate parts of something. *Rob was trying to fit the sections of the model airplane together.*

security *noun*
feeling safe or trying to keep things safe. *She locked the door for extra security.*

see sees seeing saw seen *verb*
1 When you see people or things, you look at them with your eyes.
2 To see also means to understand something. *You see what I mean?*

seed seeds *noun*
a tiny, hard part inside the flower or fruit of a plant. If you put seeds into the ground they will grow into new plants.

seek seeks seeking sought *verb*
To seek means to look for somebody or something. *The police are seeking a woman who was seen near the bank at midnight.*

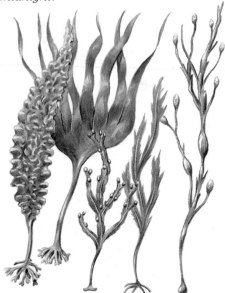

seem seems seeming seemed *verb*
To seem means to look or feel like something.

seen past of **see**.

seesaw seesaws *noun*
a thing that you ride on in a playground. One person sits at each end of a long piece of wood and you take turns going up and down.

segregate segregates segregating segregated *verb*
to not open something like a school to all people of all races.
segregation *noun*.

seize seizes seizing seized *verb*
If you seize something, you grab it. ▲ Rhymes with *freeze*. ● A word that sounds like **seize** is **sees**.

seldom *adjective*
not very often.

select selects selecting selected *verb*
When you select people or things, you choose them.
selection *noun*.

self-esteem *noun*
a good feeling about who you are and what goals you can reach. *Your compliment boosted my self-esteem.*

selfish *adjective*
A selfish person does not like to help or share things with other people.

sell sells selling sold *verb*
If people sell something to you, they give it to you and you pay them money.

semicircle semicircles *noun*
half a circle.

Senate *noun*
one of the two branches of Congress. Its members serve for six years.

send sends sending sent *verb*
To send is to make somebody or something go to another place.

senior *adjective*
older in years or more important. ■ The opposite is **junior**.

senior seniors *noun*
a student in the fourth, or last, year of high school or college.

sense senses *noun*
1 the powers that most people have to see, hear, touch, taste, and smell.
2 knowing and being careful to do the right thing.

sensible *adjective*
A sensible person thinks carefully about what he or she is doing and does not do anything silly or foolish. ■ The opposite is **foolish**.

sensitive *adjective*
1 A sensitive person cares about other people's feelings.
2 If your skin is sensitive, it is sore or it gets sore very easily.

sent past of **send**
● A word that sounds like **sent** is **scent**.

sentence sentences *noun*
a group of words that make sense together. A written sentence begins with a capital letter and ends with a period or a question mark. *Joan is late today.* and *Where is the cat?* are sentences.

separate *adjective*
If two things are separate they are not joined together. ▲ Say *sep-ur-ut*.

separate separates separating separated *verb*
to set or keep apart. *Hal separates the white from the yolk.* ▲ Say *sep-ur-rate*.

serial serials *noun*
a story that is told in parts on television or in a magazine. ● A word that sounds like **serial** is **cereal**.

series *noun*
1 a set of things of the same kind that follow each other.

2 a number of programs on radio or television on the same subject, that follow each other. *I am watching a series on dinosaurs.*

serious *adjective*
1 important or very bad. *a serious accident.*
2 A serious person is quiet and does not laugh or joke very often.

servant servants *noun*
A servant is a person who works in somebody else's house, doing such things as cooking and cleaning.

serve serves serving served *verb*
1 If people serve you in a restaurant, they bring you food and drink.
2 If people serve you in a store, they help you to look at things you want to buy.

service services *noun*
1 something useful that a person or a company does for other people. *train service.* ◆ *the postal service.*
2 A service is also a meeting in a church where people pray and sing.

session sessions *noun*
a time when people meet to do something. *a session of Congress.*

set sets *noun*
a group of things that belong together. *a china tea set.* ◆ *a chess set.*

set sets setting set *verb*
1 When something liquid like cement sets, it gets hard.
2 When the Sun sets, it goes down below the horizon and then the sky gets dark.
3 When you set a table, you put all the things on it you need for a meal such as glasses, plates, knives, and forks.
4 When you set a clock or a watch, you move the hands to a certain time. *I set my alarm clock for 7:30.*
5 To set also means to choose a date. *They set May 30th as the wedding date.*

settee settees *noun*
a long, comfortable seat for two or more people, also called a sofa.

settle settles settling settled *verb*
If you settle, you go to a place and stay there. *A ladybug settled on my hand.*
◆ *Nita and Bill have settled in Georgia.*

several *adjective*
more than two but not very many. *Several people walked by.*

severe *adjective*
very bad. *a severe headache.* ◆ *severe winter storms.*

sew sews sewing sewed sewn *verb*
When you sew, you join pieces of material together or join something to material using a needle and thread. *Can you sew this button back on my shirt, please?* ▲ Say *so.*

sewer sewers *noun*
a large pipe under the ground that takes waste away from houses and other buildings. ▲ Say *su-er.*

sex sexes *noun*
the two groups that people and animals belong to. These two groups are the *male sex* and the *female sex.*

shade *noun*
1 a place where the Sun cannot reach. *We sat in the shade of an oak tree.*
2 a cover for a lamp.
3 a variety of a color. *a dark shade of blue.*
shady *adjective.*

shadow shadows *noun*
a dark shape that you see near somebody or something that is under or in front of the light. *When you place your hands in front of a light you can have fun by making hand shadows like these.*

shake shakes shaking shook shaken *verb*
1 When you shake something, you move it up and down or backward and forward. *I shook the bottle of salad dressing.*
2 If your body shakes because you are cold or frightened, it wobbles around.
shaky *adjective,* **shakily** *adverb.*

shallow *adjective*
not very deep. *This water is shallow; it only just covers my feet.* ■ The opposite is **deep.**

shame *noun*
the guilty feeling that you have if you have done something wrong.
shameful *adjective.*

shampoo shampoos *noun*
a liquid that you use to wash your hair.

shape shapes *noun*
what you see if you draw a line around the outside of something. Circles, squares, triangles, and rectangles are different shapes. ❖ *Look at page 145*

share shares sharing shared *verb*
1 If you share something, you give some of it to somebody else. *I shared my birthday cake with my friends.*
2 To share also means to use something together with another person. *I share a bedroom with my sister.*
share *noun.*

shark sharks *noun*
a big sea fish that has lots of very sharp teeth and a big mouth.

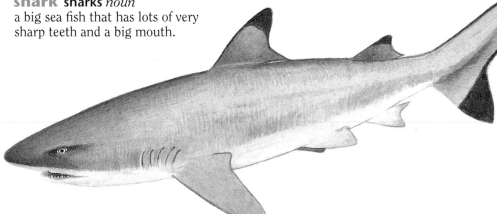

Great white shark

sharp sharper sharpest *adjective*
1 Something that is sharp has an edge or a point that is good for cutting. *Knives and scissors are usually sharp.*
2 sudden and severe. *a sharp pain.*
sharply *adverb.*

shatter shatters shattering shattered *verb*
If something such as glass shatters, it breaks into lots of little pieces.

shave shaves shaving shaved *verb*
To shave is to cut hair off the skin with a razor.

shawl shawls *noun*
a wide scarf that you wear around your shoulders.

shed sheds *noun*
a small building made of wood. *a tool shed.* ◆ *a cow-shed.*

shed sheds shedding shed *verb*
1 If an animal sheds hair, some of its hair falls out.
2 When trees shed their leaves, the leaves drop off because it is fall.

sheep sheep *noun*
an animal that farmers keep for their wool and for their meat. A male sheep is called a ram and a female sheep is called a ewe.

sheet sheets *noun*
1 a large piece of material for putting on a bed.
2 a thin, flat piece of paper, glass, or metal. *a sheet of writing paper.* ◆ *The road was like a sheet of ice.*

SHAPES

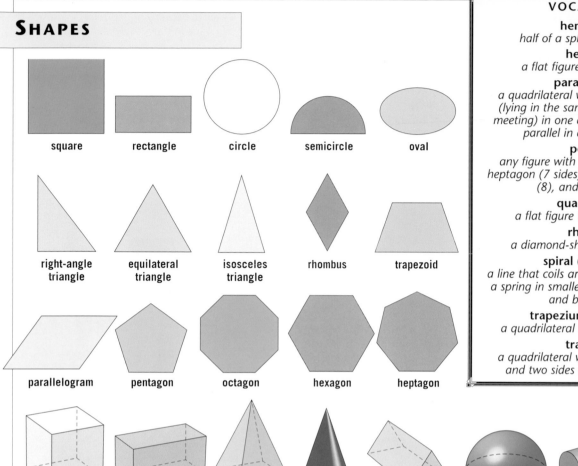

square   rectangle   circle   semicircle   oval

right-angle triangle   equilateral triangle   isosceles triangle   rhombus   trapezoid

parallelogram   pentagon   octagon   hexagon   heptagon

cube   cuboid   pyramid   cone   prism   hemisphere   cylinder   tetrahedron

COLORS

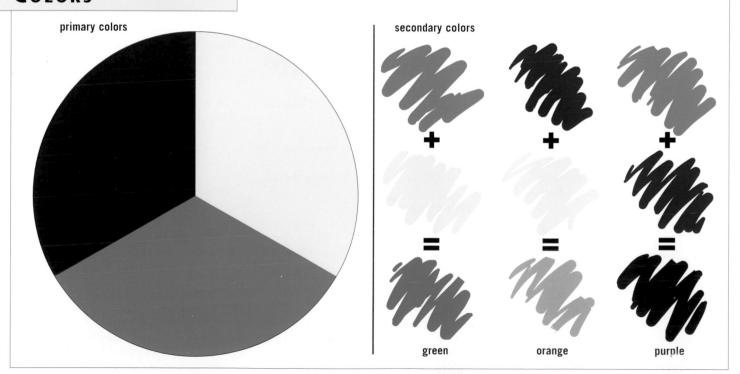

primary colors

secondary colors

+   +   +

=   =   =

green   orange   purple

A B C D E F G H I J K L M N O P Q R S T U V W X Y Z

shelf shelves *noun*
a long, flat piece of wood or glass attached to a wall or in a closet where you can put things.

shell shells *noun*
1 the hard outside part of some living things. Eggs, nuts, snails, and crabs have shells.
2 a very large kind of bullet.

shelter shelters *noun*
a covered place where you are safe from bad weather or danger.

sheriff sheriffs *noun*
a county police officer.

shield shields *noun*
a large piece of wood or metal that soldiers used to carry to protect their bodies from enemy weapons.

shin shins *noun*
Your shin is the front part of your leg between your knee and your ankle.

shine shines shining shone *verb*
When something shines, it gives out light, or is bright like silver.
shiny *adjective*
a shiny new coin.

shingle shingles *noun*
a piece of material that covers a roof.

ship ships *noun*
a big boat for carrying people and things.

shipwreck shipwrecks *noun*
a bad accident when a ship is broken up by rocks or a rough sea.

shirt shirts *noun*
a piece of clothing that you wear on the top part of your body. Shirts have a collar, sleeves, and buttons down the front.

shiver shivers shivering shivered *verb*
When you shiver, you shake because you are cold or frightened. *The rabbit was shivering with fright.*

shoal *noun*
a large group or number; a crowd. *a shoal of fish.*

shock shocks *noun*
1 a sudden and bad thing that happens to you. *The news of the plane crash was a shock.*
2 An electric shock is a sharp pain that you feel if electricity goes through your body.

shod *adjective*
wearing shoes.

shoe shoes *noun*
things that you wear on your feet. Shoes are usually made of leather or plastic.

shone past of **shine**
I polished my shoes until they shone.

shook past of **shake**.

shoot shoots shooting shot *verb*
1 To shoot means to fire bullets from a gun or to use a bow and arrow.
2 To shoot also means to kick or throw a ball at a goal in sports like basketball or soccer.
3 To shoot can also mean to move somewhere very fast. *The kitten shot under the sofa.*

shop shops *noun*
a place where you go to buy things or to have things fixed.

shop shops shopping shopped *verb*
When you shop, you go to stores to buy things. *We went shopping for food in the supermarket.*
shopper *noun*.

shore shores *noun*
the land along the edge of the sea or a lake. *We walked along the sandy shore.*

short shorter shortest *adjective*
1 not having great height. ■ The opposite is **tall**.
2 not long. *Gerald has short hair.*
3 not lasting long. *The senator made a short speech.* ■ The opposite is **long**.

4 **short for** a short way of writing or saying something. *"Phone" is short for "telephone."*

shorts *noun*
short pants that usually do not cover your knees. *Freddie and Rose are wearing matching shorts.*

shot past of **shoot**.

shoulder shoulders *noun*
Your shoulder joins your arm to the rest of your body.

shout shouts shouting shouted *verb*
If you shout, you say something in a very loud voice. *Jill had to shout so that we could hear her.*

show shows showing showed shown *verb*
1 When you show somebody something, you let them see it or you point it out to them. *Show me your photos.*
◆ *Show me the girl who hit you.*
2 When you show somebody how to do something, you explain to them how to do it. *Can you show me how to use the computer?*

show shows *noun*
1 something you see at the theater or on television. *It's time for my favorite TV show.*
2 things arranged so that people can look at them. *a dog show.*

shower showers *noun*
1 a place where you can wash by standing under water that sprays down on you.
2 A shower is also rain that falls for only a short time.

138

shrank past of **shrink**.

shred shreds *noun*
a small, thin piece that has been cut or torn from something larger.

shrimp shrimp or shrimps *noun*
a small sea animal that is related to the lobster and is good to eat.

shrink shrinks shrinking shrank shrunk or shrunken *verb*
When something shrinks, it gets smaller. *Hal's T-shirt shrank in the wash.*
shrunken *adjective*.

shut shuts shutting shut *verb*
1 If you shut something, you move a door, window, lid, or book so that it is no longer open.
2 To shut something like a store means that people cannot go into it until it opens again. *What time did you shut the restaurant?*
■ The opposite is **open**.

shuttle shuttles *noun*
1 an airplane or bus that goes backward and forward between two places. *the New York—Washington shuttle.*
2 A shuttle is also a kind of spaceship. *the Space Shuttle.*

shy shier or shyer shiest or shyest *adjective*
If somebody is shy, he or she does not feel happy or comfortable with unfamiliar people. *Sharon was shy and found it hard to talk to strangers.*

sick sicker sickest *adjective*
1 If you are sick, you are not well.
2 If you are sick, you bring food up from your stomach through your mouth.

sickness sicknesses *noun*
something such as a cold that makes you feel unwell.

side sides *noun*
1 the left or right of something. *Mom sat on my right side, Dad on my left.*
2 the flat surfaces of something.
3 the edges of something. *A square has four sides.*
4 one of the two teams that are playing against each other in a game.

sidewalk sidewalks *noun*
pavement by a street to walk on.

sieve sieves *noun*
a frame or container with a mesh bottom or with lots of tiny holes in it. You use a sieve to separate small pieces from larger pieces or a liquid from something solid. ▲ Say *siv*.

sigh sighs sighing sighed *verb*
When you sigh, you breathe out loudly because you are tired, sad, or bored.

sight sights *noun*
1 the ability to see things with your eyes. *Owls have good sight in the dark.*
2 things such as interesting old buildings that people go to see are also sights.

sign signs *noun*
1 a notice that tells you something or where to find something. *Can you see a sign to the airport?*
2 a movement you make to tell somebody something. *His sister made a sign to him to keep quiet.*
3 a mark that means something special. In math, a sign like this + means add.

sign signs signing signed *verb*
1 When you sign your name, you write it. *He signed the check.*
2 **sign up** to agree to do something. *Jack signed up for the club.*

signal signals *noun*
a sound, a light, or a movement that tells you something. *The referee blew a whistle as a signal to start the game.*

signature signatures *noun*
your name written in your own writing.

silence silences *noun*
1 no sound.
2 a very quiet state.
■ The opposite is **noise**.

silent *adjective*
not making any noise. *The house was silent and empty.*
silently *adverb*.

silk silks *noun*
a smooth, shiny material made from threads produced by an insect called a silkworm. *a silk scarf.*
silky *adjective*.

silly sillier silliest *adjective*
stupid and not sensible or smart. *You were very silly to run across the road.*

silver *noun*
a gray, shiny metal. Rings, bracelets, and necklaces are often made of silver.
silver *adjective*
the silver Moon.

similar *adjective*
If two things are similar they are almost the same.

A horse, a zebra, and a donkey are similar.

simple simpler simplest *adjective*
easy to do or understand. *These questions are simple!* ■ The opposite is **difficult**.
simply *adverb*.

sing sings singing sang sung *verb*
When you sing, you make music with your voice. *Sing that song again.* ◆ *The birds start singing very early in the morning.*
singer *noun*
Who's your favorite singer?

A B C D E F G H I J K L M N O P Q R S T U V W X Y Z

a b c d e f g h i j k l m n o p q r s t u v w x y z

single *adjective*
1 one. *I can't find a single sock anywhere!*
2 A person who is single is not married.

singular *noun*
one person or thing. *the singular of geese is goose.* ■ The opposite is **plural**.

sink sinks sinking sank *or* sunk *verb*
If something like a ship sinks, it goes under water. *The ship sank in the storm.* ◆ *The rock has sunk.*

sink sinks *noun*
a basin; a large bowl attached to water and drains.

sip sips sipping sipped *verb*
If you sip a drink, you drink it slowly, taking a little bit at a time. *She sipped her cocoa slowly because it was hot.*

sister sisters *noun*
A person's sister is a girl or woman who has the same mother and father.

sit sits sitting sat *verb*
1 When you sit somewhere you rest your bottom there. *We sat on the sofa.*
2 When a bird sits on its nest, it stays there to cover its eggs.

sitcom sitcoms *noun*
a funny television program that you see each week.

situation situations *noun*
something that is happening in a place at a particular time. *the political situation in China.*

size sizes *noun*
The size of something is how big it is. *What size shoe do you wear?*

skate skates *noun*
1 Roller skates are special boots with wheels on the bottom that you wear for moving around on smooth ground.
2 Ice skates are boots with sharp blades on the bottom that you wear for moving around on ice.
skate *verb*.

skateboard skateboards *noun*
a long piece of wood or plastic with wheels that you stand on to move along fast and to do jumps and turns.

skein skeins *noun*
a length of yarn or thread loosely coiled around a spool. ▲ Rhymes with **rain**.

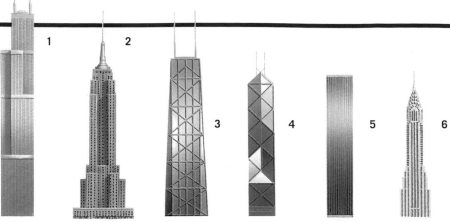

Skyscrapers: 1 Sears Tower, Chicago; 2 Empire State Building, New York City; 3 John Hancock Tower, Boston; 4 Bank of China, Hong Kong; 5 Library Tower, Los Angeles; 6 Chrysler Building, New York City

skeleton skeletons *noun*
all the bones that are joined together inside the body of a person or an animal.

sketch sketches *noun*
a picture that you draw quickly.

ski skis *noun*
long, flat pieces of plastic, wood, or metal that are attached to boots for moving over snow. ▲ Say *skee*.
ski *verb*.

skill skills *noun*
If you have a skill, you have the ability to do something very well.
skillful *adjective*.

skin *noun*
1 the natural outside covering of the bodies of people and many animals.
2 the outside covering of many fruits and vegetables. a *banana skin.*

skin diving *noun*
swimming under the water while you wear flippers, a mask, and oxygen tanks.

skip skips skipping skipped *verb*
When you skip, you move with little jumps from one foot to the other.

skirmish skirmishes *noun*
1 a small fight in a larger battle.
2 a verbal conflict.

skirt skirts *noun*
a piece of clothing that women and girls wear. A skirt hangs down from the waist.

skull skulls *noun*
Your skull is the round, bony part of your head. Your brain is in your skull.

skunk skunks *noun*
an animal with black and white fur and a full tail. It can spray a bad-smelling liquid when it is nervous.

sky skies *noun*
the space above the Earth.

skyscraper skyscrapers *noun*
a very tall building.

slam slams slamming slammed *verb*
When a door slams, it closes with a bang. *She slammed the door.*

slang *noun*
words that you use in conversation, especially with people of your own age, but not when you are writing or being polite. *"Dough" is slang for money.*

slanted *adjective*
Something that is slanted is not straight but leans in one direction.

slap slaps slapping slapped *verb*
If you slap somebody, you hit him or her with the palm of your hand.

slave slaves *noun*
a person who is kept as a prisoner and forced to work very hard for somebody else without being paid.
slavery *noun*.

sled sleds *noun*
a small, flat vehicle with runners that you ride down hills in the snow.

sleep sleeps sleeping slept *verb*
When you sleep, you close your eyes and rest your body as you do in bed at night.

sleepy sleepier sleepiest *adjective*
When you are sleepy, you feel tired.

sleeve sleeves *noun*
the part of a shirt, blouse, coat, or dress that covers your arm.

sleigh sleighs *noun*
a vehicle that you sit on to move over snow. Sleighs are usually pulled by animals such as horses or reindeer.

slept past of **sleep**.

slice slices *noun*
a thin, flat piece that has been cut from something. *a slice of cake.*

slide slides sliding slid *verb*
When something slides, it moves smoothly over a surface. *The children were sliding on the ice.*

slight *adjective*
small or not very important. *I've got a slight earache.*

slim slimmer slimmest *adjective*
If you are slim, you are thin, but not too thin. ■ The opposite is **plump**.

slingshot slingshots *noun*
a Y-shaped stick with a piece of elastic stretched over it. You pull the elastic to shoot small stones.

slink slinks slinking slunk *verb*
to move secretly or by creeping. *Jaguars slink through the rain forests.*

slip slips slipping slipped *verb*
If you slip, you slide by mistake and fall down. *I slipped on the wet floor and sprained a muscle in my back.*

slipper slippers *noun*
a soft, comfortable shoe that you wear in the house.

slippery *adjective*
Something that is slippery is very smooth and difficult to hold, or to stand on without sliding and falling over. *a slippery floor.* ◆ *a wet, slippery fish.*

slit slits *noun*
a long, thin cut in something. *They cut a slit in the material.*

slope slopes *noun*
ground that goes upward or downward. *We walked down the mountain slope.*

slot slots *noun*
a short, thin hole in something. *You put coins in the slot to use the washer.*

slow slower slowest *adjective*
Somebody or something that is slow does not move quickly. *Snails and turtles are very slow animals.* ■ The opposite is **fast**.
slowly *adverb*
We walked home slowly.

slug slugs *noun*
a small, slimy animal like a snail without a shell. Gardeners do not like slugs because they eat plants.

sly slyer slyest *adjective*
If somebody is sly, he or she is smart in a secret and not very nice way. *The sly salesman sold us rotten corn.*

small smaller smallest *adjective*
not very big. *Ants are small insects.* ◆ *My brother is smaller than me.* ■ The opposite is **big** or **large**.

small

Some words you can use instead of small:

All small animals look sweet.
☞ *baby, young* ☜

The writing is so small you need a magnifying glass to read it.
☞ *minute, tiny* ☜

Don't worry. It's only a small mistake.
☞ *unimportant, slight, minor* ☜

Centipedes have lots of small legs.
☞ *short* ☜

smart smarter smartest *adjective*
A person who is smart can learn and understand things quickly.

smash smashes smashing smashed *verb*
If something smashes, it breaks into a lot of pieces. *I dropped the plate and it smashed on the floor.*

smell smells smelling smelled or smelt *verb*
1 When you smell something, you use your nose to find out about it. *I can smell food cooking in the kitchen.*
2 When something smells, you notice it with your nose. *This rug smells.*
smelly *adjective*
smelly old socks.

smile smiles smiling smiled *verb*
When you smile, the corners of your mouth turn up to show that you are happy.

smog *noun*
fog mixed with smoke.

smoke smokes smoking smoked *verb*
When people smoke, they have cigarettes, cigars, or pipes in their mouths, and breathe the smoke in and out.

smoke smokes *noun*
the white, gray, or black stuff that you see going up in the air when something is burning.

smooth smoother smoothest *adjective*
If something is smooth, you cannot feel lumps or any rough parts when you touch it. *These vases have smooth surfaces.*

smudge smudges *noun*
a dirty mark on something.

smuggle smuggles smuggling smuggled *verb*
To smuggle means to take things such as alcohol, drugs, or cigarettes into or out of a country when it is illegal.
smuggler *noun*.

A
B
C
D
E
F
G
H
I
J
K
L
M
N
O
P
Q
R
S
T
U
V
W
X
Y
Z

snack snacks *noun*
a small amount of food that you eat when you are in a hurry. *We had a quick snack of cheese and crackers.*

snail snails *noun*
a small creature with a hard shell on its back. Snails move along very slowly.

snake snakes *noun*
a long, thin kind of animal called a reptile. Snakes have no legs and move by sliding along the ground. *Some snakes can give a poisonous bite.*
❖ *Look at page 134*

snap snaps snapping snapped *verb*
1 When something snaps, it breaks and makes a sudden sharp sound. *The pencil snapped when I stepped on it.*
2 When a dog snaps, it tries to bite somebody or something. *The dog snapped at us when we walked by.*
3 When people snap, they speak in an angry way. *"Be quiet!" she snapped.*

snatch snatches snatching snatched *verb*
If you snatch something, you take it quickly and roughly. *The thief snatched her purse.*

sneak sneaks sneaking sneaked *verb*
If you sneak somewhere, you move in a quiet and secret way. *No one saw him sneak out of the room.*

sneeze sneezes sneezing sneezed *verb*
When you sneeze, you blow air out of your nose and mouth with a sudden, loud noise. *You sometimes sneeze when you have a cold.*

sniff sniffs sniffing sniffed *verb*
When you sniff, you breathe air in through your nose in a quick and noisy way. You often sniff when you are crying or when you have a cold.

snore snores snoring snored *verb*
When people snore, they breathe noisily when they are asleep.

snorkel snorkels *noun*
a tube that you breathe through when you swim close to the surface of the water.

snow *noun*
small, white pieces of frozen water that fall from the sky when it is very cold.

snowboarding *noun*
a sport where you move down snowy hills on a piece of wood or metal that looks like a skateboard without wheels.

snowflake snowflakes *noun*
a small piece of falling snow. Snowflakes are star-shaped ice crystals.

soak soaks soaking soaked *verb*
1 When you soak something, you put it in water and leave it for a long time.
2 If you get soaked, you get very wet. *We got soaked in the rain.*

soap *noun*
a substance that can be solid, liquid, or powder that you use with water for washing. *This bar of soap smells nice.*

sob sobs sobbing sobbed *verb*
When you sob, you cry loudly.

soccer *noun*
a game played by two teams of eleven players. The teams try to score goals by kicking a ball into a net at each end of a field.

society societies *noun*
1 all the people who live in the same country or area and have the same laws and customs.
2 a kind of club for people who are involved in the same things. *our local medical society.*

sock socks *noun*
a thing that you wear on your foot inside your shoe.

soda sodas *noun*
a drink that has bubbly water in it.

sofa sofas *noun*
a long, comfortable seat for two or more people, also called a settee.

soft softer softest *adjective*
1 bending easily. ■ The opposite is **hard**.
2 not firm or stiff. *soft snow.*
3 not loud; quiet and gentle. ■ The opposite is **loud**.
softly *adverb,* **soften** *verb*

soften softens softening softened *verb*
When something softens, it becomes soft. *The butter began to soften in the heat.* ■ The opposite is **harden**.

software *noun*
the part inside a computer or on a computer disk that has the instructions that make a computer work.

soil *noun*
the brown stuff, which is also called dirt, that plants grow in.

solar *adjective*
to do with the Sun. *solar heating.*

sold past of **sell**

soldier soldiers *noun*
a person in an army. ▲ Say *sole-jer.*

sole soles *noun*
the bottom of your foot or your shoe.

solid solids *noun*
an object that is hard and not a liquid or a gas. ■ The opposite is **liquid**.

solid *adjective*
1 hard. *solid rock*.
2 with no space inside. *a solid brick wall*.
■ The opposite is **hollow**.

solve solves solving solved *verb*
1 If you solve a problem, you find the answer to it.
2 If you solve a mystery, you find out why it happened.

sombrero sombreros *noun*
a tall hat with a wide brim.

some *adjective*
being a number that you don't give or know exactly. *I need some peas*.
● A word that sounds like **some** is **sum**.

somersault somersaults *noun*
rolling your body in a circle so that your feet go over your head.

son sons *noun*
Somebody's son is a boy or man who is their child. ● A word that sounds like **son** is **sun**.

song songs *noun*
a short piece of music with words that you sing.

soot *noun*
black powder that comes from smoke after a fire.

sophomore sophomores *noun*
a student who is in the second year at a high school or college.

sore *adjective*
If a part of your body is sore, it hurts. *I've got a sore throat*.

sorrow *noun*
the feeling that you have when you are very sad. *He felt great sorrow when his mother died*. ■ The opposite is **joy**.

sort sorts sorting sorted *verb*
If you sort things, you put them into different groups. *Hal sorts the blocks into plain, colored, and patterned ones*.

sort sorts *noun*
a kind. *What sort of animal is it? It's a lizard*.

sought past of **seek**.

sound sounds *noun*
something that you can hear. *I can hear the sound of somebody playing a guitar*.

soup soups *noun*
a hot liquid food that you make by boiling vegetables or meat in water. *tomato soup*. ◆ *chicken soup*.

sour sourer sourest *adjective*
1 Something that tastes sour is not sweet. *Lemons are sour*.
2 When milk is sour, it is not fresh.

source sources *noun*
1 the place, person, or thing that something comes from. *The library is a good source of information*.
2 the place where a river starts. *The source of the river is in the mountains*.

south *noun*
the direction that is on your right if you face the Sun as it rises in the morning.
■ The opposite is **north, northern**.
south *adjective*, **southern** *adjective*
Peru is in South America. ◆ *Key West is in southern Florida*.
south *adverb*
The Arctic tern flies south from the Arctic to the Antarctic every winter.

souvenir souvenirs *noun*
something that you keep to remember a place or something that happened. *My friend bought me a Dutch doll as a souvenir of Holland*.

sow sows sowing sowed sown *verb*
When you sow seeds, you put them in the soil so that they will grow into plants. ▲ Rhymes with *low*.

space spaces *noun*
1 an empty place with nothing in it. *There is space in this closet for your clothes*. ◆ *Mom couldn't find a space to park the car*.
2 the place above the Earth where the Sun, stars, and planets are.

spacecraft *noun*
a vehicle that travels in space.

spade spades *noun*
a tool with a long handle and a wide flat blade that you use for digging.

spaghetti *noun*
a kind of pasta; long strings of dough made of flour and water that you cook by boiling them.

span spans spanning spanned *verb*
When something like a bridge spans a river, it goes across it.

spare *adjective*
Something that is spare is not being used now, but you can use it when you need to. *When my friend stayed over, he slept in the spare room*.

spark sparks *noun*
a tiny piece of fire. Sparks can be made by electricity. *Sparks from the fire flew up the chimney*.

sparkle sparkles sparkling sparkled *verb*
When something sparkles, it shines with little flashes of light. *sparkling objects*.

A B C D E F G H I J K L M N O P Q R S T U V W X Y Z

spat past of **spit**.

speak speaks speaking spoke spoken *verb*
When you speak, you say words. *Philippa was speaking to her friend on the telephone.* ◆ *Can you speak Spanish?*

spear spears *noun*
a weapon made from a long stick with a sharp point at one end.

special *adjective*
1 If something is special, it is not ordinary but better or more important than other things. *Today is a special day because it's my birthday.*
2 Special also means for a particular person or thing, or to do a particular job. *An ambulance is a special vehicle for taking people to the hospital.*
specially *adverb*
a specially designed classroom.

species *noun*
a group of animals or plants that are the same in some way. *different species of rodents.*

European hedgehog

desert hedgehog

Mindanao moonrat

moonrat

spectator spectators *noun*
a person who watches something. *There were thousands of spectators at the football game.*

speech speeches *noun*
1 the ability to talk. Speech is one of the main ways of communicating.
2 a special talk that you give to a group of people.

speed *noun*
how fast something goes or happens. *The car was traveling at a speed of 60 miles per hour.*

speedometer speedometers *noun*
an instrument that shows how fast a vehicle is traveling.

spell spells spelling spelled *verb*
When you spell a word, you say or write the letters in the right order. *"How do you spell tiger?" "T-i-g-e-r."*
spelling *noun*.

spend spends spending spent *verb*
1 When you spend money, you use it to buy something. *I must stop spending so much money on candy.*
2 When you spend time with somebody, you stay with them. *I spent a week with my aunt and uncle.*

sphere spheres *noun*
a solid shape like a ball. *The Earth is a sphere.*
spherical *adjective*.

spice spices *noun*
powder or seeds from a plant that you put in food to give it a stronger taste. *Cinnamon, ginger, and nutmeg are spices.*
spicy *adjective*.

spider spiders *noun*
a small creature with eight legs and no wings. *Spiders spin webs to catch insects.*

spike spikes *noun*
a piece of metal or wood with a sharp point at one end. *The fence has spikes along the top.*

spill spills spilling spilled or spilt *verb*
If you spill a liquid, you let it flow out of a container by mistake. *I spilled my drink on the rug.*

spin spins spinning spun *verb*
1 When something spins, it turns around and around very fast. *The ball spun through the air.*
2 To spin also means to pull cotton or wool into long, thin pieces and then twist them together to make thread or yarn.

spinach *noun*
a dark green leafy vegetable.

spine spines *noun*
1 Your spine is the row of bones down your back.
2 one of the sharp points on some animals and plants. *Porcupines and cactuses have spines.*
3 The spine of the book is the part of the cover between the front and the back.

spirit spirits *noun*
1 Your spirit is the part of you that some people believe does not die when the body dies.
2 a ghost.

spit spits spitting spat *verb*
If you spit, you send food or liquid out of your mouth. *We spat out the cherry pits.*

splash splashes splashing splashed *verb*
If you splash someone or something, you make that one wet with drops of water or some other liquid.

split splits splitting split *verb*
1 When something splits, it breaks open. *The bag split and all the groceries fell out.*
2 To split also means to share something. *We split the candy between us.*

spoil spoils spoiling spoiled or spoilt *verb*
1 If somebody spoils something, he or she makes it less good than it was before. *I spoiled my shirt when I spilled paint all over it.*
2 If people spoil a child, they give the child everything that the child wants.

spoke, spoken past of **speak**

sponge
sponges
noun
1 a soft thing that is full of holes. You use a sponge to wash yourself or to clean things. *Wendy washed the car with a sponge.*
2 A sponge is also a sea creature with a soft part inside that is full of holes.

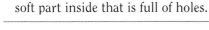
a natural sponge

sponsor **sponsors** *noun*
a person or a company that gives money to somebody or a group of people for doing something special such as walking for a charity. *A famous sportswear company is the sponsor of the city marathon.*

spooky **spookier spookiest** *adjective*
Something that is spooky is frightening.

spool **spools** *noun*
a round thing you wind film or thread on.

spoon **spoons** *noun*
a metal tool that you use for eating things such as soup and cereals.
spoonful *noun*
six spoonfuls of sugar.

sport **sports** *noun*
something that you do to keep your body strong and well and to have fun. *Football, tennis, soccer, and swimming are all sports.*

spot **spots** *noun*
1 a small, round mark. *Leopards have yellow fur with dark spots.*
2 a small red mark on your skin.
3 a place. *This is the spot where I fell off my horse.*
spotted *adjective*
a spotted horse.
spotty *adjective*
a spotty windshield.

spout **spouts** *noun*
a part of a container such as a teapot or coffeepot where the liquid comes out.

sprain **sprains spraining sprained** *verb*
When you sprain something such as your ankle or your wrist, you hurt it by twisting it suddenly.

sprang past of **spring**.

spray **sprays spraying sprayed** *verb*
When you spray something, you make lots of small drops of liquid fall on it. *Jenny sprayed the fern with water.*

spread **spreads spreading spread** *verb*
1 If you spread something such as butter, you cover something else with it. *Freddie spread honey on the waffle.*
2 When something spreads it moves all over a place. *The rain has spread to all parts of the country.*
3 When you spread your arms, you stretch them out. *The bird spread its wings.*

spring **springs** *noun*
1 the season of the year between winter and summer. *Plants start to grow in the spring.*
2 A spring is a piece of wire that is twisted around in circles. *A spring will jump back into the same shape if you press or pull it and then let it go.*

spring **springs springing sprang sprung** *verb*
To spring is to jump. *The cat sprang onto the wall.*

sprinkle **sprinkles sprinkling sprinkled** *verb*
If you sprinkle something, you throw small drops or pieces of something onto it. *She sprinkled the flowers with some water.*

sprung past of **spring**.

spun past of **spin**.

spy **spies** *noun*
a person who tries to find out secret information about another person or a country.

square **squares** *noun*
a flat shape with four straight sides that are the same length.
square *adjective*
a square table.

squash **squashes squashing squashed** *verb*
If you squash something, you press it hard and make it flat. *He sat on my hat and squashed it.*

squeak **squeaks squeaking squeaked** *verb*
To squeak is to make the small, high sound that a mouse makes. *The door squeaks when you open it.*

squeeze **squeezes squeezing squeezed** *verb*
If you squeeze something, you press it hard on the sides. *I squeezed the water out of the sponge.*

squirrel **squirrels** *noun*
a small gray animal with a big, thick tail. *Squirrels climb well and live in trees.*

squirt **squirts squirting squirted** *verb*
When something squirts, liquid comes out very fast. *I opened the bottle and lemonade squirted everywhere.*

A B C D E F G H I J K L M N O P Q R S T U V W X Y Z

stab stabs stabbing stabbed *verb*
To stab is to stick a knife or weapon into somebody or something.

stable stables *noun*
a building where horses are kept.

stadium stadiums *noun*
a large area for sports such as football or athletics. There are usually seats around the edge so that people can watch the games. *an ancient stadium.*

stage stages *noun*
1 A stage is the part of a theater where the actors perform.
2 If you do something in stages, you do it in parts. *It will take a long time to build the treehouse, so we'll have to do it in stages.*

stain stains *noun*
a dirty mark on something that is very difficult to get rid of. *Joe's football uniform was covered with grass stains.*

stair stairs *noun*
one of a set of steps for going up or down inside a building.

staircase staircases *noun*
a set of stairs inside a building.

stale staler stalest *adjective*
not fresh. *Sheri threw away the last piece of cake because it was stale.*

stalk stalks *noun*
the stem or long, thin part of a plant that flowers, leaves, and fruit grow on.

stall stalls *noun*
1 A stall is a place in a shed for one cow or in a stable for one horse.
2 A stall is also a spot on an open table in a market where you sell things.

stamp stamps *noun*
a small piece of paper with a picture and a price on it. *You have to put a stamp on a letter before you drop it into the mailbox.*

stamp stamps stamping stamped *verb*
1 If you stamp your foot, you put it down hard on the floor. *My little sister stamps her foot when she is angry.*
2 To make a mark on paper or on an object using a special tool. Stamping something often shows that you have paid for it or that you have returned it.

stampede stampedes *noun*
When cattle suddenly run fast together, they are in a stampede.

stand stands standing stood *verb*
to be on your feet.

standard standards *noun*
a measure of how good or bad something is. *a high standard.*

star stars *noun*
1 a small, bright light that you can see in the sky on a clear night.
2 a shape with five or six points. *We put a star on top of the Christmas tree.*
3 a famous person who sings, acts, or plays a sport. *a movie star.*

stare stares staring stared *verb*
If you stare at somebody or something, you look at them for a long time. *Freddie and James stared at each other.*

start starts starting started *verb*
1 When something starts, it begins. *What time does the movie start?* ■ The opposite is **end** or **finish**.

2 When you start something like a car, you make it move.

start *noun*
the beginning. ■ The opposite is **end**.

startle startles startling startled *verb*
If people or things startle you, they surprise you in a frightening way. *You startled me when you jumped out from behind the curtain.*

starve starves starving starved *verb*
If people or animals starve, they get sick and can die because they do not have enough to eat. *Many birds starve during the winter months.*
starvation *noun.*

state states *noun*
1 a country and its government. *The state runs the armed forces.*
2 a part of a country. *California is one of the western states of the United States of America.*
3 A state is also how somebody or something looks or is. *Your clothes are in a terrible state!*

station stations *noun*
1 a place where trains and buses stop and pick up passengers.
2 a building that is used for something special. *a police station.*

station wagon station wagons *noun*
a rectangular car with back seats that fold down, and a door in the back.

statue statues *noun*
a sculpture or model of a person or an animal that is made of stone or metal.

stay stays staying stayed *verb*
1 If you stay somewhere, you do not move from that place.
2 If you stay with somebody, you live in their house for a short time.

steady steadier steadiest *adjective*
Somebody or something that is steady is not moving about or shaking. *The ladder must be steady when I climb it.* ■ The opposite is **unsteady**.

steal steals stealing stole stolen *verb*
To steal is to take something that does not belong to you and keep it. *Somebody stole my purse.*

steam *noun*
Steam is the gas that water turns into when it boils. *Steam was coming out of the kettle.*

steel *noun*
a strong metal that is used for making such things as knives, tools, and machines.

steep steeper steepest *adjective*
If something such as a hill is steep, it goes up or down sharply. *This mountain is too steep to climb.*

steer steers steering steered *verb*
When you steer a car, you turn the wheel so that it goes in the direction you want it to.

stem stems *noun*
the long, thin part of a plant that grows above the ground.

step steps *noun*
1 what you do when you lift your foot and put it down in a different place. *Try to follow these dance steps.*
2 the flat part of stairs where you put your foot for going up or down.

step steps stepping stepped *verb*
To step is to lift your foot and put it down in another place as you walk. *You stepped on my foot!*

stereo *noun*
music or sound that comes from two different loudspeakers at the same time. *a stereo CD player.*

stick sticks *noun*
a long thin piece of wood. *We supported the young plants with sticks.*

stick sticks sticking stuck *verb*
1 When you stick two things together, you join them with glue. *Camille stuck a picture into her book.*
2 If something sticks, it cannot be moved. *The car is stuck in the mud.*
3 When you stick a pointed thing into something else, you push it in. *If you stick a pin into a balloon it will burst.*
sticky *adjective*
Her fingers are sticky with glue!

sticker stickers *noun*
a small piece of paper with a picture or words on it that you can attach to something. *My suitcase is covered with stickers.*

stiff stiffer stiffest *adjective*
1 If something is stiff, it does not bend easily. *a stiff piece of cardboard.*
2 not moving easily. *a stiff neck.*

still *adjective, adverb*
1 not moving. *Please stand still while I take your picture.*
2 going on and on. *It's still raining.*

sting stings stinging stung *verb*
If an insect or a plant stings you, a small sharp point goes into your skin and hurts you.
sting *noun*.

stingray stingrays *noun*
a sea animal that has a flat body and a long tail that looks like a whip. It also has a poisonous spine.

stir stirs stirring stirred *verb*
When you stir a liquid, you move a spoon around to mix it. *Rose stirred the soup.*

stitch stitches *noun*
a loop that you make when you put a needle and thread through a piece of material and bring it out again a little further along.

stock stocks *noun*
all the things that a store keeps ready to sell. *This store has a large stock of children's shoes.*

stocking stockings *noun*
a piece of clothing like a long, thin sock that women and girls wear over their legs and feet.

stole, stolen past of **steal**.

stomach stomachs *noun*
Your stomach is the place in the middle of your body where food goes after you have eaten it.

stone stones *noun*
1 a small piece of rock.
2 a large mass of rock that is used for building. *a stone wall.*

stood past of **stand**.

stool stools *noun*
a kind of chair without a back or arms.

stop stops stopping stopped *verb*
1 If you stop what you are doing, you do not do it any more. *Stop talking and listen for a moment.*
2 When something that was moving stops, it stands still. *The bus stopped.*
3 If you stop somebody from doing something, you do not allow them to do it. *I tried to stop the dog from sitting on the sofa.*
4 When a machine stops, it does not work any more. *My watch has stopped.*

stoplight stoplights *noun*
a set of red, yellow, and green lights on a street that tell you to stop, to be careful, or to go.

store stores *noun*
a shop that sells things.

store stores storing stored *verb*
If you store something somewhere, you put it there so that you can use it later. *The cans of food were stored in the pantry.*

stork storks *noun*
a big white bird with long legs and a large beak. *Storks live near water.*

storm storms *noun*
very bad weather with strong winds and a lot of rain or snow. *Many storms also have thunder and lightning.*
stormy *adjective*
stormy winter weather.

story stories *noun*
A story tells you about things that have happened. Some stories are about real things and others are made up. *I read a story about a boy who made friends with a ghost.*

story stories *noun*
all the rooms on one floor of a building. *This skyscraper has fifty stories.*

stout stouter stoutest *adjective*
1 rather fat. *a stout woman.*
2 sturdy and strong. *stout hiking boots.*

A B C D E F G H I J K L M N O P Q R S T U V W X Y Z

stove stoves *noun*
A stove has an oven inside for baking and broiling, and parts on the top that heat up for boiling and frying.

straight straighter straightest *adjective*
not bending or curving.

strain strains straining strained *verb*
1 If you strain a part of your body, you hurt it by stretching a muscle too much.
2 If you strain food, you put it through a utensil called a strainer to separate the solid part from the liquid. *James strained the can of tomatoes.*

strand strands *noun*
a long, thin piece of something. *strands of long, blond hair.*

strange stranger strangest *adjective*
1 odd or unusual. *I read a story about a strange animal that could talk.*
2 not known or seen before. *a strange house.* ■ The opposite is **familiar**.

stranger strangers *noun*
a person whom you do not know. *A complete stranger waved at me.*

strap straps *noun*
a long, thin piece of material that you use for fastening things, carrying things, or for holding things. *How many kinds of straps can you see?*

straw straws *noun*
1 the dried stems of plants like wheat. Straw is used for animals such as horses and pet rabbits to lie on. You can make hats out of straw.
2 a long, thin tube made of paper or plastic for drinking through.

strawberry strawberries *noun*
a small, soft, red fruit that grows near the ground. ❖ *Look at page 69*

streak streaks *noun*
a long, thin line of something. *There are streaks of paint on the floor.*

stream streams *noun*
1 a small, narrow river.
2 a long line of things going in one direction. *a stream of traffic.*

street streets *noun*
a road in a town or city, with houses and other buildings along each side.

strength *noun*
how strong somebody or something is. *Do you have the strength to move the table?*

stress *noun*
too much worry or work. *Stress has caused his headaches.*

stretch stretches stretching stretched *verb*
1 If you stretch something, you make it longer or wider by pulling it. *Hal's sweater has stretched.*
2 If you stretch your body, you push your arms and legs out and make yourself as tall as you can.

strict stricter strictest *adjective*
strict people expect others to do what they say and to obey rules.
strictly *adverb*.

stride strides striding strode stridden *verb*
to walk or run with long steps.

strike strikes striking struck *verb*
1 If you strike people or things, you hit them. *The ball struck me on the back of the head.*
2 When lightning strikes, it hits and goes through somebody or something. *The tree was struck by lightning.*
3 When a clock strikes, it rings a bell to show the time. *The clock struck ten.*
4 When you strike a match, you rub it on something rough to make a flame.
5 When people strike, they stop working because they want more money or because they want to protest about something.

strike strikes *noun*
when people stop working because they want more money or because they want to protest about something.

string *noun*
1 very thin rope. You use string to tie up things such as packages.
2 Musical instruments such as guitars and violins have thin wires called strings that you touch to make sounds.

strip strips *noun*
a long, thin piece of something such as paper or material.

stripe stripes *noun*
a colored line on something. *My soccer shirt has red and white stripes.*
striped *adjective*
a striped dress.

stroke strokes stroking stroked *verb*
When you stroke an animal such as a cat, you move your hand gently over its body.
stroke *noun*.

strong stronger strongest *adjective*
1 If you are strong, you have a lot of power in your muscles. ■ The opposite is **weak**.
2 not easy to break. *These toys are made of strong plastic.*
3 If a taste or a smell is strong, you can notice it easily. *This cheese has a very strong smell.*

struck past of **strike**.

struggle struggles struggling struggled *verb*
1 To struggle means to fight to get away from somebody or something. *The thief struggled to get away from the police.*
2 If you struggle to do something that is difficult, you try hard to do it. *Connie and Joe struggled to get dressed.*

stubborn *adjective*
Stubborn people do not change their minds easily and do not like doing what other people tell them to do.

stuck past of **stick**.

student students *noun*
a person who is learning something at a school, university, or college.

studio studios *noun*
1 a room where an artist or a photographer works.
2 a place where movies, television or radio programs, or records are made.

study studies studying studied *verb*
1 If you study something, you spend time learning about it. *I am studying history at school.*
2 To study something is to look at it very carefully. *David was studying the stars through his telescope.*
studious *adjective*
somebody who is studious spends a lot of time studying. *a studious girl.*

stuff *noun*
something that we don't have a word for. *What's this stuff on the floor?* ◆ *Please clean up all that stuff in your room.*

stumble stumbles stumbling stumbled *verb*
If you stumble over something, you nearly fall over it. *I stumbled over a pair of shoes on the floor.*

stung past of **sting**.

stupid stupider stupidest *adjective*
silly, not smart, bright, or sensible. ■ The opposite is **bright**.
stupidity *noun*.

style styles *noun*
the way something is done or made, or how it looks. *a new style of shoe.*

subject subjects *noun*
1 something you learn about. *My best subjects at school are English and history.*
2 what something such as a story is all about. *Animals are the subject of this book.*
3 the subject of a sentence is the person or thing that does the action. In the sentence *Katie climbed a tree.* "Katie" is the subject.

submarine submarines *noun*
a boat that can travel underwater.

substance substances *noun*
something that you can see, touch, or use for making things. *This vegetable contains a very sticky substance.*

subtract subtracts subtracting subtracted *verb*
To subtract is to take one number away from another number. *If you subtract 4 from 6, you get 2.* ■ The opposite is **add**.
subtraction *noun*

suburb suburbs *noun*
an area near a city.
suburban *adjective*.

subway subways *noun*
a railroad under city streets.

succeed succeeds succeeding succeeded *verb*
If you succeed, you do or get the thing that you wanted.

success successes *noun*
doing something well or getting what you wanted. *We wish you success in the race.* ◆ *The party was a great success.*
successful *adjective*, **successfully** *adverb*.

suck sucks sucking sucked *verb*
to pull liquid into your mouth from something. *The baby is sucking milk from a bottle.*

sudden *adjective*
happening quickly when you are not expecting it. *We ran inside to get out of the sudden rain.*
suddenly *adverb*.

suffer suffers suffering suffered *verb*
If you suffer, you feel pain because you have been hurt, are sick, or because you are unhappy. *Tom suffers a lot when he has a cold.*

suffocate suffocates suffocating suffocated *verb*
If people or animals suffocate, they die because they have no air to breathe.

sugar *noun*
something that you put in food and drinks to make them sweet. Sugar comes from sugarcane or sugar beets.

sugarcane *noun*
a tall grass with thick stems. We get sugar from the stems, called "canes."

suggest suggests suggesting suggested *verb*
If you suggest something to others, you tell them about an idea that you have for doing something. *Sophie suggested that we go to the beach.*

A B C D E F G H I J K L M N O P Q R S T U V W X Y Z

suicide *noun*
Suicide means killing yourself on purpose.

suit suits *noun*
a set of clothes made out of the same material and that you wear together. A suit can be a jacket and pants, or a jacket and a skirt.

suit suits suited *verb*
1 If clothes suit you, they look good on you. *Does this dress suit me?*
2 If something suits you, it is right for what you want or need. *This bedroom suits me.*

suitable *adjective*
right for somebody or something. *This coat is suitable for rainy weather.*

suitcase suitcases *noun*
a large box or bag with a handle that you carry your clothes in when you travel.

sulk sulks sulking sulked *verb*
If you sulk, you refuse to talk to anybody because you are angry about something. *Dominic is sulking because he's not allowed to watch any more television.*

sum sums *noun*
a result of adding numbers. *The sum of 3 + 2 is 5.* ● A word that sounds like sum is some.

summer *noun*
the season of the year between the spring and the fall. *Summer is the hottest part of the year.*

summit summits *noun*
the top of a mountain.

summon summons summoning summoned *verb*
If you summon somebody, you call that person and say to come. *We were summoned to the principal's office.*

Sun suns *noun*
the bright star that you can see in the sky during the day. The Sun gives us light and heat. ● A word that sounds like Sun is son.

sunbathe sunbathes sunbathing sunbathed *verb*
To sunbathe is to sit in the Sun and let it make your skin get darker.

sung past of **sing**.

sunglasses *noun*
special dark glasses that you wear to protect your eyes from the bright light of the Sun.

sunk past of **sink**.

sunny sunnier sunniest *adjective*
with the Sun shining brightly. *It's a sunny day—let's have a picnic!*

sunrise *noun*
the time when the Sun comes up (rises) in the morning.

sunset *noun*
the time when the Sun goes down (sets) at night.

sunshine *noun*
the light and heat from the Sun.

super *adjective, interjection*
great; excellent.

superb *adjective*
wonderful. *We had a superb vacation in Europe last year.*

superior *adjective*
better than somebody or something else. *Suzanne's drawing of the school building is superior to mine.*

supermarket supermarkets *noun*
a big store where you can buy food and lots of other things, which you pay for all at one time at a "checkout counter."

supersonic *adjective*
If an aircraft, rocket, or bullet is supersonic, it goes faster than the speed of sound.

superstitious *adjective*
A superstitious person believes that bad luck will happen if he or she does or does not do certain things. *Superstitious people think it is bad luck to walk under ladders.*

superstore superstores *noun*
a huge store that sells lots of things of one kind, like computers.

supervise supervises supervising supervised *verb*
If you supervise somebody or something, you watch them to make sure they are doing things in the right way.

supper suppers *noun*
a light evening meal.

supply supplies *noun*
an amount of something that you need. *We took a large supply of food on the camping trip.*

support supports supporting supported *verb*
1 To support is to hold somebody or something up. *Joe supported Connie when she twisted her ankle.*
2 If you support a club, a team, or some other group, you try to help and encourage it. *Which team do you support?*
support *noun* supporter *noun*.

suppose supposes supposing supposed *verb*
If you suppose that something is true, you think that it is probably true. *I suppose you are right.*

sure surer surest *adjective*
1 If you are sure about something, you know it is true. *I'm sure I packed my raincoat.*

a b c d e f g h i j k l m n o p q r s t u v w x y z

2 If you are sure that something will happen, you know it will. *I'm sure it will snow tomorrow.*
surely *adverb.*
without a doubt.

surf *noun*
the foam or white part on top of the waves on the sea.

surf surfs surfing surfed *verb*
To surf is to ride on top of the waves by standing on a long piece of wood or plastic called a surfboard.

surface surfaces *noun*
the outside part of something.

surgeon surgeons *noun*
a doctor whose job is to operate on people in a hospital.

surgery *noun*
cutting somebody's body to take out or mend a part inside. *heart surgery.*

surname surnames *noun*
your last name that shows which family you belong to. *My first name is Ben and my surname is Smith.*

surprise surprises surprising surprised *verb*
If you surprise somebody, you do something that the person does not expect. *You surprised me when you came home early.*
surprise *noun*
Don't tell Chris about the party—it's a surprise!
surprising *adjective.*

surrender surrenders surrendering surrendered *verb*
When an army surrenders, it stops fighting and gives in to the enemy.
surrender *noun.*

surround surrounds surrounding surrounded *verb*
To surround means to be or go all around something. *An island is surrounded by water.* ◆ *The police surrounded the office building.*

survive survives surviving survived *verb*
To stay alive after something very bad or dangerous has happened. *Our cat was lucky to survive after being hit by a car.*

suspect suspects suspecting suspected *verb*
If you suspect somebody of doing something wrong, you think the person did it. *The police suspected her of stealing the money and jewelry.*
suspect *noun.*

suspense *noun*
a feeling of fear or excitement that you have when you do not know what is going to happen. *We waited with suspense for the results of the election.*

suspicious *adjective*
If you are suspicious, you think that something is wrong, or you do not believe somebody. *I was suspicious when he said he had lost my money.*

swallow swallows swallowing swallowed *verb*
When you swallow food or drink, it goes down your throat.

swam past of **swim**.

swamp swamps *noun*
a marsh or an area of wet ground. There are some big swamps in the southeast of the United States.

swan swans *noun*
a big white bird with a long neck that lives on water. Young swans are gray and are called cygnets. *We saw swans swimming on the lake.*

swap swaps swapping swapped *verb*
To swap means to change something for something else. *May I swap my book for your camera?*
swap *noun.*

sway sways swaying swayed *verb*
When people or things sway, they move slowly from side to side for some time. *The daffodils were swaying on their long stems in the wind.*

swear swears swearing swore sworn *verb*
1 If people swear, they say bad or rude words.
2 If you swear, you promise something in a very serious way. *I swear that I will tell the truth.*

sweat sweats sweating sweated *verb*
When you sweat, you lose liquid from your body through your skin. *Everybody was sweating because it was so hot.*
sweat *noun.*

sweater sweaters *noun*
a piece of clothing that is knitted. You wear it to cover the top part of your body.

sweep sweeps sweeping swept *verb*
When you sweep something, you clean it with a brush. *Would you please sweep the porch?*

sweet sweeter sweetest *adjective*
1 Sweet foods and drinks have a taste like sugar. *Honey is sweet.*
2 A sweet person is gentle and kind. *It was very sweet of you to help me.*
sweetness *noun.*

swell swells swelling swelled swollen *verb*
When something swells, it gets bigger and thicker. *My ankle swelled up when I twisted it.* ◆ *The insect bite made her hand swell up.*
swelling *noun.*

swept past of **sweep**
Gerry swept the snow from the path.

swerve swerves swerving swerved *verb*
When something that is moving swerves, it goes quickly to one side. *The cyclist swerved in order to avoid being hit by the car.*

A B C D E F G H I J K L M N O P Q R S T U V W X Y Z

swim swims swimming swam swum *verb*
When you swim, you use your arms and legs to move along in water. *We are going swimming in the sea.* ◆ *We watched the fish swimming in the pond.* **swim** *noun.*

swimming pool swimming pools *noun*
a large indoor or outdoor water-filled tank for swimming and diving.

swing swings swinging swung *verb*
When something swings, it moves backward and forward through the air. *The soldiers swung their arms as they marched.*

swing swings *noun*
a seat for swinging that hangs from two strong ropes or chains. *It is relaxing to sit in a swing and move gently backward and forward.*

switch switches *noun*
a thing that you press or turn to stop or start something working. *Use the light switch to turn the light on.*

switch switches switching switched *verb*
1 To switch is to change one thing for another thing. *My friend and I switched places.*
2 When you switch something on, you use a switch to make it work. *Will you switch the lights on?*
3 When you switch something off, you use a switch to make it stop working. *Did you switch the lights off?*

swivel swivels swiveling swiveled *verb*
To swivels is to twist or turn around on the same spot.

swollen past of **swell**.

swoop swoops swooping swooped *verb*
to rush or fly downward suddenly. *The bird swooped down to catch the worm.*

sword swords *noun*
a weapon with a handle and a long metal blade with a sharp point at the end. Long ago soldiers used to fight with swords and shields. ▲ Say **sord**.

Spelling tip:
••••••••••••••••••••••••
Some words that start with the sound "s" as in "simple," are spelled with a "c" such as certain, city, cycle.

swore, sworn past of **swear**.

swum past of **swim**.

swung past of **swing**.

syllable syllables *noun*
a word or part of a word that has one sound. The word "but" has one syllable, the word "butter" has two syllables, and the word "America" has four syllables.

symbol symbols *noun*
1 a sign or mark that means something. This symbol + means add in math.
2 A symbol is also a thing that stands for something else. *The dove is a symbol of peace.*
Do you know what these symbols mean? Look at page 190 for the answers.

---

symmetrical *adjective*
If a shape is symmetrical, both sides are the same. If you draw a line through the middle of a circle, you will see that both sides are symmetrical.
symmetry *noun.*

All these shapes are symmetrical.

sympathy *noun*
If you feel or show sympathy for somebody, you are very kind to that person because he or she is hurt or sad. **sympathetic** *adjective,* **sympathize** *verb.*

symphony symphonies *noun*
a long piece of music written for a large orchestra.
symphonic *adjective.*

symptom symptoms *noun*
something that is wrong with you and shows that you are sick. *A sore throat and a temperature are symptoms of a bad cold.*

synagogue synagogues *noun*
a building where Jews go to pray. ▲ Say *sin-a-gog.*

synonym synonyms *noun*
a word that means nearly the same as another word. *Little* and *small* are synonyms. ■ A word that means opposite is **antonym**.

synthetic *adjective*
created artificially using chemicals. Nylon is a synthetic fabric.
▲ Say *sin-thet-ik.*

syringe syringes *noun*
a special needle that doctors can push into your skin when they give you an injection of medicine or when they take blood out of your body.

syrup *noun*
a sweet, sticky food made from water boiled with sugar, and often flavored.

system systems *noun*
1 an organized way of doing something. *We have changed the system for borrowing books and recordings from the library.*
2 a group of machines or other things that work together. *a computer system.* ◆ *a transportation system.*

T t

table **tables** *noun*
1 a piece of furniture with a flat top that you can put things on.
2 a set of numbers or words arranged in columns.
3 a list of the multiplication of all the numbers between 1 and 12.

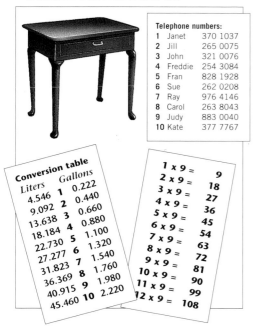

Telephone numbers:		
1	Janet	370 1037
2	Jill	265 0075
3	John	321 0076
4	Freddie	254 3084
5	Fran	828 1928
6	Sue	262 0208
7	Ray	976 4146
8	Carol	263 8043
9	Judy	883 0040
10	Kate	377 7767

Conversion table

Liters		Gallons
4.546	1	0.222
9.092	2	0.440
13.638	3	0.660
18.184	4	0.880
22.730	5	1.100
27.277	6	1.320
31.823	7	1.540
36.369	8	1.760
40.915	9	1.980
45.460	10	2.220

1 x 9 =	9
2 x 9 =	18
3 x 9 =	27
4 x 9 =	36
5 x 9 =	45
6 x 9 =	54
7 x 9 =	63
8 x 9 =	72
9 x 9 =	81
10 x 9 =	90
11 x 9 =	99
12 x 9 =	108

tablet **tablets** *noun*
a small round piece of medicine that you swallow.

table tennis *noun*
a game for two or four people who stand at each end of a table with a net across the middle and hit a very small ball to each other, bouncing it off the table, with small bats.

tackle **tackles tackling tackled** *verb*
1 If you tackle somebody when playing a game such as football, you try to get the ball away from him or her.
2 When you tackle something, you do whatever is needed, even if it is difficult.

tactful *adjective*
careful not to say anything that would hurt somebody else's feelings.
tactfully *adverb*.

tadpole **tadpoles** *noun*
a tiny animal that lives in water and that will grow into a frog or toad. Tadpoles have tails.

tail **tails** *noun*
the part at the back end of an animal, bird, or fish. *The dog wagged its tail.* ◆ *Airplanes have tails.* ● A word that sounds like **tail** is **tale**.

tailor **tailors** *noun*
a person who makes suits, jackets, and coats.

take **takes taking took taken** *verb*
1 If you take something, you get hold of it or carry it. *Can you take these books back to the library?*
2 If somebody takes you, that one drives you, or you go with them. *Dan took me to school on his way to work.*
3 If you take something, you remove it. *She took her purse out of her bag.* ◆ *Have you taken my bag?*
take off When a plane takes off, it leaves the runway and moves into the air. ■ The opposite is **land**.

tale **tales** *noun*
a story. *a tale of love and adventure.*
● A word that sounds like **tale** is **tail**.

talent **talents** *noun*
If you have a talent for something, you have a natural ability for it and can do it well. *Clive's got a real talent for acting.*
talented *adjective*.

talk **talks talking talked** *verb*
When you talk, you say words. *We talked on the phone for hours.* ▲ Say **tawk**.

tall **taller tallest** *adjective*
1 higher than usual. *She's very tall.* ◆ *a tall building.* ■ The opposite is **short**.
2 having a certain height. *He's just over five feet tall.*

tambourine **tambourines** *noun*
a small, round musical instrument that you shake or tap with your fingers.
▲ Say *tam-ber-een*.

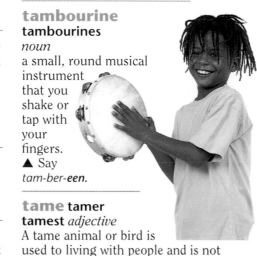

tame **tamer tamest** *adjective*
A tame animal or bird is used to living with people and is not afraid of them.
■ The opposite is **wild**.

tan *noun*
If you have a tan, your skin is a darker color than usual because you have been in the Sun.

tandem **tandems** *noun*
a special bicycle for two people.

tangled *adjective*
twisted together in knots or muddled up together untidily. *This wool is a tangled mess.*

tank **tanks** *noun*
1 a big container that holds liquid or gas.
2 a big, heavy vehicle with a gun in it that is used in a war.

tanker **tankers** *noun*
1 a very big, long ship that carries oil.
2 a big truck that carries gasoline or some other liquid.

tap **taps** *noun*
a thing that you turn on to make water or gas flow out of a pipe and turn off to stop it from flowing.

tap **taps tapping tapped** *verb*
If you tap somebody or something, you hit that one gently. *He tapped a few keys, and data came up on the screen.*

tape **tapes** *noun*
1 a long, narrow piece of material. *a tape measure.*
2 a long strip of plastic that you can record sounds or pictures on and then play back on a tape recorder or by using a VCR and a television.
tape *verb*.

tape recorder **tape recorders** *noun*
a machine that you use to play a tape or to record sounds on to a tape.

tapestry **tapestries** *noun*
a piece of material that has a picture on it made from colored threads.

A B C D E F G H I J K L M N O P Q R S T U V W X Y Z

tar *noun*
a thick, black, sticky substance that is used mainly for building roads.

tardy **tardier tardiest** *adjective*
arriving late. *tardy students.*

target **targets** *noun*
an object that people aim at or try to hit when they are shooting.

task **tasks** *noun*
a job that must be done.

taste **tastes tasting tasted** *verb*
1 When you taste something, you try a little of it to see if you like the flavor. *Please taste this fish and tell me if you like it.*
2 If something tastes good or bad, you think the flavor is good or bad. *I like that ice cream, it tastes great.* ◆ *This milk tastes funny.*

taste **tastes** *noun*
1 the ability to recognize the flavor of something by touching it with your tongue. *Sugar has a sweet taste.*
2 the way something tastes. *This bread has no taste at all.*

tattoo **tattoos** *noun*
a permanent or temporary pattern on a person's skin made by putting colored dyes under the skin using a needle or by using makeup.

taught past of **teach**
▲ Say *tawt.*

tax **taxes** *noun*
money that people have to pay to the government for running the country. *income taxes.*

taxi **taxis** *noun*
a car that will take you where you want to go if you pay the driver.

tea *noun*
a drink that you make by pouring boiling water on to the dried leaves of the tea plant.

teach **teaches teaching taught** *verb*
1 When people teach you, they tell you about a subject and help you learn about it. *Mrs. Jones teaches history.*
2 to show somebody how to do something. *I'll teach you how to surf this summer.*
teacher *noun.*

team **teams** *noun*
a group of people who work together or play a sport together. *a football team.*

teapot **teapots** *noun*
a container for making tea in with a spout for pouring it out.

tear **tears** *noun*
one of the drops of liquid that comes from your eyes when you cry. ▲ Rhymes with **here.** ● A word that sounds like **tear** is **tier.**

tear **tears tearing tore torn** *verb*
When you tear something, you pull one part away from the rest. *If you tear paper in a special way, you can make different shapes and patterns.* ▲ Rhymes with **chair.**

tease **teases teasing teased** *verb*
When you tease people, you laugh at them or make jokes about them. *Tom's friends teased him because of his new haircut.* ▲ Say *teez.*

technology **technologies** *noun*
machines or ways of doing things that have been invented because of discoveries by scientists. ▲ Say *tek-nol-o-jee.*

teenage *adjective*
between 13 and 19 years of age.
teenager *noun.*

teeth plural of **tooth.**

telephone **telephones** *noun*
an instrument that you use to speak to another person who is not in the same place as you. ▲ Say *tel-u-fone.*

telescope **telescopes** *noun*
an instrument in the shape of a tube with a lens at each end that makes things that are far away look clearer and closer when you look through it.

television **televisions** *noun*
an instrument in the shape of a box that receives programs that are broadcast and shows them in sound and pictures.

tell **tells telling told** *verb*
1 If you tell somebody something, you give the person information in words about it. *I told him how to fix a tire.* ◆ *She told me a very funny joke.*
2 If you tell somebody to do something, you say that the person must do it.

temper *noun*
1 If you have a bad temper, you get angry easily. *His temper gets bad when he loses.*
2 If you lose your temper, you get very angry.

temperature *noun*
1 how hot or cold something is. *Water freezes at a temperature of 32 degrees.*
2 If you have a temperature, your body is hotter than it should be.
▲ Say *temp-re-cher.*

temple temples *noun*
a building where some people go to pray.

temporary *adjective*
lasting for a short time. *He's got a temporary job.* ■ The opposite is **permanent**.
temporarily *adverb*.

tempt tempts tempting tempted *verb*
If something tempts you, you want it very strongly even if you know you should not have it.
temptation *noun*.

tenant tenants *noun*
a person who pays another person in order to rent and live in an apartment or a house.

tend tends tending tended *verb*
If something tends to happen, it usually happens or happens often. *I tend to miss the bus if I leave after 8 o'clock.*

tender tenderer tenderest *adjective*
1 easy to chew. *This is very tender meat.* ■ The opposite is **tough**.
2 a little sore. *My ankle is still tender from when I fell over.*
3 gentle and loving.
tenderly *adverb*
She spoke tenderly to the little girl.
tenderness *noun*.

tennis *noun*
a game for two or four players. The players hit a soft ball with rackets backward and forward to each other over a net that is stretched across the middle of an area called a court.

tense tenser tensest *adjective*
1 nervous and anxious about something.
2 If your muscles are tense, they are stiff and tight. *After running the marathon my legs were very tense.*
tensely *adverb*

tent tents *noun*
a shelter made of strong cloth that is held up by poles and ropes.

tepee tepees *noun*
The Native Americans made tepees out of skins or the bark of trees. These were their tents.

tepid *adjective*
slightly warm. *Babies have tepid baths so that they don't burn themselves.*

term terms *noun*
1 a length of time. *He served a four-year term as the President of the U.S.A.*
2 a word or phrase. *"Adagio" and "forte" are musical terms.*

terminal terminals *noun*
a building at an airport where passengers leave and arrive.

terrible *adjective*
very bad or unpleasant. *What a terrible noise!*
terribly *adverb*.

terrific *adjective*
very good indeed. *The video is terrific—I've seen it five times.*

terrify terrifies terrifying terrified *verb*
If you terrify somebody, you make that one very frightened. *The explosion terrified the horses.* ◆ *Many dogs are terrified of thunder.*

territory territories *noun*
1 land that belongs to or is controlled by a country, army, or ruler.
2 an area where an animal lives that it will fight for if another animal tries to come and live there.

terror *noun*
very great fear. *He screamed with terror when he thought he'd seen a ghost.*

test tests *noun*
1 a way of finding out what you know about something by asking you a set of questions or getting you to show what you can do. *a driver's test.* ◆ *a spelling test.*
2 a check to see if part of your body is working properly. *an eye test.*

test tests testing tested *verb*
1 When you test something, you use or examine it to see if it works well. *I'm testing the brakes to make sure they're working properly.*
2 When you test somebody, you try to find out how much he or she knows by using a test.

text texts *noun*
written words. *Books for very young children have lots of pictures and not much text.*

texture textures *noun*
the way that something feels. *This wool has a smooth texture almost like silk.*

thank thanks thanking thanked *verb*
When you thank people, you tell them how nice it was of them to do something for you or give you something. *Thank you very much for taking us all to the movies.*

thaw thaws thawing thawed *verb*
When something frozen thaws, it becomes warm enough to melt. *The Sun's out and the snow has started to thaw.*

an eye test

theater theaters *noun*
a building where people go to see plays. ▲ Say *thee-u-ter*.

theft thefts *noun*
the crime of stealing. *He was sent to jail for the crime of theft.*

theme park theme parks *noun*
a place you go to have fun where all the games and activities are to do with the same subject, for example space.

thermometer thermometers
noun
an instrument that shows what the temperature is.

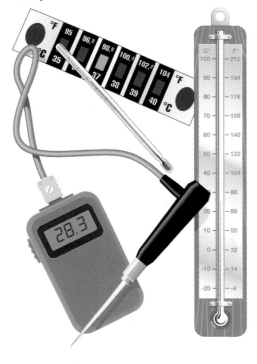

thick thicker thickest *adjective*
1 Something that is thick measures a lot from one side to the other or from top to bottom. *The castle wall was three feet thick.* ■ The opposite is **thin**.
2 A thick liquid does not flow easily. *Honey is thick.* ■ The opposite is **thin**.
3 Something that is thick is not easy to get through or to see through. *The airport shut down because of thick fog.* ◆ *a thick forest.*
thicken *verb*
The fog thickened.
thickly *adverb.*

thief thieves *noun*
a person who steals something. *Thieves broke into the store and stole all the silver and jewelry.* ▲ Say **theef**.

thigh thighs *noun*
Your thigh is the part of your leg above your knee. *Your thighs are the fattest part of your legs.*

thin thinner thinnest *adjective*
1 narrow from side to side or from top to bottom. *a thin slice of cake.* ◆ *There was a thin layer of ice on the pond.* ■ The opposite is **thick**.
2 A thin person does not have much flesh covering the bones and weighs less than most people. ■ The opposite is **fat**.
3 A thin liquid flows easily. *This soup is too thin.* ■ The opposite is **thick**.
thinly *adverb.*

think thinks thinking thought *verb*
1 When you think, you have ideas or words in your mind. *What are you thinking about?*
2 When you think something is true, you believe it. *I think Mike's plan for the party is great.*

thirsty thirstier thirstiest *adjective*
If you are thirsty, you need something to drink. *Exercise can make you thirsty.*

thistle thistles *noun*
a wild plant with very prickly leaves and purple or white flowers.

thorn thorns *noun*
a little sharp point on the stem of a plant such as a rose.
thorny *adjective.*

Blackberry bushes have thorny stems.

thorough *adjective*
complete and careful. *a thorough investigation.* ▲ Say **thu-ro**.
thoroughly *adverb.*

thought thoughts *noun*
an idea or something that you think. *Any thoughts about what you'd like for your birthday?* ▲ Say **thawt**.

thought past of **think**
I thought I could solve the problem.

thoughtful *adjective*
1 quiet and serious while you are thinking about something carefully.
2 If you are thoughtful, you think about what other people want and try to behave in a way that makes them more comfortable or happy. ▲ Say **thot-ful**.
thoughtfully, thoughtless *adverbs*
thoughtless behavior.

Hal is looking thoughtful.

thread threads *noun*
a long, thin piece of cotton, wool, or synthetic material that you use for sewing or weaving. ▲ Say **thred**.
thread *verb.*

threat threats *noun*
a warning that something bad may happen. ▲ Say **thret**.

threaten threatens threatening threatened *verb*
If somebody threatens you, that person says that he or she will do something mean if you do not do what is wanted.

three-dimensional *adjective*
Something that is three-dimensional is like a real thing with height, width, and depth, and not like a flat picture. A hologram is three-dimensional.

threw past of **throw**
● A word that sounds like **threw** is **through**.

thrill thrills *noun*
a sudden feeling of excitement or pleasure.
thrilling *adjective.*

throat throats *noun*
Your throat is the front part of your neck and the tube that goes down from inside your mouth taking food and air into your body.

throne thrones *noun*
a special chair for a king or queen.

through *preposition*
from one side to the other. *The train went through a tunnel.*◆ *Water is coming through a hole in the ceiling.* ▲ Say **throo**. ● A word that sounds like **through** is **threw**.

throw throws throwing threw thrown *verb*
When you throw something, you send it through the air from your hand. *Throw the ball up into the air and then hit it with your racket.*

thruway thruways *noun*
a big highway that usually has four lanes or more.

thumb thumbs *noun*
Your thumb is the short, thick finger at the side of your hand. ▲ Say **thum**.

thumbtack thumbtacks *noun*
a small object with a sharp point and a broad, flat head that you push into a wall to hold up notices and other paper.

thump thumps thumping thumped *verb*
If you thump somebody or something, you hit them with your fist.

thunder *noun*
the loud noise that you hear after a flash of lightning during some storms.

tick ticks *noun*
a tiny animal with eight legs that is related to the spider. It sucks blood from people and animals.

ticket tickets *noun*
a small piece of paper that shows you have paid for something. *Have you bought the movie tickets yet?* ◆ *a railroad ticket.*

tickle tickles tickling tickled *verb*
When you tickle people, you touch them very softly in a place where it makes them laugh and wriggle away.

tide tides *noun*
the movement every day of the sea coming toward land and then away from land. *The tide is coming in.*◆ *The tide is going out.*

tidy tidier tidiest *adjective*
neat; with everything in its proper place. *a tidy ship.*
tidy *verb*, **tidily** *adverb*.

tie ties tying tied *verb*
1 When you tie something, you fasten it using string or something similar. *The box was tied with red and white ribbons.* ◆ *She tied the dog to a tree.*
2 When two people or teams tie in a race or competition, they finish in an equal position. *They tied for second place.*
tie up *Ships were tied up at the dock.*

tie ties *noun*
a long, thin piece of material that you wear around the neck of a shirt. It has a knot at the front.

tier tiers *noun*
one of a series of rows or layers that are placed one above the other. *There are several tiers of seats in the theater.* ◆ *a wedding cake with three tiers.* ● A word that sounds like **tier** is **tear**, as in crying.

tiger tigers *noun*
a large wild animal in the cat family that has orange fur with dark stripes. Tigers live in Asia.

tight tighter tightest *adjective*
1 fitting very close to your body. *Connie's shoes are very tight—Joe is trying to pull them off.*
2 When something is tight, it is firmly fastened so that it will not move. *Make sure the lid is on tight.*
▲ Say **tite**. ■ The opposite is **loose**.
tightly *adverb*.

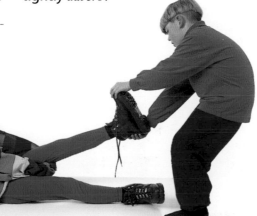

tighten tightens tightening tightened *verb*
If you tighten something, you make it tighter. If something tightens it gets tighter. ▲ Say **teye-ten**.

tightrope tightropes *noun*
a rope high up in the air that acrobats walk along in the circus. ▲ Say **tite-rope**.

tights *noun*
a thin piece of clothing that tightly covers your body, sometimes from the neck down, sometimes from the waist. ▲ Say **tites**.

tile tiles *noun*
a thin piece of hard material that you use to cover a wall, floor, or a roof. *The bathroom tiles have pictures of fish and shells on them.*

till *preposition*
until. *We had to wait two weeks till we heard the test results.*

time *noun*
1 what we measure in units such as minutes, hours, days, weeks, and years.
2 a particular point in time. *What's the time?*
3 a period of time. *Did you enjoy your time in San Francisco?*

timetable timetables *noun*
a list that shows when things are going to happen. *Let's read the timetable to find out when to board the train.*

time zone time zones *noun*
a region where the same time is used.

timid *adjective*
shy and not very brave. *A mouse is a timid creature.*
timidly *adverb*.

tin tins *noun*
a kind of silver-colored metal.

tiny tinier tiniest *adjective*
very small. *Bacteria are so tiny that you can see them only through a microscope.* ■ The opposite is **enormous** or **huge**.

tip tips *noun*
1 the end of something long and thin. *the tips of your fingers.*
2 an extra amount of money that you give to somebody such as a waiter for helping you. *Dad gave the waiter a big tip.*

A B C D E F G H I J K L M N O P Q R S T U V W X Y Z

tiptoe tiptoes tiptoeing tiptoed *verb*
to walk on your toes quietly.

tire tires *noun*
a circle of rubber around the rim of a car or bicycle wheel. ● Rhymes with **fire**.

tired *adjective*
If you are tired, you want to go to sleep.

tissue tissues *noun*
1 a thin piece of soft paper that you can use as a handkerchief.
2 a lot of tiny cells of the same kind that make up part of the body. *muscle tissue.*

title titles *noun*
1 the name of something such as a book, movie, or picture.
2 a word such as *Professor, Dr., Mrs.,* or *Ms.* that a person can have in front of the name.

toad toads *noun*
an animal like a big frog. It lives on land but lays its eggs in water.

Fire-bellied toad

Giant toad

toadstool toadstools *noun*
a poisonous fungus that looks like a mushroom.

toast *noun*
a slice of bread that has been browned on both sides to make it crunchy. **toaster** *noun*.

tobacco *noun*
the cut and dried leaves of the tobacco plant that are used in cigarettes, cigars, and pipes.

toboggan toboggans *noun*
a vehicle like a long seat fixed to two long strips of wood or metal called

runners that you use to slide downhill on snow.

toddler toddlers *noun*
a very young child who is just learning to walk.

toe toes *noun*
the five parts at the end of your foot. ● A word that sounds like **toe** is **tow**.

toilet toilets *noun*
a large bowl with a seat that you use to get rid of liquid and solid waste from your body.

token tokens *noun*
a metal disk that you can use instead of money to buy something. *a subway token.*

told past of **tell**.

toll tolls *noun*
money that you pay to use a big road.

tomato tomatoes *noun*
a soft, round, red fruit that you eat in salads.

tomb tombs *noun*
a grave or place where somebody important is buried. ▲ Say *toom*.

tongue tongues *noun*
the long, pink part inside your mouth that you use to lick something and that helps you to taste things and to speak. ▲ Say *tung*.

tonsil tonsils *noun*
Your tonsils are the two small, soft lumps at the back of your throat. They sometimes swell and hurt in a sickness called tonsillitis.

took past of **take**.

tool tools *noun*
anything that you use to help you to do a particular job. Hammers and saws are tools.

tooth teeth *noun*
1 one of the hard, white parts inside your mouth that you use to bite and to chew.
2 one of the thin parts that stick out in a row on such things as a comb, saw, or zipper.

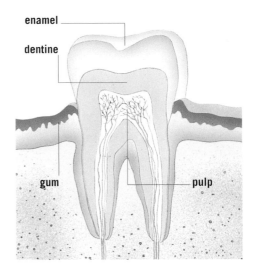

enamel

dentine

gum

pulp

toothbrush toothbrushes *noun*
a small brush with a handle that you use to brush your teeth.

toothpaste *noun*
a paste that you put on your toothbrush to brush your teeth.

top tops *noun*
1 the highest part of something. *We walked to the top of the hill.* ■ The opposite is **bottom**.
2 a lid or cover for something. *Screw the lid tightly on the jar.*

topic topics *noun*
something that is being talked about or written about. *The topic of my essay is solar energy.*

topple topples toppling toppled *verb*
If something topples, it falls over because it is too heavy at the top. *The tree toppled over in the wind.*

tore, torn past of **tear**.

tornado tornadoes *noun*
a very strong wind that travels in circles and that can do a lot of damage to buildings. ▲ Say *tor-nay-doh*.

tortilla tortillas *noun*
a flat piece of bread made with water and cornmeal. ▲ Say *tor-tee-yah*.

tortoise tortoises *noun*
a turtle that lives on land and moves very slowly. Tortoises are reptiles.
▲ Say *tor*-tus.

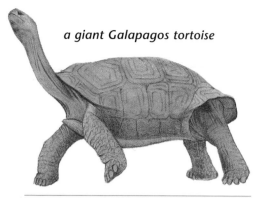

a giant Galapagos tortoise

torture tortures torturing tortured *verb*
To torture is to make somebody feel great pain as a punishment or to get information from him or her.
▲ Say *tor*-cher.

toss tosses tossing tossed *verb*
1 If you toss something, you throw it upward in a careless way. *She tossed me a pen.*
2 If something tosses, it moves around from side to side.

total *adjective*
complete. *a total disaster.*

total totals *noun*
the amount that you get when you add everything together. *If you add 12, 17, and 8, you get a total of 37.*

touch touches touching touched *verb*
1 When you touch something, you feel it with your hand or another part of you.
2 If two things touch, there is no space between them.
▲ Say *tuch.*

touchdown touchdowns *noun*
a score of six points in football made by passing or running the ball into the opponent's end zone.

tough tougher toughest *adjective*
1 strong and hard to break or damage.
2 difficult. *a tough decision.*
3 difficult to chew. *This meat is tough.*
■ The opposite is **tender.**
▲ Say *tuff.*

tour tours *noun*
a trip to different interesting places. *a tour of Chicago.* ▲ Say *tor.*

tourist tourists *noun*
a person who is visiting interesting places on vacation. ▲ Say *tor*-ist.

tournament tournaments *noun*
a competition in which a lot of matches are played until one person wins over all the others. ▲ Say *tor*-na-ment.

tow tows towing towed *verb*
To tow a vehicle is to pull it along behind another vehicle. *The car is towing a boat trailer.* ● A word that sounds like **tow** is **toe.**

towel towels *noun*
a large piece of soft, thick material that you use to dry yourself.

tower towers *noun*
a very tall, narrow building or part of a building. *the Eiffel Tower.* ◆ *the Leaning Tower of Pisa.*

the Leaning Tower of Pisa

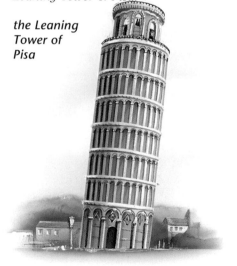

town towns *noun*
a place with streets, houses, stores, and other buildings where people live and work. *a small Midwestern town.*

toy toys *noun*
a thing for a child to play with.

trace traces tracing traced *verb*
1 When you trace a picture, you put a thin piece of paper over it and draw over the lines that show through.

2 If you trace others, you find them after looking for them. *He is trying to trace an uncle whom nobody in the family has heard from for many years.*

trace traces *noun*
a tiny amount. *Traces of garlic are in this soup.*

track tracks *noun*
1 footprints or other marks left by a person or animal that show where they have been.
2 an area of ground where races take place.
3 the rails that a train runs on.
4 one of the songs or pieces of music on a record or tape.

tractor tractors *noun*
a powerful vehicle with very large back wheels used on a farm for pulling heavy machinery and plowing.

trade *noun*
buying and selling things. *The USA has a lot of trade with Mexico.*

tradition traditions *noun*
a way of doing something that has been the same for a very long time.
traditional *adjective*
traditional songs.
traditionally *adverb.*

traffic *noun*
cars, trucks, buses, and other vehicles that are moving along the roads. *A lot of traffic goes through the city.*

tragedy tragedies *noun*
1 a very sad event. *Two of his brothers and a sister died in the tragedy.*
2 a serious play with a sad ending.
▲ Say *traj*-e-dee.
tragic *adjective*
a tragic accident.

trail trails *noun*
1 a track or path for people to follow or go along in the country. *the Appalachian Trail.*
2 marks or other signs left behind where a person or animal has been. *He left a trail of muddy footprints across the kitchen floor.*

trailer trailers *noun*
1 a vehicle that is towed behind a car or truck to carry very large or heavy things, such as a boat.
2 an advertisement that shows short scenes from a film or TV program.

A B C D E F G H I J K L M N O P Q R S T U V W X Y Z

train trains *noun*
a set of railroad cars that move along rails pulled by an engine. Some trains carry passengers and some trains carry freight.

train trains training trained *verb*
1 When you train, you practice a sport or do exercises to get fitter. *He's training for the Olympics.*
2 To train a person or animal is to teach them how to do something. *She's training the dog to shake a paw.*
3 If you train, you learn the skills you need to do a job. *Sue's training to be a doctor.*
trainer *noun*.

traitor traitors *noun*
a person who helps the enemy of his or her country.

trample tramples trampling trampled *verb*
If you trample on something, you walk on it and crush it. *Please don't trample the flowers.*

trampoline trampolines *noun*
a piece of very strong material fixed to a metal frame with springs that is used for jumping up and down in gymnastics. ▲ Say *tramp-o-leen.*

transfer transfers transferring transferred *verb*
To transfer others is to move them to a different place.

transform transforms transforming transformed *verb*
If you transform something, you change it completely. *With makeup, a wig, and good acting, he transformed himself into an old man.*

translate translates translating translated *verb*
If you translate something, you change the same thing into a different language. *Richard translated the story from Spanish into English.*

transparent *adjective*
If something is transparent, you can see through it. *Glass is transparent.*

transplant transplants *noun*
an operation in which a surgeon takes out a damaged part of the body and replaces it with one that is not damaged. *a heart transplant.*

transport transports transporting transported *verb*
To transport people or things is to take them from one place to another in a vehicle. *The boxes were transported by air.*

transportation *noun*
cars, buses, trains, and other vehicles that take people or goods from one place to another.

trap traps *noun*
a thing to catch an animal or bird. *a mousetrap.*
trap *verb.*

trapeze trapezes *noun*
a bar hanging from ropes high up in the air that acrobats in a circus swing from.

trash *noun*
things that you do not want that you throw away.

travel travels traveling traveled *verb*
When you travel, you go from one place to another. *We'll be traveling back to Fort Worth on Wednesday.*
travel *noun,* **traveler** *noun.*

trawler trawlers *noun*
a boat for catching fish by pulling a wide net behind it in the sea.

tray trays *noun*
a flat piece of wood, metal, or plastic that you carry things on.

tread treads treading trod trodden *or* trod *verb*
When you tread on something, you put your foot down on it. *Ouch! You trod on my toe!* ▲ Rhymes with **head**.

treasure treasures *noun*
a collection of very valuable objects such as gold, silver, or jewels. *The pirates hid the treasure in a cave.* ▲ Say **tre**-zure.

treat treats treating treated *verb*
1 When you treat somebody in a particular way, you behave toward that person like that. *He always treats me politely.*
2 To treat people is to give them medicine or to look after them in a way that will make them well. *The doctor treated her for an earache.*

treatment treatments *noun*
1 how a doctor treats somebody who is ill. *What's the right treatment?*
2 how somebody behaves toward a person, animal, or thing. *cruel treatment.*

tree trees *noun*
a big plant that has a thick, hard stem of wood called a trunk and branches and leaves. ❖ **Look opposite**.

tremble trembles trembling trembled *verb*
If you tremble, you shake a little because you are frightened, cold, or excited.

trend trends *noun*
the way things seem to be changing. *The trend is for people to save their money.*

trespass trespasses trespassing trespassed *verb*
If you trespass, you go on other people's land without asking them for permission.

a trawler

TREES

Hornbeam

Douglas fir

Cedar of Lebanon

Common juniper

Golden weeping willow

Hybrid black-poplar

Sea black thorn

Red oak

Spindle

Box

Pendulculate oak

Common jujube

Guelder rose

Dragon tree

Petticoat palm

VOCABULARY

broadleaf
trees with broad, flat leaves are deciduous. The leaves drop in the fall.

deciduous
trees that shed their leaves in the fall.

evergreen
conifers that keep their needle-like leaves in winter.

hardwood
the wood of slow-growing, broadleaf or deciduous trees. The wood is strong and used for making furniture.

heartwood
the oldest, hardest wood at the center of the trunk.

softwood
the wood of evergreen trees. The word is misleading as some "softwoods" are "hard."

A B C D E F G H I J K L M N O P Q R S T U V W X Y Z

trial **trials** *noun*
1 a period of time in a law court when lawyers, judge, and jury try to find out whether somebody is guilty or innocent of a crime.
2 a test to find out how good a thing is.

triangle **triangles** *noun*
1 a shape with three straight sides.
2 a small musical instrument with three metal sides that you play by hitting it with a short metal rod.
▲ Say *try-ang-gul.*
triangular *adjective*
a triangular shape.

triathlon **triathlons** *noun*
a race including swimming, bicycling, and running.

tribe **tribes** *noun*
a group of people of the same race that speak the same language and live in the same area.

trick **tricks** *noun*
1 something that is done to cheat others or to try to make them believe something that is not true.
2 something that looks as if it could not be done. *a magic trick.*

trick **tricks** **tricking** **tricked** *verb*
To trick others is to cheat them or try to make them believe something that is not true.

trickle **trickles** **trickling** **trickled** *verb*
When liquid trickles, a small amount of it flows slowly. *When Ben heard that his dog had died, tears slowly trickled down his cheeks.*

tricycle **tricycle** *noun*
a vehicle like a bicycle with three wheels. ▲ Say *try-sik-ul.*

trim **trims** **trimming** **trimmed** *verb*
If you trim something, you cut small pieces off it so that it has a better shape and looks tidy. *Connie is trimming Joe's hair.*

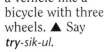

trip **trips** *noun*
a journey to a place and back again. *We went on a school trip to New York City just before Christmas.*

trip **trips** **tripping** **tripped** *verb*
If you trip, you knock your foot on something and fall over. *She tripped over the cat.*

triple *adjective*
having three parts or done three times. *He's a triple winner.* ◆ *the triple crown in horse racing.*

triplet **triplets** *noun*
one of three people or animals who have the same mother and were born at the same time.

triumph **triumphs** *noun*
a great success at something you have had to try hard to do. *The acrobat's performance was a triumph.*
▲ Say *try-umf.*

trod, trodden past of **tread.**

trolley **tolleys** *noun*
a streetcar.

trombone **trombones** *noun*
a large brass musical instrument that you play by blowing into it and moving one tube in and out of another tube to change the notes.
trombonist *noun.*

trophy **trophies** *noun*
a prize such as a silver cup that is given to a person who has won a competition or tournament. *Sarah won a big trophy at the horse show.* ▲ Say *troh-fee.*

tropical *adjective*
to do with the tropics, the very hot parts of the world near the Equator. *a tropical rain forest.*

trot **trots** **trotting** **trotted** *verb*
When a horse trots, it is moving quickly.
trot *noun.*

trouble **troubles** *noun*
a problem or a difficult or worrying situation. ▲ Say *trub-el.*
in trouble.
If you are in trouble, you have done something wrong and made somebody angry who might punish you. *If you break the window with that ball, you'll be in big trouble.*

trough **troughs** *noun*
a long narrow container that has food or water in for animals.
▲ Say *troff.*

trousers *noun*
pants.

truant **truants** *noun*
a student who stays away from school without permission.
truancy *noun.*

truck **trucks** *noun*
large motor vehicle that moves things by road.

trudge **trudges** **trudging** **trudged** *verb*
If you trudge somewhere, you walk slowly because you are tired or angry. *We trudged home through the mud.*
▲ Say *trudj.*

true **truer** **truest** *adjective*
If something is true, it is based on known facts and accurate, not made up or guessed at. *a true joke.* ■ The opposite is **false.**
truly *adverb*
very. *It was a truly funny story, and we all laughed loudly.*

trumpet **trumpets** *noun*
a brass musical instrument that you play by blowing into it.
trumpeter *noun.*

trunk **trunks** *noun*
1 the round, hard stem of a tree that the branches grow from.
2 the long nose of an elephant.
3 the main part of your body from the top of your legs to your shoulders—not your head, arms, or legs.
4 a large, strong box for carrying things in on a long trip or for storing things. *a steamer trunk.*

trust trusts trusting trusted *verb*
If you trust others, you believe that they are good and honest and will not do anything to hurt you.
trust *noun*.

truth *noun*
what is true, accurate, and correct. *I'm sure she's telling the truth*.

try tries trying tried *verb*
1 If you try to do something, you do your best to do it.
2 If you try something, you test it to see what it is like. *Try this soup and tell me if it needs more salt*.

T-shirt T-shirts *noun*
a shirt made of cotton with short sleeves and no collar or buttons that you pull over your head.

tub tubs *noun*
a big container that you take a bath in.

tube tubes *noun*
1 a long, round, hollow thing, like a pipe.
2 a long, thin container that you squeeze to get the contents out.

tuck tucks tucking tucked *verb*
If you tuck something, you push the end of it under something or in something else. *He tucked his shirt into his pants*.

tuft tufts *noun*
a clump of hair or grass.

tug tugs tugging tugged *verb*
If you tug something, you pull hard at it. *The baby kept tugging at my hair*.

tulip tulips *noun*
a plant that grows from a bulb and has a long stem and a bright flower in the shape of a cup.

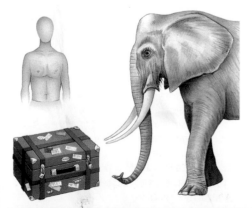

tumble tumbles tumbling tumbled *verb*
If you tumble, you fall suddenly, rolling over and over. *The child tumbled down the stairs*.

tuna tunas *noun*
a huge ocean fish. *We eat tuna in sandwiches*.

tune tunes *noun*
a series of musical notes that are nice to listen to.

tunnel tunnels *noun*
a long hole under the ground or through a hill. *the Lincoln Tunnel*.
tunnel *verb*
The moles have tunneled large burrows in the backyard.

turban turbans *noun*
a long strip of material wound around the head.

turf *noun*
short, thick grass. *After the football game, the turf was torn up*.

turkey turkeys *noun*
a large bird that does not fly and that is usually raised on a farm for its meat.

ocellated turkey

common turkey

turn turns turning turned *verb*
1 When something turns, it moves around so that it faces in a different direction or goes in a different direction. *The car turned right at the traffic lights*. ◆ *He turned around and looked behind him*.
2 When something turns, it goes around. *The wheel turned*.

3 When you turn something, you turn it around. *She turned the handle*.
4 When something turns into something else, it changes to become that thing. *A caterpillar turns into a butterfly*.

turn turns *noun*
a time when you do something that other people have done before you and that other people will do after you. *It's my turn to use the computer*.

turtle turtles *noun*
a reptile with a hard shell that lives on land or in the water.

tusk tusks *noun*
a long, pointed tooth that comes right outside the mouth of an animal such as an elephant.

TV TVs *noun*
short for television. *She's upstairs watching TV*.

twice *adverb*
two times. *I've been to see the movie twice now. How many times have you seen it?*

twig twigs *noun*
a small branch of a tree.

twilight *noun*
a time after sunset before it gets completely dark. ▲ Say *twy-lite*.

twin twins *noun*
one of two people or animals who have the same mother and were born at the same time.

twinkle twinkles twinkling twinkled *verb*
When something twinkles, it shines with little flashes of light. *The stars were twinkling*.

A
B
C
D
E
F
G
H
I
J
K
L
M
N
O
P
Q
R
S
T
U
V
W
X
Y
Z

twirl twirls twirling twirled *verb*
to turn or spin round and round. *She twirled her hair around her fingers.* **twirl** *noun.*

twist twists twisting twisted *verb*
1 If you twist something, you turn it around and around. *She twisted the screwdriver to tighten the screw.*
2 When you twist something, you bend it or turn it around. *He twisted the wires together.*

twitch twitches twitching twitched *verb*
To twitch is to make a small, quick movement. *The big rabbit's nose*
suddenly twitched.
twitchy *adjective.*

tycoon tycoons *verb*
A tycoon is a rich and powerful businessman or businesswoman.

type types typing typed *verb*
When you type, you press the keys on a keyboard to write something. ▲ Rhymes with *pipe*.

type types *noun*
1 a kind of thing. *What type of apple is that?*

2 the size and style of printed letters and numbers. *big black type.*
▲ Rhymes with *pipe*.

typewriter typewriters *noun*
a machine with keys that you press to print letters and numbers on paper.

typhoon typhoon *noun*
a violent tropical storm of wind and rain. Typhoons usually happen in the western part of the Pacific Ocean.
▲ Say *ti-foon*.

typical *adjective*
A typical thing is the most usual of that kind of thing. *a typical Midwestern town.* ◆ *a typical summer storm.*
▲ Say *tip-i-cal*.

tyrannosaur tyrannosaurs *noun*
a huge dinosaur with small front legs, a large head, and sharp teeth. It walked on its hind legs and ate meat. ❖ **Look at page 125.**

tyrant tyrants *noun*
a cruel and unfair ruler.
tyrannical *adjective.*

U u

udder udders *noun*
the part of a cow, goat, or sheep that hangs under the its body, near the back legs, and that produces milk.

ugly uglier ugliest *adjective*
not pretty. ■ The opposite is **beautiful**.

ukulele ukuleles *noun*
a four-stringed Hawaiian guitar.

umbrella umbrellas *noun*
a thing that you hold over your head to stay dry when it rains. The frame of an
umbrella is covered with a round piece of material and joined to a long handle.

uncle uncles *noun*
Your uncle is the brother of your mother or your father, or the husband of your aunt.

unconscious *adjective*
1 If you are unconscious, you are in a kind of sleep and you do not know what is happening. *When she fell downstairs and hit her head, she was unconscious for an hour.* ■ The opposite is **conscious**.

uncover uncovers uncovering uncovered *verb*
1 When you uncover something, you take off the thing or things that cover it.

He uncovered the box and looked inside.
2 To uncover also means to find something that was hidden or not known about. *A skeleton was uncovered by a farmer digging in a field.* ◆ *The plot to blow up the building was uncovered.*

underground *adjective, adverb*
below the surface of the earth. *Rabbits build their burrows underground.*

undergrowth *noun*
all the bushes and other plants that grow under trees. *thick undergrowth.*

underline underlines underlining underlined *verb*
If you underline something, you draw a line under it to make people notice it. *Please write the date and <u>underline</u> it with a ruler.*

underneath *preposition*
below or under something. *I found my shoes underneath the bed.*

underpass underpasses *noun*
a road that goes underneath a railroad or another road.

understand **understands understanding understood** *verb*
to know what something means, how it works, or why it happens.

underwear *noun*
clothing such as a T-shirt and shorts that you wear under your other clothes.

undo **undoes undoing undid undone** *verb*
If you undo a package, you open it.

undress **undresses undressing undressed** *verb*
to take off clothes. ■ The opposite is **dress**.

unemployed *adjective*
A person who is unemployed does not have a job and is not working. **unemployment** *noun*.

uneven *adjective*
not straight or level. ■ The opposite is **even**.

unfair **unfairer unfairest** *adjective*
not just or fair. ■ The opposite is **fair**.

unfold **unfolds unfolding unfolded** *verb*
to open something out so that it lies flat.

unicorn **unicorns** *noun*
A unicorn is an imaginary animal similar to a horse but with one horn sticking out of the front of its head.

uniform **uniforms** *noun*
a set of clothes that people wear to show that they belong to the same group.

union **unions** *noun*
a group of workers that come together to talk to their managers about any problems at work.

unit **units** *noun*
1 one part of something.
2 an amount used in measuring or counting. *A foot is a unit of length, a pound is a unit of weight, and a minute is a unit of time.*
▲ Say **you**-nit.

unite **unites uniting united** *verb*
If things or people unite, they join together or do something together. *The colonists united to fight for independence.*
▲ Say you-**nite**.

universe *noun*
the Earth, the Sun, the Moon, and all the other planets and stars in space.

university **universities** *noun*
a place where people can go to study things when they finish high school. *Nancy wanted to go to the same university that her mother had gone to.*

unkind **unkinder unkindest** *adjective*
not nice to others. ■ The opposite is **kind**.

unlike *preposition*
not the same as. ■ The opposite is **like**.

unlikely **unlikelier unlikeliest** *adjective*
if something is unlikely, it is probably not going to happen. ■ The opposite is **likely**.

unload **unloads unloading unloaded** *verb*
To unload is to take things off a ship or vehicle. *The cargo was unloaded at the dock last Friday.* ■ The opposite is **load**.

unlock **unlocks unlocking unlocked** *verb*
When you unlock something, you turn a key to open it. ■ The opposite is **lock**.

untie **unties untying untied**
to undo knots. *Michael had to untie a lot of ribbon to open his presents.*

until *preposition*
up to a certain time or day. *Dad is in his office until six o'clock every evening.* ◆ *I can't come out to play on Saturday until I've cleaned up my room.*

unusual *adjective*
not ordinary. ■ The opposite is **normal** or **usual**.

upper *adjective*
above or higher than another thing. *He has a cut on his upper lip.*

upright *adjective, adverb*
If something like a bottle is upright, it is standing up, with the top facing upward.

upset **upsets upsetting upset** *verb*
1 If you upset people, you make them unhappy. *She upset me when she said my idea was dumb.*
2 If you upset something like a drink, you knock it over and spill it.

upside-down *adjective, adverb*
If something is upside-down, the bottom is at the top and the top is at the bottom. *This sloth is hanging upside-down.*

upstairs *adjective, adverb*
on or to an upper floor. *My bedroom is upstairs.*

A
B
C
D
E
F
G
H
I
J
K
L
M
N
O
P
Q
R
S
U
X
Y
Z

up-to-date *adjective*
new and modern. *News is information that is up-to-date.*

upward, upwards *adverb*
going to a higher place. *The balloon moved upward.*

urgent *adjective*
so very important that it must be done immediately. *She made an urgent phone call to the doctor.*
urgency *noun.*

use **uses using used** *verb*
1 If you use something, you do a job with it. *You use scissors to cut things.* ◆ *Do you know how to use your new computer?*
2 To use also means to take something. *Don't use all the glue.* ▲ Say **youzz**.
used to
1 If you used to do something, you did it before, but you do not do it now. *I used to go swimming every Tuesday, but now I play tennis.*

2 Used to can also mean knowing somebody or something well. *We are all used to her jokes.* ▲ *Say* **yoosd**-to.

use **uses** *noun*
what you can do with something. *This bag has many uses.* ▲ Say **youss**.

useful *adjective*
If people or things are useful, they help you in some way. *Ben was very useful and he helped with the baby.*
usefulness *noun.*

useless *adjective*
If something is useless, it is not good for anything and you cannot use it. *This bag is useless because the handle has broken.* ■ The opposite is **useful**.

usual *adjective*
If something is usual, it happens often or most of the time. ■ The opposite is **unusual**.
usually *adverb*
I usually go to school by bike.

utensil **utensils** *noun*
a tool or container, especially one used for cooking.

utter **utters uttering uttered** *verb*
To make a sound or to say something. *He uttered a cry of pain.*

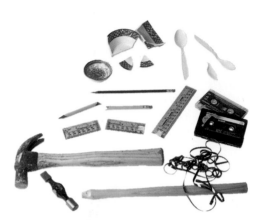

The broken objects are useless, but the others are useful, and will help you to do a job properly.

V v

vacant *adjective*
empty and not being used.
vacancy *noun*

vacation **vacations** *noun*
a time when you do not go to school or work and when you might travel to a nice place like a beach.

vaccination **vaccinations** *noun*
an injection that keeps you from getting an illness. ▲ Say *vak-si-nay-shun*.
vaccinate *verb.*

vacuum cleaner **vacuum cleaners** *noun*
a machine that sucks up dirt from rugs.

vague **vaguer vaguest** *adjective*
not clear or definite. ▲ Say **vayg**.

vain **vainer vainest** *adjective*
Vain people are too proud of themselves, especially of how they look.

valentine **valentines** *noun*
a special greeting card that you send to someone you like or love on February 14.

valley **valleys** *noun*
low land between hills or mountains.

valuable *adjective*
1 worth a lot of money. *a valuable necklace.*
2 useful and helpful. *He gave me some valuable advice.*

value *noun*
1 the amount of money that something is worth. *What is the value of your house?*
2 how useful and helpful something is. *The instructions you gave were of great value in helping me to make the machine work.*

vampire **vampires** *noun*
in stories, a dead person who drinks people's blood.

van **vans** *noun*
a small, covered motor vehicle with doors at the back and on the sides.

vandal **vandals** *noun*
a person who breaks or damages property on purpose. *Vandals have smashed the telephone booth.*

vanilla *noun*
a flavor that comes from the pod of a tropical plant and is used in sweet foods. *vanilla ice cream.*

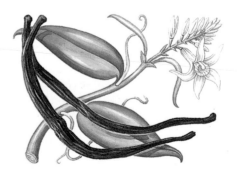

vanish **vanishes vanishing vanished** *verb*
If something vanishes, it suddenly disappears.

vanity *noun*
being vain and very proud of what you look like.

variety **varieties** *noun*
1 a number of different kinds of something. *They had a variety of skirts and dresses in the sale.*
2 a kind or sort of thing. *There are lots of different varieties of breakfast cereal.*
3 a lot of different things happening. *I like a lot of variety in my life.*
▲ Say *ver-eye-i-tee.*

different varieties of breakfast cereal

various *adjective*
several different things. *You can buy these towels in various colors.* ▲ Say *vair-ee-us.*

varsity *adjective*
A varsity team is the first, or main, team of players in a sport.

vary **varies varying varied** *verb*
If something varies, it keeps changing. *I take sandwiches to school every day, but what goes in them varies.* ▲ Say *vair-ee.*

vase **vases** *noun*
a jar or container for putting flowers in.
▲ Say *vase.*

vast **vaster vastest** *adjective*
very, very large. *The Sahara is a vast desert.*

vegetable **vegetables** *noun*
a plant that people eat. Cabbages, carrots, and potatoes are vegetables.
▲ Say *vej-te-bul.* ❖ Look at page 178

vegetarian **vegetarians** *noun*
a person who does not eat meat or fish.
▲ Say *veg-e-tair-ee-un.*

vehicle **vehicles** *noun*
a thing that takes people or goods from one place to another. Buses, cars, trucks, and trains are all vehicles.
▲ Say *vee-i-cul.*

veil **veils** *noun*
a piece of material that some women wear over their faces or heads.

vein **veins** *noun*
one of the tubes in your body that carries blood back to your heart.

velvet *noun*
cloth that is thick and soft on one side.

verb **verbs** *noun*
a word that tells you what somebody or something does or what is happening. Think, run, and cut are all verbs. *What are you thinking?*

verdict **verdicts** *noun*
what the jury, and sometimes the judge, decide at the end of a trial in a court.

verse **verses** *noun*
a part of a poem or song made of several lines.

version **versions** *noun*
1 a changed form of something. *We bought a new version of the computer game.*
2 one person's way of telling a story or what happened that is a little different from other people's. *In Harry's version of the story, the bull didn't chase her to the gate, she just ran.*

vertical *adjective*
standing straight up. *a vertical post.*
■ The opposite is **horizontal**.

vessel **vessels** *noun*
1 a ship or large boat.
2 a container for liquid.

vest **vests** *noun*
clothing with no sleeves that you wear under a jacket or over a blouse.

vet **vets** *noun*
a person whose job is to treat animals and help them to get well when they are sick or hurt.

viaduct **viaducts** *noun*
a long bridge that carries a road or railway over a valley. ▲ Say *veye-a-duct.*

vibrate **vibrates vibrating vibrated** *verb*
When something vibrates, it shakes very quickly. *The floor vibrated every time a train went past.* ▲ Say *veye-brate.*
vibration *noun.*

Vice-President **Vice-Presidents** *noun*
the second highest official in the U.S. government.
Vice-Presidency *noun.*

vicious *adjective*
cruel and violent. *a vicious attack.*
▲ Say *vish-us.*

victim **victims** *noun*
a person who has been attacked, hurt, robbed, or killed.

victory **victories** *noun*
a success in winning a battle or game.

video **videos** *noun*
a tape used to record a movie or something on television.

videocassette recorder (VCR) **videocassette recorders (VCRs)** *noun*
a machine that you use to record a TV program and play it back later.

view **views** *noun*
1 what you can see from one place. *We had a good view of the mountains.*
2 a person's opinion or what he or she thinks about something. *In my view, he fell over because he wasn't looking where he was going.* ▲ Say *vyou.*

vile **viler vilest** *adjective*
horrible. *That color is vile.*

village **villages** *noun*
a group of houses and other buildings in the country. *Villages are smaller than towns.*

villain **villains** *noun*
a very bad person, especially in a movie, story, or play. *The villain was killed at the end of the movie.* ▲ Say *vil-un.*

vine **vines** *noun*
a climbing plant that grapes grow on.

vinegar *noun*
a sour liquid used to add flavor to food.

A B C D E F G H I J K L M N O P Q R S T U V W X Y Z

VEGETABLES

1 savoy cabbage	9 broccoli	17 parsnips	25 celery
2 white cabbage	10 artichoke	18 zucchini	26 butternut squash
3 cauliflower	11 yam	19 carrot	27 green onions
4 pumpkin	12 lettuce	20 red onion	28 cucumber
5 lollo rosso	13 snow peas	21 string bean	29 sweet potato
6 leek	14 peas	22 brussels sprouts	30 rutabaga
7 corn	15 flat beans	23 potato	
8 asparagus	16 French beans	24 radish	

a b c d e f g h i j k l m n o p q r s t u v w x y z

vineyard vineyards *noun*
a place where grape vines are grown for making wine. ▲ Say **vin**-*yard*.

violent *adjective*
1 a violent person uses force or weapons to hurt somebody else.
2 very strong or rough. *a violent storm.*

violet violets *noun*
a small plant with small white or purple flowers.

violin violins *noun*
a musical instrument with strings stretched across a wooden frame. *You play a violin by holding it under your chin and moving a stick called a bow across the strings.*
violinist *noun.*

virtual reality *noun*
an image made by a computer that surrounds you and that looks real.

virtue *noun*
a kind of goodness. *Honesty is a virtue.*

virus viruses *noun*
1 a tiny germ that causes a disease. *Colds and flu are caused by viruses.*
2 a computer program that damages the data in a computer system.

visible *adjective*
If something is visible, you can see it. ▲ Say **viz**-*i-bul*. ■ The opposite is **invisible**.

vision *noun*
a person's ability to see. *He has excellent vision.* ▲ Say **vish**-*un*.

visit visits visiting visited *verb*
If you visit people somewhere, you go to see them. *Matt visited his friend Tom in the hospital.*
visitor *noun.*

vitamin vitamins *noun*
one of the substances that are in food naturally that you need to keep healthy.

vocabulary vocabularies *noun*
1 all the words that somebody knows.
2 a list of words and what they mean.

voice voices *noun*
the sound that you make when you speak or sing.

volcano volcanoes *noun*
a mountain with an opening called a crater in the top, from which very hot melted rock and gases sometimes pour out.

ash and smoke

lava

magma chamber

Earth's layers

volume volumes *noun*
1 the amount of space inside something or the amount of space that something takes up. *What's the volume of that gasoline can?*
2 a book in a set of books. *The first volume of a 20-volume encyclopedia.*
3 how loud a sound is. *Will you please turn down the volume of your radio?*

volunteer volunteers *noun*
a person who does something without being paid and without being made to do it. *hospital volunteers.*

vote votes voting voted *verb*
If you vote for people, you choose them by putting your hand up, by making a mark on a piece of paper, or by using a special machine. *Have you voted yet?*
voter *noun.*

vowel vowels *noun*
the letters a, e, i, o, u, and sometimes y are vowels.

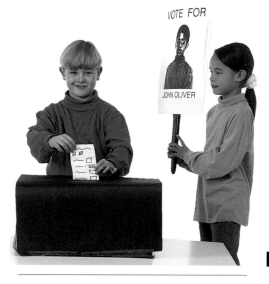

VOTE FOR

JOHN OLIVER

voyage voyages *noun*
a long journey by sea or in space. ▲ Say **voy**-*ij*.
voyager *noun.*

vulture vultures *noun*
a very large bird that eats dead animals. *The California condor is a kind of vulture.*

A B C D E F G H I J K L M N O P Q R S T U V W X Y Z

W w

wade wades wading waded *verb*
To wade is to walk through deep water. *He waded across the stream.*

wag wags wagging wagged *verb*
When a dog wags its tail, it moves it quickly from side to side and up and down.

wages *noun*
the money that people are paid for the work they do.

wagon wagons *noun*
a cart that is used to carry people and things from one place to another. It has four wheels and is usually pulled along by horses.

wail wails wailing wailed *verb*
If somebody wails, the person shouts or makes a sad cry because he or she is hurt or sad.

waist waists *noun*
Your waist is the narrow, middle part of your body. *Jack is wearing a belt around his waist.*

waistline *noun*
what your body measures around your waist.

wait waits waiting waited *verb*
If you wait, you stay where you are because you are expecting something. *We waited half an hour for the bus.*

waiter waiters *noun*
a person who brings you food in a coffee shop or restaurant.

wake wakes waking woke or waked *verb*
1 When you wake, you stop sleeping. *I woke up at seven o'clock.*
2 When you wake someone, you make them stop sleeping. *I woke him at five o'clock.*

walk walks walking walked *verb*
When you walk, you move along on your feet. *I walk to the park every day.*
walk *noun*
We took the dog for a walk.

wall walls *noun*
1 one of the sides of a building or a room. *I helped to paint my bedroom walls.*
2 A wall is also something made of bricks or stones that you can see around some gardens. *We climbed over the wall into the secret garden.*

wallet wallets *noun*
a small, flat case for keeping paper money and credit cards in.

wand wands *noun*
a stick that fairies and magicians wave when they do magic. *The fairy princess waved her magic wand.*

wander wanders wandering wandered *verb*
When you wander, you walk around slowly without going in any particular direction. *We wandered around in the woods looking for mushrooms to study in our science class.*

want wants wanting wanted *verb*
When you want something, you need it or you would like to have it. *Do you want an apple or an orange?*

war wars *noun*
a time when armies of different countries are fighting. ■ The opposite is **peace**.

ward wards *noun*
a big part of a hospital. *a surgical ward.*

wardrobe wardrobes *noun*
a person's clothes. *She has a big wardrobe of winter clothes.*

warehouse warehouses *noun*
a building where goods are kept before they are taken to stores or other places. *It took a few weeks to get our new sofa from the furniture warehouse.*

warm warmer warmest *adjective*
quite hot but not too hot. *The cat sat by the fire to keep warm.* ■ The opposite is **cool**.
warmth *noun*
I felt the warmth of the sun on my skin.

warn warns warning warned *verb*
If you warn people, you tell them about something dangerous or bad that may happen. *He warned us not to swim in the river because it was very deep.* ◆ *Dad warned us not to be late or he'd get upset.*

warning warnings *noun*
something that tells you about a danger that may happen. *The sign on the gate said, "Warning! Keep out—dangerous bull in field."*

wart warts *noun*
a hard lump on your skin. ▲ Rhymes with **sort**.

wash washes washing washed *verb*
When you wash something, you use soap and water to clean it. *He washed his face before going to bed.*

wash *noun*
laundry; clothes that you need to wash or that you have washed. *I put the wash in the washing machine.*

washing machine washing machines *noun*
a machine that washes, rinses, and spins laundry; a washer.

wasp wasps *noun*
a flying insect with a narrow middle part of its body. Wasps can sting you.

waste *noun*

1 What is left after you have digested your food and that is sent out of your body.

2 garbage and trash.

3 Something is a waste when you use too much of it, or do not use it carefully. *It's a waste to throw food away.*

waste **wastes wasting wasted** *verb*

1 If you waste something, you use more than you need. *Don't waste water by letting the hose run.*

2 To waste also means not to make good use of something. *Don't waste time watching too much TV.*

watch **watches watching watched** *verb*

If you watch something, you look at it for a long time. *We watched the football game.* ◆ *Watch how I do this trick.*

watch **watches** *noun* a small clock that you wear around your wrist.

water *noun*

the clear liquid that is in seas, lakes, and rivers. *All living things need water.*

water **waters watering watered** *verb*

When you water plants, you pour water over them to help them grow.

waterfall **waterfalls** *noun*

a place on a river where a lot of water falls over high rocks or down a mountain. *Niagara Falls is the most famous waterfall in North America.*

waterproof *adjective*

If something is waterproof, it does not let water go through it. *a waterproof jacket.*

wave **waves** *noun*

1 a curved line of water moving across a sea. *The waves crashed up onto the shore.*

2 a vibrating movement like a wave on the sea that carries sound or light. *sound waves.*

3 a curving shape in your hair.

4 a movement with your hand that you make when you say "hello" or "good-bye" to somebody.

wave **waves waving waved** *verb*

When you wave, you move your hand up and down to say hello or good-bye to somebody. *My sister waved good-bye as she got on the bus.*

wax *noun*

material that candles are made out of. Wax is hard when it is cold but it gets soft and melts when you heat it.

weak **weaker weakest** *adjective*

1 a weak person or thing has little power or strength. *She felt weak after her illness.* ◆ *weak knees.*

2 likely to break very easily. *That branch is too weak to support your weight.*

3 A weak drink has a lot of water or milk in it. *weak tea.*

■ The opposite is **powerful** or **strong**.

● A word that sounds like **weak** is **week**.

wealthy **wealthier wealthiest** *adjective*

rich. *wealthy businessmen.*

weapon **weapons** *noun*

something such as a gun, a spear, a sword, or a bow and arrow that people use to fight with.

wear **wears wearing wore worn** *verb*

1 When you wear clothes, you have them on your body. *Lindsay is wearing a blue dress.* ◆ *Steve wore jeans.*

2 When something wears out, you cannot use it any more because it is broken or too old. *These socks are worn out—they have holes in them.*

3 When something wears you out, it makes you very tired. *After running all the way to school, I was worn out.*

weather *noun*

The weather is how hot, cold, windy, rainy, or dry it is outside. *The weather forecast tells you what the weather will be like for the next few days.*

weave **weaves weaving wove woven** *noun*

1 When you weave, you make a piece of cloth using a machine called a loom. The loom has rows of thread fixed at each end and you move another thread in and out of these.

2 To weave also means to make something like a basket or a mat by twisting thin strips of wood or straw in and out of each other.

web **webs** *noun*

a net that a spider makes to catch flies.

web-footed *adjective*

having feet with a piece of skin between the toes, such as geese and ducks have.

wedding **weddings** *noun*

When two people get married, they have a ceremony called a wedding.

a
b
c
d
e
f
g
h
i
j
k
l
m
n
o
p
q
r
s
t
u
v
w
x
y
z

weed weeds *noun*
a wild plant that grows in the garden and that you do not want. *Thistles are weeds.*

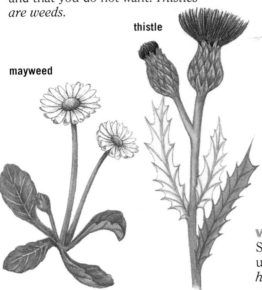

mayweed

thistle

week weeks *noun*
a measure of time. There are seven days in a week – Monday, Tuesday, Wednesday, Thursday, Friday, Saturday, and Sunday. There are 52 weeks in a year. ● A word that sounds like **week** is **weak**.

weekend weekends *noun*
Saturday and Sunday.

weep weeps weeping wept *verb*
If people weep, they cry. *She wept because her cat had died.*

weigh weighs weighing weighed *verb*
1 You weigh something on scales to find out how heavy it is.
2 Weigh also means how heavy you are. *How much do you weigh?*

weight weights *noun*
1 how heavy somebody or something is. *What's the weight of these apples?*
2 a piece of metal weighing a certain amount that you use on scales to find out how heavy something is.
weighty *adjective*
a weighty problem.

weird weirder weirdest *adjective*
Something that is very strange or unusual. *I heard a weird noise in the house last night.*

welcome welcomes welcoming welcomed *verb*
If you welcome people, you show that you are happy to see them. *She came to the door to welcome us.*

well better best *adjective, adverb*
1 When you do something well, you do it in a good way. *Gerry plays the guitar very well.*
2 If you are well, you feel healthy.

well wells *noun*
a well is a deep hole in the ground with water or oil at the bottom.

wept past of **weep**.

west *noun*
1 the direction in which the Sun sets in the evening. ■ The opposite is **east**, **eastern**.
2 The West is the part of the United States that used to be the frontier. *The West has lots of open spaces like prairies and deserts.*
west *adjective*, **western** *adjective*
west *adverb*
The boat was sailing west.

western westerns *noun*
a movie or a book about cowboys and the Wild West.

wet wetter wettest *adjective*
Something that is wet is covered with or full of water or other liquid. *You will get wet if you go out in the rain.* ■ The opposite is **dry**.

whale whales *noun*
a very large mammal that lives in the sea. Whales need air to breathe. A young whale is called a calf.

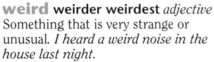

Blue whales

wheat *noun*
a plant that farmers grow. We use its seeds, called grain, to make flour.

wheel wheels *noun*
A wheel is a round thing on something like a car, truck, or bicycle. Wheels turn around and around to move things along the ground.

wheelchair wheelchairs *noun*
a special chair with wheels for somebody who cannot walk very well.

whether *conjunction*
If. *I don't know whether I can come tonight.*

whine whines whining whined *verb*
To whine is to make a long, miserable sound because you want something.

whip whips whipping whipped *verb*
1 If you whip others, you hit them with a long piece of rope or leather.
2 To whip also means to stir cream or eggs very fast until they become stiff.

whisk whisks whisking whisked *verb*
When you whisk things such as eggs or cream, you beat them very quickly. **whisk** *noun*.

whisker whiskers *noun*
one of the long hairs that cats, mice, and some other animals have on their faces.

whisper whispers whispering whispered *verb*
When you whisper, you speak very quietly so that other people cannot hear you. *She whispered in his ear.*

whistle whistles *noun*
1 an instrument that you blow into to make very high sounds. *He blew a whistle to end the football game.*
2 a high sound that you make when you blow through your lips.
whistle *verb*.

whole *adjective*
all of something. *He ate the whole cake.*
● A word that sounds like **whole** is **hole**. ■ The opposite is **part**.
whole *noun*
Two halves make a whole.

wick wicks *noun*
a piece of string that goes through the middle of a candle. When you light the wick, the candle burns.

wicked wickeder wickedest *adjective*
very bad or cruel. *In the fairy-tale, Snow White's stepmother was a wicked witch.*

wide wider widest *adjective*
1 Something that is wide measures a lot from one side to the other. *Freeways are very wide roads.*
■ The opposite is **narrow**.
2 Wide also means how much something measures. *The window is three feet wide.*

widow widows *noun*
a woman whose husband is dead.

widower widowers *noun*
a man whose wife is dead.

width *noun*
how wide something is. *He measured from side to side to find the width of the box.*

wife wives *noun*
A man's wife is the woman he is married to.

wig wigs *noun*
a thing made of hair that covers your head. Actors and bald people sometimes wear wigs.

wild wilder wildest *adjective*
1 Wild animals are animals that are not kept by people for food or as pets. Foxes and badgers are wild animals.
■ The opposite is **tame**.
2 Wildflowers and plants are not planted by people.

will wills *noun*
the part of your mind that makes you want to do things or decide what you want to do. *She has the will to win the race.* ◆ *He cleaned his bedroom against his will.*

willing *adjective*
If you are willing, you are ready and happy to do what is wanted. *Are you willing to go to the stores for me?*

willow willows *noun*
a tree with long, narrow leaves that grows near water. Weeping willows have thin branches that hang downward.

wilt wilts wilting wilted *verb*
If a plant wilts, it droops because it needs water.

win wins winning won *verb*
When you win a race or game you come first and do better than everybody else. *Karen won the marathon.*

wind winds *noun*
air that is moving very fast. *The wind blew the sailboat along.* ▲ Rhymes with **tinned**.
windy *adjective*.
windy weather.

wind winds winding wound *verb*
1 When you wind a clock or a watch, you turn a key or a knob so that it starts working.
2 When you wind something like string around another thing, you twist it around and around. *They wound the yarn into a ball.*
3 When a road or a river winds, it has lots of bends in it.
4 When you wind a film or a tape, you move it backward or forward. *Remember to wind the film on before you take the next picture.*
▲ Rhymes with **find**.

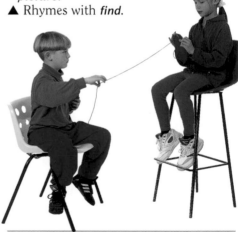

windmill windmills *noun*
a tall building with large pieces of wood, called sails, on top that turn around in the wind. As the sails turn, they make machines inside work to grind corn into flour or to make electricity.

A B C D E F G H I J K L M N O P Q R S T U V W X Y Z

window windows *noun*
a hole covered by glass in a wall of a building that lets in light and air.

windshield windshields *noun*
the window at the front of a car.

windsurf windsurfs windsurfing windsurfed *verb*
To windsurf is to ride over water on a special board with a sail.
windsurfer *noun*.

wine wines *noun*
Wine is an alcoholic drink usually made from grapes.

wing wings *noun*
1 Birds, bats, and insects like bees have wings that they flap when they fly around.
2 The wings of an airplane are the two flat parts on each side that help it move through the air.

wink winks winking winked *verb*
If you wink at somebody, you close and open one eye very quickly. *She winked at me to show that it was a joke.*

winter *noun*
the season of the year between fall and spring. Winter is the coldest part of the year.

wipe wipes wiping wiped *verb*
When you wipe something, you move a cloth over it to clean or dry it. *I wiped the table clean after dinner.*

wire wires *noun*
a long, thin piece of metal that bends easily. Copper wire is used to carry electricity. Many fences are made of wire.

wise wiser wisest *adjective*
A person who is wise knows and understands a lot about many things. *Mom says you get wiser as you get older.*
wisdom *noun*.

wish wishes wishing wished *verb*
If you wish for something, you want to have it or you want it to happen very much. *I wish I were good at sports.*
wish *noun*.

witch witches *noun*
a woman in fairy stories who has magic powers. *The prince rescued the princess from the wicked witch.*

wither withers withering withered *verb*
When a plant withers, it becomes dry and dies. *The flowers withered and died in the hot sun.*

witness witnesses *noun*
a person who sees something important happen and can tell other people about it later. The *police are looking for a witness to the accident.*

wives plural of **wife**.

wizard wizards *noun*
a man in fairy stories who has magic powers.

wobble wobbles wobbling wobbled *verb*
When something wobbles, it shakes a little from side to side. *The jelly wobbled on the plate.*
wobbly *adjective*.

woke past of **wake**.

wolf wolves *noun*
a wild animal that looks like a big dog, with a pointed nose and pointed ears. Wolves hunt in groups called packs. A young wolf is called a cub.

woman women *noun*
a grown-up female person.

won past of **win**.

wonder wonders wondering wondered *verb*
To wonder is to think about something that you do not know the answer to. *I wonder why snakes have no feet.*
wonder *noun*
They gazed with wonder at the fireworks.

wonderful *adjective*
very beautiful or very good. *We had a wonderful vacation.*

wood woods *noun*
the material that trees are made of. Tables and chairs are usually made of wood. You can also use wood to make paper.
wooden *adjective*
a wooden table.

woodpecker woodpeckers *noun*
a bird with a sharp beak. It makes holes in wood and in trees.

woods *noun*
a place where a lot of trees grow near each other.

wool wools *noun*
the soft, thick hair that grows on sheep. Wool is used for making cloth and for knitting.
woolen *adjective*
woolen gloves.
woolly *adjective*

word words *noun*
We use words when we speak or write. Words are made of letters of the alphabet and each word means something. *Angela looked up the meaning of a word in the dictionary.*

wore past of **wear**.

work works working worked *verb*
1 When you work, you do or make something as a job. *Wendy works in a fast-food restaurant.*
2 To work also means to do something that takes a lot of time and effort. *I worked hard to finish the essay.*
3 When a machine works, it does what it should do. *The radio isn't working.*
work *noun*.

world *noun*
1 the planet that we live on, and all its countries and people.
2 the universe.

worm worms *noun*
a small creature with a long, thin body and no legs. Many worms live in the dirt in gardens.

worn past of **wear**

worry worries worrying worried *verb*
If you worry, you keep thinking of bad things that might happen. *Dad worries when I'm home late from school.*

worship worships worshiping worshiped *verb*
To worship is to pray to God or Allah.

worth *adjective*
having a certain value. If something is worth $80, you could sell it for $80. *This bike is worth $80.*

wound wounds wounding wounded *verb*
To wound is to hurt or injure somebody. *He was shot and wounded in the leg.*
▲ Say **wooned**.
wound *noun*.

wound past of **wind**
▲ Say **wownd**.

wove, woven past of **weave**.

wrap wraps wrapping wrapped *verb*
If you wrap something, you cover it with paper or cloth. *He wrapped up the birthday present.* ◆ *She wrapped the baby in a light blanket.*

wreck wrecks wrecking wrecked *verb*
To wreck is to break or destroy something completely so that you cannot use it. *The fire wrecked the house.*

wreck wrecks *noun*
a car, boat, or an aircraft that has been badly damaged in an accident.

wreckage wreckages *noun*
the broken parts of something that has been badly damaged.

wrench wrenches *noun*
a tool for tightening and undoing pieces of metal.

wrestle wrestles wrestling wrestled *verb*
To wrestle is to fight with somebody and

try to push the person onto the ground.

wring wrings wringing wrung *verb*
If you wring something that is wet, you twist and squeeze it to get water out of it. *He wrung the clothes and hung them out to dry.*

wrinkle wrinkles *noun*
a crease or line in your skin. *The old man's face was full of wrinkles.*
wrinkle *verb*
He wrinkled his forehead.
wrinkled *adjective*
wrinkled skin.

wrist wrists *noun*
Your wrist is the thin part of your arm just above your hand.

write writes writing wrote written *verb*
When you write, you make words with a pen or pencil. *Tom wrote his name at the top of the paper.* ● A word that sounds like **write** is **right**.
writer *noun*.

writing *noun*
the words that you make on paper with a pen or pencil. *Rosemary has very neat writing.*

wrong *adjective*
1 If something is wrong, it is incorrect. *The answer to that problem is wrong.* ■ The opposite is **right**.
2 bad. *Being unkind to animals is wrong.*

wrung past of **wring**.

Sumo wrestlers

A B C D E F G H I J K L M N O P Q R S T U V W X Y Z

175

X x

X-ray **X rays** *noun*
a picture that shows the bones and other parts inside your body so that doctors can see if anything is broken or damaged.
X-ray *adjective,* **x-ray** *verb*

xylophone **xylophones** *noun*
a musical instrument with a row of wooden or metal bars of different lengths that you hit to give notes.
▲ Say *zy-lo-fone.*

Y y

yacht **yachts** *noun*
a large boat with sails or an engine.

yard **yards** *noun*
There are three feet in a yard.

yawn **yawns** **yawning** **yawned** *verb*
When you yawn, you open your mouth wide and breathe in as you do when you are very tired.

year **years** *noun*
a measure of time. There are 12 months in a year.
yearly *adjective, adverb*
a yearly visit.

yeast *noun*
a substance that is used to make bread rise.

yell **yells** **yelling** **yelled** *verb*
If you yell, you shout very loudly.

yogurt *noun*
a thick, slightly sour liquid made from milk. ▲ Say *yoh-gert.*

yoke **yokes** *noun*
a wooden frame that goes across the back of two oxen pulling a plow or cart to make them stay together.
● A word that sounds like **yoke** is **yolk.**

yolk **yolks** *noun*
the yellow part inside an egg.
▲ Say *yoke.*

young **younger** **youngest** *adjective*
not having lived for many years or for as many years as somebody else. *I'm younger than my grandpa.*
▲ Say *yung.*
■ The opposite is **old.**

youth **youths** *noun*
1 a time when a person is young. *He spent his youth in Oregon and in Montana.*
2 a young man.
3 all young people. *the youth of today.*
◆ *a youth program.*
▲ Say *yooth.*

Z z

zap **zapping** **zapped** *verb*
To zap is to shoot somebody or destroy something in a computer game.

zebra **zebras** *noun*
an animal like a horse with black and white stripes. Zebras live in Africa.

zero **zeros** *noun*
the number 0. You write ten with a one and a zero – 10.

zinc *noun*
a hard, blue-white metal. *A coating of zinc protects iron and steel from rust.*

Zip Code **Zip Codes** *noun*
a set of numbers at the end of your address on an envelope or a package that comes after the name of your state. It tells the Postal Service where you live.

zipper **zippers** *noun*
two long strips of fabric with metal or plastic teeth that fit together to fasten two edges of material. *Pants and skirts often have zippers.*
zip *verb*

zombie **zombies** *noun*
in stories, a dead body brought back to life by witchcraft. *Stories about zombies are used in horror movies.*

zone **zones** *noun*
an area in a town or a country used for a special purpose. *a work zone.* ◆ *a no-parking zone.*

zoo **zoos** *noun*
a place where wild animals are kept so that people can look at them.
❖ *Look opposite*

zoology *noun*
the scientific study of animals.
▲ Say *zoh-ol-uh-jee.*
zoological *adjective,* **zoologist** *noun*
zoological gardens. ◆ *Tom wanted to be a zoologist and to make a special study of animals from the rain forest.*

zoom **zooms** **zooming** **zoomed** *verb*
If something zooms, it moves very fast. *The rocket zoomed into space.*

a b c d e f g h i j k l m n o p q r s t u v w x y z

The Kingfisher
Children's
Illustrated
Thesaurus

A a

abandon *v.* forsake, give up, leave in the lurch, surrender, sacrifice ▷*leave, quit*

abate *v.* lessen, slacken, dwindle, fade

abbey *n.* monastery, priory, cloister, church

abbreviate *v.* shorten, cut, contract, reduce ▷*abridge* ★**expand**

abdicate *v.* resign, retire, renounce ▷*quit*

ability *n.* aptitude, knack, flair, talent, gift, skill ★**inability**

able *adj.* skillful, competent, talented, strong ▷*clever* ★**incapable**

abnormal *adj.* unusual, exceptional, erratic ★**normal**

abode *n.* home, residence, haunt, dwelling, lodging

abolish *v.* destroy, cancel, do away with, exterminate ★**restore**

abominable *adj.* detestable, foul, hateful, horrible, loathsome, atrocious ▷*awful* ★**desirable**

about *prep. & adv.* near, nearly, touching, concerning, around

above *prep. & adv.* over, beyond, exceeding, on high, aloft ★**below**

abridge *v.* condense, compact ▷*abbreviate*

abroad *adv.* overseas, far, away, apart, adrift ★**home**

abrupt *adj.* ① sudden, curt, blunt, brusque ② steep, hilly ★**smooth**

absent *adj.* not present, away, elsewhere, missing ★**present**

absent-minded *adj.* distracted, heedless, forgetful ★**attentive**

absolute *adj.* perfect, complete, certain, positive ▷*utter* ★**imperfect**

absorb *v.* take in, soak up, assimilate, devour, pull in, swallow, consume ★**emit**

absorbed *adj.* intent, rapt, engrossed, preoccupied

abstain *adj.* refuse, refrain, give up, keep from, avoid, forbear ★**indulge**

abstract ① *adj.* theoretical, intangible ② *v.* withdraw, steal, remove, take away

absurd *adj.* preposterous, nonsensical, foolish ▷*silly* ★**sensible**

abundant *adj.* ample, profuse, rich, plentiful, overflowing ★**scarce**

abuse ① *v.* damage, injure, spoil, maltreat, hurt, misuse ★**protect** ② *n.* mistreatment, attack

accelerate *v.* speed up, hasten, quicken, urge ▷*hurry* ★**delay**

accent *n.* ① stress, beat, rhythm, emphasis ② dialect, brogue *Eileen speaks with an Irish brogue,* drawl, pronunciation

accept *v.* receive, take, admit, adopt, take on ★**refuse**

accident *n.* chance, casualty, disaster, calamity, mishap ★**purpose**

acclaim *v.* applaud, praise, approve ★**denounce**

accommodate *v.* oblige, lodge, receive, admit, adapt ★**deprive**

accompany *v.* be with, go with, escort, attend, convoy ★**abandon**

accomplice *n.* ally, confederate, helper, partner, conspirator

accomplish *v.* perform, fulfill, finish, complete ▷*achieve* ★**fail**

accord ① *v.* agree, consent, harmonize, allow ★**differ** ② *n.* agreement, harmony

account *n.* ① bill, invoice, record, score ② tale, story *Mary told us the story of her trip to Washington,* narrative, history

accumulate *v.* collect, grow, gather, hoard, increase, amass ★**scatter**

accurate *adj.* careful, exact, faithful, precise ▷*correct* ★**defective**

accuse *v.* charge, incriminate, taunt, denounce ★**defend**

accustom *v.* acclimatize, get used to, familiarize ★**estrange**

ache ① *n.* pain, twinge ② *v.* hurt, pain, sting, smart

achieve *v.* fulfill, accomplish, reach ▷*attain* ★**fail**

achievement *n.* accomplishment, attainment, exploit, deed, completion ▷*feat*

acid *adj.* sharp, vinegarish, acrid, sour, tart ★**sweet, mellow**

a b c d e f g h i j k l m n o p q r s t u v w x y z

acknowledge *v.* admit, avow, recognize, own, accept, yield ★**disclaim**

acquaint *v.* inform, tell, teach, notify, advise ★ **deceive**

acquaintance *n.* ① friend, pal, associate ② knowledge *You will need some knowledge of Spanish if you visit Mexico,* familiarity, experience

acquainted *adj.* aware, familiar, informed

acquire *v.* gain, earn, obtain, get, capture ★**forfeit, lose**

acquit *v.* discharge, release, exonerate, dismiss, liberate ★**accuse**

acrid *adj.* bitter, harsh, sour ▷*acid* ★**mellow**

across *adj. & prep.* crosswise, athwart, slantingly, over against ★**along**

act ① *n.* deed, performance, action, step, presentation ② *v.* operate, work, function, perform *Our class will perform a play by Ibsen*

action *n.* operation, movement, feat, deed, exercise ★**rest**

actual *adj.* correct, true, positive, certain ★**possible**

acute *adj.* sharp, pointed, keen, penetrating, severe, distressing ★**blunt**

adapt *v.* fit, adjust, accommodate, suit, conform

adaptable *adj.* flexible, usable, adjustable

add *v.* ① total, combine, tote up ★**subtract** ② affix, annex, connect ★**detach**

address ① *n.* residence, place, home, domicile ② *v.* talk to, speak to, accost, call

adept *adj.* expert, adroit, handy, skillful ▷*clever* ★**clumsy**

adequate *adj.* ① sufficient, ample *The boat was small, but there was ample room for two*, plenty ② equal, able, qualified

adjacent *adj.* near, neighboring, next, bordering, touching ★**separate**

adjoin *v.* border, touch, verge, annex

adjust *v.* ① regulate, rectify, correct, amend, revise ② get used to *Our puppy quickly got used to her new home*

administer *v.* ① execute, perform, carry out, conduct, direct, manage ② give, dole out

The nurse doled out the pills each morning

admirable *adj.* praiseworthy, commendable, excellent ★**despicable**

admiration *n.* adoration, affection, approval, delight, respect ★**contempt**

admire *v.* approve, esteem, appreciate ▷*respect* ★**despise**

admit *v.* ① pass, permit, grant, concede, allow, let in, acknowledge ② confess, own up ★**deny**

ado *n.* hubbub, commotion, fuss *Let's start the meeting without any more fuss,* excitement

adopt *v.* assume, select, choose, employ, apply, take over

adore *v.* worship, idolize, admire, revere, venerate ★**despise**

adorn *v.* beautify, decorate, embellish, deck, garnish ★**deface**

adrift *adv.* loose, afloat, floating, distracted

adroit *adj.* handy, skillful, dexterous, expert ▷*adept* ★**awkward**

adult *adj.* grown-up, mature, full-grown ★**immature**

advance *v.* ① progress, increase, further, go,

Adequate

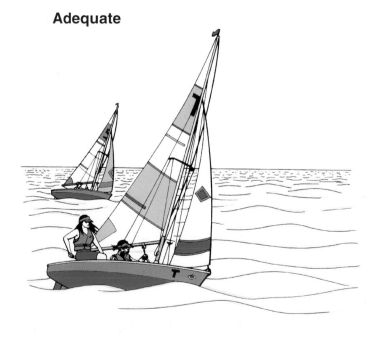

The boat was small, but there was ample room for two.

A B C D E F G H I J K L M N O P Q R S T U V W X Y Z

go on, proceed ★**retreat** ② lend *Helen said she will lend me the money,* loan

advanced *adj.* beforehand, ahead, modern

advantage *n.* benefit, upper hand, opportunity, assistance, boon ★**hindrance**

adventure *n.* experience, escapade, venture, undertaking

adversary *n.* foe, opponent, antagonist, rival ▷*enemy* ★**ally**

adverse *adj.* unfavorable, hard, hostile, unfortunate ▷*unlucky* ★**fortunate**

advice *n.* counsel, suggestion, guidance

advise *v.* counsel, urge, suggest, prompt, inform, persuade ★**deter**

afar *adv.* far, far off, away, abroad ★**near**

affable *adj.* courteous, gracious, easy, frank, open ★**haughty**

affair *n.* ① matter, business, concern ② romance, liaison

affect *v.* ① assume, adopt, feign, sham, put on airs ② influence, change, sway *Your argument did not sway my opinion*

affection *n.* desire, fondness, feeling, kindness, liking ▷*love* ★**indifference**

affectionate *adj.* warmhearted, fond, loving ▷*tender* ★**indifferent**

affirm *v.* assert, state, declare, endorse, maintain ★**deny**

affix *v.* attach, fasten, unite, append ★**detach**

afflict *v.* trouble, ail, distress, upset

afford *v.* ① be wealthy, be rich ② produce, provide *The stream provided good, clean water,* yield, bear ★**deny**

afraid *adj.* timid, cautious, frightened, alarmed ▷*fearful* ★**fearless**

after *prep.* behind, later, following, succeeding ★**before**

again *adv.* ① frequently, repeatedly, anew, afresh ② furthermore, moreover

against *prep.* opposite, over, opposing, resisting ★**for**

age ① *n.* period, date, time ② *n.* old age, senility ★**youth** ③ *v.* grow old, mature

aged *adj.* ancient, antiquated ▷*old* ★**youthful**

agent *n.* doer, actor, performer, operator,

Aircraft

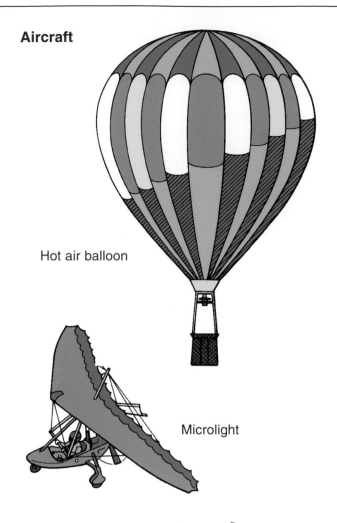

Hot air balloon

Microlight

Seaplane

worker, representative

aggravate *v.* ① increase, make worse, worsen ★**mitigate** ② irritate, annoy

aggressive *adj.* offensive, warlike, military, pushy ★**peaceful**

aghast *adj.* astonished, dumbfounded, bewildered ★**calm**

agile *adj.* nimble, active, fleet, brisk, alert ▷*lithe* ★**clumsy**

agitate *v.* disturb, trouble, excite, stir, fluster ★**smooth**

ago *adv.* past, gone, since ★**hence**

agony *n.* torture, torment, distress, pangs

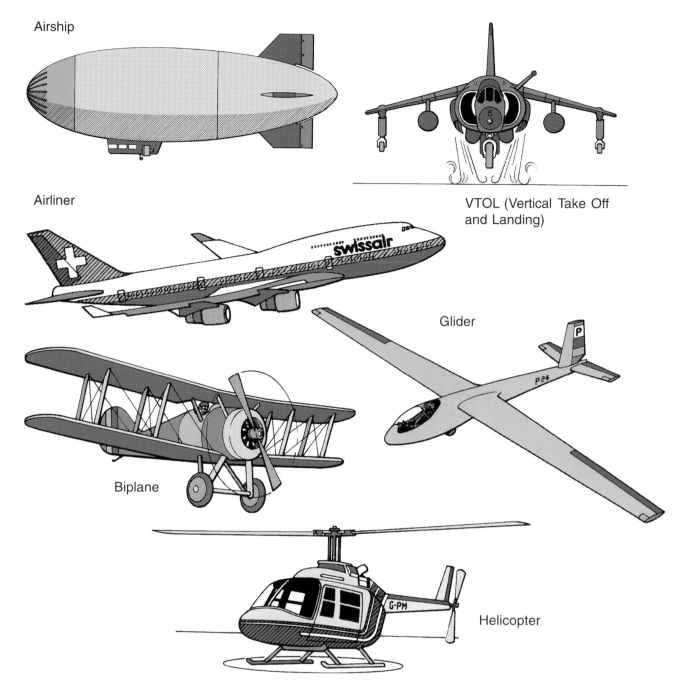

Airship

VTOL (Vertical Take Off and Landing)

Airliner

swissair

Glider

Biplane

Helicopter

G·PM

▷*pain* ★**comfort**

agree *v.* accord, fit, harmonize, combine, tally, suit ★**differ**

agreeable *adj.* obliging, welcome, acceptable, grateful ▷*pleasant* ★**disagreeable**

agreement *n.* understanding, harmony, concord ★**dispute**

ahead *adv.* ① forward, onward ② before, in advance ★**behind**

aid *v.* assist, support, encourage, serve ▷*help* ★**hinder**

aim *n.* object, goal, purpose, end, intention

aisle *n.* path, corridor, passage, way ISLE

akin *adj.* related, similar, allied, like ★**dissimilar**

alarm *v.* frighten, terrify, startle ▷*scare* ★**comfort**

alert *adj.* active, ready, wakeful, watchful ▷*agile* ★**drowsy**

alien ① *adj.* foreign, strange, remote ★**akin** ② *n.* foreigner, stranger

alike *adj.* similar, resembling, allied, like ★**unlike**

alive *adj.* living, breathing, warm, alert, brisk ★**dead**

all *adj.* whole, entire, complete, total ★**none**

allot *v.* apportion, give, allocate, dispense, grant ★**retain**

allow *v.* grant, permit, concede, owe, tolerate, entitle ★**forbid**

ally *n.* friend, companion, supporter, accomplice, colleague ★**foe**

almost *adj.* nearly, about, approximately, well-nigh

alone *adj.* lone, lonely, lonesome, forlorn ★**together**

aloud *adv.* loudly, noisily, clamorously, audibly ★**silently** ALLOWED

already *adv.* at this time, now, just now, previously

alter *v.* modify, vary, convert, transform ▷*change* ★**retain** ALTAR

altogether *adv.* completely, wholly, outright, totally ★**partially**

always *adv.* ever, forever, eternally ★**never**

amass *v.* collect, accumulate, heap, pile ★**scatter**

amaze *v.* astound, surprise, stun, dumbfound ▷*astonish*

ambition *n.* aspiration, desire, longing, zeal, aim ▷*goal*

amend *v.* revise, mend, correct, repair, improve ▷*alter*

amiable *adj.* affable, kindly, pleasant, amicable ▷*agreeable* ★**unfriendly**

amount *n.* figure, volume, sum, number, total

ample *adj.* bountiful, liberal, sufficient, plentiful ▷*abundant* ★**insufficient**

amplify *v.* increase, raise, enlarge, elaborate *Our teacher explained the problem and went on to elaborate on the details,* make louder ★**abbreviate**

amuse *v.* entertain, charm, beguile, please ★**bore**

ancestor *n.* forebear, parent, forefather, antecedent, predecessor

ancient *adj.* aged, antique, primeval, time-honored ▷*old* ★**modern**

anger *n.* wrath, ire, resentment, indignation, fury ▷*rage*

angry *adj.* wrathful, irate, resentful, furious, infuriated, indignant ★**good-tempered**

angle *n.* ① corner, bend, fork, branch ② aspect, phase, point of view *We quarreled at first, but then I saw Tom's point of view*

anguish *n.* torment, torture, pain ▷*agony* ★**ease**

announce *v.* broadcast, declare, propound,

Alphabets

Arabic

אבגד הו
Hebrew

АБВГДЕ
Cyrillic (Russian)

ลิหรูต่๑๖อ้า
Thai

Egyptian hieroglyphs

A B C D E F
Latin

ग्र ॠ ठ ग्रौ भ ङ
Sanskrit

おてふゆれづ
Japanese

ΑΒΓΔΕΖ
Greek

ᚠᚢᚦᚨᚱᚲ
Runes

reveal, herald ▷*proclaim* ★**conceal**

annoy *v.* tease, vex, irritate, disturb, harass ▷*upset* ★**soothe**

answer *n.* reply, response, solution *It was a difficult puzzle, but Emma came up with the solution* ★**question**

anticipate *v.* expect, prepare, hope for, foresee, predict

anxious *adj.* fearful, afraid, apprehensive, worried ★**carefree**

apart *adv.* away, separately, asunder, loosely ★**together**

aperture *n.* slit, hole, orifice, opening, cleft

apologize *v.* express regret, excuse, explain, plead, atone ★**insult**

apparel *n.* clothes, robes, vestments, raiment, trappings, attire

apparent *adj.* plain, conspicuous, unmistakable, clear ▷*obvious* ★**obscure**

appeal *v.* address, request, urge, entreat, invite, ask ▷*attract*

appear *v.* emerge, become visible, seem, look, come into view ★**disappear**

appearance *n.* aspect, look, shape, form, impression, likeness

appease *v.* pacify, moderate, satisfy, stay, soften ★**provoke**

appetite *n.* hunger, palate, relish, liking

applaud *v.* clap, cheer, praise, approve, encourage ★**denounce**

apply *v.* ① use, appropriate, employ ② devote, direct, dedicate *Sue was dedicated to her job and worked very hard*

appoint *v.* name, assign, nominate, engage

appreciate *v.* esteem, recognize, respect, value, enjoy

appropriate ① *v.* use, employ, adopt ② *adj.* fitting, proper *To do a job well, you should use the proper tools,* timely

approve *v.* acclaim, admire, appreciate, favor, agree ★**disapprove**

approximate *adj.* near, close, rough

apt *adj.* ① fit, clever, liable, likely ★**unfitted** ② liable, prone, inclined *Jack and Meg are both inclined to be late, so we'll wait a while*

ardent *adj.* passionate, warm, eager, fervent,

Apes

Gorilla

Gibbon

Orangutan

Chimpanzee

intense, dedicated ★**indifferent**

arduous *adj.* hard, laborious, tough, strenuous ▷*difficult* ★**easy**

area *n.* district, region, place, expanse, tract

argue *v.* ① discuss, debate, talk over ② quibble, quarrel, disagree

arid *adj.* parched, sterile ▷*dry* ★**moist**

arise *v.* ① awaken, get up ② begin, come into existence, originate, crop up, take place

army *n.* troops, legion, force, soldiery

around *adv.* about, encircling, on every side ★**within**

arouse *v.* awaken, excite, disturb, alarm ★**pacify**

arrange *v.* sort, order, dispose, deal, classify ★**confuse**

arrest *v.* seize, take prisoner, hold, detain, stop ★**release**

arrive *v.* reach, attain, land, get to, appear ★**depart**

arrogant *adj.* supercilious, proud, haughty, conceited, disdainful ★**modest**

A
B
C
D
E
F
G
H
I
J
K
L
M
N
O
P
Q
R
S
T
U
V
W
X
Y
Z

art *n.* skill, artistry, cleverness, talent

artful *adj.* cunning, knowing, crafty, wily, sly ★**innocent**

article *n.* ① thing, object, substance ② essay, treatise, typescript

artificial *adj.* invented, fictitious, fabricated, synthetic ★**real**

ascend *v.* climb, rise, go up, get up, move up, scale, mount ★**descend**

ashamed *adj.* shamefaced, abashed, confused ★**proud**

ask *v.* demand, query, inquire, appeal ▷*request* ★**answer**

aspect *n.* front, face, side, appearance, presentation, look, expression

aspire *v.* wish, long, desire, aim, hope, crave

ass *n.* ① donkey, mule ② fool, dunce, idiot, jerk, dolt

assault *v.* attack, assail, set upon, charge, invade ★**defend**

assemble *v.* meet, gather, convene, come together, muster, collect ★**disperse**

assent *v.* agree, comply, accept, consent ★**dissent**

assert *v.* pronounce, maintain, state, aver ▷*declare* ★**deny**

assess *v.* estimate, evaluate, appraise

assign *v.* appoint, name, apportion, entrust

assist *v.* aid, support, protect, maintain, sustain ▷*help* ★**obstruct**

association *n.* union, connection, companionship, society, company, club

assortment *n.* variety, kind, sort, batch, parcel, collection

assume *v.* ① believe, accept, suppose, admit ② confiscate, take, possess oneself of

assure *v.* promise, guarantee, warrant, encourage ★**deter**

astonish *v.* startle, surprise, confound, alarm, scare ▷*amaze*

astound *v.* stagger, stupefy ▷*astonish*

astray *adj.* lost, gone, vanished, missing, loose ★**safe**

astute *adj.* shrewd, brainy, knowing, sharp, acute, crafty ★**simple**

atrocious *adj.* monstrous, enormous, shameful, cruel, abominable, vile

attach *v.* fasten, append, unite, tie ▷*connect* ★**unfasten**

attack *v.* assault, invade, set upon, pounce, descend upon ★**defend**

attain *v.* extend, master, obtain, acquire, grasp ▷*reach* ★**fail**

attempt *v.* endeavor, strive, seek, tackle ▷*try* ★**abandon**

attend *v.* ① listen, heed, notice, observe, follow ★**disregard** ② be present

attentive *adj.* mindful, particular, heedful, observant ★**careless**

attire *n.* costume, robes, clothes, garments ▷*apparel*

attitude *n.* disposition, bearing, outlook, posture, position, aspect

attract *v.* ① draw, influence, tempt, prompt, pull, drag ② fascinate, enchant, captivate ★**repel**

attractive *adj.* agreeable, beautiful, handsome, pretty, tempting ★**repellent**

avail *n.* benefit, advantage, use, help, profit

available *adj.* convenient, handy, ready, attainable, accessible

avenge *v.* retaliate, revenge, pay back ★**pardon**

average *adj.* usual, ordinary, mediocre, so-so, normal, standard ★**extreme**

avid *adj.* eager, greedy, grasping

avoid *v.* shun, elude, quit, keep clear of, evade ▷*dodge* ★**seek**

awake *v.* wake, rouse, arouse, awaken, stir

award *v.* reward, give, bestow, grant, donate ★**withdraw**

aware *adj.* conscious, sensible, informed, assured ★**unaware**

away *adv.* absent, not present, afar, elsewhere ★**near**

awe *n.* fear, dread, shock, consternation, wonder

awful *adj.* fearful, terrible, alarming, dreadful ★**commonplace** OFFAL

awkward *adj.* ungainly, unwieldy, uncouth, clownish, gawky ▷*clumsy* ★**dexterous**

awry *adj.* crooked, askew, amiss, twisted, wrong ★**straight**

B b

babble v. prattle, blab, cackle, chatter, gossip

baby n. babe, infant, child, toddler, tot

back ① adj. after, rear, hind, posterior ★**front** ② v. uphold, support *The party will support Tina Johnson at the next election,* endorse, be loyal to

backer n. supporter, ally, champion

backward adj. slow, shy, reluctant, unwilling, retarded ▷*dull* ★**forward**

bad adj. ① imperfect, dreadful, unsound, awful, atrocious ② naughty, wrong, wicked, ill-behaved ③ rotten *This barrel is full of rotten apples,* spoiled ★**good**

badge n. emblem, hallmark, symbol, crest

badger v. bother, annoy, nag ▷*pester*

bad-mannered adj. impolite, boorish, uncivil ▷*rude* ★**polite**

baffle v. puzzle, perplex, frustrate, bewilder, mystify ▷*puzzle*

bag n. net, sack, pouch, purse, backpack

bail v. scoop, ladle, dip

bait ① v. tease, bother, goad, rib, needle ▷*pester* ② n. decoy, lure, snare BATE

bake v. cook, roast, harden, fire

balance v. weigh, adjust, equalize, compare

bald adj. hairless, severe, stark, bare, unadorned

balk v. hinder, baffle, thwart, obstruct, foil ★**aid**

ball n. ① dance, masquerade ② globe, orb, sphere

ballad n. song, serenade, ditty

ballot n. vote, election, franchise, poll

ban v. prohibit, forbid, deny, stop

band n. ① stripe, strip, zone, belt ② orchestra, ensemble, group BANNED

bandit n. outlaw, robber, highwayman, thief, crook

bang v. crash, slam, smash, collide

banish v. expel, eject, exclude, exile, deport, cast out ▷*dismiss* ★**welcome**

bank n. ① shore, ledge, terrace, coast, embankment ② safe, vault, treasury

banner n. ensign, standard, streamer ▷*flag*

banquet n. meal, feast, repast

banter v. chaff, tease, ridicule, joke

bar v. ① obstruct, block, blockade, forbid, shut out ② fasten, bolt, lock, latch

bare adj. ① barren, empty, void ② naked, unclothed, severe, blunt *We expected a polite reply, but got a blunt refusal,* bald BEAR

barely adv. hardly, scarcely *The well had run dry, and there was scarcely enough water for all of us,* just, simply

bargain ① n. pact, deal ② adj. low-priced, cheap

bark n. ① rind, husk, peel ② yelp, growl, cry

barrel n. cask, keg, drum, tub, cylinder

barren adj. bare, unfertile, empty ▷*arid* ★**fertile** BARON

barrier n. obstruction, obstacle, block, fence

barter v. swap, exchange, trade

base ① adj. low, sordid, cheap, corrupt ② adj. dishonorable, vile ③ adj. humble, menial ④ n. bottom, foundation ⑤ v. found *The book* Robinson Crusoe *was founded on a true story* BASS

Band

Banned

A B C D E F G H I J K L M N O P Q R S T U V W X Y Z

bashful *adj.* shy, timid, modest, coy ★**bold**

basin *n.* bowl, pot, sink, tub

batch *n.* lot, amount, assortment, collection

batter *v.* beat, strike, shatter, break, smash

battle *v.* clash, combat, fight, struggle, wrestle

bawl *v.* shout, yell, roar, bellow ★**whisper**

bay ① *n.* inlet, gulf, basin, bight ② *v.* bark, yelp BEY

be *v.* exist, live, breathe

beach *n.* shore, sands, seaside, strand BEECH

beacon *n.* signal, lamp, light, guide

beak *n.* snout, bill, nose

beam *n.* ① ray, light, streak ② plank, joist, girder

bear *v.* ① tolerate, put up with, endure, suffer ★**protest** ② bring, fetch, carry BARE

bearing *n.* manner, behavior, appearance, attitude, posture *He was a tall man with a military bearing* BARING

bearings *n.* direction, whereabouts, location *In the storm we totally lost our bearings*

beat *v.* ① strike, pound, thrash ▷*batter* ② throb, flutter, thump *My heart thumped when I heard the sound of shouting in the street* BEET

beautiful *adj.* handsome, lovely, graceful, delicate, gorgeous ▷*pretty* ★**ugly**

beauty *n.* elegance, charm, loveliness, grace ★**ugliness**

because ① *conj.* for, owing to, by reason of, since *Since Tom and Jane are here, I will stay too,* as ② *adv.* consequently

beckon *v.* signal, call, nod, summon

becoming *adj.* graceful, suitable, comely, fitting, attractive

before ① *prep.* ahead, in front of, forward, preceding ② *adv.* earlier *Here is a pie that I baked earlier,* previously ★**after**

beg *v.* ask, request, entreat, beseech, plead, pray

begin *v.* commence, initiate, found, launch ▷*start* ★**end**

beginner *n.* novice, recruit, learner, pupil

beginning *n.* start, opening, origin, outset, foundation ★**end**

behavior *n.* conduct, demeanor, manners

Bell

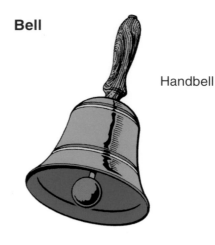

Handbell

Belfry
Bell tower
Bicycle bell
Church bell
Doorbell
Gong

▷*bearing* ★**misbehavior**

behind ① *prep.* after, following *Bill arrived to meet us, with his dog following* ② *adv.* in the rear of, later, afterward ★**before**

being *n.* creature, animal

belief *n.* faith, confidence, opinion, trust ★**disbelief**

believe *v.* trust, assent, have faith in, think, suspect ★**disbelieve**

bellow *v.* roar, shout, cry ▷*bawl*

belong *v.* relate to, pertain, be owned by

below *adv.* under, beneath, underneath ★**above**

belt *n.* strap, sash, girdle, strip

bend *v.* curve, incline, turn, yield, relax ★**straighten**

benefit *n.* advantage, profit, good, favor, aid, blessing ★**disadvantage**

beside *adv.* alongside, side by side, next to, abreast, together ★**apart**

besides *adv.* in addition, furthermore, also, moreover

best *adj.* choice, prime, unequaled, finest ★**worst**

bestow *v.* award, donate, confer, present ★**deprive**

betray *v.* deceive, dupe, expose, unmask, inform on ★**protect**

better *adj.* superior, finer, preferable *I think it would be preferable to visit the museum this afternoon instead of this morning* ★**worse**

between *prep.* amid, among, betwixt

beware *v.* be careful, refrain from, heed,

avoid, mind

bewilder *v.* confound, dazzle, mystify, confuse ▷*astonish* ★**enlighten**

beyond *adv.* over, farther, past, more, after ★**near**

bicker *v.* quarrel, dispute, wrangle, argue ★**converse**

bid *v.* proffer, present, tender, request, propose

big *adj.* ① large, great, wide, huge, bulky, fat ② important ★**small**

bill *n.* ① statement *This is a statement of your investments with us,* account, invoice, check, chit, reckoning ② beak, mouth ③ poster, advertisement

bin *n.* box, can, case, chest, crate, tub

bind *v.* tie, fasten, secure, lace, swathe ★**untie**

birth *n.* origin, beginning, source, creation ★**death** BERTH

bit *n.* morsel, piece, fragment, part, crumb ★**whole**

bite *v.* gnaw, chew, rend, chomp BIGHT

bitter *adj.* ① harsh, sour, tart ▷*acid* ② severe, stern ▷*sarcastic* ★**mellow**

blame *v.* chide, rebuke, reproach, criticize, accuse, condemn ★**praise**

bland *adj.* soft, mild, gentle, soothing, tasteless

blank *adj.* empty, bare, void, bleak ★**full**

blare *v.* blast, boom, clang, roar, sound

blast *v.* explode, split, discharge, burst

blaze *v.* burn, flare, glare, flicker

bleak *adj.* bare, open, exposed, dismal, stormy, chilly, raw, desolate *The farm was a cold and desolate place in winter* ★**sheltered**

blemish *n.* spot, stain, mark, speck, flaw, blotch

blend *v.* mix, unite, harmonize, merge, fuse, combine ★**separate**

bless *v.* hallow, praise, exalt, endow, enrich, consecrate ★**curse**

blessing *n.* advantage, boon, approval, godsend ★**curse**

blight *n.* pest, plague, disease

blind *adj.* ① eyeless, sightless *These*

salamanders live in underground caves and are sightless, unsighted, unseeing ② ignorant, uninformed

blink *v.* wink, twinkle, glitter, gleam

bliss *n.* joy, ecstasy, rapture, blessedness, happiness ★**misery**

block ① *n.* lump, mass, chunk ② *v.* obstruct, bar, arrest BLOC

bloom ① *n.* flower, blossom, bud ② *v.* blossom, flourish, flower, thrive ★**decay**

blot *n.* stain, blotch ▷*blemish*

blow ① *v.* puff, gust, blast ② *n.* shock, stroke, impact, bang

blue *adj.* azure, turquoise, indigo, navy, ultramarine, cobalt BLEW

bluff ① *adj.* frank, brusque, abrupt, outspoken *Freda Jones will never be elected mayor; she's too outspoken* ② *v.* deceive, pretend *The lion closed its eyes, pretending it had not seen the antelope,* conceal

blunder ① *n.* mistake, error, slip, fault *It was my fault that the plates were broken,* oversight ② *v.* slip, err, bungle ★**correct**

blunt *adj.* ① plain, abrupt, curt ▷*bluff* ② dull, not sharp

blush *v.* redden, color, crimson, flush

The Body

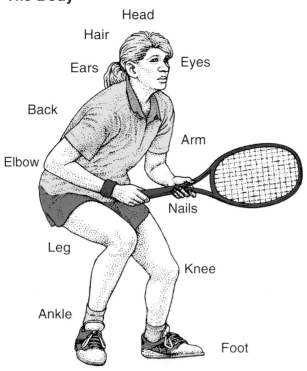

a b c d e f g h i j k l m n o p q r s t u v w x y z

board ① n. plank, table ② n. committee, council ③ v. live *The new teacher is going to live at our house,* lodge, accommodate BORED

boast v. swagger, swell, bluster ▷*brag*

boat n. ship, vessel, craft, bark, barge

body n. ① corpse, trunk, carcass ② corporation, company, society

bog n. swamp, morass, marsh, quagmire

bogus adj. fake, false, spurious, sham, counterfeit ★**genuine**

boil v. cook, steam, poach, seethe, foam

boisterous adj. tempestuous, stormy, uncontrolled, loud, noisy ★**serene**

bold adj. fearless, courageous, adventurous, valiant, daring ▷*brave* ★**fearful** BOWLED

bolt ① v. run away, take flight, flee *After the revolution, the queen had to flee the country* ② v. devour, gorge, eat ▷*gulp* ③ n. lock, latch, fastening

bond n. tie, link, joint, band, fastening

bonny adj. fair, handsome, healthy, shapely, buxom ▷*pretty* ★**plain**

bonus n. premium, benefit, award, prize

booby n. blockhead, sap, oaf, chump, nincompoop, dunce, fool, numbskull ★**oracle**

boom n. ① thunder, roar, rumble, blast ② prosperity *After the recession came years of prosperity*

boon n. blessing, windfall, advantage ▷*benefit* ★**drawback**

boorish adj. unrefined, loutish, bad-mannered, rude, clumsy ★**refined**

boost v. strengthen, raise up, heighten

border n. fringe, edge, margin, frontier

bore v. ① tire, weary, fatigue *We were fatigued by the long bus ride home* ② drill, punch, perforate BOAR

bored adj. uninterested, tired, jaded, fed-up BOARD

borrow v. take, imitate, adopt, assume, raise money ★**lend**

boss n. ① stud, knob ② chief, manager *Helen is manager of the new beauty salon,* employer

bossy adj. domineering, tyrannical, overbearing ▷*arrogant* ★**modest**

bother v. alarm, annoy, concern, distress ▷*disturb*

bottom n. underside, deepest part, floor ▷*base* ★**top**

bough n. branch, limb, shoot BOW

boulder n. rock, slab, stone

bounce v. leap, spring, bound, bump, jump

bound v. rebound, prance ▷*bounce*

boundary n. bounds, limits, border, frontier ▷*barrier*

bounty n. donation, gift, grant ▷*bonus*

bow v. bend, nod, stoop, kneel, yield, submit BOUGH

bowl n. plate, basin, dish, vessel, casserole BOLL

box ① n. carton, case, chest, coffer *The town's coffers were empty, so they had to raise taxes,* pack ② v. fight, spar, punch

boy n. lad, youth, child, youngster

brag v. crow, swagger, gloat ▷*boast*

braid v. entwine, weave, plait BRAYED

branch n. ① shoot, limb, twig ▷*bough* ② department, office, division

brand n. ① trademark, emblem, label *This label shows that the cloth is of high quality* ② blot, stigma, stain

brandish v. flourish, parade, shake, swing, wave

brash adj. brazen, foolhardy, hasty, impetuous, impudent ▷*rash*

brave ① adj. audacious, fearless, daring, dauntless, gallant, heroic ▷*bold* ★**cowardly** ② v. dare, defy, endure

break v. batter, burst, crack, snap, fracture, shatter BRAKE

breathe v. draw in, gasp, inhale, sniff, gulp, wheeze, emit

breed v. reproduce, produce, cause, bear, rear, multiply, propagate

bribe v. corrupt, buy, grease the palm, fix

brief adj. short, little, concise, terse, crisp, curt ★**lengthy**

bright adj. ① clear, cloudless, fair, airy ② cheerful, genial *We were pleased to find so many genial members in the club* ③ clever, ingenious, acute ★**dull**

Bridges

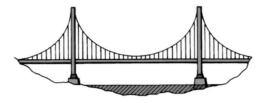

Cantilever

Suspension

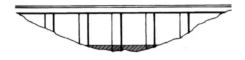

Girder

Arch

Bascule bridge
Drawbridge
Footbridge

Rope bridge
Swing span bridge
Viaduct

brilliant *adj.* ① lustrous, shining, radiant, dazzling, luminous ② clever, intelligent ★**dull**

brim *n.* edge, brink, rim, fringe

bring *v.* bear, fetch, deliver, carry, convey

bring about *v.* bring off, accomplish, achieve, cause, make happen

bring up *v.* breed, develop, raise, educate, foster

brink *n.* margin, border, boundary, limit

brisk *adj.* agile, alert, busy, energetic, active, nimble, invigorating ★**sluggish**

brittle *adj.* breakable, fragile, delicate ▷*frail*

broad *adj.* wide, expansive, roomy, open, vast, large ★**narrow**

brood *v.* sigh, agonize, dwell upon *You must try to forget your disappointment and not dwell upon it,* languish BREWED

brook *n.* stream, creek, rivulet, watercourse

brow *n.* forehead, face, front, brink, edge, summit

bruise *v.* damage, discolor, blemish, injure, wound BREWS

brusque *adj.* abrupt, discourteous, gruff ▷*blunt* ★**polite**

brutal *adj.* cruel, inhumane, savage, barbarous, bloodthirsty ★**humane**

bubble *n.* drop, droplet, blob, bead

buckle *n.* catch, clasp, clip, fastening

bud *n.* sprout, germ, shoot

budge *v.* propel, push, roll, shift, slide

build *v.* make, form, assemble, construct, erect, put up ★**demolish** BILLED

bulge *n.* bump, swelling, lump, billow

bulky *adj.* big, huge, unwieldy, massive, cumbersome *I never liked that chair; it's too big and cumbersome to move*

bully ① *n.* ruffian, tease, bruiser, tyrant, tough ② *v.* tease, harass, oppress, terrorize

bump *v.* collide, hit, knock, strike, jab, jolt

bunch *n.* batch, bundle, cluster, collection, lot

bundle *n.* group, mass, heap, pack, parcel

bungle *v.* botch, blunder, mess up, ruin, fumble ★**succeed**

burden *n.* ① load, weight ② strain, hardship *We suffered great hardship during the war*

burly *adj.* beefy, big, hefty, brawny, muscular ★**frail**

burn *v.* blaze, flare, glow, singe, scorch, char, incinerate

burst *v.* break open, crack, explode, shatter, erupt

bury *v.* inter, conceal, cover up, hide, entomb, lay to rest BERRY

business *n.* ① occupation, career, profession ② company, enterprise, firm ③ problem, duty, affair

busy *adj.* active, brisk, industrious, lively, bustling ★**lazy**

buy *v.* acquire, get, purchase, procure *If I can procure a computer, I'll do the job for you* ★**sell** BY, BYE

A
B
C
D
E
F
G
H
I
J
K
L
M
N
O
P
Q
R
S
T
U
V
W
X
Y
Z

Cc

cab *n.* taxi, taxicab, hackney carriage

cabin *n.* ① hut, chalet, cottage, shack ② berth, compartment

cabinet *n.* ① cupboard, closet ② council, committee

cackle *v.* chuckle, giggle, snicker

café *n.* restaurant, coffee shop, snack bar

cage *v.* shut up, confine, imprison ★**free**

calamity *n.* catastrophe, disaster, misadventure ▷*mishap* ★**blessing**

calculate *v.* reckon, figure, estimate ▷*count*

call *v.* ① cry out, shout, hail ② name, designate ③ summon, telephone ④ visit *We will visit you next week,* drop in

calling *n.* occupation, job, profession

callous *adj.* unfeeling, harsh, hard-bitten ★**sensitive**

calm ① *v.* soothe, ease, pacify, comfort ② *adj.* easy, composed, mild ▷*peaceful* ★**excited**

can *n.* tin can, jar, container, canister

cancel *v.* abolish, erase, put off, obliterate ★**confirm**

candid *adj.* fair, honest, open, sincere, truthful ▷*frank* ★**devious**

capable *adj.* talented, able, competent, ▷*clever* ★**incompetent**

capacity *n.* ① space, volume, extent ② ability, aptitude *Jenny has an aptitude for learning languages,* intelligence

caper ① *v.* dance, gambol, frolic ② *n.* prank, joke, jest, lark

capital ① *n.* cash, assets, funds, finance ② *adj.* chief, excellent, important

captain *n.* chief, head, commander, master, skipper

capture *v.* seize, arrest, trap ▷*catch* ★**release**

car *n.* automobile, vehicle, conveyance, carriage, coach

carcass *n.* body, corpse, skeleton

care ① *v.* take care, beware, heed, mind ② *n.* attention, protection ★**carelessness**

careful *adj.* heedful, prudent, watchful ▷*cautious* ★**careless**

careless *adj.* neglectful, slack, casual, thoughtless ★**careful**

carelessness *n.* inaccuracy, negligence, slackness ★**care**

caress *v.* hug, stroke, cuddle, embrace, pet, pat

carriage *n.* car, coach, buggy, baby buggy

carry *v.* bring, convey, lift, support ▷*bear*

carry on *v.* continue, maintain, persist

carry out *v.* perform, achieve, fulfill, do

cart *n.* wagon, pushcart, buggy, wheelbarrow

carton *n.* bin, case, package, crate ▷*box*

carve *v.* sculpt, cut, chisel, fashion, whittle ▷*shape*

case *n.* chest, bin, carton ▷*box*

cash *n.* money, coins, bills, coinage CACHE

cask *n.* barrel, keg, drum

cast *v.* ① mold, form, shape ② fling, heave, sprinkle ▷*throw* CASTE

casual *adj.* accidental, chance, random ▷*occasional* ★**regular**

catch *v.* grasp, seize, arrest ▷*capture* ★**miss**

catching *adj.* infectious, contagious

cause ① *v.* bring about, create, provoke ② *n.* reason, source, origin CAWS

caution *n.* watchfulness, heed, vigilance, prudence ▷*care* ★**recklessness**

cautious *adj.* careful, discreet, prudent ▷*watchful* ★**heedless**

cavity *n.* dent, hole, gap, hollow

cease *v.* stop, conclude, end, refrain, terminate ★**begin**

celebrate *v.* commemorate, observe, honor, glorify, rejoice, praise

cell *n.* chamber, cavity, cubicle, compartment SELL

cellar *n.* basement, vault, crypt, cave SELLER

cement ① *v.* glue, stick, bind, gum, unite ② *n.* plaster, mortar, adhesive

censor *v.* cut, examine, take out CENSER

censure *v.* blame, rebuke, reprimand, chide ▷*scold* ★**praise**

center *n.* middle, core, heart, nucleus

a b c d e f g h i j k l m n o p q r s t u v w x y z

ceremony *n.* ritual, custom, performance

certain *adj.* ① decided, definite, undoubted ▷*sure* ★**dubious** ② particular *I had a particular reason for inviting you,* special

certainty *n.* confidence, assurance, trust, sureness ★**doubt**

certificate *n.* document, permit, deed, diploma, testimonial

chafe *v.* rub, rasp, grate, irritate

chain *v.* bind, fetter, shackle, tether, bond

challenge *v.* dare, demand, dispute, defy, object to

chamber *n.* room, apartment, bedroom, compartment, hollow

champion *n.* defender, victor, master, winner ★**loser**

chance *n.* ① fortune, hazard, luck, gamble, lottery, wager ② opportunity, occasion, risk ★**certainty**

change *v.* alter, vary, turn, shift, reform, transform ★**preserve**

chant *v.* intone, drone, croon, recite ▷*sing*

chaos *n.* turmoil, confusion, disorder, pandemonium ★**order**

chapter *n.* clause, division, part, period *It was a period in my life that I will never forget,* phase

character *n.* ① letter, mark, emblem, device ② reputation *She had the reputation of being very generous,* temperament, qualities

charge *n.* ① attack, stampede, advance ② cost, amount, price ③ accusation, blame *The men were all guilty, but it was Harry Smith who took the blame,* indictment

charm *v.* please, delight, enchant, bewitch ▷*attract* ★**irritate**

charming *adj.* delightful, appealing, lovely, pleasant ▷*attractive* ★**disgusting**

chart *n.* map, sketch, diagram, plan

chase *v.* hunt, pursue, follow, run after, hurry

chaste *adj.* virgin, pure, virtuous, innocent ★**immodest** CHASED

chastise *v.* punish, whip, flog, beat, scold, tell off

chat *v.* converse, gossip ▷*talk*

chatter *v.* babble, gossip ▷*talk*

Chest

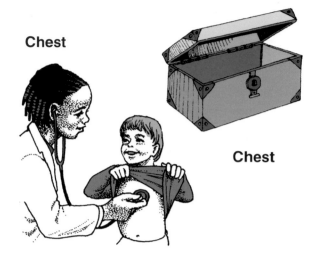

Chest

cheap *adj.* inexpensive, low-priced, bargain, reasonable, inferior ★**expensive**

cheat *v.* swindle, bilk, defraud, fleece ▷*trick*

check ① *v.* inspect, compare, examine *The customs officer examined our luggage,* make sure ② *n.* bill, invoice, reckoning

cheek *n.* audacity, boldness, impertinence, insolence

cheer *v.* ① comfort, console, elate, buck up ② applaud *The audience applauded the leading soprano,* clap, hail

cheerful *adj.* lively, bright, happy, merry, joyful ▷*happy* ★**sad**

cheery *adj.* blithe, breezy, bright, merry ★**downcast**

cherish *v.* caress, hold close, care for, shelter, treasure

chest *n.* ① case, coffer ▷*box* ② bosom, torso

chew *v.* bite, gnaw, grind, munch ▷*eat*

chide *v.* scold, criticize, blame, tell off

chief *adj.* main, principal, leading, foremost ★**minor**

child *n.* baby, infant, youth, juvenile

chilly *adj.* cool, crisp, brisk, cold, unfriendly ★**warm**

chip *v. & n.* crack, splinter, dent, flake

chirp *v. & n.* warble, trill, cheep, twitter

choice ① *n.* option *I had no option but to take the job,* preference, alternative ② *adj.* select, dainty, precious, cherished, special

choke *v.* throttle, suffocate, gag, strangle ▷*stifle*

**Churches
and Places
of Worship**

Cathedral
Chapel
Church
Mosque
Oratory
Pantheon
Synagogue
Temple

choose *v.* pick, elect, decide, prefer ▷*select*
CHEWS

chop *v.* cut, hack, clip, cleave, sever, lop

chubby *adj.* plump, buxom, portly, round,
stout ★**slim**

chum *n.* comrade, pal, friend, buddy,
companion

chuck *v.* throw, toss, fling, heave, sling

chuckle *v.* cackle, chortle, snigger, giggle,
★**laugh**

chunk *n.* piece, lump, mass, portion, slab

churlish *adj.* brusque, harsh, impolite,
morose *Dad had a headache and was in a
morose mood* ▷surly ★**polite**

circle *n.* ① ring, band ② company, group,
class

circular ① *adj.* round, disklike ② *n.*
handbill, notice, poster

circulate *v.* broadcast, distribute, publicize

cistern *n.* tank, sink, basin, reservoir

cite *v.* mention, specify, name, quote
SIGHT, SITE

civil *adj.* polite, courteous, polished
▷*affable* ★**churlish**

claim *v.* demand, ask, require, insist, call for

clamor *n.* babel, blare, din, row, hubbub,
racket ▷*noise* ★**silence**

clamp *v.* fasten, fix, hold, grasp

clap *v.* applaud, acclaim, cheer

clarify *v.* ① make clear, explain, simplify
② cleanse, purify

clash *v.* ① battle, conflict, quarrel ② bang,
crash, clang, clatter

clasp ① *v.* grasp, grip, seize, hold, fasten
② *n.* buckle, catch, pin

class *n.* category, type, sort, grade, group,
species

classical *adj.* pure, refined, scholarly,
elegant, polished, well-proportioned

classify *v.* grade, sort, arrange, catalog

clean ① *adj.* pure, fresh, spotless, unsoiled
② *v.* cleanse, scrub ▷*wash* ★**dirty**

cleanse *v.* purify, scour ▷*clean* ★**defile**

clear *adj.* ① bright, fair, fine, light ★**dim**
② distinct, audible, lucid ★**vague** ③ free,
open, empty

cleft *n.* crack, cranny, slit, split, aperture

clever *adj.* able, astute, apt, brainy, skillful,
talented ▷*expert* ★**foolish**

cliff *n.* precipice, height, bluff, crag,
overhang

climax *n.* crisis, head, summit, turning point

climb *v.* mount, scale, ascend, soar, go up

cling *v.* adhere, attach, embrace, grasp, hold

clip ① *n.* fastener, clasp ② *v.* trim, prune,
snip, cut

clog *v.* block, dam up, hinder, jam, impede

close ① *v.* (kloz) shut, bolt, bar, obstruct
*The drapes were thick and obstructed
a lot of light,* end ② *adj.* (klos) near,
neighboring, adjacent ★**far** ③ *adj.* heavy,
stuffy, uncomfortable

closet *n.* cupboard, cabinet

clothing *n.* garments, dress, attire, raiment

cloud *n.* vapor, fog, billow, haze

clown *n.* buffoon, comedian, jester, joker

club *n.* ① cudgel, stick, truncheon
② company, group, society

clue *n.* evidence, inkling, lead, sign CLEW

clump *n.* cluster, group, bunch

clumsy *adj.* awkward, gawky, ungainly,
blundering ★**graceful**

clutch *v.* snatch, clasp, grasp, seize, grip

clutter *n.* litter, muddle, mess

coach *n.* ① bus, car, carriage, vehicle
② trainer, tutor, instructor

a b c d e f g h i j k l m n o p q r s t u v w x y z

Clothing

Dresses and pants
Bermuda shorts
cocktail dress
dress
evening gown
jeans
jodhpurs
kilt
miniskirt
petticoat
sari
sarong
skirt
slacks

Coats and jackets
blazer
parka
poncho
raincoat
suit
tuxedo

Headwear *see page 228*

Tops
blouse
pullover
sweater
sweatshirt
T-shirt

Foot and legwear
boots
galoshes
moccasins
shoes
sneakers
socks
stockings

coarse *adj.* ① rough, unrefined, unpolished ② brutish, rude, uncivil ★**refined** COURSE

coat *n.* ① jacket, blazer, windbreaker ② fleece, fur, skin, hide

coax *v.* cajole, wheedle, urge, persuade, beguile *We sat for hours as Aunt Anna beguiled us with stories* ★**dissuade** COKES

coddle *v.* pamper, spoil, indulge, baby, mollycoddle

coffer *n.* casket, case, chest, treasury

cog *n.* tooth, prong

coil *v.* twist, wind, loop

coincide *v.* match, agree, accord, synchronize, tally

cold *adj.* cool, chilly, frigid, freezing, frosty, frozen ★**hot**

collapse *v.* founder, topple, break down, crumple, fall down

collect *v.* accumulate, amass, assemble, save ▷*gather* ★**scatter**

collide *v.* crash, smash, hit, strike, meet

colossal *adj.* enormous, gigantic, immense, massive ▷**huge** ★**tiny**

column *n.* ① pillar, post, shaft ② file *The file of soldiers marched on parade,* line, procession

combat *v.* battle, contend, contest, oppose, defy ★**submit**

combine *v.* unite, join, link, fuse, merge, mix ★**separate**

come *v.* arrive, appear, enter, reach, advance ★**go**

come by *v.* get, procure, acquire *I acquired a new television set in the sale*

comfort *v.* cheer, hearten, calm, soothe, console ★**torment**

comfortable *adj.* restful, convenient, cozy, agreeable ★**uncomfortable**

comforting *adj.* cheering, encouraging, consoling

command *v.* ① order, dictate, direct ② rule, dominate

commence *v.* start, begin, initiate, originate ★**finish**

comment *v.* mention, remark, observe, point out

commiserate *v.* sympathize, show pity, be sorry for

commit *v.* carry out, do, enact, perform, promise, entrust

A
B
C
D
E
F
G
H
I
J
K
L
M
N
O
P
Q
R
S
T
U
V
W
X
Y
Z

common *adj.* ① ordinary, vulgar, habitual, customary ② public, social, communal

commonplace *adj.* everyday, humdrum, ordinary, obvious ★**rare**

commotion *n.* excitement, flurry, stir, uproar ▷*fuss*

communicate *v.* tell, disclose, impart, reveal

community *n.* society, partnership, association ▷*group*

compact *adj.* dense, close, tight, firm, condensed, concise

companion *n.* comrade, friend, chum, colleague, comrade, escort ★**rival**

company *n.* association, league, alliance, business, firm

compare *v.* match, liken, equal, parallel

compartment *n.* cubicle, alcove, bay, cell, carriage

compassion *n.* kindness, mercy, sympathy, charity, understanding ▷*pity* ★**indifference**

compel *v.* make, coerce, drive, force *We could not understand the signs so we were forced to guess where to check in*, urge ★**coax**

compensate *v.* make good, refund, reimburse, repay, reward ★**injure**

compete *v.* contest, contend, rival, strive, oppose, challenge

Compel

We could not understand the signs so we were forced to guess where to check in.

competent *adj.* able, adapted, capable ▷*clever* ★**incompetent**

competition *n.* game, match, contest, tournament, rivalry, race

compile *v.* amass, put together, unite ▷*collect*

complacent *adj.* self-satisfied, contented ▷*smug* ★**diffident**

complain *v.* protest, gripe, grumble, grouse ▷*nag* ★**rejoice**

complement *v.* complete, round off, add to, supplement, match COMPLIMENT

complete ① *v.* finish, accomplish, achieve ② *adj.* finished, full, entire

complex *adj.* complicated, intricate, mixed, tangled ★**simple**

complicated *adj.* entangled, involved ▷*complex*

compliment *v.* flatter, admire, congratulate ▷*praise* ★**insult** COMPLEMENT

comply *v.* agree to, assent to, abide by, perform, yield ★**refuse**

compose ① *v.* make up, put together, form, construct, write ② calm, quell

composure *n.* assurance, calm, confidence ★**exuberance**

compound *n.* mixture, alloy, blend, combination

comprehend *v.* grasp, discern, take in ▷*understand* ★**misunderstand**

compress *v.* condense, contract, abbreviate ▷*squeeze* ★**expand**

comprise *v.* contain, consist of, include, embody, encompass

compromise *v.* ① meet halfway, strike a balance, adjust, agree ② imperil, weaken, jeopardize

compulsory *adj.* forced, necessary, obligatory *Everyone in the school has to go* *to the meeting; it's obligatory,* required ★**voluntary**

compute *v.* calculate, figure, reckon, estimate

computer *n.* calculator, word processor

comrade *n.* companion, pal, chum, buddy ▷*friend* ★**enemy**

conceal *v.* bury, camouflage, cover ▷*hide* ★**reveal**

concede *v.* allow, admit, yield, acknowledge, surrender ★**dispute**

conceit *n.* vanity, self-importance, arrogance ▷*pride* ★**modesty**

conceited *adj.* proud, vain, arrogant ★**modest**

conceive *v.* create, design, devise *We devised a way to sharpen the scissors,* form, think up, develop

concentrate *v.* focus on, centralize, heed, pay attention

concept *n.* idea, thought, theory, view

concern ① *v.* affect, touch ② *n.* affair, matter, interest, business

concerning *prep.* as regards, respecting, about

concise *adj.* brief, condensed, short ▷*compact* ★**expansive**

conclude *v.* ① finish, terminate ▷*end* ② deduce, judge, reckon, presume

conclusion *n.* result, termination, end

concoct *v.* contrive, hatch, plan, devise, invent

concord *n.* agreement, understanding, goodwill, harmony ★**discord**

concrete ① *adj.* actual, definite, real ② *n.* cement, mortar

concur *v.* approve, agree, coincide, consent ★**disagree**

condemn *v.* blame, denounce, reprove, sentence, disapprove ★**approve**

condense *v.* compress, concentrate, abridge, thicken ★**expand**

condition *n.* shape, way, state, position, plight, situation ▷*predicament*

condone *v.* overlook, disregard, forgive, excuse ★**censure**

conduct ① *n.* attitude, bearing, behavior

② *v.* guide, direct, lead, steer, pilot

confederate *n.* accomplice, ally, associate, partner

confer *v.* bestow, grant, award, give, present

conference *n.* discussion, meeting, forum

confess *v.* admit, acknowledge, own up, divulge ★**deny**

confide *v.* tell, divulge, reveal, whisper, entrust

confidence *n.* assurance, belief, boldness, firmness ★**doubt**

confident *adj.* certain, assured, poised, fearless ★**diffident**

confine *v.* restrict, limit, detain, imprison, constrain ★**free**

confirm *v.* verify, assure, approve, endorse, attest ★**deny**

confiscate *v.* seize, impound, commandeer *The house was commandeered by the army*

conform *v.* agree with, comply with, yield, adjust

confound *v.* perplex, mystify, puzzle, baffle, fluster ▷*bewilder* ★**enlighten**

confront *v.* challenge, defy, face, oppose, menace

confuse *v.* baffle, bemuse, mystify ▷*bewilder* ★**clarify**

congenial *adj.* companionable, natural, sympathetic, agreeable ▷*friendly* ★**disagreeable**

congested *adj.* jammed, crowded, clogged, packed, teeming ★**clear**

congratulate *v.* rejoice, compliment, praise, wish one joy ★**commiserate**

congregate *v.* assemble, meet, come together, converge ★**disperse**

congress *n.* meeting, assembly, council, convention

conjecture *v.* guess, surmise, suspect, imagine, assume

connect *v.* unite, join, combine, fasten, link ★**disconnect**

conquer *v.* beat, crush, overcome, overpower, triumph ▷*defeat* ★**surrender**

conscientious *adj.* moral, scrupulous, careful, diligent ▷*honest* ★**careless**

conscious *adj.* alert, alive, aware, sensible,

responsible ★**unconscious**

consecutive *adj.* chronological, in sequence, successive, continuous

consent *v.* assent, permit, concur, approve, comply ▷*agree* ★**oppose**

conserve *v.* keep, preserve, protect, save, store up, safeguard ★**waste**

consider *v.* discuss, examine, ponder, reflect *Alone on the island, I reflected on all that had happened,* take account of ★**ignore**

considerable *adj.* abundant, ample, great, large, noteworthy, important ★**insignificant**

consist of *v.* comprise, be composed of, contain, include

consistent *adj.* uniform, constant, regular, steady ★**inconsistent**

console *v.* comfort, cheer, sympathize, soothe, solace ★**upset**

conspicuous *adj.* noticeable, marked, apparent, obvious, prominent ★**inconspicuous**

conspire *v.* intrigue, scheme, plot *He was jailed for plotting against the government*

constant *adj.* ① regular, stable, uniform ▷*consistent* ② loyal, faithful, staunch, true ★**fickle**

consternation *n.* dismay, horror, fear, awe, stupefaction ▷*alarm* ★**composure**

constitute *v.* compose, comprise, set up, fix, form, establish ★**destroy**

constrict *v.* tighten, strain, tauten, draw together, choke, pinch ★**expand**

construct *v.* erect, compose, compound, assemble ▷*build* ★**demolish**

consult *v.* ask, seek advice, discuss, confer, debate

consume *v.* use up, absorb, eat up, devour

contact *n.* touch, connection, communication

contagious *adj.* catching, infectious

contain *v.* comprise, consist of, hold, accommodate, enclose

contaminate *v.* pollute, soil, stain, sully, taint, infect

contemplate *v.* think, reflect, deliberate, consider, ponder

contempt *v.* disdain, scorn, disregard, derision ★**admiration**

contend *v.* compete, contest, conflict, strive, struggle ★**concede**

content ① *adj.* (con-*tent*) satisfied, smug ② *v.* satisfy, delight, gratify ③ *n.* (*con*-tent) matter, text, subject

contest ① *n.* (*con*-test) competition, match, tournament ② *v.* (con-*test*) dispute, argue

continue *v.* go on, keep up, endure, last, persist ★**stop**

contract ① *v.* (con-*tract*) condense, lessen, shrink ② *n.* (*con*-tract) agreement, pact, understanding

contradict *v.* deny, dispute, challenge, oppose

contrary *adj.* opposed, adverse, counter, opposite ★**agreeable**

contrast ① *n.* (*con*-trast) difference, disparity, comparison ② *v.* (con-*trast*) compare, differ, oppose, distinguish

contribute *v.* donate, present, bestow, provide ★**withhold**

contrive *v.* form, fashion, construct, create, design, invent

control *v.* command, direct, dominate, lead, supervise

convene *v.* call together, rally, meet, muster *We mustered on the dock before boarding the ship,* assemble ★**dismiss**

convenient *adj.* handy, fit, helpful, suitable, accessible ★**awkward**

conversation *n.* talk, chat, communication, discussion

convert *v.* alter, change, transform, adapt

convey *v.* carry, transport, conduct, bear, transmit

convict ① *n.* (*con*-vict) prisoner, captive, criminal ② *v.* (con-*vict*) find guilty, condemn

convince *v.* assure, persuade, prove to, win over

cook *v.* boil, broil, heat, warm, steam, fry, stew, bake

cool *adj.* ① chilly, frigid ▷*cold* ② self-composed, calm, relaxed

cooperate *v.* collaborate, combine, aid,

assist, join forces

cope (with) *v.* deal, handle, struggle, grapple, manage

copy *v.* duplicate, reproduce, imitate, mimic, simulate

cord *n.* string, rope, twine, line CHORD

cordial *adj.* hearty, sincere, congenial, jovial, affable ★**hostile**

core *n.* heart, kernel, pith, crux *Now we're getting to the crux of the problem,* center CORPS

corner *n.* angle, bend, crook, cavity, cranny, niche, compartment

corpse *n.* body, carcass, remains

correct *adj.* true, actual, accurate, exact, precise ★**wrong**

correspond *v.* ① fit, harmonize, agree, coincide ② write letters

corridor *n.* hallway, passage, aisle

corroborate *v.* confirm, certify, endorse, establish ★**contradict**

corrode *v.* erode, waste, eat away, rust

corrupt ① *adj.* dishonest, fraudulent, rotten

② *v.* bribe, deprave, entice

cost *n.* ① charge, amount, price, outlay ② penalty, forfeit, sacrifice

costly *adj.* expensive, valuable, precious

costume *n.* suit, outfit, ensemble, attire, dress

cot *n.* bed, bunk, berth

cottage *n.* bungalow, cabin, chalet, shack, lodge

couch *n.* sofa, davenport, chaise longue

council *n.* assembly, committee, congress, convention COUNSEL

counsel ① *n.* lawyer, attorney, advocate ② *v.* advise, instruct, recommend COUNCIL

count *v.* add up, calculate, check, compute, reckon, tally

counter ① *n.* token, coin, disk ② *n.* bar, bench ③ *adj.* against, opposed

counterfeit *adj.* forged, fraudulent, fake, bogus *She entered the country on a bogus passport,* false

country ① *n.* nation, people, realm, state ② *adj.* rural, boondocks, sticks

A B C D E F G H I J K L M N O P Q R S T U V W X Y Z

Cooking utensils

Blender	Grill	Saucepan
Bottle	Jar	Saucer
Bowl	Juicer	Sieve
Casserole	Kettle	Skillet
Colander	Ladle	Spatula
Cup	Masher	Spoon
Cutting	Measuring	Tureen
board	cup	Urn
Dish	Pan	Waffle iron
Frying pan	Peeler	Whisk
Funnel	Plate	Wok
Grater	Pot	
Griddle	Ramekin	
	Rolling pin	

couple ① *n.* pair, brace, two ② *v.* link, yoke, unite, join, connect

courage *n.* bravery, valor, boldness, gallantry, daring, pluck ★**cowardice**

courageous *adj.* brave, bold, fearless, valiant ▷*plucky* ★**cowardly**

course *n.* ① route, channel, path, road, track, trail ② policy, plan, manner COARSE

court ① *n.* alley, courtyard, atrium, ② *n.* bar, law court, tribunal ③ *n.* palace, retinue ④ *v.* make love, woo, flatter

courteous *adj.* considerate, polite, refined, elegant ★**discourteous**

courtesy *n.* politeness, civility, manners, gentility, respect

cove *n.* inlet, bay, creek, firth

cover ① *v.* conceal, hide, secrete ② *v.* include, embody, incorporate ③ *n.* cap, case, lid, canopy

covet *v.* want, envy, fancy, hanker after, long for, crave

cow *v.* frighten, bully, terrorize, scare, subdue

coward *n.* weakling, craven, funk, sneak ★**hero** COWERED

cowardice *n.* fear, funk, faint-heartedness ★**courage**

cowardly *adj.* fearful, weak, scared,

Creature

It was a huge brute—the biggest crocodile I'd ever seen.

spineless, timid ★**courageous**

cower *v.* cringe, grovel, flinch, crouch

coy *adj.* demure, skittish, blushing, bashful, shy ★**forward**

crack ① *n.* slit, split, cleft, cranny, crevice, breach ② *v.* snap, split, splinter

craft *n.* ① cunning, deceit ② ability, cleverness, expertise ③ occupation, business ④ boat, ship, plane

crafty *adj.* cunning, artful, wily, shrewd

cram *v.* ram, stuff, squeeze, press

cramp *v.* restrict, obstruct, hinder, confine

crash *v.* bang, clash, clatter, break, fall, topple, collapse

crass *adj.* stupid, oafish, boorish, obtuse, gross, vulgar, coarse ★**sensitive**

crave *v.* long for, hanker after, need, yearn for, beg, plead

crawl *v.* creep, drag, slither, grovel

crazy *adj.* insane, mad, beserk, deranged, idiotic ★**sane**

creak *v.* grate, grind, rasp, groan CREEK

crease *n.* fold, pucker, ridge, tuck

create *v.* bring into being, compose, concoct, make, invent, devise

creation invention, handiwork, foundation, production ★**destruction**

creature *n.* animal, beast, being, brute *It was a huge brute—the biggest crocodile I'd ever seen,* person

credible *adj.* believable, likely, plausible ★**incredible**

credit *n.* ① acclaim, kudos, merit ② belief, faith, confidence

creek *n.* stream, brook, rivulet CREAK

creep *v.* crawl, slither, squirm, wriggle

crest *n.* top, crown, pinnacle

crestfallen *adj.* downcast, dejected, discouraged ★**elated**

crevice *n.* cleft, chink, crack, cranny, gap

crew *n.* team, company, party, gang

crime *n.* misdemeanor, offense, fault, felony

criminal ① *n.* culprit, convict, felon, crook ② *adj.* unlawful, wicked

cringe *v.* cower, flinch, duck, shrink, grovel

cripple *v.* disable, mutilate, paralyze, weaken, damage

Creek

Creak

crisis *n.* climax, turning point, catastrophe, disaster

crisp *adj.* brittle, crumbly, crunchy, firm, crusty

critical *adj.* crucial, all-important, acute, grave

criticize *v.* find fault with, disapprove of, condemn ★**praise**

crony *n.* accomplice, ally, confederate, comrade, chum ▷*friend*

crooked *adj.* ① bent, bowed, distorted, twisted ② dishonest, criminal

crop ① *n.* harvest, gathering, yield ② *v.* graze, shorten, browse

cross ① *adj.* angry, annoyed, crusty ② *v.* bridge, pass over ③ *n.* crucifix

crouch *v.* stoop, squat, bow, cringe

crow ① *v.* gloat, shout, brag, bluster ② *n.* blackbird, raven

crowd *n.* mob, multitude, flock, assembly, swarm, throng

crowded *adj.* jammed, packed, congested, cramped

crucial *adj.* decisive, critical, acute

crude *adj.* raw, unrefined, rustic, unpolished ▷*coarse* ★**refined**

cruel *adj.* unkind, brutal, inhuman, ruthless ▷*savage* ★**kind**

cruise *n.* voyage, trip, sail, crossing CREWS

crumb *n.* bit, morsel, seed, grain, scrap, shred

crumble *v.* decay, grind, powder, crunch

crumple *v.* crinkle, crush, wrinkle, pucker

crunch *v.* chew, grind, masticate, munch ▷*crush*

crush *v.* squash, mash, pound, compress

cry *v.* ① exclaim, call, shout, shriek ② weep, bawl, blubber, sob

cuddle *v.* hug, embrace, fondle, cosset, pet, snuggle

cue *n.* hint, key, nod, sign, signal QUEUE

cull *v.* choose, pick, thin out, amass, collect

culprit *n.* criminal, convict, felon, offender, malefactor

cultivated *adj.* refined, civilized, cultured, educated, trained ★**neglected**

cumbersome *adj.* bulky, awkward, clumsy, hefty ★**convenient**

cunning *adj.* artful, astute, crafty

curb *v.* check, tame, restrain

cure ① *n.* remedy, medicine, drug ② *v.* heal, remedy, treat, attend

curious *adj.* ① odd, peculiar, singular ② inquisitive, prying, nosy

curl *v.* coil, twist, curve, crimp

current ① *adj.* present, contemporary, topical, fashionable ② *n.* stream, course, flow, electrical flow CURRANT

curse ① *v.* swear, condemn, damn ② *n.* oath, denunciation

curt *adj.* brusque, blunt, churlish, crusty, gruff ▷*terse* ★**polite**

curtail *v.* trim, shorten, clip, truncate ▷*abbreviate* ★**lengthen**

curve *n.* loop, hook, curl, twist, wind, coil ▷*bend*

cushion *n.* pillow, bolster, pad, support

custom *n.* habit, usage, convention, rite ▷*fashion*

customer *n.* purchaser, buyer, client, patron

cut *v.* carve, whittle, chisel, cleave, sever, gash, slice

cut off *v.* disconnect, interrupt, stop

cute *adj.* charming, attractive, pretty, dainty

cutting *adj.* sharp, biting, bitter, sarcastic

A
B
C
D
E
F
G
H
I
J
K
L
M
N
O
P
Q
R
S
T
U
V
W
X
Y
Z

D d

dab *v.* blot, swab, touch, pat

dabble *v.* toy, meddle, tinker, trifle, putter

daft *adj.* crazy, silly, innocent, idiotic, cracked, dopey ★**bright**

dagger *n.* knife, dirk, bayonet, stiletto

daily ① *adj.* everyday, normal, common *It is quite common to see squirrels in the woods* ② *n.* newspaper

dainty *adj.* delicate, charming, exquisite, choice, tasty

dally *v.* play, trifle, dawdle, linger, loiter

damage *n.* harm, sabotage, vandalism, injury, hurt

damn *v.* curse, swear, condemn, criticize ★**bless**

damp *adj.* humid, clammy, dank ▷*moist* ★**dry**

damsel *n.* girl, maiden, lady, woman

dance *v.* hop, skip, jump, prance, frolic, gambol

danger *n.* peril, hazard, risk, jeopardy, menace ★**safety**

dangerous *adj.* perilous, precarious, unsafe, risky, hazardous ★**safe**

dangle *v.* hang, swing, sway

dank *adj.* sticky, muggy, moist, soggy ▷*damp*

dapper *adj.* spruce, natty, neat, stylish, trim ▷*smart* ★**scruffy**

dare *v.* brave, face, risk, defy, challenge, venture

daring *adj.* adventurous, dashing, bold, fearless ▷*brave* ★**timid**

dark *adj.* dusky, swarthy, shady, dim, dingy, shadowy ★**light**

darling *n.* pet, love, dear, favorite, beloved, precious

darn *v.* mend, sew, patch, repair

dart ① *n.* arrow, missile ② *v.* dash, hurtle *The express train hurtled through the tunnel,* charge, gallop

dash *v.* rush, gallop, run, career, fly, hasten

date ① *n.* time, point ② *n.* appointment *I have an appointment to see the doctor,* engagement ③ *v.* become old, become dated

daub *v.* plaster, spread, smear, dab, paint

daunt *v.* intimidate, terrify, scare, confront

dauntless *adj.* fearless, gallant, courageous ▷*brave* ★**discouraged**

dawdle *v.* linger, loiter, lag, waste time

Dances

Ballet	Polonaise
Bolero	Quadrille
Bop	Quickstep
Cha-cha	Rumba
Charleston	Samba
Conga	Square dance
Country dance	Tango
Disco	Tarantella
Fandango	Two-step
Flamenco	Twist
Fox-trot	Waltz
Gavotte	
Highland fling	
Jitterbug	
Jive	
Mazurka	
Minuet	
Morris dance	
Polka	

▷ *dally* ★**hurry**

dawn *n.* beginning, daybreak, daylight, morning, sunrise ★**dusk**

daze *v.* deaden, muddle, blind, dazzle ▷ *bewilder* DAYS

dazzle *v.* blind, glare, confuse ▷ *daze*

dead *adj.* deceased, departed, gone, lifeless, dull ★**alive**

deaden *v.* paralyze, blunt, muffle, drown

deadly *adj.* fatal, lethal, mortal, baleful, venomous

deaf *adj.* hard of hearing, unhearing, heedless

deal *v.* bargain, trade, market, communicate, traffic, give out

dealer *n.* merchant, trader, tradesman

dear ① *adj.* darling, beloved, loved, cherished *These old records are some of my cherished possessions* ② expensive, high-priced, costly DEER

death *n.* decease, end of life, mortality ★**life**

debate *v.* argue, discuss, dispute, question, contend

debris *n.* trash, junk ▷ *garbage*

debt *n.* obligation, debit, dues, liability ★**credit**

decay *v.* ① decompose, rot *The potatoes had been left too long and had rotted,* spoil ② decline, sink, dwindle, waste

deceive *v.* dupe, hoax, trick, cheat, mislead ▷ *betray* ★**enlighten**

decent *adj.* respectable, chaste, proper, fair, modest ★**indecent**

decide *v.* determine, rule, judge, resolve

declare *v.* avow, state, profess, proclaim, announce

decline ① *v.* descend, dwindle *The profits of the business had dwindled,* drop, fall ② *v.* refuse, say no ★**assent** ③ *n.* descent, slope, slant, dip, pitch

decorate *v.* embellish, adorn, ornament

decoy ① *v.* entice *We were enticed into the café by the smell of roasting coffee,* ensnare, mislead, tempt ② *n.* lure, bait

decrease *v.* diminish, lessen, wane, decline, reduce ★**increase**

decree *n.* law, edict, manifesto, rule, decision

decrepit *adj.* senile, infirm, crippled, feeble, frail ★**robust**

dedicate *v.* devote, apportion, assign, surrender, pledge

deduce *v.* draw, infer, conclude, glean, surmise, reason

deduct *v.* subtract, take from, remove, withdraw ★**add**

deed *n.* ① act, feat, stunt ② document, paper, contract *Michael was under contract to play ball for the team for three years*

deep *adj.* ① profound *The accident taught us a profound lesson about friendship,* bottomless, low ② learned, wise, sagacious

deface *v.* disfigure, deform, injure, mar, blemish ★**adorn**

defeat *v.* beat, conquer, overcome, vanquish ★**triumph**

defect *n.* flaw, fault, weak point, blemish, error

defective *adj.* imperfect, faulty, deficient, insufficient ★**perfect**

defend *v.* protect, guard, fortify, support, sustain, uphold ★**attack**

defer *v.* postpone, put off, adjourn, waive, yield ★**hasten**

defiant *adj.* mutinous, rebellious, resistant, aggressive ★**submissive**

deficient *adj.* wanting, imperfect, defective, faulty ★**superfluous**

defile *v.* taint, infect, pollute, sully, disgrace ★**cleanse**

define *v.* explain, interpret, designate, mark out, specify ★**obscure**

definite *adj.* clear, certain, clear-cut, distinct ▷ *sure* ★**vague**

deform *adj.* misshape, distort, contort, twist, warp

defraud *v.* fleece, swindle, embezzle, diddle ▷ *cheat*

defy *v.* resist, withstand, disregard, challenge, disobey ★**obey**

degrade *v.* humble, debase, corrupt, downgrade, cheapen ★**improve**

degree *n.* grade, step, measure, rate, scale *Our answers were scored on a scale from* *one to ten,* class

dejected *adj.* depressed, downcast, crestfallen, disheartened ▷*gloomy* ★**elated**

delay *v.* postpone, put off, detain, halt, hinder, impede ★**hurry**

deliberate ① *adj.* willful, calculated, intentional, planned ★**unintentional** ② *v.* reflect, contemplate, discuss

delicate *adj.* dainty, refined, soft, luxurious, modest, fragile, tender ★**harsh**

delicious *adj.* palatable, luscious, mellow, savory, choice ▷*scrumptious* ★**unpleasant**

delight *n.* enjoyment, pleasure, rapture, bliss ▷*happiness* ★**displease**

delightful *adj.* enjoyable, cheery, enchanting, lovely ▷*agreeable* ★**horrible**

deliver ① *v.* transfer, hand over, bear *She came bearing gifts for the whole family,* carry, convey ② free, liberate, release

delude *v.* cheat, hoax, hoodwink, mislead ▷*deceive* ★**guide**

deluge *n.* inundation, swamp, spate ▷*flood*

demand *v.* ① request, ask, appeal, entreat ② badger, pester, nag *My sister has been nagging me to take her to the park*

demeanor *n.* bearing, manner, conduct, air

demented *adj.* distracted, foolish, insane ▷*mad* ★**sane**

demolish *v.* destroy, wreck, ruin, smash, overthrow, knock down ★**build**

demon *n.* fiend, imp, devil, evil spirit

demonstrate *v.* prove, exhibit, illustrate ▷*show*

demote *v.* degrade, downgrade, relegate ★**promote**

demur *v.* hesitate, object, protest, doubt, waver ★**consent**

demure *adj.* coy, sedate, staid, sober, prudish, discreet ★**indiscreet**

den *n.* ① nest, cave, haunt, lair ② hideaway, retreat *This little room is my retreat, where I can sit and think,* study

denote *v.* designate, indicate, mean, show, point out

denounce *v.* decry, defame, attack, brand

▷*accuse* ★**praise**

dense *adj.* ① thick, solid, stout, compact ★**sparse** ② stupid, thick, stolid, obtuse ★**smart** DENTS

dent *n.* notch, cavity, chip, dimple, hollow

deny *v.* ① refuse, reject, repudiate ② disagree with *I am afraid that I disagree with what you say,* oppose, contradict ★**admit**

depart *v.* quit, go, retire, withdraw, vanish ▷*leave* ★**arrive**

department *n.* section, division, office, branch, province

depend on *v.* lean on, rely upon, trust in

depict *v.* describe, sketch, portray, outline, draw

deplorable *adj.* distressing, disastrous, shameful, scandalous ★**excellent**

deplore *v.* regret, lament, mourn ★**celebrate**

deport *v.* banish, exile, expel, oust

deposit *v.* drop, lay, place, put, bank, entrust, save ★**withdraw**

depot *n.* ① warehouse, storehouse ② terminus, station

depraved *adj.* corrupted, immoral, evil, sinful, vile *After calling me vile names, he left* ★**upright**

depreciate *v.* ① devalue, lessen, lose value *From the moment it was bought the car began losing value,* reduce ② belittle, disparage, deride ★**appreciate**

depress ① *v.* dishearten, dispirit, cast down ★**cheer** ② flatten, push down

depressed *adj.* dispirited, disheartened, despondent, fed up

deprive *v.* take away, rob, starve, divest *The traitor had been divested of all her honors* ★**bestow**

depth *n.* pit, shaft, well, chasm, gulf, abyss

deputy *n.* agent, delegate, lieutenant, assistant, councillor

derelict *adj.* abandoned, deserted *The* Mary Celeste *sailing ship was found deserted in the Atlantic,* forlorn

deride *v.* laugh at, jeer at, ridicule ▷*mock* ★**praise**

derive *v.* develop *Many English words developed from Norman-French,* obtain, arise from, originate

descend *v.* fall, drop, lower, decline, collapse ▷*sink* ★**ascend**

describe *v.* depict, portray, detail, define, tell

desert ① *n.* (*dez*-ert) wasteland, wilderness ② *adj.* desolate, arid, barren ③ *v.* (dez-*ert*) forsake, leave ▷*abandon* DESSERT

deserve *v.* be worthy of, merit, warrant, be entitled to ★**forfeit**

design *n.* drawing, painting, plan, pattern, scheme

desirable *adj.* ① agreeable, pleasing, good ② attractive, alluring, adorable

desire *v.* ① wish, require, need, want, crave ② long for, yearn after, pine for *My sister lived abroad, but always pined for home* ★**detest**

desist *v.* abstain, avoid, break off, cease, end

desolate *adj.* lonely, forlorn, miserable, wretched, alone ★**cheerful**

despair *n.* depression, misery, hopelessness, sorrow ▷*gloom* ★**hope**

desperate *adj.* drastic, reckless, frantic, rash, wild ★**hopeful**

despicable *adj.* contemptible, low, detestable, degrading ★**noble**

despise *v.* abhor, detest, loathe, look down upon ▷*hate* ★**prize**

despite *prep.* in spite of, notwithstanding

despondent *adj.* depressed, dispirited, brokenhearted ▷*miserable* ★**cheerful**

destination *n.* goal, terminus, end, objective, journey's end

destiny *n.* fate, lot, fortune, future, prospect, doom

destitute *adj.* poor, needy, bankrupt, penniless, poverty-stricken ★**wealthy**

destroy *v.* ruin, demolish, spoil, smash, exterminate ▷*wreck* ★**create**

destruction *n.* desolation, downfall, ruin, defeat, havoc ★**creation**

detach *v.* separate, part, divide, loosen, undo ★**attach**

detail *n.* item, fact, circumstance, point

detain *v.* delay, retard, restrain, arrest, hold

Dessert

Desert

up, hinder, impede ★**release**

detect *v.* notice, discover, observe, scent, track down ★**miss**

deter *v.* prevent, hold back, check, stop ▷*detain* ★**encourage**

deteriorate *v.* become worse, worsen, corrode, decline, decompose ★**improve**

determine *v.* find out, decide, identify, choose, regulate

detest *v.* abhor *Lucy was a peaceful person and abhorred violence,* loathe, despise ▷*hate* ★**adore**

devastate *v.* lay waste, ravage, overwhelm ▷*destroy*

develop *v.* mature, ripen, grow up, evolve, extend ★**restrict**

deviate *v.* diverge, differ, vary, contrast, wander ★**conform**

device *n.* apparatus, contrivance, instrument, appliance

devil *n.* imp, evil spirit, demon, fiend, Satan

devious *adj.* tricky, sly, subtle, cunning, roundabout ★**forthright**

devise *v.* contrive, fashion, form, plan, conceive

devoid *adj.* barren, empty, free, without, lacking ★**endowed**

devote *v.* allocate, allot, give, assign, dedicate

A
B
C
D
E
F
G
H
I
J
K
L
M
N
O
P
Q
R
S
T
U
V
W
X
Y
Z

devoted *adj.* dedicated, devout, loyal, caring, ardent ★**indifferent**

devour *v.* swallow, gulp, gorge, consume 3 *eat*

devout *adj.* pious, devoted, religious, faithful, passionate ★**insincere**

dexterous *adj.* able, active, deft, nimble 3 *skillful* ★**clumsy**

diagram *n.* outline, plan, sketch, draft, chart, drawing

dictate *v.* speak, utter, say, instruct, ordain, command

die *v.* expire, finish, end, pass away, perish, cease ★**live** DYE

differ *v.* ① vary, contrast, diverge *In this case, my views diverge strongly from yours* ② argue, conflict, clash

difference *n.* variance, distinctness, divergence, subtlety ★**agreement**

different *adj.* contrary, variant, distinct, original, unusual ★**same**

difficult *adj.* hard, puzzling, baffling, complex, laborious ★**easy**

difficulty *n.* trouble, bother, predicament ★**plight**

diffident *adj.* bashful, reserved, retiring, timid, unsure 3 *shy* ★**confident**

dig *v.* burrow, excavate, grub, delve, scoop

digest ① *v.* (di-*gest*) absorb, assimilate, dissolve ② *n.* (*di*-gest) abridgment, condensation, précis

digit *n.* ① number, figure, cipher ② finger, toe, thumb

dignified *adj.* grave, majestic, noble, lofty, grand ★**undignified**

dignity *n.* grandeur, merit, fame, gravity, nobility

dilapidated *adj.* neglected, unkempt, crumbling, decayed

dilemma *n.* quandary, plight, difficulty, predicament

dilute *v.* water down, weaken, reduce, thin

dim *adj.* dark, faint, pale, gloomy 3 *obscure* ★**bright**

diminish *v.* reduce, lessen, decrease, become smaller ★**enhance**

din *n.* uproar, racket, babble, commotion,

pandemonium 3 *noise* ★**quiet**

dingy *adj.* murky, dark, dreary, somber, gloomy 3 *dismal* ★**bright**

dip *v.* sink, subside, immerse, plunge

dire *adj.* alarming, appalling, awful, horrible 3 *terrible* DYER

direct ① *adj.* straight, even, blunt, candid ② *v.* aim, level, train, point

direction *n.* course, trend, way, track, route

dirt *n.* impurity, filth, grime, muck, soil

dirty *adj.* unclean, impure, filthy, sordid, squalid, nasty ★**clean**

disable *v.* cripple, lame, maim, disarm

disadvantage *n.* inconvenience, burden, damage, loss, obstacle ★**advantage**

disagree *v.* differ, revolt, decline, refuse, dissent, argue ★**agree**

disagreeable *adj.* unpleasant, obnoxious,

Dogs

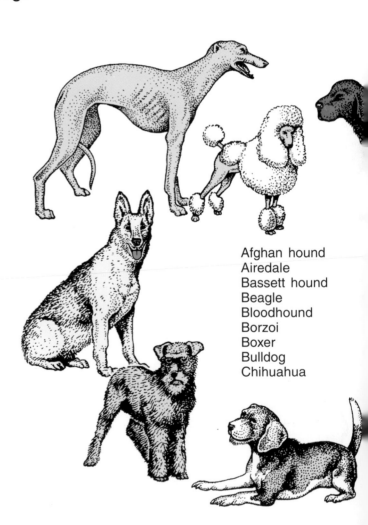

Afghan hound
Airedale
Bassett hound
Beagle
Bloodhound
Borzoi
Boxer
Bulldog
Chihuahua

unwelcome, offensive ★**agreeable**

disappear *v.* vanish, dissolve, fade, melt, depart, expire ★**appear**

disappoint *v.* frustrate, disillusion, let down, dismay, dissatisfy ★**please**

disapprove *v.* condemn, denounce, criticize, reproach ★**approve**

disaster *n.* calamity, catastrophe, accident, misfortune ★**triumph**

disbelief *n.* incredulity, distrust, doubt, suspicion ★**belief**

discard *v.* eliminate, get rid of, reject, scrap *Once we got a new car, I scrapped the old one,* throw away ★**adopt**

discern *v.* note, discover, distinguish

discharge *v.* ① dismiss, give notice to, expel ② detonate, emit, fire

disciple *n.* follower, learner, pupil, attendant

discipline *n.* correction, training, self-control, obedience

disclaim *v.* repudiate, disown, renounce, deny, reject ★**acknowledge**

disclose *v.* discover, show, reveal, expose, betray ▷*divulge* ★**conceal**

disconcert *v.* abash, confuse, confound, upset, baffle ★**encourage**

disconnect *v.* separate, detach, cut off, sever, uncouple ★**connect**

disconsolate *adj.* distressed, sad, forlorn, melancholy, desolate ▷*unhappy* ★**cheerful**

discontented *adj.* displeased, disgruntled, unsatisfied, reluctant ★**content**

discord *n.* disagreement, strife ★**concord**

discourage *v.* depress, dismay, dispirit, dishearten *I don't want to dishearten you, but our vacation is cancelled,* put off ★**encourage**

discouraged *adj.* crestfallen, daunted, depressed, downcast ★**encouraged**

discourteous *adj.* blunt, crude, churlish,

Chow chow
Collie
Dachshund
Dalmatian
Doberman pinscher
German shepherd
Golden retriever

Great Dane
Greyhound
Irish setter
Labrador
Old English
  sheepdog
Pekingese
Pointer
Poodle

Pug
St. Bernard
Saluki
Spaniel
Terrier
Whippet

A B C D E F G H I J K L M N O P Q R S T U V W X Y Z

outspoken, abrupt ★**courteous**

discover *v.* locate, surprise, unearth, uncover ▷*find* ★**conceal**

discreet *adj.* prudent, cautious, careful, tactful, sensible ★**indiscreet** DISCRETE

discriminate *v.* distinguish, penetrate, favor, judge, assess ★**confound**

discuss *v.* confer, consider, talk over, debate, argue

disdain *n.* ridicule, scorn, contempt, derision ★**admiration**

disease *n.* infection, contagion, illness, plague, ailment, sickness

disfigure *v.* blemish, deface, deform, mar, scar, spoil ★**adorn**

disgrace *n.* scandal, dishonor, shame, infamy, stigma ★**honor**

disguise *v.* conceal, mask, falsify, cloak, deceive, fake

disgust ① *n.* revulsion, loathing, distaste *The room was messy, and I entered it with distaste* ② *v.* repel, revolt, nauseate ★**admire**

dish *n.* plate, platter, bowl

dishearten *v.* depress, cast down, deter, deject ▷*discourage* ★**encourage**

dishonest *adj.* deceitful, unscrupulous, shady, crooked ★**honest**

disintegrate *v.* crumble, molder, decompose, rot, fall apart ★**unite**

dislike *v.* hate, loathe, detest, abhor, abominate ▷*despise* ★**like**

dismal *adj.* dreary, ominous, cheerless, depressing ▷*hopeless* ★**cheerful**

dismiss *v.* banish, discard, abandon, dispel, repudiate, release ★**appoint**

disobey *v.* rebel, transgress, resist, defy, ignore ★**obey**

disorder *n.* confusion, disarray, commotion, chaos ★**order**

dispel *v.* disperse, drive away, dismiss, allay, scatter ★**collect**

dispense *v.* distribute, arrange, allocate, supply, measure out ★**accept**

disperse *v.* scatter, separate, break up, spread abroad, distribute ★**gather**

display *v.* show, exhibit, unfold, expose,

flaunt *He flaunts his expensive clothes to his friends,* flourish ▷*reveal* ★**hide**

displease *v.* annoy, anger, irritate, upset, vex, offend, infuriate ★**please**

dispose *v.* arrange, place, position, regulate, order

dispose of *v.* discard, dump, destroy, eliminate, throw away ★**keep**

dispute ① *n.* conflict, quarrel, argument ② *v.* argue, refute, contend

disregard *v.* overlook, misjudge, despise, ignore, snub ★**heed**

disreputable *adj.* discreditable, dishonorable, disgraceful ▷*shameful* ★**honorable**

dissect *v.* examine, scrutinize, analyze, dismember

dissent *n.* disagreement, difference, repudiation, opposition ★**assent**

dissimilar *adj.* different, diverse, unlike, various ★**similar**

dissolve *v.* melt, thaw, break up, fade

dissuade *v.* deter, discourage, warn, put off ★**persuade**

distance *n.* extent, remoteness, range, reach, span, stretch

distinct *adj.* ① separate, independent, detached ② clear, conspicuous, lucid ★**hazy**

distinguish *v.* discern, discover, differentiate

distinguished *adj.* important, notable, great, famed, celebrated ★**ordinary**

distort *v.* deform, misshape, twist, bend, buckle

distract *v.* ① beguile, bewilder, disturb, confuse ② entertain

distress *v.* harass, embarrass, trouble, grieve ▷*worry* ★**soothe**

distribute *v.* give out, deliver, disperse, circulate ▷*dispense* ★**collect**

district *n.* area, community, locality *Pat and Mike have moved to a new locality,* neighborhood, region

distrust *v.* suspect, discredit, doubt, disbelieve ★**trust**

disturb *v.* annoy, bother, disquiet, unsettle, upset, confuse ★**calm**

a b c d e f g h i j k l m n o p q r s t u v w x y z

Domesticated Animals

Camel	Goat
Canary	Goose
Cat	Horse
Cattle	Parakeet
Chicken	Parrot
Dog	Pig
Donkey	Pigeon
Duck	Sheep
Elephant	

dither *v.* waver, hesitate, falter, oscillate

dive *v.* plunge, pitch, swoop, descend, drop

diverse *adj.* different, various, dissimilar, numerous, separate ★**identical**

divert *v.* ① alter, change, deflect ② entertain, gratify

divest *v.* disrobe, undress, strip

divide *v.* separate, dissect, part, divorce, distribute, apportion, split ★**join**

division *n.* portion, fragment, section, compartment, department

divorce *v.* annul, cancel, separate, divide, part, split up

divulge *v.* betray, disclose, tell, announce, broadcast, uncover

dizzy *adj.* giddy, confused, shaky, wobbling, muddled, staggering

do *v.* ① carry out, perform, act ② be adequate, suffice

do away with *v.* destroy, abolish, eliminate, kill

do up, *v.* fasten, tie, fix

docile *adj.* amenable, tame, meek, orderly, manageable ★**uncooperative**

doctrine *n.* article, belief, creed, dogma, teaching

document *n.* paper, deed, certificate, form

dodge *v.* avoid, parry, duck, elude, fend off

dogged *adj.* obstinate, morose, sullen, persistent, steadfast ★**docile**

doleful *adj.* dismal, woebegone, depressing, rueful, sad ▷*gloomy* ★**merry**

domestic ① *adj.* homey, household *The children always help with the household chores,* family, internal ② domesticated, tame

dominant *adj.* masterful, superior, supreme, prevalent ★**subordinate**

dominate *v.* rule, control, direct, tyrannize, overbear ★**yield**

donation *n.* gift, present, contribution

doom *n.* judgment, fate, verdict, destiny, destruction

door *n.* entrance, doorway, gate, gateway, portal

dose *n.* draft, potion, quantity, amount

doubt *v.* hesitate, waver, demur, suspect, mistrust, be dubious ★**trust**

doubtful *adj.* suspicious, dubious, indefinite, uncertain, unclear ★**certain**

dour *adj.* austere, dreary, grim, hard, severe ★**cheery**

dowdy *adj.* dull, plain, dingy, frumpish ▷*shabby* ★**elegant**

downcast *adj.* crestfallen, downhearted, dejected ▷*miserable* ★**happy**

downfall *n.* ruin, overthrow, misfortune, disgrace, failure

downright *adj.* blunt, candid, absolute, forthright, straightforward

doze *v.* snooze, slumber, sleep, nod off, drowse

A B C D E F G H I J K L M N O P Q R S T U V W X Y Z

drab *adj.* colorless, cheerless, dull, gloomy, gray ▷*dreary* ★**bright**

draft *v.* sketch, outline, draw, design, plan

drag *v.* draw, pull, haul, tug, tow, lug

drain ① *v.* draw, strain, drip, percolate, empty, dry, drink up ② *n.* conduit, sewer, pipe

dramatic *adj.* theatrical, exciting, surprising, sensational ★**ordinary**

drape *v.* hang, suspend, droop, cover

drastic *adj.* extreme, dire, desperate, harsh, radical ★**mild**

draw *v.* ① pull, tug, drag, haul ② sketch, design, depict, portray

drawback *n.* weakness, shortcoming, failing, defect, handicap ★**advantage**

dread *n.* fear, terror, horror, alarm, awe, dismay ▷*fright* ★**confidence**

dreadful *adj.* fearful, terrible, horrible, alarming ▷*awful* ★**comforting**

dream *n.* trance, vision, fancy, reverie, fantasy, illusion

dreary *adj.* dingy, gloomy, somber, cheerless ▷*dismal* ★**bright**

drench *v.* saturate, soak, steep, flood

dress ① *n.* clothing, vestments, costume, garb, apparel, attire ② *v.* wear, put on, don

dress up *v.* playact, don costumes

drift *v.* float, flow, wander, stray, meander
The little stream meandered through lush countryside

drill ① *v.* teach, exercise, train, discipline ② bore, penetrate, pierce

drink *v.* imbibe, swallow, absorb, quaff, sip

drip *v.* drop, ooze, percolate, drizzle, trickle

drive *v.* ① make, compel, force, oblige, prod, goad ② propel, direct, operate, actuate

drivel *n.* nonsense, babble, twaddle, bunkum, gibberish

drizzle *v.* dribble, mizzle, shower, spit ▷*rain*

droll *adj.* whimsical, comical, comic ▷*funny*

droop *v.* flag, sink, decline, languish, drop, bend, wilt

drop ① *v.* fall, sink, dip, plunge, plummet ② *n.* droplet, globule, drip

drown *v.* sink, immerse, swamp, submerge, extinguish

drowsy *adj.* sleepy, somnolent, dazed, tired

drudge *v.* toil, labor, struggle, plod, slave

drug *v.* dope, deaden, sedate, stupefy, poison

dry *adj.* ① arid, parched, moistureless, dried up ★**wet** ② uninteresting, boring, tedious, prosaic, dull

dubious *adj.* suspicious, fishy, suspect, untrustworthy ▷*doubtful* ★**trustworthy**

duck ① *n.* waterfowl ② *v.* plunge, submerge, dip, dodge, lurch

due *adj.* ① owing, unpaid, payable ② just, fair, proper ③ scheduled, expected DEW, DO

duel *n.* combat, contest, battle, swordplay

duffer *n.* blunderer, bungler, booby, dolt

dull *adj.* ① stupid, stolid, obtuse, dim-witted ② blunt, not sharp ③ boring, uninteresting, tedious

dumb ① *adj.* silent, speechless, mute ② foolish, stupid ▷*dull* ★**intelligent**

dummy ① *n.* mannequin, puppet, doll ② *n.* blockhead, dimwit ③ *adj.* artificial, fake, false

dump *v.* deposit, ditch, empty, throw away

dunce *n.* dimwit, dolt, blockhead, duffer, ignoramus ★**genius**

dungeon *n.* cell, prison, jail, vault

dupe *v.* cheat, defraud, deceive, outwit

duplicate *n.* copy, facsimile, replica, reproduction

durable *adj.* lasting, enduring, permanent, stable, reliable ★**fragile**

dusk *n.* twilight, nightfall, evening, gloaming ★**dawn**

dusty *adj.* grimy, dirty, filthy, grubby ★**polished**

duty *n.* ① obligation, responsibility, allegiance, trust, task ② impost, tax, excise

dwell *v.* stop, stay, rest, linger, tarry, live, reside

dwell on *v.* emphasize, linger over, harp on

dwindle *v.* diminish, decrease, decline, waste, shrink, become smaller ★**increase**

dye *n.* pigment, coloring matter, color, stain, tint DIE

a b c d e f g h i j k l m n o p q r s t u v w x y z

E e

eager *adj.* avid, enthusiastic, ambitious, ardent, zealous ▷*keen* ★**indifferent**

early *adj.* advanced, forward, soon ★**late**

earn *v.* make money, deserve, merit, rate, win, acquire ★**spend** URN

earnest *adj.* serious, sincere, determined, eager, zealous ★**flippant**

earth *n.* ① soil, dust, dry land ② world, globe, sphere

ease *n.* ① calm, repose, rest, quiet, peace ② dexterity, deftness ★**difficulty**

easy *adj.* effortless, smooth, simple, practicable ★**difficult**

eat *v.* consume, dine, chew, swallow, gorge

ebb *v.* flow back, fall back, recede, decline, wane ★**flow**

eccentric *adj.* queer, strange, odd, erratic, whimsical ▷*peculiar* ★**normal**

echo *v.* vibrate, reverberate, imitate

economical *adj.* moderate, reasonable, frugal ▷*thrifty* ★**expensive**

ecstasy *n.* joy, happiness, delight, elation ▷*bliss* ★**torment**

edge *n.* border, rim, brink, fringe, margin, tip ▷*end*

edible *adj.* eatable, comestible, safe, wholesome ★**inedible**

edit *v.* revise, correct, adapt, censor, publish

educate *v.* instruct, teach, tutor, coach, train

educated *adj.* learned, cultured, erudite, literate, well-bred ★**ignorant**

eerie *adj.* weird, unearthly, uncanny, awesome

effect ① *n.* outcome *What was the outcome of your interview?*, end, result ② *v.* cause, make, bring about, accomplish

effective *adj.* operative, serviceable, competent ★**useless**

efficient *adj.* competent, proficient, able ▷*effective* ★**inefficient**

effort *n.* exertion, toil, labor, accomplishment ▷*feat*

eject *v.* drive out, force out, expel, evict, oust, discharge

elaborate *adj.* complex, elegant, ornate, intricate ★**simple**

elated *adj.* excited, gleeful, joyous, overjoyed ▷*pleased* ★**downcast**

elderly *adj.* old, aged, ancient ★**youthful**

elect *v.* choose, determine, vote, select, pick

elegant *adj.* refined, luxurious, polished, classical ▷*graceful* ★**inelegant**

elementary *adj.* easy, effortless, basic, clear ▷*simple* ★**complex**

Eating verbs

bolt breakfast
chew chomp consume
devour dig in dine drink
eat eat up
feast feed finish off
gobble gorge gulp guzzle
imbibe
lap up lunch
masticate munch
nibble nosh
partake peck at pick at
quaff
relish
sample savor set to sip slurp
snack swallow sup swig swill
taste tuck in
wash down wine and dine
wolf down

elevate *v.* raise, erect, hoist, upraise ▷*lift* ★**lower**

eligible *adj.* qualified, suitable, acceptable, proper ▷*fit* ★**unfit**

eliminate *v.* do away with, abolish *The government has abolished many old laws,* exterminate, erase, delete ★**keep**

elude *v.* evade, avoid, depart, dodge, escape

embarrass *v.* abash, confuse, disconcert, fluster, shame

emblem *n.* badge, mark, brand, sign, crest, device

embrace *v.* ① hug, squeeze, cuddle, caress, hold ② include *The census figures include new arrivals this year,* encompass, enclose

emerge *v.* come out, exit, appear, arise, turn up ★**disappear**

emergency *n.* crisis, danger, extremity, predicament ▷*plight*

eminent *adj.* famous, noted, renowned, well-known, esteemed ▷*important* ★**unknown**

emit *v.* give off, belch, radiate, discharge, eject, vent ★**absorb**

emotion *n.* sentiment, feeling, fervor, passion

emotional *adj.* affected, sensitive, responsive, temperamental ★**cold**

emphasize *v.* accentuate, accent, intensify ▷*stress* ★**understate**

employ *v.* engage, hire, retain, apply, adopt ▷*use*

employee *n.* worker, workman, staff member, jobholder

empty ① *adj.* bare, barren, vacant *That house has been vacant for months,* hollow, unoccupied ★**full** ② *v.* discharge, drain, unload, pour out ★**fill**

enchant *v.* enthrall, bewitch, delight, gratify ▷*charm* ★**bore**

enclose *v.* surround, encircle, encompass, contain, include ★**open**

encounter *v.* come upon, meet, experience, face

encourage *v.* cheer, hearten, console, comfort, support ▷*urge* ★**dissuade**

encroach *v.* intrude, transgress, overstep, trespass, infringe

end ① *n.* conclusion, finish, limit, boundary *This river marks the boundary of the county* ② *v.* complete, close, terminate ▷*finish* ★**start**

endanger *v.* hazard, imperil, jeopardize ▷*risk* ★**protect**

endeavor *v.* aspire, aim, strive, struggle, try ▷*aim*

endless *adj.* ceaseless, continuous, everlasting, limitless

endorse *v.* undersign, uphold, support, guarantee, vouch for ★**disapprove**

endow *v.* settle upon, invest, award, bequeath, provide ▷*bestow* ★**divest**

endowed *adj.* talented, gifted, enhanced

endure *v.* bear, tolerate, suffer, go through, experience, cope with

enemy *n.* foe, adversary, rival, antagonist, opponent ★**friend**

energetic *adj.* dynamic, lively, vigorous, brisk ▷*active* ★**sluggish**

energy *n.* vigor, endurance, stamina, vitality, force, power

enforce *v.* apply, administer, carry out

engage *v.* ① employ, hire, charter, rent ② occupy *That new book has occupied my mind for weeks,* oblige, operate ③ pledge, betroth

engine *n.* machine, device, motor, turbine, appliance

engrave *v.* etch, stipple, incise, sculpture, carve, chisel

engrossed *adj.* absorbed, fascinated, enthralled ★**bored**

enhance *v.* intensify, strengthen, amplify, improve ★**decrease**

enigma *n.* riddle, puzzle, cryptogram, mystery, problem

enjoy *v.* like, be fond of, delight in, appreciate, savor ▷*relish* ★**detest**

enjoyable *adj.* likable, amusing, delicious ▷*agreeable* ★**disagreeable**

enlarge *v.* amplify, make bigger, expand, extend, magnify, increase, broaden ▷*swell* ★**shrink**

enlighten *v.* inform, teach, explain to,

Engines

Diesel engine
Internal combustion
 engine
Jet engine
Piston engine
Steam engine
Turbojet engine
Turboprop
 engine
Wankel engine

educate, instruct ★**confuse**

enlist *v.* conscript, employ, engage, muster, sign up, volunteer

enmity *n.* animosity, acrimony, bitterness, hostility, antagonism, antipathy ▷*hatred* ★**friendship**

enormous *adj.* immense, vast, tremendous, massive ▷*huge* ★**tiny**

enough *adj.* sufficient, adequate, ample, plenty ★**insufficient**

enrage *v.* aggravate, incite, incense, infuriate ▷*anger* ★**soothe**

enrich *v.* decorate, embellish, adorn, improve ★**impoverish**

enroll *v.* sign up, enlist, register, accept, admit ★**reject**

enslave *v.* bind, conquer, dominate, overpower, yoke ★**free**

ensue *v.* develop, follow, result, arise ▷*happen* ★**precede**

ensure *v.* confirm, guarantee, insure, protect, secure

entangle *v.* tangle, snarl, ensnare, complicate ▷*bewilder* ★**extricate**

enter *v.* go in, arrive, enroll, invade, commence, penetrate ★**leave**

enterprise *n.* endeavor, adventure, undertaking, concern, establishment

entertain *v.* amuse, charm, cheer, please, divert, beguile ★**bore**

enthrall *v.* captivate, charm, entrance, fascinate ★**bore**

enthusiasm *n.* fervor, ardor, interest, hobby, passion, eagerness

entice *v.* attract, beguile, coax, lead on, wheedle

entire *adj.* complete, intact, total, whole, full ★**partial**

entirely *adj.* absolutely, wholly, utterly *Our old dog came home, utterly tired and exhausted,* altogether ★**partially**

entitle *v.* ① allow, authorize, empower *As president, I am empowered to sign this document,* enable ② call, christen, term, name

entrance ① *n.* (*en*-trance) way in, access *There is an access to the garden on the far side,* doorway, gate, opening ② *v.* (en-*trance*) bewitch, captivate, charm ★**repel**

entreat *v.* beg, beseech, implore, ask

entry *n.* access, admission, admittance ▷*entrance* ★**exit**

envelop *v.* wrap, wind, roll, cloak, conceal, enfold

envious *adj.* jealous, grudging, covetous *Arlene cast a covetous eye at my new jacket,* resentful ★**content**

environment *n.* surroundings, neighborhood, vicinity, background

envy *v.* covet, grudge, desire, crave, resent

episode *n.* occasion, affair, circumstance, happening, installment

equal *adj.* ① matching, like, alike, same ★**different** ② fit *I'm not sure if Joe is really fit for this job*

equip *v.* furnish, provide, supply, fit out, rig

equipment *n.* stores, supplies, outfit, tackle *When we arrived at the lake, Sam found he'd left his fishing tackle behind,* gear

equivalent *adj.* equal, comparable, alike, similar, interchangeable ★**unlike**

era *n.* epoch, age, generation, period, time

eradicate *v.* uproot, weed out, remove, stamp out ▷*abolish*

erase *v.* cancel, rub out, obliterate, eliminate ▷*delete* ★**mark**

erect ① *adj.* upright, upstanding, rigid *The tent had a rigid metal frame* ★**relaxed** ② *v.* build, construct, put up ★**demolish**

err *v.* be mistaken, blunder, go astray,

A
B
C
D
E
F
G
H
I
J
K
L
M
N
O
P
Q
R
S
T
U
V
W
X
Y
Z

mistake, misjudge, sin

errand *n.* mission, assignment, duty, job
▷*task*

erratic *adj.* eccentric, irregular, unstable, unreliable ★**stable**

erroneous *adj.* untrue, false, faulty, inaccurate ▷*wrong* ★**correct**

error *n.* mistake, fault, flaw, fallacy, untruth ▷*blunder* ★**truth**

erupt *v.* blow up, explode, burst, vent ▷*discharge*

escape *v.* break free, get away, dodge, elude, evade ▷*flee* ★**capture**

escort ① *n.* (*es*-cort) guard, conductor, aide, attendant, procession ② *v.* (es-*cort*) accompany, conduct

especially *adv.* chiefly, principally, notably

essay *n.* ① effort, trial ② theme, manuscript, composition *Whoever writes the best composition gets a prize*

essence *n.* ① extract, juice, perfume ② substance *He spoke well, but there was no substance to his speech,* core, pith, character

essential *adj.* necessary, needed, vital, requisite ★**superfluous**

establish *v.* situate, place, station, found, organize, set up ★**upset**

estate *n.* property, land, fortune, inheritance

esteem *v.* honor, respect, admire ▷*like* ★**dislike**

estimate *v.* consider, calculate, figure, assess, reckon

estrange *v.* alienate, antagonize, separate ★**unite**

eternal *adj.* endless, ceaseless, forever, immortal, undying ★**temporary**

evacuate *v.* leave, desert, quit ▷*abandon* ★**occupy**

evade *v.* elude, avoid, get away from, escape from ★**face**

evaporate *v.* vanish, dissolve, disappear, condense, dry up

even *adj.* ① smooth, plane, flat, flush ② balanced, equal ★**uneven** ③ yet, still

evening *n.* eve, eventide, sunset ▷*dusk* ★**morning**

event *n.* occurrence, incident, happening

ever *adv.* always, evermore, perpetually, forever ★**never**

everlasting *adj.* continual, endless, permanent, lasting ★**temporary**

everyday *adj.* common, frequent, daily, familiar ★**occasional**

everything *n.* all, the whole, the lot

evict *v.* expel, eject, cast out, remove, kick out

evidence *n.* appearance, proof, sign, token, testimony

evident *adj.* obvious, apparent, plain, visible, conspicuous ★**obscure**

evil *v.* wicked, sinister, wrong, bad, hurtful, sinful ★**good**

exact *adj.* accurate, precise, definite, correct ▷*right* ★**inexact**

exaggerate *v.* magnify, overstate, overestimate, amplify ★**minimize**

examine *v.* check, inspect, scrutinize, test, quiz, question

example *n.* case, sample, specimen, pattern, model, illustration

exasperate *v.* provoke, anger, annoy, aggravate ★**soothe**

excavate *v.* mine, quarry, shovel, dig up, discover, unearth ★**bury**

exceed *v.* excel, surpass, better, beat, outstrip

excel *v.* outdo ▷*exceed*

excellent *adj.* admirable, good, superb, exquisite ▷*splendid* ★**inferior**

except *prep.* with the exception of, barring, save, saving, omitting

exceptional *adj.* unique, unusual, rare *Margaret has a rare gift for the piano,* uncommon ★**common**

excess *n.* too much, extreme, glut, extravagance, extreme ▷*surplus* ★**scarcity**

exchange *v.* trade, barter, swap, convert, change

excite *v.* inflame, inspire, provoke, rouse, thrill ★**quell**

excited *adj.* ablaze, wild, ecstatic, frantic, thrilled ★**bored**

exclaim *v.* state, say, utter, ejaculate, declare, cry out

exclude *v.* bar, shut out, prevent, boycott, forbid, leave out ★**include**

exclusive *adj.* only, personal, choice, particular, special ★**inclusive**

excuse *v.* forgive, pardon, absolve, exempt, release ★**accuse**

execute *v.* ① accomplish, do, carry out *The work was carried out just as I had expected,* achieve ② put to death, hang

exempt *v.* excuse, release, discharge, relieve, exonerate

exercise ① *n.* performance, lesson, lecture, training ② *v.* apply, train, practice *We have been practicing our tennis for months*

exert *v.* apply, exercise, strain, struggle, toil

exhale *v.* breathe out, expel, expire ★**inhale**

exhaust ① *v.* use up *We have used up all our butter,* consume, deplete, empty ② overtire, fatigue, weaken

exhibition *n.* spectacle, show, fair, pageant, display

exhilarate *v.* invigorate, animate, stimulate, thrill ★**discourage**

exile *v.* deport, banish, relegate, transport, dismiss

exist *v.* be, live, breathe, subsist, stand

exit *n.* way out, outlet, egress, door

expand *v.* inflate, spread, dilate, extend, amplify ▷*swell* ★**contract**

expansive *adj.* affable, genial, friendly, open, comprehensive

expect *v.* look out for, anticipate, assume, foresee, contemplate

expedition *n.* ① outing, excursion, exploration, quest *As a child I spent long hours in the library in the quest for knowledge* ② speed, dispatch, alacrity

expel *v.* evict, eject, discharge, throw out ★**admit**

expend *v.* spend, lay out, waste, consume, use up ▷*exhaust* ★**save**

expensive *adj.* costly, high-priced, valuable, rich ★**cheap**

experience ① *n.* training, practice, wisdom, knowledge ② *v.* encounter, try, undergo, endure

experiment *n.* trial, test, check, venture

expert *n.* specialist, master, authority, professional ★**novice**

expire *v.* ① breathe out, exhale ② die, lapse *The lease on this house will lapse at the end of the year,* run out ★**begin**

explain *v.* elucidate, spell out, define, expound, teach ★**mystify**

explanation *n.* definition, outline, answer, meaning

explode *v.* detonate, blow up, go off, burst, discharge

exploit ① *n.* deed, feat, act, stunt ② *v.* take advantage of, profit by

export *v.* ship, send out, send abroad

expose *v.* show, reveal, exhibit, present, lay bare, betray ★**cover**

express ① *v.* phrase, voice, put into words, utter ② *v.* squeeze out ③ *adj.* speedy, fast

expression *n.* ① phrase, idiom, sentence, statement ② look, countenance, appearance

exquisite *adj.* dainty, subtle, fine, refined ▷*beautiful* ★**coarse**

extend *v.* stretch, reach, lengthen ▷*expand* ★**shorten**

extent *n.* breadth, expanse, width, bulk, mass, reach, duration

exterior ① *n.* outside, surface ② *adj.* external, outer, outdoor ★**interior**

extinct *adj.* defunct, dead, exterminated ★**living**

extinguish *v.* put out, blow out, abolish, destroy, quench ★**establish**

extract *v.* take out, select, remove, withdraw ★**insert**

extraordinary *adj.* unusual, incredible, strange, uncommon, marvelous ★**common**

extravagant *adj.* wasteful, reckless, prodigal, lavish ★**stingy**

extreme *adj.* ① excessive, outrageous, intense ★**moderate** ② farthest, final, remote

extricate *v.* loose, loosen, remove, retrieve, pull out

exultant *adj.* rejoicing, jubilant, joyous, triumphant ▷*elated* ★**depressed**

F f

fable *n.* myth, legend, story, fantasy ★**fact**

fabric *n.* cloth, textile, material

fabulous *adj.* imaginary, legendary *Many tales have been passed down about the legendary deeds of Robin Hood,* mythical, marvelous ▷*wonderful*

face ① *n.* countenance, visage ② *n.* front, frontage, facade *The original facade was kept when the building was renovated* ③ *v.* confront, be opposite

facetious *adj.* frivolous, jocular, humorous, witty, comical ▷*funny* ★**serious**

facility *n.* ease, readiness, quickness, adroitness, knack

facsimile *n.* replica, copy, repro, photocopy

fact *n.* truth, deed, occurrence, event, reality, actuality ★**fiction**

factory *n.* plant, mill, works, shop

factual *adj.* true, actual, accurate, correct ▷*real* ★**false**

fad *n.* craze, fashion, passion, desire, mania *My sister has a mania for teddy bears,* vogue

fade *v.* discolor, bleach, dwindle, dim

fail *v.* collapse, fall, miss, trip, lose, flop ★**succeed**

failing *n.* frailty, weakness, fault, flaw ▷*defect*

failure *n.* collapse, crash, fiasco, downfall ★**success**

faint ① *adj.* indistinct *The writing was so indistinct that we could hardly read it,* soft, low, dim, feeble ② *v.* swoon, pass out, collapse FEINT

fair *adj.* ① just, equal, reasonable ★**unfair** ② mediocre *He was not a good piano player, just mediocre,* average, moderate ③ blonde, light-skinned, beautiful

faith *n.* trust, confidence, belief, fidelity, creed

faithful *adj.* ① loyal, constant, staunch, true ★**faithless** ② accurate, dependable *My watch is very dependable; it keeps accurate time* ★**inaccurate**

faithless *adj.* false, unfaithful, untrue ★**faithful**

fake *adj.* false, fictitious, pretended ▷*bogus* ★**genuine**

fall *v.* ① fall down, stumble, drop ② decline, dwindle *My mother's shares had dwindled and were worth much less,* lower ★**rise**

fall down *v.* stumble, lose one's balance

fall through *v.* collapse, fail, founder *The family business had foundered during the recession*

fallacy *n.* flaw, fault, mistake, illusion, deception

false *adj.* ① untrue, counterfeit, fake, inaccurate ② dishonest, disloyal ★**reliable**

falsehood *n.* lie, fiction, fable, fabrication, untruth, fib ★**truth**

falter *v.* reel, totter, stumble, waver, tremble

fame *n.* glory, distinction, honor, eminence, renown

familiar ① *adj.* common, frequent, well-known ② intimate *Joe and Mary are intimate friends of mine,* close, dear

famine *n.* scarcity, hunger, shortage, starvation

famished *adj.* hungry, starving, ravenous

famous *adj.* famed, well-known, celebrated, legendary *My grandmother was very attractive; her beauty was legendary,* notorious ★**unknown**

fan *v.* ventilate, cool, blow, stimulate

fanatic *n.* enthusiast, zealot, follower, fan

fanciful *adj.* romantic, fantastic, imaginary, unreal ★**ordinary**

fancy ① *adj.* decorative, beautiful, ornamental ② *v.* desire, hanker after *I had been hankering after a sea cruise all year,* yearn

fantastic *adj.* strange, bizarre, unfamiliar, romantic ▷*fanciful* ★**ordinary**

far *adj.* distant, faraway, remote ★**near**

fare ① *v.* manage *I managed quite well while my parents were abroad,* get along, happen ② *n.* charge, cost, fee ③ *n.* food, meals, menu

farewell *interj.* good-bye, so long, adieu *We*

bade our hosts adieu as we drove off

farm ① *v.* cultivate, raise, grow ② *n.* farmstead, homestead, ranch, holding *We owned a small holding of land in the west*

fascinate *v.* bewitch, beguile, enthrall, engross ★**bore**

fashion ① *n.* style, fad, mode, manner ② *v.* form, carve, sculpt, devise

fast ① *adj.* rapid, quick, speedy, brisk ② *v.* starve, famish, go hungry

fasten *v.* fix, tie, attach, bind, hitch, truss ★**unfasten**

fat ① *adj.* stout, corpulent *Uncle Harry was a corpulent old man* ▷*plump* ★**thin** ② *n.* grease, oil, tallow, shortening

fatal *adj.* deadly, lethal, destructive, mortal ★**harmless**

fate *n.* fortune, destiny, future, lot, portion

fathom *v.* unravel, understand, follow, comprehend

fatigue ① *n.* tiredness, weariness ② *v.* tire, exhaust, languish *The survivors of the shipwreck languished in an open boat*

fault *n.* ① defect, flaw, imperfection ② blame, responsibility, error

faulty *adj.* imperfect, defective, unreliable, unsound, broken ★**perfect**

favor ① *n.* kindness, courtesy, benefit ② *v.* indulge, prefer, approve ★**disapprove**

favorite ① *n.* choice, darling, preference ② *v.* best-liked, chosen, preferred

fawn *v.* crouch, crawl, grovel FAUN

fear ① *n.* fright, alarm, terror, panic, shock ★**courage** ② *v.* dread, be afraid, doubt

fearful *adj.* timid, anxious, alarmed, worried ▷*afraid* ★**courageous**

fearless *adj.* gallant, courageous, daring, valiant *My ailing mother made a valiant effort to keep working* ▷*brave* ★**timid**

feast *n.* banquet, repast, dinner

feat *n.* deed, exploit, achievement, performance, stunt FEET

feature *n.* mark, peculiarity, distinction, characteristic

fee *n.* charge, commission, cost

feeble *adj.* frail, faint, flimsy, puny ▷*weak* ★**strong**

Feat

Feet

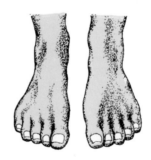

feed *v.* nourish, sustain, foster, nurture *These plants must be nurtured if they are to survive*

feel *v.* touch, handle, perceive, comprehend, know, suffer

feign *v.* fake, pretend, act, sham FAIN

feint *n.* bluff, pretense, dodge, deception FAINT

fellow *n.* companion, comrade, associate, colleague

female *adj.* feminine, womanly, girlish, maidenly ★**male**

fence ① *n.* barrier, paling, barricade ② *v.* dodge, evade, parry *The sudden attack was parried by the defenders,* duel

ferocious *adj.* fierce, savage, brutal, grim, vicious ★**gentle**

fertile *adj.* fruitful, productive, rich, abundant ★**barren**

fervent *adj.* warm, passionate, enthusiastic, zealous ▷*ardent*

festival *n.* celebration, carnival, fête, jubilee

festive *adj.* convivial, jovial, sociable, gleeful, cordial ★**somber**

fetch *v.* bear, bring, carry, deliver, convey

fête *n.* bazaar, carnival, fair, festival

fetter *v.* manacle, handcuff, shackle, restrain

feud *n.* dispute, grudge, conflict, discord ★**harmony**

fever *n.* illness, infection, passion, excitement, heat, ecstasy

few *adj.* scant, scanty, meager, paltry, not many

fiasco *n.* washout, calamity, disaster, failure

fib *n.* lie, falsehood, untruth

fickle *adj.* unstable, changeable, faithless, disloyal ★**constant**

fiction *n.* stories, fable, myth, legend, invention ★**fact**

fidelity *n.* faithfulness, loyalty, allegiance *I owe allegiance to my family and my country* ★**treachery**

fidget *v.* be nervous, fret, fuss, jiggle, squirm

field *n.* farmland, grassland, green, verdure, meadow, prairie

fiend *n.* devil, demon, imp, beast, brute

fiendish *adj.* atrocious, cruel, devilish, diabolical

fierce *adj.* barbarous, cruel, brutal, merciless ▷*savage* ★**gentle**

fiery *adj.* passionate, inflamed, excitable, flaming ★**impassive**

fight *n. & v.* conflict, argument, encounter, combat, contest, battle

figure ① *n.* symbol, character, numeral ② *n.* form, shape, model ③ *v.* calculate, reckon *Bella has reckoned the amount correctly*

filch *v.* steal, thieve, sneak, purloin *Someone has purloined the letters from our mailbox*

file ① *v.* scrape, grind, grate, rasp ② *n.* binder, case, folder

fill *v.* load, pack, cram, replenish, occupy ★**empty**

filter *v.* sieve, sift, refine, clarify, screen, percolate PHILTER

filth *n.* impurity, dirt, soil, slime, smut, grime, squalor, muck ★**purity**

filthy *adj.* unclean, impure, nasty, foul ▷*dirty* ★**pure**

final *adj.* terminal, closing, ultimate, conclusive ▷*last*

find *v.* discover, achieve, locate, obtain, perceive, meet with *Our plans met with the approval of the committee* ★**lose** FINED

fine ① *adj.* thin, minute, smooth, slender ② *adj.* excellent, sharp, keen, acute ③ *n.* forfeit, penalty

finesse *n.* skill, competence, deftness

finger ① *v.* feel, grope, handle, touch ② *n.* digit, thumb, pinkie

finish *v.* accomplish, complete, close, conclude ▷*end* ★**begin**

fire ① *n.* blaze, conflagration, heat ② *v.* ignite, light, discharge, shoot

firm ① *adj.* stable, steady, solid, substantial ② *n.* company, business

first *adj.* beginning, earliest, initial, chief, principal

fishy *adj.* suspicious, dubious, doubtful ★**honest**

fissure *n.* breach, cleft, crack, cranny FISHER

fit *adj.* ① apt, suitable, fitting, able ② trim, hale, healthy, sturdy

fitting *adj.* proper, suitable, appropriate, correct ★**unsuitable**

fix ① *v.* repair, mend, attach, fasten ② *n.* predicament, jam, pickle, plight *After the earthquake, the town was in a desperate plight*

flabby *adj.* baggy, drooping, feeble, sagging, slack

flag ① *v.* droop, languish, dwindle, fail ② banner, ensign, colors *The regimental colors were flying at half-mast*

flagrant *adj.* blatant, bold, brazen, arrant ★**secret**

flair *n.* knack, talent, faculty, ability, gift FLARE

flame *n.* fire, blaze, radiance

flap *v.* agitate, flutter, wave, swing, dangle

flare ① *v.* blaze, burn, glare, flash, glow ② *n.* signal, beacon FLAIR

flash *v.* gleam, glimmer, sparkle, twinkle,

Flags

Jack

Banner

Burgee

Signaling flags

Streamer

Standard

Ensign

Pennant

Jolly Roger

Bunting

scintillate

flat ① *adj.* level, smooth, even, horizontal ② *n.* apartment, chambers

flatter *v.* blandish, toady, soft-soap, butter up, curry favor *He gives me presents, but only to curry favor with me* ★**criticize**

flavor *n.* taste, savor, tang, aroma, quality

flaw *n.* fault, defect, blemish, mark, weakness

flawless *adj.* perfect, immaculate, faultless, sound ★**imperfect**

flee *v.* escape, abscond, run away, bolt, vanish ★**stay** FLEA

fleet ① *adj.* rapid, speedy, quick, nimble ▷*swift* ★**slow** ② *n.* navy, armada, flotilla *A flotilla of yachts sailed up the river*

fleeting *adj.* passing, brief, momentary, temporary ★**lasting**

flexible *adj.* pliant, pliable, supple, elastic

flicker *v.* blaze, glitter, flare, burn, sparkle

flimsy *adj.* slight, meager, fragile, trivial, rickety, weak, feeble ★**sturdy**

flinch *v.* cower, cringe, shrink, wince *I had twisted my ankle, and winced with pain as I climbed the hill*

fling *v.* throw, pitch, cast, heave ▷*hurl*

flippant *adj.* saucy, pert, brash, impudent, glib ★**earnest**

float *v.* drift, glide, hover, sail, swim

flock *n.* herd, drove, crush, group

flog *v.* beat, chastise, flay, lash, spank

flood *v.* deluge, engulf, inundate *The town was inundated when the river overflowed*, drown, swamp

floor *n.* deck, base, bottom, platform, level, story

flop *v.* flap, fall, drop, droop, fall flat

florid *adj.* ruddy, flushed, red, ornate ★**pale**

flounce *v.* bounce, fling, jerk, spring, bob

flounder ① *v.* bungle, fail, falter, fumble ② *n.* flatfish

flour *n.* meal, bran, farina FLOWER

Flower

Flour

flourish *v.* ① shake, brandish, flaunt ② blossom, bloom, prosper ▷ *thrive*

flow *v.* run, stream, glide, sweep, swirl ▷ *gush* FLOE

flower *n. & v.* blossom, bloom, bud FLOUR

fluent *adj.* vocal, facile, articulate *Sally is very articulate and has a great command of language,* flowing, fluid

fluid *adj.* watery, flowing, liquid, runny ★**solid**

flummox *v.* baffle, confuse, fluster, confound ▷ *bewilder* ★**enlighten**

flush ① *v.* glow, bloom, blush ② *v.* douse, drench, rinse ③ *adj.* level, even

fluster *v.* bother, confuse, perturb ▷ *fuss* ★**calm**

flutter *v.* wave, flap, flop, flitter, hover, flit

fly ① *v.* take flight, glide, soar, float ② *v.* escape, hasten ③ *n.* winged insect

foam *n.* froth, scum, lather, suds, surf

foe *n.* enemy, opponent, rival, adversary ★**friend**

fog *n.* mist, vapor, haze, cloud

foil ① *v.* defeat, overcome, elude ② *n.* sheet metal, tinfoil, film, flake

fold *n. & v.* crease, hem, seam, crimp, pleat FOALED

follow *v.* ① pursue, succeed, come after ② understand, catch on to

folly *n.* silliness, foolishness, absurdity, craziness ▷ *nonsense* ★**wisdom**

fond *adj.* tender, loving, caring ▷ *affectionate* ★**hostile**

fondle *v.* pet, stroke, cuddle, caress, coddle

food *n.* nourishment, nutriment, provender, provisions, fare

fool ① *n.* idiot, dunce, clown, blockhead, simpleton ② *v.* deceive, trick, swindle

foolhardy *adj.* reckless, impetuous, madcap ▷ *rash* ★**cautious**

foolish *adj.* absurd, ridiculous, daft ▷ *silly* ★**wise**

for *prep.* on behalf of, toward, because of ★**against** fore, four

forbid *v.* bar, ban, prohibit, deter, hinder, prevent ★**allow**

force ① *n.* energy, strength, might, power ② *v.* make, compel, coerce *It's no use, you can't coerce me into flying home,* push

fore *adj.* first, front, leading FOR, FOUR

forecast *v.* foresee, predict, foretell, prophesy

foreign *adj.* alien, strange, remote, exotic, outlandish ★**domestic**

foremost *adj.* chief, leading, principal, uppermost

forfeit *v.* abandon, give up, lose, relinquish, sacrifice ★**reward**

forge *v.* ① counterfeit, falsify, copy, imitate ② construct, form, make, fashion

forgery *n.* fake, dud, counterfeit, imitation, phony

forget *v.* overlook, neglect, lose sight of ★**remember**

forgive *v.* pardon, absolve, reprieve, let off, overlook ★**blame**

forlorn *adj.* lonely, desolate, miserable, wretched ★**hopeful**

form ① *v.* make, fabricate, fashion, contrive, create ② *n.* manner, fashion, style ③ *n.* shape, figure *I made a clay figure of a pirate*

formal *adj.* stiff, solemn, ceremonial, ritualistic, aloof ★**informal**

former *adj.* earlier, previous, prior ★**later**

formidable *adj.* awful, terrible, alarming, terrifying, serious ★**trivial**

forsake *v.* abandon, give up, desert, discard, leave ▷*quit* ★**resume**

forth *adv.* ahead, forward, onward, outward

forthright *adj.* frank, candid, direct, bald, blunt ★**devious**

forthwith *adv.* immediately, directly, at once, instantly ★**soon**

fortify *v.* ① strengthen, confirm, corroborate, hearten ② garrison, protect, buttress *The old house was crumbling and the walls needed to be buttressed* ★**weaken**

fortitude *n.* courage, endurance, bravery, composure ▷*strength* ★**cowardice**

fortunate *adj.* happy, felicitous, auspicious, rosy ▷*lucky* ★**unfortunate**

fortune *n.* ① affluence, wealth, treasure ② chance, destiny, fate

forward ① *adv.* onward, forth, ahead, before ② *adj.* progressive, bold, audacious ★**modest** ③ *v.* advance, send, transmit

foster *v.* ① help, promote, aid ② care for, cherish, nurse

foul *adj.* mucky, nasty, filthy, dirty, murky ★**fair** FOWL

found *v.* create, build, erect, establish

foundation *n.* establishment, base, basis, groundwork *You will pick up Spanish easily, for you already have the groundwork*

fountain *n.* spring, well, reservoir, source

fowl *n.* bird, chicken, poultry FOUL

foxy *adj.* crafty, slick, cunning, tricky ▷*artful* ★**naive**

fraction *n.* portion, part, division ▷*fragment*

fracture *n.* break, cleft, crack, fissure, opening ▷*split*

fragile *adj.* brittle, frail, delicate, dainty ▷*flimsy* ★**robust**

fragment *n.* portion, bit, chip, morsel, piece ▷*fracture*

fragrance *n.* aroma, smell, odor ▷*scent*

frail *adj.* weak, feeble, infirm ▷*fragile*

frame *n.* framework, casing, shape, mount, chassis

frank *adj.* sincere, candid, open, honest, blunt ▷*truthful* ★**insincere**

frantic *adj.* excited, furious, distracted, wild, mad ▷*frenzied* ★**calm**

fraud *n.* deceit, fake, extortion, swindle ▷*forgery*

fraudulent *adj.* sham, fake, counterfeit ▷*bogus* ★**genuine**

fray *n.* combat, contest, battle, brawl ▷*rumpus*

freak *adj.* abnormal, bizarre *A snowstorm in the tropics would be bizarre,* odd, unusual ★**common**

free ① *adj.* unhindered, at liberty, liberated, unrestricted ② *adj.* gratuitous, gratis, without cost ③ *v.* let loose, unleash, release

freeze *n.* ice, frost, refrigerate FREES, FRIEZE

frenzied *adj.* agitated, excited, furious, hysterical *Lisa became hysterical when she saw the house on fire* ▷*frantic* ★**placid**

frequent *adj.* repeated, numerous, recurrent, common ▷*regular* ★**rare**

frequently *adv.* often, many times, commonly ★**rarely**

fresh *adj.* new, young, vigorous, blooming, recent, wholesome ★**stale**

fret *v.* worry, harass, irritate, torment ▷*vex* ★**calm**

friction *n.* ① rubbing, grating, contact, abrasion ② ill-feeling, discord, dispute

friend *n.* companion, associate, ally, crony *On Saturdays, my father plays golf with some of his cronies,* pal ▷*chum*

friendly *adj.* affable, amicable, kindly, cordial ▷*genial* ★**hostile**

friendship *n.* affection, fellowship, fondness, harmony ▷*concord* ★**enmity**

A
B
C
D
E
F
G
H
I
J
K
L
M
N
O
P
Q
R
S
T
U
V
W
X
Y
Z

fright *n.* alarm, dread, dismay, terror ▷*fear* ★**calm**

frighten *v.* daunt, dismay, scare, alarm ▷*terrify* ★**reassure**

frightful *adj.* alarming, shocking, ghastly ▷*horrible* ★**pleasant**

frigid *adj.* cool, chilly, icy, frozen, wintry ★**warm**

fringe *n.* edge, border, limits, outskirts

frisky *adj.* lively, spirited, playful, active ★**quiet**

frivolous *adj.* frothy, facetious, flippant, foolish ▷*trivial* ★**serious**

frock *n.* robe, dress, gown, smock

frolic *v.* gambol, caper, frisk, sport

front *n.* fore, brow, forehead, face, facade, beginning ★**back**

frontier *n.* border, boundary, edge, limit

frosty *adj.* chilly, frigid, frozen, freezing ▷*cold* ★**warm**

froth *n.* scum, bubbles ▷*foam*

frown *v.* glower, grimace, glare ▷*scowl* ★**smile**

frugal *adj.* thrifty, economical, careful, sparing *We were poor in the old days and needed to be sparing with our money* ▷*meager* ★**wasteful**

fruitful *adj.* fertile, productive, flourishing

Futile

It was hopeless, the bear was too big for Zak to carry.

★**barren**

fruitless *adj.* unprofitable, sterile, barren, pointless ★**fruitful**

frustrate *v.* thwart, balk, foil, hinder, defeat ★**fulfill**

fugitive *n.* escapee, runaway, deserter

fulfill *v.* perform, render, please, accomplish, achieve ★**frustrate**

full *adj.* loaded, packed, laden, charged, abundant, complete ★**empty**

fumble *v.* grope, spoil, mismanage, flail ▷*bungle*

fun *n.* sport, frolic, gaiety, jollity, entertainment, amusement

function ① *n.* service, purpose, activity ② *n.* affair, party, gathering ③ *v.* act, operate, work

fund *n.* stock, supply, pool, store, treasury *The city treasury has a small surplus this year*, reserve

fundamental *adj.* basic, essential, primary, rudimentary ★**unimportant**

funny *adj.* comical, droll, amusing, ridiculous ▷*humorous* ★**solemn**

furious *adj.* agitated, angry, fierce, intense ▷*frantic* ★**calm**

furnish *v.* ① supply, provide, offer ② equip

furrow *n.* groove, channel, hollow, seam, rib

further ① *adj.* extra, more, other, supplementary, ② *v.* advanced, aid, hasten

furtive *adj.* secretive, sly, hidden ▷*stealthy* ★**open**

fury *n.* anger, frenzy, ferocity, passion ▷*rage* ★**calm**

fuse *v.* melt, smelt, combine, merge, solder, weld, integrate ▷*join*

fuss *n.* stir, excitement, tumult, bustle, bother, commotion ▷*ado* ★**calm**

fussy *adj.* busy, faddish, fastidious, finicky, exacting ★**plain**

futile *adj.* useless, in vain, hopeless *It was hopeless, the bear was too big for Zak to carry*, barren, forlorn, ineffective ★**effective**

future *adj.* forthcoming, coming, impending, eventual

fuzzy *adj.* murky, foggy, misty, unclear

G g

gain *v.* get, win, acquire, attain, profit

gale *n.* storm, wind, hurricane, tornado, cyclone

gallant *adj.* courageous, noble, chivalrous ▷*brave*

gallop *v.* dash, run, career, rush

gamble *v.* bet, risk, wager, chance GAMBOL

gambol *v.* prance, romp, frisk, frolic ▷*jump* GAMBLE

game *n.* ① sport, pastime, contest, competition ★**work** ② quarry, prey

gang *n.* crew, team, troop, crowd, cluster, party

gap *n.* space, blank, hole, break, cranny, chink, opening, crack, interval

gape *v.* yawn, stare, gaze, gawk ▷*look*

garbage, *n.* trash, rubbish, refuse, waste, slop

garden *n.* flower bed, vegetable patch, patio, park

garment *n.* clothes, dress, attire, robe, costume ▷*clothing*

garret *n.* attic, loft, cupola

gas *n.* vapor, fume, mist, smoke

gasp *v.* gulp, pant, choke ▷*breathe*

gate *n.* door, portal, gateway GAIT

gather *v.* ① collect, pick up, pick, draw, amass, assemble, flock, hoard, acquire ★**disperse** ② understand *I understand that you have been elected treasurer of the club,* assume, judge

gathering *n.* meeting, assembly, function, affair, company, collection

gaudy *adj.* flashy, cheap, tawdry, loud, showy

gaunt, *adj.* thin, lean, skinny, spare ▷*haggard* ★**robust**

gauge ① *n.* measure, meter, rule ② *v.* judge, measure, estimate *We must estimate the number of beans in the jar,* probe GAGE

gaze *v.* stare, look, regard, contemplate

gear *n.* tackle, array, accessories, machinery, harness, equipment

gem *n.* jewel, stone, treasure

general *adj.* normal, usual, habitual, customary, total, whole ★**local**

generous *adj.* free, liberal, kind ★**selfish**

genial *adj.* cheerful, cheery, sunny, hearty, cordial, pleasant ▷*jolly* ★**cold**

genius *n.* brilliance, prowess, talent, power, skill, cleverness, brains ★**stupidity**

genteel *adj.* refined, polished, civil, courteous, well-bred, polite, elegant ★**boorish**

gentle *adj.* ① easy, mild, soft, kind, moderate, tender, humane ② gradual, faint, feeble, slight *The field had a slight slope as it came down to the river*

genuine *adj.* ① real, authentic, true, sound ② sincere, honest, candid, frank ★**false**

germ *n.* microbe, seed, embryo, nucleus

gesture *n.* sign, signal, motion, nod, shrug, movement

get *v.* ① acquire, obtain, gain, win, receive, secure, achieve, inherit ★**forfeit** ② understand, catch on *It took Johnny quite a while to catch on to what I meant,* fathom, figure out, learn

get up *v.* arise, awake, awaken

get rid of *v.* discard, reject, throw away, scrap

ghastly *adj.* shocking, hideous, horrible, fearful, terrible, frightful

ghost *n.* spook, spirit, specter, banshee, phantom, apparition

ghostly *v.* uncanny, haunted, eerie, weird

giant *adj.* mammoth, huge, colossal, enormous, tremendous, immense ▷*big, gigantic* ★**tiny**

gibber *v.* gabble, prattle, jabber

gibberish *n.* nonsense, drivel, garbage

gibe *v.* jeer, sneer, scoff, deride ▷*taunt*

giddy *adj.* dizzy, whirling, reeling, unsteady, wild, reckless

gift *n.* ① present, donation, bounty, boon ② talent, skill *Her skill was so great that I knew she must have been born with it,* ability, power

gigantic *adj.* stupendous, titanic, colossal ▷*giant* ★**minute**

giggle *v.* chuckle, chortle, cackle, snicker ▷*laugh*

gingerly *adv.* carefully, daintily, warily, cautiously

girder *n.* rafter, joist, beam

girl *n.* maid, maiden, miss, damsel, young woman, lass, wench

girlish *adj.* maidenly, dainty, feminine

girth *n.* circumference, perimeter, fatness, breadth

gist *n.* essence, substance, kernel, nub, pith, significance

give *v.* ① donate, grant, distribute, bestow ② bend, yield *The wooden footbridge suddenly yielded under his weight and crashed into the stream,* relax, recede ③ produce, yield ④ pronounce, utter, emit ★**take**

give back *v.* return, restore

give forth *v.* emit, send out, radiate

give in *v.* surrender, quit, yield

give off *v.* belch, emit, exude

give up *v.* surrender, give in, relinquish, hand over

giver *n.* donor, bestower, presenter

glad *adj.* joyful, joyous, delighted, pleased ▷*happy* ★**sorry**

gladden *v.* make happy, gratify, delight, elate ▷*please* ★**grieve**

gladly *adv.* freely, readily, cheerfully, willingly

glamour *n.* romance, interest, fascination, attraction, enchantment

glance ① *n.* look, glimpse, peep ② *v.* peer, notice ③ brush, shave, graze, *The bullet merely grazed his head*

glare ① *v.* blaze, glow, flare, sparkle, dazzle ② frown, glower, stare

glaring *adj.* ① sparkling, dazzling ② blatant, notorious, conspicuous

glass *n.* tumbler, goblet, beaker, mirror, looking glass

glaze *v.* polish, gloss, burnish, varnish

gleam *v.* sparkle, glitter, flash, glisten, twinkle

glee *n.* jollity, gaiety, elation, triumph ▷*happiness*

glib *adj.* fluent, slick, smooth, slippery, facile, talkative

glide *v.* slide, slither, slip, soar, sail, skate, skim

glimmer *v.* sparkle, scintillate, flicker, glow, gleam

glimpse *v.* spy, spot, glance, view

glisten *v.* shine, glitter, glow, gleam

glitter *v.* gleam, sparkle, flash, glint, glisten, scintillate

gloat *v.* whoop, exult, crow, revel, triumph

globe *n.* ball, sphere, planet, earth, world

gloom *n.* darkness, gloaming, dusk, shadow, dimness, bleakness ★**light**

gloomy *adj.* cheerless, black, dark, bleak, cloudy, overcast, dismal, dour, glum, melancholy ▷*dreary* ★**happy**

glorious *adj.* brilliant, lustrous, noble, exalted, renowned ▷*splendid*

glory *n.* brilliance, radiance, pride ▷*splendor*

gloss *n.* luster, sheen, shimmer, polish ▷*glaze*

glossy *adj.* shiny, burnished, sleek, slick, polished

glow *n. & v.* glare, glitter, bloom, blush, flush, shine, gleam, twinkle

glower *v.* frown, stare, scowl, glare

glue ① *n.* paste, gum, cement, mucilage, adhesive, rubber cement ② *v.* stick, fasten

glum *adj.* sullen, sulky, morose, miserable, dejected, downcast ▷*gloomy*

glut *n.* abundance, plenty, too much, surplus

glutton *n.* gorger, stuffer, crammer, pig, gormandizer, gourmand

gnash *v.* grind, chomp, bite, crunch

gnaw *v.* chew, nibble, bite, champ, consume

go *v.* ① walk, pass, move, travel, depart, proceed ② stretch, reach, extend *The prairie extended as far as the mountain range*

go after *v.* pursue, chase, follow

go ahead *v.* progress, proceed, continue

go away *v.* leave, depart, vanish, disappear

go back *v.* return, resume, withdraw

go by *v.* pass, elapse, vanish

go in *v.* enter, advance, invade, penetrate

go in for *v.* enter, take part, participate, compete

go off *v.* explode, blow up, depart

go on *v.* continue, advance, proceed, move ahead, keep up

go up *v.* climb, mount, rise ▷*ascend*

goad *v.* prod, incite, impel, drive, urge, sting, worry

goal *n.* target, ambition, aim, object, destination

gobble *v.* devour, gorge, swallow, gulp, bolt

goblin *n.* sprite, demon, gnome, elf

God *n.* the Creator, the Father, the Almighty, Jehovah, the Divinity, the Holy Spirit, King of Kings, the Supreme Being

godless *adj.* unholy, unclean, wicked, savage, profane ★**righteous**

golden *adj.* excellent, precious, brilliant, bright

good *adj.* ① excellent, admirable, fine ② favorable, *The calm weather provides favorable conditions for waterskiing,* advantageous, profitable ③ righteous, moral, true *A true friend can forgive your mistakes* ④ clever, skillful, expert ⑤ fit, proper, suited ★**bad**

goodness *n.* excellence, merit, worth, honesty, kindness ▷*virtue* ★**evil**

goods *n.* wares, commodities, cargo, load, material, belongings

gorge ① *v.* swallow, gulp, devour ▷*eat* ② *n.* canyon, glen, valley

gorgeous *adj.* beautiful, ravishing, stunning, superb, magnificent

gossip *v.* chat, chatter, prattle, tittle-tattle

gouge *v.* excavate, groove, dig out

govern *v.* rule, reign, manage, direct, guide, control, conduct, command

government *n.* rule, administration, supervision, parliament

governor *n.* director, manager, leader, chief, overseer, head of state

gown *n.* robe, dress, frock

grace *n.* elegance, refinement, polish, symmetry ▷*beauty*

graceful *adj.* beautiful, lovely, shapely, refined ▷*elegant*

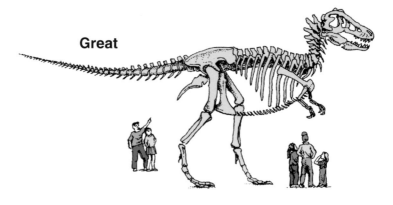
Great

Grate

gracious *adj.* amiable, kind, suave, urbane, affable, elegant ★**churlish**

grade *n.* ① class, rank, degree ② slope, gradient, incline, slant

gradual *adj.* by degrees, step-by-step, continuous, little by little ★**sudden**

graft ① *v.* splice, insert, bud, plant ② *n.* bribery, corruption

grain *n.* fiber, crumb, seed, particle, atom, bit, drop

grand *adj.* splendid, impressive, stately, magnificent, wonderful, superb

grandeur *n.* magnificence, splendor, majesty, lordliness

grant ① *n.* bounty, award, subsidy ② *v.* bestow, donate *We all donated some money to help the earthquake victims,* confer, give

grapple *v.* struggle, tussle, wrestle, seize, grasp, clutch

grasp *v.* ① grip, seize, take, grab, hold ② understand, comprehend

grasping *adj.* greedy, avaricious, covetous, miserly ★**generous**

grate ① *v.* rasp, file, jar, clash, rub, grind ②

annoy, irritate, vex ③ *n.* fireplace GREAT

grateful *adj.* thankful, appreciative, obliged, indebted

gratify *v.* delight, satisfy, please, content, enchant, indulge, favor ★**displease**

gratitude *n.* thankfulness, appreciation, obligation

grave ① *adj.* solemn, sober, momentous, dignified, majestic ② essential, important *I have important news to tell* ③ *n.* tomb, vault, shrine

gravity *n.* ① seriousness, solemnity, importance, significance ② force, gravitation, weight

graze *v.* ① scrape, brush, shave, glance ② browse, crop, bite GRAYS

grease *n.* fat, suet, tallow, oil

great *adj.* ① large, considerable, bulky, huge, ample ② important, elevated, noted *Here is a list of noted citizens of this town* ③ main, chief, principal GRATE

greedy *adj.* gluttonish, voracious, grasping, selfish, acquisitive ★**unselfish**

green *adj.* ① emerald, jade, turquoise ② ungrown, immature, raw *During the war, many raw recruits were drafted into the army,* untrained ★**expert**

greet *v.* welcome, accost, hail, salute, salaam, address

grief *n.* woe, sadness, regret, distress, anguish ▷*sorrow* ★**joy**

grievance *n.* injury, hardship, complaint, wrong, trial ★**boon**

grieve *v.* lament, deplore, mourn, sorrow, be sad, afflict, hurt ★**rejoice**

grievous *adj.* lamentable, deplorable, grave, critical, severe, mortal

grill ① *v.* fry, broil ② *n.* grating, grid

grim *adj.* ① serious, stern, harsh, solemn, dour, forbidding ② horrid, dreadful, terrible ▷*somber* ★**mild**

grime *n.* filth, soil, dust, soot ▷*dirt*

grin *n. & v.* smile, beam, smirk, simper

grind *v.* ① scrape, file, crush, powder ② sharpen, whet, grate

grip *v.* grasp, grab, snatch, clasp, seize ▷*hold* ★**loosen**

Groups of Animals

a drove of cattle
a flock of birds
a herd of elephants
a mob of kangaroos
a pack of wolves
a pride of lions
a school of porpoises
a sloth of bears
a swarm of bees
a troop of monkeys
a colony of seals
a cete of badgers
a skulk of foxes

grisly *adj.* horrid, horrible, dreadful, ghastly ▷*grim*

grit *n.* ① powder, dust, sand, gravel ② nerve, mettle, pluck ▷*courage*

groan *v.* moan, complain, grumble, creak GROWN

groom ① *n.* husband, bridegroom ② *n.* stable boy, servant, hostler ③ *v.* spruce, tidy, preen

groove *n.* furrow, ridge, corrugation, channel, rut, score

grope *v.* feel, handle, finger, manipulate, touch, pick

gross *adj.* ① large, bulky, unwieldy, massive ② coarse, vulgar, crude ③ outrageous,

Growls, grunts, and other animal noises

Bees buzz	Lions roar
Cats meow	Mice squeak
Cows moo	Owls hoot
Dogs bark	Pigs grunt
Dogs also growl	Roosters crow
Ducks quack	Snakes hiss
Horses neigh	Wolves howl

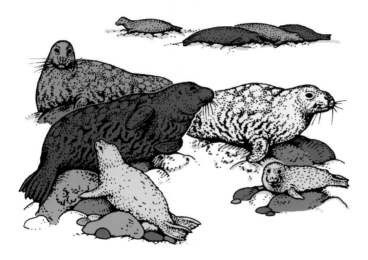

glaring, flagrant *The driver was arrested for a flagrant disregard of the speed limit*

grotesque *adj.* deformed, malformed, misshapen, freakish, abnormal, bizarre

ground *n.* ① dry land, soil, earth, dust ② bottom, base, foundation

grounds *n.* ① foundation, cause, basis, excuse ② dregs, sediment, silt ③ gardens, parkland, estate

group *n.* ① division, section, branch ② gang, throng, cluster, bunch, class, set

grovel *v.* fawn, crouch, crawl, toady, cringe, wallow, cower

grow *v.* ① increase, advance, expand, extend, develop, raise ② sprout, germinate, shoot

growl *v.* snarl, snap, threaten, thunder

growth *n.* expansion, development, advance ▷*increase*

grow up *v.* mature, develop, ripen

grubby *adj.* messy, dirty, mucky

grudge *n. & v.* hate, envy, dislike, spite

gruesome *adj.* frightful, hideous, ghastly ▷*grisly*

gruff *adj.* husky, throaty, croaky, blunt, churlish, crusty, curt ★**affable**

grumble *v.* complain, snivel, murmur, growl, protest

grumpy *adj.* disgruntled, dissatisfied, surly, sour, irritable, sullen ★**affable**

grunt *n. & v.* snort, groan ★**growl**

guarantee *n.* warranty, assurance, security, pledge

guard ① *n.* protector, sentry, guardian, watchman ② *v.* protect, defend, watch over, shelter, shield

guess *v.* surmise, conjecture, judge, think, suspect, suppose

guest *n.* visitor, caller GUESSED

guide ① *n.* pilot, director, leader, controller ② *v.* steer, navigate, lead, direct, manage, conduct *Our teacher conducted us to the bus and we all climbed aboard*

guild *n.* club, trade union, association, federation, fellowship, band, society

guile *n.* knavery, foul play, trickery, deceit, cunning, fraud ★**honesty**

guilty *adj.* blameworthy, sinful, wicked, wrong ★**innocent**

guise *n.* garb, pose, posture, role, aspect *The motel manager's aspect was a little too friendly; we did not trust him,* appearance GUYS

gulch *n.* valley, gully, ravine

gulf *n.* ① bay, basin, inlet ② chasm, opening, abyss, depths

gullible *adj.* credulous, innocent, naive, trusting

gully *n.* trench, ditch, channel, ravine

gulp *v.* swallow, consume, guzzle, devour

gun *n.* rifle, cannon, revolver, pistol, automatic, shotgun

gurgle *v.* ripple, murmur, purl, babble

gush *v.* stream, spurt, spout, flow, run, pour out

gust *n.* blast, blow, squall, wind

gusto *n.* relish, zest, eagerness, zeal, pleasure

gutter *n.* moat, ditch, dike, drain, gully, channel, groove

guzzle *v.* gulp, imbibe, drink, swill, quaff

H h

habit *n.* ① custom, practice, routine, way, rule ② mannerism *One of his annoying mannerisms is drumming his fingers on the table,* addiction, trait

hack *v.* chop, mangle, gash, slash

hackneyed *adj.* stale, trite, commonplace, tired ★**new**

hag *n.* crone, harridan, witch, virago *I know I have a temper, but Julia is a real virago*

haggard *adj.* drawn, wan, pinched, thin ▷*gaunt* ★**hale**

haggle *v.* bargain, barter, bicker, dispute ★**yield**

hail ① *v.* salute, call to, accost, welcome, greet ② *n.* sleet, frozen rain, ice storm HALE

hair *n.* locks, mane, tresses, strand

hale *adj.* hearty, robust, sound, fit ▷*healthy* ★**ill** HAIL

half *n.* division, fraction, segment

hall *n.* entrance, foyer, corridor, lobby, vestibule *There is a coat rack and an umbrella stand in the vestibule of her house* HAUL

hallow *v.* sanctify, consecrate, bless, dedicate, make holy

hallucination *n.* illusion, fantasy, delusion, mirage, dream ★**reality**

halt *v.* end, pause, rest, cease ▷*stop* ★**start**

halting *adj.* faltering, hestitating, wavering, awkward ★**fluent**

hammer ① *v.* beat, pound, bang ② *n.* mallet, gavel *The leader banged his gavel on the desk and called for order*

hamper ① *v.* hinder, interfere, impede, curb ★**aid** ② *n.* basket, creel *The fisherman carried a creel to put his catch in,* crate

hand ① *v.* give, pass, present, yield ② *n.* fist, palm

handicap *n.* defect, disability, drawback, restriction ★**advantage**

handicraft *n.* skill, hobby, art, workmanship, craft, occupation

handle ① *n.* shaft, holder, grip ② *v.* feel,

Habitations

Apartment	Igloo
Bungalow	Lodge
Cabin	Mansion
Castle	Palace
Chalet	Ranch
Chateau	Shack
Cottage	Shanty
Duplex	Villa
Estate	
Flat	
Hacienda	
Hut	

touch, finger, work, wield

handsome *adj.* ① good-looking, graceful, attractive ② generous, lavish *Aunt Betsy is always lavish with presents for the children* HANSOM

handy *adj.* ready, convenient, deft, skilled ★**clumsy**

hang *v.* dangle, suspend, sag, droop, swing

hanker for *v.* long for, yearn for, crave, desire ★**dislike**

haphazard *adj.* accidental, random, aimless, casual ▷*chance* ★**deliberate**

hapless *adj.* ill-fated, luckless, unlucky ▷*miserable* ★**lucky**

happen *v.* occur, take place, come about, result

happening *n.* event, incident, occurrence, occasion

happiness *n.* delight, ecstasy, gaiety, joy, enjoyment ▷*bliss* ★**unhappiness**

happy *adj.* cheerful, blithe, content, joyous, jubilant ▷*merry* ★**unhappy**

harass *v.* beset, annoy, upset, bother

▷*distress* ★**assist**

harbor ① *n.* port, anchorage, mooring ② *n.* refuge, shelter, safety *At last we were back in the safety of our home* ③ *v.* give shelter to

hard *adj.* ① firm, stony, rocky, solid ★**soft** ② difficult, tough *I had a very tough problem to solve,* perplexing ★**easy** ③ stern, severe, callous, ruthless

hardly *adv.* seldom, rarely, scarcely, slightly

hardship *n.* trouble, suffering, want ▷*difficulty* ★**ease**

hardy *adj.* rugged, sturdy, tough, healthy, stout, sound ▷*robust* ★**weak**

hark *v.* listen, hear ▷*listen*

harm ① *n.* damage, mischief, ruin, wrong, abuse, sin ② *v.* abuse, blemish, hurt *I'm sorry, I didn't mean to hurt you,* injure ★**benefit**

harmful *adj.* injurious, evil, wicked, damaging ★**harmless**

harmless *adj.* safe, gentle, innocuous, innocent ★**harmful**

harmony *n.* agreement, conformity, accord, unity, goodwill ★**discord**

harp ① *n.* lyre, stringed instrument ② *v.* harp on, dwell on *I tried to forget our quarrel, but Carol continued to dwell on it,* allude to

harrow *v.* agonize, taunt, distress, torture, harry ▷*harass* ★**hearten**

harsh *adj.* ① jarring, coarse, rough ② severe, strict, ruthless ★**mild**

harvest *v.* plow, harrow, reap, pluck

hash *n.* ① mess, confusion, muddle ② stew, goulash, meat loaf

hassle *n.* argument, bother, difficulty, squabble, struggle

haste *n.* rush, bustle, dispatch, urgency, swiftness ▷*hurry* ★**delay**

hasten *v.* hurry, hustle, quicken, accelerate, speed up ★**dawdle**

hasty *adj.* hurried, rushed, abrupt, indiscreet ★**deliberate**

hate *v.* abhor, detest, loathe ▷*despise* ★**love**

hateful *adj.* abominable, loathsome, odious, despicable ★**pleasing**

haughty *adj.* arrogant, disdainful, scornful, snobbish ★**humble**

haul *v.* pull, draw, tug, drag, heave HALL

have *v.* possess, occupy, own, receive, take in

haven *n.* harbor, port, refuge, retreat, sanctum, shelter

havoc *n.* wreckage, ruin, destruction, disorder, mayhem

hay *n.* pasture, silage, grass, straw HEY

haze *n.* cloud, vapor, fog, mist HAYS

hazy *adj.* foggy, misty, murky, vague, uncertain ★**clear**

head ① *n.* visage, skull, cranium, pate ② *adj.* chief, main, principal

heading *n.* caption, headline, title, inscription

headlong *adj.* rough, dangerous, reckless ▷*rash*

heal *v.* soothe, treat, cure, mend, restore HEEL, HE'LL

healthy *adj.* fine, fit, hearty, sound, vigorous ▷*hale* ★**sick**

heap *n.* pile, mass, mound, collection

hear *v.* listen to, hearken, overhear HERE

hearten *v.* assure, encourage, embolden, inspire ★**dishearten**

heartless *adj.* brutal, callous, cold ▷*unkind* ★**kind**

hearty *adj.* cordial, sincere, earnest, honest, jovial ★**cold**

heat *n.* ① warmth, temperature ② passion, ardor, fervor *She spoke with great fervor about what she believed*

heave *v.* fling, cast, hurl, hoist, pull, tug

heavenly *adj.* beautiful, blessed, divine, lovely ★**hellish**

heavy *adj.* weighty, hefty, ponderous, loaded ★**light**

hectic *adj.* excited, fast, frenzied, wild ▷*frantic* ★**leisurely**

heed *v.* listen, pay attention, follow, respect, obey ★**ignore**

heedless *adj.* thoughtless, reckless, unwary, rash ▷*careless*

height *n.* ① altitude, stature ② top, apex, peak, zenith ★**depth**

A
B
C
D
E
F
G
H
I
J
K
L
M
N
O
P
Q
R
S
T
U
V
W
X
Y
Z

Headgear

Balaclava	Helmet	Stetson
Beret	Homburg	Tam-o'-shanter
Boater	Hood	Top hat
Bonnet	Kepi	Toque
Cap	Panama	Trilby
Derby	Shako	Turban
Fedora	Sombrero	Tyrolean hat
Fez	Sou'wester	Yarmulke

hellish *adj.* abominable, awful, inhuman, fiendish ★**heavenly**

help ① *n.* aid, support, assistance ② *v.* lend a hand *We all lent a hand in building the hut,* aid, assist ★**hinder**

helpful *adj.* caring, considerate ▷*useful* ★**useless**

helping *n.* ration, portion, piece, serving, helping *Mike would like a second helping. He's still hungry,* share

helpless *adj.* incapable, powerless, unfit, forlorn ▷*weak* ★**strong**

hem *n.* edge, border, fringe, margin

hence *adv.* accordingly, thus, therefore, henceforward

herd *n.* crowd, crush, flock, group, mass, mob, horde HEARD

here *adv.* present, attending, hereabouts, in this place HEAR

heritage *n.* inheritance, legacy, birthright, tradition

hermit *n.* recluse, solitary, monk

hero *n.* champion, daredevil, star, idol, conqueror ★**villain**

heroic *adj.* bold, fearless, lion-hearted, gallant ▷*brave* ★**cowardly**

heroine *n.* celebrity, goddess *Marilyn Monroe was a goddess of the silver screen,* idol, star, lead

hesitate *v.* falter, dither, doubt, wait

hew *v.* chop, cut, fashion, carve, sculpt HUE

hidden *adj.* concealed, covered, veiled, unseen ★**open**

hide *v.* conceal, cover, obscure, bury, cloak ★**reveal** HIED

hideous *adj.* repulsive, unsightly, gruesome, horrible ▷*ugly* ★**beautiful**

hiding *n.* beating, thrashing, caning

high ① *adj.* tall, towering, lofty, elevated ② shrill *The referee blew a shrill blast on his whistle,* treble, strident ③ expensive, costly ★**low**

highbrow *adj.* brainy, educated, intellectual

hijack *v.* raid, kidnap, seize, snatch, steal

hike *v.* walk, ramble, tramp

hilarious *adj.* amusing, gleeful, jocular,

entertaining ▷*funny* ★**serious**

hill *n.* hummock, rise, climb, height, elevation, slope

hinder *v.* hamper, impede, obstruct, retard, frustrate ▷*handicap* ★**help**

hindrance *n.* impediment, obstruction, check, barrier ★**aid**

hint *n.* clue, inkling *We had just an inkling of what was in store,* whisper, tip, suggestion

hire *v.* charter, rent, lease, retain, engage ★**dismiss** HIGHER

hiss *v.* boo, hoot, jeer, deride, whistle ▷*ridicule* ★**applaud**

history *n.* narration, account, saga, story, chronicle *The new book is a chronicle of the progress of equal rights*

hit ① *v.* strike, slap, beat, batter, whack ② *v.* collide, strike, clash ★**miss** ③ *n.* stroke, collision, blow, success, triumph

hitch ① *v.* attach, connect, fasten ② *n.* delay, holdup, problem, snag *The work went smoothly for hours, until we hit a snag*

hoard *v.* accumulate, save, collect, treasure ★**squander** HORDE

hoarse *adj.* raucous, croaky, husky, throaty ★**mellow** HORSE

hoax *n.* trick, deception, fraud, joke, spoof, lie

hobble *v.* dodder, falter, shuffle, stagger

hobby *n.* pastime, amusement, recreation, interest

hoist *v.* lift, raise, erect, heave

hold ① *v.* have, possess, own, retain, keep, grasp ② *v.* contain, accommodate *This cabin can accommodate four people* ③ *v.* stop, arrest ④ *n.* fortress, keep, storeplace HOLED

hole *n.* aperture, slot, perforation, opening, cavity WHOLE

hollow ① *adj.* concave, empty, vacant ② *adj.* insincere, artificial ③ *n.* basin, depression *Water had accumulated in a small depression,* crater, channel

holy *adj.* sacred, pure, consecrated, blessed, hallowed ★**wicked** WHOLLY

home *n.* house, dwelling, homestead

homely *adj.* ① humble, unpretentious, comfortable, modest ② ordinary, plain, simple ③ unattractive, plain

honest *adj.* upright, fair, sincere, honorable ★**devious**

honesty *n.* integrity, honor, sincerity, morality ★**dishonesty**

honor *n.* morality, honesty, reputation, integrity, uprightness ★**disgrace**

honorable *adj.* honest, respectable, highminded, virtuous ★**dishonest**

hook *n.* clasp, link, catch, fastener, barb *The fishhook ended in a number of small barbs*

hoop *n.* loop, ring, band, circle

hoot *v.* call, cry, howl, shout, shriek, yell

hop *v.* jump, leap, skip, spring, vault, caper

hope *v.* anticipate, envision, envisage, desire, expect, foresee ★**despair**

hopeful *adj.* expectant, confident, optimistic ★**pessimistic**

hopeless *adj.* despairing, desperate, downhearted, unattainable ★**hopeful**

horde *n.* crowd, gang, band, throng, swarm *We were suddenly attacked by a swarm of hornets,* HOARD

horrible *adj.* awful, atrocious, frightful, ghastly ▷*horrid* ★**agreeable**

horrid *adj.* beastly, bloodcurdling, dreadful, frightening ▷*horrible* ★**pleasant**

horror *n.* dread, fear, fright, outrage, panic, loathing ★**attraction**

horse *n.* mount, charger, hack, stallion, mare, filly, colt, foal HOARSE

hose *n.* ① tubing, pipe ② socks, stockings HOES

hospitable *adj.* sociable, neighborly, charitable, welcoming ★**hostile**

host *n.* ① entertainer, master-of-ceremonies, sponsor ② army, band, legion, horde

hostile *adj.* unfriendly, antagonistic, alien, malevolent ★**friendly**

hot ① *adj.* warm, fiery, scalding, roasting, heated ★**cold** ② pungent, peppery, sharp

hotel *n.* inn, hostelry *The stagecoach pulled in to a local hostelry for refreshment,* tavern, motel, resort

house *n.* home, residence, dwelling, abode

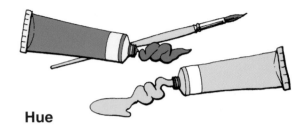

Hue

A hue is a tint or variety of a color.
Blue: aquamarine beryl turquoise indigo azure sapphire ultramarine
Brown: amber chocolate dun fawn beige khaki auburn chestnut
Green: apple emerald jade moss olive pea sea
Purple: violet lilac heliotrope amethyst mauve magenta
Orange: carrot tangerine sandy
Red: crimson scarlet cherry cerise terracotta salmon pink cardinal
Yellow: sulfur primrose apricot saffron citron canary lemon

hovel *n.* cabin, shed, den, shack, shanty

hover *v.* fly, float, hang, dally, linger

howl *v.* hoot, cry, bellow, shriek ▷*scream*

hub *n.* center, axis, focal point, pivot

hubbub *n.* babel, bedlam, chaos, clamor, uproar ▷*row* ★**calm**

huddle *v.* cluster, flock, gather, herd, nestle ★**separate**

hue *n.* color, dye, shade, tinge, tint HEW

huff *n.* anger, passion, mood, pique *My cousin stormed off in a fit of pique* ▷*sulk*

hug *v.* clasp, embrace, enfold ▷*cuddle*

huge *adj.* enormous, monstrous, colossal, immense ▷*vast* ★**tiny**

hum *v.* drone, croon, buzz, pulsate, throb

human *adj.* reasonable, understandable, mortal ▷*humane* ★**inhuman**

humane *adj.* benign, forgiving, gentle, lenient, kind ★**inhumane**

humble *adj.* low, lowly, meek, unassuming ▷*modest* ★**arrogant**

humbug *n.* bluff, bunkum, claptrap *The salesman's goods were cheap and he talked a lot of claptrap about them,* quackery, trickery

humdrum *adj.* monotonous, commonplace, everyday, boring ▷*dreary* ★**exceptional**

humid *adj.* clammy, damp, moist, wet, vaporous ★**dry**

humiliate *v.* embarrass, humble, abash, degrade, deflate ★**boost**

humor ① *n.* comedy, fun, banter, whimsy ② *v.* flatter, coax, pamper, spoil

humorous *adj.* amusing, droll, comical, whimsical ▷*funny* ★**serious** HUMERUS

hunch ① *n.* feeling, guess, idea, inkling ② *v.* crouch, curl up, squat *We squatted in the long grass, where we were out of sight*

hunger ① *n.* craving, desire, starvation ② *v.* crave, desire, hanker

hungry *adj.* famished, starving, voracious

hunt *v.* chase, seek, scour, search, stalk, trail

hurdle *n.* barrier, fence, hedge, obstruction

hurl *v.* cast, fling, heave, pitch, throw, propel, toss

hurry *v.* dash, hustle, quicken, accelerate ▷*hasten* ★**dally**

hurt ① *v.* harm, wound, pain, sting, suffer ② *v.* upset, annoy, distress ③ *adj.* rueful, sad, offended

hurtful *adj.* cutting, cruel, distressing, wounding ★**kind**

hurtle *v.* chase, charge, dash, rush, speed, tear

hush *v.* calm, quiet down, soothe ★**disturb**

husky *adj.* croaking, gruff, harsh ▷*hoarse*

hustle *v.* bustle, speed, hasten ▷*hurry*

hut *n.* cabin, shelter, shanty, shack

hymn *n.* anthem, chant, carol, psalm HIM

hypnotize *v.* mesmerize, fascinate, spellbind *We stood spellbound as we watched the trapeze artist,* bewitch

hypocrite *n.* fraud, deceiver, impostor, mountebank

hysterical *adj.* ① distraught, mad, delirious, beside oneself ② comical, hilarious, farcical ★**calm**

I i

icy *adj.* freezing, frozen, cold, frigid, frosty

idea *n.* notion, thought, belief, fancy, impression, image

ideal *adj.* perfect, absolute, supreme, best, model, complete

identical *adj.* same, alike, twin, duplicate, equal ★**different**

identify *v.* detect, recognize, know, distinguish, spot

identity *n.* existence, self, singularity, individuality

idiot *n.* imbecile, moron, fool, dimwit, dolt

idiotic *adj.* crazy, stupid, simple, fatuous ▷*foolish* ★**sane**

idle *adj.* ① unoccupied, unemployed, unused ② lazy, frivolous, sluggish ★**active** IDOL

idol *n.* ① image, icon, god, fetish ② hero, favorite, star *Buster Keaton was a star of the silent movies* IDLE

ignite *v.* kindle, set light to, spark off, catch fire

ignorant *adj.* unknowing, ill-informed, unread, stupid, dumb ★**wise**

ignore *v.* disregard, neglect, omit, overlook, pass over ★**note**

ill *adj.* ① ailing, diseased, frail, infirm, sick, poorly ★**well** ② hostile, malicious *Cinderella's sisters were cruel and malicious,* evil, harmful

ill-mannered *adj.* coarse, crude, boorish, uncivil ▷*rude* ★**polite**

ill-tempered *adj.* bad-tempered, curt, irritable ★**good-tempered**

ill-treat *v.* abuse, harm, injure, neglect, oppress ★**care for**

ill will *n.* animosity, hard feelings, dislike, hatred, hostility ▷*malice* ★**good will**

illegal *adj.* unlawful, wrong, villainous, illicit, contraband ★**legal**

illegible *adj.* unreadable, indecipherable, obscure, indistinct ★**legible**

illegitimate *adj.* illegal, unlawful, improper, wrong ★**legitimate**

illiterate *adj.* uneducated, unlearned, unlettered, unread, untaught ★**literate**

illness *n.* ailment, attack, complaint, disease, disorder

illuminate *v.* brighten, clarify, enlighten, light up ★**darken**

illusion *n.* apparition, fancy, fantasy, mirage, deception ★**reality**

illustration *n.* picture, drawing, explanation, sketch

image *n.* likeness, effigy, portrait, replica, reflection, double

imaginary *adj.* unreal, fanciful, fictitious, visionary ★**real**

imagination *n.* idea, notion, thought, illusion, conception, fancy, vision, impression ★**reality**

imagine *v.* assume, believe, invent, pretend, think up ▷*visualize*

imbecile *n.* blockhead, fool, idiot, bungler, dolt

imitate *v.* emulate, follow, reproduce, simulate, mock ▷*copy*

immaculate *adj.* clean, spotless, faultless, stainless ▷*pure* ★**soiled**

immature *adj.* callow, raw, crude, childish, unripe ★**mature**

immediate *adj.* ① instant, instantaneous, prompt ② nearest, next, neighboring *As children, my mother and father lived in neighboring houses* ★**distant**

immediately *adv.* at once, directly, without delay, forthwith

immense *adj.* tremendous, enormous, vast ▷*huge* ★**tiny**

immerse *v.* plunge, dip, douse, submerge ▷*sink*

imminent *adj.* impending, approaching, looming, close

immobile *adj.* at rest, at a standstill, motionless ★**moving**

immodest *adj.* shameless, barefaced, indelicate, improper ★**modest**

immoral *adj.* evil, unscrupulous, vicious, vile, depraved ▷*wicked* ★**moral**

immortal *adj.* undying, eternal, everlasting, constant ★**mortal**

A B C D E F G H I J K L M N O P Q R S T U V W X Y Z

immune *adj.* exempt, resistant, safe, protected ★**susceptible**

imp *n.* rascal, urchin, elf

impact *n.* blow, shock, stroke, collision, crash, knock

impair *v.* damage, spoil, devalue, cheapen, harm ▷*hinder* ★**enhance**

impart *v.* communicate, render, bestow, disclose *I am unable to disclose where I heard that story* ▷*tell*

impartial *adj.* unbiased, candid, fair-minded, impersonal ★**biased**

impatient *adj.* intolerant, irritable, hasty, curt ★**patient**

impede *v.* hamper, interfere with, obstruct ▷*hinder* ★**aid**

impel *v.* goad, incite, urge, actuate, push ▷*drive* ★**dissuade**

impending *adj.* approaching, coming, forthcoming, looming ★**remote**

imperfect *adj.* defective, unsound, blemished, flawed ▷*faulty* ★**perfect**

imperial *adj.* august, majestic, lofty, regal, royal, grand

imperious *adj.* arrogant, domineering, overbearing ★**humble**

impersonal *adj.* aloof, detached, remote, neutral, cold ★**friendly**

impersonate *v.* imitate, mimic, masquerade as, pose as, portray

impertinent *adj.* insolent, impudent, discourteous ▷*saucy* ★**polite**

impetuous *adj.* sudden, unexpected, impulsive, spontaneous ▷*hasty* ★**careful**

implement ① *v.* accomplish, bring about, fulfill *I was able to fulfill my dream of going to Japan* ② *n.* instrument, tool, gadget

implicate *v.* connect, entangle, involve, throw suspicion on ★**absolve**

implicit *adj.* implied, indicated, understood, tacit

implore *v.* beseech, entreat, beg, crave, plead

imply *v.* hint at, intimate, insinuate ▷*suggest* ★**declare**

impolite *adj.* discourteous, ill-mannered ▷*rude* ★**polite**

import ① *v.* bring in, carry in ② *n.* meaning, purport *When I grew old enough I realized the purport of my mother's advice,* sense

important *adj.* significant, essential, serious, substantial ▷*great* ★**trivial**

imposing *adj.* impressive, massive, magnificent ▷*stately* ★**modest**

impossible *adj.* hopeless, not possible, unworkable, unacceptable ★**possible**

impostor *n.* impersonator, masquerader, deceiver, fraud, pretender, quack

impoverish *v.* bankrupt, diminish, weaken, ruin, beggar ★**enrich**

impractical *adj.* impossible, unworkable, idealistic, unusable ★**practical**

impress *v.* ① influence, affect, sway, inspire ② emboss *She wore a crown of gold embossed with diamonds,* engrave, indent

impression *n.* ① belief, concept, fancy, effect ② dent, imprint, stamp, printing *The book had sold 5,000 copies, and a new printing was planned*

imprison *v.* jail, lock up, confine, ★**free**

improbable *adj.* doubtful, unlikely, implausible ▷*dubious* ★**probable**

impromptu *adj.* improvised, spontaneous, ad lib, unrehearsed ★**planned**

improper *adj.* ① erroneous, false, unsuitable ② immoral *My parents always taught me that lying and cheating were immoral,* indecent ▷*wrong* ★**proper**

improve *v.* make better, repair, restore, improve upon, refine ★**diminish**

impudent *adj.* impertinent, audacious, brazen, disrespectful ▷*rude* ★**polite**

impulse *n.* motive, drive, force, inclination, urge, wish

impulsive *adj.* sudden, unexpected, reckless ▷*impetuous* ★**cautious**

impure *adj.* contaminated, corrupted, foul, corrupt ★**pure**

inaccessible *adj.* remote, isolated, unattainable ★**accessible**

inaccurate *adj.* erroneous, incorrect, imprecise ▷*faulty* ★**accurate**

inactive *adj.* inert, static, dormant, quiet, unoccupied ★**active**

inadequate *adj.* deficient, unequal, incapable ▷*unfit* ★**adequate**

inane *adj.* absurd, ridiculous, stupid, senseless ▷*silly* ★**sensible**

inappropriate *adj.* improper, wrong, incorrect, unsuitable, unfitting ★**appropriate**

inattentive *adj.* unheeding, indifferent, careless, neglectful ★**attentive**

incapable *adj.* helpless, inadequate, unable, unfit, weak ★**capable**

incense ① *v.* (in-*cense*) enrage, infuriate, annoy ② *n.* (*in*-cense) fragrance *We walked through fields where the fragrance of wild flowers was wonderful,* aroma, perfume

incentive *n.* motive, impulse, drive, spur, lure

incident *n.* event, happening, episode, circumstance, occurrence

incidental *adj.* casual, chance, accidental, random, minor

incite *v.* encourage, urge, drive, goad, impel, provoke ▷*prompt* ★**restrain**

incline ① *n.* (*in*-cline) slant, slope, grade, gradient ② *v.* (in-*cline*) tend, verge, lean to, bias, favor

inclined *adj.* liable, prone, disposed, favorable

include *v.* contain, cover, incorporate, embody, comprise ★**exclude**

inclusive *adj.* comprehensive, all-embracing ★**exclusive**

income *n.* earnings, royalty, revenue, receipts, profits ★**expenses**

incomparable *adj.* brilliant, first-class, superb ▷*unrivaled* ★**ordinary**

incompetent *adj.* incapable, inadequate, inept, helpless ▷*clumsy* ★**competent**

incomplete *adj.* unfinished, partial, imperfect, wanting ★**complete**

incomprehensible *adj.* unintelligible, perplexing, puzzling ★**comprehensible**

inconceivable *adj.* incredible, unlikely, strange ▷*extraordinary* ★**comprehensible**

inconsiderate *adj.* tactless, careless, insensitive ▷*thoughtless* ★**considerate**

inconsistent *adj.* incongruous, unstable, unpredictable ★**consistent**

inconspicuous *adj.* indistinct, faint, hidden, ordinary ★**conspicuous**

inconvenient *adj.* annoying, awkward, difficult, troublesome ★**convenient**

incorrect *adj.* erroneous, imprecise, mistaken ▷*wrong* ★**correct**

increase ① *v.* add to, boost, magnify, heighten ② *n.* addition *We heard the news today that Emily has had an addition to her family,* rise, enhancement ★**decrease**

incredible *adj.* unbelievable, amazing, farfetched, wonderful ★**ordinary**

incriminate *v.* implicate, accuse, indict ▷*blame* ★**acquit**

indecent *adj.* immodest, improper, impure, coarse ★**decent**

indeed *adv.* actually, truly, really, very much, positively

indefinite *adj.* uncertain, unsure, unreliable, dubious ▷*vague* ★**certain**

indelicate *adj.* coarse, immodest, indecent ▷*unseemly* ★**delicate**

independent *adj.* free, self-reliant, separate, self-governing ★**dependent**

indicate *v.* show, point out, denote, suggest, symbolize, flag, signal

indifference *n.* disinterest, unconcern, apathy, coldness ★**interest**

indifferent *adj.* uninterested, cold, casual, apathetic, listless ★**interested**

indignant *adj.* annoyed, resentful, wrathful ▷*angry* ★**pleased**

indirect *adj.* devious, roundabout, incidental ★**direct**

indiscreet *adj.* incautious, thoughtless, ill-advised ▷*hasty* ★**discreet**

indiscriminate *adj.* confused, bewildered, careless ▷*random* ★**deliberate**

indispensable *adj.* necessary, crucial, vital ▷*essential* ★**unnecessary**

indistinct *adj.* faint, dim, unclear, obscure, murky ▷*vague* ★**distinct**

individual ① *adj.* single, odd, special, exclusive ② *n.* person, being *Sharon enjoys the company of other human beings,*

A
B
C
D
E
F
G
H
I
J
K
L
M
N
O
P
Q
R
S
T
U
V
W
X
Y
Z

creature

indulge *v.* gratify, humor, pamper, satisfy, spoil

industrious *adj.* busy, hard-working, diligent, conscientious ★**lazy**

inedible *adj.* deadly, poisonous, harmful, uneatable ★**edible**

inefficient *adj.* negligent, incapable ▷*incompetent* ★**efficient**

inelegant *adj.* awkward, ungainly, crude, coarse ▷*clumsy* ★**elegant**

inept *adj.* awkward, absurd, unskilled ▷*clumsy* ★**skillful**

inert *adj.* inactive, passive, static, sluggish, listless, dead ★**alive**

inevitable *adj.* unavoidable, certain, sure, necessary ★**uncertain**

inexact *adj.* imprecise, inaccurate ▷*erroneous* ★**exact**

inexpensive *adj.* low-priced, reasonable, economical ▷*cheap* ★**expensive**

inexperienced *adj.* inexpert, unskilled, untrained ▷*inept* ★**experienced**

infallible *adj.* perfect, unerring, faultless ▷*reliable* ★**faulty**

infamous *adj.* notorious, shady, scandalous, shameful, disgraceful ★**glorious**

infant *n.* baby, child, little one, toddler

infatuated *adj.* in love, beguiled, charmed, fascinated, smitten

infect *v.* contaminate, blight, defile, pollute

infectious *adj.* catching, contagious

infer *v.* reason, conclude, judge, understand

inferior *adj.* second-rate, lesser, lower, poor, mediocre, imperfect ★**superior**

infinite *adj.* eternal, unending, endless, immense, unbounded

infirm *adj.* weak, feeble, frail, senile, decrepit ★**healthy**

inflame *v.* inspire, provoke, excite, stimulate, arouse ★**cool**

inflate *v.* expand, dilate, swell, pump up, blow up ★**deflate**

inflict *v.* apply, burden, deal, deliver, force

influence ① *n.* authority, control, guidance, force ② *v.* affect, impress, inspire *After Annie visited her old neighborhood, she was inspired to write a poem,* prejudice

inform *v.* tell, let know, acquaint, warn, enlighten

informal *adj.* casual, easy, familiar, relaxed, simple ★**formal**

information *n.* knowledge, news, intelligence, advice

infrequent *adj.* unusual, uncommon, occasional ▷*rare* ★**frequent**

infringe *v.* disobey, violate, encroach, trespass, flout

infuriate *v.* anger, enrage, madden, incense, vex ▷*annoy* ★**calm**

ingenious *adj.* clever, resourceful, shrewd, adroit, inventive ★**clumsy**

ingenuous *adj.* honest, open, simple, trusting, sincere ★**artful**

ingratiate *v.* curry favor, flatter, grovel, toady *We distrusted Tim, he was always trying to ingratiate himself with the teacher*

Ingratiate

We distrusted Tim, he was always trying to ingratiate himself with the teacher.

ingredient *n.* component, element, part, factor

inhabit *v.* live in, dwell in, reside in, dwell, occupy

inhale *v.* breathe in, inspire, sniff, suck in ★**exhale**

inherit *v.* succeed to, acquire, take over, receive

inhospitable *adj.* unfriendly, desolate, unkind, unsociable ★**hospitable**

inhuman *adj.* barbaric, brutal, beastly, heartless, savage

inhumane *adj.* callous, cruel, pitiless, ruthless ▷*inhuman* ★**humane**

initiate *v.* start, launch, teach, instruct, train ▷*begin*

initiative *n.* ambition, drive, enterprise, resourcefulness

inject *v.* inoculate, infuse, vaccinate

injure *v.* hurt, mar, spoil, wound, blemish, deform, disfigure

inkling *n.* suspicion, impression, notion, clue

inlet *n.* bay, gulf, basin, bight, estuary, harbor

inn *n.* hotel, motel, lodge, tavern IN

innocent *adj.* guiltless, faultless, stainless, virtuous, blameless ★**guilty**

inoffensive *adj.* harmless, safe, gentle, quiet ▷*innocent* ★**malicious**

inquire *v.* ask, examine, inspect, check, question

inquisitive *adj.* nosy, snooping, eager, inquiring, ▷*curious*

insane *adj.* demented, mad, frenzied, crazy, wild, lunatic ★**sane**

inscribe *v.* write, stamp, cut, carve, etch

inscription *n.* heading, caption, legend, epitaph, label

insecure *adj.* perilous, unsafe, hazardous, dangerous, unconfident, uncertain ★**secure**

insensible *adj.* ① unconscious, stunned, knocked out *The reigning champion was knocked out in the third round* ② insensitive, numb, stupefied

insensitive *adj.* impassive, indifferent, thick-skinned, unruffled, insensible ★**sensitive**

inseparable *adj.* indivisible, devoted, intimate, close

insert *v.* put in, inset, introduce, place, interleave ★**remove**

inside *adv.* indoors, inner, inward, within ★**outside**

insight *n.* awareness, intelligence, judgment, knowledge ▷*wisdom*

insignificant *adj.* unimportant, non-essential, meager, irrelevant ▷*humble* ★**important**

insincere *adj.* pretended, deceptive, dishonest, two-faced, false ★**sincere**

insinuate *v.* suggest, imply, signify, get at, intimate

insipid *adj.* tasteless, flat, flavorless, bland, banal ★**tasty**

insist *v.* assert, maintain, request, require, demand, persist ★**waive**

insolent *adj.* impudent, impertinent, discourteous, insulting, fresh, rude ★**respectful**

inspect *v.* examine, check, oversee, supervise, superintend

inspiration *n.* motive, stimulus, brain wave, ▷*encouragement*

inspire *v.* hearten, prompt, provoke, excite ▷*encourage* ★**deter**

install *v.* establish, plant, set, position, fix, introduce

instance *n.* example, case, occasion, occurrence INSTANTS

instant ① *adj.* immediate, instantaneous *I pressed the button, and there was an instantaneous explosion,* rapid ② *n.* moment, minute, flash, jiffy

instantly *adv.* at once, right away, immediately, now ▷*forthwith* ★**later**

instead *adv.* alternatively, preferably, rather

instead of *adv.* in place of, in one's place, on behalf of

instinct *n.* ability, knack, intuition, feeling, sixth sense

institute ① *n.* association, college, establishment, organization ② *v.* begin, start *The people raised enough money to start a new program to help the poor,* found, open

A B C D E F G H I J K L M N O P Q R S T U V W X Y Z

Musical Instruments

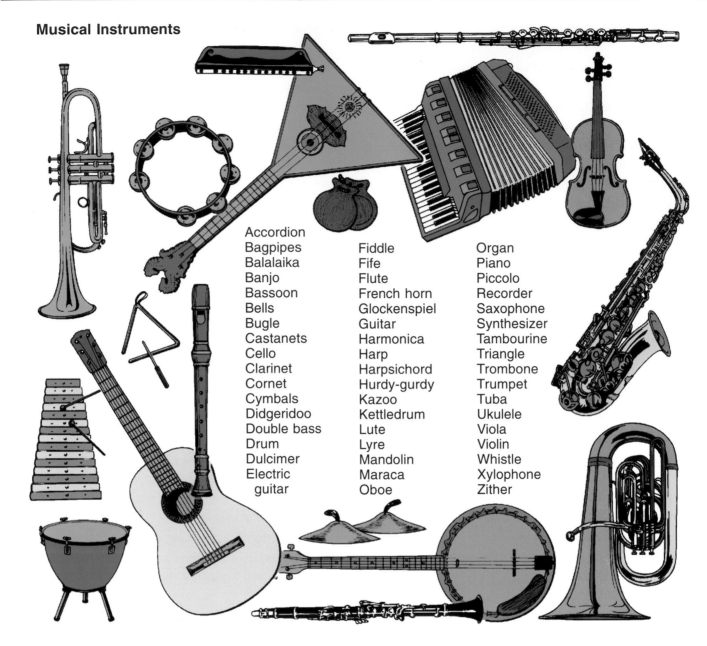

Accordion
Bagpipes
Balalaika
Banjo
Bassoon
Bells
Bugle
Castanets
Cello
Clarinet
Cornet
Cymbals
Didgeridoo
Double bass
Drum
Dulcimer
Electric
  guitar

Fiddle
Fife
Flute
French horn
Glockenspiel
Guitar
Harmonica
Harp
Harpsichord
Hurdy-gurdy
Kazoo
Kettledrum
Lute
Lyre
Mandolin
Maraca
Oboe

Organ
Piano
Piccolo
Recorder
Saxophone
Synthesizer
Tambourine
Triangle
Trombone
Trumpet
Tuba
Ukulele
Viola
Violin
Whistle
Xylophone
Zither

instruct *v.* teach, direct, order, educate, coach, drill, train

instrument *n.* device, gadget, implement, contraption, tool

insufferable *adj.* unbearable, intolerable, impossible ★**tolerable**

insufficient *adj.* inadequate, lacking, scanty, wanting ▷*sparse* ★**sufficient**

insulate *v.* protect, shield, isolate, set apart

insult *n. & v.* slander, slight, snub, abuse, outrage ★**compliment**

insure *v.* guarantee, protect, warrant, assure

intact *adj.* whole, unharmed, uncut, complete, in one piece, sound ★**damaged**

integrity *n.* honor, uprightness, honesty, goodness, purity ★**dishonesty**

intellectual *adj.* scholarly, studious, thoughtful ▷*intelligent* ★**foolish**

intelligent *adj.* acute, astute, brainy, brilliant, intellectual ▷*clever* ★**stupid**

intend *v.* mean, aim, determine, ordain, plan, project

intense *adj.* extreme, ardent, earnest, forcible, passionate ▷*keen* ★**mild** INTENTS

intention *n.* aim, intent, project, design, notion, end, goal

intercept *v.* stop, arrest, confiscate, delay, obstruct ▷*thwart*

interest *n.* appeal, fascination, zest, activity, concern ★**boredom**

interesting *adj.* appealing, fascinating, absorbing, entertaining ★**boring**

interfere *v.* meddle, intrude, interrupt, butt in, tamper ★**assist**

interior *adj.* internal, inner, inside, inward ★**exterior**

interlude *n.* pause, interval, intermission, spell, recess

internal *adj.* inner, inward ▷*interior* ★**external**

interpret *adj.* explain, define, construe

interrogate *v.* question, examine, ask, inquire, quiz ▷*investigate*

interrupt *adj.* break in, butt in, interject, disturb, hold up, suspend

interval *n.* space, period, term, intermission ▷*interlude*

intervene *v.* break in, interrupt, intrude, mediate, arbitrate ▷*interfere*

interview *n.* conference, inquiry, meeting, consultation, talk

intimate ① *adj.* near, close, familiar, private, secret ★**distant** ② *v.* hint at, suggest *The evidence suggests that the defendant has not been telling the truth* ▷*insinuate*

intimidate *v.* daunt, overawe, cow, bully, frighten, browbeat ★**persuade**

intolerant *adj.* bigoted, unfair, small-minded, dogmatic ★**tolerant**

intoxicated *adj.* drunk, inebriated, tipsy

intrepid *adj.* daring, heroic, unafraid, bold, gallant ▷*fearless*

intricate *adj.* complex, complicated, elaborate, tricky ★**simple**

intrigue ① *n.* plot, scheme, affair, liaison ② *v.* attract, enchant *The old man enchanted us with his stories,* captivate, scheme

introduce *v.* ① put in, insert, inject ② acquaint, present

intrude *v.* interrupt, interfere, invade, trespass ★**withdraw**

inundate *v.* flood, deluge, engulf, immerse, submerge, swamp *We advertised for a new assistant and were swamped with replies*

invade *v.* break in, penetrate, assault, assail ▷*enter* ★**withdraw** INVEIGHED

invalid ① *adj.* (in-*val*-id) null, void *These tickets are void, for they are more than a year old,* useless ② *n.* (*in*-val-id) patient, sufferer, sick person, disabled person

invaluable *adj.* precious, costly, priceless, valuable ★**worthless**

invent *v.* fabricate, conceive, devise, make up, originate, concoct

invention *n.* creation, gadget, contrivance, discovery

investigate *v.* explore, examine, research, inquire, search, study

invisible *adj.* hidden, concealed, out of sight, unseen, masked ★**visible**

invite *v.* ask, beckon, attract, summon, urge, encourage ★**force**

involve *v.* comprise, complicate, entangle, include, take in

inward *adj.* hidden, inner, internal, secret, inside ★**outward**

irate *adj.* incensed, cross, annoyed, furious, infuriated ▷*angry* ★**calm**

irksome *adj.* annoying, irritating, disagreeable ★**pleasing**

ironic *adj.* satirical, derisive, mocking, scornful

irregular *adj.* uncertain, unsettled, disordered, singular ▷*odd* ★**regular**

irrelevant *adj.* immaterial, unnecessary, unrelated ★**relevant**

irresistible *adj.* charming, compelling, overpowering, fascinating ★**resistible**

irresponsible *adj.* undependable, unreliable, feckless, flighty ★**responsible**

irritable *adj.* bad-tempered, edgy, fretful, peevish ▷*cross* ★**cheerful**

irritate *v.* annoy, vex, irk, offend, provoke ▷*bother* ★**please**

island *n.* isle, islet, key, atoll, cay

issue ① *v.* flow, ooze, bring out, circulate, publish ② *n.* edition, printing, publication *My book of poems was ready for publication,* impression ③ problem, question, concern

itch ① *v.* prickle, tingle, irritate ② *n.* impulse, motive, desire *I have always had a strong desire to work in a hospital*

item *n.* point, particular, thing, object, article

A B C D E F G H I J K L M N O P Q R S T U V W X Y Z

J j

jab *v.* poke, prod, push, stab, dig

jabber *v.* chatter, gabble, mumble, babble

jacket *n.* coat, jerkin, cover, case, sheath

jagged *adj.* rough, broken, snagged, notched, uneven ★**smooth**

jail *n.* prison, penitentiary, lockup, brig

jam ① *n.* jelly, preserves, conserve, marmalade ② *v.* crowd, pack *All the buses were full, and we were packed in like sardines,* crush, squeeze JAMB

jar ① *n.* jug, beaker, ewer, vase, pitcher, pot ② *v.* jog, rattle, grate *That singer's voice really grates on me,* grind

jaunt *n. & v.* trip, journey, cruise, travel, tour

jaunty *adj.* lighthearted, showy, dapper, spruce, debonair

jealous *adj.* envious, covetous, grudging

jealousy *n.* envy, covetousness, distrust, spite

jeer *v.* laugh at, deride, mock, ridicule, insult ▷*taunt*

jeopardy *n.* peril, risk, hazard, plight ▷*danger* ★**safety**

jerk *n. & v.* yank, pull, drag, jog, jolt, tug

jersey *n.* pullover, sweater

Jewels

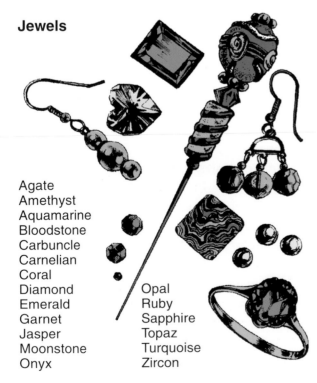

Agate
Amethyst
Aquamarine
Bloodstone
Carbuncle
Carnelian
Coral
Diamond
Emerald
Garnet
Jasper
Moonstone
Onyx

Opal
Ruby
Sapphire
Topaz
Turquoise
Zircon

jest *n.* joke, jape, spoof, banter, chaff

jester *n.* clown, buffoon, merry-andrew, prankster, comedian

jet *n. & v.* spurt, squirt, flow, gush

jetty *n.* wharf, dock, quay, pier

jewel *n.* gem, stone, trinket, charm, locket

jibe *v.* mock, scoff, scorn, sneer, taunt ▷*jeer*

jiffy *n.* instant, flash, minute, moment

jilt *v.* abandon, brush off, desert, drop, forsake

jingle *v.* tinkle, clink, chink, ring, jangle

job *n.* task, work, chore, place, office, post, position

jocular *adj.* gleeful, hilarious, witty, humorous, jolly ▷*funny* ★**serious**

jog *v.* ① prod, nudge, shove, shake ② run, sprint, canter, trot, exercise

join *v.* ① unite, link, combine, connect, attach ★**separate** ② enlist, sign up *Gaby and Bill have signed up for tennis lessons*

joint ① *n.* junction, knot, union, connection ② *adj.* shared, united, mutual *It's in our mutual interest to keep expenses down*

joke *n.* gag, trick, frolic, lark, jape, game, prank ▷*jest*

jolly *adj.* jovial, cheerful, blithe, frisky ▷*merry* ★**sad**

jolt *n. & v.* jar, shock, shove, rock, jerk, bump

jostle *v.* push, shove, shoulder, thrust, elbow

jot ① *n.* atom, bit, grain, particle ② *v.* note, scribble, take down

journal *n.* ① ledger, account book ② diary, newspaper, magazine *I've just become editor of the natural history society's magazine*

journey *n.* excursion, trip, tour, jaunt, ramble

jovial *adj.* jolly, festive, cordial, affable, cheerful ▷*merry* ★**sad**

joy *n.* rapture, enchantment, delight, pleasure, charm ▷*bliss* ★**sorrow**

joyful *adj.* joyous, enjoyable, pleasurable, happy, jovial, delighted ★**sorrowful**

jubilant *adj.* exultant, gleeful, happy, overjoyed, excited ★**depressed**

judge ① *n.* justice, magistrate, referee, umpire ② *v.* assess *We can ask the jeweler to assess the value of these pearls,* decide, find, appraise, estimate

judgment *n.* ① decision, opinion, verdict *The*

K k

Key

Keys

jury gave a verdict of "not guilty," decree, finding ② intelligence, understanding, valuation

judicious *adj.* prudent, discreet, expedient, wise ★**indiscreet**

jug *n.* beaker, ewer, urn, vase ▷*jar*

juggle *v.* conjure, manipulate

juice *n.* essence, extract, sap, fluid, nectar

jumble *n.* medley, mixture, muddle, tangle, clutter

jump *v.* spring, bound, hop, skip, vault, ▷*leap*

junction *n.* ① union, combination, joint, connection ② crossroads, intersection, juncture, crossing

jungle *n.* forest, bush, wilderness

junior *adj.* lesser, lower, younger, subordinate ★**senior**

junk *n.* trash, debris, rubbish, waste, clutter, litter, scrap, garbage, refuse

just ① *adj.* sound, regular, orderly, exact, fair, honest, impartial ② *adv.* exactly, precisely ③ *adv.* only, merely, simply

justice *n.* equity, impartiality, fairness, right ★**injustice**

justify *v.* vindicate, acquit, condone, uphold, legalize

jut *v.* bulge, extend, stick out, overhang, project *We took shelter where the cliff projects over the path* ★**recede**

juvenile ① *adj.* adolescent, youthful, young, childish ★**mature** ② *n.* boy, girl, child, youngster, youth

keen ① *adj.* eager, ardent, earnest, diligent ② sharp *Her wit is as sharp as a razor,* acute, fine ★**dull**

keep ① *v.* hold, retain, collect, possess ★**abandon** ② *v.* care for, maintain, shelter *We have arranged to shelter the refugees* ③ *n.* tower, dungeon, castle, fort, stronghold

keeper *n.* jailer, warden, attendant, caretaker, janitor, custodian

keeping *n.* compliance, obedience, accord

keep on *v.* continue, go on, endure, persist ★**give up**

keepsake *n.* souvenir, token, memento, reminder, relic

keg *n.* barrel, cask, tub, drum, container

ken *n.* grasp, grip, understanding, mastery, knowledge

kerchief *n.* scarf, headscarf, shawl, neckcloth

kernel *n.* core, heart, hub, center, gist, nub COLONEL

kettle *n.* boiler, cauldron, cooking pot, teakettle

key ① *n.* opener ② *n.* solution, clue, answer ③ *n.* cay, isle, island, atoll ④ *adj.* essential, fundamental, vital, critical QUAY

kick *v.* ① boot, strike with the foot, punt, hit ② complain, grumble, rebel *The people rebelled against the harsh rule of the new king,* resist

kidnap *v.* abduct, capture, seize, snatch, steal, hijack

kill *v.* slay, assassinate, destroy, massacre, slaughter ▷*murder*

killjoy *n.* spoilsport, wet blanket *I don't want to be a wet blanket, but I'm tired and want to go home,* grouch, complainer ★**optimist**

kin *n.* race, kindred, offspring, kind, family, relative

kind ① *adj.* gentle, kindly, genial, good-natured, amiable ★**unkind** ② *n.* style, character, sort, variety

kindle *v.* ① light, ignite, set fire to ② inflame

A B C D E F G H I J K L M N O P Q R S T U V W X Y Z

A Little Knowledge is a Dangerous Thing—and Other Misquotes

Many of the familiar quotations we use from literature, history, or the world of entertainment are incorrect adapations of the original. Greta Garbo did not say "I want to be alone." Her true words were: "I like to be alone." Shakespeare did not say "Discretion is the better part of valor." The correct quotation is: "The better part of valor is discretion." Here are some more, with the correct original version printed in italic type:

From Shakespeare

Alas, poor Yorick: I knew him well.
Alas, poor Yorick; I knew him,
Horatio: a fellow of infinite jest.
(Hamlet)

O Romeo. Romeo! wherefore art thou, Romeo?
O Romeo. Romeo! wherefore art thou
Romeo? (Romeo and Juliet)
(Note the position of the comma.
"Wherefore" means "why" not "where.")

To gild the lily . . .
to gild refined gold, to paint the lily . . .
(King John)
Screw your courage to the sticking-point
But screw your courage to the sticking-
place (Macbeth)

All that glitters is not gold
All that glisters is not gold
(The Merchant of Venice)
Discretion is the better part of valor.
The better part of valor is discretion.
(King Henry IV, part I)

From the King James Bible

Pride goes before a fall
Pride goeth before destruction and an
haughty spirit before a fall (Proverbs)

Money is the root of all evil
For the love of money is the root of
all evil (Timothy)

To go the way of all flesh
And, behold, this day I am going the
way of all the earth (Joshua)

The mayor's words only inflamed the
people even more, excite, provoke, rouse

kindness *n.* good nature, charity, amiability, affection, tenderness ★**cruelty**

king *n.* monarch, sovereign, majesty, ruler, emperor

kink *n.* ① knot, loop, bend, coil ② freak, eccentricity, whim *This strange tower was built as the result of a whim by the eccentric designer*

kiss *v.* salute, embrace, smooch, buss

kit *n.* set, outfit, baggage, effects, gear, rig

knack *n.* flair, talent, ability, genius, gift ▷*skill*

knave *n.* cheat, rascal, villain, scamp, scoundrel ▷*rogue* NAVE

knead *v.* form, squeeze, mold, shape, press NEED

kneel *v.* bend the knee, genuflect *The nun genuflected before the altar, then said her rosary,* bow down, worship

knife *n.* scalpel, blade, dagger, cutter

knight *n.* cavalier, champion, soldier, warrior, baronet NIGHT

knit *v.* weave, crochet, spin, twill, link, loop

knob *n.* boss, bump, handle, opener, button

knock *v.* hit, slap, punch, bang, smite, strike

knock out ① *v.* stun, make insensible, render

L l

Water, water, everywhere, and not a drop to drink
Water, water, everywhere, Nor any drop to drink (The Rime of the Ancient Mariner)

A little knowledge is a dangerous thing *A little learning is a dang'rous thing* (Alexander Pope)

Tomorrow to fresh fields and pastures new *Tomorrow to fresh woods, and pastures new* (Paradise Lost)

They shall not grow old as we that are left grow old
They shall grow not old, as we that are left grow old (Laurence Binyon)

Play it again, Sam (Humphrey Bogart, in the film *Casablanca*)

Play it, Sam. Play "As Time Goes By" (Ingrid Bergman, in the film *Casablanca*)

unconscious ② *n.* success, hit, triumph

knoll *n.* barrow, hill, mound, hillock

knot *n.* ① tie, bond, join, loop, kink, snarl, tangle ② cluster, group NOT

know *v.* perceive, discern, notice, identify ▷*understand* NO

know-how *n.* skill, knowledge, talent

knowing *adj.* astute, knowledgeable, intelligent, perceptive ★**ignorant**

knowledge *n.* understanding, acquaintance, learning, wisdom, scholarship, information, sapience ★**ignorance**

kudos *n.* prestige, distinction, fame, glory, recognition

label *n.* badge, tag, ticket, sticker, docket, slip

labor *n. & v.* toil, work, drudge, strain, struggle

laborious *adj.* ① hard-working, diligent ② strenuous, arduous *Digging potatoes is arduous work,* hard ★**easy**

lack ① *n.* need, want, absence, deficiency, scarcity *During the hot weather there was a scarcity of water* ② *v.* need, require, want, miss

laconic *adj.* terse, curt, brief, concise ★**wordy**

lad *n.* boy, fellow, kid, youth, chap

laden *adj.* loaded, burdened, hampered, weighed down ★**empty**

ladle *v.* dip, scoop, dish, shovel

lady *n.* woman, female, dame, damsel, matron, mistress

lag *v.* dawdle, loiter, tarry, saunter ▷*linger* ★**lead**

lagoon *n.* pool, pond, lake, basin

lair *n.* den, nest, retreat, hideout, hole

lake *n.* lagoon, loch, pond, spring, reservoir

lam *v.* beat, hit, clout, knock ▷*strike*

lame *adj.* ① crippled, hobbled, disabled ② weak, feeble *That's a feeble excuse for missing school,* inadequate, unconvincing

lament *v.* deplore, mourn, grieve, sorrow ▷*regret* ★**rejoice**

lamp *n.* lantern, light, flare, torch, flashlight

lance ① *n.* spear, pike, javelin, shaft ② *v.* puncture, pierce, cut

land ① *n.* country, district, tract, area, nation, region ② *v.* alight, arrive, carry, touch down *We had engine trouble, so the aircraft touched down in the desert*

landlord *n.* host, hotelier, innkeeper, owner

landmark *n.* milestone, milepost, beacon, monument, signpost

landscape *n.* scenery, view, prospect, countryside, panorama

lane *n.* alley, drive, passage, way LAIN

language *n.* tongue, speech, utterance, dialect, jargon

languid *adj.* leisurely, unhurried, sluggish, slow, easy ★**lively**

languish *v.* decline, droop, flag, pine, suffer, yearn ★**flourish**

lanky *adj.* tall, rangy, gangling, scrawny ★**squat**

lantern *n.* lamp, flashlight, torch

lap ① *v.* lick, drink, sip, sup ② *n.* circuit, course, distance ③ *n.* thighs, knees

lapse *v.* expire, die, pass, elapse, go by, deteriorate LAPS

larder *n.* pantry, storeroom, cellar

large *adj.* big, ample, substantial, great, broad ▷*huge* ★**small**

lark *n.* adventure, escapade, spree, joke, frolic, gambol

lash ① *v.* beat, cane, whip, flay, flog ② *n.* prod, goad, drive, whip

lass *n.* girl, maiden, maid, young woman

last ① *adj.* final, concluding, latest, utmost, aftermost ★**first** ② *v.* remain, linger *The foggy weather lingered for most of the morning,* endure, stay

latch *n.* bolt, bar, padlock, fastener

late *adj.* tardy, behindhand, departed, slow ★**early**

lately *adv.* recently, latterly, formerly

lather *n.* suds, foam, bubbles, froth

latter *adj.* final, last, latest, recent, closing ★**former**

laud *v.* compliment, praise, applaud, glorify ★**blame**

laugh *v.* chuckle, giggle, guffaw, snicker ★**cry**

launch ① *v.* start, begin, commence, establish, initiate ② *n.* motorboat

lavish ① *adj.* abundant, generous, liberal, extravagant ② *v.* waste, squander *My parents left me a small fortune, but I squandered it all,* give

law *n.* rule, ordinance, regulation, edict, decree

lawful *adj.* legal, legitimate, rightful ★**illegal**

lawyer *n.* attorney, counsel, jurist, barrister, solicitor, advocate

lax *adj.* careless, casual, slack, relaxed, vague ★**strict** LACKS

lay ① *v.* put, set *It's time for dinner; let's set the table,* deposit, place, spread ② *v.* impute, charge ③ *adj.* nonprofessional, amateur

layer *n.* seam, sheet, thickness, tier

lazy *adj.* idle, inactive, slothful, slow, sluggish ★**active**

lead *v.* conduct, guide, escort, direct, command ★**follow**

leader *n.* guide, pilot, conductor, chief, head, master

leaf *n.* frond, blade, sheet LIEF

league *n.* band, association, society, guild, group

leak *v.* trickle, ooze, seep, exude, flow out LEEK

lean ① *adj.* spare, slim, thin, skinny *Lina has no flesh on her; she is very skinny,* ② *v.* bend, curve, tilt, incline LIEN

leap *v.* spring, bound, jump, hop, skip

learn *v.* find out, ascertain, determine, acquire knowledge, understand

learned *adj.* cultured, educated, scholarly, literate ★**ignorant**

learning *n.* scholarship, education, knowledge ▷*wisdom* ★**ignorance**

least *adj.* fewest, smallest, slightest, lowest, tiniest ★**most** LEASED

leave ① *v.* abandon, desert, forsake, quit, go ② bequeath, bestow ③ *n.* vacation, furlough *Jack is on a furlough from the army,* permission

lecture *n.* talk, speech, address, sermon

ledge *n.* shelf, ridge, step

legacy *n.* bequest, inheritance, gift

legal *adj.* legitimate, lawful, valid, sound ★**illegal**

legend *n.* ① fable, myth, tale, fiction ② inscription *The box bore a brass plate with an inscription,* heading, caption

legible *adj.* clear, readable, understandable, distinct ★**illegible**

legitimate *adj.* legal, lawful, proper, rightful ▷*genuine* ★**illegal**

a b c d e f g h i j k l m n o p q r s t u v w x y z

Lights

Arc lamp
Candle
Chandelier
Desk lamp
Electric light
Flashlight
Fluorescent lamp
Footlights
Gaslight
Headlight
Lantern
Nightlight
Reading light
Spotlight
Sunlamp
Table lamp
Torch

leisurely *adj.* unhurried, slow, easy, carefree, tranquil **★hectic**

lend *v.* loan, advance, provide, supply, grant, lease **★borrow**

lengthen *v.* extend, elongate, stretch, draw out, prolong **★shorten**

lengthy *adj.* long, drawn out, longwinded ▷*tedious* **★short**

lenient *adj.* tolerant, merciful, sparing, forbearing, indulgent **★severe**

less *adj.* lesser, smaller, inferior, lower

lessen *v.* reduce, cut, become smaller, diminish, decrease **★increase** LESSON

lesson *n.* instruction, lecture, information, teaching, exercise LESSEN

let ① *v.* allow, permit, suffer, authorize *The mayor authorized our school to hold the celebrations in the park,* grant ② lease

let down *v.* ① lower, take down ② betray, abandon, disappoint **★satisfy**

letter *n.* ① dispatch, communication, epistle, message ② character *The book was printed in Hebrew characters,* sign, symbol

level ① *n.* plane, grade ② *adj.* even, flat, smooth **★uneven** ③ *v.* aim, direct, point ④ *v.* demolish *Many houses were demolished*

during the earthquake, destroy

liable ① *adj.* answerable, accountable, responsible ② apt *My parents are apt to be annoyed if I play loud music,* prone, inclined

liar *n.* deceiver, fibber, teller of tales LYRE

libel *v.* slander, malign, blacken, defame, slur **★praise**

liberal *adj.* open-handed, generous, open-hearted, free, lavish

liberate *v.* set free, save, release, **★restrict**

liberty *n.* freedom, independence **★slavery**

license *v.* allow, permit, entitle **★ban**

lie ① *n.* untruth, falsehood ② *v.* recline *I shall recline on the sofa for the afternoon,* lounge, repose ▷*loll* ③ *v.* tell a lie, fib, invent LYE

life *n.* being, existence, activity, energy, **★death**

lift *v.* raise, erect, hoist, elevate, hold up **★lower**

light ① *n.* radiance, glow, shine, glare, brightness ② *n.* lamp, beacon, flame ② *v.* ignite, illuminate, kindle *The scouts kindled a fire to cook their food* ③ *adj.* fair, light-colored, sunny **★dark** ④ lightweight, buoyant, airy **★heavy**

like ①*adj.* similar, resembling, akin **★unlike**

② *v.* admire, love, adore, cherish, prize ★**dislike**

likely *adj.* probable, expected, possible

likeness *n.* ① resemblance, appearance ② photograph *That's a wonderful photograph of my grandmother,* portrait

likewise *adv.* also, too, furthermore, further

limb *n.* leg, arm, extension, branch, shoot, bough

limit ① *n.* barrier, boundary, border, edge, end, restraint ② *v.* reduce, restrict *The heavy rain was restricted to the hilly country,* confine ★**free**

limited *adj.* restricted, reduced, narrow, confined ★**unrestricted**

limp ① *adj.* flabby, flimsy, flexible ② *v.* hobble, falter, shuffle

line *n.* ① stripe, streak, dash, bar ② cord, thread ③ row, queue, file ④ calling *Being an opera singer is a noble calling but a difficult one,* occupation

linger *v.* loiter, lag, dally, tarry, delay ▷*dawdle* ★**speed**

link ① *n.* bond, tie, connection, joint ② *v.* unite, join, couple, bracket ★**separate**

liquefy *v.* liquidize, melt

liquid *n.* fluid, liquor, solution, juice

list ① *n.* schedule, table, catalog, register ② *v.* tilt, lean, heel *The yacht heeled over as it turned into the wind,* careen, slope

listen *v.* hear, hearken, hark, heed

listless *adj.* languid, dull, lethargic, lifeless ▷*sluggish* ★**lively**

literally *adv.* actually, faithfully, precisely, really ★**loosely**

literate *adj.* educated, well-educated, learned, lettered ★**illiterate**

lithe *adj.* agile, nimble, flexible, supple ★**stiff**

litter *n.* clutter, jumble, rubbish, mess, refuse

little ① *adj.* small, tiny, short, slight, trivial, petty ▷*small* ★**large** ② *adv.* hardly, rarely, seldom

live ① *adj.* alive, living, existing, active, alert ★**dead** ② *v.* be, subsist, breathe, exist

lively *adj.* active, brisk, vivacious, animated, agile ★**listless**

livid *adj.* ① angry, enraged, furious, mad ② ashen *We were really scared, and Bob's face was ashen,* grayish, pale, leaden

living ① *adj.* alive, existing ② *n.* job, occupation, work, livelihood

load ① *n.* freight, cargo, goods, burden ② *v.* fill, pack, burden, pile up, stack LODE, LOWED

loaf ① *v.* waste time, idle, dally, dawdle ② *n.* block, cube, lump, cake

loan ① *n.* credit, advance, allowance ② *v.* allow, lend, advance *The bank advanced me the money to pay the mortgage* LONE

loath or **loth** *adj.* reluctant, disinclined, opposed

loathe *v.* abhor, detest, despise, dislike ▷*hate* ★**like**

lobby *n.* hallway, entrance, vestibule, foyer

local *adj.* regional, district, provincial

locate *v.* find, discover, detect, unearth

lock ① *n.* bolt, fastener, latch, clasp ② *v.* bolt, fasten, secure ③ *n.* floodgate, weir ④ *n.* curl, braid, tress *I kept a tress of her hair in a locket*

lodge ① *v.* stay at, put up, shelter, get stuck *A fishbone got stuck in his throat,* remain ② *n.* inn, hotel

lofty *adj.* ① tall, high, noble, great ② proud, exalted, arrogant ★**modest**

logical *adj.* fair, justifiable, reasonable, sound ★**illogical**

loiter *v.* lag, trail, linger, dally, dawdle, hang around

loll *v.* recline, sprawl, lounge, lie, rest, flop

lone *adj.* single, sole, lonely, separate, unaccompanied LOAN

lonely *adj.* alone, forsaken, friendless, remote, forlorn, lonesome

long ① *adj.* lengthy, extended, expanded ★**short** ② *v.* crave, hanker, yearn, desire

look ① *v.* appear, seem ② *v.* peer, glance, watch, behold ③ *n.* appearance, glance, gaze *Her gaze fell upon me, and I had to answer the next question*

loom *v.* menace, portend, rise, emerge, appear

loop *n.* bend, circle, coil, noose, twist

loophole *n.* escape, way out, excuse, get-out

loose *adj.* ① slack, separate, apart, flimsy, flabby, baggy ② free, relaxed, ③ vague, indefinite

loosely *adv.* freely, separately, vaguely

loosen *v.* slacken, relax, undo, detach, release, unfasten ★**tighten**

Loot

Lute

loot *n.* booty, haul, swag, spoils, plunder LUTE

lord *n.* noble, ruler, duke, marquess, earl, viscount, baron

lose *v.* ① mislay, misplace, miss ★**find** ② be defeated, suffer defeat *The rebels suffered defeat at the hands of the army,* fail ★**win**

loser *n.* failure, dud, flop ★**winner**

loss *n.* damage, harm, forfeit, ruin, misfortune ★**gain**

lost *adj.* mislaid, missing, gone, vanished, strayed, ruined ★**found**

lot *n.* ① group, batch, assortment ② fate, portion, fortune ③ plot, patch, land

lotion *n.* balm, salve, ointment, cream, liniment

loud *adj.* ① noisy, blatant, shrill, blaring, deafening ② gaudy, vulgar, tasteless ★**quiet**

lounge ① *v.* recline, lie, loll, sprawl, laze ② *n.* lobby *Tea was served in the hotel's lobby,* reception room, waiting room

lout *n.* oaf, clod, boor, lummox

lovable *adj.* winsome, charming, attractive, fascinating ★**hateful**

love ① *v.* adore, idolize, worship, dote on, cherish, treasure ② *n.* affection, passion, devotion, ardor ★**hate**

lovely *adj.* charming, delightful, beautiful, adorable ★**hideous**

low *adj.* ① base, vulgar, crude, improper ② not high, flat, level ③ soft, faint, muffled, deep ④ humble, modest, lowly ⑤ cheap, inexpensive ★**high** LO

lower ① *v.* let down, fall, descend ② *v.* debase, disgrace, degrade ③ *adj.* inferior, lesser, smaller, minor

loyal *adj.* constant, staunch *Bill was Kathy's staunch friend for years,* true ▷*faithful* ★**disloyal**

lucid *adj.* clear, obvious, intelligible, bright ▷*transparent* ★**murky**

luck *n.* chance, fortune, success, windfall ★**misfortune**

lucky *adj.* fortunate, successful, blessed, charmed, favored ★**unlucky**

ludicrous *adj.* absurd, foolish, silly, outlandish, ▷*ridiculous*

lug *v.* pull, draw, drag, haul, tow, heave

luggage *n.* baggage, suitcases, trunks, boxes

lull ① *v.* calm, dwindle, cease, slacken, subside ② *n.* calm, hush, respite

lumber ① *n.* timber, wood, boards, logs ② *v.* plod, shuffle, stomp

luminous *adj.* shining, radiant, bright

lump *n.* bit, piece, chunk, block, knob, swelling *I noticed a rather mysterious swelling on my arm*

lunatic *n.* insane person, maniac, psychopath

lunge *v.* push, thrust, plunge, charge, pounce

lurch *v.* lean, list, reel, rock, stagger, stumble

lure *v.* attract, draw, decoy, ensnare, invite ▷*tempt* ★**repulse**

lurid *adj.* ghastly, disgusting, grim, grisly, melodramatic, sensational

lurk *v.* slink, skulk, crouch, hide, prowl, snoop

luscious *adj.* juicy, succulent, mellow, delicious, scrumptious ★**nauseous**

lush *adj.* wild, luxuriant, green, rich, abundant

lust *n.* desire, passion, craving, greed

luster *n.* brightness, brilliance, gleam, sheen

lusty *adj.* hale, hearty, vigorous, energetic, rugged, tough ★**weak**

luxury *n.* affluence, wealth, richness, comfort, bliss

lyre *n.* harp, zither LIAR

A B C D E F G H I J K L M N O P Q R S T U V W X Y Z

M m

macabre *adj.* ghastly, grisly, hideous, horrible ▷ghostly

machine *n.* engine, contrivance, device

mad *adj.* ① angry, furious ② lunatic, crazy ▷*insane* ★**sane**

madcap *adj.* flighty, reckless, thoughtless, impulsive

magazine *n.* ① periodical, publication ② storehouse, depot, arsenal

magic ① *n.* wizardry, witchcraft, sorcery, conjuring ② *adj.* bewitching *She greeted me with a bewitching smile,* fascinating, miraculous

magician *n.* conjuror, wizard, witch, sorcerer, juggler

magistrate *n.* judge, justice, bailiff

magnanimous *adj.* forgiving, generous, charitable, liberal ★**paltry**

magnate *n.* industrialist, merchant, tycoon, VIP, leader MAGNET

magnet *n.* lodestone, attraction, bait, draw MAGNATE

magnetic *adj.* attracting, attractive, absorbing, entrancing, alluring, mesmerizing ▷*charming* ★**repulsive**

magnificent *adj.* majestic, noble, grand, brilliant, superb ▷*splendid* ★**modest**

magnify *v.* enlarge, increase, exaggerate ▷*enhance* ★**diminish**

maid *n.* ① maiden, virgin, miss, damsel ② maidservant, domestic help, waitress MADE

mail *n.* ① letters, post, correspondence, epistles ② armor *The knight's armor was made of breastplates and chain mail,* shield MALE

maim *v.* mutilate, injure, mangle, crush ▷*disable* ★**heal**

main ① *adj.* leading, principal, head, chief, central *Such important matters are dealt with at our central office,* ② *n.* channel, duct, line, pipe

mainly *adv.* chiefly, generally, mostly, on the whole, usually

Mail

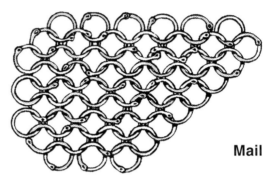

Mail

maintain *v.* ① sustain, keep, support, provide for ② affirm, advocate *The chairman advocated an increase in charges,* assert

majestic *adj.* dignified, grand, noble, august, elevated ▷*magnificent* ★**unimportant**

major ① *adj.* senior, chief, leading, more important, greater ★**minor** ② *n.* officer, soldier

majority *n.* greater number, most part, bulk, mass ★**minority**

make *v.* ① build, construct, fabricate, fashion ② compel, drive, coerce ③ designate *Two days after her boss retired Liz was designated as the new head of the department,* appoint

make up *v.* ① invent, fabricate, create ② forgive and forget, bury the hatchet *At last, my brother and sister stopped arguing and decided to bury the hatchet*

makeshift *adj.* improvised, temporary, stopgap *I fixed the car engine, but it was only a stopgap repair* ★**permanent**

malady *n.* illness, sickness, ailment, affliction, disease

malevolent *adj.* malign, baleful, venomous, malicious ▷*hostile* ★**benevolent**

malice *n.* bitterness, rancor, spite, enmity ▷*hatred* ★**kindness**

malicious *adj.* malignant, spiteful, resentful, bitter ▷*hateful* ★**kind**

maltreat *v.* bully, harm, abuse, injure ▷*hurt* ★**assist**

mammoth *adj.* giant, colossal, enormous, massive ▷*huge* ★**small**

man ① *n.* male, sir, mankind, gentleman ② *n.* valet, manservant ③ *v.* equip, fit out, arm, crew

manage *v.* ① direct, control, administer ② get along *I get along quite well on my own,* fare, cope with ★**fail**

manager *n.* director, superintendent, overseer, supervisor, boss

mandate *n.* authority, command, instruction, warrant

maneuver *v.* direct, drive, guide, handle ▷*manipulate*

mangle *v.* crush, deform, destroy, maul ▷*maim*

mania *n.* madness, delirium, craze, fad, enthusiasm, passion

manifest *v.* signify, suggest, demonstrate, display ▷*show* ★**hide**

manipulate *v.* work, handle, wield, use, conduct, control ▷*operate*

manly *adj.* male, masculine, brave, bold, strong ▷*fearless*

manner *n.* fashion, style, form, mode, demeanor, bearing, way MANOR

manor *n.* estate, country house, château, hall MANNER

mansion *n.* house, castle, residence ▷*manor*

mantle *n.* canopy, cape, covering, hood, shroud, cloak MANTEL

mantel *n.* fireplace shelf, mantelpiece MANTLE

manual ① *adj.* hand-operated, physical *We found the electric typewriter easier to use than the manual typewriter* ② *n.* guide, guidebook, handbook

manufacture *v.* make, build, fabricate, create, produce ▷*construct*

manuscript *n.* ① script, article, essay, theme ② handwriting, autograph

many *adj.* numerous, varied, various, frequent, countless ★**few**

map *n.* chart, plan, diagram, outline

mar *v.* deface, disfigure, injure, blemish, damage ▷*spoil* ★**enhance**

march *v.* stride, walk, pace, step, file, trek

margin *n.* edge, border, rim, side, boundary, brim, brink ★**center**

mariner *n.* seaman, sailor, seafarer, deckhand, tar, seadog

mark ① *n.* feature, emblem, impression *The letter had a hand-stamped impression on it,* blemish ② *v.* scratch, blemish, stain ③ *v.* take notice of, observe

marked *adj.* noticeable, conspicuous, apparent, clear, striking ★**slight**

market *n.* grocery store, supermarket, bazaar

maroon *v.* desert, beach, strand, abandon, cast away ★**rescue**

marry *v.* wed, get married, espouse, mate, unite ★**separate**

marsh *n.* swamp, mire, moor, morass, bog

marshal *v.* gather, group, deploy, assemble MARTIAL

martial *adj.* military, militant, hostile, warlike ★**peaceful** MARSHAL

marvel *n.* miracle, wonder, spectacle, sensation

marvelous *adj.* wonderful, wondrous, fabulous, spectacular ▷*remarkable* ★**ordinary**

masculine *adj.* manlike, manly, strong, robust, strapping ▷*male* ★**feminine**

mash *v.* crush, squash, pulverize, grind

mask ① *n.* camouflage, veil, domino ② *v.* conceal, disguise *Aladdin went to the marketplace disguised as a beggar,* shield ★**uncover**

mass *n.* batch, combination, hunk, load, quantity, lump

massacre *v.* exterminate, butcher, murder, slaughter, kill

massive *adj.* big, large, bulky, enormous ▷*huge* ★**small**

master ① *n.* controller, director, leader, captain, champion ② *v.* tame *Our job on the*

A B C D E F G H I J K L M N O P Q R S T U V W X Y Z

ranch was to tame the wild horses, control, defeat, subdue

match ① *n.* light, fuse, taper, lucifer ② *v.* copy, pair, equal, tone with

mate ① *n.* spouse, husband, wife, companion, chum, comrade ② *v.* breed, join, wed, yoke

material ① *n.* fabric, textile, cloth, stuff, matter ② *adj.* actual, real, concrete *There was concrete evidence of the prisoner's innocence*

maternal *adj.* motherly, parental, kind, affectionate, protective

matter ① *n.* affair, concern, subject, topic ② *n.* stuff, material, substance *This rock contains some sort of mineral substance* ③ *n.* trouble, distress ④ *v.* signify, count, affect

mature *adj.* ripe, mellowed, seasoned, developed, grown-up, adult ★**immature**

maul *v.* batter, beat, molest, paw ▷*mangle*

maxim *n.* saying, motto, axiom, proverb

maximum *adj.* supreme, highest, most, greatest, top, largest ★**minimum**

maybe *adv.* possibly, perhaps, perchance

maze *n.* labyrinth, puzzle, tangle, confusion ▷*muddle* MAIZE

meadow *n.* grassland, field, mead, pasture

meager *adj.* thin, spare, slight, flimsy, sparse ▷*scanty* ★**substantial**

meal *n.* repast, dinner, lunch, breakfast, supper ▷*feast*

mean ① *v.* signify, denote, express, suggest ② *adj.* cruel, base, low, paltry, miserly ★**generous** ③ average, medium mien

meaning *n.* significance, explanation, sense

means *n.* ① resources, money, wealth ② technique, ability *She has the ability to become a professional player,* method

measure ① *n.* meter, gauge, rule ② *n.* limit, extent, amount ③ *v.* estimate, value, quantify *It is hard to quantify how much damage has been done*

meat *n.* flesh, viands, victuals, food, muscle,

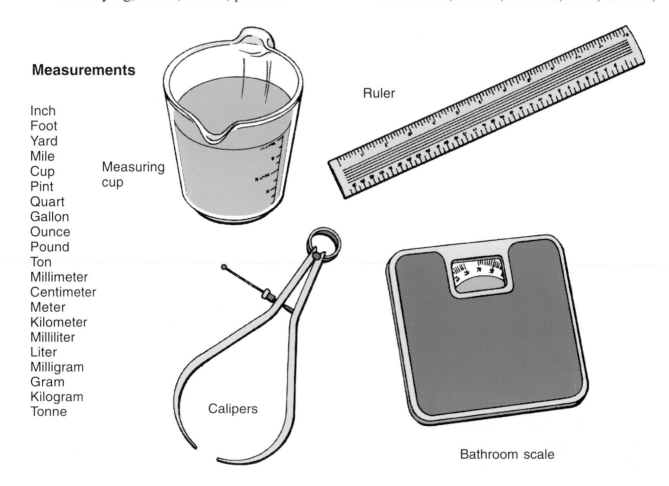

Measurements

Inch
Foot
Yard
Mile
Cup
Pint
Quart
Gallon
Ounce
Pound
Ton
Millimeter
Centimeter
Meter
Kilometer
Milliliter
Liter
Milligram
Gram
Kilogram
Tonne

Measuring cup

Ruler

Calipers

Bathroom scale

brawn MEET, METE

mechanical *adj.* ① automatic, machine-driven ② routine, unthinking

medal *n.* award, decoration, ribbon, prize, trophy MEDDLE

meddle *v.* interfere, intervene, intrude, tamper MEDAL

medicine *n.* remedy, cure, physic, medicament, nostrum, drug

mediocre *adj.* average, common, inferior, middling ▷*ordinary* ★**excellent**

meditate *v.* ponder, puzzle over, think, reflect, contemplate

medium ① *n.* means, agency, center ② *n.* conditions, setting, atmosphere *I like school because it has such a wonderful atmosphere of learning* ③ *adj.* average, fair ▷*mediocre*

medley *n.* assortment, jumble, collection, hodgepodge

meek *adj.* docile, humble, quiet, patient, uncomplaining ▷*mild* ★**arrogant**

meet *v.* come together, converge, join, flock, assemble, encounter MEAT, METE

meeting *n.* gathering, assembly, convention

melancholy *adj.* glum, gloomy, unhappy, sad ▷*miserable* ★**cheerful**

mellow *adj.* ① ripe, rich, full-flavored ★**unripe** ② jovial, cheerful ③ smooth, soothing, delicate *The wine had a smooth, delicate flavor*

melodious *adj.* sweet, mellow, silver-toned, rich, resonant ★**harsh**

melody *n.* tune, air, lay, song, chant, theme

melt *v.* dissolve, liquefy, soften, thaw ★**solidify**

member *n.* ① fellow, associate, representative, comrade ② limb, part, portion, leg, arm

memorable *adj.* unforgettable, fresh, indelible, noticeable, striking ▷*conspicuous*

memorial *n.* monument, memento, relic, mausoleum *The emperor was buried in the state mausoleum*

memorize *v.* learn, commit to memory, remember

memory *n.* recall, recapture, recollection, renown ▷*fame*

menace *v.* threaten, intimidate, frighten, alarm ▷*bully*

mend *v.* restore, correct, promote, improve, rectify, heal ▷*repair* ★**damage**

menial ① *adj.* servile, ignoble, base ② *n.* flunky, underling, lackey

mental *adj.* intellectual, theoretical *Edward's knowledge of music is purely theoretical; he can't play or sing,* abstract ★**physical**

mention *v.* declare, announce, observe, disclose, speak of, say

mercenary ① *adj.* acquisitive, grasping, greedy ▷*selfish* ② *n.* soldier of fortune *The men who were killed were not patriots, but soldiers of fortune,* freelance, hireling

merchandise *n.* wares, goods, commodities, cargo, freight, stock

merchant *n.* dealer, trader, marketeer, vender, retailer, tradesman

merciful *adj.* humane, clement, lenient, compassionate, sparing, forgiving ★**merciless**

merciless *adj.* callous, cruel, pitiless, unrelenting, inhuman ★**merciful**

mercy *n.* compassion, clemency, forgiveness,

Metals

Aluminum
Brass
Bronze
Chromium
Copper
Gold
Iron and Steel
Lead
Manganese
Mercury
Nickel
Platinum
Silver
Tin
Zinc

Trophy

Girder

A B C D E F G H I J K L M N O P Q R S T U V W X Y Z

forbearance, grace ▷*pity* ★**cruelty**

mere *adj.* pure, unmixed, absolute, unaffected, simple, paltry

merge *v.* mix, mingle, combine, fuse, blend, weld ▷*unite*

merit ① *n.* excellence, quality, virtue, worth, caliber ▷*talent* ★**failing** ② *v.* deserve, be worthy of

merry *adj.* jolly, gleeful, cheerful, mirthful, sunny ▷*happy* ★**melancholy**

mesh *n.* net, lattice, snare, netting, tangle, trap, web

mess ① *n.* muddle, confusion, clutter, jumble, chaos ▷*plight* ★**order** ② dining hall, mess hall, dining room

message *n.* communication, letter, missive, notice, note, dispatch *The reporter sent a dispatch to her paper in Lisbon*

messenger *n.* courier, runner, agent, bearer, carrier, herald

mete *v.* measure, apportion, distribute, divide, deal MEAT, MEET

meter *n.* ① measure, gauge, rule ② cadence *He recited some of his poems, which had a peculiar cadence to them,* rhythm, lilt, swing

method *n.* routine, usage, way, means, system, rule, manner ▷*mode*

mettle *n.* spirit, life, fire, animation, ardor, boldness ▷*courage*

middle ① *n.* center, heart, midst ② *adj.* medium, average, normal

midget ① *n.* dwarf, gnome, pygmy ② *adj.* little, miniature, small ▷*tiny* ★**giant**

mien *n.* appearance, air, look, manner, expression MEAN

miffed *adj.* annoyed, nettled, offended, hurt ▷*upset* ★**delighted**

might ① *n.* strength, ability, power, force, energy ② *v. past tense of* **may** *She might not have gone had she known it would snow* MITE

mighty *adj.* strong, powerful, potent, stupendous ▷*hefty* ★**weak**

mild *adj.* moderate, calm, gentle, genial, docile ▷*meek* ★**harsh**

military *adj.* martial, soldierly, warlike

mill ① *n.* grinder, works, factory, plant ② *v.* crush, grind, pulverize *The rock was pulverized and used for making roads,* grate, pound

mimic *v.* impersonate, copy, simulate, imitate

mince *v.* shred, chop, crumble, grind, hash MINTS

mind ① *n.* brain, intellect, soul, spirit ② *v.* listen to, obey, follow orders ③ *v.* take care of, look after ④ *v.* be careful, watch out for

mine ① *n.* quarry, colliery, shaft, deposit, tunnel ② *n.* bomb, explosive ③ *v.* excavate, dig out ④ *pron.* belonging to me *This store is mine*

mingle *v.* mix, blend, combine ▷*merge*

miniature ① *adj.* tiny, small, dwarf, midget, minute ② *n.* small portrait

minimum *adj.* least, smallest, lowest, slightest ★**maximum**

minister *n.* ① clergyman, vicar, priest ② ambassador, diplomat *My aunt was a diplomat working in the Brazilian embassy* ③ secretary, cabinet member

minor *adj.* lesser, smaller, lower, junior, trivial, trifling ★**major** MINER

mint ① *v.* stamp, forge, cast ② *adj.* new, perfect, untarnished ③ *n.* peppermint, plant

minute ① *n.* (*min*-it) flash, instant, moment ② *adj.* (my-*nyute*) slight, tiny, small ▷*miniature* ★**huge**

miracle *n.* marvel, wonder, phenomenon

miraculous *adj.* supernatural, amazing, wondrous, prodigious ★**ordinary**

mire *n.* slime, muck, ooze, mud

mirror ① *n.* looking glass, reflector ② *v.* imitate, simulate, reflect *The essay reflected my feelings about my old home,* copy

mirth *n.* hilarity, laughter, jocularity, fun, frolic, jollity ★**melancholy**

misbehave *v.* do wrong, disobey, offend, be naughty ★**behave**

miscellaneous *adj.* various, varied, divers, sundry, mixed, jumbled

mischief *n.* roguery, pranks, damage, hurt, annoyance, harm

mischievous *adj.* rascally, villainous, naughty, destructive, spiteful ★**good**

misconduct *n.* misbehavior, wrongdoing, naughtiness, rudeness

miser *n.* niggard, skinflint, scrooge, pennypincher, tightwad ★**spendthrift**

miserable *adj.* forlorn, wretched, pitiable, desolate, suffering ★**cheerful**

misery *n.* sorrow, woe, grief, anguish, distress ▷*unhappiness* ★**happiness**

misfit *n.* eccentric *Professor Jones is something of an eccentric and comes to lectures in her slippers,* drop-out, oddball, nonconformist

misfortune *n.* adversity, bad luck, hardship, evil, calamity ▷*disaster* ★**luck**

misgiving *n.* distrust, mistrust, doubt, apprehension, anxiety ▷*qualm* ★**confidence**

mishap *n.* misadventure, blow, accident ▷*misfortune*

misjudge *v.* underestimate, overestimate, overrate, underrate ▷*mistake*

mislay *v.* lose, misplace, miss

mislead *v.* deceive, lead astray, hoodwink, take in, outwit ▷*bluff*

miss ① *v.* fail, fall short of, skip, pass over, mistake ② *v.* grieve over, yearn for, lament ③ *n.* girl, young woman, damsel

missile *n.* projectile, arrow, dart, pellet, shot, rocket

mission *n.* errand, task, assignment, object, objective, end, aim ▷*quest*

mist *n.* moisture, dew, vapor, fog, cloud MISSED

mistake ① *n.* error, fault, lapse, blunder, oversight ② *v.* slip up, misunderstand, confuse

mistaken *adj.* erroneous, untrue, false, fallacious ▷*wrong* ★**correct**

mistrust *v.* disbelieve, distrust, doubt, fear ▷*suspect* ★**trust**

misunderstand *v.* mistake, misinterpret, take wrongly ★**grasp**

misuse *v.* exploit, abuse, corrupt

mite *n.* ① grain, atom, morsel, particle ② bug, parasite *The plants were infested with parasites* MIGHT

mitigate *v.* allay, ease, abate, moderate, justify ★**aggravate**

mix *v.* blend, whip, mingle, combine ▷*stir*

mix up *v.* confuse, confound, muddle, jumble ▷*bewilder*

mixture *n.* miscellany, medley, jumble, blend

moan *v.* wail, groan, grouse, grumble, grieve

mob *n.* crowd, mass, gang, flock, rabble, company, throng

mobile *adj.* active, portable, wandering, movable ★**immobile**

mock ① *v.* mimic, imitate, jeer at, laugh at, ridicule ▷*flatter* ② *adj.* pretended, artificial

mode *n.* fashion, style, vogue, manner, way, form ▷*method* MOWED

model *n.* ① pattern, original, prototype *This car is a prototype, and we will produce many like it* ② mannequin ③ replica, representation

moderate *adj.* reasonable, medium, gentle, mild, quiet, modest ▷*fair*

modern *adj.* new, up-to-date, modish, stylish, recent

modest *adj.* bashful, demure, diffident, unassuming, humble ★**vain**

modesty *n.* humility, diffidence, reserve, shyness, decency ★**vanity**

modify *v.* transform, convert, change, alter, revise, redesign

moist *adj.* damp, humid, watery, clammy, dank ▷*wet* ★**dry**

moisture *n.* damp, dampness, liquid, wetness

mold ① *v.* form, shape, fashion, cast, create ② *n.* pattern, matrix ③ *n.* earth, loam

moldy *adj.* mildewed, putrid, bad

molest *v.* annoy, bother, pursue, attack, torment ▷*harry*

moment *n.* ① second, instant, twinkling ② importance, worth, weight *I think your argument has some weight, and I agree with you*

momentous *adj.* notable, outstanding, decisive, important ★**insignificant**

monarch *n.* king, sovereign, ruler, emperor, prince *The head of state in Monaco is a prince*

A
B
C
D
E
F
G
H
I
J
K
L
M
N
O
P
Q
R
S
T
U
V
W
X
Y
Z

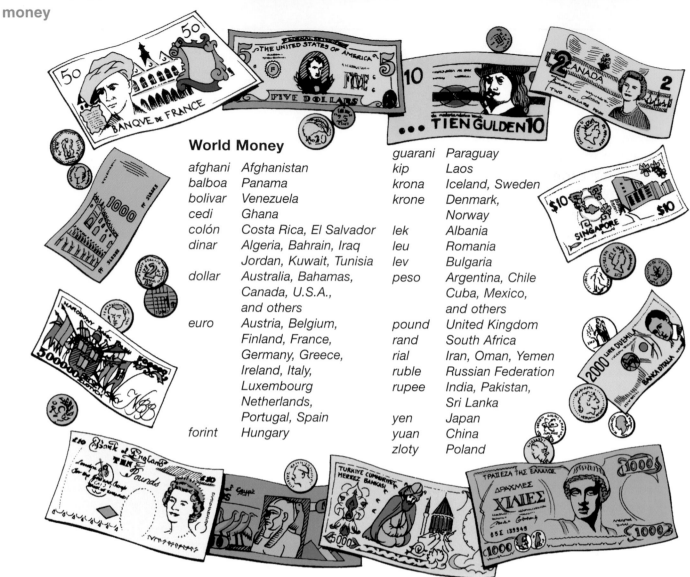

World Money

afghani	Afghanistan	guarani	Paraguay
balboa	Panama	kip	Laos
bolivar	Venezuela	krona	Iceland, Sweden
cedi	Ghana	krone	Denmark,
colón	Costa Rica, El Salvador		Norway
dinar	Algeria, Bahrain, Iraq	lek	Albania
	Jordan, Kuwait, Tunisia	leu	Romania
dollar	Australia, Bahamas,	lev	Bulgaria
	Canada, U.S.A.,	peso	Argentina, Chile
	and others		Cuba, Mexico,
euro	Austria, Belgium,		and others
	Finland, France,	pound	United Kingdom
	Germany, Greece,	rand	South Africa
	Ireland, Italy,	rial	Iran, Oman, Yemen
	Luxembourg	ruble	Russian Federation
	Netherlands,	rupee	India, Pakistan,
	Portugal, Spain		Sri Lanka
forint	Hungary	yen	Japan
		yuan	China
		zloty	Poland

money *n.* wealth, cash, coin, legal tender

mongrel *n.* hybrid, mixed, crossbreed, dog

monitor ① *n.* listener, auditor, watchdog, prefect ② *v.* check, supervise, oversee

monologue *n.* lecture, oration, speech, recitation, sermon

monopolize *v.* control, take over, appropriate ▷*dominate* ★**share**

monotonous *adj.* tedious, uninteresting, dull, prosaic *His speech was so prosaic that I almost dropped off to sleep,* repetitive ▷*tiresome*

monster *n.* beast, fiend, villain, brute

monstrous *adj.* hideous, frightful, dreadful, terrible, criminal ▷*wicked*

mood *n.* state of mind, humor, temper, disposition *My grandmother's gentle disposition won her many friends*

moody *adj.* morose, sulky, sullen, peevish, cantankerous *I didn't like Uncle Harry; he*

was a cantankerous old man ★**cheerful**

moor ① *v.* tether, picket, tie, chain, anchor, secure ② *n.* heath, moorland MORE

mop *n.* ① sponge, swab, towel ② hair, tresses, locks, mane

mope *v.* be dejected, grieve, moon, pine, sulk

moral *adj.* virtuous, good, honest, honorable ▷*upright* ★**immoral**

morbid *adj.* gruesome, macabre, melancholy

more ① *adj.* in addition, also, beyond, extra, further ② *adv.* better, again, longer MOOR

morning *n.* dawn, daybreak, daylight, cockcrow *I rose at cockcrow, saddled my horse, and was off to Richmond,* sunrise ★**evening** MOURNING

morose *adj.* glum, sullen, sulky, broody, taciturn ▷*moody* ★**cheerful**

morsel *n.* bit, bite, piece, scrap, nibble

mortal *adj.* ① human, feeble, ephemeral ② fatal, final, deadly, severe

most ① *adj.* greatest nearly all ② *adv.* mostly, chiefly, mainly, utmost

mostly *adv.* as a rule, principally, usually, normally

mother ① *n.* female parent, mom, mommy, mama ② *v.* nurse, protect, rear, care for

motherly *adj.* caring, comforting, loving, maternal, gentle

motion *n.* ① movement, locomotion, action, passage ② proposal *I vote that we accept the proposal,* suggestion

motionless *adj.* stationary, still, transfixed, stable, inert ★**moving**

motive *n.* reason, purpose, occasion, impulse, cause ▷*spur*

mottled *adj.* speckled, spotted, pied, piebald

motto *n.* saying, slogan, watchword, maxim *My mother's maxim was "Always look on the bright side,"* proverb

mound *n.* hillock, pile, knoll, rise, mount

mount *v.* ascend, climb, rise, vault

mourn *v.* lament, deplore, sorrow, regret, weep ▷*grieve* ★**rejoice**

mournful *adj.* doleful, somber, cheerless, sorrowful ▷*melancholy* ★**joyful**

mouth *n.* aperture, opening, entrance, orifice, inlet, jaws

mouthful *n.* bite, morsel, sample, taste, tidbit

move *v.* ① march, proceed, walk, go ② propose, suggest, recommend ③ propel, drive, impel

moving *adj.* touching, affecting, stirring *The band played a stirring rendition of "Amazing Grace,"* emotional

much ① *adj.* abundant, considerable, ample ② *adv.* considerably, greatly, often ③ *n.* lots, loads, heaps, plenty

muck *n.* dirt, filth, mire, ooze, mud, scum

muddle ① *n.* confusion, clutter, jumble, mix-up ② *v.* bungle, tangle, confound ▷*bewilder*

muff *v.* botch, mismanage, miss, spoil ▷*muddle*

muffle *v.* ① deaden, mute, muzzle, silence ② wrap, envelop, wind, swaddle

mug ① *n.* face, looks ② *n.* cup, beaker, tankard ③ *v.* attack, beat up, rob

muggy *adj.* clammy, dank, damp, humid, close ★**dry**

mull *v.* meditate *I meditated over the weekend before deciding what to do,* consider, study, think about

multiply *v.* increase, spread, grow, extend, intensify ★**decrease**

multitude *n.* crowd, legion, throng, swarm, horde ★**handful**

mum *adj.* dumb, silent, quiet, mute

munch *v.* crunch, chew, bit, nibble ▷*eat*

murder *v.* slay, assassinate, butcher, destroy, slaughter ▷*kill*

murky *adj.* foggy, cloudy, dark, gloomy, dull, misty ★**bright**

murmur *n. & v.* whisper, mutter, mumble, drone

muscular *adj.* brawny, athletic, burly, beefy, powerful ▷*robust* ★**puny**

muse *v.* meditate, ponder, puzzle over, brood, deliberate

must ① *v.* ought to, should, be obliged to ② *n.* duty, necessity, requirement

muster *v.* marshal, collect, assemble, rally *The troops rallied and prepared to attack again,* enroll

musty *adj.* moldy, rank, mildewy, decayed

mute *adj.* silent, speechless, voiceless, soundless ★**loud**

mutilate *v.* injure, hurt, cut, damage, hack ▷*maim*

mutiny *n. & v.* protest, revolt, strike, riot

mutter *v.* mumble, grouse, grumble ▷*murmur* ★**exclaim**

mutual *adj.* common, reciprocal, interchangeable ▷*joint* ★**one-sided**

mysterious *adj.* obscure, unrevealed, unexplained, secret ▷*hidden* ★**clear**

mystery *n.* puzzle, enigma, secrecy, riddle, problem

mystify *v.* confuse, bamboozle, hoodwink, puzzle, mislead ▷*baffle* ★**enlighten**

myth *n.* fable, legend, supposition, fabrication, tradition, fantasy ★**fact**

mythical *adj.* fabulous, fabled, legendary, traditional, imaginary ★**true**

A B C D E F G H I J K L M N O P Q R S T U V W X Y Z

N n

nab *v.* arrest, apprehend, seize, catch, capture, grab

nag ① *v.* pester, hector, heckle, badger, annoy, henpeck, scold *My parents scolded me for coming home late* ② *n.* horse, pony

nail ① *n.* brad, peg, pin, spike, tack ② *v.* hammer, fix, tack, peg ③ *v.* capture, catch, seize

naive *adj.* innocent, unworldly, unsophisticated, simple, trusting ★**cunning, sophisticated**

naked *adj.* nude, bare, unclothed, undressed ★**clothed**

name ① *n.* title, description, designation ② *n.* character, reputation *A good reputation is very important to me,* distinction ③ *v.* christen, style, term, entitle

nap ① *v.* sleep, doze, drowse, rest ② *n.* down, fiber, fuzz *Velvet is a cloth with a kind of fuzz on the surface*

narrate *v.* describe, tell, recite, yarn

narrow *adj.* slender, fine, small ▷*thin* ★**wide**

nasty *adj.* dirty, mucky, foul, offensive, unpleasant ▷*squalid* ★**nice**

national *adj.* civil, governmental, public, general

native *adj.* natural, inborn, aboriginal, domestic, local

natural *adj.* frank, genuine, innate, instinctive, ordinary, usual

naturally *adj.* absolutely, certainly, frankly, normally

nature *n.* ① temper, personality, disposition ② the world, the outdoors, landscape

naughty *adj.* mischievous, rascally, wicked, disobedient ▷*bad* ★**well-behaved**

nauseous *adj.* disgusting, sickening, repulsive, revolting ★**pleasant**

nautical *adj.* maritime *Ancient Greece was a great maritime nation,* seamanlike, naval, sailing

navigate *v.* voyage, cruise, sail, guide, pilot

navy *n.* ships, fleet, armada, flotilla

near *adj.* close, nearby, adjacent, bordering, beside ▷*nigh* ★**remote**

nearly *adv.* about, almost, all but, thereabouts, roughly

neat *adj.* ① tidy, spruce, smart, stylish ★**untidy** ② skillful, clever, adroit *I admire your adroit handling of that tricky situation,* ingenious

necessary *adj.* needed, essential, basic, required, compulsory ★**optional**

need ① *v.* require, want, crave ▷*demand* ★**have** ② *n.* distress, want, necessity, deprivation *During the long war, the people suffered many deprivations* KNEAD

needed *adj.* wanted, desired, lacking ▷*necessary* ★**unnecessary**

needless *adj.* pointless, unnecessary, superfluous, useless ★**necessary**

needy *adj.* destitute, down-and-out, deprived ▷*poor* ★**well-off**

neglect *v.* overlook, ignore, scorn, slight, disregard ▷*spurn* ★**cherish**

neglected *adj.* unkempt, abandoned, dilapidated, uncared for ★**cherished**

negligent *adj.* neglectful, forgetful, slack, indifferent ▷*careless* ★**careful**

negotiate *v.* bargain, deal, treat, haggle, mediate

neighborhood *n.* vicinity, surroundings, district, area, locality *There are many fine houses in this locality*

neighborly *adj.* hospitable, friendly, kind, obliging ▷*helpful*

nerve *n.* ① mettle, guts, pluck, courage ② audacity, impudence *Mr. Thompson already owes us money and yet he has the impudence to ask for more*

nervous *adj.* tense, taut, jumpy, flustered, anxious, timid ★**confident**

nest *n.* den, burrow, haunt, refuge, resort

nestle *adj.* cuddle, snuggle, huddle, nuzzle

net ① *v.* catch, trap, lasso, capture ② *n.* mesh, lattice, trap, web, lace *I have some new lace curtains* ③ *adj.* clear *I made a clear $15,000 after taxes,* final, lowest

nettle *v.* exasperate, annoy, ruffle,

National and Religious Holidays

Advent, All Saints' Day, Ascension Day, Ash Wednesday, Australia Day, Bastille Day, Canada Day, Candlemas, Carnival, Christmas, Columbus Day, Commonwealth Day, Diwali, Day of the Dead, Easter, Father's Day, Gandhi's Birthday, Good Friday, Guy Fawkes Day, Halloween, Hanukkah, Independence Day, Kwanzaa, Labor Day, Lent, Mardi Gras, Martin Luther King Day, Memorial Day, Mother's Day, Muhammad's Birthday, New Year's Day, Palm Sunday, Passover, Pentecost, Presidents' Day, Purim, Ramadan, Rosh Hashanah, Saint Patrick's Day, Shavuot, Sukkot, Thanksgiving Day, Valentine's Day, Veterans' Day, Yom Kippur

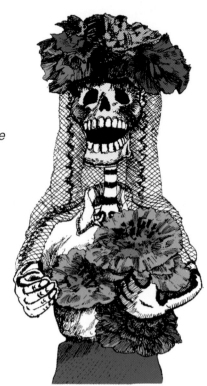

A puppet from the Mexican Day of the Dead Festival

pique ▷*vex*

neutral *adj.* impartial, unbiased, fair-minded, unprejudiced ★**biased**

never *adv.* at no time, not at all, under no circumstances ★**always**

new *adj.* recent, just out, current, latest, fresh, unused ▷*novel* ★**old** GNU, KNEW

news *n.* information, intelligence, tidings, account, bulletin

next *adj.* ① following, succeeding, after, later ② adjacent, adjoining *I live on Park Street, and my friend lives on the adjoining street,* beside

nibble *v.* bite, peck, gnaw, munch ▷*eat*

nice *adj.* ① pleasant, agreeable, amiable, charming, delightful ★**nasty** ② precise, accurate, fine, subtle

niche *n.* compartment, hole, corner, recess, place

nick *v.* dent, score, mill, cut, scratch

nigh *adj.* next, close, adjacent, adjoining ▷*near* ★**distant**

night *n.* dark, darkness, dusk, evening ★**day** KNIGHT

nimble *adj.* active, agile, spry, lithe, skillfull ▷*deft* ★**clumsy**

nip *v.* cut, snip, pinch, twinge, bite

no ① *adj.* not any, not one, none ② *adv.* nay, not at all KNOW

noble *adj.* dignified, lofty *My aunt is very important and has a lofty position on the council,* generous, grand, stately, elevated ★**base**

nod *v.* ① beckon, signal, indicate, salute ② sleep, doze, nap

noise *n.* din, discord, clamor, clatter, hubbub, tumult, uproar ★**silence**

noisy *adj.* loud, boisterous, turbulent, rowdy, clamorous ★**quiet**

nominate *v.* appoint, assign, elect, choose, propose, suggest

nonchalant *adj.* casual, unperturbed, calm, blasé *We enjoyed the new musical, but Sue has been to so many shows she was very blasé about it,* cool, detached ★**anxious**

nondescript *adj.* commonplace, colorless, dull, ordinary ▷*plain* ★**unusual**

none *pron.* not one, not any, not a part, nil, nobody NUN

nonsense *n.* absurdity, balderdash, drivel, rot, garbage, twaddle ★**sense**

nook *n.* compartment, hole, corner, alcove,

A
B
C
D
E
F
G
H
I
J
K
L
M
N
O
P
Q
R
S
T
U
V
W
X
Y
Z

crevice, cubbyhole, cranny ▷*niche*

noose *n.* loop, bight, snare, rope, lasso

normal *adj.* usual, general, average, sane, lucid, rational, standard ★**abnormal**

nose *n.* ① beak, bill, neb, snout ② prow, stem, bow, front

nosy *adj.* inquisitive, curious, prying, snooping, intrusive

nostalgia *n.* homesickness, longing, pining, regret, remembrance

notable *adj.* eventful, momentous, outstanding, great, celebrated ▷*famous* ★**commonplace**

notch *n.* dent, nick, score, cut, cleft, indentation

note *n.* ① letter, message, communication ② remark, record, report ③ fame, renown, distinction ④ banknote, bill

noted *adj.* eminent, renowned, celebrated, great ▷*famous* ★**obscure**

nothing *n.* zero, naught, null, nil, zip ★**something**

notice ① *n.* announcement, advice, sign, poster ② *v.* note, remark, observe *After observing that his bike had a flat tire, Joel knew he would have to walk to school,* perceive, make out, see ★**ignore**

notify *v.* inform, tell, intimate, announce, declare ★**withhold**

Notice

After observing that his bike had a flat tire, Joel knew he would have to walk to school.

notion *n.* idea, conception, opinion, belief, judgment

notorious *adj.* infamous, questionable, scandalous, blatant

notwithstanding *adv.* nevertheless, nonetheless, however, despite

nourish *v.* feed, sustain, nurture, comfort, support ★**starve**

nourishing *adj.* beneficial, healthful, nutritious, wholesome

novel ① *adj.* fresh, unusual, original, unique, rare, uncommon ② *n.* fiction, story, book, romance, tale

novice *n.* beginner, learner, apprentice, tyro, pupil ★**expert**

now *adv.* at this moment, at present, at once, instantly, right away

now and then *adv.* from time to time, sometimes, occasionally

nude *adj.* bare, naked, unclothed, stripped, undressed

nudge *v.* poke, push, prod, jog, shove, dig

nuisance *n.* offense, annoyance, plague, trouble, bore, pest, irritation

nullify *v.* annul, invalidate, cancel, quash ▷*abolish* ★**establish**

numb *adj.* deadened, insensible, dazed, stunned, unfeeling ★**sensitive**

number ① *n.* figure, amount, volume, quantity, sum ② *n.* crowd, throng, multitude *The new president's visit to the town was watched by a multitude of people* ③ *n.* figure, symbol ▷*numeral* ④ *v.* count, reckon, tally

numeral *n.* symbol, figure, character, cipher

numerous *adj.* many, divers, several, plentiful ▷*abundant* ★**few**

nun *n.* sister, religious, abbess, prioress NONE

nurse ① *v.* attend, care for, foster, support, sustain ② *n.* hospital attendant, caretaker

nursery *n.* ① children's room, baby's room ② greenhouse, hothouse, garden

nurture *v.* feed, nourish, cherish, foster, tend ▷*nurse*

nutritious *adj.* healthful, substantial, health-giving ▷*nourishing* ★**bad**

O o

oaf *n.* brute, lout, blockhead, dolt, ruffian, lummox

obedient *adj.* respectful, obliging, lawabiding, servile, dutiful ★**rebellious**

obey *v.* comply, conform, submit, heed, mind, behave ★**disobey**

object ① *v.* (ob-*ject*) protest, complain, argue, oppose, refuse ★**agree** ② *n.* (*ob*-ject) thing, article, commodity, item ③ *n.* mission, purpose *The purpose of my visit is to end this conflict,* end,

objectionable *adj.* displeasing, distasteful, disagreeable, repugnant ★**pleasant**

obligation *n.* responsibility, liability, commitment ★**choice**

oblige *v.* ① require, compel, force, make ② gratify, please, help ▷*assist* ★**displease**

obliging *adj.* helpful, polite, agreeable, courteous ▷*willing* ★**unkind**

obliterate *v.* blot out, efface, erase, wipe out, destroy

oblivious *adj.* unmindful, absentminded, heedless, unaware ★**aware**

obnoxious *adj.* repulsive, revolting, offensive ▷*unpleasant* ★**pleasant**

obscene *adj.* dirty, unclean, vile, filthy, nasty, immoral, indecent ★**decent**

obscure ① *adj.* indistinct, dim, vague, hidden, confusing *The language of a legal document can be very confusing* ▷*doubtful* ★**clear** ② *v.* conceal, hide, cloud, darken, cover ▷*hide* ★**clarify**

observant *adj.* attentive, watchful, heedful ▷*alert* ★**inattentive**

observation *n.* ① attention, study, supervision ② utterance, comment, remark, statement *The police issued a statement*

observe *v.* ① abide by *I intend to abide by the laws of this country,* adhere to, carry out, keep up ② note, notice, perceive, watch ▷*see* ③ utter, remark, mention

obsolete *adj.* dated, outmoded, unfashionable, out-of-date ★**current**

obstacle *n.* obstruction, barrier, bar, hindrance ▷*drawback* ★**advantage**

obstinate *adj.* determined, dogged, unyielding, perverse *As a child I upset my parents by my perverse behavior* ▷*stubborn* ★**docile**

obstruct *v.* hinder, impede, block, bar, choke ▷*restrain* ★**help**

obstruction *n.* hindrance, restraint, impediment, snag

obtain *v.* acquire, achieve, gain, procure, attain ▷*get* ★**lose**

obtuse *adj.* dull, stupid, unintelligent, stolid, thick, blunt ★**bright**

obvious *adj.* plain, evident, self-evident, explicit, apparent ▷*clear* ★**obscure**

occasion *n.* ① affair, episode, occurrence, circumstance ② reason, purpose, motive

occasional *adj.* casual, rare, infrequent, periodic ★**frequent**

occult *adj.* hidden, unrevealed, secret, mysterious, supernatural *Edgar Allan Poe wrote tales of the supernatural* ★**open**

occupant *n.* owner, resident, proprietor, tenant

occupation *n.* ① activity, employment, calling, job ② possession, tenancy, residence

occupied *adj.* ① busy, employed, active ② settled, populated, peopled ★**unoccupied**

occupy *v.* inhabit, live in, reside, dwell in, own, possess, hold

occur *v.* take place, befall, turn out, come to pass, result ▷*happen*

occurrence *n.* happening, affair, circumstance, incident, occasion ▷*event*

ocean *n.* sea, main *The pirates of the Spanish Main were the curse of shipping,* deep, tide

odd *adj.* ① single, unmatched ② singular,

Oceans and Waters

Antarctic	Bay	Sound
Arctic	Fjord	Straits
Atlantic	Gulf	
Indian	Lagoon	
Pacific	Loch	

peculiar, quaint, queer ★**ordinary** ③
surplus, left over, remaining

odds and ends *n.* leavings, debris *The police found the debris of the crashed airplane,* leftovers, oddments, remains

odious *adj.* hateful, offensive, detestable ▷*abominable* ★**pleasant**

odor *n.* ① scent, aroma ▷*fragrance* ② stink, stench, reek ▷*smell*

odorous *adj.* fragrant, perfumed, aromatic, sweet-smelling

off ① *adv.* away from, over, done ② *prep.* along, against, opposite, distant ★**on** ③ *adj.* bad, moldy, rotten

offend *v.* ① insult, hurt, wound, outrage, displease ② transgress, sin ★**please**

offense *n.* insult, outrage, attack, crime, hurt

offensive *adj.* insulting, offending, rude, repugnant, hurtful, distasteful

offer ① *v.* propose, proffer, present, tender, attempt ② *n.* bid, endeavor, proposal

offering *n.* sacrifice, donation, gift, present

offhand *adj.* ① brusque, casual, curt, informal, abrupt ② informal, improvised, impromptu *My sister, who is a singer, gave an impromptu performance* ★**planned**

office ① *n.* bureau, department, room ② position, appointment, post

officer *n.* ① official, administrator, functionary, executive ② military rank, policeman, minister *A minister from the French Embassy called*

official ① *adj.* authorized, authentic, proper, formal ★**unofficial** ② *n.* executive, officeholder, bureaucrat *The city bureaucrats take months to get a job done*

officious *adj.* interfering, meddlesome, self-important

offspring *n.* child, children, descendant, heir, family

often *adv.* frequently, regularly, recurrently, time after time, repeatedly ★**seldom**

ointment *n.* lotion, salve, cream, balm, embrocation, liniment

old *adj.* ① ancient, antique, aged, antiquated ② crumbling, decayed *Beneath the ivy were the decayed remains of the castle wall,*

decrepit ★**new** ③ out-of-date, old-fashioned, passé ④ aged, mature, elderly ★**young**

ominous *adj.* menacing, threatening, foreboding, sinister

omit *v.* leave out, neglect, let go, overlook, skip ★**include**

once *adv.* formerly, at one time, previously

one ① *adj.* sole, alone, lone, whole ② *n.* unit, single thing

one-sided *adj.* unequal, unfair, unjust, biased

only ① *adj.* exclusive, single, sole, lone, solitary ② *adv.* solely, barely, exclusively

onset *n.* start, outbreak, assault, attack, onslaught

onslaught *n.* charge, attack, bombardment

ooze ① *n.* mire, muck, slime ② *v.* bleed, discharge, emit, exude, leak

open ① *v.* uncover, unlock, unfasten ② *v.* start, commence, begin ③ *adj.* uncovered, clear, evident, apparent ★**closed** ④ *adj.* frank, honest, candid, fair

opening *n.* ① aperture, mouth, crevice, recess, hole ② commencement, beginning

openly *adv.* candidly, frankly, plainly, sincerely ★**secretly**

operate *v.* function *Despite its age, the old millwheel continued to function,* work, manipulate, drive, ▷*perform*

operation *n.* performance, movement, action, motion, proceeding

opinion *n.* view, concept, judgment, belief, point of view

opponent *n.* antagonist, rival, competitor, contestant, foe ▷*enemy* ★**ally**

opportune *adj.* timely *It had started to rain, thus the timely arrival of the bus was welcome,* convenient, fortunate, suitable ★**untimely**

opportunity *n.* occasion, chance, opening, scope, moment

oppose *v.* withstand, resist, obstruct, confront, hinder ▷*defy* ★**support**

opposite *adj.* ① facing, fronting ② conflicting, opposing, contrary, adverse ★**same**

opposition *n.* antagonism, defiance, hostility, difference ▷*resistance* ★**cooperation**

oppress *v.* crush, depress, harass, overpower, overwhelm

optimist *n.* hopeful person, perfectionist ★**pessimist**

optimistic *adj.* hopeful, cheerful, confident, positive ★**pessimistic**

option *n.* preference, choice, alternative

optional *adj.* possible, voluntary, unforced, open ★**compulsory**

opulent *adj.* rich, affluent, prosperous, well-to-do ▷*wealthy* ★**poor**

oration *n.* sermon, lecture, speech, discourse

orb *n.* globe, ball, sphere

orbit *n.* ① path, passage, trajectory ② province, realm, domain *The river, the forest, and the castle were all within her domain*

ordeal *n.* trial, nightmare, torment, agony

order ① *n.* arrangement, pattern, grouping, organization ② *n.* command, law, rule, decree *A decree was issued forbidding the killing of deer* ③ *n.* shipment, consignment ④ *v.* direct, instruct, command ⑤ *v.* arrange, control, conduct

orderly *adj.* regular, methodical, trim, neat, well-mannered ★**messy**

ordinary *adj.* common, usual, commonplace, general, customary ★**extraordinary**

organization *n.* ① association, group, institute, establishment ② structure, arrangement, system

organize *v.* arrange, form, structure, establish, classify ★**disorganize**

origin *n.* beginning, start, basis, foundation, root, source ★**end**

original *adj.* ① first, aboriginal, ancient, former, primary ② fresh, new, novel *Traveling by camel was a novel experience*

originate ① *v.* create, conceive, compose ② arise, begin ▷*start* ★**end**

ornament ① *n.* decoration, adornment, tracery, pattern ② trinket, curio, knick-knack

ornate *adj.* decorated, adorned, flowery,

Original

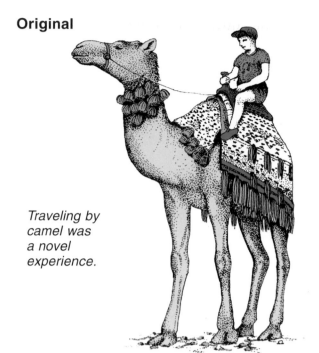

Traveling by camel was a novel experience.

embellished, showy, garish ★**plain**

oust *v.* expel, eject, evict, dismiss, propel ▷*overthrow*

out ① *adj.* away, outside, absent ★**in** ② *adj.* open, revealed, uncovered ③ *adv.* loudly, aloud, audibly

out of order *adj.* broken, not working

out of sorts *adj.* sick, ill, poorly, gloomy, fed up

outbreak *n.* epidemic *An epidemic of cholera had hit the village,* rebellion, eruption, explosion, flare-up

outburst *n.* eruption, explosion ▷*outbreak*

outcast *n.* exile, castaway *Robinson Crusoe was a castaway on a desert island,* derelict, refugee

outcome *n.* effect, consequence, conclusion, result

outcry *n.* commotion, row, uproar, tumult, shouting, hue and cry ▷*clamor*

outdated *adj.* old, antique, old-fashioned, unfashionable, obsolete ★**modern**

outdo *v.* surpass, excel, beat, outclass, eclipse

outfit *n.* ensemble, set *My mother bought a new set of dishes in the sale for half price,* rig, equipment, gear

outing *n.* excursion, picnic, expedition, trip, ramble

outlandish *adj.* strange, erratic, odd, queer, quaint, bizarre ★**ordinary**

outlaw *n.* bandit, highwayman, hoodlum, desperado *Billy the Kid was a desperado in the Wild West,* robber

outlet *n.* exit, egress, way out, vent, spout, nozzle, opening ★**inlet**

outline ① *n.* diagram, plan, blueprint, sketch, framework, summary ② *v.* draw, sketch, describe

outlook *n.* view, prospect, forecast, attitude, aspect, prognosis

output *n.* yield, product, produce, achievement, manufacture

outrage ① *n.* disgrace, injury, offense, affront ② *v.* offend, insult, shock, violate

outrageous *adj.* insulting, offensive, exorbitant, monstrous ★**acceptable**

outright ① *adj.* complete, thorough, absolute, wholesale ② *adv.* at once, completely, entirely, altogether

outset *n.* first, opening, beginning ▷*start* ★**finish**

outside ① *n.* exterior, surface, front ② *adj.* exterior, external, outward, surface

outsider *n.* stranger, foreigner, alien, misfit *Gulliver was something of a misfit in the land of the tiny Lilliputians*

outskirts *n.* limits, bounds, boundary, outpost, suburb

outspoken *adj.* frank, open, straightforward, blunt, direct ▷*candid* ★**tactful**

outstanding *adj.* striking, pronounced, conspicuous, notable ▷*exceptional* ★**ordinary**

outward *adj.* exterior, outside, outer, superficial *From a distance, my father and Bill Jones look alike, but it's really just superficial*

outwit *v.* get the better of, swindle, defraud, dupe ▷*cheat*

over ① *adj.* concluded, ended, done with, settled ② *prep.* above, more than, exceeding ③ *adv.* aloft, above, beyond, extra

overall ① *adj.* complete, inclusive, total, broad ② *adv.* by and large, on the whole

overbearing *adj.* domineering, dictatorial, haughty, pompous ▷*arrogant* ★**modest**

overcast *adj.* cloudy, heavy, dark, murky, dull ★**bright**

overcome *adj.* overwhelm, conquer, crush, defeat, vanquish ▷*subdue*

overdo *v.* overwork, exaggerate, go too far *I didn't mind your eating one of my apples, but taking all four was going too far*

overdue *adj.* delayed, belated, late, behindhand ★**early**

overflow *v.* swamp, deluge, inundate, submerge, soak, spill

overhaul *v.* ① repair, mend, fix, inspect, examine ② overtake, pass, gain on

overhead *adv.* above, upward, aloft, on high ★**below**

overhear *v.* listen, eavesdrop, snoop, spy

overjoyed *adj.* elated, jubilant, rapturous ▷*delighted* ★**disappointed**

overlap *v.* overrun, go beyond, coincide, overlay

overlook *v.* ① disregard, pardon, condone, ignore ② neglect, miss, pass over ③ inspect, check, examine

overpower *v.* conquer, crush, master, subdue, vanquish ▷*defeat*

overseas *adj.* abroad, foreign ★**domestic**

overseer *n.* inspector, supervisor, boss, manager, master, mistress

oversight *n.* omission, blunder, error, fault, lapse ▷*mistake*

overtake *v.* catch up, pass, outdo, outstrip, pass ▷*overhaul*

overthrow *v.* defeat, beat, topple ▷*overpower*

overture *n.* ① (in music) prelude, opening, introduction ② offer, proposal, invitation

overwhelm *v.* overcome, stun, shock, overpower, deluge, inundate *The reply to our advertisement was huge; we were inundated with letters*

overwhelming *adj.* all-powerful, formidable, breathtaking, shattering ★**insignificant**

owe *v.* be in debt, incur, be due

own ① *v.* possess, occupy, hold ② *v.* admit, confess, grant ③ *adj.* individual, personal, private

owner *n.* proprietor, possessor, landlord

P p

pace ① *n. & v.* step, tread, stride ② *n.* speed, rate, velocity, tempo

pacify *v.* appease, calm, moderate, tranquilize ▷*soothe* ★**aggravate**

pack ① *n.* bundle, bunch, swarm, crowd, group ② *v.* cram, load, fill, throng

package *n.* parcel, packet, bundle, box, carton

packet *n.* bag, pack, container, parcel ▷*package*

pact *n.* contract, treaty, agreement, arrangement PACKED

pad ① *n.* tablet, notepad, jotter ② *n.* foot, paw ③ *v.* fill, pack, shape, stuff, cushion

paddle ① *n.* oar, sweep, scull ② *v.* row, steer, propel ③ *v.* wade, splash, swim

pagan *n.* heathen, idol-worshiper, infidel

page *n.* ① sheet, leaf, paper ② boy, attendant, bellhop, messenger

pageant *n.* fair, parade, procession, exhibition, masque ▷*show*

pail *n.* bucket, churn, tub, container PALE

pain ① *n.* ache, pang, throb, twinge, spasm, cramp ② *v.* hurt, sting, ache ▷*ail* PANE

painful *adj.* aching, throbbing, sore, agonizing ★**painless**

painstaking *adj.* scrupulous *Carly kept a scrupulous record of all she spent,* careful, diligent, particular ★**negligent**

paint *v.* color, draw, daub, varnish, stain

painting *n.* drawing, illustration, picture, mural, design

pair *n.* couple, brace, two, twins, twosome PARE, PEAR

pal *n.* chum, friend, buddy, crony ▷*comrade* ★**enemy**

palace *n.* castle, château, stately home *In England you can visit stately homes belonging to the aristocracy,* mansion

pale *adj.* pallid, ashen, pasty, colorless, faint, feeble, white ★**ruddy** PAIL

pallid *adj.* ashen, colorless, livid *The man had a livid scar across his forehead,*

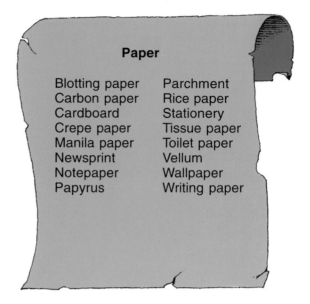

Paper

Blotting paper	Parchment
Carbon paper	Rice paper
Cardboard	Stationery
Crepe paper	Tissue paper
Manila paper	Toilet paper
Newsprint	Vellum
Notepaper	Wallpaper
Papyrus	Writing paper

waxen ▷*pale*

paltry *adj.* petty, mean, shabby, trifling, pitiable, trashy ★**significant**

pamper *v.* humor, indulge, coddle, fondle ▷*spoil* ★**neglect**

pan *n.* container ▷*pot*

pandemonium *n.* uproar, clatter, row, rumpus, din, chaos *The ice storm reduced the airline schedale to total chaos* ▷*noise* ★**calm**

pander *v.* indulge, pamper, please, give in to

pane *n.* panel, glass, window PAIN

panel *n.* ① pane, rectangle, insert ② jury, group, committee, forum *There will be a forum of all the candidates before the election*

pang *n.* ache, throe, twinge, throb ▷*pain*

panic ① *n.* fright, alarm, fear, terror ② *v.* scare, frighten, startle, stampede ★**relax**

pant *v.* puff, snort, blow, gasp, heave

pantry *n.* larder, buttery, storeroom, cupboard

paper *n.* stationery, document, deed, article, dossier *The police have a dossier on all known criminals in this town*

parade ① *n.* procession, march, display ▷*pageant* ② *v.* display, exhibit, flaunt, show off

paralyze *v.* cripple, disable, incapacitate, deaden, stun

paramount *adj.* leading, chief, supreme, outstanding ▷*foremost* ★**minor**

paraphernalia *n.* baggage, equipment, gear

parasite *n.* sponger, hanger-on, leech, scrounger

parcel *n.* batch, bundle, lot ▷*package*

parched *v.* arid, scorched, withered, dry, thirsty

pardon *v.* excuse, forgive, acquit, condone, absolve ★**condemn**

pare *v.* skin, peel, uncover, strip, scrape, shave PAIR, PEAR

parent *n.* father, mother, guardian, originator

park ① *n.* garden, green, grounds, playground, woodland ② *v.* leave *You can leave your car outside our house,* position, station

parlor *n.* drawing room, living room, sitting room

parody *n.* caricature, burlesque, satire, imitation

parry *v.* avoid, avert, fend off, rebuff, repel

parsimonious *adj.* niggardly *The factory workers received a niggardly sum for their work,* sparing, miserly, stingy ▷*frugal* ★**generous**

part ① *n.* piece, fragment, portion, scrap ② *n.* character, role *My sister has a leading role in the play,* duty ③ *v.* separate, divide, detach ④ *v.* depart, quit, leave

partial *adj.* ① imperfect, limited, part, unfinished ② biased, favorable to, inclined

partially *adv.* incompletely, somewhat, in part

participate *v.* take part, share, cooperate

particle *n.* morsel, atom, bit, seed, crumb, grain, scrap

particular *adj.* ① choosy, fastidious, scrupulous ② strange, odd, peculiar ③ special, distinct, notable *Old John Cotton was one of the notable citizens of our city*

partly *adv.* in part, incompletely, to some degree, up to a point ★**totally**

partner *n.* colleague, associate, ally, helper

party *n.* ① function, celebration, festivity, social ② group, faction *A small faction on the committee wanted the park to be closed,* body

pass ① *v.* exceed, overstep, outstrip ② *v.* experience *He experienced little pain after the operation,* suffer, undergo ③ *v.* neglect, ignore ④ *n.* permit, ticket, passport ⑤ *n.* defile, gap, notch, passage

passage *n.* ① corridor, pathway, alley ② journey, cruise, voyage ③ sentence, paragraph, clause

passenger *n.* traveler, commuter, wayfarer

passing *adj.* casual, fleeting, hasty, temporary, brief ★**permanent**

passion *n.* desire, ardor, warmth, excitement, zeal ▷*emotion* ★**calm**

passionate *adj.* ardent, impetuous, fiery, earnest, enthusiastic ★**indifferent**

past ① *adj.* finished, ended, former, gone ★**present** ② *prep.* after, exceeding, beyond ③ *n.* history, yesterday ★**future** PASSED

paste *n.* glue, cement, gum, adhesive

pastime *n.* recreation, sport, fun, hobby, amusement

pasture *n.* grass, field, meadow, mead

pat ① *v.* tap, caress, fondle, stroke, touch ② *adv.* timely, exactly *Celia arrived at exactly the right moment,* precisely

patch *v.* mend, patch up, sew, darn, cobble

path *n.* way, track, road, route, course, footway

pathetic *adj.* pitiable, sad, wretched, miserable, poor, puny *We picked out the*

Paths and Passageways

Alley	Highway	Path
Avenue	Lane	Road
Boulevard	Mountain	Sidewalk
Freeway	pass	Street
Drive	Passage	Thoroughfare

puniest pup in the litter for a pet

patience *n.* endurance, perseverance, composure, calmness, restraint ★**impatience** PATIENTS

patient *adj.* forbearing, long-suffering, persevering, understanding ★**impatient**

patriotic *adj.* loyal, nationalistic, public-spirited, jingoistic

patrol *v.* police, watch, guard, protect, tour

patronize *v.* ① assist, encourage, foster, buy from ② talk down to, condescend

pattern *n.* ① model, standard, prototype ② arrangement, decoration, ornament

pause ① *v.* halt, cease, suspend, stop, delay ② *n.* lull, intermission, break, interruption, breather, rest PAWS

pay ① *v.* reward, award, support, compensate, discharge ② *n.* payment, salary, wages, compensation

peace *n.* harmony, calm, concord, serenity, quiet, tranquility *We spent the day in total tranquility down by the lake* ★**tumult** PIECE

peaceful *adj.* serene, quiet, restful, harmonious ▷*tranquil* ★**disturbed**

peak *n.* summit, apex, top, crown, pinnacle

peal *v.* ring, strike, clamor, chime, resound, toll, clang PEEL

peasant *n.* farmer, rustic, sharecropper, countryman, yokel

peculiar *adj.* ① singular, odd, curious, unusual, uncommon, strange ② unique, private, special, distinctive

peddle *v.* sell, hawk, canvas, trade, vend, retail

peddler *n.* hawker, street trader, trader

pedestal *n.* base, stand, plinth, support

peek *n. & v.* glimpse, blink, look ▷*peer*

peel ① *v.* skin, strip, pare, scale ② *n.* skin, covering, rind, coat PEAL

peer ① *v.* peep, stare, look, gaze ② *n.* aristocrat, lord, noble ③ *n.* equal, fellow, counterpart PIER

peerless *adj.* unequaled, unique, beyond compare, unbeatable

peevish *adj.* cross, childish, grumpy, crusty, irritable ▷*testy* ★**good-tempered**

peg *n.* hook, knob, pin, post, hanger, fastener

pelt ① *v.* beat, bombard, thrash, throw ② *v.* rain cats and dogs, teem, pour ③ *n.* skin, hide, fleece, fur

pen ① *n.* quill, ballpoint ② *n.* cage, coop, hutch, stall ③ *v.* write, autograph, scribble

penalty *n.* fine, forfeit, punishment, price ★**reward**

pending *adj.* awaiting, unfinished, doubtful, uncertain, undecided

penetrate *v.* ① pierce, perforate, stab, permeate *The aroma of lilacs and roses permeated the house* ② discern, see through, comprehend

penetrating *adj.* ① sharp, perceptive, understanding ② shrill, stinging

pennant *n.* flag, streamer, bunting, banner

penniless *adj.* destitute, needy, poverty-striken ▷*poor* ★**wealthy**

pensive *adj.* thoughtful, reflective, wistful, preoccupied

people ① *n.* folk, society, the public, populace, inhabitants ② *v.* populate, inhabit, settle

pep *n.* punch, energy, high spirits, vigor ▷*vitality*

peppery *adj.* ① biting, caustic *I'm afraid your essay wasn't very good; the teacher made some very caustic comments,* hot-tempered, angry ② hot, pungent, sharp

perceive *v.* feel, sense, observe, notice, make out, understand ▷*see*

perch ① *v.* alight, light, sit, squat, roost ② *n.* rod, pole, staff, roost ③ *n.* fish

perfect ① *adj.* (*per*-fect) absolute, ideal, sublime, excellent, splendid, faultless ★**imperfect** ② *v.* (per-*fect*) complete, finish, fulfill, refine

perforate *v.* puncture, drill, punch, penetrate

perform *v.* ① carry out, do, fulfill, accomplish ② play, act, stage, present *The local drama group will present a new play next week*

performer *n.* actor, player, singer, entertainer, artist

perfume *n.* scent, essence, aroma, odor

perhaps *adv.* possibly, perchance, maybe, conceivably

peril *n.* hazard, jeopardy, menace, risk, insecurity ▷*danger* ★**safety**

period *n.* spell, time, duration, term, interval, course, span, age

periodical ① *n.* magazine, publication, journal, gazette, review ② *adj.* regular, routine, recurring, repeated

perish *v.* die, pass away, wither, disintegrate, expire, shrivel

perky *adj.* bouncy, bright, cheerful, lively ▷*sprightly* ★**dull**

permanent *adj.* endless, ageless, timeless, constant ▷*durable* ★**fleeting**

permission *n.* authorization, sanction, privilege, warrant *The police have a warrant for your arrest* ★**prohibition**

permit ① *v.* (per-*mit*) allow, grant, agree, empower ② *n.* (*per*-mit) warrant, license, pass

perpendicular *adj.* upright, erect, sheer, steep, vertical ★**horizontal**

perpetrate *v.* commit, do, inflict, perform, practice, execute

perpetual *adj.* everlasting, ceaseless, eternal, never ending ▷*endless* ★**fleeting**

perplex *v.* mystify, baffle, bewilder, confound ▷*puzzle* ★**enlighten**

persecute *v.* harass, molest, plague, badger ▷*bother* ★**pamper**

persevere *v.* persist, hold out, hang on, endure, continue ★**give up**

persist *v.* remain, stand fast, abide, carry on ▷*persevere* ★**stop**

persistent *adj.* tenacious, relentless, stubborn, obstinate ★**weak**

person *n.* individual, human, being, somebody, personage, character

personal *adj.* individual, intimate, private, special, peculiar

personality *n.* individuality, character, disposition, nature

perspective *n.* outlook, aspect, proportion

perspire *v.* sweat, exude, ooze

persuade *v.* convince, wheedle, blandish, entice, cajole *I cajoled my mother into buying me a new swimsuit,* induce ▷*coax* ★**discourage**

pert *adj.* saucy, flippant, jaunty, cheeky, brash ★**shy**

perturb *v.* upset, disturb, trouble, distress, fluster ▷*bother* ★**reassure**

peruse *v.* read, study, pore over, browse, inspect, scrutinize, examine

pervade *v.* penetrate, permeate, spread, saturate, soak

perverse *adj.* contrary, wayward, opposite, disobedient ▷*stubborn* ★**reasonable**

pessimist *n.* defeatist, killjoy, wet blanket, cynic *Uncle Bert is a real cynic; he even thinks the lottery is fixed* ★**optimist**

pessimistic *adj.* cynical, dismal, fatalistic, defeatist, downhearted ★**optimistic**

pest *n.* nuisance, plague, blight, curse, vexation, bug

pester *v.* nag, hector, badger, annoy, disturb, harass ▷*bother*

pet ① *v.* fondle, caress, baby, cosset, cuddle ② *n.* favorite, beloved, dear ③ *adj.* endearing, cherished, dearest

petition *n.* plea, appeal, entreaty, round robin, request

petrified *adj.* spellbound, frightened, scared, terrified

petty *adj.* ① paltry, cheap, inferior, trifling ▷*trivial* ★**important** ② mean, measly, stingy

petulant *adj.* fretful, displeased, querulous, irritable ▷*peevish*

phantom ① *n.* apparition, specter, spook, ghost ② *adj.* spooky, ghostly, imaginary

phase *n.* aspect, appearance, angle, view, period, point FAZE

phenomenal *adj.* remarkable, outstanding, marvelous, miraculous, incredible

phenomenon *n.* marvel, rarity, curiosity, sensation, spectacle

philanthropic *adj.* charitable, kind, generous, humane, benevolent, bountiful, public-spirited ★**selfish**

philosophical *adj.* calm, cool, logical, thoughtful, impassive, unruffled

phobia *n.* dread, fear, awe, neurosis, hang-

Pine

The flowers in the pot are languishing from lack of water.

up *My father has a hang-up about bats; he can't stand them,* horror

phrase *n.* expression, idiom, saying, utterance, sentence FRAYS

physical *adj.* ① material, substantial, solid, concrete ② bodily, personal, sensible

pick ① *v.* select, choose, single out, gather ② *n.* pike, pickax

picket ① *n.* patrol, scout, sentinel, lookout, guard ② *n.* post, rail, panel, fence ③ *v.* strike, demonstrate

pickle ① *n.* preserve ② *n.* difficulty, predicament ③ *v.* cure, salt, preserve, souse

picture ① *n.* painting, tableau, portrait, illustration, drawing ② *n.* movie, film ③ *v.* illustrate, imagine, fancy

picturesque *adj.* attractive, artistic, pictorial, scenic

piece *n.* portion, fragment, lump, morsel, bit ▷*scrap* PEACE

pier *n.* wharf, dock, quay, jetty PEER

pierce *v.* perforate, drill, bore ▷*penetrate*

piercing *adj.* ① loud, deafening, shrill, penetrating ② keen, sharp, cutting

pigment *n.* color, dye, hue, paint, stain

pile *n. & v.* heap, mass, stack, load, store

pilfer *v.* purloin, rifle, rob, filch ▷*steal*

pilgrim *n.* traveler, wanderer, wayfarer

pilgrimage *n.* excursion, journey, mission, tour, trip, crusade

pillage *v.* plunder, ravage, loot, ransack *Thieves broke into the museum and ransacked all the cases,* rifle

pillar *n.* column, shaft, tower, obelisk, monument

pillow *n.* cushion, bolster, support

pilot *n.* ① guide, steersman, coxswain, helmsman ② aviator, flyer

pimple *n.* zit, blemish, swelling, boil

pin ① *n.* fastener, clip, spike, peg ② *v.* fix, fasten, attach, join, tack

pinch ① *v.* nip, squeeze, crush, tweak ② *v.* pilfer, steal ③ *n.* dash, drop, splash ④ *n.* crisis, difficulty, jam

pine *v.* hanker, yearn, long for, languish *The flowers in the pot are languishing from lack of water,* sicken

pinnacle *n.* summit, top, crest, peak, apex

pioneer *n.* founder, leader, trailblazer, explorer, innovator

pious *adj.* devout, godly, holy, moral, religious, virtuous

pipe ① *n.* tube, duct, passage, hose, conduit ② whistle, flute

piquant *adj.* appetizing, spicy, tangy, savory, pungent

pique *v.* annoy, displease, irritate, affront, vex PEAK

pirate ① *n.* corsair *In days of old the ships in the Mediterranean were often raided by corsairs,* buccaneer, privateer, sea-rover ② *v.* copy, plagiarize, steal

pistol *n.* gun, revolver, automatic PISTIL

pit *n.* ① hole, hollow, crater, trench, mine ② dent, dimple, depression

pitch ① *v.* fling, throw, cast, sling, toss ② *v.* fall, drop, descend ③ *v.* raise, set up, erect ④ *n.* angle, slope, degree ⑤ *v.* sales message

pitcher *n.* jar, beaker, crock, jug, ewer, vessel

piteous *adj.* pitiful, heartbreaking, mournful ▷*pathetic*

pitiless *adj.* merciless, unmerciful, cruel, unrelenting ★**merciful**

pity ① *n.* mercy, compassion, charity, tenderness ② *v.* spare, forgive, grieve for, sympathize with

pivot ① *n.* axle, axis, hinge, turning point, spindle, swivel ② *v.* revolve, rotate, turn, spin

placate *v.* appease, pacify, soothe, satisfy ▷*humor* ★**infuriate**

place ① *n.* spot, locality, site, situation, position ② *n.* house, apartment, residence ③

A B C D E F G H I J K L M N O P Q R S T U V W X Y Z

Planets

The nine planets of our solar system travel around a star we call the Sun.

Earth
Jupiter
Mars
Mercury
Neptune
Pluto
Saturn
Uranus
Venus

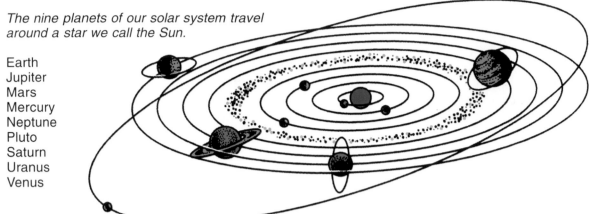

a b c d e f g h i j k l m n o p q r s t u v w x y z

v. put, deposit, establish, allocate, arrange

placid *adj.* peaceful, quiet, serene, mild ▷*restful* ★**ruffled**

plague ① *n.* epidemic, disease, contagion, pest, blight ② *v.* persecute, pester *We were pestered by flies,* infest, annoy ▷*badger*

plain ① *adj.* unadorned, simple ② *adj.* obvious, clear, apparent ③ *adj.* blunt, direct, candid ④ *adj.* smooth, level, flat ⑤ *n.* prairie, plateau, tableland PLANE

plan ① *n.* design, chart, diagram, drawing ② *n.* project, proposal, arrangement, scheme ③ *v.* design, prepare, arrange, invent

plane ① *adj.* level, even, flat, smooth ② *n.* aircraft ③ *n.* smoothing tool PLAIN

planned *adj.* prepared, ready, arranged

plant ① *v.* sow, scatter, implant ② *v.* place, set, establish ③ *n.* herb, shrub, vegetable ④ *n.* equipment, machinery, factory

plaster ① *n.* cement, mortar, paste ② *n.* bandage, dressing ③ *v.* spread, smear, daub

plastic ① *adj.* moldable, pliable, malleable, soft, supple ② *n.* thermoplastic

plate ① *n.* dish, platter, palette ② *n.* sheet, panel ③ *v.* laminate, cover, gild, anodize

platform *n.* rostrum *I was called up to the rostrum to receive my prize,* stage, stand, dais

plausible *adj.* believable, credible, convincing, glib, persuasive ★**unlikely**

play ① *v.* sport, gambol, frisk, romp, frolic ② *v.* perform, act, represent ③ *n.* drama, performance ④ *n.* sport, amusement, recreation

player *n.* actor, sportsman, artist, musician, performer, contestant

playful *adj.* frisky, frolicsome, larky, lively, sportive ★**serious**

plead *v.* appeal, argue, ask, implore, request, beseech

pleasant *adj.* affable, agreeable, cheerful, nice ▷*charming* ★**unpleasant**

please *v.* ① gratify, enchant, amuse, entertain ▷*delight* ② like, choose, wish, prefer

pleased *adj.* delighted, gratified, satisfied ▷*contented* ★**annoyed**

pleasing *adj.* agreeable, enchanting, entertaining ▷*satisfying* ★**unpleasant**

pleasure *n.* delight, joy, amusement, entertainment, enjoyment ▷*fun* ★**trouble**

pledge ① *n.* promise, vow, undertaking, warrant, oath ② *v.* bind, contract, promise, undertake

plentiful *adj.* lavish, ample, profuse, bountiful ▷*abundant* ★**scanty**

plenty *n.* enough, profusion, affluence ▷*abundance* ★**scarcity**

pliable *adj.* supple, flexible, pliant, malleable, moldable, bendy ★**rigid**

plight *n.* predicament, difficulty, condition, dilemma *We made it to the train station on time, but when we realized we had forgotten our tickets we were in a real dilemma,* jam

plod *v.* toil, labor, drudge, slog, grind

plot ① *n.* scheme, plan, intrigue ② *n.* story, narrative ③ *v.* hatch, intrigue, scheme

pluck ① *v.* gather, pick, pull, yank, catch ② *n.* courage, determination, bravery

plucky *adj.* courageous, daring, heroic, hardy 3*brave* ★**feeble**

plug ① *n.* stopper, cork, bung ② *v.* stop, block, choke, cork ③ *v.* publicize, boost, promote, push

plum ① *n.* prize, bonus, treasure ② *adj.* best, choice, first-class

plump *adj.* buxom, stout, chubby, rotund, pudgy ★**skinny**

plunder ① *n.* booty, loot, swag, spoils ② *v.* fleece, rob, ransack, pillage, loot

plunge *v.* dive, pitch, submerge, duck, immerse, swoop, hurtle

poach *v.* ① pilfer, steal, filch, purloin ② steam, cook

pocket ① *n.* compartment, pouch, sack, bag ② *v.* filch, pinch, steal

poem *n.* ode, verse, rhyme, ballad, lyric

poetic *adj.* artistic, elegant, graceful, flowing, lyrical

poignant *adj.* moving, touching, pathetic, biting, penetrating

point ① *n.* spike, barb, pike, prong, end, tip ② *n.* locality, place, spot ③ *n.* aspect, object, aim, purpose ④ *n.* headland, cape ⑤ *v.* aim, direct, level, train

pointless *adj.* meaningless, senseless, silly, vague, feeble 3*absurd* ★**significant**

poise ① *n.* confidence, assurance, dignity, self-possession, balance ② *v.* stand, hover, brood over

poison ① *n.* venom, virus, toxin ② *v.* taint, fester, corrupt, infect

poisonous *adj.* deadly, evil, lethal *Don't touch those red berries; they're lethal,* noxious, toxic, venomous

poke *v.* jab, push, nudge, jostle, ram, thrust, stab, prod 3*shove*

pole *n.* stick, stave, stake, rod, post, bar, mast, shaft, spar

policy *n.* course, action, practice, rule, procedure, guidelines

polish ① *v.* burnish, buff, smooth, brighten, clean ② *n.* gloss, glaze, shine ③ *n.* refinement, grace, culture

polished *adj.* ① glossy, burnished, shiny ② refined, cultivated, cultured

polite *adj.* courteous, attentive, civil, well-bred, elegant, discreet ★**impolite**

poll ① *n.* election, vote, count, census, ballot ② *v.* survey, canvas, vote

pollute *v.* adulterate, debase, befoul, taint, poison, corrupt ★**purify**

pomp *n.* ceremony, show, splendor, pageantry, magnificence ★**simplicity**

pompous *adj.* showy, self-important, bombastic 3*pretentious* ★**modest**

ponder *v.* meditate, consider, reflect, deliberate, think about

pool ① *n.* lagoon, pond, lake ② *n.* accumulation, funds, reserve, kitty ③ *v.* combine, contribute, share

poor *adj.* ① destitute, penniless, miserable ★**rich** ② low quality, faulty, feeble, shoddy *That shirt may be cheap, but it's shoddy and won't last* ★**superior** PORE, POUR

poorly ① *adj.* ailing, ill, sick, seedy ② *adv.* badly, inexpertly, crudely ★**well**

pop *v.* ① bang, burst, crack, explode ② slide, slip, insert

popular *adj.* ① well-liked, favorite, in favor, fashionable ② current, common, vulgar, prevailing

Poisonous Plants

Aconite
Baneberry
Belladonna
Black nightshade
Deadly nightshade
Foxglove
Hellebore
Hemlock
Henbane
Larkspur
Nux vomica
Poison ivy

A B C D E F G H I J K L M N O P Q R S T U V W X Y Z

pore *v.* scan, examine, peruse, scrutinize
POOR, POUR

portable *adj.* lightweight, convenient, transportable ▷*handy* ★**awkward**

portion *n.* piece, fragment, share, fraction ▷*part*

portly *adj.* plump, stout, fat, burly, bulky

portrait *n.* likeness, painting, picture, profile

portray *v.* describe, depict, represent, picture, illustrate, impersonate

pose ① *v.* stand, poise, posture, position ② *n.* position, stand, guise, stance *If you want to learn to play golf well, you need a good stance*

position *n.* ① spot, situation, location, place, site ② job, post ③ posture, attitude ④ rank, standing, status

positive *adj.* ① certain, sure, confident ★**doubtful** ② real, true, absolute ★**negative** ③ precise, definite, unmistakable

possess *v.* have, own, hold, occupy ★**lose**

possessions *n.* wealth, assets, property, goods

possible *adj.* conceivable, imaginable, likely, feasible, attainable ★**impossible**

possibly *adv.* perhaps, maybe, perchance conceivably

post *n.* ① rail, pole, beam, banister, stake ② position, employment, job ③ mail

poster *n.* placard, bill, advertisement, sign

posterior *adj.* hind, behind, after, rear ★**front**

postpone *v.* put off, defer, shelve, adjourn ▷*delay* ★**advance**

posture *n.* bearing, stance, attitude, carriage

pot *n.* basin, bowl, pan, vessel, container, jar

potential ① *adj.* possible, probable, latent *The professor discovered that I had a latent talent for languages,* dormant, budding ② *n.* ability, talent, capacity ▷*flair*

potion *n.* beverage, medicine, mixture, tonic, brew

pouch *n.* bag, poke, sack, purse, pocket, wallet

pounce *v.* strike, lunge, spring, swoop, fall upon ▷*attack*

pound ① *v.* beat, batter, crush, hammer ② *n.* enclosure, compound, pen ③ *n.* weight

pour *v.* spout, jet, gush, spill, cascade, rain
PORE, POUR

pout *v.* grimace, glower, sulk, scowl, mope ★**smile**

poverty *n.* ① distress, need, bankruptcy, privation ▷*want* ② scarcity, shortage ★**plenty**

powder ① *n.* dust, sand, ash, grit, bran ② *v.* pulverize, crunch, grind

power *n.* ① authority, command, control, ability ② energy, force, strength

powerful *adj.* mighty, vigorous, forceful ▷*strong* ★**weak**

practical *adj.* ① useful, effective, workable ② experienced, qualified, trained ▷*skilled* ★**impractical**

practice *n.* ① custom, habit, usage ② work, conduct, performance, action ★**theory** ② *v.* carry out, apply, do, execute ▷*perform*

praise ① *v.* acclaim, applaud, glorify, exalt ★**criticize** ② *n.* applause, flattery, compliment, approval ★**criticism** PRAYS, PREYS

prance *v.* gambol *I love to watch the lambs gambol in the spring,* frolic, romp, caper, swagger

prank *n.* trick, joke, antic, lark, jape, stunt

prattle *n. & v.* chatter, jabber, gossip, drivel, babble

pray *v.* beg, beseech, entreat, implore, request PREY

prayer *n.* petition, entreaty, worship, devotion, supplication

preach *v.* lecture, moralize, advocate *The president advocated a program to feed the poor,* urge, proclaim

precarious *adj.* perilous, hazardous, insecure, dangerous ▷*risky* ★**safe**

precaution *n.* forethought, provision, anticipation, care, providence ▷*prudence*

precede *v.* lead, head, usher, go before, preface ★**follow**

Prey

Pray

precious *adj.* valuable, cherished, treasured, dear, beloved ▷*costly* ★**worthless**

precise *adj.* ① definite, exact, pointed, accurate ② formal, particular, strict ★**vague**

precisely *adv.* absolutely, just so, exactly, correctly

precision *n.* exactitude, accuracy, care, detail

precocious *adj.* fast, smart, clever ★**backward**

predicament *n.* situation, state, condition, embarrassment, fix ▷*plight*

predict *v.* foresee, foretell, prophesy, presage, divine

predominant *adj.* leading, main, powerful, superior, ruling, controlling ★**minor**

preen *v.* prance, swagger, strut, spruce up, doll up, groom

preface *n.* introduction, prelude, prologue, preamble, foreword

prefer *v.* choose, select, desire, like better, fancy ▷*favor* ★**reject**

prejudice ① *n.* bigotry, intolerance, bias, discrimination ② *v.* influence, warp, twist, distort, undermine ★**benefit**

prejudiced *adj.* biased *My opinion of Jessica is biased; she was very cruel to me once*, bigoted, one-sided, unfair, intolerant ★**fair**

preliminary *adj.* introductory, preparatory, opening, initial ★**final**

premature *adj.* untimely, previous, early, immature ★**late**

premeditated *adj.* calculated, planned, prearranged, intentional ★**spontaneous**

premier ① *n.* prime minister, first minister, head of government ② *adj.* chief, first, head, leading, principal

premises *n.* grounds, house, building, lands

prepare *v.* arrange, adapt, provide, get ready, concoct, plan ★**demolish**

preposterous *adj.* absurd, ridiculous, laughable ▷*unreasonable* ★**reasonable**

prescribe *v.* indicate, order, propose, recommend, specify

presence *n.* ① existence, appearance, aspect ② nearness, neighborhood, proximity

PRESENTS

present ① *n.* (*pres*-ent) gift, donation, bounty, favor ② (*pres*-ent) *adj.* here, on the spot, ready, current ③ *v.* (pre-*sent*) offer, tender, bestow, award, exhibit

presently *adv.* soon, shortly, before long, immediately

preserve ① *v.* protect safeguard, conserve, shield ▷*keep* ② *n.* jam, jelly, relish

press ① *v.* bear down, depress, clamp, jam, compress, flatten ② *n.* printing machine ③ *n.* newspapers, reporters, journalism

pressure *n.* ① strain, tension, stress, urgency ② weight, compression, force

prestige *n.* repute, authority, weight, power

presume *v.* infer *I infer from your smile that you have passed your exam,* suppose, grant, take for granted, assume

presumptuous *adj.* arrogant, bold, audacious, insolent ▷*forward* ★**modest**

pretend *v.* ① make believe, simulate, sham, feign, masquerade ② aspire, claim, strive for

pretext *n.* excuse, pretense, guise, device

pretty *adj.* attractive, beautiful, comely,

A
B
C
D
E
F
G
H
I
J
K
L
M
N
O
P
Q
R
S
T
U
V
W
X
Y
Z

dainty, bonny ▷*lovely* ★**ugly**

prevail *v.* obtain, overcome, predominate ▷*triumph* ★**lose**

prevalent *adj.* current, common, popular, in use, accepted ★**uncommon**

prevent *v.* avert, forestall, ward off, discourage, stop ▷*hinder* ★**help**

previous *adj.* former, prior, earlier, premature, untimely ★**later**

prey *n.* quarry, chase, booty, victim PRAY

prey on *v.* plunder, fleece, oppress, terrorize

price *n.* cost, amount, expense, payment, value, worth

priceless *adj.* ① invaluable, precious, cherished, costly ② amusing, comic, humorous, hilarious *The clown's antics were hilarious*

prick *v.* jab, jag, puncture, stab, pierce

pride *n.* conceit, arrogance, vanity, egotism, self-importance, honor, exaltation, pleasure PRIED

prim *adj.* puritanical, demure, starchy, priggish ★**informal**

primary *adj.* first, original, chief, essential, fundamental

prime *adj.* ① principal, chief, basic, original ② best, finest, choice

primitive *adj.* ① simple, austere, crude ② uncivilized, savage, barbarous

principal ① *adj.* main, chief, head, leading, foremost ② *n.* head, leader, boss, director PRINCIPLE

principle *n.* ① law, regulation, rule, doctrine ② virtue, worth, integrity, rectitude *The president of the club was honored by the mayor as a "person of high moral rectitude"* ★**wickedness** PRINCIPAL

print ① *v.* impress, stamp, brand, publish ② *n.* impression, printing, imprint

prior ① *adj.* previous, former, earlier, preceding ② *n.* abbot, monk

prison *n.* jail, penitentiary, dungeon, lock up

private *adj.* ① particular, personal, special, own ② solitary, remote *He spent his vacations in a remote cabin,* quiet ★**public**

privilege *n.* ① advantage, benefit, exemption

Printing

- Collotype
- Computer-setting
- Cylinder press
- Flatbed press
- Intaglio
- Letterpress
- Linotype
- Lithography
- Monotype
- Photogravure
- Rotary press
- Silk screen
- Type
- Web offset

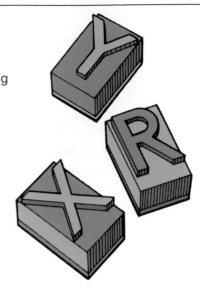

② right, authority, entitlement, prerogative *It was the emperor's prerogative to pardon offenders*

prize ① *n.* reward, premium, trophy, honor ② *n.* booty, spoils, plunder ③ *adj.* best, champion, winning ④ *v.* value, appreciate, cherish ⑤ *v.* force, lever, pry, lift, raise PRIES

probable *adj.* likely, presumable, reasonable, possible ★**improbable**

probe *v.* ① poke, prod ② examine, investigate, scrutinize

problem ① *n.* puzzle, question, riddle, poser, quandary ② difficulty, dilemma, snag, predicament, complication

proceed *v.* ① advance, continue, go on, progress ★**recede** ② arise, flow, spring, emanate *A strong sulfurous odor emanated from the crater of the volcano*

process ① *n.* procedure, operation, movement, system, method ② *v.* convert, alter, handle, refine

procession *n.* parade, pageant, march, cavalcade

proclaim *v.* declare, announce, advertise, publish, expound

procure *v.* secure, acquire, win, gain, attain, get ★**lose**

prod *v.* goad, poke, nudge, incite, urge, shove

prodigal *adj.* extravagant, reckless, lavish ▷*spendthrift* ★**thrifty**

prodigious *adj.* ① miraculous, abnormal, amazing, remarkable ▷*extraordinary*

★ordinary ② huge, mighty ▷*enormous* **★tiny**

produce ① *n.* (*pro*-duce) product, output, yield, crop, harvest ② *v.* (pro-*duce*) provide, yield, create, deliver, put forward

product *n.* output, crop, harvest, return, merchandise, commodity

profane *adj.* impious, blasphemous, unholy, worldly, sinful **★sacred**

profess *v.* declare, avow, acknowledge, own

profession *n.* ① occupation, career, job, calling, employment ② avowal, admission

professional *adj.* skilled, efficient, experienced ▷*expert* **★amateur**

proffer *v.* present, offer, tender, submit

proficient *adj.* competent, able, skilled, trained ▷*expert* **★clumsy**

profit ① *n.* benefit, gain, advantage, acquisition **★loss** ② *v.* improve, gain, reap, acquire **★lose** PROPHET

profound ① *adj.* deep, penetrating, fathomless ② wise, shrewd, learned, sagacious *The leader of the tribe was old, wise, and sagacious* **★shallow**

profuse *adj.* bountiful, extravagant, exuberant, prolific, sumptuous ▷*lavish* **★sparse**

progress ① *n.* (*prog*-ress) advancement, growth, development **★decline** ② *v.* (pro-*gress*) advance, proceed, go, forge ahead, travel, grow

prohibit *v.* forbid, bar, deny, ban, obstruct, hinder ▷*prevent* **★permit**

project ① *n.* (*pro*-ject) work, affair, plan, scheme, undertaking ② *v.* (pro-*ject*) propel, hurl, jut, protrude ③ *v.* contrive, scheme, plan ④ *v.* protrude, bulge, stick out

prolific *adj.* fruitful, creative, productive, fertile **★scarce**

prolong *v.* lengthen, stretch, draw out, spin out ▷*extend* **★shorten**

prominent *adj.* ① famous, notable, distinguished **★minor** ② projecting, standing out, bulging, jutting

promise ① *n.* commitment, undertaking, warrant, pledge ② *v.* agree, guarantee, vow

promote *adj.* ① cultivate, advance, assist ▷*encourage* ② dignify, elevate, upgrade, honor **★degrade**

prompt ① *adj.* punctual, timely, quick, smart, ready **★tardy** ② *v.* hint, remind, urge ▷*encourage* **★deter**

prone *adj.* ① inclined, apt, liable, disposed **★unlikely** ② prostrate *The poor fellow lay prostrate on the ship's deck,* face down, recumbent **★upright**

pronounce *v.* ① speak, utter, say, articulate ② declare, decree, proclaim

pronounced *adj.* outstanding, striking, noticeable ▷*distinct* **★vague**

proof *n.* evidence, testimony, confirmation, criterion, scrutiny **★failure**

prop *n.* & *v.* stay, brace, truss, support

propel *v.* start, push, force, impel, send ▷*drive* **★stop**

proper *adj.* ① correct, without error, right, accurate, exact ② respectable, decent, becoming, seemly **★improper** ③ personal, own, special **★common**

property ① *n.* possessions, wealth, chattels, buildings, belongings ② quality, virtue, characteristic, peculiarity

prophecy *n.* forecast, divination, prediction, prognostication

prophesy *v.* predict, foretell, foresee, declare

proportion ① *n.* ratio, percentage, part, fraction ② adjustment, arrangement

proposal *n.* proposition, offer, outline

propose *v.* ① put forward, offer, suggest ② ask for the hand of, ask to marry, pop the question

proprietor *n.* owner, possessor, landlady, landlord

prosaic *adj.* factual, tedious, uninteresting, boring, unimaginative, everyday, dull, mundane, ordinary **★interesting**

prosecute *v.* ① indict, put on trial, summon, sue ② continue, pursue, carry on, conduct **★abandon**

prospect *n.* ① outlook, forecast, promise, expectation ② view, landscape, vista, aspect

prosper *v.* succeed, flourish, grow **★fail**

prosperous *adj.* affluent, wealthy, rich, successful, thriving **★unsuccessful**

A B C D E F G H I J K L M N O P Q R S T U V W X Y Z

protect *v.* defend, preserve, guard, secure, shelter, support ★**endanger**

protest ① *v.* (pro-*test*) complain, object, dispute, challenge ★**accept** ② *n.* (*pro*-test) objection, complaint, dissent, outcry

protracted *adj.* extended, drawn out, lengthy, prolonged ★**shortened**

protrude *v.* project, bulge, jut ★**recede**

proud ① *adj.* arrogant, haughty, supercilious, boastful ★**humble** ② lofty, majestic, noble, splendid ★**mean**

prove *v.* show, demonstrate, authenticate, confirm, verify ★**disprove**

provide *v.* supply, furnish, equip, contribute, afford ★**withhold**

province *n.* ① realm, sphere, orbit, place, department ② region, state, county

provoke *v.* prompt, incite, excite, enrage, inflame ▷*aggravate* ★**appease**

prowess *n.* ability, strength, might, bravery ▷*valor* ★**clumsiness**

prowl *v.* stalk *Somewhere in the darkness a large gray cat stalked its prey,* roam, slink

prudent *adj.* careful, cautious, discreet, shrewd ▷*thrifty* ★**rash**

prudish *adj.* straitlaced, narrow-minded, demure, priggish ▷*prim*

prune ① *v.* cut, shorten, trim, crop ② *n.* dried plum

pry *v.* snoop, peep, meddle, intrude

public ① *adj.* communal, civil, popular, social, national ② *n.* the people, the populace, society

publish *v.* broadcast, distribute, circulate, communicate, bring out

pucker *v.* fold, crease, cockle, furrow, wrinkle ★**straighten**

puerile *adj.* callow, immature, juvenile

puff *v.* inflate, swell, blow, pant, distend

pull *v.* ① haul, drag, tow, heave ★**push** ② gather, pluck, detach, pick

pump *v.* ① inflate, expand, swell, inject, siphon ② interrogate, question, grill

punch *v.* ① strike, beat, hit, cuff ② puncture, pierce, perforate, bore

punctual *adj.* prompt, on time, precise, exact, timely ★**tardy**

puncture *n.* perforation, hole, leak, wound

pungent *adj.* sharp, bitter, poignant, biting ▷*acrid* ★**mild**

punish *v.* chastise, correct, discipline, chasten, reprove, scold

puny *adj.* feeble, weak, frail, small, petty, stunted, insignificant ★**large**

pupil *n.* student, scholar, schoolchild, learner

puppet *n.* ① doll, marionette ② cat's-paw *The prisoner was not the true culprit, but only the ringleader's cat's-paw,* figurehead, pawn

purchase ① *v.* buy, procure, secure, obtain, get ▷*buy* ★**sell** ② *n.* bargain, investment

pure *adj.* ① immaculate, spotless, stainless, clear ▷*clean* ★**impure** ② virtuous, chaste, honest, blameless

purely *adv.* simply, barely, merely, only

purge *v.* ① purify, clean, cleanse, scour ② liquidate, exterminate, kill

purify *v.* clean, clarify, wash, purge

purloin *v.* rob, thieve, take, filch, pilfer ▷*steal*

purpose *n.* intent, design, will, goal, target

purse ① *n.* handbag, wallet, pouch, reticule, ② *v.* pucker, crease, compress, wrinkle

pursue *v.* ① follow, track, trace ▷*chase* ② practice, maintain, work for

pursuit *n.* ① hunt, chase, follow, hue and cry ② occupation, hobby, interest *Stamp collecting has always been one of my main interests*

push ① *v.* shove, thrust, press, drive, propel ② *n.* advance, assault, drive

put *v.* ① set, place, deposit, repose, lay ② express, propose, state

put down *v.* ① write, jot down, record, note ② crush, humiliate, subdue, insult

put off *v.* ① postpone, defer, delay, adjourn ② dishearten, unsettle, perturb

putrid *adj.* decomposed, rotten, rancid, rank, stinking ★**wholesome**

putter *v.* dabble, fiddle, tinker, mess around

puzzle ① *v.* baffle, confuse, mystify, perplex ▷*bewilder* ② *n.* conundrum, brainteaser, problem, dilemma

puzzling *adj.* baffling, curious, strange, bewildering ▷*peculiar*

Q q

quack *n.* impostor, charlatan *She pretended to tell fortunes by cards, but she was nothing but a charlatan,* humbug, fake

quaff *v.* imbibe, swallow ▷*drink*

quagmire *n.* bog, mire, marsh ▷*swamp*

quail *v.* tremble, flinch, shrink, cower, succumb ★**withstand**

quaint *adj.* curious, whimsical, fanciful, singular, old-fashioned, droll

quake ① *v.* tremble, quaver, shiver, quiver, shudder ② *n.* shock, convulsion, tremor *The tremors from the earthquake were felt hundreds of miles away*

qualification *n.* ① fitness, capacity, ability, accomplishment ② restriction, limitation, modification *The engineer's design was accepted with certain modifications*

qualify *v.* ① empower, enable, fit, suit ② moderate, limit, restrict

quality *n.* ① characteristic, condition, power ② excellence, worth, goodness

qualm *n.* doubt, misgiving, hesitation

quandary *n.* difficulty, doubt ▷*dilemma*

quantity *n.* amount, number, volume, sum

quarrel ① *n.* dispute, squabble, wrangle, disagreement ★**harmony** ② *v.* argue, bicker, brawl, squabble ★**agree**

quarry *n.* ① game, prey, object, victim, target ② mine, excavation, pit

quarter *n.* ① area, territory, place, district ② one-fourth ③ mercy *The commander of the invading army showed no mercy to the local defenders,* grace, lenience

quarters *n.* lodgings, dwelling, billet, rooms

quash *v.* abolish, nullify, suppress, overthrow, subdue

quaver *v.* shake, tremble, shiver, shudder, vibrate, oscillate, quake

quay *n.* pier, dock, wharf, landing, jetty KEY

queasy *adj.* bilious, squeamish, sick, faint

queer *adj.* strange, odd, whimsical, peculiar

quell *v.* crush, stifle, extinguish, defeat

quench *v.* ① douse *We carefully doused our campfire before leaving the site,* put out, cool, check ② slake *The cattle rushed to the river and slaked their thirst,* cool, allay

query ① *n.* question, doubt, objection ② *v.* ask, inquire, question, doubt ★**accept**

quest *n.* chase, hunt, search, pursuit, venture

question ① *n.* query, inquiry, interrogation, ② *n.* topic, problem, issue ③ *v.* ask, inquire, interrogate ★**answer**

questionable *adj.* doubtful, uncertain, undecided, unbelievable ★**certain**

queue *n.* ① row, line, procession, lineup ② pigtail, coil, braid, ponytail CUE

quibble *v.* argue, trifle, split hairs, carp *If you like our plan, don't carp about the details*

quick *adj.* ① speedy, rapid, express, swift ▷*fast* ② alert, active, agile, lively ★**slow** ③ clever, intelligent, acute ★**dull** ④ hasty, sharp, touchy ★**mild**

quicken *v.* accelerate ▷*hasten* ★**delay**

quiet ① *adj.* silent, soundless, noiseless, hushed ★**noisy** ② *adj.* placid, smooth, undisturbed ★**busy** ③ *n.* peace, rest, tranquility, silence ★**tumult**

quilt *n.* blanket, cover, comforter, eiderdown

quip *n.* joke, gag, gipe, jest, wisecrack, retort

quirk *n.* pecularity, curiosity, foible *Despite his age and one or two foibles, old Uncle Fred was very agile,* mannerism ▷*habit*

quit *v.* ① cease, desist, stop ② leave, depart, relinquish ③ give up, surrender

quite *adv.* absolutely, altogether, wholly

quits *adj.* even *If I pay what I owe, it makes us even,* all square, level, equal

quiver ① *v.* tremble, quake, shiver, shudder ② *n.* holster, scabbard, sheath

quiz ① *v.* question, ask, examine, grill ② *n.* test, examination, contest *Barbara was the winner in the spelling contest*

quizzical *adj.* ① incredulous, skeptical, suspicious ② whimsical, teasing, amused

quota *n.* allowance, allocation, ration

quotation *n.* ① extract, selection, passage ② cost, estimate, price

quote *v.* recite, cite, recount, recollect, tell, mention

R r

rabble *n.* crowd, mob, scum, riffraff

race ① *n.* competition, contest, chase, dash ② *n.* people, nation, folk, stock, breed, tribe ③ *v.* run, speed, hurry, scamper, gallop, sprint

rack ① *n.* shelf, stand, frame, framework ② *v.* distress, strain, torment, pain WRACK

racket *n.* ① uproar, noise, hubbub, tumult ▷*din* ② fraud, deception, swindle

racy *adj.* ① pungent, piquant, zestful ② spirited, smart, lively

radiant *adj.* ① brilliant, bright, luminous, shining ② splendid, glorious, happy ★**dull**

radiate *v.* ① gleam, sparkle, beam, shine ② emit, spread, diffuse

radical *adj.* ① extreme, fanatical, deep-seated ② original, fundamental *The new teacher made some fundamental changes in our lessons,* natural ★**superficial**

raffle *n.* draw, sweepstakes, lottery

rafter *n.* joist, girder, beam, support

ragamuffin *n.* scarecrow, urchin ▷*waif*

rage ① *n.* wrath, fury, ferocity, passion, madness ▷*anger* ② *v.* rave, fret, fume *The mad bull was fuming with rage as we leaped over the fence,* storm, flare up

ragged *adj.* shabby, seedy, shaggy, rough, torn ★**smart**

raid ① *n.* invasion, attack, strike, sortie ② *v.* attack, invade, ransack, plunder, maraud *The ship was attacked and plundered by pirates* RAYED

rail ① *n.* post, picket, fence, railing ② *v.* scold, rant, blast, reproach

rain *n. & v.* deluge, drizzle, flood, shower, torrent REIGN, REIN

raise *v.* ① elevate, lift, erect, hoist *The flag was hoisted as the ship came into port* ★**lower** ② excite, awaken, rouse ③ promote, increase, advance ④ cultivate, grow, breed RAZE

rake *v.* grope, scrape, collect, gather, assemble

rally *v.* ① meet, assemble, convene *The members of the club will convene next month* ★**disperse** ② encourage, restore, reunite

ram *v.* ① cram, crowd, push, pack, stuff, poke, wedge ② charge, beat, crash, drive

ramble *v.* ① stroll, meander, saunter, roam, rove ② chatter, digress *Joe's speech was very long, as he kept digressing from the point,* dodder

ramp *n.* gradient, slope, incline, grade

rampage ① *n.* storm, rage, riot, uproar, tumult ② *v.* rave, rush, run wild *Someone left the gate open, and the pigs ran wild in the cabbage patch*

ramshackle *adj.* unstable, shaky, unsteady, flimsy, rickety ▷*decrepit* ★**stable**

rancid *adj.* sour, curdled, rank, putrid, musty

rancor *n.* spite, grudge, animosity, hatred ▷*malice* RANKER

random *adj.* haphazard, vague, casual, accidental ▷*chance* ★**deliberate**

range ① *n.* extent, length, span, magnitude, area ② *n.* kind, sort, class, order ③ *v.* wander, rove, roam, stray

rank ① *n.* grade, class, position, level ② *adj.* foul, musty, offensive, coarse ③ *adj.* luxuriant, fertile, dense *The whole county was covered with dense forest*

rankle *v.* burn, smolder, fester, be embittered

ransack *v.* plunder, pillage, search, scour

ransom ① *n.* release, deliverance, payoff, price ② *v.* rescue, redeem *Jill was lazy at school to begin with, but later redeemed herself with hard work,* liberate

rant *v.* rave, declaim, bluster, roar, shout

rap *v.* tap, pat, strike, knock

rape *v.* violate, abuse, assault, attack

rapid *adj.* speedy, quick, swift ▷*fast* ★**slow**

rapt *adj.* engrossed, intent, captivated, fascinated, delighted RAPPED, WRAPPED

rapture *n.* bliss, ecstasy, delight ▷*joy* ★**sorrow**

rare *adj.* ① unusual, uncommon, scarce, occasional ② valuable, fine, precious ★**common** ③ underdone, lightly cooked

rascal *n.* rogue, knave, villain, scamp, scoundrel, blackguard ★**gentleman**

rash ① *adj.* headstrong, audacious, hasty,

foolhardy ▷*reckless* ★**cautious** ② *n.*
eruption, outbreak, epidemic *There has
been an epidemic of chicken pox in our
neighborhood*

rashness *n.* audacity, carelessness,
hastiness, recklessness ★**carefulness**

rasp ① *v.* file, grate, grind ② *v.* irk, irritate,
vex ③ *n.* file, tool

rate ① *n.* pace, tempo *It took us a while to
get used to the tempo of life in the city,*
velocity, speed ② *n.* tax, charge, cost ③ *v.*
appraise, assess, estimate, merit, value

rather *adv.* ① somewhat, to some extent, sort
of ② first, preferably, sooner

ration ① *n.* portion, share, allotment, helping
② *v.* allocate, allot, restrict, control

rational *adj.* ① sensible, sound, wise,
intelligent, sane ★**irrational** ② reasonable,
fair, proper ★**absurd**

rattle *v.* ① jangle, jingle, vibrate ② muddle,
confuse, daze ▷*bewilder*

raucous *adj.* harsh, hoarse, rough, strident,
gutteral

ravage *v.* devastate, destroy, pillage,
ransack, desolate, wreck

rave *v.* ① rant, ramble *The old man rambled
on for hours about his youth,* roar, rage,
storm ② favor, be ecstatic about

ravenous *adj.* hungry, starving, famished,
voracious ▷*greedy*

ravishing *adj.* beautiful, bewitching,
delightful, charming ▷*enchanting*

raw *adj.* ① uncooked ② unripe, green *I was
pretty green during the first six months in
the job,* inexperienced ③ sensitive, painful,
tender ④ cold, exposed, chilly

ray *n.* beam, gleam, glimmer, shaft, stream,
spark

raze *v.* demolish, destroy, flatten, obliterate,
ruin RAISE, RAYS

reach ① *v.* arrive at, gain, get to, attain,
grasp ② *v.* stretch, extend ③ *n.* extent,
length, grasp, distance, scope

react *v.* respond, reverberate *The sound of
the church bell reverberated through the
village,* behave, respond

read *v.* ① peruse, pore over, study, browse,

Read

Reed

understand ② recite, orate REED

readily *adv.* easily, eagerly, freely, gladly,
promptly ★**reluctantly**

ready *adj.* ① prepared, alert, prompt, willing
★**reluctant** ② convenient, handy ★**remote**
③ skillful, facile, expert ★**clumsy**

real *adj.* ① genuine, authentic, factual
★**false** ② substantial, existent, actual
★**imaginary** REEL

realistic *adj.* ① authentic, lifelike
② practical, down-to-earth *Sue is a real
romantic type, but her boyfriend is much
more down-to-earth,* unromantic,
businesslike, pragmatic ★**fanciful**

realize *v.* ① understand, comprehend, feel
② earn, gain, obtain, acquire

really *adv.* truly, indeed, actually, absolutely

realm *n.* domain, province, sphere *My
mother has taken up writing and is very
involved in the sphere of books,* region,
territory, field

reap *v.* harvest, gather, obtain, realize,
derive, gain ★**squander**

rear ① *n.* back, end, tail, behind, posterior
② *adj.* hind, after, following ③ *v.* foster,
breed, educate ④ *v.* lift, raise, elevate

reason ① *n.* purpose, motive, basis, cause,
explanation ② *n.* wisdom, sense, intellect ③
v. consider, think, argue

reasonable *adj.* ① sensible, valid, rational
★**absurd** ② moderate, fair, just, modest ③
inexpensive, low-priced *Everything in the
new supermarket is low-priced* ★**excessive**

A
B
C
D
E
F
G
H
I
J
K
L
M
N
O
P
Q
R
S
T
U
V
W
X
Y
Z

reassure v. inspire, hearten, convince ▷*encourage* ★**discourage**

rebate n. refund, repayment, discount, allowance

rebel ① v. (re-*bel*) revolt, mutiny, disobey, resist ② n. (*reb*-el) revolutionary, mutineer *Fletcher Christian was the leader of the mutineers on the* Bounty, traitor

rebellious adj. defiant, disobedient, mutinous, resistant ★**obedient**

rebuke v. reprimand, reproach, scold, tell off ★**praise**

recall v. ① recollect, remember ② cancel, overrule, countermand *We were just about to pull down the building when our orders were countermanded,* call back

recede v. ebb, retreat, flow back, decline, shrink, withdraw, return ★**proceed**

receipt n. acknowledgment, voucher

recent adj. late, new, fresh, novel, modern, current ★**out-of-date**

recently adv. lately, currently, latterly

receptacle n. container, holder, vessel, bowl

reception n. ① entertainment, function, party ② acceptance, acknowledgment

recess n. ① alcove, corner, socket, niche, slot, nook ② intermission, interlude, pause

recession n. slump, stagnation, depression ★**boom**

recipe n. formula, method *I'll show you my secret method of making angel food cake; it never fails,* prescription

recite v. recount, chant, speak, declaim, relate, describe

reckless adj. unwary, incautious, daring, brash, heedless ▷*rash* ★**cautious**

reckon ① v. calculate, figure, count, tally *I have checked the accounts and my figures tally with yours,* account ② judge, expect, believe, guess, surmise

reclaim v. recover, redeem, reform, retrieve, restore, salvage

recline v. lounge, sprawl, lie, rest, loll, repose

recognize v. ① recall, recollect, remember, identify, know ② see *I will explain my idea slowly and you will see what I mean,* comprehend, understand

recoil v. ① rebound, backfire, boomerang ② falter, flinch, shrink, quail *My little brother quailed at the sound of the thunder*

recollect v. recall, recognize, place ▷*remember* ★**forget**

recommend v. suggest, advise, propose, commend, approve ★**veto**

recompense ① n. payment, compensation, remuneration ② v. reimburse, repay ▷*reward*

reconcile v. ① accept, harmonize, pacify, placate ★**estrange** ② adjust, settle, square

record ① v. (re-*cord*) note, register, enter, inscribe, list ② n. (*rec*-ord) album, disk, platter, CD, LP ③ chronicle, archive, almanac *We'll get hold of the almanac and check the time of high tide,* register ④ performance, championship

recount v. ① (re-*count*) relate, tell, recite, describe ② (*re*-count) count again

recover v. ① reclaim, retrieve, redeem, regain ② get better, recuperate, revive ★**worsen**

recreation n. pastime, sports, amusement, fun

recruit ① n. trainee, beginner, apprentice ② v. enlist, enroll, draft, mobilize

rectify v. correct, put right, repair, remedy, restore, adjust, reset

recuperate v. get better, rally, improve, mend ▷*recover* ★**worsen**

recur v. return, reappear, come back, repeat, revert

redden v. crimson, color, flush ▷*blush*

redeem v. ① buy back, compensate for, exchange ② save, liberate, free

reduce v. ① lessen, diminish, curtail, contract ② overcome, defeat, humiliate

reek v. smell, stink, fume, exhale, smoke

reel ① v. roll, rock, shake, stagger, falter, totter ② n. spool, bobbin, spindle REAL

refer v. relate, connect, associate, assign, belong

referee n. umpire, arbitrator, judge

reference n. ① allusion, insinuation, innuendo *From your innuendo, it seems that you think I'm joking!* ▷*hint* ② testimonial, recommendation, credentials

refine v. clarify, purify, filter, process, cultivate

refined *adj.* ① civilized, cultivated, cultured ▷*polite* ② purified, pure, clarified ★**coarse**

reflect *v.* ① think, contemplate, deliberate, consider ② mirror, copy, imitate, image

reform *v.* ① improve, correct ▷*rectify* ② remodel, reorganize, revamp

refrain ① *v.* avoid, abstain, forbear, resist, keep from ② *n.* chorus, melody, tune

refresh *v.* rejuvenate, renew, restore, cheer, enliven ★**exhaust**

refrigerate *v.* chill, cool, freeze

refuge *n.* haven, harbor, asylum, sanctuary ▷*shelter*

refugee *n.* exile, fugitive, emigrant

refund *v.* repay, rebate, reimburse *I must reimburse you for everything you spent on my behalf,* pay back, return

refuse ① *v.* (re-*fuze*) decline, say no, demur, repudiate ② *n.* (*ref*-use) trash, garbage, rubbish, waste

refute *v.* deny, dispute, disprove, discredit ★**prove**

regain *v.* recover, get back, retrieve, redeem

regal *adj.* royal, princely, majestic, noble, stately

regard ① *v.* esteem, revere, honor, respect ★**dislike** ② *v.* notice, observe, see, gaze ③ *n.* affection, esteem, fondness, repute ★**contempt**

regardless ① *adj.* heedless, neglectful, indifferent ★**careful** ② *adv.* anyhow, anyway, in any case

region *n.* area, zone, territory, locality, province, country

register ① *n.* roll, roster, record, archives *We can trace the town's history from the ancient archives* ② *v.* enter, record, inscribe, enroll, sign on

regret ① *v.* repent, rue, deplore, lament, mourn, apologize ★**welcome** ② *n.* remorse, sorrow, apology, grief

regular *adj.* ① normal, customary, periodical, formal ★**unusual** ② orderly, steady, unchanging ★**variable**

regulate *v.* ① control, manage, govern, determine ② adjust, measure, time, correct

regulation *n.* ① rule, law, command, bylaw

Rain

Rein

The club bylaws require us to elect a new secretary ② order, control, government

rehearse *v.* repeat, practice, drill, prepare, run through

reign ① *n.* rule, sway, power, control ② *v.* govern, rule, dominate, command RAIN, REIN

rein *v. & n.* bridle, hold, check, harness RAIN, REIGN

reinforce *v.* support, strengthen, toughen, harden, stiffen ★**weaken**

reject ① *v.* (re-*ject*) discard, get rid of, throw out, refuse, repel, deny ② *n.* (*re*-ject) cast-off, scrap

rejoice *v.* glory, exult, cheer, please, triumph ▷*delight* ★**lament**

relapse ① *v.* revert, backslide, turn back, recede ② *n.* repetition, recurrence, setback

relate *v.* describe, recount, tell, mention, detail

related *adj.* associated, allied, connected, linked, akin ★**different**

relative ① *n.* kinsman, kinswoman, cousin, relation, sibling *I have four siblings—three sisters and one brother* ② *adj.* comparative, approximate, relevant

relax *v.* diminish, loosen, ease, reduce, relieve, unwind ★**tighten**

relaxed *adj.* composed, cool, easygoing, mellow ▷*casual* ★**tense**

A B C D E F G H I J K L M N O P Q R S T U V W X Y Z

release *v.* let go, loose, liberate, acquit, discharge ▷*free* ★**detain**

relent *v.* relax, soften, yield, ease, give in, unbend ★**harden**

relentless *adj.* unmerciful, remorseless, grim, pitiless ▷*cruel* ★**humane**

relevant *adj.* applicable, pertinent, appropriate, apt ▷*suitable* ★**irrelevant**

reliable *adj.* dependable, trustworthy, responsible, honest ▷*sound* ★**unreliable**

relic *n.* fragment, vestige, antique, keepsake, memento *This brooch is a memento of my great-grandmother; she wore it often*

relief *n.* aid, assistance, respite, support, succor ▷*help* ★**aggravation**

relieve *v.* release, support, comfort, lighten, relax, console ★**aggravate**

religious *adj.* pious, devout, orthodox, devoted, God-fearing, faithful

relinquish *v.* renounce, let go, waive, disclaim, give up ▷*abandon* ★**retain**

relish ① *v.* enjoy, like, approve ▷*appreciate* ★**loathe** ② *n.* savor, flavor, tang, gusto *The fried chicken was a great success; everyone ate with enormous gusto,* zest, sauce

reluctant *adj.* hesitant, averse, loth, disinclined, squeamish ★**willing**

rely on *v.* depend on, count on, believe in

remain *v.* ① stay, tarry, dwell, wait, rest ★**depart** ② persist, last, endure

remainder *n.* remnant, residue, leavings

remark *v.* ① utter, observe, state, mention ▷*say* ② notice, perceive, note ▷*see*

remarkable *adj.* unusual, surprising, curious, prominent ▷*outstanding* ★**ordinary**

remedy ① *n.* cure, restorative, medicine ② *n.* relief, solution, treatment, corrective ③ *v.* relieve, heal, cure, put right

remember *v.* recollect, recognize, think back ▷*recall* ★**forget**

remind *v.* suggest, hint, cue, prompt

remit *v.* ① relax, desist, slacken, modify, excuse, forgive ② pay, square, settle up

remnant *n.* residue, remains, rest ▷*remainder*

remorse *n.* regrets, contrition, pity

remote *adj.* ① distant, far, isolated ★**near** ② unrelated, alien, foreign ★**significant**

remove *v.* dislocate, take away, transfer, withdraw, carry off

rend *v.* split, fracture, tear apart, sever, break

render *v.* ① give, present, surrender, deliver ② play, execute, perform

renew *v.* ① modernize, mend, prolong, renovate ② reissue *Next week we start to reissue some of the old silent movies,* revive

renounce *v.* disown, disclaim, give up, repudiate, forsake ★**retain**

renowned *adj.* eminent, noted, famed, notable ▷*celebrated* ★**obscure**

rent ① *v.* hire, lease, let, charter ② *n.* tear, rip, break, crack, fissure ③ *n.* fee, payment

repair ① *v.* fix, mend, correct, remedy, rectify *We are sorry there was an error in your account; we will rectify it right away* ② *n.* restoration, adjustment

repast *n.* meal, food, snack, spread

repay *v.* ① refund, reimburse, pay ② avenge, retaliate, revenge, punish

repeal *v.* revoke, annul, abolish, quash *The man's innocence was proved and his sentence was quashed* ▷*cancel* ★**establish**

repeat *v.* duplicate, renew, reiterate, do again

repel *v.* ① repulse, deter, reject, push back ② revolt, disgust, nauseate ★**attract**

repellent *adj.* distasteful, hateful, discouraging ▷*repulsive* ★**attractive**

repent *v.* sorrow, deplore, grieve ▷*regret*

replace *v.* ① supersede, succeed, follow, substitute ② put back, reinstate, restore

replenish *v.* fill, refill, restock, furnish, provide, top up ★**empty**

replica *n.* facsimile, copy, likeness, duplicate

reply ① *v.* answer, respond, rejoin, retort, acknowledge ② *n.* answer, response, acknowledgment, riposte

report ① *n.* statement, account, message, communication, tidings ② *n.* noise, explosion, bang ③ *v.* tell, disclose, reveal, expose

repose ① *v.* rest, settle, lie down, sleep, recline ② *n.* ease, peace, quiet, tranquility ★**tumult**

represent *v.* ① depict, picture, portray, illustrate ② stand for, mean, denote

representative ① *n.* agent, delegate, envoy, deputy ② *adj.* typical, figurative

repress *v.* restrain, suppress, bottle up, smother, stifle

reprimand ① *v.* admonish, blame, rebuke ▷*chide* ② *n.* reproach, talking-to, scolding ★**praise**

reproach *v.* scold, reprove, reprimand, blame ▷*rebuke* ★**approve**

reproduce *v.* ① copy, duplicate, imitate, simulate ② breed, multiply, generate

reprove *v.* reproach, reprimand ▷*rebuke* ★**approve**

repudiate *v.* renounce, disown, disavow, disclaim ★**acknowledge**

repugnant *adj.* unattractive, disagreeable, offensive ▷*repulsive,* ★**pleasant**

repulse *v.* repel, rebuff, drive back, reject ▷*spurn* ★**attract**

repulsive *adj.* obnoxious, disgusting, loathsome ▷*repugnant* ★**attractive**

reputation *n.* standing, position, esteem, honor, good name

request ① *v.* demand, beg, entreat, beseech ▷*ask* ② *n.* petition, entreaty, invitation

require *v.* ① need, want, demand, crave ② expect, cause, instruct

rescue ① *v.* save, set free, liberate, recover, release ② *n.* liberation, deliverance, salvation *Salvation for the shipwrecked crew came when the coast guard lifted them to safety* ★**capture**

research *v.* examine, explore, investigate, inquire ▷*study*

resemble *v.* look like, mirror, take after, be like ★**differ**

resent *v.* resist, begrudge, dislike, take exception to ★**like**

resentful *adj.* offended, bitter, piqued, huffy ▷*indignant* ★**contented**

reserve ① *v.* hoard, retain, withhold ▷*keep* ② *n.* modesty, shyness, restraint ③ *n.* supply, backlog, stock

reservoir *n.* lake, spring, pool, container

reside *v.* live, occupy, inhabit, lodge ▷*dwell*

residence *n.* house, home, habitation, dwelling, mansion RESIDENTS

resign *v.* retire, abdicate, step down, give notice, abandon ▷*quit* ★**join**

resign oneself to *v.* accept, comply, reconcile *Robinson Crusoe became reconciled to loneliness on his island,* yield, give in ▷*submit* ★**resist**

resist *v.* withstand, oppose, defy, refrain, hinder ▷*thwart* ★**submit**

Rescue

Salvation for the shipwrecked crew came when the coast guard lifted them to safety.

resistance *n.* defiance, obstruction, opposition, hindrance ★**acceptance**

resolute *adj.* determined, resolved, obstinate, stubborn, dogged *Despite the bad weather, the climbers were dogged in their will to reach the peak* ★**weak**

resolve ① *v.* determine, intend, decide ② *v.* decipher, unravel, disentangle ③ *n.* resolution, purpose, will

resort ① *v.* frequent, haunt, visit ② *n.* alternative, chance, course ③ *n.* spa, watering place, hotel, vacation spot

resourceful *adj.* clever, ingenious, bright

respect ① *n.* esteem, honor, regard, repute, dignity ② *v.* esteem, honor, revere, venerate *The names of the pioneers and explorers will always be venerated*

respectable *adj.* decent, admirable, honest, honorable, proper ★**disreputable**

respectful *adj.* deferential, courteous, polite, dutiful ★**disrespectful**

respite *n.* break, halt, interval, lull, recess, letup

respond *v.* answer, reply, retort, tally, accord, agree ★**differ**

A B C D E F G H I J K L M N O P Q R S T U V W X Y Z

responsible *adj.* ① accountable, dependable, sensible 3*reliable* ★**unreliable** ② liable, guilty

rest ① *n.* repose, relaxation, peace, tranquillity ② *n.* break, pause, respite, spell ③ *n.* remainder, residue, balance ④ *v.* repose, settle, sleep, relax WREST

restful *adj.* peaceful, quiet, calm, placid ★**disturbing**

restless *adj.* uneasy, fitful, agitated, nervous, fretful ★**calm**

restore *v.* ① replace, reinstate, return ② refurbish, recondition, renovate *We renovated this old sofa which we found in a junk shop*

restrain *v.* stop, prevent, hold back, subdue 3*check* ★**encourage**

restrict *v.* confine, limit, cramp, handicap 3*regulate* ★**free**

result ① *n.* effect, consequence, outcome, end ★**cause** ② *v.* ensue, happen, turn out, follow, emerge, occur

resume *v.* renew, recommence, start again, go back to 3*continue* ★**interrupt**

retain *v.* hold, restrain, withhold, detain 3*keep* ★**relinquish**

retaliate *v.* avenge, reciprocate, fight back, repay, retort ★**submit**

retire *v.* ① retreat, go back 3*withdraw* ★**advance** ② abdicate, resign, relinquish

retort ① *n.* riposte, reply, rejoinder ② *v.* return, answer, reply

retract *v.* recant, deny, disavow, take back, revoke ★**maintain**

retreat ① *v.* retire, depart, shrink 3*withdraw* ★**advance** ② *n.* sanctuary *This section of the park is being made into a bird santuary,* shelter, den, haven

retrieve *v.* redeem, recover, regain, rescue 3*salvage* ★**lose**

return ① *v.* rejoin, come back, reappear ② *v.* restore, give back, repay, refund ③ *n.* form, tax form, document, list

reveal *v.* disclose, expose, show, display, uncover, divulge ★**hide**

revel ① *v.* make merry, celebrate, have fun ② *n.* celebration, gala, party, spree

revenge ① *n.* vengeance, reprisal, retaliation ② *v.* avenge, get one's own back

revenue *n.* income, receipts, earnings

revere *v.* honor, esteem, regard, adore, venerate, respect ★**despise**

reverse ① *v.* cancel, change, overrule, repeal, revoke ② *n.* adversity, disaster, bad luck, misfortune ③ *adj.* backward, contrary, opposite *We turned the car around and drove back in the opposite direction*

review ① *v.* reconsider, examine, survey ② *n.* inspection, examination ③ *n.* synopsis, journal, magazine REVUE

revise *v.* edit, amend, improve, rewrite, alter

revive *v.* awaken, rally, recover, refresh, restore, invigorate 3*rouse*

revoke *v.* repeal, abolish *The principal refuses to abolish the school dress code,* cancel, quash, reverse, withdraw

revolt ① *v.* rebel, mutiny, riot ② *v.* nauseate, sicken, disgust ③ *n.* rebellion, uprising, revolution

revolting *adj.* obnoxious *The chemical factory's chimney was giving off obnoxious fumes,* repulsive, offensive 3*repugnant* ★**pleasant**

revolve *v.* rotate, spin, gyrate, turn

reward ① *n.* award, payment, benefit, bonus, profit ★**punishment** ② *v.* compensate, repay, remunerate ★**punish**

rhyme *n.* verse, poem, ditty, ode RIME

rhythm *n.* beat, pulse, throb, stroke, timing

ribald *adj.* smutty, vulgar, coarse, gross

rich *adj.* ① wealthy, prosperous, affluent, opulent ★**poor** ② fertile, loamy, fruitful, abundant ★**barren** ③ delicious, sweet, luscious, delicate

rid *v.* get rid of, unburden, expel, free

riddle ① *n.* puzzle, cryptogram, enigma ② *v.* puncture, bore, perforate, pierce

ride ① *v.* sit, travel, drive, journey ② *n.* journey, jaunt, lift, trip

ridge *n.* ① groove, furrow, fold ② highland, chain, range *A range of hills could be seen in the distance*

ridicule ① *n.* scorn, derision, travesty, sarcasm, mockery ② *v.* deride, mock, jeer,

Rivers and Waterways

Arroyo
Brook
Canal
Channel
Creek
Lake
Loch
Pool
Pond
River
Spring
Strait
Stream
Surf
Waterfall

banter *His banter can be amusing, but he doesn't know when to stop and sometimes offends people*

ridiculous *adj.* laughable, absurd, foolish, preposterous ▷*silly* ★**sensible**

rife *adj.* common, current, frequent, prevalent ▷*widespread* ★**scarce**

rifle ① *v.* loot, rob, plunder ▷*ransack* ② *n.* gun, musket, firearm

rift *n.* ① fissure, breach, crack ② disagreement, clash, break

right ① *adj.* correct, proper, true ★**incorrect** ② *adj.* honest, upright, fair ③ *adj.* seemly, fit, suitable, becoming ★**improper** ④ *n.* truth, justice, honesty ★**wrong** RITE, WRITE

righteous *adj.* honorable, upright, moral

rigid *adj.* ① stiff, firm, inflexible ② stern, austere, harsh ★**flexible**

rigorous *adj.* stern, severe, strict, rigid

rim *n.* border, margin, edge, verge *We knew we were on the verge of disaster,* brink

ring ① *n.* circle, band, collar ② *n.* bell, chime, tinkle ③ *v.* chime, strike, jingle, sound WRING

riot ① *n.* uproar, tumult, brawl, broil ★**calm** ② *v.* revolt, rampage, rebel

ripe *adj.* ① mellow, mature, seasoned ② developed, adult, full-grown

rise ① *v.* ascend, mount, soar, arise, grow ★**fall** ② *v.* appear, occur, happen ★**vanish** ③ *n.* ascent, advance, increase ★**fall**

risk ① *v.* chance, dare, hazard, gamble ② *n.* adventure, peril, danger, jeopardy ★**safety**

risky *adj.* perilous, chancy, dangerous, tricky, uncertain ★**safe**

rite *n.* custom, ritual, practice RIGHT

rival ① *adj.* opposing, competing, conflicting ② *n.* opponent, adversary ★**associate**

river *n.* stream, waterway, brook, torrent *Before the rains came, this torrent was only a trickle*

road *n.* street, avenue, drive, lane, highway, freeway, route, way RODE, ROWED

roam *v.* rove, ramble, range, stroll, wander

roar *v.* bellow, bawl, yell, blare, cry

rob *v.* cheat, defraud, loot, plunder ▷*steal*

robber *n.* bandit, brigand, thief, crook

robe *n.* costume, dress, gown, habit

robust *adj.* strong, healthy, lusty, sturdy ▷*vigorous* ★**delicate**

rock ① *n.* stone, boulder, cobble, pebble, crag, reef ② *v.* totter, reel, sway, falter ③ *v.* quiet, still, tranquilize, soothe

rod *n.* baton, stick, stave, pole, perch, cane

rogue *n.* rascal, blackguard, scamp, knave ▷*scoundrel* ★**gentleman**

role *n.* character, post, duty, function *At the end of the party, my function will be to clear up*

roll ① *n.* record, register, list ② *n.* spool, scroll, reel ③ *v.* revolve, rotate, turn ④ *v.* smooth, level, press ⑤ *v.* lurch, reel, pitch, ROLE

romance *n.* ① love story, novel, love affair ② adventure, excitement, fantasy, glamour

romantic *adj.* ① amorous, passionate, loving ② visionary, fanciful *Many people have a fanciful idea of how things were in the old days,* fantastic, extravagant ★**ordinary**

romp *v.* gambol, caper, frolic, prance, play

roof *n.* ceiling, covering, cover, canopy

room *n.* ① apartment, chamber, area, compartment, salon ② space, capacity

A B C D E F G H I J K L M N O P Q R S T U V W X Y Z

root *n.* ① seed, source, radicle ② basis, element, stem, origin

rope *n.* cable, cord, hawser, line, lasso

rosy *adj.* ① cheerful, encouraging, hopeful, optimistic ② pink, flesh-colored

rot ① *v.* corrupt, crumble, decay, perish ② *n.* bunkum *The last speaker at the meeting was talking a lot of bunkum,* balderdash, bosh

rotate *v.* revolve, turn, spin, pivot, gyrate

rotten *adj.* ① decayed, putrid, decomposed, fetid ② deplorable, despicable, nasty, vicious ③ sick, ill, poorly

rough *adj.* ① wrinkled, craggy, coarse, shaggy, broken ② rude, crude, imperfect ③ blunt, gruff, brusque, discourteous RUFF

round ① *adj.* circular, rotund, spherical ② *n.* ring, circle, loop

rouse *v.* ① waken, arouse, excite, disturb ② anger, inflame, incite ★**calm**

rout *v.* crush, defeat, conquer, overthrow

route *n.* road, track, way, journey, direction

routine *n.* usage, practice, formula, technique, method, habit *After being alone for so long, I have gotten into the habit of talking to myself*

rove *v.* tramp, roam, wander, stroll, drift

row ① *n.* (ro) string, line, queue, rank, column ② *v.* paddle, scull ROE ③ *n.* (rhymes with *now*) fight, squabble, noise, quarrel, argument, dispute ★**calm**

rowdy *adj.* rough, unruly, boisterous, noisy, wild ★**quiet**

royal *adj.* sovereign, princely, stately, majestic ▷*regal*

rub *v.* stroke, brush, scrub, wipe, polish

rubbish *n.* debris, trash, junk, garbage

rude *adj.* ① coarse, primitive, ill-bred, impolite, boorish, bad-mannered ② crude, formless, shapeless ★**polished**
ROOD, RUED

rue *v.* be sorry for, deplore, grieve ▷*regret*

ruffian *n.* hoodlum, hooligan, lout, scoundrel, rogue, ▷*rascal*

ruffle *v.* ① fluster, worry, excite, agitate ② crumple, rumple, crease

ruffled *adj.* upset, worried, flustered,

Rulers, Monarchs, and Leaders

Caesar	Prime
Czar	Minister
Czarina	Prince
Emperor	Princess
Empress	Queen
King	Rajah
Mikado	Sultan
Mogul	
Pharaoh	
President	

harassed, bothered, irritated

rugged *adj.* ① rough, craggy, shaggy, ragged ② rigorous, robust, strong, strenuous

ruin *v.* ① demolish, wreck, damage, smash ② bankrupt, impoverish, overwhelm

rule ① *v.* control, govern, command, manage, direct ② *v.* decide, determine, judge ③ *n.* law, regulation ④ *n.* straightedge

ruler ① *n.* leader, director, king, queen, monarch, governor ② rule, straightedge

rumble *v.* roar, thunder, boom, roll

rumor *n.* hearsay, report, gossip, scandal *The bribery scandal, added to high taxes, brought down the government*

rumpus *n.* uproar, racket, riot, commotion, hurly-burly ★**calm**

run ① *v.* hurry, hasten, speed, sprint ★**saunter** ② *v.* leak, flow, ooze ③ *v.* operate, propel, drive ④ *n.* race, course

run away *v.* escape, flee, bolt, abscond ★**stay**

rupture *v. & n.* break, burst, puncture, split

rural *adj.* rustic, countrified, pastoral ★**urban**

ruse *n.* dodge, hoax, scheme, trick, ploy RUES

rush *v. & n.* dash, speed, hurry, scramble, stampede, rampage ★**saunter**

rust *n.* corrosion, mold, blight, mildew, stain, deterioration

rustic *adj.* rural, pastoral, country, homely, simple

rustle *n. & v.* crackle, swish, murmur, whisper

rut *n.* furrow, channel, groove, score, track

ruthless *adj.* cruel, savage, harsh, ferocious, pitiless ★**merciful**

S s

sack ① *n.* bag, pouch, pack ② *v.* rob, plunder, pillage ③ discharge, dismiss, lay off SAC

sacred *adj.* holy, blessed, hallowed, spiritual, consecrated, revered ★**profane**

sacrifice ① *n.* offering ② *v.* forfeit, give up, relinquish ▷*abandon*

sad *adj.* sorrowful, melancholy, unhappy, mournful, woeful ▷*sorry* ★**happy**

sadden *v.* mourn, grieve, distress, lament, dishearten, disappoint ★**please**

safe ① *adj.* secure, protected, sure ★**unsafe** ② *n.* vault, coffer, cashbox, strongbox

safety *n.* shelter, security, sanctuary, protection, refuge ★**danger**

sag *v.* bend, slump, curve, bow, decline, flag ▷*droop* ★**bulge**

sage ① *adj.* wise, sensible, shrewd, sagacious ★**foolish** ② *n.* wise person, savant *We were taught by an old savant of the university, Professor Hankins,* philosopher ★**fool**

said *adj.* expressed, stated

sail *v.* cruise, voyage, navigate, float, skim SALE

sailor *n.* seafarer, mariner, pilot, shipmate, captain, jack tar, seadog SAILER

sake *n.* motive, reason, purpose, object, principle

salary *n.* pay, earnings, reward, wages, income

sale *n.* auction, transaction, selling, trade, disposal SAIL

sally *n.* jest, joke, crack, riposte ▷*quip*

salute ① *v.* greet, accost, welcome, hail, honor ② *n.* greetings, welcome, acknowledgment

salvage *v.* save, conserve, rescue, restore, reclaim ▷*preserve* ★**abandon**

same *adj.* ① identical, duplicate, alike, similar ② aforesaid, aforementioned *I leave all my possessions to my wife, the aforementioned Angela Gomez*

sample ① *n.* specimen, example, model, pattern, illustration ② *v.* inspect, try, taste

sanction *v.* permit, allow, authorize, approve

sanctuary *n.* retreat, shelter, shrine, asylum, haven ▷*refuge*

sane *adj.* normal, rational, reasonable, lucid ▷*sensible* ★**insane**

sap *v.* bleed, drain, exhaust, reduce, weaken ★**strengthen**

sarcastic *adj.* biting, cutting, sardonic, cynical, ironic, caustic *My cousins made some caustic remarks after I played the violin*

satire *n.* invective, sarcasm, burlesque, ridicule, parody

satisfaction *n.* contentment, delight, gratification, compensation ★**grievance**

satisfy *v.* gratify, fulfill, appease, suit, please ▷*delight* ★**disappoint**

saturate *v.* soak, steep, drench, souse, waterlog *I am afraid that old canoe is too waterlogged ever to be used again*

saucy *adj.* forward, pert, impudent, cheeky, disrespectful ★**civil**

saunter *v.* roam, loiter, wander, linger, dawdle, amble ▷*stroll* ★**hasten**

savage ① *adj.* barbaric, wild, uncivilized, ferocious, brutal ★**civilized** ② *n.* brute, oaf, barbarian

save *v.* ① liberate, set free, rescue, protect,

Sacred Books

Apocrypha	Koran
Bhagavad-Gita	Talmud
Bible	Torah
Book of Mormon	Tripitaka
Book of Common Prayer	Upanishad
Granth	Veda

guard ② keep, preserve, salvage, hoard, put aside ★**squander**

savory *adj.* appetizing, flavorful, luscious, agreeable ★**tasteless**

say *v.* speak, utter, state, pronounce, talk, tell, assert

saying *n.* proverb, statement, adage, idiom, maxim, aphorism

scale ① *n.* measure, balance, calibration ② *n.* crust, plate, flake ③ *n.* clef, key *I will play this next piece in the key of C,* mode ④ *v.* climb, ascend, clamber up

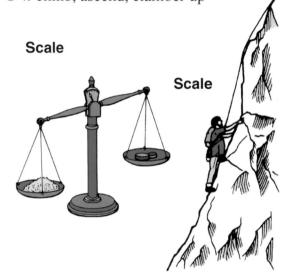

Scale

Scale

scamp *n.* knave, rogue, rascal, scoundrel, scalawag *Someone rang our doorbell, but when I opened the door, the scalawag had gone*

scamper *v.* hurry, run, scurry, hasten, sprint, scoot ▷*rush*

scan *v.* examine, glance at, scrutinize, pore over ▷*check*

scandal *n.* disgrace, libel, slander, offense, infamy, rumor, discredit ★**honor**

scanty *adj.* meager, insufficient, sparse, inadequate, poor, scant ★**plenty**

scar ① *n.* blemish, mark, stigma, wound ② *v.* brand, damage, disfigure

scarce *adj.* rare, infrequent, sparse, scanty, uncommon ★**common**

scarcity *n.* lack, deficiency, dearth, rarity, infrequency ★**abundance**

scare *v.* frighten, startle, shock, alarm, dismay ★**reassure**

scatter *v.* spread, disperse, strew, broadcast,

disseminate ▷*sprinkle* ★**collect**

scene *n.* sight, spectacle, vision, view, exhibition, landscape SEEN

scent ① *n.* aroma, tang, fragrance, smell, odor ② *v.* detect, sniff, smell CENT, SENT

schedule *n.* timetable *We checked the timetable before buying our train tickets,* program, catalog, diary

scheme *n.* plot, plan, project, design, proposal, idea

scholar *n.* ① pupil, student, schoolchild, learner ② intellectual *That café is a favorite gathering place for intellectuals,* savant, academic

scholarly *adj.* learned, educated, literate, cultured ★**illiterate**

scoff *v.* sneer, mock, deride, jeer, ridicule ★**respect**

scold *v.* rebuke, admonish, reprove, find fault with ▷*chide* ★**praise**

scoop ① *v.* bail, ladle, spoon, excavate, gouge, hollow ② *n.* exclusive, inside story, coup

scope *n.* extent, margin, compass, range, latitude, field

scorch *v.* sear, burn, singe, blister, shrivel

score *v.* ① cut, mark, scratch ② register, record, win

scorn ① *n.* mockery, disdain, ridicule, disregard ② *v.* despise, mock, spurn, slight ★**respect**

scoundrel *n.* rascal, knave, thief, rogue, villain ▷*vagabond* ★**gentleman**

scour *v.* ① cleanse, rinse, scrub, purge ② search, seek, ransack, rake

scourge ① *v.* beat, whip, thrash, cane ② *n.* curse, evil, misfortune, plague ★**blessing**

scowl *v. & n.* frown, glower, grimace, glare ★**smile**

scramble ① *v.* clamber, climb ② *v.* jostle, struggle, swarm, push ③ *n.* turmoil, bustle, confusion ★**order**

scrap ① *n.* piece, morsel, bit, portion, fragment, grain ② *v.* abandon, discard, junk

scrape ① *v.* scratch, groove, abrade, file, grate, scour ② *n.* predicament, fix, difficulty

scratch *v. & n.* wound, cut, mark, score

scream *v. & n.* screech, cry, shriek, howl, yell

screen ① *n.* awning *Before the ceremony, an awning was erected over the entrance to the hotel,* canopy, shade, protection ② *v.* protect, hide, conceal, veil

screw *v.* twist, turn, wrench, tighten, compress

scribble *v.* write, scrawl, scratch

scribe *n.* writer, penman, clerk, historian

script *n.* handwriting, manuscript, text, words, libretto *Sir Arthur Sullivan wrote the music for* The Mikado, *and W. S. Gilbert wrote the lyrics and libretto*

scrub ① *v.* scour, brush, mop, cleanse ② *n.* brushwood, undergrowth

scruffy *adj.* messy, dirty, frowzy, seedy, shabby, sloppy ▷*slovenly* ★**neat**

scrumptious *adj.* delightful, delicious, appetizing, exquisite

scrupulous *adj.* painstaking, particular, rigorous, strict, conscientious ★**careless**

scrutinize *v.* examine, inspect, peruse, study

scuffle *v. & n.* tussle, skirmish, fight, struggle, squabble

scum *n.* dross, foam, froth, dregs, crust

scuttle *v.* ① scramble, scamper, scoot, hurry ② destroy, smash, wreck

seal ① *n.* signet, stamp ② *n.* cork, bung, closure ③ *n.* sea mammal ④ *v.* fasten, close, shut

seam ① *n.* ridge, scar, lode, furrow ② hem, pleat, tuck SEEM

search ① *v.* seek, quest, hunt, trail, track, scour, explore ② *n.* exploration, investigation, quest, pursuit

season ① *n.* period, time, occasion, term ② *v.* accustom, acclimatize, mature ③ *v.* flavor, spice, salt

seat ① *n.* bench, chair, stool, sofa, couch, throne ② *n.* headquarters, place, site ③ *v.* accommodate, locate, place

secret *adj.* mysterious, hidden, concealed, obscure, private ★**public**

section *n.* division, group, department, segment, portion

secure ① *adj.* safe, protected ② *adj.* confident, certain, sure, stable ★**uncertain** ③ *v.* fasten, protect, close, lock ★**unfasten** ④ *v.* acquire, procure, obtain ★**lost**

sedate *adj.* staid, sober, demure, earnest ▷*steady* ★**flippant**

see *v.* ① behold, witness, sight, observe ② heed, examine, watch, note ③ understand, comprehend, know SEA

seedy *adj.* shabby, squalid, poor, grubby, unkempt ▷*slovenly* ★**spruce**

seek *v.* look for, search, inquire, endeavor, hunt

seem *v.* appear, look like, sound like, look as if SEAM

seemly *adj.* fit, suitable, proper, decent, decorous ★**unseemly**

seethe *v.* simmer, fizz, bubble, boil, foam

seize *v.* grasp, snatch, take, clutch, arrest ▷*grab* ★**abandon** SEAS, SEES

seldom *adv.* rarely, infrequently, hardly, scarcely ★**often**

select ① *adj.* choice, preferred, fine, prime *All the fruit on the trees in the orchard is in its prime,* first-class ★**common** ② *v.* choose, pick out, single out, prefer

selfish *adj.* greedy, self-centered, narrow, illiberal ▷*stingy* ★**generous**

sell *v.* vend, market, retail, trade, peddle ★**buy**

send *v.* transmit, dispatch, forward, mail, direct ★**detain**

send for *v.* command, order, summon, request ★**dismiss**

sensation *n.* ① feeling, perception, impression, awareness ② excitement, commotion, scandal

sensational *adj.* exceptional, scandalous, lurid ▷*exciting* ★**ordinary**

sense *n.* ① sensation, impression, feeling ② understanding, mind, tact, intellect ③ wisdom, significance, meaning CENTS, SCENTS

senseless *adj.* silly, stupid, absurd ▷*foolish* ★**sensible**

sensible *adj.* ① wise, intelligent, astute, shrewd ② reasonable, rational ③ conscious, aware, mindful ★**senseless**

sensitive *adj.* ① susceptible, responsive, acute, impressionable *Because Rachel is at such an impressionable age, her mother does not want her to see the movie* ② thin-

A
B
C
D
E
F
G
H
I
J
K
L
M
N
O
P
Q
R
S
T
U
V
W
X
Y
Z

skinned, touchy

sentence *n.* ① phrase, clause ② judgment, decision, condemnation, doom

sentimental *adj.* romantic, tender, emotional

separate ① *adj.* disconnected, apart, detached ★**united** ② *v.* detach, part, divide, break, disconnect ★**unite**

sequel *n.* continuation, consequence, result, outcome

serene *adj.* tranquil, calm, peaceful, undisturbed, clear ★**tempestuous**

series *n.* sequence, progression, succession, run, string

serious *adj.* grave, earnest, solemn, thoughtful, severe, grim ★**trivial**

serve *v.* attend, assist, aid, oblige, help, officiate, act

service *n.* ① aid, help, assistance, attendance, employment ② ceremony, rite *Stuart is at college studying the marriage rites of the Incas*

set ① *n.* group, pack, outfit, series ② *v.* settle, put, place, seat, locate ③ *v.* stiffen, congeal, harden ④ *adj.* decided, resolved, determined, fixed

setback *n.* defeat, delay, problem, snag, holdup ★**advantage**

settle *v.* ① establish, regulate, fix ② pay, liquidate, finish ③ populate, colonize ④ live, dwell, reside

several *adj.* various, numerous, sundry, separate

severe *adj.* strict, rigid, unkind, hard, austere ▷*stern* ★**lenient**

sew *v.* stitch, tack, baste, fasten, seam so, sow

shabby *adj.* torn, ragged, mean, shoddy, tacky ▷*squalid* ★**neat**

shack *n.* hut, cabin, shanty, shed, hovel

shackle *v. & n.* manacle, handcuff, chain, rope, fetter

shade *n.* ① shadow, gloom, darkness, dusk ② blind, awning, screen ③ color, tint, hue, tone ④ ghost, spirit, wraith *Out of the darkness, a wraithlike figure loomed up before us*

shadow ① *n.* shade ② *v.* follow, stalk, tail

shady *adj.* ① shadowy, shaded ★**sunny** ②

crooked, infamous, disreputable ★**honest**

shaft *n.* ① pillar, column, support ② hilt, handle, rod ③ mine, pit, well, tunnel

shaggy *adj.* hairy, tousled, unkempt, rough ★**smooth**

shake *v.* flutter, tremble, throb, shudder ▷*quiver*

shallow *adj.* ① not deep ② trivial, empty, silly, empty-headed ★**profound**

sham *adj.* false, imitation, counterfeit, forged ▷*bogus* ★**genuine**

shame *n. & v.* dishonor, discredit ▷*disgrace*

Ships and Boats

Gondola

Catamaran

Kayak

shameful *adj.* disgraceful, scandalous, outrageous ▷*disreputable* ★**honorable**

shape ① *n.* form, structure, outline, pattern ② *v.* form, fashion, make, create

share ① *v.* allot, divide, participate, co-operate ② *n.* portion, allotment, allowance

sharp *adj.* ① acute, keen, pointed ② clear, distinct, clean-cut ③ painful, severe, intense ④ pungent, acrid, acid ⑤ alert, shrewd, acute ▷*clever* ★**dull**

shatter *v.* smash, wreck, break, fracture, ruin ▷*destroy*

shave *v.* shear, crop, slice, shred, graze, trim

shear *v.* fleece, strip, cut ▷*shave* SHEER

sheath *n.* scabbard, quiver, holster, holder, case, casing

shed ① *n.* hut, barn, lean-to, shanty ② *v.* cast off, molt *Our parrot is molting and is leaving feathers all over the carpet,* spill ③ *v.* beam, radiate

sheepish *adj.* timid, diffident, foolish, embarrassed, shamefaced ★**unabashed**

sheer *adj.* ① absolute, simple, pure, unmixed ② transparent, filmy, thin ③ steep,

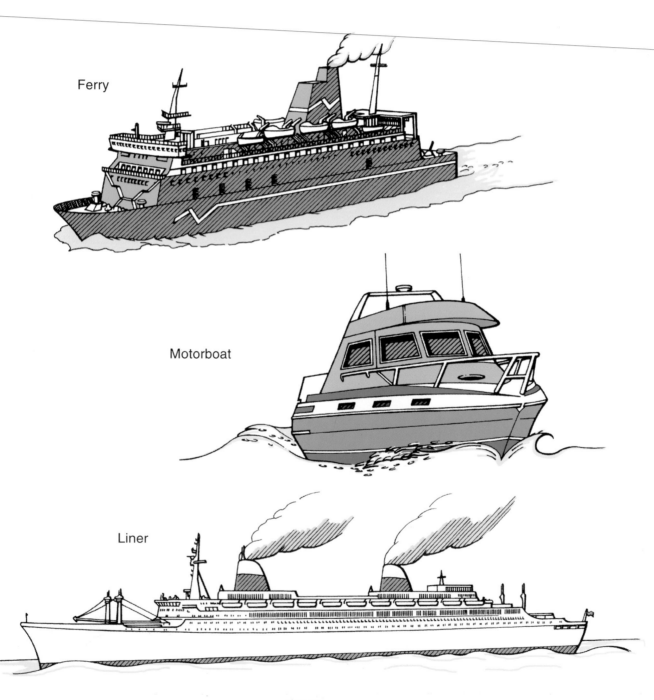

Ferry

Motorboat

Liner

A
B
C
D
E
F
G
H
I
J
K
L
M
N
O
P
Q
R
S
T
U
V
W
X
Y
Z

abrupt, perpendicular *The trail ended at the foot of a huge, perpendicular cliff* SHEAR

shell *n.* pod, case, husk, hull, shuck, crust

shelter ① *n.* roof, sanctuary, safety, home, retreat, cover ② *v.* shield, cover, protect, screen ★**expose**

shield *n. & v.* guard, screen, safeguard ▷*shelter*

shift ① *v.* alter, move, change, displace, remove ② *n.* turn, spell, stint

shifty *adj.* untrustworthy, devious, treacherous ▷*wily* ★**honest**

shine *v. & n.* glow, gleam, glitter, sparkle, flash

ship ① *n.* boat, barge, craft, vessel ② *v.* export, send, transport *(see page 114)*

shirk *v.* dodge, avoid, shun, evade, slack

shiver *v.* quaver, quiver, shake, shudder ▷*tremble*

shock ① *n.* blow, jolt, clash, collision ② *n.* scare, start, turn ③ *v.* stupefy, daze, stun

shocking *adj.* scandalous, awful, frightful ▷*horrible* ★**agreeable**

shoot *v.* ① fire, discharge, bombard, propel ② *v.* germinate *We grew some beans in a glass jar and watched them germinate,* grow, bud, sprout ③ *n.* bud, twig, sprout CHUTE

shop ① *n.* store, market, emporium ② *v.* buy, market, purchase

shore ① *n.* beach, coast, strand, seashore, seaside ② *v.* prop, support, bolster up, brace

short *adj.* ① brief, concise, condensed ★**long** ② deficient, incomplete, scanty ★**full** ③ sharp, severe, bad-tempered ④ small, puny, squat, diminutive, tiny ★**tall**

shortcoming *n.* defect, fault, flaw, inadequacy, ▷*weakness*

shorten *v.* cut, crop, abbreviate, lessen ▷*diminish* ★**lengthen**

shortened *adj.* abbreviated, abridged, condensed ★**enlarged**

shortly *adj.* presently, soon, before long, directly

shout *n. & v.* cry, scream, roar, shriek, cheer, whoop, bellow

shove *v.* push, jostle, prod, nudge, move, propel ★**pull**

show ① *v.* display, parade, exhibit, flaunt, reveal ★**hide** ② *v.* prove, testify to, demonstrate ③ *v.* explain, teach, instruct ④ *n.* exhibition, display, ceremony, play

shower ① *v.* scatter, spray, sprinkle, rain ② *n.* downpour, cloudburst ③ *n.* barrage, volley, discharge

shred ① *n.* particle, piece, scrap, tatter, fragment ② *v.* tear, rip, strip

shrewd *adj.* profound, deep, discerning ▷*wise* ★**obtuse**

shriek *n. & v.* screech ▷*shout*

shrill *adj.* treble, high-pitched, screeching, ear-piercing

shrink *v.* ① contract, dwindle, shrivel, become smaller ② flinch, cringe, recoil, withdraw

shrivel *v.* wither, contract, wrinkle, decrease, pucker, parch ▷*wilt*

shudder *v.* shake, quake, tremble ▷*quiver*

shuffle *v.* ① mix, jumble, rearrange ② hobble, limp

shun *v.* avoid, elude, ignore, spurn, steer clear of ★**accept**

shut *v.* fasten, close, secure, slam, bar, latch, lock ★**open**

shut up *v.* ① imprison, cage, intern ② be silent, hold one's tongue, be quiet

shy ① *adj.* bashful, diffident, timid, wary, shrinking ★**bold** ② *v.* flinch, quail, recoil

sick *adj.* ① ill, poorly, ailing, unwell, feeble ② weary, fed up, displeased ③ nauseated

side *n.* ① border, edge, flank, margin, half ② party, sect, group, team SIGHED

sift *v.* strain, drain, separate, screen, sieve, riddle

sigh *v.* ① grieve, lament, moan, complain ② wheeze, breathe

sight ① *n.* appearance, spectacle, scene, mirage ② *n.* seeing, perception, visibiity ③ *v.* behold, glimpse, observe CITE, SITE

sign ① *n.* symbol, emblem, mark ② *n.* omen, token ③ *n.* signboard, signpost, placard ④ *v.* endorse, autograph, inscribe

signal ① *n.* beacon *As soon as the ships*

were sighted, beacons were lit all along the coast, sign, flag, indicator ② *adj.* distinguished, impressive, outstanding

significant *adj.* symbolical, meaningful, weighty ▷*important* ★**unimportant**

signify *v.* denote, indicate, suggest, imply ▷*mean*

silence *n.* quiet, hush, peace, tranquility ★**noise**

silent *adj.* hushed, noiseless, soundless, still, mute ▷*quiet* ★**noisy**

silly *adj.* absurd, senseless, stupid, fatuous ▷*foolish* ★**wise**

similar *adj.* resembling, alike, harmonious, common ▷*like* ★**different**

simple *adj.* ① elementary, plain, uncomplicated ▷*easy* ② trusting, open, naive ★**intricate**

simply *adv.* merely, purely, barely, solely, only

sin ① *n.* misdeed, wrong, vice, evil, wickedness ② *v.* err, offend, trespass, stray, do wrong

since ① *conj.* because, as, for, considering ② *prep.* subsequently, after

sincere *adj.* true, unaffected, frank, open, truthful ▷*genuine* ★**insincere**

sing *v.* vocalize, warble, yodel, trill, croon, chant, carol, hum, chirp

singe *v.* scorch, burn, scald, sear, char

singer *n.* vocalist, minstrel, songster, chorister, crooner

single *adj.* ① one, only, sole ② solitary, alone, separate ③ unmarried, celibate *The priests of the Roman Catholic Church are celibate*

singular *adj.* odd, peculiar, curious, surprising ▷*unusual* ★**ordinary**

sinister *adj.* menacing, threatening, unlucky, disastrous ▷*evil* ★**harmless**

sink ① *v.* drop, dip, descend, decline ▷*fall* ★**rise** ② *n.* basin, drain

sit *v.* perch, seat, squat, roost, rest, settle

site *n.* spot, plot, locality, place, station, post ▷*situation* CITE, SIGHT

situation *n.* ① position, location, place, site, whereabouts, standpoint ② predicament, plight, state

Singers

Alto
Baritone
Bass
Basso profundo
Cantor
Chorister
Contrabass
Contralto
Countertenor
Mezzo-soprano
Prima donna
Soprano
Tenor
Treble
Vocalist

size *n.* ① dimensions, proportions, measurement ② magnitude, bulk, volume, weight SIGHS

skeptical *adj.* doubtful, unbelieving, incredulous ▷*dubious* ★**convinced**

sketch ① *n.* drawing, picture, cartoon ② *n.* draft, blueprint, outline ③ *v.* draw, portray, depict, outline

skillful *adj.* adroit, able, adept, dexterous, expert, competent ▷*clever* ★**clumsy**

skill *n.* ability, expertness, knack, facility ▷*talent*

skim *v.* brush, touch, graze, float, glide

skimp *v.* stint, scrimp, economize, scrape

skin *n.* peel, rind, hide, husk, pelt

skinny *adj.* thin, lean, scraggy, weedy ★**fat**

skip *v.* ① jump, hop, dance, caper ② pass over, miss, disregard, omit

skirmish *n. & v.* scuffle, fight, affray, scrap, combat, clash

skirt ① *n.* petticoat, kilt ② *n.* border, hem, edge, margin ③ *v.* border, flank, evade, avoid

skulk *v.* lurk, hide, cower, slink, sneak

slab *n.* board, stone, boulder, piece, chunk

slack *adj.* ① limp, flabby, loose, relaxed ★**tight** ② lazy, sluggish ▷*idle* ★**busy**

slander *v.* libel, malign, accuse, abuse ▷*defame* ★**praise**

slant ① *v. & n.* incline, angle, cant ▷*slope*

slap *v.* smack, whack, strike, hit, spank

slash *v. & n.* cut, slit, gash, hack, rip

slaughter *v.* slay, butcher, massacre ▷*kill*

slave ① *n.* bondsman, bondswoman, serf, vassal, drudge, captive ② *v.* drudge, toil, labor, grind

slavery *n.* bondage, enslavement, serfdom, servility, drudgery, captivity ★**freedom**

slay *v.* murder, massacre ▷*kill* SLEIGH

sleek *adj.* shiny, smooth, glossy, slick

sleep *v. & n.* snooze, nap, doze, drowse, repose, slumber

slender *adj.* ① narrow, thin, fine, slight ▷*slim* ★**thick** ② trivial, inadequate, meager

slice ① *v.* shred, shave, cut, strip, segment ② *n.* segment, piece, cut, slab

slick *adj.* ① shiny, smooth ▷*sleek* ② glib, suave, plausible

slide *v.* slip, slither, glide, skim, skate

slight ① *adj.* delicate, tender ▷*slender* ② *adj.* small, little, meager, trifling, trivial ★**significant** ③ *n. & v.* snub, insult, disdain

slim *adj.* fine, slight ▷*slender* ★**fat**

slime *n.* mire, ooze, mud, filth

sling ① *v.* hurl, toss, throw ② *n.* loop, bandage, strap, support

slink *v.* prowl, creep, sidle, sneak ▷*skulk*

slip ① *v.* slide, slither, glide ② *v.* fall, lurch, drop, slip over ③ *v. & n.* blunder, slip up

slippery *adj.* ① smooth, glassy ② tricky, untrustworthy, cunning ▷*shifty* ★**trustworthy**

slit *v.* gash, cut, rip ▷*slash*

slogan *n.* motto, catchword, war cry, saying

slope ① *n.* slant, grade, gradient, incline, ascent, descent, rise ② *v.* lean, incline, descend, ascend

sloppy *adj.* ① careless, slipshod, inattentive ▷*slovenly* ② dowdy, messy, tacky ③ dingy, dirty

slot *n.* recess, opening, hole, groove

slovenly *adj.* slipshod, careless, negligent, disorderly, sloppy, untidy, dowdy

slow ① *adj.* inactive, tardy, late, slack, leisurely ▷*sluggish* ★**fast** ② *v.* slow down, slacken, lose speed, relax ★**accelerate** SLOE

sluggish *adj.* slothful, lazy, inactive, languid, indolent, lifeless ▷*idle* ★**brisk**

slumber *v.* snooze, doze ▷*sleep* ★**awaken**

sly *adj.* cunning, tricky, furtive, sneaky, artful ▷*wily* ★**frank**

smack *v.* slap, strike, spank ▷*hit*

small *adj.* ① minute, tiny, slight, diminutive ▷*little* ★**large** ② trivial, petty, feeble, paltry, inferior

smart ① *adj.* alert, bright ▷*intelligent* ② *adj.* elegant, neat, spruce, dressy ★**dull** ③ *v.* sting, burn, throb ▷*ache*

smash *v.* break, hit, destroy, wreck, demolish

smear *v.* plaster, daub, coat, varnish, cover, spread, smudge

smell *n.* aroma, fragrance, scent, perfume, stink, stench, odor, tang

smile *v.* grin, simper, smirk, beam ▷*laugh*

smoke ① *n.* vapor, mist, gas ② *v.* fume, reek, whiff, smolder, vent

smooth ① *adj.* level, even, flat, plain, sleek ★**rough** ② *v.* flatten, level, press

smother *v.* choke, throttle, stifle, restrain

smudge *n. & v.* mark, smear, blur, stain, blight

smug *adj.* self-satisfied, content, complacent, conceited

smut *n.* dirt, smudge, blot, spot, smear

snack *n.* lunch, repast, morsel, bite

snag *n.* catch, complication, drawback, hitch

snap *v.* ① break, crack, snip ② snarl, growl

snare ① *v.* trap, catch, seize, net ② *n.* trap, noose, pitfall

snatch *v.* seize, grab, clutch, grip, take, pluck, grasp

sneak ① *v.* slink, prowl, crouch ▷*skulk* ② *n.* wretch, coward, informer

sneer *v.* jeer, scoff, gibe, scorn, ridicule, taunt

sniff *v.* smell, breathe in, inhale, scent

snivel *v.* weep, cry, blub, sniffle

snobbish *adj.* condescending, snooty, lofty, patronizing, stuck-up

snoop *v.* pry, eavesdrop, peep, peek, sneak

snooze *v.* doze, nap, slumber ▷*sleep*

snub *v.* slight, slur, spurn, cut ▷*humiliate*

snug *adj.* cozy, sheltered, secure, safe,

restful ▷*comfortable*

so *adv.* accordingly, thus, therefore, likewise SEW, SOW

soak *v.* moisten, wet, douse, saturate, steep

soar *v.* glide, fly, rise, hover, tower SORE

sob *v.* lament, cry, sigh ▷*weep*

sober *adj.* temperate, abstemious *Uncle Arthur was very abstemious and never drank anything alcoholic,* calm, composed, serious, somber ★**excited**

sociable *adj.* companionable, affable, friendly, genial ★**withdrawn**

social *adj.* neighborly, civic, public ② convivial ▷*sociable*

soft *adj.* ① pliable, plastic, flexible, supple ★**hard** ② kind, gentle, mild ▷*tender* ★**harsh** ③ low, faint, quiet ★**loud**

soften *v.* ① melt, dissolve, mellow ★**solidify** ② moderate, diminish, quell

soil ① *n.* earth, dirt, mold ② *v.* foul, dirty, sully, taint

sole *adj.* only, single, lone, one SOUL

solemn *adj.* ① grim, serious ▷*somber* ② impressive, stately, sedate ★**frivolous**

solid *adj.* ① steady, firm, stable, sturdy ② dense, compact, hard ★**soft**

solidify *v.* congeal, harden, clot, cake, set ★**soften**

solitary *adj.* alone, lonely, remote, separate, only

solution *n.* ① blend, mixture, brew, fluid ② answer, explanation

solve *v.* unravel, untangle, elucidate ▷*explain* ★**complicate**

somber *adj.* dark, serious, solemn, grim, gloomy, funereal ★**bright**

some *adj.* any, more or less, about, several SUM

sometimes *adv.* at times, from time to time, occasionally

somewhat *adv.* in part, a little, not much

song *n.* air, tune, carol, ballad, ode, ditty *The new pop song was based on an old sailors' ditty*

soon *adv.* presently, shortly, before long

soothe *v.* pacify, appease, mollify, ease, lull, comfort ★**irritate**

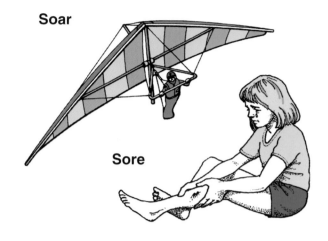

Soar

Sore

sordid *adj.* shabby, miserable, dirty, base ▷*squalid*

sore ① *adj.* tender, aching, painful, inflamed ② *adj.* annoyed, upset, grieved ③ *n.* ulcer, boil, carbuncle SOAR

sorrow ① *n.* grief, woe, remorse, anguish ★**joy** ② *v.* mourn, grieve, lament ★**rejoice**

sorrowful *adj.* sad, disconsolate, mournful, dejected ★**joyful**

sorry *adj.* ① pained, grieved, hurt, dejected, doleful ★**glad** ② wretched, mean, poor, shabby ★**delighted**

sort ① *n.* kind, type, variety, group, class ② *v.* sift, arrange, catalog, classify

soul *n.* spirit, substance, mind, vitality, fire, essence SOLE

sound ① *n.* noise, din, tone ★**silence** ② *v.* blare, blast *We were startled by a blast from the trumpets,* blow ③ *adj.* hearty, virile, whole, perfect ▷*healthy* ★**unfit**

sour *adj.* ① tart, rancid, bitter, acid ★**sweet** ② morose, peevish ▷*harsh* ★**genial**

source *n.* origin, spring, fount, cause, beginning

souvenir *n.* token, memento, keepsake, reminder, relic

sow ① *n.* (rhymes with *how*) female pig ② *v.* (rhymes with *mow*) *v.* plant, scatter, strew SEW, SO

space *n.* ① extent, expanse, capacity, room, accommodation ② the universe, the heavens, firmament

spacious *adj.* roomy, extensive, commodious, broad, wide ★**restricted**

span ① *n.* stretch, reach, extent, length ② *v.*

A B C D E F G H I J K L M N O P Q R S T U V W X Y Z

cross, bridge, link, connect

spare ① *adj.* extra, reserve, surplus ② *adj.* bare, meager, poor, scanty ▷*sparse* ③ *v.* afford, preserve, give, allow

sparkle *v.* glitter, glow, gleam, glint, twinkle

sparse *adj.* scanty, thin ▷*meager* ★**dense**

spate *n.* flood, flow, deluge, rush, torrent

speak *v.* say, utter, talk, pronounce, lecture, express

spear *n.* pike, javelin, lance

special *adj.* distinct, different, unique, individual ▷*particular* ★**common**

species *n.* breed, kind, sort, class, family

specific *adj.* definite, exact, precise ▷*special*

specimen *n.* sample, example, type, model, pattern

speck *n.* dot, speckle, spot, particle

spectacle *n.* sight, scene, exhibition, presentation ▷*display*

spectacles *n.* glasses, eyeglasses

spectacular *adj.* wonderful, fabulous, surprising ▷*marvelous*

spectator *n.* onlooker, witness, observer

speech *n.* ① talk, tongue *The people spoke a strange tongue we had never heard,* language ② address, lecture

speed *n.* velocity, rapidity, dispatch, pace, tempo *The tempo of life in the quiet seaside town was much too slow for us*

speedy *adj.* swift, rapid, fleet, quick, lively ▷*fast* ★**slow**

spell ① *n.* charm, magic, witchcraft ② *n.* period, term, space, time ③ *v.* form words, write out

spend *v.* ① expend, lay out, lavish, pay, disburse ② exhaust, use up

spendthrift *n.* wastrel, squanderer, prodigal ★**miser**

sphere *n.* ① globe, ball, orb, planet ② realm, orbit, domain, field

spice *n.* seasoning, flavoring, zest, relish, savor

spill *v.* pour, stream, run, overflow, spurt, upset

spin *v.* revolve, rotate, turn, whirl, make thread

spine *n.* backbone, needle, quill *The porcupine is covered in sharp quills,* ridge

spirit *n.* ① essence, substance, nature, character ② soul, air, breath ③ vigor, energy, courage ④ phantom, specter, ghost

spiritual *adj.* ① religious, divine, unworldly, holy ② pure, immaterial

spite ① *n.* malice, rancor, hostility, hatred ② *v.* grudge, annoy, offend, injure

spiteful *adj.* vicious, malicious, vindictive ▷*hateful* ★**kind**

splash *v.* wet, spatter, shower, sprinkle

splendid *adj.* grand, brilliant, magnificent, showy, glorious ▷*sumptuous* ★**ordinary**

splendor *n.* glory, pageantry, brilliance ▷*pomp*

split *v.* cleave, sever *Our family quarreled with our cousins and severed relationships for years,* crack, snap, splinter

spoil *v.* ① hurt, injure, harm ② deface, disfigure, destroy ③ rot, decompose, putrefy, decay

spoiled *adj.* decayed, rotten, broken up, corroded

spontaneous *adj.* natural, impulsive, self-generated, voluntary

spoof *n.* ① hoax, joke, bluff, prank, satire ② quip, jest, wisecrack

sport ① *n.* game, amusement, fun, athletics, recreation ② *v.* play, frolic, gambol, romp

Spices

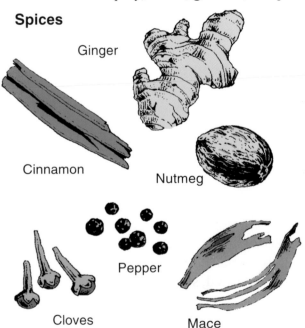

Ginger

Cinnamon

Nutmeg

Pepper

Cloves

Mace

spot ① *n.* dot, speck, mark, stain, blemish ②
v. espy, notice, recognize, distinguish

spotless *adj.* pure, clean, unstained,
faultless, perfect

sprawl *v.* recline, stretch, extend, lie
▷*lounge*

spray *v.* sprinkle, squirt, splash, shower

spread *v.* ① scatter, strew, sow, circulate ②
extend, stretch, expand, open

sprightly *adj.* lively, vivacious, cheerful,
agile ▷*brisk* ★**sluggish**

spur *v.* arouse, drive, urge, incite

spurious *adj.* fake, counterfeit, false
▷*bogus* ★**genuine**

spurn *v.* reject, scorn, disdain, disregard
▷*snub* ★**respect**

spurt *v.* ① stream, squirt, emerge, gush ②
hurry, hasten, rush

spy ① *n.* agent, detective, observer, snooper,
scout ② *v.* see, glimpse, pry, peek, spot

squabble ① *n. & v.* quarrel, clash, fight,
row ▷*dispute*

squad *n.* group, company, troop, force,
band, team

squalid *adj.* foul, dirty, untended, poverty-
stricken ▷*sordid* ★**clean**

squall ① *n.* blast, gust, blow, tempest ② *v.*
blubber, cry, bawl, howl

squander *v.* misspend, waste, fritter, lavish

squash *v.* ① mash, crush, squelch, pound ②
quell, suppress, humiliate

squat ① *adj.* dumpy, stocky, tubby, plump ②
v. crouch, sit, roost, perch

squeal *v.* squawk, squeak, cheep, grunt, cry

squeamish *adj.* fastidious, delicate, finicky,
nauseous

squeeze *v.* compress, press, constrict, force,
pinch

squirm *v.* wriggle, fidget, flounder, twist
▷*writhe*

squirt *v.* spray, splash ▷*spurt*

stab *v. & n.* cut, jab, puncture, wound, thrust

stable ① *adj.* firm, steady, solid, constant,
durable, lasting ★**unstable** ② *n.* barn,
cowshed, shed, stall

stack ① *n.* pile, pack, bundle, sheaf, heap ②
v. assemble, pile up, amass

staff *n.* ① stick, cane, pole, rod ② team,
workers, force, personnel

stage ① *n.* platform, dais, scaffold, podium
*The famous conductor stood on the podium
and raised his baton,* arena ② *n.* step,
degree, position ③ *v.* perform, produce,
present, put on

stagger *v.* reel, totter, waver, lurch

stagnant *adj.* motionless, inactive, still,
quiet, sluggish

staid *adj.* serious, steady, earnest, sober,
demure ▷*sedate* ★**frivolous** STAYED

stain ① *n.* blemish, blur, spot, blot ② *n.*
disgrace, shame ③ *v.* tarnish, sully, blemish,
defile

stair *n.* step, rung, spoke, footrest STARE

stake ① *n.* stick, stave, paling, spike, pole
▷*staff* ② *n.* bet, claim, wager, involvement
③ *v.* prop, secure, support STEAK

stale *adj.* ① musty, old, tasteless, faded ②
common, trite, banal, flat ★**fresh**

stalk *v.* ① hunt, chase, follow, pursue,
shadow ② swagger, strut, stride, parade

stall ① *v.* tarry, delay, hedge, obstruct,
hamper ★**advance** ② *n.* compartment,
booth, stand, bay

stalwart *adj.* rugged, sturdy, stout, lusty
▷*valiant* ★**timid**

stamina *n.* endurance, vitality, strength,
power, energy ★**weakness**

stammer *v.* stutter, falter, hesitate, stumble

stamp ① *v.* print, imprint, mark, impress ②
n. impression, mark, print, brand ③ *n.* kind,
make, genus, cast ④ *n.* seal, sticker

stand ① *n.* board, counter, table, platform
▷*stall* ② *v.* rest, put, locate, place ③ *v.*
tolerate, put up with, abide, endure
★**oppose** ④ *v.* arise, get up, be erect ★**sit**

standard ① *adj.* normal, regular, uniform ②
n. pattern, criterion, norm ③ *n.* flag,
banner, ensign

staple *adj.* main, principal, important,
leading

stare *v.* gaze, gape, look, peer STAIR

stark *adj.* severe, plain, downright, bare,
absolute

start ① *v.* commence, begin, found, initiate

A B C D E F G H I J K L M N O P Q R S T U V W X Y Z

② *v.* depart, set out, leave ③ *v.* startle, jump, wince ④ *n.* beginning, commencement ⑤ *n.* shock, scare, fit

startle *v.* frighten, alarm, scare, surprise ▷*start*

starve *v.* be hungry, famish, want

state ① *n.* condition, situation, position ② *n.* country, nation, commonwealth ③ *v.* declare, say, express, utter ▷*speak*

stately *adj.* imposing, grand, dignified ▷*magnificent* ★**commonplace**

statement *n.* ① declaration, utterance, remark, motto ② bill, account, invoice

station ① *n.* post, spot, site, position, terminal ② *v.* park, place, put, establish *We got there early to establish our place in the line*

stationary *adj.* still, unmoving, standing, fixed ★**mobile** STATIONERY

stationery *n.* paper, envelopes, ink, pens, pencils STATIONARY

statue *n.* carving, bust, figure

staunch *adj.* constant, faithful, true, firm

Stationery

Stationary

▷*loyal* ★**unfaithful**

stay ① *v.* endure, last, remain, stand, linger ② *v.* check, curb, prevent ③ *n.* halt, wait ▷*stop*

steady ① *adj.* firm, fixed, established, constant ▷*staunch* ★**uncertain** ② *v.* brace, stabilize, stiffen

steal *v.* ① thieve, pilfer, filch, swipe ▷*rob* ② slink, flit, creep ▷*prowl* STEEL

stealthy *adj.* furtive, sneaky, sly, secret ▷*underhanded* ★**open**

steep ① *adj.* sheer, sharp, hilly, precipitous ② *v.* bathe, soak, souse, submerge

steer *v.* guide, direct, pilot, control

stem ① *n.* stalk, shoot, stock, trunk ② *v.* arise from, flow from ③ *v.* check, resist, restrain

step ① *n.* pace, tread, stride, gait ② *n.* action, method, deed ③ *v.* walk, skip, trip, pace STEPPE

sterile *adj.* ① barren, unfertile, arid ② sanitary, disinfected

stern ① *adj.* strict, severe, harsh, grim ▷*austere* ★**mild** ② *n.* aft end, rear, poop *The name of the ship was displayed in large letters on the poop*

stew *v.* ① cook, simmer, boil ② worry, fuss

stick ① *n.* stave, pole, rod, cane, staff ② *v.* adhere, cling, cleave, glue, paste, seal

sticky *adj.* gluey, gummy, adhesive

stick out *v.* project, bulge, extrude ▷*jut* ★**recede**

stiff *adj.* ① inflexible, firm, stable, unyielding ▷*rigid* ★**flexible** ② formal, stilted, prim, precise ★**yielding**

stifle *v.* suffocate, throttle, gag, muzzle ▷*smother*

stigma *n.* ① blot, blur, scar ▷*blemish* ② disgrace, dishonor ▷*shame* ★**credit**

still ① *adj.* fixed, stable, static ② *adj.* calm, quiet, serene, tranquil, noiseless, hushed ▷*peaceful* ★**agitated** ③ *v.* quiet, hush, muffle ▷*calm* ★**agitate**

stimulate *v.* inspire, provoke, arouse, motivate ▷*excite* ★**discourage**

sting *v.* prick, wound, pain, hurt, injure

stingy *adj.* miserly, tightfisted, selfish,

niggardly ▷*tight* ★**generous**

stink *v.* smell, whiff, reek

stint ① *n.* job, task, chore ② *n.* turn, spell, share, quota ③ *v.* limit, stop, scrimp, restrict ★**squander**

stir ① *v.* move, excite, spur, agitate ▷*stimulate* ② *v.* whisk, mix, blend ③ *v.* waken, arouse ★**calm** ④ *n.* flurry, fuss, uproar

stock ① *adj.* standard, regular, established, normal ② *n.* reserve, hoard, supply ③ *v.* provide, supply, equip, hoard

stocky *adj.* thickset, chunky, sturdy, pudgy ▷*squat* ★**willowy**

stodgy *adj.* dull, heavy, tedious, boring

stolid *adj.* stupid, dull, mindless, unintelligent ▷*stodgy* ★**quick**

stoop *v.* bend, crouch, kneel, bow

stop ① *v.* cease, desist, end, terminate, halt ★**start** ② *v.* prevent, forestall, avoid ③ *v.* arrest, hold, fix ④ *n.* pause, end, cessation *A cessation of hostilities came into force after the peace agreement*

store ① *v.* put by, reserve, hoard, save ★**use** ② *n.* stock, supply, reserve ③ *n.* market, shop, emporium

story *n.* ① yarn, tale, narrative, account, anecdote ② untruth, lie, fib ③ floor, landing, level, flight, deck

storm ① *n.* tempest, gale, cyclone, hurricane, tornado ★**calm** ② *n.* turmoil, upheaval, attack ③ *v.* rage, rant, fume, attack

stout *adj.* ① sturdy, tough, robust ▷*strong* ★**weak** ② fat, corpulent ▷*plump* ★**thin**

stow *v.* deposit, store ▷*pack*

straight *adj.* ① right, undeviating, unswerving ▷*direct* ② frank, candid, truthful ▷*honest* ★**crooked** STRAIT

straightforward *adj.* open, outspoken, reliable, trustworthy ★**devious**

strain ① *n.* tension, fatigue, exertion ▷*stress* ★**relaxation** ② *n.* melody, tune, air ③ *v.* struggle, labor ▷*toil* ★**relax** ④ *v.* wrench, injure ⑤ *v.* filter, sift, separate

strait *n.* channel, sound, narrows STRAIGHT

straitlaced *adj.* prim, prudish, strict, puritanical *My family was rather puritanical and we were not allowed to play any games on Sundays*

strand ① *n.* coast, beach, shore ② *n.* hair, fiber, tress, lock ③ *v.* desert, maroon, abandon

strange *adj.* ① unusual, incredible, extraordinary, curious ▷*odd* ★**commonplace** ② foreign, alien, remote

stranger *n.* outsider, foreigner, visitor, newcomer ▷*alien* ★**acquaintance**

strangle *v.* constrict, choke, garrote, throttle

strap *n.* belt, harness, thong, leash

stray *v.* ① wander, deviate, depart, rove ② sin, err, do wrong

streak *n.* stroke, stripe, band, line, bar, strip

stream ① *n.* current, course, drift, brook, creek, run ② *v.* flow, gush, spurt, pour

strength *n.* ① power, force, might ▷*energy* ② boldness, nerve, intensity ★**weakness**

strenuous *adj.* laborious, resolute, determined ▷*earnest* ★**weak**

stress ① *n.* tension, force, effort ▷*strain* ② *n.* accent, emphasis ③ *v.* emphasize, accentuate

stretch *v.* expand, reach ▷*extend* ★**shorten**

strict *adj.* ① severe, rigorous, rigid, austere ▷*stern* ★**lenient** ② scrupulous, punctilious, accurate ▷*precise* ★**inaccurate**

stride *n. & v.* walk, step, tread, parade, march

strife *n.* struggle, contest, quarrel, friction ▷*conflict* ★**peace**

strike ① *v.* beat, smite, collide, knock ▷*thump* ② *v.* discover, unearth ③ *n.* assault, thrust, attack ④ *n.* walkout, boycott

striking *adj.* eye-catching, wonderful ▷*extraordinary* ★**commonplace**

strip ① *v.* take off, peel, skin, shave, remove ② *n.* ribbon, stroke, streak, line

stripe *n.* streak, band, bar, chevron *Soldiers in the army have chevrons on their sleeves to indicate their rank*, rule ▷*strip*

strive *v.* endeavor, attempt, aim, compete

A
B
C
D
E
F
G
H
I
J
K
L
M
N
O
P
Q
R
S
T
U
V
W
X
Y
Z

▷*try* ★**yield**

stroke ① *n.* shock, blow, knock, thump ② *n.* seizure, fit, convulsion ③ *v.* pat, rub, caress, smooth, comfort

stroll *v. & n.* walk, promenade, saunter, tramp, ramble

strong *adj.* ① powerful, vigorous, hardy, muscular ▷*robust* ② solid, secure, fortified ★**weak** ③ potent, hot, spicy ▷*pungent*

structure *n.* ① building, edifice, erection ② construction, organization, composition

struggle ① *v.* endeavor, labor, battle, wrestle ★**yield** ② *n.* conflict, battle ▷*fight* ③ *n.* distress, trouble ▷*effort*

strut ① *n.* support, mainstay, prop ② *v.* parade, prance, swagger

stubborn *adj.* ① dogged, persistent, tenacious ② pigheaded, perverse, willful ▷*obstinate* ★**docile**

stuck-up *adj.* vain, conceited ▷*snobbish* ★**modest**

studious *adj.* scholarly, learned, thoughtful ▷*diligent* ★**thoughtless**

study ① *v.* read, peruse, research, scrutinize, examine, train ▷*learn* ② *n.* learning,

Structures

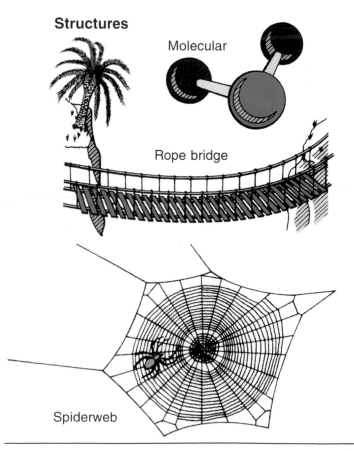

Molecular

Rope bridge

Spiderweb

meditation, thought, contemplation ▷*research*

stuff ① *v.* fill, congest, pack, crowd ② *n.* textile, fabric, material, goods

stumble *v.* ① stagger, lurch, fall ▷*trip* ② stammer, falter ▷*stutter*

stump ① *v.* perplex, mystify, confuse ▷*bewilder* ② *n.* stub, tip, log, root

stun *v.* knock out, overpower, stupefy, dumbfound ▷*confound*

stunt *n.* deed, feat, achievement, performance ▷*exploit*

stupefy *v.* daze, muddle, bewilder, astonish, flabbergast ▷*shock* ★**revive**

stupendous *adj.* astounding, amazing, overwhelming ▷*wonderful* ★**ordinary**

stupid *adj.* simple, stolid, dull, senseless ▷*foolish* ★**clever**

stupidity *n.* inanity, silliness, feebleness, foolishness ★**brilliance**

sturdy *adj.* rugged, stalwart, tough, strapping ▷*hardy* ★**weak**

stutter *v.* stumble, falter ▷*stammer*

style ① *n.* mode, vogue, fashion, way, manner, form ② *v.* name, call, christen STILE

suave *adj.* agreeable, elegant, polite, pleasant, sophisticated *After living in the city for many years, my sister had developed very sophisticated tastes*

subdue *v.* suppress, soften, tame, tone down, moderate, mellow ▷*repress*

subject ① *n.* (*sub*-ject) matter, topic, theme ② *n.* subordinate, dependant ③ *adj.* dependent, subordinate, liable ④ *v.* (sub-*ject*) rule over, subdue, subjugate

submerge *v.* plunge, immerse, sink ★**raise**

submissive *adj.* yielding, servile, meek ▷*obedient* ★**obstinate**

submit *v.* ① yield, give in, accede, surrender, hand over ② offer, tender, present

subordinate *adj.* junior, minor, subject, dependent, secondary ★**superior**

subscribe *v.* sign, enroll, register, agree, assent

subsequent *adj.* later, following, succeeding, after ★**former**

subside *v.* decline, peter out, decrease,

diminish, wane *I used to go mountaineering but my interest waned after some years* ▷*abate* ★**rise**

substance *n.* ① matter, object, stuff, material ② essence, kernel, meaning ▷*gist*

substantial *adj.* ① steady, sturdy, firm ▷*stable* ② ample, large, real, solid ★**imaginary**

substitute ① *n.* alternative, makeshift, stopgap ② *v.* swap, change, replace, duplicate

subtle *adj.* ① shrewd, fine, delicate ② clever, crafty, perceptive

subtract *v.* take away, withdraw, deduct, remove ★**add**

succeed *v.* ① flourish, prosper, thrive, triumph ★**fail** ② follow, inherit, replace ★**precede**

success *n.* prosperity, triumph, victory, achievement ★**failure**

successful *adj.* victorious, prosperous, fortunate, thriving ★**unlucky**

suck *v.* inhale, take in, draw in, imbibe

sudden *adj.* unexpected, abrupt, impulsive, swift, prompt ★**gradual**

suffer *v.* ① bear, endure, put up with ② encounter, undergo ▷*sustain*

sufficient *adj.* adequate, ample, plenty ▷*enough* ★**deficient**

suffocate *v.* smother, choke ▷*stifle*

suggest *v.* recommend, advise, submit, hint, intimate

suit ① *v.* fulfill, gratify, please, suffice, accommodate, befit ② *n.* ensemble, outfit, costume

suitable *adj.* fitting, appropriate, correct, proper, becoming ★**unsuitable**

suite *n.* ① set, series, succession ② apartment, rooms

sulk *v.* pout, grouch, brood, mope

sulky *adj.* glum, morose, churlish, moody ▷*sullen* ★**genial**

sullen *adj.* gloomy, heavy, dismal, cheerless ▷*sulky* ★**cheerful**

sum *n.* amount, total, whole, entirety SOME

summary *n.* synopsis, précis, abstract, summing-up, outline, analysis

summit *n.* peak, pinnacle, top, apex, zenith ★**base**

summon *v.* call, beckon, command, invite, muster ★**dismiss**

sumptuous *adj.* profuse, costly, gorgeous, splendid ▷*lavish* ★**frugal**

sundry *adj.* different, separate, several ▷*various*

sunny *adj.* bright, cheerful, light, clear ▷*radiant* ★**gloomy**

superb *adj.* magnificent, stately, gorgeous ▷*grand* ★**commonplace**

supercilious *adj.* contemptuous, haughty, arrogant ▷*snobbish* ★**modest**

superficial *adj.* slight, imperfect, shallow, skin-deep ▷*trivial* ★**profound**

superfluous *adj.* in excess, inessential, spare ▷*surplus* ★**essential**

superior *adj.* ① better, greater, higher, loftier ▷*excellent* ② eminent, conspicuous, principal ★**inferior**

supersede *v.* succeed, replace, displace, suspend, usurp *The president's authority was usurped by the military* ★**continue**

supervise *v.* superintend, control, manage ▷*direct*

supple *adj.* lithe, pliable, flexible, bending

supplement ① *n.* addition, complement, sequel, postscript ② *v.* supply, add, fill

supply ① *v.* provide, furnish, yield, contribute, purvey ★**retain** ② *n.* hoard, reserve ▷*stock*

support ① *v.* uphold, bear, sustain, maintain, help ▷*favor* ★**oppose** ② *v.* hold up, prop, strut, brace ③ *v.* endure, tolerate, suffer ④ *n.* maintenance, upkeep

suppose *v.* assume, presume, believe, imagine, imply ▷*consider*

suppress *v.* restrain, extinguish, destroy, stop ▷*quell* ★**incite**

supreme *adj.* dominant, highest, greatest, maximum ★**lowly**

sure *adj.* ① certain, positive, definite ② secure, steady, safe ③ permanent, abiding, enduring ★**uncertain**

surface *n.* ① area, expanse, stretch ② outside, exterior, covering ★**interior**

A B C D E F G H I J K L M N O P Q R S T U V W X Y Z

surge ① *v.* swell, rise, heave, rush ② *n.* ripple, billow, wave SERGE

surly *adj.* morose, cross, testy, touchy, crusty ▷*sullen* ★**affable**

surmise *v.* guess, speculate, conjecture, suspect ▷*presume* ★**know**

surpass *v.* eclipse, outdo, outstrip, excel, exceed ▷*beat*

surplus *n.* excess, remainder, balance, residue ★**shortcoming**

surprise ① *v.* startle, astonish, amaze ▷*astound* ② *n.* amazement, astonishment ▷*wonder*

surrender *v.* quit, give up, yield, submit ▷*relinquish*

surround *v.* enclose, encircle, encompass

survey ① *v.* (sur-*vey*) look at, examine, scrutinize ▷*study* ② *v.* estimate, measure ③ *n.* (*sur*-vey) assessment, appraisal

survive *v.* live, exist, continue, outlast, abide ★**surrender**

susceptible *adj.* sensitive, impressionable, inclined, capable ★**insensitive**

suspect ① *v.* (sus-*pect*) disbelieve, doubt, distrust ② *adj.* (*sus*-pect) unbelievable, questionable, dubious

suspend *v.* ① interrupt, delay, arrest, adjourn, postpone ▷*stop* ★**continue** ② expel, throw out ③ swing, dangle ▷*hang* ★**drop**

suspense *n.* anticipation, waiting, abeyance *The club couldn't decide on a new leader, so the matter was left in abeyance,* stoppage, uncertainty ▷*tension* ★**decision**

suspicious *adj.* incredulous, skeptical, doubtful, suspecting ★**trustful**

sustain *v.* ① uphold, keep, maintain, provide for ② suffer, undergo, experience ③ nourish, nurture, feed

swagger *v.* ① parade, prance ▷*strut* ② brag, bluster ▷*boast*

swallow ① *v.* absorb, consume, eat, digest, devour, drink ▷*gulp* ② *n.* mouthful, gulp ③ *n.* bird

swamp ① *n.* fen, bog, marsh, morass, quagmire ② *v.* submerge, submerse, overflow, deluge ▷*drench*

swap *v.* exchange, switch, trade, barter

swarm ① *n.* throng, horde, shoal, flock, crowd ② *v.* teem, abound, jam, mass, crowd, cluster

swarthy *adj.* dusky, dark, brown, tawny

sway ① *v.* swing, rock, totter, lean, incline ▷*waver* ② *n.* rule, authority, control ▷*influence*

swear *v.* ① promise, warrant, affirm, attest ② curse, damn, blaspheme

sweat *v.* perspire, ooze, leak, exude, swelter *During that time of the year it was very hot and we sweltered all day*

sweep *v.* brush, scrub, clean, scour

sweet *adj.* ① sugary, syrupy, luscious ★**sour** ② melodic, tuneful, musical, mellow ★**discordant** ③ gentle, tender, mild, lovable ★**unpleasant** ④ fragrant, pure, clean, fresh, wholesome, aromatic ★**putrid**

swell *v.* expand, distend, inflate, bulge ▷*enlarge* ★**contract**

swerve *v.* veer, deviate, skid, skew, lurch ▷*waver*

swift *adj.* speedy, rapid, quick ▷*fast* ★**slow**

swill ① *v.* swig, consume, imbibe, tipple ▷*gulp* ② *n.* refuse, garbage, waste

swim *v.* bathe, wade, paddle, float, glide

swindle ① *n.* trick, fraud, blackmail, racket ② *v.* hoodwink, deceive, hoax, dupe, rip off ▷*cheat*

swine *n.* pig, boar, sow, porker, hog

swing ① *v.* hang, suspend, dangle, lurch, reel ② *n.* tempo, time

switch ① *v.* change, exchange, alter, trade, substitute, swap ② *n.* lever, pedal, control, button

swivel *v.* pivot, spin, rotate, revolve, turn

swoop *v.* pounce, descend, stoop, plummet, plunge

sword *n.* rapier, blade, foil, épée, cutlass, saber, steel SOARED

symbol *n.* character, figure, numeral, letter, sign, token, emblem CYMBAL

sympathetic *adj.* thoughtful, understanding, kind, affectionate ★**indifferent**

system *n.* ① method, plan, order, scheme, arrangement, routine ② network, organization: *a hierarchical system*

T t

table *n.* ① board, stand, slab, tablet, counter, stall ② list, catalog, schedule, index, statement

tablet *n.* ① pill, capsule, lozenge ② board, table, pad

tack ① *n.* thumbtack, nail, pin, brad ② *n.* aim, direction, set ③ *v.* affix, fasten, join, stitch

tackle ① *n.* outfit, gear, rig, harness ② *v.* grasp, halt, intercept, seize ③ *v.* deal with *I dealt with the problem of the school fund shortage,* undertake, set about

tact *n.* diplomacy, judgment, skill, discretion *If you want your secret to be kept, you had better not rely on his discretion* TACKED

tactful *adj.* diplomatic, wise, subtle, prudent ▷*discreet* ★**tactless**

tactics *n.* strategy, campaign, method, procedure

tactless *adj.* inconsiderate, gauche, clumsy, boorish ▷*inept* ★**tactful**

tag *n.* label, ticket, docket, slip, sticker

taint *v.* sully, tarnish, infect, stain, soil, contaminate ▷*defile* ★**purify**

take *v.* ① grasp, grab, seize, procure ② receive, accept, obtain ③ carry, convey, lead, conduct ④ interpret, understand

take place *v.* occur, happen, befall *Our parents were concerned about what might befall us when we left school*

tale *n.* story, fable, anecdote, yarn, narrative TAIL

talent *n.* knack, genius, gift, ability, aptitude ★**stupidity**

talk ① *v.* speak, say, utter, gossip ② *v.* describe, comment on, talk about ③ *n.* speech, chatter, conversation ④ *n.* lecture, speech, discourse

tall *adj.* lanky, lofty, big, high, towering, giant ★**short**

tally *v.* ① count, enumerate, compute ② agree, conform, coincide ★**disagree**

tame ① *adj.* domesticated, gentle, mild, docile *Although we found it in the woods, the kitten was docile* ★**savage** ② *adj.* flat, dull, boring, tedious ③ *v.* train, discipline, domesticate

Tame

Although we found it in the woods, the kitten was docile

tamper with *v.* meddle, interfere, damage, tinker

tang *n.* smell, scent, aroma, flavor, savor, taste

tangible *adj.* concrete, solid, substantial, real, material ★**spiritual**

tangle *n. & v.* twist, muddle, jumble, knot

tantalize *v.* tease, taunt, thwart, disappoint ▷*frustrate* ★**satisfy**

tantrum *n.* rage, fit, hysterics, storm

tap ① *v.* pat, hit, knock, rap, strike ② *n.* faucet, spout, cock, nozzle, bung

tape *n.* ribbon, filament, braid, strip, riband

taper *v.* dwindle, narrow, contract, decline, wane, narrow ★**widen** TAPIR

tardy *adj.* slow, sluggish, reluctant, slack ▷*late* ★**prompt**

target *n.* goal, aim, ambition, purpose, butt, end, victim

tariff *n.* tax, rate, toll, duty, payment, schedule of fees

tarnish *v.* stain, sully *Mark's reputation at school was sullied after he was accused of stealing,* spot, darken, blemish, rust ★**brighten**

tarry *v.* delay, stall, wait, loiter ▷*linger* ★**hurry**

tart ① *adj.* acid, sour, sharp, pungent ② *n.* pie, quiche, pastry, flan

task *n.* job, stint, chore, assignment, undertaking

taste ① *n.* bite, mouthful, flavor, savor, tang ② *v.* try, sip, sample, relish

tasteful *adj.* artistic, graceful, elegant, smart ▷*refined* ★**tasteless**

tasteless *adj.* ① flavorless, insipid ② gaudy, inelegant ▷*vulgar* ★**tasteful**

tasty *adj.* appetizing, piquant, savory ▷*delicious* ★**disgusting**

tattle *v.* gossip, tittle-tattle, blab, prattle

taunt *v.* jibe, reproach, rebuke, ridicule, scoff at ▷*sneer* ★**compliment**

taut *adj.* tense, tight, stretched ▷*rigid* ★**relaxed** TAUGHT

tawdry *adj.* flashy, loud, gaudy, showy ▷*vulgar* ★**superior**

tax ① *n.* levy, duty, impost, tithe, toll ② *v.* load, oppress, overburden TACKS

teach *v.* instruct, educate, tutor, coach, guide, train, drill

teacher *n.* educator, professor, lecturer, schoolmaster, schoolmistress, coach, tutor

team *n.* party, group, gang, crew, company TEEM

tear *v.* ① rip, rend, tatter, shred ② dash, bolt, rush, sprint TARE

tearful *adj.* weepy, moist, wet, sobbing, sad

tease *v.* annoy, harass, vex, irritate, torment ▷*tantalize* ★**soothe** TEAS, TEES

tedious *adj.* wearisome, tiresome, irksome, exhausting ▷*boring* ★**fascinating**

teem *v.* abound, swarm, overflow, increase, be full ★**lack** TEAM

tell *v.* ① disclose, speak, state, talk, utter ② discern, discover, distinguish

temper ① *n.* temperament, disposition, nature, humor ② *n.* anger, annoyance, passion ③ *v.* moderate, soften, weaken, restrain

temporary *adj.* short, limited, impermanent, brief ★**permanent**

tempt *v.* entice, invite, attract, persuade ▷*lure* ★**deter**

tenacious *adj.* ① stubborn, firm, obstinate, unwavering ★**weak** ② adhesive, glutinous

tenant *n.* occupant, householder, occupier

tend *v.* ① take care of, manage, serve, guard ★**neglect** ② affect, lean, incline, verge

★**diverge**

tendency *n.* disposition, leaning, inclination, bent ★**aversion**

tender ① *adj.* delicate, soft ▷*fragile* ② *adj.* mild, kind, sympathetic ▷*gentle* ③ *adj.* raw, painful, sore ④ *v.* proffer *Charlotte proffered her services as a babysitter,* present, volunteer, bid

tense *adj.* tight, strained, taut, nervous, edgy ★**relaxed** TENTS

tension *n.* strain, stress, rigidity, suspense, worry ★**relaxation**

term ① *n.* expression, denomination, title, phrase ② *n.* time, season, spell *We stayed in Hong Kong for a spell during our trip to the Far East,* duration ③ *v.* entitle, call, dub

terminate *v.* cease, stop, end, conclude ▷*finish* ★**begin**

terrible *adj.* frightful, terrifying, fearful, dreadful ▷*horrible* ★**superb**

terrify *v.* petrify, shock, appall, alarm ▷*frighten* ★**reassure**

territory *n.* region, area, expanse, dominion, land ▷*country*

terror *n.* alarm, panic, horror, dismay ▷*fright* ★**confidence**

terse *adj.* brief, concise, short, pithy, abrupt ▷*curt* ★**long-winded**

test ① *n.* examination, trial, check, proof, experiment ② *v.* examine, try out, check, quiz, analyze

testy *adj.* irritable, bad-tempered, touchy, peevish ▷*cross* ★**genial**

tether *n.* rope, cord, lead, leash, chain

text *n.* contents, reading, passage, clause

thanks *n.* gratitude, credit, appreciation

thaw *v.* ① melt, fuse, liquefy, soften ★**freeze** ② unbend, relax

theft *n.* robbery, fraud, larceny, plundering

theme *n.* subject, text matter, topic

theory *n.* idea, supposition, concept, hypothesis

therefore *adv.* consequently, hence, accordingly, thus

thick *adj.* ① dense, solid, bulky, compact ② stiff, set, congealed ③ viscous, gummy, stodgy ★**thin**

thief *n.* crook, robber, burglar, bandit, pirate

thin *adj.* ① slender, slim, slight, lean, skinny ★**fat** ② waferlike, delicate, flimsy ③ watery, dilute, unsubstantial ★**thick**

thing *n.* article, object, something, being, substance

think *v.* ① ponder, consider ▷*reflect* ② conceive, imagine ▷*fancy* ③ surmise, conclude ▷*reckon*

thirsty *adj.* parched, dry, craving, burning

thorn *n.* barb, prickle, bramble, thistle

thorough *adj.* outright, absolute, complete, utter ★**haphazard**

though *conj.* although, even though, notwithstanding, however, yet

thought *n.* reflection, consideration, study, concept, deduction

thoughtful *adj.* ① pensive, studious, contemplative ② considerate, kind, heedful, careful ★**thoughtless**

thoughtless *adj.* heedless, careless, rash, neglectful ▷*indiscreet* ★**thoughtful**

thrash *v.* ① whip, flog, hit ② stir, pitch *The sea was rough—each wave pitched the small boat closer to the rocks,* toss

thread *n.* filament, twist, yarn, fiber

threadbare *adj.* ① shabby, ragged, worn ② commonplace, hackneyed, stale ★**fresh**

threaten *v.* intimidate, bully, blackmail ▷*menace* ★**reassure**

Thrash

The sea was rough—each wave pitched the small boat closer to the rocks.

thrifty *adj.* frugal, careful, economical, saving, sparing ★**wasteful**

thrilling *adj.* exciting, gripping, stimulating

thrive *v.* prosper, flourish, succeed, grow, increase ★**decline**

throb ① *n.* tick, beat, palpitation ② *v.* beat, palpitate, vibrate

throng ① *n.* crowd, horde, mob ② *v.* pack, crowd, swarm, fill

throttle *v.* choke, smother ▷*strangle*

through *prep.* by way of, by means of, as a result of

throw *v.* fling, cast, hurl, project, propel, thrust ★**keep** THROE

thrust *v. & n.* push, project, drive, force, prod

thug *n.* hoodlum, bandit, assassin, mugger, ruffian

thump *v. & n.* beat, hit, knock, bang, wallop

thunderstruck *adj.* open-mouthed, amazed, astounded, staggered

thus *adv.* accordingly, so, therefore, consequently

thwart *v.* frustrate, balk, baffle, hinder, obstruct ★**assist**

ticket *n.* pass, label, card, coupon, token

tickle *v.* ① caress, stroke, pat, brush ② titillate, convulse, amuse ③ delight, gratify

tidbit *n.* delicacy, morsel, dainty, snack, treat

tide *n.* stream, current, drift, ebb, flow TIED

tidings *n.* information, intelligence, report, advice ▷*news*

tidy *adj.* ① neat, well-kept, spruce, orderly ② ample, large, substantial

tie ① *v.* join, attach, secure *Be sure to secure the gate so the dogs can't get out,* unite ▷*fasten* ② *n.* cravat, necktie, bow tie ③ *n.* bond, connection

tight *adj.* ① fast, close, compact, tense ▷*taut* ★**loose** ② miserly, tightfisted ▷*stingy* ★**generous**

tighten *v.* strain, tauten, constrict, cramp, crush ▷*squeeze* ★**loosen**

till ① *prep.* until, up to, as far as ② *v.* plow, cultivate, tend ③ *n.* cash drawer, cash register

tilt *v. & n.* slant, slope, incline, lean, list, tip

time *n.* ① period, duration, season, age, era, term, span ② meter, measure, tempo, rhythm THYME

timid *adj.* fearful, afraid, timorous, diffident, modest ▷*shy* ★**bold**

tinge *v. & n.* color, tincture, tint, stain, shade

tingle *v.* thrill, throb, tickle, vibrate

tinker *v.* meddle, fiddle *Bill fiddled with the old clock for ages, trying to make it work,* patch up, putter, trifle

tinkle *v.* jingle, jangle, ring, clink

tint *n.* dye, hue, tinge, shade ▷*color*

tiny *adj.* small, diminutive, puny, wee ▷*little* ★**huge**

tip ① *n.* apex, peak, point, extremity ▷*top* ② *n.* gratuity, gift, donation, reward ③ *n.* information, hint, tip-off ④ *v.* list, lean, tilt ▷*slope*

tipsy *adj.* inebriated, drunk, drunken

tire *v.* exhaust, bore, fatigue, harass, weaken

tiresome *adj.* wearisome, tedious, boring ▷*humdrum* ★**interesting**

title *n.* ① name, denomination, term, style, designation ② claim, interest *When my father died, I was left an interest in his business,* ownership

toady *v.* fawn, crawl, grovel, crouch, cringe

toast ① *n.* pledge, compliment, salutation ② *v.* brown, roast, heat

together *adv.* collectively, jointly, simultaneously, at the same time ★**separately**

toil ① *v. & n.* struggle, labor, travail ▷*work* ★**relaxation**

token *n.* memento, keepsake, symbol, omen ▷*souvenir*

tolerable *adj.* endurable, supportable, bearable, passable ★**unbearable**

tolerant *adj.* forbearing, indulgent *Sally's parents are very indulgent with her and buy her whatever she wants,* liberal, easygoing ▷*lenient* ★**intolerant**

tolerate *v.* accept, bear with, put up with, endure, suffer ▷*allow* ★**resist**

toll ① *v.* ring, strike, chime, clang ② *n.* charge, duty, tax, levy

tone *n.* ① pitch, loudness, noise, note ② emphasis, accent, inflection ③ temper, manner, attitude ④ color, cast, hue, shade

too *adv.* ① also, as well, besides ② extremely, very, unduly

tool *n.* ① implement, utensil, machine, agent ② pawn, puppet, cat's-paw, stooge TULLE

top *n.* ① summit, pinnacle, peak ② lid, cover, stopper, cap ③ upper surface ★**bottom** ④ *n.* spinning toy ⑤ *adj.* highest, best, uppermost *After climbing for four days, we reached the uppermost part of the range*

topic *n.* subject, motif, question ▷*theme*

topical *adj.* contemporary, popular, up-to-date

topple *v.* collapse, founder, overturn, totter ▷*fall*

topsy-turvy *adj.* upside-down, overturned, confused, chaotic

torment *v. & n.* pain, distress ▷*torture* ★**ease**

torrent *n.* flood, stream, cascade, cataract, waterfall ★**trickle**

torture *v.* agonize, rack, anguish ▷*torment*

toss *v.* fling, hurl, pitch, cast, project, heave ▷*throw*

total ① *n.* aggregate, whole, sum, completion ② *v.* add, tot up, reckon ③ *adj.* complete, entire

totally *adv.* completely, absolutely, entirely, utterly ★**partially**

touch ① *v.* feel, finger, fondle, handle, stroke ② *v.* move, affect, concern ③ *v.* beat, hit, collide with ④ *v.* adjoin *Our house is situated at a spot where three counties adjoin,* meet, border ⑤ *n.* tinge, hint, suspicion

touchy *adj.* peevish, petulant, snappish ▷*moody* ★**genial**

tough ① *adj.* hard, strong, vigorous, rugged, sturdy ② *adj.* arduous, difficult ③ *n.* hoodlum, hooligan, bruiser, bully

tour *n.* trip, journey, jaunt, excursion, voyage, ride, visit

tournament *n.* contest, championship, competition ▷*match*

tow *v.* haul, drag, tug, haul, heave ▷*pull* TOE

Titles

admiral	lord
ambassador	madame
archbishop	maharajah maharani
baron baroness	major
brigadier	marshal
cardinal	mayor
chancellor	mogul
colonel	monsieur
commodore	pope
count countess	priest
czar czarina	prince princess
dame	professor
dean	queen
duchess duke	rabbi
earl	senator
emir	señor señora
emperor empress	sergeant
general	shogun
governor	signor signora
infanta	shah
kaiser	sheik
khan	sheriff
king	sultan sultana
knight lady	
lama	
lieutenant	

A B C D E F G H I J K L M N O P Q R S T U V W X Y Z

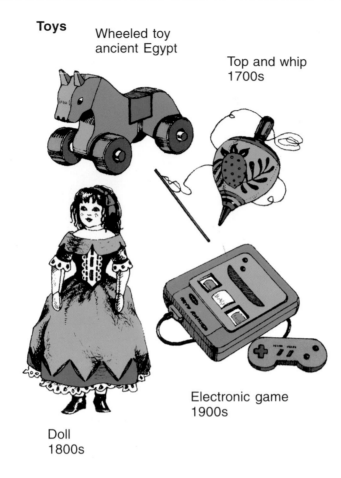

Toys

Wheeled toy
ancient Egypt

Top and whip
1700s

Electronic game
1900s

Doll
1800s

tower ① *v.* soar, dominate, surmount ② *n.* turret, spire, belfry

toy ① *n.* plaything, doll, game ② *v.* play, tinker, fiddle, twiddle

trace ① *v.* trail, track, follow, pursue, discover ② *v.* sketch, draw, copy ③ *n.* trail, track, spoor ④ *n.* drop, speck, vestige

track *v.* search out, follow ▷*trace*

tract *n.* ① area, space, extent, plot ② booklet, leaflet, pamphlet TRACKED

trade ① *v.* barter, exchange, buy, sell, patronize ② *n.* occupation, work, livelihood, business

tradition *n.* custom, convention, practice

traffic ① *n.* business, barter ▷*trade* ② transportation, vehicles, movement

tragedy *n.* catastrophe, disaster, adversity ▷*calamity* ★**comedy**

tragic *adj.* disastrous, catastrophic, miserable, wretched ▷*deplorable* ★**comic**

trail *n.* spoor, track ▷*trace*

train ① *v.* teach, educate, instruct, drill, school ② *n.* chain, procession, series

traitor *n.* rebel, mutineer, renegade, quisling, betrayer

tramp ① *n.* vagabond, wanderer, vagrant, bum, hobo ▷*beggar* ② *n.* jaunt, stroll, ramble ③ *v.* roam, rove, range, walk, travel

trample *v.* tread on, walk on, flatten ▷*crush*

tranquil *adj.* peaceful, placid, serene, restful ▷*calm* ★**restless**

transaction *n.* business, performance, dealing, negotiation, proceeding

transfer *v.* move *My sister is being moved to the head office after her promotion,* displace, change ▷*exchange*

transmit *v.* dispatch, forward, relay ▷*send* ★**receive**

transparent *adj.* clear, lucid, crystal, diaphanous

transport ① *v.* carry, convey, conduct, transfer ▷*move* ② *n.* transportation

trap ① *v.* ensnare, catch, net ② *n.* snare, pitfall, noose, decoy ▷*ambush*

trash *n.* garbage, junk, debris, rubble ▷*rubbish* ★**treasure**

travel ① *v. & n.* trek, voyage, cruise ▷*journey*

treacherous *adj.* ① traitorous, unfaithful, false, deceptive ▷*disloyal* ★**faithful**

tread *v.* ① dangerous, risky, precarious, tricky ★**reliable** ② step, walk, tramp, march, go ③ stride, gait, walk, step

treason *n.* treachery, betrayal, sedition

treasure ① *n.* hoard, fortune, riches, wealth ② *v.* appreciate, esteem ▷*value*

treat ① *v.* deal with, handle, manage, serve ② *v.* regale, entertain ③ *v.* doctor, attend ④ *n.* banquet, entertainment, fun

treaty *n.* agreement, covenant, alliance

tremble *v.* quake, quaver, shudder, flutter ▷*shake*

tremendous *adj.* ① immense, enormous ▷*huge* ② terrible, dreadful, awful

tremor *n.* quiver, shake, flutter, ripple ▷*vibration*

trench *n.* ditch, moat, trough, gully, gutter

trend *n.* tendency, inclination, direction

trespass ① *v.* infringe, overstep, intrude ② *n.* offense, sin, transgression

a b c d e f g h i j k l m n o p q r s t u v w x y z

trial *n.* ① endeavor, testing, experiment ② ordeal, grief, suffering ③ essay, proof ④ hearing, lawsuit

tribe *n.* clan, family, race, group, set

tribute *n.* ① ovation, compliment, praise ② dues, toll, tithe, tax

trick ① *n.* fraud, artifice, wile, cheat, deception ② *n.* jape, prank, frolic ③ *n.* juggling, stage magic, conjuring ④ *v.* deceive, defraud

trickle *v.* leak, ooze, seep, drip, drop, dribble

trifle ① *n.* bauble, plaything, foolishness, nonsense ② *v.* dabble, idle, play with

trifling *adj.* paltry, petty, worthless, slight ▷*trivial* ★**important**

trim ① *v.* prune, clip, shorten, crop ② *v.* ornament, smarten, decorate ③ *adj.* tidy, neat, orderly ★**scruffy**

trinket *n.* bauble, bead, jewel, ornament, toy

trip *n.* ① journey, excursion, jaunt ▷*tour* ② *v.* stumble, fall, slip

tripe *n.* garbage, trash, nonsense, twaddle *This is a silly story; I've never read such twaddle*

trite *adj.* hackneyed, ordinary, corny ▷*stale* ★**novel**

triumph *n.* victory, success, achievement ▷*conquest* ★**defeat**

trivial *adj.* trifling, common, unimportant, ordinary, useless ▷*trite* ★**important**

troop ① *n.* band, gang, group, pack, team, unit ② *v.* flock, crowd, swarm TROUPE

trophy *n.* prize, award, cup, souvenir

trot *v.* canter, jog, scamper, scurry

trouble ① *n.* disturbance, annoyance, calamity, misfortune ▷*misery* ② *v.* disturb, annoy, harass ▷*distress* ★**delight**

true *adj.* ① accurate, precise, factual, correct ★**inaccurate** ② faithful, loyal, constant ③ pure, real ▷*genuine* ★**false**

trunk *n.* ① body, torso, stem, stalk ② chest, case, box ③ proboscis *The tapir's proboscis is not as large as the elephant's trunk,* nose, snout

truss *v.* fasten, secure, strap, tie ▷*bind* ★**untie**

trust ① *n.* faith, confidence, belief ② *v.* believe in, credit, depend on ★**doubt** TRUSSED

trustful *adj.* trusting, innocent, naive ▷*gullible* ★**cautious**

trustworthy *adj.* dependable, credible, honorable ▷*reliable* ★**unreliable**

truth *n.* ① reality, fact, precision ▷*accuracy* ★**falsehood** ② integrity, faith, honor ▷*fidelity* ★**deceit**

truthful *adj.* reliable, frank, open ▷*honest* ★**false**

try ① *v.* endeavor, attempt ▷*strive* ② *v.* examine, try out ▷*test* ★**abandon** ③ *n.* trial, attempt, effort

trying *adj.* bothersome, annoying, troublesome ▷*irksome*

tub *n.* basin, bowl, pot, barrel, keg, tun

tube *n.* pipe, spout, duct, hose, shaft

tuck *v.* stow, fold, pack, pleat, hem

tug *v.* drag, tow, haul, heave ▷*pull* ★**push**

tumble *v.* drop, descend, trip, topple, stumble ▷*fall*

tumult *n.* noise, rumpus, racket, uproar, disturbance, disorder ★**peace**

tune *n.* melody, harmony, air, strain ▷*song*

tunnel *n.* subway, shaft, passage, gallery

turn ① *v.* spin, revolve, whirl ▷*rotate* ② *v.* bend, curve ▷*twist* ③ *v.* change, alter ▷*convert* ④ *v.* spoil ▷*sour* ⑤ *n.* stint, spell, chance ⑥ *n.* rotation ▷*revolution* TERN

twaddle *n.* balderdash, nonsense, drivel, rigmarole, piffle ▷*bunkum* ★**sense**

twinge *n.* pain, pang, spasm, gripe ▷*ache*

twinkle *v.* glitter, gleam, glisten, glimmer ▷*sparkle*

twist *v.* ① bend, curve, turn ② warp, contort, writhe ③ wind, intertwine *The octopus intertwined its legs around the large clam,* encircle

twitch *v.* jerk, jump, jiggle, blink, flutter

type ① *n.* kind, sort, character, description ② *n.* prototype, model, pattern ③ *n.* letter, symbol ④ *v.* typewrite, keyboard

typical *adj.* characteristic, symbolic, regular, stock, representative ★**abnormal**

tyrant *n.* despot, autocrat, dictator, martinet

A
B
C
D
E
F
G
H
I
J
K
L
M
N
O
P
Q
R
S
T
U
V
W
X
Y
Z

U u

ugly *adj.* unsightly, ungainly, frightful, ghastly, hideous, horrid, nasty ★**beautiful**

ultimate *adj.* furthest, farthest, most distant, extreme, eventual ▷*final*

umpire *n.* referee, judge, mediator

unabashed *adj.* brazen, unconcerned, undaunted ▷*composed* ★**sheepish**

unable *adj.* helpless, incapable, powerless ★**able**

unaccustomed *adj.* inexperienced, unfamiliar ▷*strange* ★**familiar**

unaffected *adj.* natural, sincere, true, artless ▷*naive* ★**impressed**

unafraid *adj.* courageous, dauntless, intrepid ▷*fearless* ★**afraid**

unanimous *adj.* harmonious, consenting, agreeing ▷*united*

unassuming *adj.* diffident, reserved, quiet, simple ▷*modest* ★**forward**

unattached *adj.* single, free, loose ▷*separate* ★**committed**

unattended *adj.* alone, unwatched, ignored ▷*abandoned* ★**escorted**

unavoidable *adj.* inevitable, irresistable, certain ▷*necessary* ★**uncertain**

unaware *adj.* ignorant, unheeding, unknowing, forgetful ▷*oblivious* ★**aware**

unbalanced *adj.* ① top-heavy, lopsided, uneven ② insane, unhinged *He seems to have become unhinged ever since he lost his job,* crazy, eccentric

unbearable *adj.* unacceptable, intolerable ▷*outrageous* ★**acceptable**

unbiased *adj.* impartial, fair, just ▷*neutral* ★**prejudiced**

uncanny *adj.* weird, ghostly, unearthly, creepy ▷*eerie*

uncertain *adj.* doubtful, vague, chancy, indefinite ▷*dubious* ★**certain**

uncivilized *adj.* primitive, barbaric, coarse, gross ▷*vulgar* ★**civilized**

uncomfortable *adj.* awkward, embarrassed, cramped, self-conscious ★**comfortable**

uncommon *adj.* rare, scarce, infrequent, extraordinary ▷*unusual* ★**common**

unconscious *adj.* ① ignorant, unheeding ▷*unaware* ② insensible, senseless, stunned ★**conscious**

unconventional *adj.* unorthodox, peculiar *I have my own peculiar way of looking at things,* individualistic ▷*eccentric* ★**conventional**

uncouth *adj.* crude, coarse, clumsy, vulgar ▷*boorish* ★**polite**

uncover *v.* expose, discover, show, divulge ▷*reveal* ★**conceal**

under ① *adv.* underneath, below, beneath ② *prep.* less than, lower than, subject to

undergo *v.* endure, tolerate, bear, suffer ▷*sustain*

underground *adj.* secret, concealed, private, hidden, subversive

underhand *adj.* stealthy, undercover, deceitful ▷*sneaky* ★**honest**

underneath *adj.* beneath, under ▷*below* ★**above**

underrate *v.* undervalue, understate, disparage, belittle ★**exaggerate**

understand *v.* comprehend, appreciate, grasp, sympathize ▷*realize* ★**misunderstand**

understudy *n.* stand-in, deputy, substitute, reserve, replacement

undertake *v.* attempt, commence, contract, embark on ▷*tackle*

undesirable *adj.* objectionable, distasteful ▷*unpleasant* ★**desirable**

undignified *adj.* improper, inelegant, clumsy ▷*unseemly* ★**graceful**

undo *v.* unfasten, disentangle, unravel, free ▷*release* ★**fasten**

undress *v.* disrobe, strip, remove, take off ▷*divest* ★**dress**

unearthly *adj.* eerie, uncanny, supernatural ▷*ghostly*

uneasy *adj.* uncomfortable, restive, self-conscious, edgy ★**calm**

unemployed *adj.* unoccupied, redundant, out of work

uneven *adj.* irregular, rough, bumpy,

lopsided, unequal ★**even**

unexpected *adj.* abrupt, impulsive, chance, surprising ▷*sudden* ★**normal**

unfair *adj.* prejudiced, one-sided, partial, unjust ★**fair**

unfaithful *adj.* faithless, untrue, dishonest ▷*false* ★**faithful**

unfamiliar *adj.* alien, obscure, fantastic, bizarre ▷*strange* ★**familiar**

unfasten *v.* release, open, unlatch, untie ▷*undo* ★**fasten**

unfinished *adj.* incomplete, imperfect, lacking, crude ★**finished**

unfit *adj.* unqualified, unsuitable, incapable, unsuited ★**suitable**

unfold *adj.* open, expand, develop, reveal, disclose, unwrap ☆**withhold**

unforeseen *adj.* surprising, sudden, accidental ▷*unexpected* ★**predictable**

unforgettable *adj.* memorable, impressive, noteworthy, exceptional

unfortunate *adj.* deplorable, lamentable, adverse, hapless ▷*unlucky* ★**fortunate**

unfriendly *adj.* antagonistic, surly, cold ▷*hostile* ★**friendly**

ungainly *adj.* gawky, awkward, graceless, unwieldly ▷*clumsy* ★**graceful**

ungrateful *adj.* thankless, selfish, ungracious, ill-mannered ★**grateful**

unhappiness *n.* depression, misery, sadness

unhappy *adj.* miserable, dismal, luckless *Try as he might, the luckless Tom was almost last in the race,* melancholy ▷*sad* ★**happy**

unhealthy *adj.* ① unwholesome, harmful ② sick, ill, diseased ★**healthy**

uniform ① *n.* regalia, livery *It was a very grand affair, with the footmen in full livery,* costume, dress ② *adj.* stable, steady, unchanging, level ★**varied**

unimportant *adj.* puny, trivial, insignificant ▷*petty* ★**important**

unintentional *adj.* inadvertent, involuntary, unwitting ▷*accidental* ★**deliberate**

union *n.* ① alliance, association, league ② agreement, accord, harmony ③ fusion, blend, compound

unique *adj.* original, exceptional, exclusive,

single, sole ★**commonplace**

unit *n.* entity, single, one, individual

unite *v.* join, combine, connect, merge, blend, fuse ★**separate**

united *adj.* joined, combined, undivided ▷*unanimous* ★**separated**

unity *n.* union, harmony, uniformity, agreement ★**disagreement**

universal *adj.* general, all-embracing, entire, worldwide *Our company has products that are sold worldwide*

unjust *adj.* partial, prejudiced, unfair, wrong ▷*biased* ★**just**

unkempt *adj.* disheveled, shabby, sloppy, slovenly, ungroomed ▷*scruffy* ★**neat**

unkind *adj.* inhuman, heartless, brutal, callous ▷*cruel* ★**kind**

unknown *adj.* hidden, mysterious, undiscovered, dark ★**familiar**

unless *conj.* if not, except when

unlike *adj.* unrelated, dissimilar, distinct ▷*different* ★**similar**

unlikely *adj.* rare, improbable, doubtful, incredible, unheard of ▷*dubious* ★**likely**

unlucky *adj.* unfortunate, luckless, ill-fated, unhappy ★**lucky**

unnatural *adj.* ① artificial, stilted, strained

Uniform

It was a very grand affair, with the footmen in full livery.

A
B
C
D
E
F
G
H
I
J
K
L
M
N
O
P
Q
R
S
T
U
V
W
X
Y
Z

② inhuman, cruel ▷*heartless* ★**natural**

unnecessary *adj.* nonessential, excess, superfluous ▷*needless* ★**necessary**

unoccupied *adj.* ① uninhabited, empty, deserted ▷*vacant* ② idle, spare ▷*unemployed* ★**occupied**

unpleasant *adj.* disagreeable, displeasing, objectionable ▷*offensive* ★**pleasant**

unpopular *adj.* obnoxious *I was glad to leave the party, for I had been forced to talk to some obnoxious people,* detested, shunned, rejected ▷*disliked* ★**popular**

unqualified *adj.* ① unable, incompetent, inadequate ▷*unfit* ② complete, thorough, absolute

unreal *adj.* imaginary, fictional, artificial, false, fanciful ★**real** UNREEL

unreasonable *adj.* ① extravagant, excessive, extreme ★**moderate** ② far-fetched, absurd, foolish ★**rational**

unreliable *adj.* untrustworthy, undependable, irresponsible ▷*fickle* ★**reliable**

unrest *n.* ① defiance, disquiet, protest, rebellion ② anxiety, distress, worry ★**calm**

unrestricted *adj.* unrestrained, unlimited, open, free, unhindered ★**limited**

unripe *adj.* green, immature, callow *I was just a callow youth in those days, but I hope I have learned something since then,* unseasoned, unready ★**ripe**

unrivaled *adj.* inimitable, unequaled, matchless, peerless ★**inferior**

unruly *adj.* disorderly, troublesome, restive ▷*rowdy* ★**orderly**

unseemly *adj.* incorrect, indecent, improper, unbecoming, shocking ★**seemly**

unselfish *adj.* generous, liberal, charitable, hospitable ▷*kind* ★**selfish**

unstable *adj.* unsteady, shaky, inconstant, fickle, volatile ★**stable**

unsuitable *adj.* improper, unacceptable, unfitting, inconsistent ★**suitable**

untidy *adj.* bedraggled, disorderly, muddled, messy ▷*slovenly* ★**tidy**

untie *v.* unfasten, unravel, free, release ▷*undo* ★**tie**

until *prep.* till, as far as, up to

untimely *adj.* inopportune, ill-timed, premature ★**opportune**

unusual *adj.* strange, queer, exceptional, quaint, curious ▷*odd* ★**normal**

unwilling *adj.* averse, disinclined, grudging, opposed ▷*reluctant* ★**willing**

upheaval *n.* disturbance, disruption, overthrow, turmoil

uphold *v.* sustain, keep up, endorse ▷*support*

upkeep *n.* maintenance, care, conservation, support, expenses ★**neglect**

upper *adj.* higher, superior, elevated, uppermost ★**lower**

upright *adj.* ① sheer, steep, perpendicular ★**horizontal** ② honorable *Josephine was one of the most honorable people I ever met,* ethical, virtuous ★**dishonest**

uproar *n.* hubbub, noise, disorder, tumult, turmoil ▷*clamor*

upset ① *v.* bother, perturb, unsettle, annoy ② *v.* overthrow, overturn, topple ③ *adj.* disturbed, confused, worried

upside-down *adj.* ① overturned, upturned ② chaotic, muddled, jumbled

urge ① *v.* goad, plead, spur, beseech ★**deter** ② *n.* encouragement, compulsion ▷*impulse*

urgent *adj.* important, earnest, intense, vital ★**trivial**

use ① *v.* employ, practice, apply ② *v.* consume, exhaust, deplete, expend ③ *n.* usage, wear

useful *adj.* valuable, favorable, practical, beneficial ★**useless**

useless *adj.* trashy, paltry, futile *Trying to train a cat to fetch is a futile activity,* inefficient ▷*worthless* ★**useful**

usual *adj.* common, general, habitual, familiar ▷*normal* ★**exceptional**

utensil *n.* tool, implement, instrument, apparatus, device

utilize *v.* employ, apply, exploit ▷*use*

utmost *adj.* extreme, supreme, greatest, ultimate, last, distant

utter ① *adj.* thorough, absolute, complete ② *v.* declare, pronounce, speak ▷*say*

utterly *adv.* extremely, completely, entirely, fully, wholly

V v

vacant *adj.* ① empty, unoccupied, exhausted ★**occupied** ② stupid, blank, expressionless, mindless

vacation *n.* holiday, rest, recess

vagabond *n.* vagrant, tramp, loafer, beggar, rover, bum, hobo

vague *adj.* indefinite, imprecise, inexact, uncertain ▷*obscure* ★**certain**

vain *adj.* ① conceited, arrogant ▷*proud* ★**modest** ② fruitless, useless, worthless ▷*futile* VANE, VEIN

valiant *adj.* stout, valorous, worthy, gallant ▷*brave* ★**cowardly**

valid *adj.* genuine, authentic, official *No one is allowed into the meeting without an official pass,* proper

valley *n.* gorge, dale, dell, glen, vale

valor *n.* courage, fortitude, heroism, gallantry ▷*bravery* ★**cowardice**

valuable *adj.* ① costly, precious, priceless, expensive ★**worthless** ② meritorious *She was awarded the medal for meritorious service during the war,* righteous, worthy

value ① *n.* worth, benefit, merit, price ② *v.* appreciate, esteem, prize, treasure ③ *v.* appraise, assess, rate, estimate

van *n.* truck, vehicle, wagon, cart

vandalize *v.* damage, sabotage, harm, ruin

vanish *v.* ① disappear, fade, dissolve ★**appear** ② exit, depart, go

vanity *n.* pride, conceit, pretension ★**modesty**

vanquish *v.* conquer, defeat, overpower, subdue ▷*beat*

vapor *n.* steam, fog, mist, moisture, smoke

variable *adj.* changeable, fickle, unsteady, fitful, wavering ★**invariable**

varied *adj.* various, diverse *She was a woman of diverse interests,* miscellaneous, mixed, assorted ★**uniform**

variety *n.* ① assortment, array, mixture, medley *The singers entertained us with a medley of popular songs* ② sort, type, kind, class, category, breed, brand

Vehicles

Ambulance	Stagecoach	Skateboard
Automobile	Surrey	Streetcar
Bicycle	Tank	Wagon
Bulldozer	Taxi	Wheelchair
Bus	Tractor	
Cab	Tram	
Car	Trap	
Cart	Trolley	
Chariot	Truck	
Fire engine		
Go-cart		
Hearse		
Jeep		
Limousine		
Motorcycle		
Rickshaw		
Roller skates		
Scooter		
Sedan		

various *adj.* mixed, different, many ▷*varied*

vary *v.* differ, alter, change, diversify, diverge

vase *n.* jug, jar, beaker ▷*pitcher*

vast *adj.* great, enormous, extensive, huge, wide ▷*immense* ★**narrow**

vault ① *n.* grave, mausoleum, cellar, crypt, dungeon ② *v.* jump, clear, bound, leap, hurdle

veer *v.* swerve, skid, turn, tack, deviate, change

vehement *adj.* impassioned, fiery, passionate, ardent, eager, zealous ▷*strong* ★**indifferent**

vehicle *n.* ① automobile, car, conveyance, carriage, cart ② agency, means, expedient

veil ① *n.* cloak, cover, wimple, curtain ② *v.* hide, conceal, shade, screen ★**expose** vale

vein *n.* ① seam, strain, streak, stripe, thread, course ② disposition, mood, style, phrasing VAIN

velocity *n.* rate, pace, tempo, rapidity, impetus *After I won the school prize, I had greater impetus to follow my studies* ▷*speed*

venerable *adj.* respectable, revered, august,

dignified, honored ▷*sage*

vengeance *n.* reprisal, retaliation ▷*revenge* ★**pardon**

venomous *adj.* ① poisonous, toxic, vitriolic ② spiteful, malicious, hostile ▷*vindictive*

vent ① *v.* discharge, emit, express, let fly, release ② *n.* aperture, duct, opening, outlet

ventilate *v.* ① aerate, cool, fan, blow ② express, debate, discuss, examine

venture ① *n.* enterprise, undertaking, endeavor ② *v.* risk, bet, hazard ▷*chance*

verbal *adj.* stated, said, expressed, spoken, unwritten ★**written**

verdict *n.* decision, judgment, finding, conclusion, opinion

verge ① *n.* border, brink, edge, boundary ② *v.* incline, tend, border, come close to

verify *v.* confirm, declare, authenticate, corroborate *The witness corroborated the story told by the defendant* ★**discredit**

versatile *adj.* adaptable, variable, adjustable, handy ★**inflexible**

verse *n.* poem, rhyme, stave, canto, jingle, doggerel *Call this stuff poetry? It's just doggerel!*

version *n.* account, form, interpretation, adaptation, type

vertical *adj.* upright, erect, sheer, perpendicular, steep ★**horizontal**

very ① *adv.* extremely, exceedingly, greatly, intensely, absolutely ② *adj.* exact, real, true, actual, genuine

vessel *n.* ① bowl, pot, canister, container, basin, jar ② craft, ship, boat

vestige *n.* remains, remnant, hint, glimmer, residue, trace

veteran ① *n.* old timer, master, old hand, expert ★**novice** ② *adj.* experienced, practiced, adept ★**inexperienced**

veto ① *v.* ban, reject, prohibit, stop, forbid ★**approve** ② *n.* embargo *The United Nations placed an embargo on the selling of arms to the two countries,* prohibition, disapproval ★**assent**

vex *v.* annoy, provoke, trouble, irritate, harass ▷*displease* ★**soothe**

vibrate *v.* shake, quiver, oscillate, fluctuate

▷*tremble*

vice *n.* evil, failing, fault ▷*sin* ★**virtue**

vicinity *n.* area, environs, neighborhood ▷*surroundings*

vicious *adj.* evil, sinful, malignant, immoral, vile ▷*wicked* ★**virtuous**

victim *n.* sufferer, scapegoat, martyr, prey, pawn, dupe

victor *n.* winner, conqueror, champion, prizewinner ★**loser**

victory *n.* success, triumph, achievement ▷*conquest* ★**defeat**

view ① *n.* landscape, sight, panorama, spectacle ② *n.* estimation, belief, theory, opinion ③ *v.* watch, see, behold, witness

vigilant *adj.* attentive, wary, alert, guarded ▷*watchful* ★**lax**

vigor *n.* energy, vim, stamina, might, power ▷*strength* ★**weakness**

vigorous *adj.* forceful, energetic, powerful, dynamic ▷*active* ★**weak**

vile *adj.* low, wretched, contemptible, miserable, nasty, evil ▷*despicable* ★**noble**

villain *n.* blackguard, knave *You are nothing but a knave who is out to steal my money,* sinner, rascal ▷*rogue* ★**hero**

vim *n.* stamina, zip, strength ▷*vigor*

vindicate *v.* warrant, sustain, support, defend, establish ▷*justify* ★**accuse**

vindictive *adj.* vengeful, unforgiving, grudging, spiteful ▷*malicious* ★**merciful**

violate *v.* ① disobey, oppose, defy, resist, infringe ★**obey** ② abuse, defile, outrage, desecrate

violent *adj.* furious, rabid, rampant, forcible, tempestuous ★**calm**

virile *adj.* manly, masculine, vigorous, vibrant ▷*strong* ★**weak**

virtually *adv.* almost, nearly, practically, substantially

virtue *n.* goodness, honesty, chastity, purity ▷*quality* ★**vice**

virtuous *adj.* chaste, innocent, honorable, moral ▷*righteous* ★**wicked**

visible *adj.* perceptible, discernible, apparent, exposed, obvious ★**invisible**

W w

vision *n.* ① apparition, specter, ghost, mirage ② concept, revelation, foresight

visit ① *n.* call, sojourn, stay, excursion ② *v.* call on, drop in, tarry, stay

visitor *n.* guest, company, tourist, caller

visual *adj.* seeable, observable, visible

vital *adj.* ① essential, indispensible, critical, crucial 3*necessary* ② alive, vibrant, virile, dynamic *Our team won a number of games after we had been trained by the new dynamic coach,* energetic

vitality *n.* stamina, virility, vigor 3*strength*

vivacious *adj.* lively, spirited, vital, animated, merry 3*sprightly* ★**languid**

vivid *adj.* ① clear, bright 3*brilliant* ② vigorous, strong, lucid ★**dull**

vocal *adj.* articulate, eloquent, spoken, strident, vociferous ★**quiet**

vocation *n.* occupation, calling, job, mission, career, pursuit

vogue *n.* style, fashion, mode, popularity

voice ① *n.* speech, articulation, utterance ② *n.* choice, preference, opinion ③ *v.* utter, express, proclaim, pronounce

void ① *adj.* bare, barren, empty ② *adj.* invalid, canceled, useless ③ *n.* cavity, chasm, space, opening, nothingness

volatile *adj.* ① lively, changeable, fickle, giddy ② elusive, fleeting, evaporable

volley *n.* discharge, fusillade, barrage, shower

volume *n.* ① bulk, capacity, mass, quantity 3*amount* ② loudness, amplitude ③ book, edition, tome

voluntary *adj.* free-willed, optional, intended, gratuitous ★**compulsory**

vomit *v.* spew, disgorge, puke, throw up

vote ① *n.* ballot, election, poll, referendum ② *v.* ballot, poll, choose, elect

vow ① *v.* promise, swear, assure, vouch, testify ② *n.* oath, pledge, promise

voyage *n.* journey, cruise, passage, trip

vulgar *adj.* ① common, coarse, crude, indelicate, rude ★**elegant** ② native, ordinary, common

vulnerable *adj.* unprotected, unguarded, exposed, defenseless, tender ★**strong**

wad *n.* bundle, chunk, block, plug

waddle *v.* wobble, totter, shuffle, toddle

wag ① *v.* waggle, shake 3*vibrate* ② *n.* wit, humorist, joker

wage ① *n.* fee, pay, salary, remuneration ② *v.* carry out, fulfill, undertake

wager ① *v.* gamble, bet, speculate, chance, hazard ② *n.* pledge, stake, bet

wagon *n.* cart, truck, van 3*vehicle*

waif *n.* orphan, stray, foundling *In the old days, children were abandoned in the streets, but some people set up homes for such foundlings*

wail ① *v.* deplore, weep, grieve, lament 3*cry* ★**rejoice** ② *n.* lamentation, weeping, grief, moan, howl

wait *v.* ① expect, await, bide, stay, stop 3*linger* ② attend, serve WEIGHT

waive *v.* relinquish, disclaim, disown, forego, defer 3*renounce* WAVE

wake *v.* awaken, stimulate, excite 3*arouse*

wakeful *adj.* ① restless, awake ② alert, wary, watchful

walk ① *v.* advance, march, step, progress, move ② *n.* stroll, hike 3*ramble* ★**run** ③ *n.* lane, alley, way ④ *n.* sphere, field, career *I started my career in journalism, but I later went into politics,* interest

wallow *v.* ① flounder, stagger, tumble ② delight, enjoy, revel

wan *adj.* pale, ashen, feeble, sickly, pallid 3*weak* ★**robust**

wand *n.* mace, baton, stick, scepter, rod

wander *v.* stray, meander, roam, stroll, deviate

wane *v.* droop, decline, decrease, lessen, ebb *As the little boat neared the rocks, Fred's courage ebbed away,* sink ★**wax** WAIN

wangle *v.* fiddle, contrive, fix, arrange

want ① *v.* desire, covet, crave, need, require ② *n.* need, necessity, demand ③ *n.* dearth, deficiency 3*scarcity* ★**plenty**

wanton *adj.* ① unscrupulous, irresponsible

② playful, frolicsome, wild ③ dissolute, immoral

war *n.* hostilities, fighting, bloodshed, enmity, strife ★**peace** WORE

ward *n.* ① pupil, minor, charge ② district, quarter WARRED

ward off *v.* prevent, forestall, avoid, stop ▷*avert*

wardrobe *n.* ① locker, cupboard, closet ② outfit, clothes, apparel

warm ① *adj.* tepid, hot, lukewarm ② *adj.* sympathetic ▷*warmhearted* ③ *adj.* eager, hot, zealous ④ *v.* heat, bake, cook, prepare

warn *v.* caution, admonish, advise, alert, apprise WORN

warning *n.* caution, admonition, forewarning, alarm, tip

warp *v.* contort, bend, twist, kink, deform ★**straighten**

warrant ① *v.* guarantee, certify, justify, permit, allow ② *n.* assurance, permit, license, authority *She produced documents that showed her authority on the board of directors*

wary *adj.* cautious, alert, careful, heedful ▷*prudent* ★**rash**

wash ① *v.* bathe, scrub, rinse, cleanse, wet ② *n.* washing, cleaning

waste ① *n.* garbage, debris, trash, rubbish ② *v.* squander, spend, lavish, fritter ③ *v.* wither, decay, shrivel, perish WAIST

wasteful *adj.* lavish, prodigal, spendthrift ▷*extravagant* ★**economical**

watch ① *v.* note, observe, guard ★**ignore** ② *v.* inspect, look at, oversee ③ *n.* timepiece ④ *n.* guard, sentry, watchman

watchful *adj.* attentive, observant, vigilant ▷*wary* ★**inattentive**

water *v.* wet, bathe, wash, douse, drench, sprinkle, spray

wave ① *v.* brandish, flourish, waft, swing ② *n.* breaker, billow, undulation WAIVE

waver *v.* falter, hesitate, vacillate *There's no time to vacillate; make up your mind* ★**decide**

wax *v.* increase, rise, grow, expand, enlarge ★**wane**

way *n.* ① route, road, path, passage, track ② technique *The company introduced a new technique for making glass,* procedure, method, style WEIGH

wayward *adj.* contrary, perverse, obstinate ▷*stubborn* ★**docile**

weak *adj.* ① feeble, frail, puny, helpless, delicate ② foolish, soft, senseless, stupid ③ thin, watery, insipid ④ fragile, flimsy, tumbledown ★**strong** WEEK

weaken *v.* enfeeble, relax, sag, flag ▷*languish* ★**strengthen**

weakness *n.* defect, fault, frailty, flaw ★**strength**

wealth *n.* riches, luxury, prosperity, money, opulence ★**poverty**

wealthy *adj.* rich, affluent, prosperous, opulent ★**poor**

wear *v.* ① dress in, don ② rub, scrape, waste, consume ③ last, endure, remain WARE

weary ① *adj.* exhausted, tired, fatigued ★**fresh** ② *v.* exhaust, tire, bore ★**refresh**

weather *n.* climate, clime, conditions

weave *v.* braid, plait, unite, blend

web *n.* net, tissue, webbing, textile, netting

wed *v.* marry, join, link, splice, tie the knot

wedge ① *n.* block, chock, lump, chunk ② *v.* crowd, force, jam, push, thrust, squeeze

wee *adj.* little, small, minute ▷*tiny* ★**large**

weep *v.* blubber, snivel, sob, whimper *The lost puppy was found at last, whimpering in a corner* ▷*cry* ★**rejoice**

weigh *v.* balance, estimate, ponder, examine, consider WAY

weight *n.* ① load, pressure, burden, heaviness ② importance, onus, significance, gravity WAIT

weighty *adj.* heavy, hefty, ponderous, onerous ★**trivial**

weird *adj.* eerie, supernatural, unearthly, mysterious ▷*uncanny*

welcome ① *adj.* pleasing, desirable ▷*agreeable* ② *v.* greet, accost, hail, salute ③ *n.* greeting, salutation, acceptance

welfare *n.* well-being, comfort, happiness, benefit, advantage ★**harm**

well ① *adj.* robust, healthy, hearty, sound

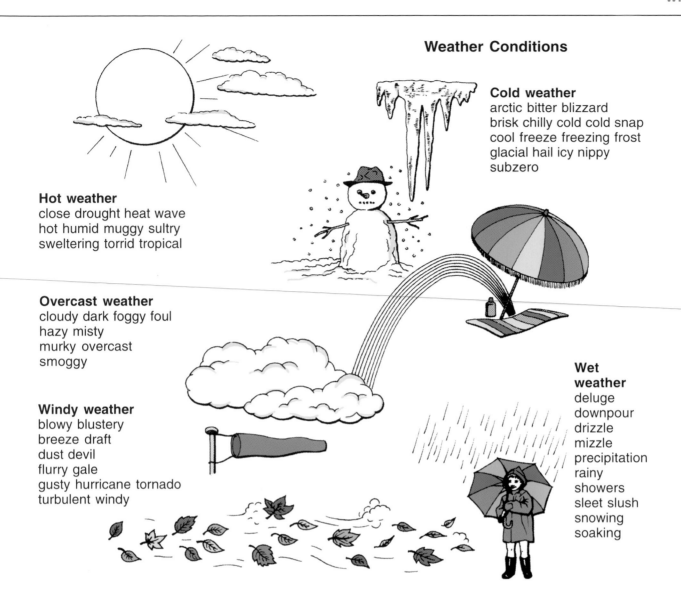

Weather Conditions

Hot weather
close drought heat wave
hot humid muggy sultry
sweltering torrid tropical

Cold weather
arctic bitter blizzard
brisk chilly cold cold snap
cool freeze freezing frost
glacial hail icy nippy
subzero

Overcast weather
cloudy dark foggy foul
hazy misty
murky overcast
smoggy

Windy weather
blowy blustery
breeze draft
dust devil
flurry gale
gusty hurricane tornado
turbulent windy

Wet weather
deluge
downpour
drizzle
mizzle
precipitation
rainy
showers
sleet slush
snowing
soaking

★**ill** ② *adv.* properly, suitable, adequately, accurately ★**badly** ③ *n.* fountain, spring

well-off *adj.* comfortable, prosperous ▷*wealthy* ★**poor**

wet *adj.* ① moist, damp, watery, drenched ② *adj.* drizzling, showery, raining ③ *v.* soak, moisten, dampen

wheedle *v.* coax, cajole, inveigle *We were inveigled into buying some of the local lace,* persuade ★**coerce**

whet *v.* ① sharpen, hone, strop ★**blunt** ② excite, stimulate, rouse ★**dampen**

whim *n.* fancy, humor, desire, urge, notion, impulse

whine *v.* ① howl, wail, whimper, moan ② complain, grouse, grumble

whip *v.* ① flog, lash, thrash, chastise, spank ② whisk, mix, blend

whirl *v.* twirl, spin, rotate, revolve, whir ▷*twist*

whisk *v.* beat, brush, hasten, hurry, sweep ▷*whip*

whisper ① *n.* murmur, hint, suggestion, breath ② *v.* breathe, murmur, divulge, buzz, intimate ★**shout**

whistle *n. & v.* cheep, chirp, warble, call

whole *adj.* ① all, entire, total, intact ② sound, complete, unbroken ★**part** HOLE

wholesome *adj.* healthful, nutritious, beneficial, sound, good ★**noxious**

wicked *adj.* infamous, corrupt, depraved, unrighteous, sinister, sinful ▷*evil* ★**virtuous**

wickedness *n.* corruption, depravity, iniquity, sinfulness, villainy ▷*evil*

wide *adj.* broad, ample, extended, spacious,

A B C D E F G H I J K L M N O P Q R S T U V W X Y Z

roomy, extensive, vast ★**narrow**

widespread *adj.* prevalent, far-flung, extensive, sweeping, universal *The use of a universal language would be of great help in the United Nations* ★**limited**

wield *v.* ① brandish, flourish, manipulate ② control, command, exert, maintain

wild *adj.* ① savage, ferocious, fierce, untamed ★**tame** ② violent, unrestrained, boisterous ★**civilized** ③ careless, insane, reckless ★**sane**

wilderness *n.* desert, jungle, wasteland, wilds, outback

will ① *n.* resolution, decision, zeal, accord ② *n.* order, wish, command, request, demand ③ *n.* legacy, testament ④ *v.* choose, desire, elect

willful *adj.* temperamental, headstrong, deliberate ▷*obstinate* ★**docile**

willing *adj.* disposed, zealous, ready, earnest ▷*agreeable* ★**unwilling**

wilt *v.* wither, waste, sag, dwindle ▷*ebb*

wily *adj.* cunning, sly, tricky, deceitful ▷*crafty* ★**sincere**

win *v.* succeed, gain, get, acquire, procure ▷*triumph* ★**lose**

wince *v.* shrink, quail, flinch *My little sister didn't flinch once when she had her vaccination,* start ▷*cringe*

wind (rhymes with *pinned*) *n.* breeze, blast, gust, gale

wind (rhymes with *mind*) *v.* coil, turn, twist, bend WINED

wink *n. & v.* blink, flutter, flicker, glint

winner *n.* champion, master ▷*victor*

wipe *v.* clean, brush, mop, remove, swab

wire *n.* ① cable, telegraph, telegram ② cable, cord

wisdom *n.* judgment, discretion, tact, thought, reason ★**folly**

wise *adj.* sensible, profound, astute, subtle, discreet ▷*sage* ★**foolish**

wish ① *v.* desire, crave, want, hanker for, long for ② *n.* command, will, desire, liking

wistful *adj.* ① pensive, musing, wishful ② forlorn, melancholy, soulful

wit *n.* ① fun, humor, levity, pleasantry ②

brains, sense, judgment, intelligence ★**stupidity**

witch *n.* enchantress, sorceress, crone, hag

withdraw *v.* ① retire, retreat, depart, leave ▷*flee* ② extract, take out

withdrawn *adj.* unsociable, retiring, reclusive, aloof, solitary ★**sociable**

wither *v.* waste, fade, pine, languish ▷*shrivel*

withhold *v.* retain, reserve, restrain, hold back ▷*keep* ★**grant**

within *adj.* inside, interior, inner

withstand *v.* resist, oppose, confront ▷*defy* ★**support**

witness ① *n.* spectator, onlooker, bystander *One of the bystanders at the accident came forward to give evidence,* signatory ② *v.* behold, observe, see, attest

witty *adj.* funny, jocular, waggish, amusing ▷*comical* ★**dull**

wizard *n.* sorcerer, magician, conjurer

woe *n.* sorrow, sadness, grief, misery, trouble ★**joy**

woman *n.* lady, girl, female, wife

wonder ① *n.* marvel, miracle, rarity, curiosity ② *n.* bewilderment, surprise, amazement ▷*awe* ③ *v.* speculate, question, marvel, muse

wonderful *adj.* marvelous, fabulous, spectacular, superb ▷*splendid* ★**commonplace**

woo *v.* make love, court, pursue

wood *n.* ① lumber, timber, planks ② forest, woods, copse, woodland, grove, thicket WOULD

word *n.* ① expression, term, utterance ② pledge, promise ③ tidings, news, information

work ① *n.* toil, drudgery, labor, grind ② *n.* task, job, stint, chore ③ *v.* operate, function, manipulate, run, drive

world *n.* globe, earth, sphere, planet

worry ① *v.* bother, annoy, disturb ▷*trouble* ★**soothe** ② *n.* vexation, anxiety, concern, fear ★**delight**

worsen *v.* aggravate, decline, deteriorate, degenerate ★**improve**

Borrowed Words

Boomerang

lemming
ombudsman
ski

Italian
balcony
cameo
fiasco
influenza

German
blitz
delicatessen
dollar
kindergarten

Dutch
boss
brandy
decoy
landscape

Modern French
police
rendezvous
liaison
menu

Scandinavia
fjord
geyser

Chinese
kowtow
sampan
typhoon
wok

Japanese
bonsai
judo
karate
origami

Turkish
coffee
kiosk

Spanish
armada
fiesta
macho
patio
siesta
sombrero

Afrikaans
aardvark
apartheid

boer
trek
veldt

Inuit
anorak
igloo
kayak
parka

Gaelic
blarney
bog
brat
brogue
smithereens

Aztec
avocado
cocoa
tomato

Arabic
admiral
alcohol
algebra
alkali
sherbet
sofa
zero

Aboriginal languages
boomerang
dingo
budgerigar
kangaroo

Persian
bazaar
caravan
divan
paradise

tulip
turban

Hindi
bungalow
chintz
cot
pajamas
thug
veranda

Native American
chipmunk
moccasin
moose
papoose
wigwam

---

worship ① *v.* revere, adore, esteem, honor, praise ★**despise** ② *n.* adoration, devotion, reverence

worth *n.* value, benefit, merit, caliber *This year's students were of a high caliber,* dignity

worthless *adj.* valueless, paltry, trifling, useless ▷*cheap* ★**valuable**

worthwhile *adj.* valuable, helpful, useful, beneficial ★**useless**

worthy *adj.* upright, admirable, excellent, honest, fine ★**vile**

wound ① *v.* hurt, injure, gash, pain, distress ▷*harm* ★**heal** ② *n.* injury, bruise, harm

wrangle *v. & n.* squabble, fight, row, scrap ▷*quarrel* ★**accord**

wrap *v.* fold, envelop, enclose, cover, clothe, conceal ★**unfold** RAP

wrath *n.* fury, ire, rage, passion ▷*anger* ★**pleasure**

wreck ① *v.* demolish, smash, ruin, destroy, spoil, ravage ★**repair** ② *n.* derelict, hulk, shipwreck, ruin

wrench *v.* twist, wring, strain, sprain, pull

wrestle *v.* struggle, battle, combat, grapple, tussle ▷*fight*

wretch *n.* vagabond, blackguard, villain, rogue ▷*scoundrel*

wretched *adj.* ① dejected, abject, miserable ▷*despicable* ② saddening, pathetic ▷*pitiful* ★**joyful**

wriggle *v.* twist, writhe, squirm, worm *My hamster wormed his way under the couch and it took some time before we could get him back out,* dodge

wring *v.* choke, squeeze, throttle, strangle, twist RING

wrinkle *n. & v.* crease, pucker, ruffle, rumple, crinkle, furrow

write *v.* inscribe, pen, sign, scrawl, scribble RIGHT, RITE, WRIGHT

writer *n.* ① scribe, penman, clerk ② author, essayist, narrator, playwright, poet, dramatist

writhe *v.* wind, twine, weave, twist ▷*wriggle*

written *adj.* recorded, set down, documentary, transcribed

wrong ① *adj.* unjust, unfair, immoral, wicked ② *adj.* false, mistaken, erroneous ③ *v.* injure, hurt, abuse ④ *n.* offense, atrocity, iniquity, sin, injustice ★**right**

wry *adj.* crooked, askew, awry, aslant, twisted, distorted ★**straight** RYE

A B C D E F G H I J K L M N O P Q R S T U V W X Y Z

Y y

yank *v.* draw, pull, snatch ▷*jerk*

yap *v.* ① bark, yelp ② prattle, blather, gossip, jaw

yard ① *n.* lawn, garden, courtyard, court, quadrangle ② three feet

yarn *n.* ① story, account, tale, narrative ② thread, wool, linen, twist

yawn *v.* gape, open

yearly *adj.* ① annual, perennial, per annum *We shall pay a salary of $50,000 per annum* ② *adv.* every year, annually

yearn *v.* ache, crave, desire, pine, hunger for ★**dislike**

yell *v.* shriek, squawk, whoop, screech, shout ▷*bellow* ★**whisper**

yield ① *v.* produce, provide, furnish, supply ② *v.* surrender, give in, submit ★**withstand** ③ *v.* abdicate, resign, renounce ④ *n.* crop, harvest, product, output

yielding ① *adj.* obedient, submissive, unresisting ★**stubborn** ② plastic, malleable, flexible ★**solid**

yoke ① *v.* join, couple, link, harness ② *n.* chain, bondage *The children of Israel moved out of bondage in the land of Egypt,* enslavement YOLK

yokel *n.* bumpkin, rustic, boor, peasant

young *adj.* youthful, tender, juvenile, junior, little ★**old**

youngster *n.* child, youth, boy, girl, kid, lad, adolescent

youth *n.* ① adolescence, prime, salad days ★**age** ② lad, boy ▷*youngster*

youthful *adj.* boyish, girlish, young, spry, juvenile, lively ★**aged**

Yule *n.* Christmas

Z z

zany *adj.* crazy, nutty, droll, goofy, eccentric, wacky, loony, loopy ▷*funny* ★**serious**

zeal *n.* devotion, eagerness, enthusiasm, keenness, ardor ★**apathy**

zealous *adj.* devoted, fervent *Dave was a fervent supporter of the school's football team,* fanatical, earnest ▷*eager* ★**apathetic**

zenith *n.* climax, height, apex, peak

zero *n.* nothing, nada, zip, naught, nil, nullity, aught

zest *n.* ① relish, gusto, appetite, keenness ② flavor, piquancy, taste ③ rind, peel

zone *n.* area, district, region, tract, sector

zoom *v.* flash, fly, shoot, streak, hurtle, whizz

a b c d e f g h i j k l m n o p q r s t u v w x y z

Our 50 states and their capitals

State	Capital	State	Capital	State	Capital
Alabama:	Montgomery	Louisiana:	Baton Rouge	Ohio:	Columbus
Alaska:	Juneau	Maine:	Augusta	Oklahoma:	Oklahoma City
Arizona:	Phoenix	Maryland:	Annapolis	Oregon:	Salem
Arkansas:	Little Rock	Massachusetts:	Boston	Pennsylvania:	Harrisburg
California:	Sacramento	Michigan:	Lansing	Rhode Island:	Providence
Colorado:	Denver	Minnesota:	St. Paul	South Carolina:	Columbia
Connecticut:	Hartford	Mississippi:	Jackson	South Dakota:	Pierre
Delaware:	Dover	Missouri:	Jefferson City	Tennessee:	Nashville
Florida:	Tallahassee	Montana:	Helena	Texas:	Austin
Georgia:	Atlanta	Nebraska:	Lincoln	Utah:	Salt Lake City
Hawaii:	Honolulu	Nevada:	Carson City	Vermont:	Montpelier
Idaho:	Boise	New Hampshire:	Concord	Virginia:	Richmond
Illinois:	Springfield	New Jersey:	Trenton	Washington:	Olympia
Indiana:	Indianapolis	New Mexico:	Santa Fe	West Virginia:	Charleston
Iowa:	Des Moines	New York:	Albany	Wisconsin:	Madison
Kansas:	Topeka	North Carolina:	Raleigh	Wyoming:	Cheyenne
Kentucky:	Frankfort	North Dakota:	Bismarck		

Our presidents and their native states

President	Native State	President	Native State
George Washington:	Virginia	Grover Cleveland:	New Jersey
John Adams:	Massachusetts	Benjamin Harrison:	Ohio
Thomas Jefferson:	Virginia	William McKinley:	Ohio
James Madison:	Virginia	Theodore Roosevelt:	New York
James Monroe:	Virginia	William Howard Taft:	Ohio
John Quincy Adams:	Massachusetts	Woodrow Wilson:	Virginia
Andrew Jackson:	South Carolina	Warren G. Harding:	Ohio
Martin Van Buren:	New York	Calvin Coolidge:	Vermont
William Henry Harrison:	Virginia	Herbert Hoover:	Iowa
John Tyler:	Virginia	Franklin D. Roosevelt:	New York
James K. Polk:	North Carolina	Harry S. Truman:	Missouri
Zachary Taylor:	Virginia	Dwight D. Eisenhower:	Texas
Millard Fillmore:	New York	John F. Kennedy:	Massachusetts
Franklin Pierce:	New Hampshire	Lyndon B. Johnson:	Texas
James Buchanan:	Pennsylvania	Richard M. Nixon:	California
Abraham Lincoln:	Kentucky	Gerald R. Ford:	Nebraska
Andrew Johnson:	North Carolina	Jimmy (James Earl) Carter:	Georgia
Ulysses S. Grant:	Ohio	Ronald Reagan:	Illinois
Rutherford B. Hayes:	Ohio	George Bush:	Massachusetts
James A. Garfield:	Ohio	Bill (William Jefferson) Clinton:	Arkansas
Chester A. Arthur:	Vermont	George W. Bush:	Texas

a b c d e f g h i j k l m n o p q r s t u v w x y z

How our states got their names

Alabama—Indian for tribal town.

Alaska—Originally an Eskimo word, *alakshak*, meaning "peninsula," "great lands," or "land that is not an island."

Arizona—Spanish version of Pima Indian word for "little spring place," or Aztec *arizuma*, meaning "silver-bearing."

Arkansas—French name for Quapaw—"downstream people"—a Siouan people.

California—Name given by the Spanish conquistadors. It was the name of an imaginary island in a Spanish romance written in the sixteenth century.

Colorado—From Spanish for "red."

Connecticut—From Mohican and other Algonquin words meaning "long river place."

Delaware—Named after Lord De La Warr, an early governor of Virginia.

Florida—Named by Ponce de Leon on "Flowery Easter," or Pasqua Florida, Easter Sunday 1513.

Georgia—Named for King George II of England.

Hawaii—Possibly from the native word for homeland: *Hawaiki* or *Owhyhee*.

Idaho—Said to be an invented name meaning "gem of the mountains." May also be a Kiowa Apache term for the Comanche.

Illinois—French for *Illini* or "land of *Illini*," an Algonquin word meaning "men" or "warriors."

Indiana—Means "land of the Indians."

Iowa—Indian word translated as "here I rest" or "beautiful land."

Kansas—Sioux word for "south wind people."

Kentucky—Indian word translated as "dark and bloody ground," "land of tomorrow," or "meadowland."

Louisiana—Named after the French King Louis XIV, who first claimed the territory.

Maine—Named after an ancient French province. It is also a descriptive term that refers to the mainland rather than the coastal islands.

Maryland—After Queen Henrietta Maria, wife of King Charles I of England.

Massachusetts—From an Indian tribe named after "large hill place."

Michigan—From Chippewa words, *mici gama*, meaning "great water."

Minnesota—From Dakota Sioux word meaning the "cloudy water" or "sky-tinted water" of the Minnesota River.

Mississippi—Probably Chippewa; *mici zibi,* "great river" or "gathering-in of all the waters." Also an Algonquin word: *messipi.*

Missouri—An Algonquin Indian term meaning "river of the big canoes."

Montana—Latin or Spanish for "mountainous."

Nebraska—From an Omaha or Otos Indian word meaning "broad water" or "flat river."

Nevada—A Spanish word meaning "snow-clad."

New Hampshire—Named in 1629 by Capt. John Mason, after his home county in England.

New Jersey—Named after England's Isle of Jersey.

New Mexico—Spaniards in Mexico applied this term to land north and west of Rio Grande in the sixteenth century.

New York—Named in 1644 after the Duke of York and Albany.

North/South Carolina—Named after King Charles I of England.

North/South Dakota—Dakota is a Sioux word for "friend or "ally."

Ohio—Iroquois word for "fine or good river."

Oklahoma—Choctaw word meaning "red man."

Oregon—Possibly named after the words on a French map: *"Ouaricon-sint."*

Pennsylvania—Named after William Penn, who had first suggested calling the region "Sylvania," which means "woodland."

Rhode Island—Possibly named *Roode Eylandt,* meaning "red clay," by a Dutch explorer.

Tennessee—*Tanasi* was the name of Cherokee villages on the Little Tennessee River.

Texas—Variant of word used by Caddo and other Indians to mean "friends" or "allies."

Utah—From a Navajo word meaning "upper," or "higher up." The Spanish form is Yutta.

Vermont—From French words *vert* (green) and *mont* (mountain).

Virginia—Named by Sir Walter Raleigh, in honor of Queen Elizabeth, who was known as the Virgin Queen of England.

Washington—Named after George Washington.

West Virginia—Took this name when the western counties of Virginia refused to secede from the U.S. in 1863.

Wisconsin—An Indian name believed to mean "grassy place" in Chippewa.

Wyoming—From the Algonquin words for "large prairie place," "at the big plains," or "on the great plain."

a b c d e f g h i j k l m n o p q r s t u v w x y z